Daily National Intelligencer

Washington
District of Columbia

Marriage and Death Notices

January 1, 1851 to December 30, 1854

Wesley E. Pippenger

HERITAGE BOOKS
2008

HERITAGE BOOKS
AN IMPRINT OF HERITAGE BOOKS, INC.

Books, CDs, and more—Worldwide

For our listing of thousands of titles see our website
at
www.HeritageBooks.com

Published 2008 by
HERITAGE BOOKS, INC.
Publishing Division
100 Railroad Ave. #104
Westminster, Maryland 21157

Copyright © 1999 Wesley E. Pippenger

All rights reserved. No part of this book may be reproduced or transmitted in any form or by any means, electronic or mechanical, including photocopying, recording or by any information storage and retrieval system without written permission from the author, except for the inclusion of brief quotations in a review.

International Standard Book Numbers
Paperbound: 978-1-58549-020-2
Clothbound: 978-0-7884-7731-7

Daily National Intelligencer
Washington, District of Columbia

MARRIAGE AND DEATH NOTICES
January 1, 1851 to December 30, 1854

WESLEY E. PIPPENGER

Daily National Intelligencer
(Washington, District of Columbia)

MARRIAGE AND DEATH NOTICES
January 1, 1851 - December 30, 1854

INTRODUCTION

The first issue of this newspaper was published in Washington, D.C., October 31, 1800, by a Philadelphian named Samuel Harrison Smith, under the title *National Intelligencer and Washington Advertiser*. The business office was first located on New Jersey avenue between D and E streets, southeast, and in 1801, moved to the south side of Pennsylvania avenue, between sixth and seventh streets, northwest. Early distribution was tri-weekly and semi-weekly. About May 1810, Smith was assisted by Joseph Gales, Jr. (1786-1860), who bought the newspaper upon Smith's retirement later that year. Mr. Gales shortened the title to *National Intelligencer*. In October 1812, Gales partnered with William Winston Seaton (1786-1866), who was previously working for the *Raleigh Register*, and the two soon began a fruitful publishing business known as Gales & Seaton.

Daily publication (except Sunday) began January 1, 1813, and the paper's name changed again— this time to the *Daily National Intelligencer*. By 1814, the newspaper office was located at the corner of 9th and E streets, N.W. (see cover illustration). The last issue of this newspaper was printed January 10, 1870. Before their demise, both Gales and Seaton served as Mayor of the city of Washington. A comprehensive article about the National Capital's first newspaper, written by William E. Ames, was published by the University of North Carolina Press, Chapel Hill, in 1972.

The first series of abstracts of marriage and death notices from the *National Intelligencer* was made by Frank J. Metcalf, and published in the *National Genealogical Society Quarterly*, beginning in June 1938. George A. Martin checked the abstracts for the earlier period and continued his own abstracts. Publication of Martin's abstracts appeared in the *Quarterly* from 1948 through 1975, covering newspaper items up through 1836 only. Martin's abstracts that were not published in the *Quarterly* were presented, along with a name index prepared by Margaret Elliott Higgins, in microfilm form. The three reels of microfilm, released in 1976 by the National Genealogical Society as its Publication Number 41, cover abstracts from 1800 to 1850.

The present work continues with transcripts of marriage and death notices from the *Daily National Intelligencer*, for the period January 1, 1851 to December 30, 1854. The District of Columbia began keeping public death records on January 1, 1855.

This work includes notices that are specifically found under the headings "Marriages" or "Deaths" in the local news portion of the newspaper. An unknown number of marriages or deaths that can be inferred from information in other parts of the newspaper, including chancery notices and health department reports, are not typically presented here. Spelling and punctuation have been preserved in most cases. A difference is made in indexing of ministers as a subject of the notice rather than the officiating clergyman, by an asterisk (*).

Wesley E. Pippenger
Arlington, Virginia
April 1999

Daily National Intelligencer, Marriage and Death Notices, 1851-1854

❖ ❖ ❖ 1851 ❖ ❖ ❖

MARRIAGE. In Rockingham county, on the 19th inst., by the Rev. Mr. Dodson, Miss HENRIETTA W., daughter of the Hon. Thos. Settle, and Hon. DAVID S. REID, Governor elect of North Carolina. (2 JAN 1851)

MARRIAGE. On the 1st ins., by the Rev. Mr. Chenowith, of Baltimore, Mr. JOHN E. BUCKINGTON, of Washington, to Miss MARGARET E. ASHTON, of Baltimore. (2 JAN 1851)

DEATH. Was killed in the city of Philadelphia, on the 22d ult., by falling from the cars, HENRY HOEKE, a native of Germany, but for the last 12 years a respected citizen of this place, aged about 45 years. The friends and acquaintances are invited to attend his funeral, on Sunday next, at 2 o'clock from his late residence near the Navy Yard. (3 JAN 1851)

DEATH. Suddenly, at her residence at Oatland, near Brookeville, in Montgomery Co., Md., at 4 o'clock A.M. on the 1st of January 1851, MARGARET D. BOWIE, in the 47th year of her age, sister of the Hon. R.J. BOWIE of the House of Representatives. (3 JAN 1851)

DEATH. On the 3d inst., after a long and painful illness, Mrs. MARGARET COLEMAN, in the 47th year of her age. Her friends and acquaintances are respectfully invited to attend her funeral, from her late residence, south B street, Capitol Hill, on Sunday, (tomorrow) at 2 o'clock. (4 JAN 1851)

DEATH. On the 3d inst., ELIZABETH DONNELLY, wife of James Donnelly, late of N.Y., aged 23 years. Her funeral will take place on Sunday afternoon, at 3 o'clock, from her late residence, corner of 12th and South C street, (Island). (4 JAN 1851)

DEATH. On the evening of the 2d inst., PATRICK BOYLE, aged 75 years. His funeral will take place from the residence of C. Gautier on 11th street, near Pa. ave., this morning, the 4th inst., at 9 o'clock. The friends of the family are invited to attend. (4 JAN 1851)

MARRIAGE. On Thurs. the 2d inst. by the Rev. Mr. Gorsuch, COVINGTON O. WEST, of Griegsville, Preston Co., Va., to Miss ATHARIA BARKER, of Washington. (6 JAN 1851)

MARRIAGE. In this city on the 2d inst. by the Rev. Mr. Lanahan, J. FENWICK YOUNG, of this District, to Miss NORA CARROLL LIVINGSTON, youngest daughter of the late Hon. Robert LeRoy Livingston, of the State of N.Y. (6 JAN 1851)

MARRIAGE. On the 1st inst., by the Rev. Mr. Chenowith, of Baltimore, Mr. JOHN E. BUCKINGHAM, of Washington, to Miss MARGARET J. ASHTON, of Baltimore. (6 JAN 1851)

MARRIAGE. At Esperance Plantation, Louisiana, on the 24th December, by the Rev. W.O. Preston, BENJAMIN W. FRAZIER, Jr. to CAROLINE E., daughter of Dr. J.H. Loughborough. (6 JAN 1851)

MARRIAGE. At Mt. Oak, on the 10th ult., by the Rev. Owen Thackara, ROBERT BOWIE, Esq., of Cedar Hill, to ELEANOR B. MAGRUDER, eldest daughter of John B. Mullikin, Esq., all of Prince George's Co., Md. (6 JAN 1851)

MARRIAGE. At Georgetown, D.C. on the 3d inst., CHARLES E. ECKLE, aged 68 years, an old and respectable citizen of that place. (6 JAN 1851)

DEATH. At Marysville, Yuba Co., Calif., on the 1st of November 1850, WILLIAM H. DIETZ, of Washington City. He had been a resident of this place for 14 years, and during that period commanded the respect of all, and the warmest regards of his more immediate friends... (6 JAN 1851)

Daily National Intelligencer, Marriage and Death Notices, 1851-1854

DEATH. In Georgetown, D.C. on the 3d inst., in the 7th year of his age, FRANKLIN BLAKE, son of William A. and Glorvina Gordon. (6 JAN 1851)

MARRIAGE. At St. Peter's Church, Capitol Hill, on the 31st ult., by the Rev. Mr. Lanahan, Mr. J.A.C. IARDELLA to Miss MARGARET A. BULGER, both of this city. (7 JAN 1851)

MARRIAGE. On Monday, the 6th inst., by the Rev. Mr. Donelan, Hon. RANSOM HALLOWAY, member of the House of Representatives for the 8th Congressional District of N.Y., to Miss ELIZA GENEVIEVE WARING, daughter of the late Col. Waring, of Mt. Pleasant, Prince George's Co., Md. (8 JAN 1851)

DEATH. In Cambridge, Mass., on the 6th ult., Mrs. MARTHA HOMANS, aged 84, relict of Benjamin Homans, formerly Chief Clerk in the Navy Department. (8 JAN 1851)

MARRIAGE. On Saturday morning the 4th inst. by the Rev. Mr. Morgan, Mr. WILLIAM G. BISHOP, of N.Y., to Miss EMELINE, youngest daughter of Daniel Pierce, of this city. (9 JAN 1851)

MARRIAGE. On Tuesday evening the 31st ult., by the Rev. Mr. Lanahan, M.P. MOHUN to Miss ROSELLA A. BRAWNER, both of this city. (9 JAN 1851)

DEATH. In this city, on the 7th inst., JABEZ GORE, Esq., an assistant clerk in the office of the House of Representatives of the U.S., in the 40th year of his age. He was an efficient officer, and highly respected and esteemed by his associates for his excellent traits of character. (9 JAN 1851)

DEATH. At her residence in Prince George's Co., Md., on the 6th inst., Mrs. CHARLOTTE COX, wife of Wm. Cox, Sr., in the 75th year of her age. (9 JAN 1851)

MARRIAGE. In Christ Church, Washington, by the Rev. Mr. Hodges, on Thursday the 9th inst., JOHN B. SPRIGG to Miss MARTHA R. STANSBURY, all of the District of Columbia. (10 JAN 1851)

DEATH. On the 11th inst. in the 5th year of her age, of disease of the brain, ELIZA B. WATKINS, daughter of George S. and Caroline Watkins, of this city. (13 JAN 1851)

MARRIAGE. In Frederick, on the 7th inst., by the Rev. Mr. Julledy, JOHN J. McCOLLAM, of this city, to Miss DRUCILLA BALDERSTON, of the former place. (14 JAN 1851)

DEATH. On Friday, the 3d inst., at Mt. Pleasant (the residence of the Rev. E.L. Childs), Charles Co., Md., in the 20th year of her age, BETTIE M., consort of Francis Price, Esq., and daughter of the late Noble Barnes. (14 JAN 1851)

MARRIAGE. In Norfolk, in St. Paul's Church, by the Rev. Mr. Jackson, Lt. Col. R.E. DeRUSSEY, U.S. Army, to Miss HELEN A. MAXWELL, of that city. (15 JAN 1851)

MARRIAGE. By the Rev. Mr. Moore, on the 12th inst., Mr. GEO. H. KENDRICK, of Washington, to Miss VIRGINIA BRIDWELL, of Va., daughter of Timothy Bridwell, Esq. (15 JAN 1851)

DEATH. On the evening of the 13th inst., in the 16th year of her age, VICTORIA, only dau. of Capt. Joseph Smoot, U.S. Navy. The friends and acquaintances of the family are invited to attend her funeral this day at one o'clock from the residence of her father, No. 3 Franklin Row. (15 JAN 1851)

DEATH. In this city, yesterday evening, at 4 o'clock, Miss ELLEN ADAMS, late of Emmittsburg, Md., of typhoid fever, in the 22d year of her age... Her funeral will take place tomorrow, from the residence of Mr. Gustavus A. Clarke, at 3½ o'clock, from the City Hall, The friends and acquaintances of the family are respectfully invited to attend. (15 JAN 1851)

Daily National Intelligencer, Marriage and Death Notices, 1851-1854

DEATH. At the Blockley Hospital, near Phila., on Thursday, January 2, DANIEL W. DAVIS, son of Barnabas Davis, Esq., of this place, aged 41 years. (15 JAN 1851)

MARRIAGE. On the 14th inst. by the Rev. Mr. Gossage, WM. CAMMACK, Jr. to MARGARET E. TAYLOR, all of this city. (16 JAN 1851)

MARRIAGE. On the 15th inst. by the Rev. Mr. Gilliss, Capt. WM. H. HULL, to Miss NANNIE J., dau. of Col. Jas. J. Randolph, all of this city. (16 JAN 1851)

DEATH. In this city, yesterday afternoon, in the 20th year of her age, MARY ANN SAGE, dau. of Mr. G.A. Sage, after an illness of but a few days. The friends of the family are invited to attend her funeral tomorrow morning at 10 o'clock from her father's residence, corner of Third and East Capitol streets. (16 JAN 1851)

MARRIAGE. On the 16th inst., by the Rev. John J. Murray, WM. CLABAUGH, of Georgetown, to ELIZABETH CISSEL, dau. of Thos. Cissel, of Washington. (17 JAN 1851)

DEATH. On the 15th inst., at Gloucester, N.J., Mr. JOSHUA A. FOLLANSBEE, aged 52. (17 JAN 1851)

DEATH. At his residence, near the town of Opelousas, Louisiana, on the 24th November 1850, the Hon. GEORGE KING, aged 82 years. The deceased was a native of Stafford Co., Va., removed to Kentucky in 1784, and thence to New Orleans in 1795. For 36 years he discharged the onerous and responsible duties of Parish Judge, in the Parish of his last residence. The deceased was the father of Judge King, late of the bench of the Supreme Court of Louisiana. (17 JAN 1851)

DEATH. In this city, of scarlet fever, on the 15th inst., aged 5 years, JAMES, son of B.J. Barbour, of Orange Co., Va., and grandson of the late Gov. James Barbour. (17 JAN 1851)

MARRIAGE. On the 16th inst., at the [F Street] First Presbyterian Church, by the Rev. Dr. Lawrie, Hon. GEORGE G. KING, of Newport, R.I., to Miss ELIZABETH C. SEAVER, dau. of Jonathan Seaver, Esq., of this District. (18 and 22 JAN 1851)

DEATH. In this city, on the 16th inst., after a painful and protracted illness, which she bore with Christian resignation, Mrs. AMANDA GREEVES, in the 35th year of her age, wife of John Greeves and dau. of Robert Boyd. She leaves a numerous circle of relatives and friends to mourn her loss. The friends of the family are invited to attend her funeral from her father's residence, on Seventh street, this afternoon, at 3 o'clock. (18 JAN 1851)

MARRIAGE. In Nashville, Tenn., on the 10th inst., by the Rev. Mr. Tomes, THOMAS PLATER, Esq., formerly of Washington, to Miss SARAH B. BUCHANAN, of Nashville, Tenn. (20 JAN 1851)

DEATH. On the 18th inst., of quinsy, at the residence of her grandson, John L. Wirt, on Capitol Hill, north side, Mrs. ELIZABETH McCARDLE, aged 87 years, a devout Christian, and member of the Roman Catholic Church. She was one of the early settlers and oldest inhabitants of this city. Her funeral will take place at 3 o'clock P.M. on Monday, the 20th inst. from the residence of J.L. WIRT. The friends and acquaintances of the family are invited to attend. (20 JAN 1851)

DEATH. In Georgetown, on the evening of the 18th inst., after a lingering illness, Mrs. MARY LUTZ, in the 72d year of her age, wife of the late John Lutz, Esq. (20 JAN 1851)

DEATH. On the 20th inst., JULIAN MONTANDON, in the 67th year of his age. His friends are invited to attend his funeral tomorrow evening at 3 o'clock from his late residence on Pa. ave., between 12th and 13th streets. (21 JAN 1851)

Daily National Intelligencer, Marriage and Death Notices, 1851-1854

DEATH. On the 20th inst., JOHN NOBLE, aged 33 years. His friends and acquaintances are invited to attend his funeral, without further notice, from A. Bennett's, 9th street, opposite Mr. Gideon's Printing Office, on Wednesday, at 11 o'clock. (21 JAN 1851)

DEATH. Yesterday morning, at 9 o'clock, Mrs. JANE C. RICHARDS, aged 25 years, wife of Alfred Richards, formerly of Charles Co., Md. Friends and acquaintances are respectfully invited to attend her funeral today, the 23d inst., at 3 o'clock, from her late residence, on N street, between First and South Capitol street, Washington. (23 JAN 1851)

MARRIAGE. In Christ Church, on Thursday the 23d inst., by the Rev. Mr. Hodges, Mr. ROBERT H. BROOM, to Miss MARIA MEEHAN, all of this city. (24 JAN 1851)

DEATH. On the 22d inst., at the residence of her uncle, Col. J. Brooks, near Washington, ELIZABETH A. BROOKS, aged 19 years. The funeral will take place this (Friday) morning, at 11 o'clock, to which the friends of the family are respectfully invited. (24 JAN 1851)

DEATH. On Tuesday, the 21st inst., at her residence in Indian town, near Port Tobacco, Charles Co., Md., Mrs. JNO. D. FREEMAN, aged 46 years, leaving an affectionate husband and seven children to mourn her loss. (24 JAN 1851)

DEATH. On the 23d inst., after a long and severe illness, which she bore with Christian fortitude and resignation, Mrs. ANN MARIA MARYMAN, in the 31st year of her age. The deceased has left a disconsolate husband and children to mourn her irreparable loss. The friends and acquaintances of the deceased are respectfully invited to attend her funeral today (Friday) at 10 o'clock A.M. at her late residence on East Capitol street, Capitol Hill. (24 JAN 1851)

DEATH. On the 23d inst., after a short illness, HAMILTON, son of James B. and Mary C. Phillips, aged 1 years, 11 months and 12 days. The friends and acquaintance(s) are invited to attend the funeral this afternoon at 3 o'clock, corner of 6th and H streets. (24 JAN 1851)

MARRIAGE. On Thursday evening, the 23d inst. at Brentwood, near Washington, by the Rev. Mr. Pyne, Lt. CARLILE PATTERSON, U.S. Navy, to ELIZA WORTHINGTON, dau. of the Hon. Joseph Pearson. (25 JAN 1851)

MARRIAGE. At Cape Island, N.J., on Sunday evening, 19th inst., by the Rev. J.M. Church, Mr. RICHARD R. THOMPSON, late of this city, to Miss ANNA S. HAND, of the former place. (27 JAN 1851)

DEATH. In this city, at the residence of her son, Mr. John L. Clubb, on the 25th inst., Mrs. ELIZABETH CLUBB, in the 70th year of her age. Her funeral will take place this (Monday) afternoon at 2 o'clock, to which the friends are respectfully invited. (27 JAN 1851)

DEATH. In Princeton, N.J., on the 21st inst., Dr. J. IRWIN DUNN, formerly of this city. (27 JAN 1851)

MARRIAGE. At Newark, N.J. on the 21st inst., by the Rev. Samuel L. Southard, WM. H. HEISS, of Phila., to Miss HARRIET WHALEY, only dau. of Thomas Whaley, deceased, of N.Y. (28 JAN 1851)

DEATH. On the 7th of March last, in Stockton, Calif., Dr. JAMES WASHINGTON PARSONS, only son of Mr. Bernard Parsons, of this city, in his 46th year. The deceased was a resident citizen of Guayaquil, South America, for a number of years, and lately of the former place. (28 JAN 1851)

MARRIAGE. On Tuesday the 28th inst., by the Rev. P.B. O'Flannigan, ANDREW GODDARD, Esq., to Miss MARIA C. GOLDSBOROUGH, both of Georgetown, D.C. (29 JAN 1851)

Daily National Intelligencer, Marriage and Death Notices, 1851-1854

MARRIAGE. On the 28th inst., by the Rev. Mr. Edwards, JOHN E. HUDDLESTON, of Prince George's Co., Md., to Miss M.L. WARRING, of this city. (29 JAN 1851)

MARRIAGE. At Cincinnati, on the 16th inst., by the Rev. Mr. Nicholson, SOLOMON W. ROBERTS, of Phila., Chief Engineer of the Ohio and Pa. Railroad, to ANNA S., dau. of R.H. Rickey, Esq., of Cincinnati. (29 JAN 1851)

MARRIAGE. At Alexandria, on Thursday 23d inst., by the Rev. Mr. Danforth, WILLIAM P. GUNNELL, M.D., of Fairfax C.H., to Miss MARTHA A. LINDSEY, of Alexandria. (29 JAN 1851)

DEATH. Yesterday morning in this city, Mrs. PRISCILLA DODSON, in the 72d year of her age, relict of the late Capt. Joseph Dodson, of Cambridge, Eastern Shore, Md. She died in the full triumphs of the Christian faith, in which she had lived for near 60 years. Her friends and those of the family are respectfully invited, without further notice, to attend her funeral, from the residence of her daughter, Mrs. Adams, tomorrow (Thursday) morning, at 11 o'clock. (29 JAN 1851)

DEATH. Yesterday morning (Tuesday 28th), between 5 and 6 o'clock, Mr. RICHARD E. CROPLEY, at his residence, Third street, Georgetown, D.C., in the 42d year of his age. The funeral will take place this afternoon at 3 o'clock. (29 JAN 1851)

DEATH. At Buffalo, N.Y., on the 17th inst., Mrs. CATHARINE B. PETER, wife of James F. Peter, and second dau. of James J. Baldwin, of that city, aged 26 years. (29 JAN 1851)

MARRIAGE. On the 27th inst., by the Rev. Mr. Lanahan, WM. E. HUTCHINSON, to Miss ANN CATHARINE HARRISON, all of this city. (30 JAN 1851)

DEATH. Suddenly, on Thursday morning, the 30th inst., Mrs. MARY HOLLAND, in the 69th year of her age, relict of Edward Holland. The friends of the family are invited to attend her funeral on Saturday afternoon, at 2 o'clock, from her late residence, corner of 11th and G streets. (31 JAN 1851)

DEATH. Death of Mr. KAUFMAN (of Texas). It is our painful duty to announce the decease of the Hon. DAVID S. KAUFMAN, a Representative in Congress from the State of Texas. About two o'clock yesterday he was in his seat in the House of Representatives, but, feeling a painful sensation about the region of the heart, he returned in a carriage to his lodgings at the U.S. Hotel. He there lay upon his bed for some time, in apparent tranquil repose, in the presence of his wife. About sunset he spoke, in reply to an observation from his child, and suddenly expired. His disease was an affection of the heart... (1 FEB 1851)

MARRIAGE. On the 29th of January, by the Rev. Mr. Tinkle, Mr. FRANCIS T. HERBST to Miss CAROLINE C. ARNY, both of Georgetown. (1 FEB 1851)

DEATH. Yesterday morning (Friday, 31st ult.), Mrs. MARY MAGDALEN, consort of JACOB SEUFFERELE, in the 63d year of her age, a native of Würtemburg, Germany, and for the last 16 years a resident of this city. The friends of the family are respectfully invited to attend her funeral from her late residence, on tomorrow (Sunday) evening, at 3 o'clock. (1 FEB 1851)

DEATH. On Thursday evening, the 31st inst., JOHN LAURENCE, in the 64th year of his age. The friends of the family are invited to attend his funeral on this (Saturday) afternoon, at 2 o'clock, from his late residence, corner of Fayette and Second streets, Georgetown. (1 FEB 1851)

DEATH. On Friday morning, 31st inst., WILLIAM D. TALLEY, in the 62d year of his age. The friends of the family are invited to attend his funeral on this (Saturday) morning at 11 o'clock, from his late residence on 11th street. (1 FEB 1851)

Daily National Intelligencer, Marriage and Death Notices, 1851-1854

DEATH. At New York, on the 21st ult., ALEXANDER GARDINER, Clerk of the U.S. Circuit Court, and U.S. Commissioner, in the city of New York, and brother-in-law of ex-President Tyler. The name of this gentleman is familiar to the country for his prompt execution of the fugitive slave law, recently passed by Congress... (4 FEB 1851)

DEATH. In Charles Co., Md., on the 1st inst., at the residence of his father, Col. Theodore Mudd, after a lingering and painful illness, which he bore with a Christian fortitude, ROBERT IGNATIUS MUDD, in the 16th year of his age. The deceased, although cut off so early in life, had evinced many noble traits of character, which had won for him the respect and esteem of all who knew him. (4 FEB 1851)

MARRIAGE. In this city, on Saturday morning, the 1st inst., by the Rev. Mr. Morgan, Mr. JAMES ORR, of Decatur, Ala., to Miss SARAH JANE SHERMAN, of Saratoga Co., N.Y. (5 FEB 1851)

MARRIAGE. In this city, on the 3d inst., by the Rev. Mr. Edwards, L.F. BEELER, of Cumberland, Md., to Miss AMANDA FILLINS, of Prince George's Co., Md. (5 FEB 1851)

MARRIAGE. At Milton, Del., on Wednesday evening, the 29th January 1851, by the Rev. John L. McKim, JOHN E. PARKER, of Georgetown, Del., and Miss ELIZA B., eldest daughter of Dr. WM. W. WOLFE, of the former place. (5 FEB 1851)

DEATH. At Wheeling, Va. on the 1st inst., Mrs. MARY ELLEN, consort of Mr. Thomas Wheat, aged 66 years. (5 FEB 1851)

MARRIAGE. On the 3d inst., by the Rev. Dr. Butler, BICKERTON SAUNDERS, Esq., to Miss NANCY BARRETT, both of Louisa Co., Va. (6 FEB 1851)

DEATH. On the 5th inst., Mrs. SUSAN A. SNIFFIN, aged 37 years. The friends of the family are respectfully invited to attend her funeral tomorrow afternoon, at 2 o'clock, from her late residence, on Garrison street, opposite the Marine Barracks. (6 FEB 1851)

MARRIAGE. In this city, on the 6th inst., by Rev. S.A. Roszell, ROYAL A. MILLER, to Miss SUSAN E. PERRIE, all of this city. (7 FEB 1851)

DEATH. Yesterday morning, at the residence of Mr. J.T. Sullivan, of this city, JOHN K. TOWNSEND, M.D., of Philadelphia, Pa. (7 FEB 1851) The funeral of John K. Townsend, M.D., late of Philadelphia, will take place from the residence of John T. Sullivan, Esq., on 7th street, this morning at 11 o'clock, to which his friends and those of the family are invited. (8 FEB 1851)

DEATH. On Saturday, the 1st inst., ARABELLA FLORINDA LITTLE, aged 3 months, daughter of James and Araminta Little. (7 FEB 1851)

MARRIAGE. On Thursday, the 6th inst., at the Church of the Epiphany, by the Rev. John W. French, Mr. ALEXANDER H. BROWN, of Md., and Miss MARY J. MURRAY, daughter of the late A.B. Murray, Esq., of Baltimore. (8 FEB 1851)

MARRIAGE. In Christ's Church, on Thursday, the 6th inst., by the Rev. Mr. Hodges, JOHN T. PHELPS to SARAH ELIZABETH KIDWELL, all of this city. (8 FEB 1851)

DEATH. In this city, of consumption, at midnight of the 6th proximo, Mrs. ANNA M. ADAMS, of New Haven, Conn., wife of C.B. Adams, of the Treasury Department. Her remains have been taken North for interment. (8 FEB 1851)

DEATH. In this city, on Saturday evening, the 8th inst., ELEANOR D., daughter of Andrew and Ann ROTHWELL, in the 17th year of her age. In her day of youth and health, she had given her heart to her

Daily National Intelligencer, Marriage and Death Notices, 1851-1854

Saviour... The friends of the family are invited to attend the funeral this morning at 11 o'clock from her father's residence. (10 FEB 1851)

DEATH. On Sunday (yesterday) evening, Miss HANNA WOOD, a native of Philadelphia. Her funeral will take place on Tuesday, at 3 o'clock, from the residence of her brother-in-law, Richard Cruit, on Penn. ave., between 4½ and 6th streets. The friends of the family are respectfully invited to attend. (10 FEB 1851)

DEATH. On the 8th inst., at 7 o'clock in the evening, in Georgetown, D.C., Mrs. SARAH REBECCA COLLINS, daughter of Capt. Tucker, of West River, Anne Arundel Co., Md., and the wife of Jos. Henry Collins, Esq. Of the deceased it may be truly said that she lived the life of the righteous and died the triumphant death of the Christian. "Blessed are the dead who die in the Lord." (10 FEB 1851)

DEATH. On the night of the 4th inst., at the residence of his father, in Warrenton, Va., Dr. RICHARD H. MOORE, in the 31st year of his age. (10 FEB 1851)

DEATH. In this city, on Saturday evening, the 8th inst., JAMES, infant son of James and Susan JACK, aged 28 days. (10 FEB 1851)

DEATH. Died, at Cincinnati, on Thursday, January 30th, THOS. WORTHINGTON KING, second son of the late Edward King, Esq., in the 32d year of his age. A native of Ohio, he was educated at Harvard University, where he was graduated in 1840. On leaving college he entered the counting-house of the late Richard Alsop, of Philadelphia, and, after several years of preparation in the routine of his office, in voyages to South America and China, and a short residence in New Orleans, he entered into mercantile business at Cincinnati in 1845. During the few years which have since elapsed, he had already won an elevated character and position among the merchants of that enterprising city, and bade fair to become one of their most useful and distinguished members, when, in the full vigor of early manhood, his career was closed in death... (11 FEB 1851)

DEATH. Departed this life, on the 24th ult., after a short and severe illness, at the residence of Mrs. Sarah C. Waring, his mother-in-law, in Prince George's Co., Md., Dr. RICHARD H. CLAGETT, aged 42. In the death of the subject of this obituary notice, it may be truly said, society has sustained a loss and the profession to which he belonged, and in which in early life he had attained a distinguished rank, been deprived of a skillful and efficient member. The deceased had been compelled, from feeble health, to withdraw from the practice of his profession for some time before his health... (11 FEB 1851)

DEATH. The aged and venerable Dr. McWHIR, whose name is familiar to most of our readers, died, we regret to state, on the 31st ult. An Irishman by birth, Dr. McWhir emigrated to this country about the year 1783, settled soon after at Alexandria, Va., where he taught school for several years, and thence removed to Georgia, with a view to take charge of the Richmond county academy, but finally settled at Sunbury, at which place and its vicinity he continued successfully the profession of a teacher, preaching at the same time to destitute places within his reach. He never had any regular pastoral charge in Georgia, but continued to preach at different places, as occasion offered, until a very advanced age. Whilst living at Alexandria, he was often the inmate of Gen. Washington's house, at Mt. Vernon, and was also the instructor of two of the General's nephews. Dr. McWhir was a ripe classical scholar, and his name has long been associated with public instruction in Georgia. He died at Mr. Roswell King's in Liberty county, in his 92d year. *Savannah Republican.* (11 FEB 1851)

DEATH. On Saturday, the 8th inst., FANNIE ELLEN, daughter of Thomas J. and Mary A. GALT, aged 2 years and 4 months. (11 FEB 1851)

DEATH. On the 9th inst., at 1½ o'clock P.M., in Georgetown, D.C., CHARLES BURNETT, son of Thomas A. and Sarah A. LAZENBY, aged 16 months. (11 FEB 1851)

Daily National Intelligencer, Marriage and Death Notices, 1851-1854

MARRIAGE. In this city, last evening, by the Rev. Joseph White, Mr. JOHN CLAPHAM, U.S. Navy, to Miss ANN M. BARBER, of Fauquier Co., Va. (12 FEB 1851)

MARRIAGE. On Sunday, the 9th inst., by Rev. Mr. Marks, Mr. WM. VENABLE to Miss MARY EDELIN, of Prince George's Co., Md. (12 FEB 1851)

MARRIAGE. On Sunday evening, 9th inst., by the Rev. O.B. Brown, Mr. MILTON CLARK to Mrs. SUSAN BEARDSLEY. (12 FEB 1851)

DEATH. At Piqua, Ohio on the 2d inst., of erysipelas, in the 35th year of her age, Mrs. CATHERINE B., wife of the Rev. C.W. FITCH, of that place, and daughter of the late Thomas C. Wright, Esq., of Georgetown, D.C. (12 FEB 1851)

MARRIAGE. In Christ Church, Washington, on Tuesday, the 11th inst., by the Rev. Mr. Hodges, ANDREW F. BEEDLE to Miss EMMA HODGE, all of this city. (13 FEB 1851)

MARRIAGE. In this city, on the 11th inst., by the very Rev. Wm. Matthews, JOSEPH N. YOUNG to JOANNA FRANCES, daughter of Major Parke G. Howle, U.S.M.C. (13 FEB 1851)

MARRIAGE. In Charlestown, Jefferson Co., Va., on the 5th February, by the Rev. Dudly Tyng, Mr. P.C. LITTLE, of Georgetown, D.C., to Miss JULIA ROBERTS, formerly of Massachusetts. (13 FEB 1851)

MARRIAGE. On Tuesday evening last, by the Rev. C.A. Davis, EDWARD MAGRUDER, of Prince George's Co., to LAURA E., daughter of Thomas Wilson, Esq., of Montgomery Co., Md. (13 FEB 1851)

DEATH. Yesterday morning [12 FEB 1851], ALBERT A., infant son of James and Mary WILLIAMSON, aged eight months. The friends of the family are respectfully requested to attend the funeral from the residence of its parents, Capitol Hill, this evening at 3 o'clock. (13 FEB 1851)

MARRIAGE. On Thursday, the 13th instant, at St. Patrick's Church, Washington, by the Rev. Mr. Slattery, JAMES WM. NORTON to Miss LUCRETIA HARPER, of Montgomery Co., Maryland. (14 FEB 1851)

DEATH. At his farm, in Charles Co., Md., on Friday last, the 7th inst., W. BRUCE WILSON, aged 52 years, second son of the late James Wilson, Esq., of Alexandria. (14 FEB 1851)

MARRIAGE. On the 13th inst., at St. Mary's Church, by the Rev. Mr. Alig, Mr. JOSEPH MEYER, of Rockville, Md., to JANE WELCH, of this city. (15 FEB 1851)

MARRIAGE. On the 9th inst., by the Rev. Mr. Alig, Mr. MICHAEL O'CONNER to Miss MARY O'CONNER. (15 FEB 1851)

MARRIAGE. On the 2d of January, by Rev. Mr. Alig, PATRICK FITZGERALD to Miss ELLEN COLLINS. (15 FEB 1851)

MARRIAGE. On the 25th of November, by Rev. Mr. Alig, Mr. PETER SCHAEFER to Miss MARY CATHARINE SCHLATTMAN. (15 FEB 1851)

MARRIAGE. On the 29th of November, by Rev. Mr. Alig, EDWARD CORRIDAN to HONORA LEEHY. (15 FEB 1851)

DEATH. In this city, on Friday morning, February 14, in the 83d year of his age, THOMAS H. GILLISS, late and for many years Chief Clerk in the Fourth Auditor's Office. His funeral will take place from the Church of the Ascension, on Sunday next, at 2 P.M. (15 FEB 1851)

Daily National Intelligencer, Marriage and Death Notices, 1851-1854

MARRIAGE. On the 13th inst., at St. Matthew's Church, by Rev. J.B. Donelan, Mr. THOMAS A. DODD, of Norfolk, Va., to Miss AMANDA A. NORRIS, of this city. (17 FEB 1851)

MARRIAGE. On Thursday, 30th ult. [30 JAN 1851], in Christ Church, Baltimore, by the Rev. Dr. Johns, JOHN H. SMOOT, of Georgetown, D.C., to JULIA, daughter of Col. Daniel Duvall, late of Frederick Co., Md. (17 FEB 1851)

MARRIAGE. On the 29th ult. [29 JAN 1851], by the Rev. D.A. Tyng, LAWSON BOTTS, Esq., to BETTIE, youngest daughter of James L. Ranson, all of Jefferson Co., Va. (17 FEB 1851)

MARRIAGE. In Baltimore, on the 13th inst., by Rev. Mr. Roley, WILLIAM D. WILLIAMS, to MARY ANN BEERS. (17 FEB 1851)

DEATH. At Pensacola Navy Yard, on the 4th inst., MARY L., wife of Lieut. Wm. D. Hurst, U.S.N., and third daughter of the late Col. John M. Gamble, U.S.M.C. (17 FEB 1851)

DEATH. On Saturday evening, the 15th inst., after a short but painful illness, KATE, youngest daughter of Thomas and Matilda Bayne. The friends and acquaintances of the family are invited to attend her funeral this (Monday) afternoon, 17th inst., at 2 o'clock, from the residence of her parents near the Navy Yard, without further notice. (17 FEB 1851)

MARRIAGE. On Tuesday, 19th inst., at Lake Drummond, (N.C.), BENJAMIN F. WILKINS, of this city, to Miss EMMA JANE BINGHAM, of Portsmouth, Va. (20 FEB 1851)

MARRIAGE. In Baltimore, on Tuesday evening, 18th inst., at St. Alphonsus Church, by Rev. A. Schmid, C.S.S.R., V.L. ERNEY, of York, Pa., to Miss CATHARINE MATILDA SMITH, of this city, formerly of Adams Co., Pa. (20 FEB 1851)

DEATH. On the 18th inst., MARGARET, daughter of Thomas and Margaret Robbins, aged ten years. The friends and acquaintances of the family are requested to attend the funeral this afternoon, between the hours of two and three o'clock, without further notice, corner of 12th street and Massachusetts avenue. (20 FEB 1851)

MARRIAGE. On Thursday, the 20th inst., by the Rev. Mr. Hodges, THOMAS THORNLEY to Miss MARTHA E. McCOMB, all of Washington. (22 FEB 1851)

DEATH. At Willard's Hotel, in this city, on Wednesday, the 19th inst., Major RICHARD POLLARD, of Alta Vista, Albemarle Co., Va. Universal gentleness and dignity of deportment, scrupulous integrity in every worldly transaction, and affectionate devotedness to his family and friends, render the memory of Major Pollard precious to all who held relations with him, whether near or distant. He was highly connected in his native Virginia, and had been invested with offices of importance, from which he retired with spontaneous praises even from political opponents. His military career in early life, his conduct as the representative of his Government for a long term at Chili, and the manner in which he acquitted himself when delegated from the State of his birth to a National Convention at Baltimore, are sufficient attestations of his claim to public respect. The anguish of a bereaved wife and children, and the sadness of many less closely allied mourners, tell how deeply and how extensively he deserved personal regard. The remains of Major Pollard have been removed for interment to the family burial place at Oak Ridge, Nelson Co., Va. (22 FEB 1851)

DEATH. On the 20th inst., Dr. JOHN P. VANTINE, aged 44 years. His friends and relatives are particularly invited to attend his funeral this (Saturday) afternoon, at 3 o'clock, from his late residence, 13½ street. (22 FEB 1851)

Daily National Intelligencer, Marriage and Death Notices, 1851-1854

DEATH. On Thursday evening, the 20th inst., FRANCIS WILLIAM, son of W.H. and Catharine Thomas, aged 18 months. The friends of the family are invited to attend the funeral this (Saturday) afternoon, at 3 o'clock, from the residence of Mr. Levi Pumphrey, on C street. (22 FEB 1851)

DEATH. At Philadelphia, on Thursday morning, the 20th inst., at twenty minutes past 7 o'clock, aged 23 years, MARY KATE, wife of James R. Smith, and eldest daughter of W.G.W. White, of this city. (22 FEB 1851)

DEATH. At Lyme, Conn., on the 2d inst., Miss SUSAN MITCHEL, 82 years of age. Also, on the 4th inst., Miss DESIRE MITCHEL, aged 87. The above were members of a very aged and singular family of five persons, whose united ages amount to 403 years, viz: Desire, aged 87; Samuel, 84; Susan, 82; John and Louis, twins, 75 each; they were children of John Mitchel, who died in the year 1818, age 87. The mother died in 1776, 75 years of age. This singular family have always lived on the same place where there father and grandfather lived; they have remained single, and lived bachelor and maiden lives, have been a very happy and peaceable family, without a known enemy, and have always enjoyed good health; the oldest having lived 86 years without the need of a physician, which is accounted for by their temperate habits and plain living. They always raised what they consumed, and manufactured all their own clothing and bedding from the flax and wool, by hand, their hats from straw, and their shoes from the leather. Their house is in the oldest style, without plastering, stoves, or carpets. They use the same shovels and tongs that their grandmother used; in fact the particulars of this singular family would fill a small volume.--*Saybrook Mirror*. (22 FEB 1851)

OBITUARY. In the death of the late venerable THOMAS H. GILLISS, Esq., this city has lost one of its oldest and most respected citizens, and the Church of which he was a member one of its earliest, most active, and efficient friends. He was followed to the grave by the hearts of an entire community who were the witnesses of the daily beauty of his life. Mr. GILLISS was born in Somerset Co., Md., in December, 1768. In 1798 he received the appointment of Chief Clerk to the Navy Accountant, as he was then called, now the Fourth Auditor of the Treasury. He removed to Washington with the Government, in 1800, and continued in the same office until June of last year, when the infirmities of his great age compelled him to resign. On a visit to his native country last summer he met with the accident — the fracture of his leg — which occasioned the protracted illness which caused his death. The remainder of his life was patience, and the end of it was peace. The prominent traits of the character of this venerable man were recognized at once by all who approached him. He was a man of a naturally equable, systematic, affectionate, and gentle character. From an early period a devoted and active member of the Protestant Episcopal Church, his whole nature was manifestly brought under the new creating power of the grace of God, and his heart, then "baptized in the pure fountain of eternal love," exhibited through his long life singularly winning and beautiful characteristics. Old age was, in his case, not only venerable, but lovely [text continues]. (22 FEB 1851)

MARRIAGE. On the 20th inst., in St. Paul's Church, Baltimore, by Bishop WHITTINGHAM, Dr. LOUIS MACKALL, to Miss MARY L., daughter of Major Thos. Bonce, all of Prince George's Co., Md. (24 and 25 FEB 1851)

DEATH. On Sunday morning, about 7 o'clock, COLUMBIA SAPHRONIA McDUELL, aged nineteen years. The friends and relatives of the family are requested to attend her funeral at the Foundry Church, on Tuesday morning, at 11 o'clock. (24 FEB 1851)

DEATH. On the 23d inst., Mr. LUCIAN CARTER BROWNE, a native of Gloucester Co., Va., aged 26 years. His relatives and friends are respectfully invited to attend his funeral, from the residence of his father-in-law, Mr. GEORGE MATTINGLY, south F street, (Island,) on Tuesday, the 25th inst., at 3½ o'clock. (24 FEB 1851)

Daily National Intelligencer, Marriage and Death Notices, 1851-1854

DEATH. At Red Hill, in the county of Granville, North Carolina, on Tuesday, the 18th of February, Mrs. MARY GRACE DANIEL, eldest daughter of Hon. A.W. Venable, in her twenty-third year. (24 FEB 1851)

DEATH. At Jamaica Island, of cholera, CHAS. ALBERT, son of Dr. Albert Dorman, of this city. (24 FEB 1851)

DEATH. On the 14th inst., at Glen Wallace, Madison Co., Va., MICHAEL WALLACE, Esq., in the seventy-fourth year of his age. (25 FEB 1851)

DEATH. At Sandusky City, Ohio, on the 24th inst., MARY POWERS, sister of Mrs. Millard Fillmore. (26 FEB 1851)

DEATH. Yesterday, in the 28th year of his age, ROBERT ROSE FITZHUGH, son of Samuel Fitzhugh, of this city. His friends and those of the family are invited to attend his funeral, at the residence of his father, on 7th near K street, on Thursday afternoon at 3 o'clock. (26 FEB 1851)

DEATH. On the 24th inst., WM. E.E. RANDOLPH, aged about forty-two years, formerly of Petersburgh, Va. (27 FEB 1851)

MARRIAGE. On Tuesday, 25th inst., in Georgetown, D.C., by Rev. Mr. Atkinson, WARREN TILTON, of Boston, to SARAH A., daughter of the late Robert Ould, of the former place. (28 FEB 1851)

DEATH. Yesterday morning, after a short illness, A.B. LINDSLEY, aged 64 years, lately of Frankfort, Mo. (1 MAR 1851)

DEATH. On the 26th February, after a short illness, at the residence of his grandfather, Alexander Ray, ROBERT H., infant son of Robert H. and Ellen L. Leslie, aged 10 months. (1 MAR 1851)

DEATH. In Georgetown, D.C., on the 27th February, Mrs. ELEANOR RAY, in the 77th year of her age. The friends of the family and of her son, Alexander Ray, of this city, are invited to attend her funeral from her late residence on Gay street, this day (Saturday) at 4 o'clock. (1 MAR 1851)

DEATH. In Baltimore, on the 15th instant, Thomas WANNALL, in his 68th year, formerly of Washington. (1 MAR 1851)

MARRIAGE. At Frederick, (Md.) on the 26th February, by the Rev. W.N. Pendleton, CHARLES E. TRAIL, Esq., to Miss ARIANA, youngest daughter of Col. John H. McElfresh, all of that city. (3 MAR 1851)

MARRIAGE. At Martinsburg, Berkeley Co., Va., on the 25th ult., by the Rev. Joseph H. Plunkett, JEREMIAH HARRIS, Esq., of Jefferson Co., Va., to Miss SUSAN MARTHA, daughter of Capt. Charles Boarman, U.S. Navy. (3 MAR 1851)

DEATH. Yesterday morning, after a lingering illness, in the sixty-third year of his age, IGNATIUS MUDD, Esq., Commissioner of the Public Buildings. Mr. Mudd was a native of Charles Co., Md., and for thirty years a resident of this city, highly esteemed by all who knew him as an honorable, intelligent, and most worthy gentleman. The remains of the deceased will be removed from his late residence, on Maryland avenue, on Tuesday evening, the 4th inst., at 3 o'clock P.M., to St. Patrick's Church, where the funeral services will be performed. (3 MAR 1851)

MARRIAGE. On the 3d inst., by the Rev. J.B. Donelan, JAMES R. BRENT, of Charles Co., Md., to Miss ANNE ELIZA LINDENBERGER, of this city. (4 MAR 1851)

Daily National Intelligencer, Marriage and Death Notices, 1851-1854

MARRIAGE. In this city, on the 3d inst., by the Rev. Mr. Slattery, Mr. MICHAEL R. SHYNE to Miss CATHARINE O'BRYAN. (4 MAR 1851)

DEATH. On the 2d inst., after a short and painful illness, ROSANNA A., consort of Fred'k. W. DeKrafft, and daughter of the late Dr. Chas. A. Beatty, of Georgetown, D.C. Her friends and acquaintances are invited to attend the funeral from her late residence, High street, Georgetown, at 4 o'clock this (Tuesday) afternoon. (4 MAR 1851)

DEATH. At the residence of Richard Ronaldson, Philadelphia, ELLEN DUANE STEEDMAN, aged 3 years, daughter of Lieut. Charles Steedman, of the U.S. Navy. (4 MAR 1851)

MARRIAGE. On the 27th ult., by the Rev. Mr. Morgan, EVERET WROE, of Washington, to Miss MARGARET E. DUVALL, daughter of the late Marshur Duvall, of Prince George's Co., Md. (5 MAR 1851)

MARRIAGE. On Monday, the 3d inst., by the Rev. Mr. Gillis, JOHN W. BADEN, of Washington, to MARY A.K. WALLACE, youngest daughter of the late Robert Wallace, of Montgomery Co., Md. (5 MAR 1851)

DEATH. On Monday night, at 11½ o'clock, after a lingering illness, ISABEL C., youngest daughter of John H. and Jane C. Batman. The friends and acquaintances of the family are respectfully invited to attend her funeral at 3 o'clock today, from the residence of her father, on 7th street east. (5 MAR 1851)

DEATH. On the 17th of February, at the residence of Miss Sarah O. Hilleary, Prince George's Co., Md., Mr. TILGHMAN HILLEARY, Sr., in the 62d year of his age. (5 MAR 1851)

MARRIAGE. On Tuesday, the 4th inst., by the Rev. Mr. Donelan, RICHARD TONGE to Miss ELLEN CLARK, both of this city. (6 MAR 1851)

MARRIAGE. In Annapolis, on the 4th inst., by the Rev. Mr. Griffith, Mr. ELIAS G. HYDE, to Miss FRANCES ANN RIDGELY, all of that city. (6 MAR 1851)

DEATH. Of cholera, in the city of Houston, Tex., on the 5th of January last, Dr. WILLIAM G. LEWIS, in the 44th year of his age. Dr. L. was a native of Philadelphia, but latterly a citizen of Texas. (6 MAR 1851)

DEATH. In St. Louis, on Wednesday, the 5th March inst., of consumption, Miss Mary Harriet, youngest daughter of the late Rev. Alexander McAlister, in the 19th year of her age. (6 MAR 1851)

DEATH. On Tuesday, March 4th, at Buena Vista, Newcastle Co., Del., after a brief but painful illness of a week, in the 28th year of his age, JAMES F. CLAYTON, son and sole surviving child of the Hon. John M. Clayton, late Secretary of State under President Taylor. Youth, health, a warm heart, and generous and hopeful spirit, were all at once struck down by a calamity which has rendered one hearth desolate and inflicted sorrow on many hearts. (7 MAR 1851)

DEATH. On the 6th inst., ADA AUGUSTA, only child of William S. and Mary A. Jackson. The funeral will take place this (Friday) afternoon, at three o'clock, from the residence of her aunt, Mrs. Howison, Ninth street, between E and F. (7 MAR 1851)

MARRIAGE. On the 20th ult., by the Rev. Wm. B. Edwards, Mr. WM. P. DAWSON to Miss MARY FRANCES WHITE, all of this city. (8 MAR 1851)

DEATH. In this city, on Saturday, the 8th inst., Mrs. MARY INGLE, consort of Joseph Ingle, deceased, formerly of Alexandria, Va., in the seventy first year of her age. Her funeral will take place from her late

Daily National Intelligencer, Marriage and Death Notices, 1851-1854

residence, north of the Jail, at three o'clock today, at which the friends and acquaintances of the family are respectfully invited to attend. (10 MAR 1851)

DEATH. On Saturday morning, the 8th inst., at the residence of his mother, on Congress street, Georgetown, Mr. JAMES O'REILLY, aged 32 years. His funeral will take place at 10 o'clock this (Monday) morning. The friends of the family are respectfully requested to attend. (10 MAR 1851)

DEATH. On the 1st inst., in Frederick Co., Md., WILLIAM HENRY, son of James and Sarah Elizabeth Owner, of Washington, D.C., aged 7 months and 21 days. (10 MAR 1851)

DEATH. On yesterday, the 10th inst., of consumption, at the residence of his father, A.C. Brown, in the village of Bladensburg, ROBERT T. BROWN, late of this city. His friends are respectfully invited to attend his funeral. (11 MAR 1851)

MARRIAGE. On Tuesday evening, by the Rev. John C. Smith, ISAAC H. WAILES, Esq., of this city, to Mrs. MARTHA NUGENT, of Columbia, Pa. (13 MAR 1851)

DEATH. At his residence, in Jefferson City, Mo., on the 21st ult., of pneumonia, Col. WILLIAM G. MINOR, formerly of Spotsylvania Co., Va., in the 45th year of his age. Col. Minor emigrated to Missouri in 1840, and, establishing himself at Jefferson City, entered upon the practice of his profession in the circuit of which Cole county forms a part. He at once took a prominent position among the bar of Missouri, and enjoyed to the close of his life a large and respectable practice, both in the Circuit and Supreme Courts of the State. During the greater part of the last eleven years he was editor of the *Jefferson Inquirer*. As one of the Commissioners appointed by the Supreme Court of the United States to survey and fix the boundary between this State and Iowa, he was engaged during the greater part of the past season, and, while thus busied, his health received a shock, from which, in the opinion of his friends, it had not fully recovered when his recent illness seized him. (13 MAR 1851)

DEATH. On Wednesday morning, 12th inst., at 3 o'clock, WILLIAM THOMAS, in the 10th year of his age, only son of Wm. S. and Ann W. Dove. The friends of the family are requested to attend his funeral this afternoon, at 4 o'clock, from the residence of his father, between 21st and 22d streets. (13 MAR 1851)

DEATH. In this city, on Friday evening, March 7, at 11 o'clock, MARY GERTRUDE JENKINS, aged ten months and ten days, only child of the late Leoline and Rosina L. Jenkins. (13 MAR 1851)

MARRIAGE. On Wednesday, the 12th inst., by the [Rev.] S.A.H. Marks, Mr. SYLVESTER F. GATES to Miss MARY JANE HOLROYD, all of Washington. (14 MAR 1851)

DEATH. On the 9th inst., Mrs. ELIZABETH BURFORD, aged 53 years. (14 MAR 1851)

DEATH. On Thursday morning, after a short illness, THOMAS SHIELDS, aged thirty-five years. His friends, and those of the family, are requested to attend his funeral on Saturday morning at ten o'clock, from the residence of his brother-in-law, Mr. J.P. McKean, on Second, between B and C streets. (14 MAR 1851)

DEATH. On Wednesday evening, the 13th inst., of croup, AMELIA JANE, daughter of J.T. and Louisa M. Quisenberry, of this city. The funeral will take place at 3 o'clock to-day, from the residence of her parents, corner of 15th street and Massachusetts avenue. (14 MAR 1851)

DEATH. On the evening of the 12th inst., JOSEPH E. LEWIS, son of Washington and Rachel Lewis, in the fourth year of his age. The funeral will take place from the residence of his parents, on Saturday morning, at ten o'clock. (14 MAR 1851)

Daily National Intelligencer, Marriage and Death Notices, 1851-1854

MARRIAGE. On Thursday evening, the 13th inst., by the Rev. Edmund C. Bittinger, U.S. Navy, E.T. CHAPPELL, Esq. to Miss HANNAH A. PLANT, both of this city. (15 MAR 1851)

DEATH. At Ash Grove, Fairfax Co., Va., on Wednesday morning, 12th inst., Mr. WILLIAM HERBERT, in the 65th year of his age. (15 MAR 1851)

DEATH. On Monday morning, the 17th inst., of croup, LOUISA MATILDA, daughter of J.T. and Louise Quisenberry, of this city. The funeral will take place this afternoon at 3 o'clock from the residence of her parents, corner of 15th and N streets and Massachusetts avenue. (18 MAR 1851)

DEATH. At Annapolis, on Sunday last, ALEXANDER RANDALL, Jr. son of Alexander and Catharine W. Randall, after a short and painful illness, in the second year of his age. (18 MAR 1851)

MARRIAGE. On the 18th inst., by the Rev. Mr. Woods, Mr. CHARLES EVERETT, Jr. to Miss HARRIET DUNDAS, daughter of William H. Dundas, Esq., all of Washington, D.C. (19 MAR 1851)

DEATH. At the residence of her son, in the vicinity of New York, on the 24th of February last, Mrs. ANN W. EVANS, for many years a resident of this city, but originally of Portsmouth, N.H., and the widow of the Hon. Richard Evans, of the latter place, deceased in 1816. It is richly due to the subject of this record, and also to the religious and intellectual world, to say that she sustained in life a character for the highest worth and for a superior understanding. She has left, besides her children, many relations and friends, who will cherish her memory with that priceless affection which rests on esteem. (19 MAR 1851)

MARRIAGE. On the 8th inst., at St. Louis, (Mo.) by the Very Rev. A. O'Regan, Lieut. JAMES A. HARDIE, 3d Regiment U.S. Artillery, to MARGARET HUNTER, niece of the late Gen. R.B. Mason, U.S. Army. (20 MAR 1851)

DEATH. At the Highlands, on Wednesday morning, the 19th inst., Major CHARLES L. NOURSE, late of the U.S. Army. The funeral will take place at Rock Creek Church, this (Thursday) afternoon, at 4 o'clock. (20 MAR 1851)

DEATH. At his residence in Harper's Ferry, (Va.) on the 12th inst., HENRY STIPES, Esq., in the 55th year of his age. He was one of the oldest citizens of that place, and was loved and respected by all who knew him. He lived and died a true Christian, and in the hope of a blessed immortality. (20 MAR 1851)

DEATH. At the Washington Infirmary, PETER HAUSENPFLUTE, aged 50 years, a native of Germany, and for some years past a resident of Harrisburg, Pa. (20 MAR 1851)

DEATH. Yesterday, at her residence in this city, after a brief illness, Madame CARVALLO, the excellent and universally respected consort of Don Manuel Carvallo, the esteemed Minister of the Republic of Chile. (21 MAR 1851)

DEATH. On Thursday, the 20th inst., of consumption, Mr. ALLEN A. THOMPSON, Printer, in the 51st year of his age. The funeral will take place tomorrow morning, at 10 o'clock, from his late residence on F, between 13th and 14th streets. The relatives and friends of the family are respectfully invited to attend. (21 MAR 1851)

DEATH. At Georgetown, on the 20th inst., after protracted illness, JANE ANNA GUY, in the 24th year of her age. Her funeral will take place from the residence of her brother-in-law, LEVI DAVIS, on Market street, at half-past 3 o'clock, this afternoon. (21 MAR 1851)

DEATH. At The Hive, near Hagerstown, Md., on Tuesday, the 18th inst., of bilious pleurisy, WILLIAM H. FITZHUGH, eldest son of the late Col. WILLIAM FITZHUGH, of Livingston Co., N.Y. "*Earth is embittered to us that Heaven may be endeared.*" (21 MAR 1851)

Daily National Intelligencer, Marriage and Death Notices, 1851-1854

DEATH. On Thursday, the 20th inst., Mrs. ELIZABETH D. THOMPSON, in the 73d year of her age. Her friends and those of her family are respectfully invited to attend her funeral, to take place at the residence of her son, Henry Thompson, on Sunday, at 3 o'clock. (22 MAR 1851)

DEATH. In this city, yesterday, about eight o'clock, Mrs. CATHARINE ADAMS, consort of Mr. Leonard Adams, in the sixty-ninth year of her age. Her funeral will take place on Sunday morning, at twelve o'clock, from the residence of her husband, on New York avenue, between 12th and 13th streets, where her friends and acquaintances are invited to attend punctually. (22 MAR 1851)

DEATH. At his lodgings in this city, on Saturday last, after a lingering illness, of pulmonary consumption, Hon. ISAAC HILL, of New Hampshire, formerly Governor of that State, and during six years a Senator from it in Congress. (24 MAR 1851)

DEATH. On Sunday morning, the 23d, after a painful illness of several months, which he bore with Christian fortitude, JOHN CLAXTON, in the 77th year of his age. The deceased was a native of Norfolk, England, but for the last thirty-five years a citizen of Georgetown, D.C. The funeral will take place from his late residence on Bridge street this afternoon, at 4 o'clock, at which time the friends and acquaintances of the family are invited to attend. (24 MAR 1851)

DEATH. In this city, at half-past nine o'clock on Saturday morning, (22d inst.,) Mr. William Ward, aged seventy-five years. He was a native of Ireland, and for nearly half a century a resident of this city. The funeral services will be performed today (Monday) at St. Patrick's Church, at nine o'clock, where the friends of the family are invited to attend. (24 MAR 1851)

DEATH. On the 12th inst., at the residence of Doctor SAMUEL WILSON, in the county of Surry, Va., Mrs. ANNIE ELIZA HUNNICUTT, wife of John A. Hunnicutt, in the 34th year of her age. (24 MAR 1851)

DEATH. On the 22d inst., at an advanced age, Hon. SAMUEL GREEN, formerly Judge of the Superior Court of the State of New Hampshire, and for the last twelve years a clerk in the office of the Secretary of the Treasury. (24 MAR 1851) The funeral of the late Judge SAMUEL GREEN will take place from the house of Miss Briscoe, corner of 7th street and Pennsylvania avenue, today, at half-past 3 o'clock. His friends are respectfully requested to attend without further invitation. (25 MAR 1851)

MARRIAGE. On the 18th inst., by the Rev. Mr. French, LEOPOLD NEUMEYER to MARGARET A., eldest daughter of Josiah Eagleson, of Baltimore. (25 MAR 1851)

DEATH. On the 22d inst., THEODORE F., aged 5 years 2 months and 12 days, only son of John M. and Adeline Mankins, after a short but painful illness. The friends and acquaintances of the family are respectfully invited to attend his funeral from the residence of his grandfather, on 19th street, this morning at 10 o'clock. (25 MAR 1851)

DEATH. On Sunday, March 23d, JAMES TAYLOR, a native of England, in the 41st year of his age. (26 MAR 1851)

MARRIAGE. At New York, on the 18th inst., by the Rev. Mr. Carder, Lieut. HENRY W. STANTON, U.S. Dragoons, to Miss SARAH MACOMB, daughter of the late Major General Macomb, U.S. Army. (27 MAR 1851)

DEATH. In the city of Richmond, Va., after a few hours illness, the Rev. JOHN SCHERMERHORN, in the 65th year of his age. He was an officer under Gen. Jackson's administration as Indian agent in the Western States, and was at the time of his death attending to some lands he had recently gained by a suit in Richmond. This notice is given that his family and friends may learn of his death, and that he had every attention paid him in his last hours. (28 MAR 1851)

Daily National Intelligencer, Marriage and Death Notices, 1851-1854

DEATH. At his residence, in Prince George's Co., Md., on the 25th inst., CLEMENT BADEN, Esq., in the 69th year of his age. During the late war with England, he held a commission in the service of his native State, and was frequently called into active service. In later life he filled for many years the office of magistrate, with credit to himself and usefulness to the public. In the various relations which he sustained to society and to his family, as citizen, magistrate, husband, and father, he was noted for the propriety, urbanity, and dignity of his manners — but above all, for his unflinching integrity and good faith. He has left a numerous and highly respectable family, with a wide circle of friends. to mourn his loss. (29 MAR 1851)

DEATH. In New Orleans, on the 12th of March, JAMES W. DOUGHTY, a highly respectable and esteemed merchant of St. Louis, Mo., aged thirty-five years. (29 MAR 1851)

DEATH. In Washington, JAMES CAUSTEN, infant son of Manuel and Mary deCarvallo, of Chile; born on the 16th and died on the 30th of March, 1851 — ten days after his mother. (31 MAR 1851)

DEATH. On Sunday morning, March 30th, Mrs. ELENOR HARBAUGH, consort of Joseph Harbaugh, in the 69th year of her age. The friends and acquaintances of the family are invited to attend her funeral on Tuesday morning at 10 o'clock. (31 MAR 1851)

DEATH. On Saturday evening last, 29th inst., SALLY BOGAN OTT, in the twelfth year of her age, third daughter of John D. and Mary Ann Ott, of this city. The friends of the family are respectfully invited to attend the funeral of the deceased from the residence of her father, on Vermont avenue, between H and I streets, at 3 P.M. (Monday) this day. (31 MAR 1851)

DEATH. On the 31st of March, at 9 o'clock A.M., THOMAS DIXON, son of John and Marry [sic] Ann Hands, aged 8 years. His funeral will take place from his father's residence on 4½ street, at 4 o'clock this (Tuesday) afternoon. (1 APR 1851)

DEATH. Yesterday morning, the 1st inst., LAURA VIRGINIA, infant daughter of Wm. A. and Wilmina E. Richardson. (2 APR 1851)

MARRIAGE. On Wednesday, 2d inst., at St. John's Church, Baltimore, by the Rev. Mr. Webster, Mr. GEORGE R.P. BRITT, to Miss GEORGIANNA H. MITCHELL, both of Baltimore, Maryland. (3 APR 1851)

DEATH. On the morning of the 3d inst., after a painful illness, which was borne with Christian fortitude, Capt. CHARLES BRADFORD, of Duxbury, Mass., in the 85th year of his age, long a respected citizen of Alexandria, and for some years past of Washington. May he rest in peace! The friends of the family are respectfully invited to attend his funeral, from the residence of his son-in-law, S. Masi, on E street, between 9th and 10th streets, of half-past 3 o'clock this afternoon. (4 APR 1851)

DEATH. At Keokuk, Iowa, on the 27th of March, GEORGE PIERCY, son of the late Capt. John McKnight, of Alexandria, Va. (4 APR 1851)

DEATH. March the 30th, at his residence, Locust Grove, Prince George's Co., Md., in his forty-ninth year, BENJAMIN M. DUCKETT, after a brief but violent attack of inflammatory fever. The deceased was extensively known and universally respected. The writer of this tribute of love to the memory of the departed, sincerely believes that he died without one single enemy. He was liberal, disinterested, frank and sincere. His heart was open to sympathy and pity for the misfortunes and necessities of his fellow man, and the needy and unfortunate never appealed to him in vain. He was a man of the strictest integrity and veracity, his word was universally known to be his bond, and he would have infinitely preferred death to falsehood, deceit, fraud, or dishonor. His mind was vigorous and active, and his judgment clear, and had he preferred the exciting career of a politician to the quiet and peaceable pursuit of agriculture, he would have discharged honestly, faithfully, and prudently the duties of any office or trust that might have been confided in his care. He was devoted to the wants of his family in the various relations of husband, father, and master. He left a devoted wife and five children, with many relatives, friends, and acquaintances, to mourn his loss. (5 APR 1851)

DEATH. On Saturday morning, the 5th inst., Commodore ALEXANDER S. WADSWORTH, of the U.S. Navy, in the 61st year of his age. The Funeral will take place from his late residence, Franklin Row, at 12 o'clock M. on Tuesday. Officers of the Navy and Army, and the friends of the family, are respectfully invited to attend. (7 APR 1851)

DEATH. On the 5th inst., after a painful and protracted illness, which she bore with Christian resignation, Mrs. HARRIET KNOBLOCH, in the 43d year of her age. Her Funeral will take place from her late residence on 19th street, near H, this (Monday) afternoon, at 3 o'clock. (7 APR 1851)

MARRIAGE. On the 31st March, at Columbia, Fluvanna Co., Va., by the Rev. Mr. Clover, JAMES M. ESTES, of Palmyra, to SUSAN R., daughter of Joseph Hodgson. (8 APR 1851)

DEATH. In Georgetown, on the evening of the 8th inst., of consumption, Miss MARY MILLER, daughter of William Parsons, Esq. The friends of the family are respectfully invited to attend her funeral this afternoon, at 3 o'clock, from the residence of her father, on High street. (10 APR 1851)

MARRIAGE. On Tuesday evening, the 1st inst., at Solona, Fairfax Co., Va., by the Rev. F.N. Whaley, JAS. T. CLOSE, Esq. of Saratoga Co., N.Y., to Miss A. ELIZA SHERMAN. (11 APR 1851)

DEATH. At his residence, in Bladensburg, on yesterday, the 10th inst., the Rev. JOHN SMITH, of the Methodist Episcopal Church. His funeral will take place tomorrow morning, at 10 o'clock. (11 APR 1851)

MARRIAGE. On Thursday evening, April 10th, by the Rev. Mr. Morgan, Mr. THOMAS W. SNAPE, of England, to Miss MARY A. PIERCE, of this city. (12 APR 1851)

MARRIAGE. On Tuesday evening, the 11th February, by the Rev. Mr. Tillinghast, Mr. CHARLES ALLEN to Mrs. MARY E. BAGGETT, both of Georgetown. (12 APR 1851)

DEATH. On the evening of 10th April, Mrs. ELEANORA FALCONER, widow of the late Elisha Falconer, of Frederick Co., Md., in the 64th year of her age. Her funeral will take place from the residence of her son, (Mr. R.J. Falconer,) 7th street, on Saturday afternoon at 3½ o'clock, at which time all the relatives and friends of the family are respectfully invited to attend without further notice. (12 APR 1851)

DEATH. On Friday morning, April 11th, JOHN WINGERD, second son of John P. and Ann Wingerd. His friends, and those of the family, are requested to attend his funeral from the residence of his parents on Green street, near Gay, Georgetown, this (Saturday) afternoon at 3 o'clock. (12 APR 1851)

DEATH. On Friday night last [11 APR 1851], Mr. JAMES CARBERY, aged about 59 years. His funeral will take place from his late residence on Saturday evening, at 3 o'clock. His friends are invited to attend. (12 APR 1851)

MARRIAGE. In Georgetown, on the 7th inst., by the Rev. F.G. Binney, ADONIS L. YERBY, of Washington, to MARY S., daughter of Joseph Radcliffe, Esq., of the former place. (16 APR 1851)

DEATH. At the residence of his nephew on C street, between 12th and 13th streets, Mr. JOSEPH KNOX BOYD, a resident of this city for the last nineteen years. His funeral will take place on Thursday afternoon, the 17th inst., at 3 o'clock. The relatives and friends of the family are respectfully invited to attend. (16 APR 1851)

Daily National Intelligencer, Marriage and Death Notices, 1851-1854

DEATH. At New York, on Sunday morning, MARIA GRAHAM, wife of Commander John S. Chauncey, U.S. Navy, and eldest daughter of the late David Graham, Esq. (16 APR 1851)

MARRIAGE. At Rochester, N.Y., on the 12th inst., at St. Luke's Church, by the Rev. H.W. Lee, Major E.S. SIBLEY, U.S. Army, to Miss CHARLOTTE H., youngest daughter of the late Seth Saxton, of that city. (17 APR 1851)

OBITUARY. In announcing the death of the late JOSEPH KNOX BOYD, a few words may not be inappropriate, as a matter of justice to the deceased, showing one action in his life sufficient to give honor to the longest life, and, as the councils of his country have never given him a token of his merit, it rests with his friends to show their appreciation of it. The daring and bold exploit of the burning of the frigate *Philadelphia* in the harbor of Tripoli, to prevent the Turks from availing themselves of their prize, at night, and within musket-shot of their batteries, must be fresh in the minds of his countrymen. So hazardous an enterprise could not be undertaken in the course of regular naval duty; it was only to be accomplished by volunteers--by ready hands and willing hearts. Seventy brave men instantly offered their services, (the deceased was among the first.) Forward they moved to what must have appeared inevitable death; but, acted upon by the purest spirit of patriotism and the courage of brave men, they determined to effect their purpose or meet a noble death. The sequel is known--it is recorded upon the brightest page of history. One by one these gallant men have descended to their graves. A few days since but two remained; and now the gallant Commodore Morris is the sole survivor of that patriotic seventy. Few men have ever won brighter laurels, and their names should belong to the history of that country in whose service they performed this brilliant achievement. (18 APR 1851)

MARRIAGE. On Tuesday, the 15th inst., by the Rev. Mr. Gorsuch, Mr. EDWARD S. ALLEN to Miss MARTHA CAMMACK, daughter of Mr. Wm. Cammack, all of this city. (18 APR 1851)

DEATHS. In this city, on the 16th inst., GEORGE STRICKLAND. His friends and acquaintances are invited to attend his funeral this day, (Friday,) at 9 o'clock A.M., at the dwelling of Mrs. James, F street, between 12th and 13th. (18 APR 1851)

DEATH. On the evening of the 16th inst., at 10½ o'clock, ERNEST, son of Z.D. and H.P. GILMAN, in the 3d year of his age. (18 APR 1851)

DEATH. On the 18th inst., at one P.M., MARY, consort of Stephen Pleasonton, Esq., Fifth Auditor of the Treasury, in the 67th year of her age. The friends and acquaintances of the family are requested to attend her funeral on Tuesday next, at 12 o'clock, M. (19 APR 1851)

DEATH. On the 18th inst., Major ERASTUS T. COLLINS, of the Pension Office, in the 58th year of his age. The friends of the family are invited to attend his funeral, from the residence of Mr. Tingle, corner of 12th and F streets, on Sunday, at 3 o'clock P.M. (19 APR 1851)

DEATH. At White Sulphur Springs, Greenbrier Co., Va., a few days ago, JAMES CALDWELL, Esq., after a few hours' illness, in the 78th year of his age. He was a native of Maryland, and for many years a merchant in Baltimore, but since 1818 he was the popular proprietor of the White Sulphur Springs, where he died generally respected and highly esteemed. (19 APR 1851)

DEATH. In Frederick Co., Md., on the 14th inst., after a severe illness, which he bore with Christian patience, THOS. C. FARQUHAR, aged 31 years and 10 months. (19 APR 1851)

DEATH. In this city, yesterday morning, Mrs. AMELIA DUNN, in the 81st year of her age. The friends of the family are invited to attend her funeral this afternoon (Monday) at 3 o'clock, from her late residence over the Bank of Washington. (21 APR 1851)

Daily National Intelligencer, Marriage and Death Notices, 1851-1854

MARRIAGE. In Trinity Church, in this city, on Wednesday the 16th inst., by Rev. Dr. C.M. Butler, Mr. JAMES C. WALKER, of Tennessee, to Miss CAROLINE C. CHRISTIAN, of Virginia. (22 APR 1851)

MARRIAGE. On Monday evening, by the Rev. John C. Smith, Mr. JAMES FORD to Miss SARAH DOVE, all of this city. (23 APR 1851)

MARRIAGE. On Monday, the 21st inst., in the Church of the Ascension, by the Rev. L.J. Gilliss, the Rev. HENRY J. WINDSOR, Rector of East New Market Parish, Dorchester Co., Md., to Miss SUSAN HARRIET, daughter of the late Cephas W. Benson, Esq., of Prince George's Co., Md. (23 APR 1851)

MARRIAGE. On the 22d inst., by the Rev. James B. Donelan, CHARLES EDWARD THOMAS, of Norfolk, Va., to Miss JANE ELIZABETH, daughter of Ephraim French, of New Milford, Conn. (24 APR 1851)

MARRIAGE. In Baltimore, on the 22d inst., by the Rev. Mr. Berry, Dr. LOUIS MARSHALL, Jr. to MARGARET W. McVEAN, all of Georgetown, D.C. (24 and 25 APR 1851)

DEATH. In Georgetown, D.C., April 22d, of pulmonary consumption, Miss MARIA BOOTES, eldest daughter of the late Samuel Bootes. The friends of the family are respectfully invited to attend her funeral on Thursday afternoon at 5 o'clock, from her late residence on Bridge street. (24 APR 1851)

DEATH. On Wednesday, 23d inst., ROSE FRANCES TRENHOLM, aged nine months. The friends of the family are requested to attend the funeral this afternoon at 3½ o'clock, from the residence of her parents, on E street near 10th. (24 APR 1851)

MARRIAGE. On Tuesday, the 22d inst., at St. Matthew's Church, by the Rev. James B. Donelan, Mr. JAMES C. ESLIN, of Washington Co., D.C., to Miss HARRIET E. LANHAM, of Prince George's Co., Md. (25 APR 1851)

DEATH. The following notice will convey sad intelligence to numerous relatives and friends in Baltimore and Alexandria. Mrs. LAWRASON was previous to her marriage Miss Carson. The writer of this has known her for fifty years, and a more lovely girl was not in the town she lived in, or a more affectionate devoted wife, kind mother, or generous friend. *From the New Orleans Commercial Bulletin of 14th April.* Died, on Friday morning, the 11th inst., after a short illness, at the residence of her son, in this city, in the sixtieth year of her age, Mrs. ELIZABETH LAWRASON, wife of the late Thomas Lawrason, of Alexandria, Va. (25 APR 1851)

DEATH. On the 22d inst., CHARLES EUGENE Van VALLENBURG, aged one year and three months. The friends of the family are requested to attend the funeral from the residence of his parents, on 12th street, between G and H, today at three o'clock. (25 APR 1851)

MARRIAGE. On the 24th inst., by the Rev. C.M. Butler, Mr. JOHN WILEY, formerly of Philadelphia, to Miss EMILY F. BROWN, of Washington. (26 APR 1851)

MARRIAGE. On the 24th inst., at St. Mary's Church, by the Rev. Mr. Alig, JOHN BOHN to ELIZABETH MARTELL. (26 APR 1851)

MARRIAGE. On the 10th inst., Mr. MICHAEL BRICK to MARGARET CRAY. (26 APR 1851)

MARRIAGE. On the 10th inst., JEREMIAH NOLEN to MARTHA GORDEN. (26 APR 1851)

MARRIAGE. On the 8th of March, TIMOTHY HOURLY to JULIANA HOURLY, all of this city. (26 APR 1851)

Daily National Intelligencer, Marriage and Death Notices, 1851-1854

DEATH. At his residence in this city, on Thursday, the 24th inst., Dr. CHARLES BEALE HAMILTON, in the 60th year of his age. Dr. Hamilton entered the navy in 1811 as surgeon's mate, and served under Commodore Warrington during the whole of the last war with Great Britain, with distinguished usefulness and ability. After the close of the war he continued in the naval service for several years as surgeon, and finally resigned his commission to practice his profession, in which he had acquired eminent skill and experience, both as a surgeon and physician. Preferring the pleasing and active pursuits of agriculture, however, to the profession of medicine, he abandoned the practice, except within a very limited circle, and purchased a farm a few miles from Washington, to which, by his industry and science, he gave in a few years a beauty and fertility that attracted every eye. Dr. Hamilton was a gentleman of high moral character; just, humane, benevolent, and useful; high-minded and honorable in no ordinary degree; and in all the relations of life most exemplary. He sinks into the grave with a memory embalmed in the affections of all who knew him--for "none knew him but to love him"--leaving behind him an afflicted widow to lament her irreparable loss, and to mourn over her melancholy bereavement. The Funeral of Dr. Hamilton will take place at 12 o'clock today, from his late residence on south B street, Capitol Hill. The friends of the family are respectfully requested to attend the funeral. (26 APR 1851)

DEATH. On Thursday afternoon, the 24th inst., SAMUEL THOMAS PETTIT, son of Charles Pettit, in the 26th year of his age. The friends and acquaintances of the family are requested to attend his funeral tomorrow (Sunday) afternoon, at 3 o'clock, from the residence of his father, on E street, between 5th and 6th streets. (26 APR 1851)

DEATH. At Philadelphia, on Thursday, Brevet Major THOMAS B. LINNARD, of the Corps of Topographical Engineers, U.S. Army, in the 41st year of his age. (26 APR 1851)

DEATH. At the St. Charles Hotel, on the 25th inst., JEANET St. CLAIR, infant daughter of George A.D. and Mary V. Clarke. (26 APR 1851)

MARRIAGE. On the 23d inst., at Trinity Church, by the Rev. Mr. Pyne, ALBERT RAY to AMANDA J., daughter of Capt. R.E. CLARY, United States Army. (28 APR 1851)

MARRIAGE. On Thursday last, at the Theological Episcopal Seminary, Alexandria Co., Va., by the Rev. Mr. Lockwood, FELIX RICHARDS, Esq. to Miss ANN AMELIA H. MACRAE, all of said county. (28 APR 1851)

MARRIAGE. In St. Peter's Church, Baltimore, on the 10th inst., by the Rev. Mr. Williams, RICHARD H. HAGNER, Esq. to ANNIE M., daughter of the late Dr. HUNGERFORD, all of Calvert Co., Md. (28 APR 1851)

DEATH. On Wednesday, April 23d, at the Infirmary, GEORGE HOMEWOOD, a native of England, but for the last eighteen or twenty years a resident of Washington. (29 APR 1851)

DEATH. At Hopeten, on the 26th inst., of scarlet fever, BENJAMIN ERNEST, aged two years one month and two days, son of Joseph C. and Mary K. Lewis. (29 APR 1851)

OBITUARY. From the *Philadelphia Inquirer* of April 23 [1851]. Died, at Washington, on Friday last, MARY PLEASANTON, wife of STEPHEN PLEASONTON, Esq., and daughter of the late John Hopkins, Esq., of Lancaster Co., Pa. In the death of this estimable lady, her family has experienced a severe bereavement, and a wide-spread circle of friends an afflicting loss. It is the lot of few in this world to garner up such stores of affection and esteem as were bestowed upon her, and the lot of few so richly to deserve them. A peaceful self-possession of mind, a warm and generous heart, a sound discriminating judgment, a firm but affectionate sense of duty, regulated all her actions. The poor have lost in her a kind and sympathetic friend; the stranger, whom duty or pleasure brought within her sphere, a generous entertainer. Her hospitality was as unaffected and refined as her association was pleasing and instructive. Her intelligence of character is amply recorded in the minds of a large portion of the most distinguished of the land. Her peaceful virtues will ever be remembered with gratitude by the poor and humble. To the partner of her bosom and her surviving children, she has left a rich legacy of virtues to be cherished. May the remembrance of these in some measure soothe the anguish which her loss has occasioned! This humble memorial is the heartfelt tribute of a friend, who, in a long course of years, has witnessed what he has recorded, and felt what he desires may not be easily forgotten. (29 APR 1851)

MARRIAGE. At Baltimore, on Monday morning, the 28th inst., by the Rev. Dr. Pyne, of St. John's Church, Washington, His Excellency ALPHONSE DE BORBOULON, Minister from France to China, to KATHARINE, youngest daughter of Alexander Norman MacLeod, Esq., formerly of Isle Harris, Scotland. (30 APR 1851)

DEATH. In Washington, on Wednesday, 30th April, at the residence of her daughter, Mrs. Louisa Delany, on Missouri avenue, at half-past 12 o'clock A.M., Mrs. MARY ANN VILLARD, widow of the late R.H.L. VILLARD, of Georgetown, D.C., in the 53d year of her age. Her funeral will take place this (Thursday) morning, at 11 o'clock, from Trinity Church, (corner of Third and C streets,) at which time and place her friends and acquaintances are requested to attend. (1 MAY 1851)

DEATH. Sudden and Melancholy Death. — We learn that Mr. JOHN C. MULLAY, of Pennsylvania, a clerk in the Indian Bureau, was, at eleven o'clock Tuesday morning, taken with an apoplectic or epileptic attack, and, notwithstanding the presence and utmost endeavors of several eminent medical gentlemen, he died within a few hours. His wife was promptly summoned, and was by his side when he expired. Mr. Mullay was in the 38th year of his age, and greatly respected for his general intelligence and high qualifications for his official trust, to which he had been but recently promoted. His funeral will take place this afternoon at 4 o'clock, from his late residence on H street, near 18th street. The friends of the family are invited to attend without further notice. (1 MAY 1851)

OBITUARY. Departed this life, at Jackson Court-house, Va., on the 16th of March, 1851, Mrs. JANE H., consort of Fleet Smith, Esq., (late of Washington, D.C.) in the 66th year of her age. The deceased was retiring and unobtrusive in her deportment. She had many friends and relatives, whose sympathy will be freely afforded to those relatives who compose the domestic circle of which she was so lately a member. She had for the greater portion of her life been a communicant in the Presbyterian Church, and cherished in her old age, when bowed down by continued infirmity and disease, the hopes of that blessed immortality beyond the grave, where "the wicked cease from troubling, and the weary are at rest." (1 MAY 1851)

MARRIAGE. On the 30th ult., by the Rev. Mr. Morgan, Mr. HENRY F.B. PARDON, of England, to Miss VIRGINIA C.M. BARRON, of this city. (2 MAY 1851)

MARRIAGE. At Haddock's Hills, near Washington, on Tuesday, the 29th ult., by the Rev. Daniel Lynch, of Georgetown College, JOHN F. BOONE, of Washington, to HENRIETTA H. DYER, of the same place, daughter of the late Capt. Joseph Tarbel, of the U.S. Navy. (2 MAY 1851)

DEATH. On Tuesday, 29th of April, at a quarter before 8 o'clock P.M., JOHN BLACKSTON RILEY, aged 23 years, third son of the late Thos. R. Riley, of this city. His funeral will take place on Friday, May 2d, at 4 o'clock P.M., from the late residence of his father, corner of Ninth and H streets, Island. Friends of the family are invited to attend. (2 MAY 1851)

MARRIAGE. Philadelphia, on the 1st inst., by the Rev. J.Y. Ward, Mr. JOHN B. WARD, of this city, to Miss LOUISA P., daughter of E.W. David, Counsellor at Law, of the former city. (3 MAY 1851)

MARRIAGE. On the 29th April, at Baltimore, by the Rev. George W. Burnap, HENRY ROLANDO, U.S.N., to ANN ELIZABETH, daughter of Dr. Jno. Buckler. (5 MAY 1851)

DEATH. On Friday, the 2d inst., JOHN GEORGE, son of J.G. and Lydia Weaver, aged two years, four months and nine days. (5 MAY 1851)

Daily National Intelligencer, Marriage and Death Notices, 1851-1854

OBITUARY. The Late Major LINNARD. This distinguished and accomplished officer, whose decease in the full meridian of manhood has just occurred in Philadelphia, was a native of that city. He graduated at the Military Academy, and was commissioned a Lieutenant in the Second Regiment of Artillery in 1830 [text continues]. (5 MAY 1851)

OBITUARY. The late Mrs. MARY ANN VILLARD was a native of Philadelphia, but had been a resident of the District of Columbia for the last thirty-five years. She has passed into "the rest that remaineth for the people of God," after protracted and dreadful sufferings [text continues]. (6 MAY 1851)

OBITUARY. Died, at Woodsfield, Ohio, on the 1st inst., after a short but severe illness, Mr. ENOS M. MORRIS, in the 24th year of his age, son of the Hon. Joseph Morris... During the administration of President Polk the deceased was a resident of Washington, and by his gentlemanly and amiable deportment won the affection and esteem of all who made his acquaintance. But he is gone, and we humbly trust to the fruition of a well-spent life. (6 MAY 1851)

DEATH. On Saturday, the 3d inst., of dropsy in the chest, BENJAMIN FRANKLIN, son of Martha Jane and the late Benjamin Franklin Coston, aged five years and four months. (6 MAY 1851)

MARRIAGE. On Tuesday morning, the 6th inst., in the Church of the Ascension, by the Rev. L.J. Gilliss, ELIJAH W. DAY, Esq., of Port Tobacco, Md., to Miss MARY LATIMER, of this city. (7 MAY 1851)

MARRIAGE. On the 29th April, at St. Mary's Church, by the Rev. Mathias Alig, JOHN FREEMAN to Miss CAROLINA WALTER, both of this city. (8 MAY 1851)

MARRIAGE. On the 4th of May, by the Rev. Mathias Alig, THOS. DONOHO to Miss JANE MURTER, of this city. (8 MAY 1851)

MARRIAGE. On the 6th inst., by the Rev. Mr. French, JOHN F. MULLOWNY, Esq., late U.S. Consul at Tangiers, to Miss AMANDA L. TURPIN, of this city. (8 MAY 1851)

DEATH. In the city of Jackson, Miss., on the 18th ult., in the 44th year of her age, Mrs. ANN ALIZA JOHNSON, consort of the Rev. W.P.C. Johnson, of St. Andrew's Church of that city, leaving several children and numerous friends to mourn her loss. Mrs. Johnson was a native of Fairfax Co., Va., and a niece of the late Judge Bushrod Washington, under whose hospitable roof at Mt. Vernon she spent much of her youth. Her character was adorned with all Christian and feminine graces, and her death exhibited a bright example of the triumph of religious hope. (8 MAY 1851)

DEATH. On board the sloop-of-war *Warren*, off San Francisco, on the 15th March, Lieut. WM. H. THOMPSON, of the U.S. Navy. (8 MAY 1851)

MARRIAGE. On Thursday morning, at Wesley Chapel, by Rev. Mr. Kenny, THOMAS W. GRAYSON, Esq., Editor of *Washington (Pa.) Examiner*, to Miss MAY ELIZABETH, daughter of Mr. A. Green, of this city. (9 MAY 1851)

DEATH. In this city yesterday, in the 72d year of her age, Mrs. CATHARINE GOLDSBOROUGH, relict of the late C.W. Goldsborough. Her funeral will take place tomorrow, at 3 o'clock P.M., from her late residence at Mrs. Ford's, corner of F and 19th streets, which her friends and acquaintants are respectfully invited to attend. (10 MAY 1851)

DEATH. On Friday afternoon, the 9th inst., MARY A. HOLLAND, daughter of John E. and Susannah Holland, in the 10th year of her age. The friends of the family are invited to attend her funeral from the residence of her father, on H street, between 6th and 7th streets, on Sunday afternoon at 2 o'clock. (10 MAY 1851)

Daily National Intelligencer, Marriage and Death Notices, 1851-1854

MARRIAGE. In Brooklyn, N.Y., by the Rev. Doctor Bethune, on Wednesday, the 7th inst., at the residence of her father, Miss CAROLINE ELIZABETH, youngest daughter of Robert Speir, Esq., to LEONARD CASSELL McPHAIL, M.D., late Surgeon U.S. Army. (12 MAY 1851)

DEATH. On the evening of the 28th of March, at Memphis, Tenn., WILLIAM LANPHIER, in the 78th year of his age. He was born in Fairfax Co., Va., and was a descendant of the Huguenots. His grandfather and father emigrated from Ireland to this country in 1732, and settled at Port Tobacco, Md. Since 1784 he had been a resident of Alexandria, Va., until he moved to Memphis in 1845. (12 MAY 1851)

DEATH. On the 14th of April last, at the residence of her son-in-law, P.D.G. Hedgman, Esq., in Stafford Co., Va., Mrs. HANNAH B. HEDGMAN, relict of John G. Hedgman, Esq., for many years delegate from that county, in the 72d year of her age. Her spirit had been severely tried by peculiarly afflicting bereavements, but she bore them with the resignation and fortitude of a true and zealous Christian. (12 MAY 1851)

DEATH. Yesterday morning, at two o'clock, after an illness of nine weeks, WILLIAM W. BILLING, the only son of the late WILLIAM W. BILLING, aged twelve years and five months. His funeral will take place from the residence of his mother, on H street north, near 6th street, this (Monday) evening at 4 o'clock. (12 MAY 1851)

DEATH. On the 10th inst., after a few hours' illness, EMMA ELBERTA, aged two years ten months and two days, youngest daughter of Greenberry and Thomazine M. Rowzee. (12 MAY 1851)

MARRIAGE. In Trinity Church, Washington, on Tuesday, the 13th inst., by the Rev. Dr. Butler, MATHEW HARRISON, Esq., of Virginia, to HARRIETTE L., daughter of General Walter Jones. (14 MAY 1851)

MARRIAGE. In Baltimore Co., Md., on Thursday, the 8th inst., by the Rev. Mr. Hamner, SAMUEL B. BEYER, of Washington, D.C., to Miss SARAH A., daughter of James Reeside, Esq., of Baltimore county. (14 MAY 1851)

DEATH. In Cincinnati, Ohio, on the 29th ult., of typhoid fever, CHARLES H. GOLDSBOROUGH, second son of the late Charles W. Goldsborough, of this city. (14 MAY 1851)

The funeral of Mrs. CATHARINE V. DAY will take place this afternoon, at 2 o'clock, from the residence of her father, George W. Freedley, on D street north, between 13th and 13½ streets. The friends and acquaintances of the family are respectfully invited to attend. (14 MAY 1851)

MARRIAGE. In Wesley Chapel, Washington, on Wednesday morning, the 14th inst., by the Rev. G.W. Israel, JAMES WILLIAMS, Esq., of Montgomery Co, Md., to MARTHA A. ISRAEL, of the former place. (15 MAY 1851)

DEATH. At Baltimore, on Tuesday last [6 MAY 1851], after a short illness, in the 62 year of his age, Gen. WILLIAM H. MARRIOTT, long a respected resident of that city, and formerly the Collector of the port of Baltimore. (15 MAY 1851)

MARRIAGE. On Thursday evening [15 MAY 1851], by the Rev. John C. Smith, BUSHROD JOLLY, Esq., to Miss LUCINDA J. BREWER, both of Upperville, Va. (17 MAY 1851)

DEATH. On Thursday evening [15 MAY 1851], at quarter past 6 o'clock, ADELAIDE CAROTHERS, daughter of John T. and Emily S. Given, aged 4 years and 9 months. (17 MAY 1851)

MARRIAGE. On Thursday, the 15th inst., by the Rev. Mr. Massey, J.T. RADCLIFF, of Washington, to LOUISA HARRISON, daughter of the late Joseph Harrison, of Talbot Co., Md. (19 MAY 1851)

Daily National Intelligencer, Marriage and Death Notices, 1851-1854

MARRIAGE. On Thursday, the 15th inst., by the Rev. Mr. Hodges, Mr. STARK B. TAYLOR, to Miss MARY ELLEN NORRIS, all of Washington. (19 MAY 1851)

MARRIAGE. On Wednesday evening last [7 MAY 1851], by the Rev. C.A. Davis, THOMAS SHACKLEFORD to FRANCES DAVIS, both of Prince William Co., Va. (19 MAY 1851)

MARRIAGE. On Thursday evening [15 MAY 1851] by Rev. C.A. Davis, HENRY YEATMAN to SUSAN AMELIA THOMPSON, all of that city [Prince William Co.]. (19 MAY 1851)

MARRIAGE. On the 17th inst., by the Rev. O.B. Brown, CHAS. G. GRIFFITH, Esq., of Baltimore, to Miss FRANCES, daughter of HAZARD KNOWLES, Esq., of Washington. (21 MAY 1851)

DEATH. On the 18th inst., of scarlet fever, CLARENCE S.M., aged 4 years 6 months and 15 days, son of J.G. and Lydia Weaver. (21 MAY 1851)

DEATH. At Buffalo, 11th inst., EBENEZER F. NORTON, aged 77 years. Mr. Norton, some twenty five years ago, represented [this] district in Congress. (21 MAY 1851)

DEATH. At Poughkeepsie, N.Y., on the 13th inst., MARY ELIZABETH CUNNINGHAM, eldest daughter of Gen. Walter Cunningham, of that city. (21 MAY 1851)

DEATH. On Tuesday evening, after a painful illness, which he bore with Christian resignation, THOMAS GREEVES, in the 68th year of his age. Truly, his end was peace! His friends are invited to attend his funeral this evening, at 4 o'clock, from his late residence on Fifth street, between M and N streets. (22 MAY 1851)

MARRIAGE. In Georgetown, on the 20th inst., by the Rev. Dr. Ryder, WM. G. HARDY, M.D., to Mrs. MATILDA HILL, both of the District. (23 MAY 1851)

MARRIAGE. On the 22d inst., at the Foundry M.E. Church, by the Rev. L.F. Morgan, Rev. ROBERT KELLEN, of Concord Biblical Institute, to Miss EUPHEMIA JANE, eldest daughter of Abner Young, Esq., of this city. (23 MAY 1851)

MARRIAGE. At Smithtown, Long Island, N.Y., on Sunday, the 18th inst., by the Rev. J.C. Edwards, J. CRUTCHETT, Esq., to Miss MARCIA AUGUSTA SMITH, daughter of the late Richard Smith, Esq. of Smithtown. (23 MAY 1851)

DEATH. On Thursday morning, 22 inst., after a long and painful illness, Mrs. ELEANOR MARIA McINTOSH, (daughter of the late Thomas Foote, of London,) wife of J.M. McIntosh, formerly of Virginia, but for the last twelve years a resident of this city. She died in the fullness of the Christian faith, and in the hope of a blessed immortality beyond the grave. The relatives and friends of the family are requested to attend her funeral on this (Friday) morning, at 10 o'clock, from the residence of her husband, on the corner of 10th and L streets. (23 MAY 1851)

MARRIAGE. At Elmwood, near Princess Anne, on Wednesday, the 30th ult. [30 APR 1851], by the Rev. John Crosdale, Mr. GEORGE S. ATKINSON, to Miss ELIZABETH JACKSON, second daughter of the late Col. Arnold E. Jones, of Somerset Co., Md. (24 MAY 1851)

DEATH. In this city, at 4 o'clock yesterday morning, (23d May,) LETITIA McCREERY WALKER, Daughter of the late Samuel Purviance Walker. The relatives and Friends of the Family are respectfully requested to attend the Funeral of the deceased from the residence of her Mother, on Sixth street, at 4 o'clock this afternoon. (24 MAY 1851)

Daily National Intelligencer, Marriage and Death Notices, 1851-1854

DEATH. Yesterday, WM. THOMAS, son of Edward and Mary A. Gallant, aged five years. The friends and acquaintances of the family are requested to attend the funeral tomorrow, (Sunday,) from the residence of his father, on 6th street west, between O and P streets north, at 5 o'clock in the evening. (24 MAY 1851)

DEATH. On Friday evening last [23 MAY 1851], JAMES, infant son of J.W. and Sidney J. Moorhead, of this city. (26 MAY 1851)

OBITUARY.--[Communicated.]. Died in Staunton, Va., on the 14th inst., Mrs. FANNY PEYTON BROWN, widow of the late Gen. John Brown, first Chancellor of the Staunton district, aged 88 years. FANNY PEYTON was the daughter of Henry PEYTON and Margaret SALLAHUE, and was born at Milford, in Prince William Co., in the Colony of Virginia, in 1762. She was in many respects a most remarkable woman. Her mind was naturally strong, active, and perspicacious, was highly cultivated by early education, and was well stored with useful and valuable information. She grew up amid the trying scenes of the revolution, in which her family was actively engaged and suffered severely. She lost three brothers in its conflicts. When the intelligence was brought to her father, HENRY PEYTON, that his third and last son was also slain, he walked from the messenger agonized with grief, but suddenly, stifling his emotions, he turned and said, "Sir, much as I deplore the loss of my poor boy, I would to God I had another to supply his place, though he likewise perished in the cause of his country." She was a close observer of all the national events since that period, and enjoyed a personal acquaintance with most of the distinguished men whom Virginia has given to the nation. Her mind and memory were unimpaired by her great age, and she retained her buoyant and cheerful spirits to the last hour of her life, which rendered her conversation remarkably interesting and instructive. (27 MAY 1851)

DEATH. On Monday, 26th inst., Mrs. MARGARET KELLY, in the 17th year of her age, after a painful and most distressing sickness of four weeks, but borne with the fortitude and resignation of a Christian. The friends and acquaintances of the family are respectfully requested to attend her funeral from the residence of her father, Mr. Edward McCubbin, on Eighth street, near Pennsylvania avenue, this day, Tuesday, at 2 o'clock P.M. (27 MAY 1851)

DEATH. At College Hill, D.C., on the morning of the 26th inst., after a very short illness of congestion of the brain, LEMUEL P. BACON, son of the Rev. Joel S. Bacon, D.D., President of Columbia College, aged 12 years. The funeral services will take place at 4 o'clock P.M. this day, (May 27th,) in the College Chapel. The friends of the family are invited to attend. (27 MAY 1851)

DEATH. On the 18th inst., in Warrenton, Va., (where she had gone but a few days previous,) Mrs. CATHARINE POWELL, the widow of the late Major Burr Powell, deceased, of Middleburg, Va. (27 MAY 1851)

MARRIAGE. By the Rev. Wm. B. Edwards, on Tuesday morning, the 27th inst., AMMON GREEN, to Miss ANN MARIA LAZENBY, all of that city. (28 MAY 1851)

DEATH. Suddenly, at Louisville, Ky., on the 19th inst., Mrs. ADELA CULVER, consort of Dr. F.B. Culver, and second daughter of Hon. Amos Kendall. (28 MAY 1851)

MARRIAGE. On Tuesday evening last [20 MAY 1851], by the Rev. O.B. Brown, Mr. JOHN KEITHLEY, to Miss MARY RIGSBY, all of this city. (29 MAY 1851)

DEATH. On Wednesday, the 28th inst., LUCINDA ALBERTER, youngest daughter of J.C. and Cecelia Maria Cook, aged six years four months and two days. The friends and acquaintances of the family are respectfully invited to attend her funeral at 9 o'clock this (Thursday) morning, at her father's residence, Maryland avenue, corner of 7th street. (29 MAY 1851)

Daily National Intelligencer, Marriage and Death Notices, 1851-1854

MARRIAGE. On Thursday afternoon, in the Fourth Presbyterian Church, by the Rev. John C. Smith, Mr. JOHN H. WALKER, of Baltimore, to Miss ROSANNA E. PHILLIPS, of this city. (30 MAY 1851)

MARRIAGE. In Baltimore, on the 28th inst., by the Rev. Mr. Ross, ERICKSON H. TANEYHILL to MARY E. TANEYHILL, both of Calvert Co., Md. (30 MAY 1851)

DEATH. On the 30th inst., ABRAHAM DeCAMP, of the city of New York, from congestion of the brain, aged 52 years. The funeral will take place tomorrow at 2 o'clock, from the residence of his brother, on D, between 9th and 10th streets. (31 MAY 1851)

DEATH. At Baltimore, on Wednesday evening, the 27th inst., IDA LESLIE, only child of A. Ross and Eliza L. Ray, aged 19 months and 17 days. (31 MAY 1851)

OBITUARY.--[Communicated.]. At Eastern Hill, D.C., on Tuesday, the 20th inst., after a brief existence of a few hours, the infant daughter of Dr. W.A. and R.C. Manning. And also, at the same place, on the Monday following, (the 26th inst.,) Mrs. ROSETTE CAROLINE MANNING, wife of Dr. W. Wilfred A. Manning, and daughter of Major Ignatius Manning, after a short period of great suffering, which she bore with marked firmness and Christian resignation, aged 33 years 9 months and 10 days. This devoted wife and fond parent has thus early, by the relentless hand of death, been summoned to the angelic choir, already adorned by three most interesting infants, co-heirs of heaven, leaving a most disconsolate husband and heart-stricken relatives and friends to mourn their irreparable loss. (31 MAY 1851)

OBITUARY. Death of ROBERT E. HORNOR, Doorkeeper of the U.S. House of Representatives, died at Queenston, near Princeton, on Thursday [29 MAY 1851] afternoon, about half-past two o'clock [text continues]. (2 JUN 1851)

DEATH. At Cedar Hill, near Frankfort, Ky., on the 12th of May, Mrs. ANNA INNIS, relict of the Hon. Henry Innis, and mother of Mrs. J.J. Crittenden [text continues]. (2 JUN 1851)

DEATH. On Tuesday evening, the 27th inst., after an illness of only five hours, of effusion on the brain, MARY, infant daughter of Eustace E. and Rebecca O'Brien, aged 1 year 7 months and 18 days. (2 JUN 1851)

MARRIAGE. On the 22d ult., at Evermay, Claiborne Co., Miss., by the Rev. Wm. Baxter, ALEXANDER C. BULLITT, Esq., one of the editors and proprietors of the *New Orleans Picayune*, and late editor of the *Republic*, to Miss FANNY SMITH, daughter of the late Benjamin Smith, Esq., of Kentucky. (3 JUN 1851)

DEATH. In Duxbury, Mass., 2d ult. [2 MAY 1851], Capt. JOSHUA BREWSTER, of that place, aged eighty-eight years. He was a descendant of Elder William Brewster, one of the Pilgrims who came over in the *Mayflower*, and landed at Plymouth in 1620. (3 JUN 1851)

MARRIAGE. On the 28th May, at Scranton, Pa., the residence of Dr. Throop, by the Rev. Mr. Mitchell, S.W. THOMPSON, to SARAH HALE, second daughter of J.W.N. Throom, of this city. (4 JUN 1851)

MARRIAGE. On Tuesday, the 3d inst., by the Rev. Mr. Hodges, JOHN C. METCALF, to JULIETTA M. MASSOLETTI, all of Washington. (4 JUN 1851)

DEATH. In Philadelphia, on the morning of the 30th May, HENRY TURK, infant son of Thomas H. and Ellen Lane, of this city. (4 JUN 1851)

MARRIAGE. At Baltimore, on Tuesday morning, by the Rev. Mr. Killen, JOHN T. MASON, Surgeon U.S. Navy, to MARY, daughter of the late Thomas R. Johnson, of St. Mary's Co., Md. (5 JUN 1851)

Daily National Intelligencer, Marriage and Death Notices, 1851-1854

DEATH. On Tuesday afternoon, June 3, WILLIAM HARRISON WARD, in the 37th year of his age. His friends and those of the family are invited to attend his funeral, which will take place this (Thursday) afternoon from the E Street Baptist Church, at 4 o'clock. (5 JUN 1851)

DEATH. Yesterday, after a painful illness, Mr. WILLIAM LINKINS, Sr., in the 64th year of his age. His friends and acquaintances are invited to attend his funeral, from his late residence, on L street, near Eighteenth street, this afternoon, at 4 o'clock. (5 JUN 1851)

DEATH. On Tuesday, the 3d inst., HARVEY L., aged one year and four months, son of William and Mary A. Phillips. The friends and acquaintance of the family are invited to attend the funeral on this (Thursday) afternoon, at 4 o'clock, from his parents' residence, on Seventh street near the Northern Market. (5 JUN 1851)

MARRIAGE. On Tuesday, the 3d inst., by the Rev. Mr. Lenaghan, Mr. JOHN JOHNSTON, to Mrs. ELIZABETH ANN MULLIKEN, both of this city. (6 JUN 1851)

DEATH. On the 5th inst., NATHANIEL PLANT, aged 62 years. The funeral this evening, from his late residence, at the corner of C and 13th street, at 4 o'clock. His friends and acquaintance are respectfully invited to attend. (7 JUN 1851)

DEATH. At his residence, Stony Arbor Farm, Prince George's Co., Md., on Wednesday, the 28th ult., Mr. RAPHAEL C. EDELEN. The deceased was an exemplary Christian, an accomplished gentleman, and a kind friend. He has left an interesting family to mourn his loss, and a large circle of friends, to whom he was endeared by his many virtues. (7 JUN 1851)

MARRIAGE. On the 5th inst., by the Rev. John Lanahan, SOLOMON STOVER, Esq., of Frederick Co., Md., to Miss HESTER A. TRAVERS, daughter of Capt. JABEZ TRAVERS, of Washington. (9 JUN 1851)

MARRIAGE. In Georgetown, on Thursday morning last, at 7 o'clock, by the Rev. J.J. Murray, W.H. DOUGAL, Esq., of Washington, to Miss M. VIRGINIA, daughter of MORRIS ADLER, of the former place. (9 JUN 1851)

MARRIAGE. At Goodwood, Prince George's Co., Md., on Wednesday the 4th inst., by the Rev. Mr. Mackenheimer, FRANCIS M. HALL to ROSALIE EUGENIA, eldest daughter of Charles H. CARTER, Esq. (9 JUN 1851)

DEATH. On the 11th February 1850, in the region of the Great Salt Lake, Mr. RICHARD J.A. CULVERWELL, in the 49th year of his age. The deceased was a native of Baltimore, Md., but for the last 15 years a resident of this city. He leaves a wife and several children to mourn his loss. (9 JUN 1851)

MARRIAGE. On the 5th inst., by the Rev. Mr. Callahan, ALLEN J. DORSEY to Miss MARGARET R. SHREEVE, all of this city. (10 JUN 1851)

MARRIAGE. On the 3d inst., by the Rev. Smith Pine, CHARLES VINSON, of the Treasury Department, to Mrs. H.R.F., widow of the late Capt. E.A. CAPRON, 1st Artillery, U.S.A. (10 JUN 1851)

DEATH. Yesterday [9 JUN 1851], AGNES CUSHING, infant daughter of James and Mary F. Greenough, aged 5 months. (10 JUN 1851)

MARRIAGE. At Georgetown, on the 2d inst., by the Rev. Mr. Lanahan, Mr. GEORGE N. BEALE to Miss ELIZABETH B., daughter of Col. J.H. WHEELER, of North Carolina. (11 JUN 1851)

DEATH. On Saturday, the 7th inst., MARION ECKFORD, the wife of Lieut. F. STANLY, U.S. Navy, and daughter of F.R. TILLOU. (12 JUN 1851)

Daily National Intelligencer, Marriage and Death Notices, 1851-1854

DEATH. On the 3d inst., WILLIAM E. McCLASKY, son of Wm. T. McClasky, aged 7 months. (12 JUN 1851)

DEATH. Yesterday morning [11 JUN 1851], Mr. GEO. BEAN, in the 54th year of his age. The funeral will take place today, at 2 o'clock P.M. The friends of the family are invited to attend. (12 JUN 1851)

MARRIAGE. On Tuesday evening, June 10, by the Rev. Mr. Nelson, JOHN MARBURY, Jr., of Georgetown, D.C., to JULIET, daughter of the late A.B. MURRAY, formerly of Baltimore. (13 JUN 1851)

MARRIAGE. On Tuesday evening, the 10th inst., at Martinsburg, Va., by the Rev. D. Francis Sprigg, GEORGE F. HARRISON, Esq., of Elkora, Cumberland Co., Va., to Miss REBECCA HOLMES CONRAD, second daughter of David Holmes Conrad, Esq. (13 JUN 1851)

DEATH. In this city, on the 12th of June, in the 29th year of her age, LOUISA PEMBERTON, wife of CHARLES W. FORREST, and daughter of the late Chas. J. Nourse. The friends of the family are respectfully invited to attend her funeral this (Friday) afternoon, at 4 o'clock. (13 JUN 1851)

DEATH. In this city, on Monday, the 26th of May, MIRIAM PHILLIPS, daughter of Thomas and Emily G. Blagden, aged seven months and ten days. "Ere sin could blight, or sorrow fade, Death came, with friendly care, The opening bud to Heaven convey'd, And bade it blossom there." (13 JUN 1851)

DEATH. On the 12th inst., after a long and painful illness, which she bore with Christian resignation, Mrs. CATHARINE MINITREE, in the 65th year of her age. The friends and acquaintances of the family are requested to attend the funeral this day (Saturday) from the residence of her son, on Maryland Ave., between 4½ and 6th streets, at 10 o'clock A.M. (14 JUN 1851)

DEATH. On Thursday morning, the 12th inst., MARGARET MARIAH EDWARDS, daughter of the Rev. Wm. B. and Elizabeth A. Edwards, of this city, in the 9th year of her age. The funeral will take place from the Wesley Chapel on Sunday afternoon, at three o'clock. The friends of the family are invited to attend. (14 JUN 1851)

DEATH. On the 11th inst., in this city, EMMA, only daughter of William and Cordelia Mitchell, aged 22 months. (14 JUN 1851)

MARRIAGE. On Thursday, the 11th inst., Mr. JAMES LEWIS to Miss ELLEN ELIZABETH DUBANT, all of this city. (16 JUN 1851)

DEATH. On Friday evening [13 JUN 1851], MARIA S., only child of Mrs. H. Ulerich. The friends of the family are requested to attend her funeral this afternoon, at 4½ o'clock, at the residence of her mother, 15th street. (16 JUN 1851)

MARRIAGE. In Rockville, Md., on the 27th May, by the Rev. Basil Barry, Mayor MATTHEW MARKLAND, of this city, (formerly of Kentucky,) to Miss CAROLINE S. HALL, daughter of the late Dr. E.J. Hall, of Baltimore Co. (17 JUN 1851)

DEATH. At Madison, Conn., on Monday evening, the 9th inst., EMILY JOANNA HAND, youngest daughter of the late Joseph W. Hand, of this city, aged 11 years. (17 JUN 1851)

DEATH. In this city, on Sunday, June 15th, at her father's residence, on G street, FRANCES ELIZABETH HENRY McDOWELL, third daughter of Gov. James McDowell, Representative in Congress from Virginia. (17 JUN 1851)

Daily National Intelligencer, Marriage and Death Notices, 1851-1854

DEATH. On the 16th inst., in the 8th year of his age, WILLIAM, an interesting son of William and Catharine Begman. Funeral this morning at 10 o'clock, at his father's house on 13th street, between E and F. (17 JUN 1851)

DEATH. On Monday, 16th inst., JESSE WILLIAM, infant son of Elias and Rachel Yulee, aged 9 months. The friends of the family are invited to attend the funeral, which will take place today, at 5 o'clock P.M., from Mrs. Rice's boarding-house, on Capitol Hill. (17 JUN 1851)

MARRIAGE. At [Burli]ngton, Ver., on Tuesday evening, June 10, by the Rev. Bishop Hopkins, JAMES G. RUMSEY, Esq., of Detroit, Mich., and AUGUSTA J., eldest daughter of Gen. John A. Arthur, of Burlington. (18 JUN 1851)

DEATH. On the [?]th inst., at the residence of Dr. Garnett, of this city, [?]CER SERGEANT WISE, infant son of the Hon. Henry Wise, of Virginia. (18 JUN 1851)

DEATH. On the 17th inst., FURMAN BLACK, Jr., aged 7 years and 5 months, only son of Furman and Sarah A. Black. The friends of the family are invited to attend the funeral this (Thursday) afternoon at 4 o'clock, at the National Hotel. (19 JUN 1851)

DEATH. At Terre Haute, Ind., on the 6th inst., JOHN M. WHEAT, in the 49th year of his age, son of the late John Wheat, of Greenleaf's Point, Washington. (19 JUN 1851)

MARRIAGE. At Baltimore, on Wednesday morning, by the Rev. Mr. Foley, at the residence of H.B. Majesty's Consul, Lieut. D. AMMEN, U.S. Navy, to MARIA CATHARINE JACKSON. (20 JUN 1851)

DEATH. At San Francisco, (California,) on the 8th May, Mr. THOMAS McCALLA, son of John M. McCala, Esq., late Second Auditor of the Treasury Department. (20 JUN 1851)

DEATH. On the 19th inst., HENRY STANFORD, infant son of Wm. H. and Sarah E. Stanford. His funeral will take place this (Friday) morning, the 20th inst., from his father's residence, Capitol Hill, north Capitol street. The friends and acquaintances are invited to attend. (20 JUN 1851)

DEATH. On the morning of the 17th inst., AUGUSTUS, son of Caroline and L.A. Fleury, late of the Quartermaster General's office, aged 15 months. (20 JUN 1851)

DEATH. On Thursday, the 19th inst., GEORGE W., infant son of JAMES and MARGARET SELDEN, aged 4 months and 13 days. (20 JUN 1851)

DEATH. In Alexandria, Va., of scarlet fever, on Sunday, the 8th inst., GEORGE DASHIEL, aged 18 months; and on Sunday, the 15th inst., CAROLYN DENNIS, in the 7th year of his age, only sons of George D. and Sarah Ellen Fowle. (20 JUN 1851)

MARRIAGE. On the 19th inst., by the Rev. Mr. Morgan, Mr. A.F. HINES to Miss SARAH A. FICKETT, all of this city. (21 JUN 1851)

MARRIAGE. On Thursday, the 19th inst., by the Rev. Mr. Gilliss, Mr. EDWARD A. SMITH to Miss ELIZABETH DAVIS, all of this city. (21 JUN 1851)

DEATH. On the 2d inst., of cholera, on the plains, about 90 miles from Ft. Leavenworth, Dr. ALFRED W. KENNEDY, Surgeon in the U.S. Army. Also, of the same disease, and about the same time, his son [WESLEY], in the 4th year of his age. Dr. Kennedy, accompanied by his wife and children, was on the line of march to New Mexico, with a detachment of U.S. troops that had been concentrated from different military posts at Ft. Leavenworth. The cholera first broke out among the troops at the Fort on the 29th or 30th ult., and before leaving that post 11 of the soldiers had died. Dr. Kennedy, who had just arrived from

Daily National Intelligencer, Marriage and Death Notices, 1851-1854

Ft. Scott to accompany the regiment as surgeon, continued unremitting in his self-sacrificing exertions to alleviate the sufferings of the afflicted and dying, until he fell himself a noble victim of the pestilence, in the prime of manhood and in the midst of his career of usefulness. In 1840 he was commissioned Assistant Surgeon in the U.S. Army, and received the "first honor" among a large number of applicants examined at the same time. Since that period he has been almost constantly in active service in Florida and Mexico with Gen. Taylor, during the whole of the war, and afterwards he had charge of the hospital at Baton Rouge, which was filled to overflowing with soldiers broken down in the Mexican campaign, and all of whom looked up to him with reverence and gratitude. (21 JUN 1851)

DEATH. On Thursday, the 19th inst., Miss SUSAN WRIGHT, daughter of Mrs. Sarah Wright, of this city. (21 JUN 1851)

DEATH. At Baltimore, yesterday [20 JUN 1851], the Rev. DANIEL McJILTON, long an active Clergyman of the Methodist Church, in the 70th year of his age. (21 JUN 1851)

DEATH. In this city, on the 20th inst., Mrs. MARY M. TELFAIR, formerly of Rhode Island. (21 JUN 1851)

DEATH. On the 21st June inst., T. EGERTON BROWNE, Esq., of the Post Office Department, in the 59th year of his age. (23 JUN 1851)

DEATH. In Upperville, Va., on the 19th inst., MARY ELIZABETH, daughter of Rev. HENRY W. DODGE, aged 2 years and 6 months. (23 JUN 1851)

MARRIAGE. On Tuesday, June 17, at Sing Sing, N.Y., by the Rev. Dr. J. McVickar, PETER BERRY, of Georgetown, D.C., to PRISCILLA, daughter of the late Roderick McLeod. (24 JUN 1851)

DEATH. In St. Louis, Mo., on the 13th inst., of pulmonary consumption, JAMES BROOKS, aged 28 years. Deceased was a native, and for a considerable period a resident, of this city, where he leaves a number of relatives and friends to lament his early death. (24 JUN 1851)

DEATH. On board the steamer *Fremont*, at sea, on Sunday, the 6th of April, when 8 days out from Rio de Janerio, on her way to California, Mrs. MARIA C. McLANE, wife of Allan McLane, U.S. Navy, and daughter of the late Richard Bache, of Philadelphia. It will be comforting to her friends to know that her death was calm and peaceful, as her life had been pure and happy. She was buried at Valparaiso, in the Foreign Burial Ground. (24 JUN 1851)

DEATH. At his residence, in Prince George's Co., on the night of the 20th of June, Mr. ANTHONY C.W. PAGE, in the 36th year of his age. (24 JUN 1851)

MARRIAGE. On Monday evening [23 JUN 1851], by the Rev. John C. Smith, Mr. CALVIN T. HARTMAN to Miss ANN H. WALKER, all of this city. (25 JUN 1851)

MARRIAGE. On Thursday evening, 19th inst., by the Rev. Mr. Cushman, JNO. OBER to Miss FRANCES L. CLARKE, (youngest daughter of the late Robt. Clarke, Esq.,) all of Washington. (25 JUN 1851)

DEATH. Suddenly, at West Point, N.Y., on the morning of June 19th, Mrs. ELIZA GAITHER, of Montgomery Co., Md., relict of the late Henry C. Gaither, and mother of Gen. Wm. Lingan Gaither, President of the Senate of Md. Mrs. Gaither had accompanied her son to West Point, where he, as a member of the Board of Visitors, was in attendance on the annual examination at the Military Academy; and this trip was looked to as calculated to improve her health, which had been for some time seriously impaired... (25 JUN 1851)

Daily National Intelligencer, Marriage and Death Notices, 1851-1854

DEATH. At Philadelphia, early on Sunday morning, CHARLES N. BUCK, Esq., in the 76th year of his age, a native of Hamburg, but for 55 years a resident of that city, and Consul-General from the Government of the city of Hamburg. (25 JUN 1851)

DEATH. At the residence of its grandfather, Thomas Mustin, in this city, on Friday night last, 20th inst., MARY SOPHIA, infant daughter of the Rev. Thomas and Annie S. Jones, of Newville, Va. (25 JUN 1851)

DEATH. At Maple Hill, near this city, on Monday evening, June 23, ROBERT S.P. son of George and Harriet McCeney, in the second year of his age. The friends of the family are invited to attend his funeral from the residence of his parents this day, (Wednesday,) at 10 o'clock A.M. (25 JUN 1851)

MARRIAGE. At Newport, R.I., on the 19th inst., at the Catholic Chapel, by Rev. James Fitton, Chevalier BANUELOS, Spanish Secretary of Legation of this country, to Miss MARY A. THORNDIKE, of Boston. (26 JUN 1851)

DEATH. In this city, on the 24th inst., GEORGE TAYLOR, in the 91st year of his age. The friends of the family are invited to attend his funeral, which will take place at 10 o'clock this morning, from Mrs. Clare's boarding-house, corner of Louisiana avenue and C street. (26 JUN 1851)

DEATH. On Tuesday, the 24th inst., GEORGE, son of the late Florence S. and Wenefred McCarthy, aged 18 years. The funeral will take place this (Thursday) afternoon, at 4 o'clock, from his late residence, on F street, between 6th and 7th streets, to which the friends of the family are invited. (26 JUN 1851)

MARRIAGE. On Tuesday, the 24th, by the Rev. James B. Donelan, Mr. AUGUSTUS VOSS to Miss LUCY AMANDA FRANCES MANN, all of this city. (27 JUN 1851)

MARRIAGE. On Tuesday evening, the 17th inst., by the Rev. Mr. Tillinghast, Dr. WM. W. EUSTACE, of Richmond, Va., to Miss MARTHA VIRGINIA LAUB, of Washington. (27 JUN 1851)

MARRIAGE. Last evening, by the Rev. Mr. Davis, Mr. J.W. JORDON to Miss MARY ELIZABETH WESTERFIELD, all of this city. (27 JUN 1851)

DEATH. On the morning of the 26th inst., after a sudden illness, PORTER GILLET, infant son of the Rev. R.R. and E.M. Gurley. Their friends are invited to attend the funeral this day, at half-past 3 o'clock, from the residence of his parents, on 12th street. (27 JUN 1851)

OBITUARY. Were the pen that now writes capable of tears, it would weep while it records that Miss MARY L.K. STRIDER, only daughter of Samuel Strider, of Jefferson Co., Va., is no more. She took cold during the Christmas holydays; it fell upon her bust and lungs, slightly at first, but afterwards the inflammation attacked the brain with a fierceness that baffled the skill of the best physicians and the watchful care of the most attentive nurses, and despite of every effort that experience, vigilance, and love could suggest, she fell a victim to death January 22d, 1851, in the 17th year of her age, at the Wesleyan Female College, at Wilmington, Del. [continues]. (28 JUN 1851)

DEATHS. At Fayetteville, N.C., on the 21st inst., Dr. THOMAS NASH CAMERON, a native of Virginia, but who had resided in Fayetteville for 55 years. Dr. Cameron had been often chosen to the highest municipal office of the town, and had also more than once represented the county in the Legislature of the State. (28 JUN 1851)

DEATH. At Nashville, Tenn., on the 20th inst., Mrs. JANE ELLEN CHEATHAM, consort of Col. E.S. Cheatham, of Springfield, Tenn., and eldest daughter of Hon. E.H. Foster, aged 29 years. (28 JUN 1851)

Daily National Intelligencer, Marriage and Death Notices, 1851-1854

DEATH. At Kent Island, Queen [Anne's] Co., Md., on Tuesday, the 24th inst., in the 23d year of her age, Miss MARIA LOUISA GIBSON, after an illness of only a few days, which she bore with Christian fortitude and perfect resignation. (28 JUN 1851)

DEATH. In this city, on the 27th inst., HANNAH, in the 27th year of her age, consort of the late DENNIS BUCKLEY, of Baltimore, a native of Cork, Ireland. Her funeral takes place on Sunday morning, at 5½ o'clock, from her late residence on 11th street, near Maryland avenue, where her friends and acquaintances are requested to attend, without further invitation. (28 JUN 1851)

DEATH. Yesterday morning [27 JUN 1851], at his residence on Rock Creek, ABNER C. PIERCE. The funeral will take place tomorrow (Sunday) at 3½ o'clock. (28 JUN 1851)

MARRIAGE. On Thursday evening [26 JUN 1851], in the 4th Presbyterian Church by the Rev. John C. Smith, Mr. JAMES A. JOHNSON to Miss CASSANDRA VIRGINIA BANGS, all of this city. (30 JUN 1851)

MARRIAGE. On Thursday morning, 26th inst., by the Rev. Mr. Edwards, EDWARD HALL and SUSAN LOWNDES, daughter of Wm. B. Jackson, Esq., all of this city. (30 JUN 1851)

MARRIAGE. In St. Louis, on the 18th inst., Lieut. JOHN W. DAVIDSON, Adjutant First Dragoons U.S. Army, to Miss CLARA B., daughter of Geo. K. McGunnegle, Esq., of St. Louis. (30 JUN 1851)

MARRIAGE. On the 24th, by the Rev. James Todd, Mr. GEORGE B. LAIRD to Miss VIRGINIA F., daughter of Hon. HENRY J. MILLER, of Rockingham Co., Va. (30 JUN 1851)

DEATH. At Dwight Mission, (Cherokee Nation,) on Sabbath morning, June 8th, Rev. DANIEL S. BUTRICK, for more than 30 years a faithful and useful missionary of the American Board of Foreign Missions among the Cherokee people. (30 JUN 1851)

DEATH. On Friday, June 27th, ELEANOR JANE BEDINGFELD, only daughter of O. Bedingfeld Queen (now in California) and Sarah Queen, aged 18 months and 10 days. (1 JUL 1851)

DEATH. On Sunday evening, 29th ult., of congestion of the brain, MARY LINCOLN, eldest and only daughter of J. James and Mary F. Greenough. (1 JUL 1851)

DEATH. At Baltimore, on the 1st inst., after a few days illness, Mrs. ANNA JANE MEIERE, wife of Professor J. Meiere, and daughter of the late Rev. Christopher MacAllister, D.D.T.C.D. (2 JUL 1851)

DEATH. On Tuesday, the 1st inst., of congestive intermittent, WILLIAM MARION, son of William Q. and Elizabeth A. Force, aged six months. The friends of the family are invited to attend the funeral this day, (Wednesday,) at 10 o'clock. (2 JUL 1851)

MARRIAGE. On the morning of the 1st inst., at the Church of the Epiphany, by the Rev. Mr. French, D.R. GOODLOE, Esq., of North Carolina, to Miss MARY E. WARING, of Georgetown, D.C. (3 JUL 1851)

MARRIAGE. In Pitt Co., N.C., on the 25th inst. [25 JUN 1851], by the Rev. Mr. Croghan, WILLIAM GRIMES to Miss ELIZABETH, daughter of Thomas Hannahan, Esq. (3 JUL 1851)

DEATH. On the 23d of June, at the residence of her father, in Waterford, Saratoga Co., N.Y., FLORILLA, daughter of the Hon. Hugh White, M.C., in the 21st year of her age... (3 JUL 1851)

DEATH. On the 30th ult., LAWRENCE SMITH, infant son of John and Mary C. [Dahlgren], aged 7 months and 16 days. (3 JUL 1851)

Daily National Intelligencer, Marriage and Death Notices, 1851-1854

MARRIAGE. On Wednesday evening, by the Rev. John C. Smith, Mr. HENRY FISHER to Miss ELLEN ANN BARRETT, all of this city. (4 JUL 1851)

MARRIAGE. On Thursday morning, 3d inst., by the Rev. Mr. Marks, Mr. JOSEPH FOWLER, of Anne Arundel Co., Md., to Miss MARY ANN VIRGINIA BROWN. At the same time, by the same, Mr. JULIUS HENRY PILES to Miss HARRIET SANSBURY. (4 JUL 1851)

MARRIAGE. At Fredericksburg, Va., on the 26th June, 1851, by the Rev. G.W. McPhail, H.M. HIESKELL, U.S. Navy, to Miss EMILY L.H. BADGER, of that place. (4 JUL 1851)

MARRIAGE. On Saturday afternoon [5 JUL 1851], by the Rev. John C. Smith, Mr. THOMAS MULLONE to Mrs. ANN O'MEARA, all of this city. (7 JUL 1851)

MARRIAGE. On the 3d inst., by the Rev. James B. Donelan, Mr. JOHN S. EVERETT to Miss REBECCA FREEMAN, all of this city. (7 JUL 1851)

DEATH. On the 4th inst., in this city, aged 45 years, Mrs. DOROTHY MATTINGLY, after a long and painful sufferings, which she bore with meek submission. (7 JUL 1851)

DEATH. On the 3d inst., in Richmond, Va., after a protracted illness, HENNINGHAM H. LYONS, consort of James Lyons, Esq., in the 52d year of her age. (7 JUL 1851)

DEATH. On the 25th ult., at Poplar Run, Orange Co., Va., GARLAND BALLARD, Esq., at about 55 years of age. (7 JUL 1851)

DEATH. On the 30th ult., at the residence of her son, in Waynesburg [sic], Va., Mrs. RACHAEL HINES, of this city, in the 58th year of her age, after a long illness of 8 days, in the hope of a blissful immortality. Her friends and acquaintances are respectfully notified that her funeral will take place on Tuesday next, at 5 o'clock P.M., at the Foundry Church without further notice. (7 JUL 1851)

DEATH. On the 29th ult., at the residence of his grandfather, Wm. G. Yerby, in Upperville, Va., OSCAR, infant son of A. Oscar and Bettie Yerby, of Essex Co., Va., aged 14 months. (7 JUL 1851)

MARRIAGE. On Sunday, the 22d of June, by the Rev. James P. Donelan, of St. Matthew's Church, JOHN C. SEIBEL to Miss SARAH R. ROSS, both of Washington. (9 JUL 1851)

MARRIAGE. On the 6th inst., by the Rev. Dr. Morgan, MARTIN L.B. JOSETTI, of Washington, to Miss ANNA BERRY, of Prince George's Co., Md. (9 JUL 1851)

DEATH. On Friday, the 4th inst., WILLIAM L. OGDEN, in the 66th year of his age. (9 JUL 1851)

DEATH. At Annapolis, on the 2d inst., MARY T., second daughter of the Hon. John Johnson, in the 17th year of her age. A severe attack of bilious fever carried this young and beautiful plant from her native soil to those mansions eternal in the skies, where the blessed rest from their labors. It is there the good and virtuous and gentle enter into immortal joy; and now [prose continues]. (9 JUL 1851)

MARRIAGE. On Tuesday evening, by the Rev. John C. Smith, Mr. WILLIAM CAREY to Miss ELIZABETH KERR, all of this city. (10 JUL 1851)

MARRIAGE. At Baltimore, July 8th, by the Rev. Dr. Wyatt, Dr. WILLIAM BOTELER, of Frederick Co., Md., to MARIA SIDNEY, daughter of the late Geo. A. Hughes. (10 JUL 1851)

MARRIAGE. At Baltimore, July 8th, by the Rev. Dr. Wyatt, ANTHONY KENNEDY, of Martinsburg, Va., to MARGARET SMITH, daughter of the late Hon. Christopher Hughes. (10 JUL 1851)

Daily National Intelligencer, Marriage and Death Notices, 1851-1854

MARRIAGE. In Alexandria, Va., on the 10th inst., by the Rev. C.B. Dana, Dr. WM. KLEIPSTEIN to Miss MARY A., daughter of Rebecca Taylor, all of that place. (11 JUL 1851)

DEATH. On the 10th inst., Mrs. MARIA H. WALLER, wife of J.D. Waller. The friends of the family are invited to attend her funeral this (Friday) evening, at 3 o'clock, without further notice. (11 JUL 1851)

DEATH. On Thursday morning, 10th inst., at half-past 7, GEO. WASHINGTON, infant son of Maria P. and Wm. E. Spalding, aged 4 months and 18 days. The friends of the family are respectfully invited to attend the funeral this (Friday) afternoon, at 5 o'clock, from their residence on H, between 21st and 22d streets. (11 JUL 1851)

DEATH. On the morning of the 11th inst., HELEN PARRIS GILMAN, wife of Z.D. Gilman. Her funeral will take place on Sunday afternoon at 4 o'clock, from the residence of her husband, corner of C and Third streets. (12 JUL 1851)

DEATH. On Sunday morning, 13th inst., Mrs. MARY ATTRIDGE, in the 79th year of her age. Her funeral will take place this afternoon at 4 o'clock from the residence of her son-in-law (Mr. Abraham Butler) on 13th street. (14 JUL 1851)

DEATH. On the 10th inst., at the residence of his grandfather, Agricola Favier, of hydrocephalus, AGRICOLA ARMAND, aged 7 months and 11 days, son of Armand and Honorine Jardin. (14 JUL 1851)

DEATH. At Philadelphia, on the 3d inst., in the 19th month of her age, ANNIE, only daughter of Jas. R. Smith, and grand-daughter of Wm. G.W. White, of this city. (14 JUL 1851)

DEATH. On Sunday evening, the 13th inst., RITTENHOUSE, aged 11 months, infant son of Levi D. and Jennie Slamm. The friends and acquaintances of the family are invited to attend the funeral this (Tuesday) morning, the 15th inst., at 10 o'clock, from the residence of his grandfather, B.K. Morsell, Esq., Pennsylvania Avenue. (15 JUL 1851)

DEATH. In Georgetown, on the 12th inst., of a short illness, at the residence of his father, in the 28th year of his age, JOHN H., son of Henry C. Matthews. (15 JUL 1851)

MARRIAGE. On the 15th inst., by the Rev. Jas. Rider, President of Georgetown College, EDWARD C. DYER to BETTIE ELTON BELT, both of this city. (16 JUL 1851)

MARRIAGE. On the 10th inst., by the Rev. Wm. Edwards, Mr. GEORGE M. HEAD to Miss BARBARA TILLEY, both of this city. (16 JUL 1851)

DEATH. At Kent Island, on Saturday, the 12th inst., of bilious dysentery, in the 6th year of his age, Wm. G.W., eldest son of Jas. L. White, of this city. (16 JUL 1851)

DEATH. At Poplar Hill, Montgomery Co., Md., (the residence of Thos. Connelly, Esq.) on the 10th inst., SALLIE ELLIS, only daughter of Samuel C. and Lydia A. Espey, of this city, aged 9 months. (16 JUL 1851)

DEATH. On the 15th inst., CHRISTOPHER COLUMBUS, son of Christopher and Frederick Hager, aged 1 year 3 months and 21 days. The funeral will take place today (Wednesday) at 4 o'clock P.M. (16 JUL 1851)

DEATH. On the 15th inst., MARY ALICE, youngest daughter of John A. and Catharine P. Kirkpatrick, aged 18 months. The friends of the family are respectfully invited to attend the funeral this evening at 4 o'clock, from the residence of her father, on D, near 13½ streets. (16 JUL 1851)

Daily National Intelligencer, Marriage and Death Notices, 1851-1854

OBITUARY. Departed this life on Friday, the 11th inst., in the 44th year of his age, Dr. JNO. H. SELLMAN, of Anne Arundel Co., Md. [Davidsonville, July 14, 1851] (17 JUL 1851)

DEATH. In this city, yesterday [16 JUL 1851], Mr. MARCELLUS SIMPSON, in the 52d year of his age. His funeral will take place from the residence of Louis Marceron, on Pennsylvania avenue, near the Navy Yard, this evening, at 4 o'clock. The friends and relatives of the family are respectfully invited to attend. (17 JUL 1851)

DEATH. At Galveston, Tex., on the 14th ult., JOSEPH ELLIS WHITALL, late of Iberville Parish, La., eldest son of Samuel Whitall, Esq., of Georgetown, D.C. (17 JUL 1851)

DEATH. At Cairo, in Egypt, on the 10th of June, on his return from China, DAVID W.C. OLYPHANT, Esq., of New York, in the 63d year of his age. (17 JUL 1851)

DEATH. In this city, on the 16th inst., after an illness of only three days, JAMES LAWRENCE, son of James L. White, aged 6 months and 16 days. Funeral this morning at 10 o'clock. (17 JUL 1851)

DEATH. In this city, on Thursday last, Mrs. AMELIA POSTON, aged 70 years. She was for many years a resident of Alexandria. (18 JUL 1851)

DEATH. At St. Louis, Mo., July 9th, RICHARD H. SIMMS, of this city, in the 23d year of his age. (18 JUL 1851)

DEATH. At Philadelphia, on Monday, the 14th inst., Commander THOMAS J. LEIB, U.S. Navy, in the 49th year of his age. (18 JUL 1851)

DEATH. At the Naval Asylum, Philadelphia, on Saturday, the 12th inst., THOMAS JOHNSON, seaman, aged above 100 years. This old tar is believed to have been the last survivor of the gallant crew who so well sustained Paul Jones in his desperate conflict with the Serapis in 1779. (18 JUL 1851)

DEATH. At Sandy Spring, Md., on the 14th inst., CALEB BENTLEY, in the 90th year of his age. Few comparatively attain the age of four-score and ten; and perhaps still fever even of that number have passed through so active and varied a life. and maintained throughout a more unblemished reputation, and the respect and love of an extended circle of relatives and friends. (18 JUL 1851)

DEATH. On the 13th inst., at the residence of her son, Thomas Henderson, in Fauquier Co., Va., Mrs. ORRA M. HENDERSON, relict of the late Richard H. Henderson, Esq., of Leesburg, Va., in the 66th year of her age. (19 JUL 1851)

DEATH. On the 19th inst., Miss MARGARET DAYLY, aged 14 years. The friends of the family are invited to attend her funeral today, at 10 o'clock, from 10th street, between E and F streets. (19 JUL 1851)

DEATH. At Providence, R.I., on the 13th inst., Hon. CALEB EARLE, in the 81st of his age. Gov. Earle was one of the oldest and most respectable citizens of Providence. He was for several years a Representative in the Legislature, was formerly Lieutenant Governor of Rhode Island, and in 1824, and in 1828, an Elector of President of the United States. (19 JUL 1851)

DEATH. At Aintab, in Syria, on the 3d ult. [3 JUN 1851], of lung fever, Rev. AZARIAH SMITH, M.D. Missionary of the A.B.C.F.M. to the Armenians, aged 34. (19 JUL 1851)

DEATH. On Thursday evening, the 17th inst., of scarlet fever, after an illness of 11 days, MARION ANN MUIRHEAD, the precious and lovely daughter of the Rev. R.R. and E.M. Gurley, aged 6 years and 9 months. Her brief life was one sunny hour of joy and goodness, and to her parents and friends she never caused pain but when she sickened and died. Funeral from the residence of her parents, on 12th street,

Daily National Intelligencer, Marriage and Death Notices, 1851-1854

this morning, 9½ o'clock. (19 JUL 1851)

MARRIAGE. At Baltimore, the 2d inst., J.W. NICHOLLS, of Nashville, Tenn., to Miss MARY A., daughter of the late Dr. Morgan P. Pitts, of Norfolk Co., Va. (21 JUL 1851)

DEATH. At the residence of her son-in-law, W.D. Porter, U.S. Navy, Mrs. E.A. BEALE, the widow of the late George Beale, Sr. The friends of the family are requested to attend the funeral on this (Monday) morning at 11 o'clock, on F, near 6th street. (21 JUL 1851)

DEATH. In this city, on Saturday afternoon, the 19th inst., in the 35th year of her age, Mrs. MARY ANN WORTHEN, wife of Charles Worthen, leaving him and five children to mourn her loss. The funeral will take place at four o'clock this afternoon, from the family residence on 10th street, between L and M streets north. (21 JUL 1851)

DEATH. Yesterday afternoon [20 JUL 1851], of a lingering illness, in the 49th year of his age, Mr. HENRY HOWARD. His friends are invited to his funeral this afternoon at three o'clock, from his late residence, on Fifth street west, between Massachusetts avenue and K street north. (21 JUL 1851)

MARRIAGE. In Raleigh, N.C., on the 25th ult., by the Rev. Dr. Mason, BRADLEY T. JOHNSON, of Frederick, Md., to JEANNIE C., daughter of Hon. R.M. Saunders. (22 JUL 1851)

DEATH. On Wednesday, 16th inst., at Georgetown, D.C., CHARLES B. LUCAS, in his 31st year, son of Wm. and Eliza Lucas. (22 JUL 1851)

DEATH. At Ft. Leavenworth, Mo., June 21, 1851, THOMAS F., infant son of Mary T. and Dr. Joseph K. Barnes, U.S. Army. (22 JUL 1851)

MARRIAGE. On Monday evening, 21st inst., by Rev. John W. French, S. POWHATAN CARTER, U.S. Navy, to CAROLINE C., daughter of Samuel J. Potts, Esq. (23 JUL 1851)

DEATH. At Concord, N.H., on the 14th inst., of consumption, CHARLOTTE PACKARD, youngest daughter of Capt. Joseph Manahan, for many years a resident of this city, aged 16 years and one month. (23 JUL 1851)

DEATH. In the city of Raleigh, N.C., on Saturday, 21st ult., in the 80th year of his age, Mr. WM. PECK, a merchant of fifty years' standing. Mr. Peck was born in the borough of Norfolk, Va., on the 1st April 1772; soon after removed to Petersburg, where he resided until 8th February 1798, at which time he came to North Carolina and located as a merchant in our city... *Raleigh Register*. (23 JUL 1851)

MARRIAGE. On the 22d inst., by the Rev. Mr. Slattery, Mr. WASHINGTON F. DARNES to Miss ANN COLUMBIA MAY, all of this city. (25 JUL 1851)

MARRIAGE. At St. Mary's Church, by the Rev. Mr. Alig, on the 22d July, Mr. WILLIAM CORD to Miss MARY THERESA SCHLATMANN, both of this city. On the 14th, by the same, MICHAEL ULRICK, Esq., of Pennsylvania, to Miss MARY ELLEN McKELYUTTE, of this city. On the 12th of June, by the same, Mr. WM. SULLIVAN to Miss EMMA FITZPATRICK, both of this city. (25 JUL 1851)

DEATH. At Louisville, Ky., on Monday, the 21st inst., PETER JULME, aged about 40 years, a resident of Philadelphia, but known and valued here as elsewhere. (25 JUL 1851)

DEATH. Suddenly, on the 20th July, at the Grove, Prince William Co., Va., Mr. SAMUEL LATIMER, in the 46th year of his age, in the full possession of his mind, and resigned and peaceful, leaving an affectionate wife and a large family of children, and a numerous circle of friends and relatives to mourn his loss. Mr. W.

fell a victim thus early in life to a cancer, which, less than a year ago, appeared to be entirely removed by the knife. (25 JUL 1851)

MARRIAGE. On the 24th inst., at Washington, by the Rev. Wm. Hodge, Mr. THOS. A. MITCHELL, of Annapolis, Md., to Miss ISABELLA C. MAYO, of Richmond, Va. (26 JUL 1851)

DEATH. On the 25th inst., ANNIE BOOTH, aged 22 months and 19 days, youngest daughter of John B. and Sarah A. Turton. The friends of the family are invited to attend the funeral on this (Saturday) afternoon at 4 o'clock, from their residence on H street, between 21st and 22d streets. (26 JUL 1851)

DEATH. At New York, on the 24th inst., in the 34th year of his age, CHARLES HENRY OAKLEY, M.D., U.S. Navy. (28 JUL 1851)

DEATH. On the 16th inst., at the residence of Bernard Jones, Jr., Collinsville, Ill., DAVID W. FOUTZ, of Virginia. His effects are in the possession of Mr. Jones, who desires to hear from his family. (28 JUL 1851)

LOCAL ITEM. We regret exceedingly to learn that Mrs. Durham, wife of Mr. James H. Durham, who a few evenings since was severely burnt by the explosion of a camphine lamp, died at an early hour yesterday morning. Mrs. D. was an excellent lady, and her family has the sympathies of a large circle of acquaintances. (29 JUL 1851)

DEATH. In this city, on the 28th inst., in the 51st year of her age, Mrs. NANCY W. DURHAM, wife of Mr. James H. Durham. The friends of the family are requested to attend her funeral this morning, at 10 o'clock, from the residence of her husband, on Capitol Hill. (29 JUL 1851)

MARRIAGE. On Monday, the 28th inst., in Christ Church, Washington, by Rev. Mr. Hodges, CANRATT SCOTOOZSLER to Miss LOUISA LAPOLT, all of this city. (30 JUL 1851)

MARRIAGE. In Ryland Chapel, on Monday evening, the 28th inst., by the Rev. J.S. Gorsuch, Mr. WASHINGTON O. BERRY to Miss AMY HART. (30 JUL 1851)

MARRIAGE. At St. Mary's church, on the 29th inst., by the Rev. Mr. Alig, Mr. PHILIP MILLER to Miss LOUISA GRAMLICH, all of this city. (30 JUL 1851)

MARRIAGE. In this city, on the 28th inst., by the Rev. James Laurie, D.D., WILLIAM B. HALE, of Winchester, N.H., and HARRIET AMELIA, daughter of Mr. Wright Porter, of Hartford, Ver. (30 JUL 1851)

MARRIAGE. On Tuesday, the 22d inst., by the Rev. Mr. Edwards, JOHN WM. EARP to Miss MATILDA GARDNIER, both of this city. (30 JUL 1851)

DEATH. In Mobile, Ala., on the 18th July, in the 31st year of his age, Mr. GEORGE W. WALLACE, formerly of this city. (30 JUL 1851)

DEATH. On Tuesday, 29th inst., at 5 o'clock A.M., CHARLES VERNON, aged 14 months and 8 days, only child of S.J. and Hannah Ober. Friends and acquaintances are invited to attend the funeral from Messrs. Adams's, at 10 o'clock this day. (30 JUL 1851)

DEATH. On the 29th inst., after a lingering illness, Mrs. MARY F. OWEN, wife of Edward Owen, of this city. The friends of the family are requested to attend her funeral this afternoon, at 5 o'clock, from her residence, on South B street, opposite the Smithsonian Institution. (31 JUL 1851)

DEATH. In this city, on Tuesday evening last, Mrs. LOUIS ADELLVIG. The deceased was a native of Germany, but for several years a resident of this city, in the 82d year of her age. The funeral will take place this afternoon at 4 o'clock from the residence of her son-in-law, Wm. Grupe, on Pennsylvania avenue, between 4½ and 3d streets. The friends and relatives of the family are respectfully invited to attend. (31 JUL 1851)

MARRIAGE. On the 29th ult., by the Rev. Jos. S. Collins, Mr. ORFORD BOUCHER to Miss MARGARETTA SKIDMORE, both of Georgetown, D.C. (1 AUG 1851)

DEATH. On Thursday, the 31st ult., MARY O'LEARY, wife of John O'Leary, of consumption, in the 27th year of her age. Her friends and those of the family will please attend her funeral from the residence of her husband, on 4½ street, near Maryland avenue, on tomorrow, (Saturday,) at 3 o'clock, without further notice. (1 AUG 1851)

DEATH. On the 29th of July, in the 30th year of her age, FRANCES, the beloved wife of JOHN G. DEEBLE, a native of Ireland, but for the last two years a resident of this city. Her disease was consumption, which she bore with Christian fortitude. (1 AUG 1851)

DEATH. At Baltimore, on the evening of the 30th ult., of paralysis, after an illness of two weeks, PETER FOY, in the 71st year of his age. (1 AUG 1851)

DEATH. On the 31st ult., HENRIETTA, infant daughter of James C. and Henrietta Greer, aged 2 years and 4 months. The funeral will take place this day, at 2 o'clock P.M., from the residence of Wm. Greer, 10th street. The friends of the family are requested to attend. (1 AUG 1851)

DEATH. At Leesburg, Va., on the 30th ult., aged 1 year and 10 days, HOWARD S., second son of Alpheus L. Edwards, of this city, late of Chattanooga, Tenn. (2 AUG 1851)

DEATH. At the village of Stoke Newington, near London, England, on the 16th of July, in the 66th year of her age, JANE, the wife of Pishey Thompson, formerly and for many years a resident of this city. "*None knew her but to love her, None nam'd her but to praise.*" (4 AUG 1851)

DEATH. On Sunday evening, the 3d inst., after a lingering illness, HARRIET, aged 54 years, wife of Jacob A. Bender. Funeral today (Tuesday) at 4 o'clock, from her late residence on F street south, near 7th. The friends of the family are respectfully invited. (5 AUG 1851)

DEATH. At his residence, near Fairfax Court-House, on the 29th ult., HIRAM FULLER, Esq., Editor of the *Fairfax News*. Mr. Fuller was born at South Salem, N.Y., but in the spring of 1844 he purchased a farm in Fairfax Co., and removed there with his family. In August 1849, he became the editor and proprietor of the *Fairfax News*, which he conducted with credit and ability, and with considerable success, from that time until his death. (5 AUG 1851)

DEATH. At his residence, near Ft. Smith, Ark., after a few hours' illness, July 12th, of cholera, Col. WILLIAM DUVALL, in the 69th year of his age. A few hours previous to his death he enjoyed his usually vigorous health; but the disease had marked him as its victim, and his long and useful life was terminated without a murmur or a groan. Col. D. was a native of Frederick Co., Md., and was the oldest surviving member of a noble Huguenot family. He removed with his family to Ft. Smith (to fill an important office under Government) about 22 years since. His remains were interred in his family vault beside his excellent wife, near the residence of his son-in-law, Maj. Rector. (5 AUG 1851)

DEATH. At Ft. Hamilton, N.Y. harbor, on Saturday, the 19th ult., BETTIE BLANEY, daughter of Lieut. Col. J.H. Eaton, U.S. Army, aged 10 months. (5 AUG 1851)

DEATH. At Santa Fe, N.M., of erysipelas, on the 6th of May last, in the 19th year of his age, ALEXANDER GORDON BEALL, son of Col. Benjamin L. Beall, U.S. Army, and grandson of the late venerable George Taylor, of this city. (6 AUG 1851)

Daily National Intelligencer, Marriage and Death Notices, 1851-1854

DEATH. On Tuesday, the 29th ult., in Prince George's Co., Md., of dysentery, LUCY FAIRFAX, only daughter of Lieut. A.B. Fairfax, and the late Sarah C. Fairfax, his wife, aged 1 year and 5 months. (6 AUG 1851)

DEATH. On Wednesday, the 6th inst., at 4 o'clock A.M., MARY ELIZABETH, daughter of John and Caroline Granenger, aged 3 years 9 months and 10 days. The friends of her family are respectfully invited to attend the funeral, from the residence of her uncle, Chas. E. Rison, K street, near 13th street, this afternoon at 2 o'clock, without further notice. (7 AUG 1851)

DEATH. On the 6th inst., of dropsy, RICHARD H. HARRINGTON, in the 48th year of his age. His friends and the friends and acquaintances of the family are invited to attend his funeral, from his late residence on Garrison street, near the Navy Yard, this (Friday) afternoon, at 3 o'clock. (8 AUG 1851)

DEATH. On Wednesday [6 AUG 1851], between the hours of 7 and 8 o'clock, MARY FRANCES, only daughter of B. Birch, in the 18th year of her age. Her friends and those of the family are invited to attend her funeral, from the residence of her father, on 14th street, between F and G streets, this evening, at 4½ o'clock. (8 AUG 1851)

DEATH. On Friday morning, August 8th, MEURY WHITE, eldest daughter of M.H. and Susan B. Stevens, aged 3 years 9 months and 10 days. The funeral will take place from the residence of Mrs. Adams, on Pennsylvania avenue, this (Saturday) morning at 10 o'clock. The friends and relatives of the family are invited to attend. (9 AUG 1851)

MARRIAGE. At Mobile, Ala., on the 19th ult., R. CARRESE BRENT, of Maryland, to Miss JANET MILLER, of Mobile, Ala. (11 AUG 1851)

DEATH. On Tuesday morning, 5th inst., in Baltimore, Mrs. B. COTTRINGER, relict of Garrett Cottringer, Esq., formerly of Philadelphia, and confidential friend of the late Robert Morris, Secretary of Finance of the U.S., and ex-Secretary of the North American Land Company, Philadelphia. She and her daughter were well and favorably known and their merits appreciated in this city, during some years' residence, and in conducting a Female Academy. (11 AUG 1851)

DEATH. On the 21st ult. [21 JUL 1851], at Prospect Hill, Montgomery Co., Md., JAMES MASON, son of Ebenezer Peyton and Mary E. Piggott, aged 22 months. (11 AUG 1851)

MARRIAGE. On Monday, July 28, by the Rev. Dr. Bunting, Mr. REMIGIUS BURCH, of Washington, to Miss ANN BERNARD, of Little Hackney, St. Mary's Co., Md., daughter of the late Bernard Blackiston. (12 AUG 1851)

DEATH. On the 1st of August, after a protracted illness of severe suffering, which he bore with Christian fortitude and submission, GEORGE, youngest son of Gold S. Silliman, of Brooklyn, L.I. (12 AUG 1851)

DEATH. [Communicated]. At Chicago, Ill., after a few hours' illness', of cholera, WALTER BUTLER, brother of Benjamin F. and Chas. Butler, of New York city. Mr. Butler was the oldest member of the family, and removed from the State of New York to Chicago, after the monetary embarrassments of 1842. His oldest (and third) daughter, accompanied by his eldest son, were absent on their bridal tour, having been married three weeks previous. His second daughter (also married) was ill, and unable to reach her father's bedside to receive his blessing. Thus died, in the full vigor of manhood, one eminently qualified with every virtue to command the admiration of men and the approval of God. (12 AUG 1851)

DEATH. On the 4th inst., at the residence of the Hon. Andrew Stewart, Uniontown, Pa., ELIZABETH STEWART, daughter of Charles E. and Mary E. Swearingen, of Washington, D.C., aged 1 year and 11 months. (12 AUG 1851)

Daily National Intelligencer, Marriage and Death Notices, 1851-1854

MARRIAGE. In the Catholic Church at Harper's Ferry, on the 9th inst., by Rev. Mr. Plumnkitt, Miss APOLLONIA JAGIELLO, late of Lithuania, Poland, and Maj. GASPAR TOCHMAN, formerly of Warsaw, Poland. (13 AUG 1851)

MARRIAGE. On the 11th inst., by the Rev. Mr. Donelan, JOHN E. HERRILL to HENRIETTA Q. MAHORNEY. (13 AUG 1851)

DEATH. In this city, on the 11th inst., MARGARET BEATLEY, wife of C. Beatley, in the 42d year of her age. The friends and acquaintances of the deceased are requested to attend the funeral from her late residence, on 22d street, between B and C streets, this evening, 13th inst., at 4 o'clock. (13 AUG 1851)

DEATH. At Norfolk, Va., on Sunday, the 3d inst., Mrs. CHLOE ANN, wife of the Rev. William McKenney, Chaplain U.S. Navy. (13 AUG 1851)

DEATH. In this city, on Saturday afternoon last [9 AUG 1851], PORTIA, daughter of Robert A. and Anne Sommerville, aged 2 years 1 month and 19 days. (13 AUG 1851)

DEATH. At Appleby, in Harford Co., Md., CATHARINE SCOTT, wife of William Murray Maynadier, in the 68th year of her age. (13 AUG 1851)

MARRIAGE. On the 13th inst., by the Rev. U. Ward, JOHN S. HOPKINS, of Georgetown, to Miss HESTER E. DASHIELL, of the same place. (14 AUG 1851)

DEATH. At Burnside, his residence, in Granville Co., N.C., on the 28th of June, PATRICK HAMILTON, Esq., in the 63d year of his age. (14 AUG 1851)

DEATH. At 27 Paterson street, Kingston, Glasgow, (in Scotland,) on the 27th July, MARY KATHERINE, daughter of David Munroe, Esq., of Washington, D.C. (15 AUG 1851)

DEATH. At Sacramento City, Calif., on the 30th of June last, ALFRED HOWELL TIDBALL, in the 24th year of his age, youngest son of the late Alexander S. Tidball, of Winchester, Va. (15 AUG 1851)

MARRIAGE. On Thursday evening, by the Rev. John C. Smith, Mr. JOSEPH A. BLAU to Miss LAURA V. FREEMAN, all of this city. (16 AUG 1851)

MARRIAGE. At the Mansion House [Hotel], Alexandria, Va., on the 12th inst., by the Rev. Elias Harrison, Major THOMAS A. HARRIS, of the U.S. Army, to Miss IMOGEN PORTER, daughter of the late Comm. Porter, U.S. Navy. (16 AUG 1851)

DEATH. At "Stony Harbor," her late residence, near Piscataway, Md., on Monday the 4th inst., after a painful illness of 7 months, which she bore with truly Christian fortitude, Mrs. SARAH ANN EDELEN, consort of the late Raphael C. Edelen, Esq., in the 53d year of her age. (16 AUG 1851)

DEATH. On the 14th inst., in Bladensburg, Md., PHILIP T. BROWN. The friends of the family are requested to attend his funeral, from the residence of his father, at 10 o'clock A.M. today. (16 AUG 1851)

MARRIAGE. At Baltimore, on the 14th inst., by Rev. Mr. Tarring, E. DORSEY ETCHISON, of that city, to Miss RACHEL A. STEPHENS, of Washington. (18 AUG 1851)

DEATH. Departed this life, on the 15th inst., of typhoid fever, EDMUND B. DARNALL, in the 20th year of his age, youngest son of Francis L. and Mary Darnall, Prince George's Co., Md. (18 AUG 1851)

Daily National Intelligencer, Marriage and Death Notices, 1851-1854

DEATH. At Powhatan Hill, the residence of Col. Edward T. Tayloe, in King George Co., Va., on the 12th inst., after a protracted illness, in the 23d year of her age, Mrs. LOUISA R.T. JENIFER, the wife of James L. Jenifer, Esq., and daughter of Wm. H. Tayloe, of Mt. Airy. (18 AUG 1851)

DEATH. At Shepherd's Hill, in Caroline Co., Va., on Friday, the 11th of July, 1851, JOHN WOOLFOLK, after an illness of 15 days, in the 47th year of his age. (19 AUG 1851)

MARRIAGE. ON the 19th inst., by Rev. W.T. Eva, COLVILLE TERRETT, U.S. Navy, and Miss M. ANNA F. MATHEWS, eldest daughter of the late Capt. William P. Mathews, of Baltimore, Md. (21 AUG 1851)

MARRIAGE. On the 14th ult., at Oakwood, near Fayette, Mo., by the Rev. Dr. Dunn, HORACE EVERETT, Esq., of Gainesville, Ala., to MARY, eldest daughter of A. Leonard, Esq., of the former place. (21 AUG 1851)

MARRIAGE. On the 13th inst., at the seat of Capt. O.H. Berryman, Fauquier, Va., by the Rev. A. Compton, FENTON MERCER EWELL, Esq., to Miss ALBERTA OTWAYANNA REYNOLDS. (21 AUG 1851)

DEATH. Suddenly, at Georgetown, D.C., on the evening of the 15th ult., to the inexpressible regret of his family and a large circle of friends and associates, Dr. WILLIAM SOTHORON, in the 65th year of his age. (21 AUG 1851)

DEATH. At Ft. Snelling, Minnesota Territory, on the 5th day of August, SARAH R. HENDRICKSON, wife of Capt. T. Hendrickson, U.S. Army. (21 AUG 1851)

DEATH. On Tuesday morning, 19th August, SARAH ELLEN, infant daughter of William Henry and Margaret Kelly, and grandchild of Edward and Susan McCubbin, of this city. (21 AUG 1851)

MARRIAGE. On Thursday evening, 21st inst., by the Rev. Wm. B. Edwards, WM. H. JONES to MARY F., second daughter of Chas. L. Coltman, Esq., all of this city. (23 AUG 1851)

DEATH. On Friday morning, 22d inst., DOROTHY H., widow of Jno. Storer, in the 81st year of her age. Her funeral will take place from the residence of her son-in-law, J.K. Hanson, Esq., this afternoon at 4 o'clock, when her friends and those of the family are invited to attend. (23 AUG 1851)

DEATH. On Tuesday, 19th inst., at the residence of the Rev. C.M. Callaway, Jefferson Co., Va., SARAH VIRGINIA, youngest daughter of Samuel D. and Matilda S. King, aged 3 years and 27 days. (23 AUG 1851)

DEATH. On Saturday evening, the 23d inst., by accidental drowning, CHARLES S. WEST, aged 29 years. The funeral will take place today, (Monday,) at 3 o'clock P.M., from the residence of his father, Mr. John West, on 7th street, opposite Centre Market. The friends and acquaintances of the family are requested to attend. (25 AUG 1851)

MARRIAGE. On Sunday morning, the 24th inst., by Rev. L.F. Morgan, Mr. A.H. MARKLAND, of Kentucky, to Miss M.L. SIMMS, daughter of Sampson Simms, of this city. (26 AUG 1851)

DEATH. At the residence of P.F. Bacon, Esq., WASHINGTON F. MURRAY, of Louisville, Ky., aged 28 years. The funeral will take place this afternoon at 4 o'clock. His acquaintance and the friends of the family are invited to attend. (26 AUG 1851)

MARRIAGE. On Sunday afternoon, by the Rev. Mr. Marks, Mr. CHARLES W. SMITH to Miss ELIZABETH BRIGHTWELL, both of Prince George's Co., Md. (27 AUG 1851)

Daily National Intelligencer, Marriage and Death Notices, 1851-1854

MARRIAGE. At St. Louis, 14th inst., Lieut. A. READ, U.S.N., to Miss CONSTANCE, daughter of Major E. Steen, U.S.A. (27 AUG 1851)

MARRIAGE. On the 23d inst., by the Rev. Mr. Alig, TIMOTHY MURPHY and MARGARET DONOHUE. (27 AUG 1851)

DEATH. On the 25th inst., PRISCILLA FRASER, in the 63d year of her age. She has been a resident of Washington for 45 years. Her friends are respectfully requested to attend her funeral on this (Wednesday) afternoon, at 2 o'clock, from her late residence on Half street west, near the Eastern Branch. (27 AUG 1851)

DEATH. At Louisville, Ky., on Thursday evening, the 14th inst., after 9 hours' illness of cholera, WILLIAM THOMPSON, aged nearly 13, eldest son of Martha F. and Samuel Campbell, formerly of Middleburg, Va. (27 AUG 1851)

DEATH. On the 14th inst., in the Navy Yard at Pensacola, after a long illness, GEORGE LYNDALL, formerly of this city. A large circle of friends mourn his loss, and deeply sympathize with his afflicted widow and children. (27 AUG 1851)

DEATH. On Saturday, the 23d inst., EFFIE KATE, youngest child of Robert T. and Susan Bassett, aged one year. (27 AUG 1851)

DEATH. At Fredericksburg, Va., on the 21st inst., JAMES D. HARROW, Esq., in the 60th year of his age. He was the Editor of the *Virginia Herald*, one of the oldest papers in the country, and with which he became connected early in the present century. The *Fredericksburg News* says of him: "As an individual or an editor the deceased had no enemies. Most quiet and unobtrusive he passed through life, infringing on no one's rights, and no one disposed to trespass on his. Remarkable for taciturnity, he never gave offence. He wrote but little and that little never offensive or tinged with personality. For many years he was a member of the Presbyterian Church, and lived a Christian life." (28 AUG 1851)

MARRIAGE. On the 26th inst., by the Rev. J.G. Butler, WM. G.F. TABLEMAN to Miss SOPHIA L. SMITH, both of this city. (29 AUG 1851)

MARRIAGE. On the 28th inst., by the Rev. J.R. Eckard, GEO. WM. YERBY to MARY E. PHILLIPS, of Harrisburg, Pa. (29 AUG 1851)

DEATH. At his residence, near Rock Creek Church, on Friday, the 29th inst., Major GEORGE A. WALKER, Paymaster U.S. Marine Corps, in the 51st year of his age. The friends of the family are respectfully invited to attend his funeral on Sunday next, at 10 o'clock A.M. (30 AUG 1851)

DEATH. At Fayetteville, N.C., on the 22d inst., Capt. WILLIAM H. BAYNE, for 11 years past the Editor of the *North Carolinan*. The deceased was a native of Washington, D.C., but has been a resident of Fayetteville since the 4th of July 1840, at which time he took charge of the "Carolinan." He left a wife and five small children to mourn the loss of a kind protector and friend. (30 AUG 1851)

NATIONAL INTELLIGENCER. — The publishers of this paper desire to purchase a file of the *National Intelligencer* for the years 1800 to 1806, both inclusive. A liberal price will be given for the whole or any one of the above years, if early application is made. Address the Editors. (30 AUG 1851)

MARRIAGE. In this city, the 1st inst., by the Rev. J.W. French, Lieut. Col. BENJAMIN P. LARNED, Deputy Paymaster General U.S. Army, to ELIZABETH R. LARNED, of this city. (2 SEP 1851)

MARRIAGE. On the 2d inst., in this city, by the Rev. Dr. Ducachet, of Philadelphia, SOMMERVILLE NICHOLSON, of the U.S. Navy, to HANNAH MARIA, daughter of Dr. Wm. Jones. (4 SEP 1851)

MARRIAGE. On the morning of the 1st inst., at the E Street Baptist Church, by the Rev. Mr. Kempton, Mr. BENJAMIN S. MYERS and Miss EMMA BROWN, formerly of New York. (4 SEP 1851)

MARRIAGE. At the University of Virginia, on the 2d inst., by the Rev. R.K. Meade, the Rev. WILLIAM McGUFFEY, Professor of Moral Philosophy in the University, to LAURA P., daughter of Prof. Henry Howard. (5 SEP 1851)

OBITUARY. [Communicated.] DIED, at his residence near Nottingham, Md., on Saturday evening last [30 AUG 1851], very suddenly, of apoplexy, MICHAEL B. CARROLL, Esq., aged about 54... The writer of this was present, and was struck with the deep grief exhibited by the Negroes belonging to Mr. Carroll, of whom there were nearly a hundred [text continues]. (5 SEP 1851)

DEATH OF JUDGE WOODBURY. A telegraph despatch [Portsmouth, N.H.] yesterday announced the demise of the Hon. Levi Woodbury, an Associate Justice of the Supreme Court of the United States [text continues]. (6 SEP 1851)

MARRIAGE. In Georgetown, on Tuesday morning, the 2d inst., by the Rev. Chas. McElfresh, Mr. BENJ. R. MAYFIELD to Miss CHARLOTTE L. BROWN, both of that place. (8 SEP 1851)

MARRIAGE. At New York, on Thursday [4 SEP 1851], at Calvary Church, by the Rev. Francis L. Hawks, Lieut. EDWARD HIGGINS, U.S. Navy, to ANNA MARIA, daughter of John C. Zimmerman, Esq., of that city. (8 SEP 1851)

DEATH. Near Taneytown, Carroll Co., Md., on Thursday the 28th ult., Mrs. MARGARET GALT, wife of Sterling Galt., Esq., in the 53d year of her age. (8 SEP 1851)

DEATH. In Germantown, Pa., on the morning of the 4th inst., Mrs. MARGARET PROVEST, widow of the late Alexander Provest, in the 74th year of her age. In the death of this amiable lady we are called upon to chronicle the loss of a devoted mother and a firm and consistent Christian. Her death will leave a void not easily filled in the community of which she was so long a member, and to whom she was endeared by her many shining virtues. (8 SEP 1851)

DEATH. Near Ft. Washita, 3d ult., Lieut. P.A. FARRELLY, 5th Inf. U.S. Army. On the Thursday before his death Lieut. F. was thrown from a horse, his head striking a stump, which affected the skull and brain, and which is supposed to have caused his death. (8 SEP 1851)

DEATH. On the 29th of August 1851, ANN ELIZA, daughter of James and Jane Keck, aged 11 years and 9 months. (8 SEP 1851)

DEATH. On the 5th day last, the 4th inst., at the residence of his father adjoining this city, JONATHAN M. SEAVER, a member of the Religious Society of Friends. (9 SEP 1851)

DEATH. On the 8th inst., after a long and painful illness, Mrs. ELIZABETH RUFF, in the 61st year of her age. The funeral will take place this afternoon, at 3 o'clock, from the residence of her son, on E street, between 5th and 6th. The friends of the family are invited to attend without further notice. (9 SEP 1851)

DEATH. On Sunday, the 7th inst., WILLIAM WATERS, Boatswain in the U.S. Navy, in the 50th year of his age. The funeral will take place this (Tuesday) afternoon at two o'clock, at the Navy Yard, where the friends and acquaintances of the deceased are invited to attend. (9 SEP 1851)

DEATH. On the 8th inst., Capt. SAMUEL KILLMON, aged 63 years, a native of Dorchester Co., Md., but for the last 30 years a resident of this city, and a most estimable and worthy citizen. The funeral will move from the late residence of the deceased, 13th street, this morning at 10 o'clock. (9 SEP 1851)

Daily National Intelligencer, Marriage and Death Notices, 1851-1854

OBITUARY. [Communicated.] Departed this life, at Jackson Court-house, Va., on the 19th day of August 1851, FLEET SMITH, Esq., late of this city. The deceased was for a long time a resident of Leesburg, Va., and practised the profession of the law in Loudoun and the neighboring counties. He was licensed to practice by Edmund Pendleton, Spencer Roane, and Robert White, Judges of the General Court of Virginia, in the year 1798. He removed to Washington in 1820, where he pursued for many years successfully the practice of his profession. He also resided for a few years in the county of St. Mary's, Md. He was a gentleman of the old school, was remarkable for his integrity, for a high sense of honor, for candor, and for a great fund of humor, and for many fine qualities which adorn the walks of private life. He met death with calmness and composure, and although he had reached a period of existence when in the course of nature the sands of life were fast running out, yet the loss to the surviving relatives of his family will long be deplored, and felt with the keenest anguish, whilst time must only afford to them a balm to heal the wound inflicted by the hand of Death. (9 SEP 1851)

MARRIAGE. On the 9th inst., by the Rev. Thos. F. Lockett, Mr. JOS. FOWLER to Miss ALCUZERA BARNHOUSE, all of this city. (10 SEP 1851)

DEATH. On the 9th inst., after a protracted illness, which she bore with the patience and resignation of a humble and pious Christian, MARY ANN HURLEY, aged 34 years, widow of John Hurley, and eldest daughter of William and Susan Dant. *Requiescat in pace!* The funeral will take place at four o'clock this (the 10th) afternoon from her father's, on D, between 2d and 3d streets. (10 SEP 1851)

OBITUARY. [Communicated.] Died, near Greensboro, Ala., in the 33d year of his age, Rev. JAMES SOMERVELL MARBURY, eldest son of John Marbury, Esq., of Georgetown, and late Rector of St. Paul's Church, Greensboro [text continues]. (11 SEP 1851)

MARRIAGE. At Philadelphia, on Tuesday evening, the 9th inst., by the Rev. H.W. Ducachet, D.D., ROBERT LeROY, of New York, to AMELIA, second daughter of William D. Lewis, Esq., of the former city. (12 SEP 1851)

MARRIAGE. At Westwood, in the vicinity of Nashville, Tenn., on the evening of the 3d inst., by the Rev. Dr. Edgar, Dr. THOMAS R. JENNINGS and Miss MARY COURTNEY, eldest daughter of Col. M. Courtney. (13 SEP 1851)

OBITUARY. [Communicated.] Died, at Santa Fe, N.M., Capt. W.H. SAUNDERS, a native of Leesburg, Va., and late of the 2d regiment of U.S. Dragoons... Served with distinction through the Florida war under Generals Taylor and Worth. Subsequently he participated in the brilliant victories upon the Rio Grande and siege of Vera Cruz, which resulted in the complete discomfiture of the Mexican forces, and the consequent triumph of American army [text continues]. (13 SEP 1851)

DROWNING. A case of drowning took place early on Friday evening [12 SEP 1851], near the Long Bridge. A child named Jenkins, a light mulatto or quadroon, about 6 years of age, was gathering chips and fragments of bark on the wharf where the schooner *Robert Armstrong*, of Washington, was discharging her load of wood. By some mischance he fell into the water between the *Armstrong* and the wharf... [15 SEP 1851)

MARRIAGE. On the 13th inst., by the Rev. Dr. Laurie, Dr. LEOPOLD DOVILLIERS, of St. Louis, Mo., to PHILLIPPA, second daughter of Mr. Nathaniel Carusi, of this city. (15 SEP 1851)

MARRIAGE. On the 1st inst., at Georgetown, D.C., by the Rev. Mr. Rumley, JOSEPH S. DUCKWALL, Esq., to VIRGINIA M., youngest daughter of John W. Bronaugh, deceased, late of Stafford Co., Va. (15 SEP 1851)

Daily National Intelligencer, Marriage and Death Notices, 1851-1854

DEATH. In this city, on Sunday the 14th inst., PHILIP ENNIS, in the 64th year of his age, a native of county Wexford, Ireland, and for the last 30 years a resident of this city. His funeral will take place from his late residence, on 6th street, on Tuesday, the 16th inst., at 4 o'clock P.M. (15 SEP 1851)

DEATH. On Saturday evening last [13 SEP 1851], Mrs. MARY CORCORAN, wife of Mr. Jno. Corcoran. Her remains will be taken from her residence, corner of 7th and H streets, at 3 o'clock this afternoon, to St. Patrick's Burial-Ground. The friends of the family are invited to attend. (15 SEP 1851)

MARRIAGE. On Sunday evening last [14 SEP 1851], by the Rev. Mr. [Alig], Mr. JOHN CASEY to Miss MARY ANN FLANNEGAN, all of this city. (16 SEP 1851)

DEATH. At Floyd Courthouse, Va., on the 6th inst., Mr. Nathaniel Henry, about 60 years of age, son of the famous Patrick Henry. (16 SEP 1851)

MARRIAGE. On the 16th inst., at St. Peter's Church, in this city, by the Rev. Peter Laneghan, PETER T. MARCERON to ELIZABETH F.X. GARTLAND, both of this city. (17 SEP 1851)

MARRIAGE. On the 16th inst., by the Rev. J. Geo. Butler, JOHN McLANE BUEL to Miss MARY ELLEN, daughter of John C. Roemmelle, Esq., all of this city. (18 SEP 1851)

DEATH. On the 17th inst., Mrs. LYDIA WOOD, wife of Henry S. Wood, in the 51st year of hear age. The funeral will take place from her late residence, Capitol Hill, Fourth street east, near Pennsylvania avenue, on Friday (tomorrow) afternoon, at 2 o'clock, where her friends and acquaintances will attend without further notice. (18 SEP 1851)

DEATH. In this city, on the 16th of September, after a long illness, which he bore with fortitude and resignation, Mr. ZACHARIAH HAZEL, in the 82d year of his age. The friends and acquaintances of the deceased are respectfully invited to attend his funeral at his late residence, on Capitol Hill, on Tuesday, at 2 o'clock P.M. (18 SEP 1851)

MARRIAGE. On the 15th inst., at St. Mary's Church, by the Rev. Mr. Alig, MICHAEL RAGAN to MARY AGNES ELDER, both of this city. (19 SEP 1851)

MARRIAGE. On the 16th inst., at St. Mary's Church, by the Rev. Mr. Alig, MARTIN YUNGANZ to MARGARET BOTT, both of this city. (19 SEP 1851)

MARRIAGE. On the 18th inst., by the Rev. Mr. Alig, Mr. WILLIAM HAMMEL to Miss BARBARA VONDERLEHR, both of this city. (19 SEP 1851)

DEATH. The funeral of SAMUEL MUNDELL, aged fourteen years, will take place from the residence of his parents, Marine Barracks, this afternoon, at 4 o'clock. The friends of the family are respectfully invited to attend. (19 SEP 1851)

DEATH. On the 18th inst., MARY ALICE DAVIS, daughter of M.A. Davis, aged three years and 10 months. The friends of the family are invited to attend the funeral today, at 4 o'clock, on Pennsylvania avenue, between 4½ and 6th streets. (20 SEP 1851)

DEATH OF REV. LEVI R. REESE. We have just learned that this distinguished minister of the Methodist Protestant Church died, after a short illness, at five o'clock this morning, on the Eastern Shore of Maryland, whither he had gone on a visit. Mr. Reese is too well known in this community to require any eulogium at our hands. He had the honor of being selected at several sessions as one of the Congressional Chaplains. He was twice elected President of the Maryland Conference, and in every station to which he has been called he has brought with him a mind well stored with practical knowledge, and a firm determination to discharge the duties imposed upon him with fidelity to those by whom he had been selected. We sympathize with his friends in this sudden and unexpected bereavement. — *Baltimore Argus*. (20 SEP 1851)

MARRIAGE. On the 18th inst., at Broad Creek House, Prince George's Co., Md., by the Rev. J. Martin, T.S. EVERETT, U.S. Army, to Miss ELIZA, daughter of the late Col. Thomas C. Lyles. (22 SEP 1851)

MARRIAGE. At Salisbury, N.C., September 17th, by Rev. Prof. Morgan, his Daughter, Miss CHARLOTTE ELIPHEL MORGAN, to E. DELAFIELD SMITH, Esq.,. Counsellor at Law of New York. (23 SEP 1851)

MARRIAGE. On the 20th inst., by the Rev. Mr. Hodges, EDWIN WATERMAN to MARIA AMOS LINDSAY, all of Washington. (24 SEP 1851)

DEATH. At New York, on Monday [22 SEP 1851], while on his way to the Eastward, Capt. JOHN A. BLAKE, in the 54th year of his age. He has been a resident of this city about 20 years, and leaves a family and many friends to mourn his sudden death. His funeral will take place tomorrow morning, at 10 o'clock, from his late residence, on 11th, near E street. (24 SEP 1851) Funeral by the Odd Fellows, of which Mr. Blake was a member, with burial in Congressional Cemetery. (see 26 SEP 1851)

DEATH. On Saturday, the 20th inst., Mrs. MARGARET ANN YOUNG, aged 64 years, consort of Ezekiel Young. The deceased was for many years a resident of this city. She was an exemplary and upright Christian, and her death is lamented by a large family and numerous friends. (24 SEP 1851)

DEATH. On Friday, the 19th inst., at Harper's Ferry, Va., at the residence of her grandson, the Rev. Horace Stringfellow, Jr., Mrs. MILLEY STROTHER, in the 81st year of her age. (24 SEP 1851)

DEATH. At New Brunswick, N.J., on Sunday, the 21st inst., MARY H., wife of C.L. Hardenbergh, Esq., and daughter of the late John G. Warren, of New York city. (24 SEP 1851)

DEATH. On Wednesday, the 24th inst., at Mt. Hope, Georgetown, D.C., the residence of Wm. Robinson, Esq., Passed Midshipman, WM. H. WEAVER, U.S. Navy, in the 25th year of his age. His friends and the friends of the family are invited to attend his funeral, on Friday afternoon, at half-past 4 o'clock, from the above-named residence, without further notice. (25 SEP 1851)

DEATH. In Alexandria, Va., on Saturday, the 13th inst., after a long and painful illness, ESTHER D., wife of Wm. Fowle, Esq., of that place, in the 62d year of her age. (27 SEP 1851)

DEATH. Suddenly, in Winchester, on Wednesday week [17 SEP 1851], MARY BROCKENBROUGH, second daughter of the Hon. Willoughby Newton, of Westmoreland, Va., in the 18th year of her age. (27 SEP 1851)

DEATH. At White Sulphur Springs, Va., on Wednesday, the 17th inst., Mrs. COLUMBIA CALWELL, wife of Wm. B. Calwell, and daughter of Robert T. Gwathmey, of Richmond. (27 SEP 1851)

DEATH. On Tuesday, the 16th inst., at Willow Glen, the residence of her father-in-law, Hezekiah Brawner, in Charles Co., Md., MARY JANE, wife of Jas. T. Brawner, in the 23d year of her age. (27 SEP 1851)

MARRIAGE. On Thursday evening, 25th inst., by Rev. S.A.H. Marks, Mr. JOSEPH JOHNSON to Miss ELIZABETH CHAUNCEY, both of Alexandria, Va. (29 SEP 1851)

MARRIAGE. On Thursday evening, 25th inst., by the Rev. Wm. B. Edwards, Mr. FRANCIS J. GIBSON, of Philadelphia, to Miss SARAH JANE HALL, of this city. (29 SEP 1851)

Daily National Intelligencer, Marriage and Death Notices, 1851-1854

MARRIAGE. On Wednesday, the 24th of September, at Grace Church, Brooklyn, by the Rev. Dr. Croswell, of New Haven, Rev. EDWARD O. FLAGG, Rector of Trinity Church, Norwich, (Conn.) and ELIZA W., daughter of Gen. Wm. Gibbs MacNeill, of New York. (29 SEP 1851)

DEATH. On the night of the 27th inst., in Georgetown, SUSAN E., second daughter of the late A.B. Murray, formerly of Baltimore, Md. (29 SEP 1851)

MARRIAGE. On Thursday, the 25th inst., by the Rev. L.F. Morgan, Mr. WILLIAM BRENT MICKUM, to Miss SARAH PRISCILLA OGDEN, all of this city. (1 OCT 1851)

DEATH. In this city, on Saturday evening last [27 SEP 1851], EDWIN C. WEED, in the 57th year of his age, late of Fairfax, Va., and formerly of Greenfield, Saratoga Co., N.Y., in which county, as well as in Rensaelaer, he was extensively and favorably known as an efficient man of business. (1 OCT 1851)

DEATH. In Georgetown, D.C., September 30, Mrs. ELLEN O. FARRELL, aged 75 years, formerly of Donegaltown county, Ireland, but for the last three years a resident of this town. Her friends and the friends of the family are requested to attend her funeral on this day, the 2d October, at 4 o'clock, from the residence of her son-in-law, Wm. Burns, on Bridge street, between Potomac and Market streets. (2 OCT 1851)

MARRIAGE. On the 2d ult., in Georgetown, by the Rev. Joseph S. Collins, EDWARD WAITE, formerly of New York, to MARY A. STETSON, late of Alexandria, Va. (3 OCT 1851)

MARRIAGE. On Tuesday morning, 30th September, by Rev. L.F. Morgan, Mr. JNO. P. BROWN and MARY ELIZABETH McBAIN, all of this city. (3 OCT 1851)

MARRIAGE. On Wednesday evening, October 1st, by Rev. Mr. MacElfresh, RICHARD EARL to Miss HANNAH DAVISON, all of this city. (3 OCT 1851)

DEATH. At his residence, in Lincoln Co., N.C., on the 25th ult., the Hon. JAMES GRAHAM, in the 57th year of his age. Mr. Graham was the second son of the late Gen. Joseph Graham, and the last surviving Brother of the present Secretary of the Navy. He was educated at the university of his native State, and bred to the profession of the law, which he practiced successfully for several years. He was frequently a member of the Legislature of N.C., and was widely known to the country as one of her most faithful and devoted Representatives in Congress for a period of 12 years. His social nature, and courteous, frank, and manly character attracted to him a large circle of friends among his associates in public life and the visitors and residents of this metropolis, while his kindly sympathies and affections endeared him to those with whom he was more nearly connected. (3 OCT 1851)

DEATH. Of the Asiatic cholera, on the 15th September, at Burlington, Ver., CHARLES S. McGUFFEY, in his 60th year, only son of the Rev. Wm. H. McGuffey, Professor of Moral Philosophy in the University of Virginia. (3 OCT 1851)

DEATH. On Sunday, the 21st ult., in the 21st year of her age, Mrs. MARY FRANCES MARSHALL, wife of Jaquelin A. Marshall, Jr., Esq., of Fauquier, and the eldest daughter of Joseph H. Sherrard, Esq., of Winchester, Va. (4 OCT 1851)

DEATH. On the morning of the 3d inst., PHEBE, wife of J. Bartram North. The friends of the family are invited to attend her funeral from the residence of her husband, on New Jersey avenue, at half-past 3 o'clock on Sunday afternoon. (4 OCT 1851)

DEATH. At her residence near Charlotte Hall, Md., on the 28th ult., of a short illness, ELIZABETH B. MATTHEWS, aged 61 years. (4 OCT 1851)

Daily National Intelligencer, Marriage and Death Notices, 1851-1854

DEATH. On the 20th September last, near Memphis, Tenn., on her way home from the North, Mrs. EMILY WRIGHT, wife of Benjamin D. Wright, Esq., U.S. Navy Agent at Pensacola, Fla. (4 OCT 1851)

DEATH. On Thursday night, the 2d inst., in the sixth year of her age, ANNIE H.R., daughter of John and America Willey. The funeral services will take place at the Foundry Church, on Sunday afternoon, the 5th inst., at 3 o'clock, where the friends and acquaintances are invited to attend. (4 OCT 1851)

MARRIAGE. At Meadville, Pa., Sept. 16th, by the Rev. John Barker, D.D., President of Allegheny College, Lieut. GEORGE HURST, U.S. Navy, to Miss CLARA VAN TASSEL, formerly of Erie. (6 OCT 1851)

DEATH. At Mendota, Minn., on the 20th ult., HENRY HASTINGS, only son of Hon. Henry H. Sibley, aged four years. (6 OCT 1851)

DEATH. On the 20th of September, at Deep Falls, the residence of his grandmother, Mrs. Eliza Thomas, HENRY, aged 6 years and 6 months, son of Dr. James and Ann M. Waring, of Chaptico, St. Mary's Co., Md. (7 OCT 1851)

DEATH OF JAMES BEATTY. The *Baltimore Patriot* of Monday [6 OCT 1851] announces the death of the venerable JAMES BEATTY, at the advanced age of 81 years. Mr. Beatty but a few short weeks since lost the companion of his youth and the soother of his old age, and now he too has gone to that bourn whence none return. There was no man nor merchant (says the *Patriot*) more highly esteemed in our city than James Beatty. He formerly, and for some time, filled the office of Navy Agent in Baltimore, and has long been the proprietor of extensive powder mills on Jones's Falls, and was perhaps the oldest merchant of Baltimore at his death. (8 OCT 1851)

MARRIAGE. On the 8th inst., WILLIAM G. TEMPLE, U.S. Navy, to CATLYNA, second daughter of General Totten. (8 OCT 1851)

MARRIAGE. On Thursday evening, the 2d inst., by the Rev. F.S. Evans, Mr. EDWIN E. TRUE to Miss MARY ELLEN ANGEL. (8 OCT 1851)

MARRIAGE. On the 2d inst., by the Rev. Mr. Hodges, JAMES M. ROBERTSON to MARGARET ISABELLA MARTIN, all of Washington. (8 OCT 1851)

MARRIAGE. At Louisville, Ky., on the morning of the 5th inst., in St. Paul's Church, by the Rev. W.T. Rooker, the rector thereof, GEORGE FRANCIS TRAIN, of Boston, Mass., to HENRIETTA WILHELMINA WILKINSON, daughter of Col. Geo. T.M. Davis, of the former place. (10 OCT 1851)

MARRIAGE. At Baltimore, on the 7th inst., by the Rev. Dr. Plumer, Dr. HENRY WM. WILSON and ELIZA KELSO HOLLINGSWORTH, all of that city. (10 OCT 1851)

DEATH. On Wednesday evening, October 8th, FRANCIS DODGE, in his 70th year. His funeral will take place on Friday, the 10th, at 4 o'clock P.M., (this afternoon,) from his late residence on Congress street, Georgetown. The friends and acquaintances of the family are respectfully invited to attend. (10 OCT 1851) He died at residence in Georgetown, was attached to the Presbyterian Church in Georgetown, of which he was a regular attendant till his last illness, and always a firm supporter. He died in the 69th year of his age. (13 OCT 1851)

DEATH. On Friday, the 10th inst., after a lingering illness of several weeks, Mrs. ELIZABETH H., wife of Mr. Matthew McLeod, and daughter of Ignatius Manning, deceased, in the 43d year of her age, leaving four small children and a disconsolate husband to mourn their irreparable loss. Her funeral will take place from her late residence, opposite the Convent, Georgetown, this afternoon, at 4 o'clock P.M., when and where her friends are respectfully invited to attend. (11 OCT 1851)

Daily National Intelligencer, Marriage and Death Notices, 1851-1854

MARRIAGE. On Thursday evening, the 9th inst., by the Rev. Mr. Morgan, Mr. JOHN W. CONNELL to Miss ELIZABETH A.M. DULANEY, all of this city. (13 OCT 1851)

DEATH. On Sunday morning, the 12th inst., at fifteen minutes past five o'clock, Commodore LEWIS WARRINGTON, in his 69th year. The friends of the family are respectfully requested to attend his funeral from St. John's Church on Tuesday, the 14th inst., at 12 o'clock. (13 OCT 1851)

MARRIAGE. On the 2d inst., by the Rev. W.H. Foote, D.D., at the residence of her father, C.J. CUMMINGS, Esq., of Abingdon, Va., to Miss ELIZA J.A. GIBSON, daughter of Col. David Gibson. (14 OCT 1851)

DEATH. On the 13th inst., Mrs. ALIEY SPIGNUL, in the 56th year of her age. Her friends and acquaintances are respectfully invited to attend her funeral this (Tuesday) evening, at 3 o'clock, at the residence of her son, Wm. B. Spignul, corner of New York avenue and 7th street. (14 OCT 1851)

DEATH. On Wednesday, the 8th inst., in St. Mary's Co., Md., the Rev. THOMAS CORNELIUS, of the Baltimore Annual Conference, in the 28th year of his age. (14 OCT 1851)

DEATH. In Winchester, Ky., on the 1st of September 1851, WILLIAM FLANAGAN, Esq., in the 47th year of his age. Mr. F. was a graduate of the U.S. Military Academy. After his appointment to the Army, his health failing him, he resigned his position in the Army, and retired to the pursuits of private life. He filled, during his civil life, many important public trusts, all of which he discharged with great fidelity. (14 OCT 1851)

MARRIAGE. On Tuesday, the 7th inst., by the Rev. Mr. Alig, Mr. MEINARD MENKE to Miss ELIZABETH E. EICHHORN, all of this city. (15 OCT 1851)

MARRIAGE. On the 24th September, at the Thoroughfare, Prince William Co., Va., by the Rev. Mr. Towles, JOSEPH HORNER, of Warrenton, Va., to LOUISA, daughter of the late George Chapman, of the former place. (15 OCT 1851)

MARRIAGE. On Tuesday evening, the 7th inst., at Bowling Green, Ky., by the Rev. A.C. Dickerson, JEANIE, daughter of the Hon. J.R. Underwood, and GEORGE CLARKE ROGERS, Esq. (15 OCT 1851)

MARRIAGE. On Thursday, the 9th inst., in this city, by the Rev. O.B. Brown, Mr. WILLIAM MOSS to Miss ELIZABETH LOMAX. (15 OCT 1851)

DEATH. On the 5th September, in Livingston Co., N.Y., Dr. CHARLES DOUGLAS, late Commissioner of Public Buildings in this city. (15 OCT 1851)

MARRIAGE. On Tuesday evening, the 14th inst., by the Rev. Wm. Hamilton, Mr. R. LAIDLER HAWKINS to Miss JANE ELIZABETH WINEBERGER, all of this city. (16 OCT 1851)

MARRIAGE. On Wednesday, the 15th inst., at St. Paul's English Lutheran Church, by the Rev. Wm. H. Smith, of Pennsylvania, Rev. J. GEORGE BUTLER, Pastor of said Church, to Miss CLARA E., daughter of Lewis Smith, Esq., of Georgetown, D.C. (16 OCT 1851)

MARRIAGE. In St. George's Church, Ramsgate, England, September 22, ALFRED LOWE, Esq., United States Consul at Civita Vecchia, Roman States, to MARY ANN, eldest daughter of Paul Balme, Esq., of Mile-end, Middlesex, and Romford, Essex. (16 OCT 1851)

DEATH. At his residence in this city on Tuesday night last [14 OCT 1851], after a brief illness, MOSES POOR, Esq., in the 79th year of his age. Mr. Poor was for many years a resident of Washington, and was much esteemed for his upright, exemplary, and amiable character. He has left a large and respected

Daily National Intelligencer, Marriage and Death Notices, 1851-1854

family circle and numerous friends to lament his death. His funeral will take place this afternoon, at 3 o'clock, from his late residence on F street. (16 OCT 1851)

MARRIAGE. On the 15th inst., by the Rev. W.T. Eva, JOHN B. RIDDLEMOSER, of Baltimore, and HANNAH MELVILLE BEVERIDGE, of this city. (17 OCT 1851)

MARRIAGE. On the 2d of October, at the Chapel of Grace, New York city, by the Rev. Thomas Gallaudet, Mr. JOHN W. COMPTON, of Washington, to Miss ANNA MEAD, daughter of Charles Wayland, Esq., of the former place. (20 OCT 1851)

DEATH. On the 6th October, at the residence in New Geneva, Pa., JAMES W. NICHOLSON, in the 79th year of his age. He was the only son of the late Commodore Nicholson, was a Christian and a gentleman, beloved and respected by all who knew him. (20 OCT 1851)

DEATH. On the morning of the 19th, Mrs. MARGARET SLATER, in the 47th year of her age, wife of Wm. Slater, and daughter of the late Isaac Cooper, of this city. The friends of the family are invited to attend the funeral from her late residence on New Jersey avenue, at 2 o'clock today. (21 OCT 1851)

MARRIAGE. At Pensacola, on the 8th inst., by the Rev. P. Donan, Gen. DAVID E. TWIGGS, of the U.S. Army, to Mrs. TABITHA HUNT. (22 OCT 1851)

DEATH. At New Orleans, on the 11th inst., Brevet Major P.W. McDONALD, U.S. Army. The deceased graduated with distinction at the Military Academy in 1841, and was commissioned in the Second Dragoons, in which regiment he saw much active service on the Western frontier and in Texas. Early in the Mexican war he was appointed aid-de-camp of Gen. Twiggs, in whose staff he served with credit and efficiency throughout the war. He was present at nearly all the engagements of both lines, and was twice breveted for gallantry and good conduct. (22 OCT 1851)

MARRIAGE. In Philadelphia, on the 21st inst., by the Rev. Mr. Howe, J. MUNROE CHUBB, of this city, to CAROLINE AUGUSTA, daughter of Amos Leland, Esq., of the former city. (23 OCT 1851)

MARRIAGE. On Wednesday evening, 22d inst., by the Rev. Mr. Marks, JAMES HUGHES to Mrs. MARY DOWNEY. At the same time, by the same, WM. MARTIN to Miss JANE HOOPER, all of this city. (24 OCT 1851)

MARRIAGE. On Thursday, the 23d inst., by Rev. Mr. Hodges, at the residence of her father, Miss ANNE E. RICHARDS, of Washington, to Mr. ELIJAH WELLS, of Port Tobacco, Md. (24 OCT 1851)

DEATH. At her residence, in this city, at 4 o'clock last evening [23 OCT 1851], after a most painful illness, Mrs. GEORGE ANN PATTERSON, widow of the late Commodore Daniel T. Patterson, of the U.S. Navy, aged about 66 years. The death of this most excellent lady, who was endeared to a large circle of friends by her most estimable character and disposition, will be severely felt by those to whom she was best known, while to her family it will create a void and an affliction which the healing hand of time only can assuage. Her funeral will take place from her dwelling, at the corner of I and 21st street, tomorrow (Saturday), at 11 o'clock, which her friends are invited to attend without further notice. (24 OCT 1851)

DEATH. At Thomaston, Me., Mrs. CAROLINE F. HOLMES, widow of the late Hon. John Holmes, and youngest daughter of Gen. Knox, of Revolutionary memory. (24 OCT 1851)

DEATH. At Fairfield, Me., on the 11th inst., Hon. JONATHAN G. HUNTOON, formerly Governor of the State of Maine, aged 70 years. (24 OCT 1851)

DEATH. REV. ARCHIBALD ALEXANDER, D.C., of the Princeton Theological Seminary, died at Princeton on Wednesday morning [22 OCT 1851], in the 81st year of his age. He was one of the oldest and most

Daily National Intelligencer, Marriage and Death Notices, 1851-1854

distinguished clergymen of the Presbyterian Church in the U.S. In 1811, when the Theological Seminary at Princeton was first established, he was elected a Professor, and continued in office up to the hour of his death. (24 OCT 1851)

DEATH. On Friday morning [24 OCT 1851], CHARLES RICHARD ADAMS, infant son of John and America Willett. The friends and acquaintances of the family are invited to attend the funeral this afternoon at 3 o'clock, from the residence of his grandfather, Thomas Adams, on 11th street, between G and H streets. (25 OCT 1851)

DEATH. On the 23d inst., HARRIET REBECCA, daughter of James M. and Mary Rebecca Wright, aged 3 years. The friends and acquaintances of the family are invited to attend the funeral from the residence of her parents on 4th street west, this day (Saturday) at 2 o'clock P.M. (25 OCT 1851)

DEATH. On the 25th inst., EDWIN K., son of Dr. S.C. and Emma Smoot, aged 15 months and 23 days. The funeral will take place this afternoon at 2 o'clock from the residence of his father, on Pennsylvania avenue, between 19th and 20th streets. (27 OCT 1851)

DEATH. On Thursday, October 9th, in the Parish of Avoyelles, La., ELENORE O'NEIL, aged 51 years, consort of Capt. Wm. H. Bassett, formerly of Washington. (28 OCT 1851)

DEATH. On Monday morning, the 27th inst., THOMAS MacGILL, in the 60th year of his age. His friends are invited to attend his funeral this (Tuesday) afternoon, at 4 o'clock, from his late residence on 8th street, between G and H streets. (28 OCT 1851)

MARRIAGE. On Thursday, October 30th, by the Rev. Jas. B. Donelan, JOSEPH REDFERN to JOSEPHINE VIVANS, all of this city. (31 OCT 1851)

MARRIAGE. On the 28th inst., by the Rev. Stephen P. Hill, HENRY RUSSELL, of Loudoun Co., Va., to JOANNA LOUISA HANNAN, of Washington. (31 OCT 1851)

MARRIAGE. In Cincinnati, on the 9th inst., by the Rev. P.B. Wilber, ELECTA V. MITCHELL, formerly of Mount Morris, Ill., and ANDREW M. HIRT, of this city. (31 OCT 1851)

DEATH. Suddenly, at her residence in this city, on the morning of the 29th inst., of a hemorrhage of the lungs, Miss BARBARA LOWE, in the 85th year of her age. She has been a resident of Washington for the last forty years. This estimable lady was the grand aunt of the present Governor of Maryland, the Hon. E.L. Lowe, and through her long life maintained the character of a sincere and zealous Christian, a kind and indulgent mistress, and a useful member of society. Her heart was ever open to the calls of the suffering and afflicted, and her "piety gave ere charity began"... Her funeral will take place on this afternoon, the 31st inst., a 2 o'clock, from her late residence, at the corner of 4th street east and M street south, which her friends and those of her family are requested to attend. (31 OCT 1851)

DEATH. On the 21st inst., at the residence of Robt. Y. Conrad, Esq., Winchester, Va., Mrs. BETTY CARR HARRISON, aged 22 years, wife of Dr. Edward Jaquelin Harrison, of Cumberland Co., Va., and eldest daughter of David Holmes Conrad, Esq., of Martinsburg. The aged must die; but oh how cruel does death seem when he snatches from amongst us the young, the lovely, the innocent, and pure in heart. (31 OCT 1851)

MARRIAGE. In Boston, on the 28th ult., by the Rt. Rev. Bishop Fitzpatrick, Capt. L.A.B. WALBACK, U.S. Ordnance Corps, to Miss PENELOPE R., daughter of Samuel K. Williams. (1 NOV 1851)

MARRIAGE. On Thursday, the 30th ult., by the Rev. A. Holmead, BENJAMIN T. GREENFIELD, formerly of Maryland, to Miss LOUISA V. HEPBURN, of this city. (3 NOV 1851)

Daily National Intelligencer, Marriage and Death Notices, 1851-1854

DEATH. On the 2d inst., Mrs. ELIZABETH MAYHUE, in the 73d year of her age. The friends of the family are respectfully invited to attend the funeral this afternoon at 2 o'clock, from the residence of her son, on East Capitol street, near the Eastern Branch. (3 NOV 1851)

MARRIAGE. On Tuesday, the 4th inst., by the Rev. Jas. B. Donelan, Mr. GEORGE E. SENSENEY, one of the Editors of the *Winchester Republican*, to MARY HELEN, daughter of John S. Gallaher, Esq., Third Auditor of the Treasury. (5 NOV 1851)

DEATH. On Tuesday, at half-past 6 o'clock P.M., Mrs. MARY H. WILSON, in the 62d year of her age. Her friends and acquaintance are respectfully invited to attend her funeral on Thursday morning, at 10 o'clock, from the residence of her daughter, Mrs. Hill, Pennsylvania avenue, between 9th and 10th streets. (5 NOV 1851)

MARRIAGE. On Tuesday evening [4 NOV 1851], by the Rev. John C. Smith, Mr. WM. W.S. KERR to Miss MARY JANE BASSETT, all of this city. (6 NOV 1851)

MARRIAGE. On Tuesday, the 4th inst., by the Rev. David Kerr, Rector of "Rock Creek Parish," Mr. ALB'T CHARLES, of the District of Columbia, to Miss ANNA VIRGINIA FAY, of this city. (7 NOV 1851)

DEATH. At Hancock, Delaware Co., N.Y., on the 20th ult., Gen. DAVID PHELPS, in the 83d year of his age. Gen. P. was born in Hebron, Conn., in 1768. He graduated at Yale College in 1793. He studied law in Sharon, in his native State, and in Poughkeepsie, N.Y. In 1796 or 1797 he came into Colchester, and lived there more than 50 years. He moved, with his son, a little more than a year since, to Hancock. (7 NOV 1851)

DEATH. On Friday morning, the 7th inst., of consumption, ADOLPH FORNARO, draughtsman in the office of the U.S. Coast Survey, aged 37 years. He was a native of Switzerland, and held the rank of Major in the corps of Topographical Engineers of that country. His friends and acquaintances are respectfully invited to attend his funeral half-past two o'clock P.M. on Sabbath, the 9th inst., from Mrs. Langston's, Capitol Hill. (8 NOV 1851)

MARRIAGE. On the 6th inst., by the Rev. L.S. Morgan, WM. D. SERRIN to Miss SARAH A. CUMBERLAND, all of this city. (12 NOV 1851)

DEATH. In Baltimore, on Monday night last [10 NOV 1851], WILLIAM C. RADCLIFF, son of Mr. Joseph Radcliff, of this city, after a short attack of congestive fever succeeding an extreme nervous affection, in the 23d year of his age. His funeral will take place from the residence of his father, corner of 6th and F streets, this afternoon at 2 o'clock, where the friends of the family are respectfully invited to attend. (12 NOV 1851)

MARRIAGE. In Alexandria, Va., on the 11th inst., by the Rev. George King, JOSEPH T. MITCHELL, Esq., of Kent Co., Md., to Miss KATE L., daughter of the late Gov. Kent, of Maryland. (13 NOV 1851)

DEATH. At his residence, in the county of Washington, on the 6th inst., ROBERT L. BEALL, in his 95th year — one of that glorious band who fought to gain the liberties we now enjoy. (13 NOV 1851)

DEATH. At Avondale, near St. Charles, Mo., on the 25th ult., aged 54 years and 21 days, Mrs. MAY ANN CLOUGH, wife of Mr. William Clough, formerly instructor of the Mayhew School in the city of Boston, and more recently instructor of one of the State Normal schools of Massachusetts. As a wife, a mother, a daughter, a sister, a neighbor, the deceased had no superior; and her dying moments were among the most blissful, perhaps, that were ever witnessed by man. (13 NOV 1851)

MARRIAGE. In this city, on Tuesday evening, the 11th inst., by Rev. Mr. Slattery, Mr. ALFRED RICKERBY to Miss JANE TERESA ROGERS, both formerly of Baltimore. (14 NOV 1851)

Daily National Intelligencer, Marriage and Death Notices, 1851-1854

MARRIAGE. On Tuesday evening, the 11th inst., by the Rev. William Hamilton, Mr. M.M. HITCHCOX, of Virginia, to Miss COLUMBIA V. HAWKINS, of this city. (14 NOV 1851)

MARRIAGE. In Georgetown, on Thursday evening [13 NOV 1851], by the Rev. John C. Smith, Mr. THOMAS E. REED to Miss MARGARET ELLEN, daughter of Mr. Samuel Cunningham, all of that place. (14 NOV 1851)

MARRIAGE. On Sabbath evening [9 NOV 1851], by the Rev. John C. Smith, Mr. WILLIAM HENRY TEMPS to Miss VIRGINIA ELIZABETH CARROLL, all of this city. (14 NOV 1851)

MARRIAGE. On Tuesday, the 11th inst., by the Rev. Nicholas D. Young, Miss SARAH T. YOUNG and Mr. JOHN CARROLL BRENT, both of this city. (14 NOV 1851)

DEATH. In this city on the 12th inst., DENNIS HIGGINS, a native of the county of Cork, Ireland, aged 78 years. His funeral will take place from the residence of his son-in-law, Mr. Curry, on East Capitol street, Capitol Hill, this afternoon, at 3 o'clock, at which time the friends of the family are invited to attend. (14 NOV 1851)

DEATH. On the 8th inst., Mrs. MARGARET SUTTON, in the 63d year of her age. (14 NOV 1851)

MARRIAGE. On Thursday evening, the 13th inst., by the Rev. C.M. Butler, Mr. BENJAMIN KLOPFER to Miss SOPHIA HENDLEY, all of this city. (15 NOV 1851)

MARRIAGE. On Tuesday, the 11th inst., at the Church of the Epiphany, in this city, by the Rev. J.W. French, Mr. REUBEN C. JOHNSON, of Gorham, Me., to Miss CAROLINE ALEXANDER, of Philadelphia. (15 NOV 1851)

DEATH. On the 9th inst., at Petersburg, Va., Mrs. FRANCES MARIA TRACEY, aged 49 years, formerly of Mt. Erin, Fairfax Co., Va., the widow of the late Jas. Francis Tracey, both natives of Dublin, Ireland. She was the daughter of Matthew McDonald, of Dublin, Ireland. (15 NOV 1851)

DEATH. At Corpus Christi, Tex., on the 18th ult. [18 OCT 1851], Capt. S.M. PLUMMER, of the U.S. Army. (15 NOV 1851)

MARRIAGE. On the 5th inst., by the Rev. Mathias Alig, WM. HANNEFIN to MARY DONOHOUGH. (17 NOV 1851)

MARRIAGE. On the 13th inst., by the Rev. Mathias Alig, Mr. THOS. FITZGERALD to Miss JULIA CONNELL. (17 NOV 1851)

MARRIAGE. On the 12th inst., by the Rev. Mr. French, SAM'L V. NILES to MARY GORDON, all of this city. (17 NOV 1851)

DEATH. In this city, on the 14th inst., at the residence of his parents, ALBERT MORGAN, aged 2 years and 11 months and 13 days, only son of Chas. E. and Mary Jane Walker. (17 NOV 1851)

MARRIAGE. On the 4th inst., at Bowling Green, Ky., by the Rev. Mr. Tomes, LIGHT UNDERWOOD, Daughter of Hon. J.R. Underwood, and ARTHUR MIDDLETON RUTLEDGE, of Nashville, Tenn. (18 NOV 1851) At Bowling Green, Ky., on the 4th of November, 1851, by the Rev. Charles Tomes, ARTHUR MIDDLETON RUTLEDGE, Esq., to Miss ELIZA, daughter of the Hon. Judge Underwood, U.S. Senator from Kentucky. (20 NOV 1851)

Daily National Intelligencer, Marriage and Death Notices, 1851-1854

MARRIAGE. At Keene, N.H., on the 12th inst., by the Rt. Rev. Carleton Chase, Bishop of New Hampshire, JOHN SHERWOOD, Esq., of New York, to Miss MARY ELIZABETH, eldest daughter of the Hon. James Wilson, of New Hampshire. (18 NOV 1851)

MARRIAGE. In Alexandria, Va., on the 11th inst., by Rev. Geo. King, JOSEPH T. MITCHELL, Esq., of Kent Co., Md., to KATE L., daughter of the late Gov. Kent, of Maryland. (18 NOV 1851)

DEATH. On the evening of the 16th inst., Mrs. MARY VIRGINIA MASON, wife of Mr. Maynadier Mason, of Fairfax Co., aged 40 years. The friends and acquaintances of the family are respectfully invited to attend her funeral this afternoon, at 2 o'clock, from the residence of her aunt, Miss Clark, on the Heights of Georgetown. (18 NOV 1851)

DEATH. On Wednesday, the 27th of August, at the residence of his brother, Edward J. Heard, on Lake Catahoula, in the parish of St. Marin, La., Capt. JOSEPH HEARD, in the 85th year of his age. (18 NOV 1851)

DEATH. On Saturday evening, the 15th inst., of pseudo-membranous croup, GEORGE, youngest son of Joseph and Julia A. Radcliffe, in the fourth year of his age. (18 NOV 1851)

DEATH. On the 17th inst., at 3 o'clock, P.M., JAMES THOMAS, son of James and Mary E. Frasier, aged two years and five months. The funeral will take place at 3 o'clock this day, at the residence of his father, on G street, near the corner of 7th street. (18 NOV 1851)

DEATH. On the morning of the 18th inst., TERESA FRANCES, in the fourth year of her age, daughter of Francis and Mary Reilly. The friends and acquaintances of the family are respectfully invited to attend the funeral from their residence, Eighth street, near the Navy Yard, this (Wednesday) afternoon at two o'clock. (19 NOV 1851)

MARRIAGE. In this city, on Tuesday evening, the 18th inst., by the Rev. Mr. Pyne, Dr. BERNARD M. BYRNE, U.S. Army, to Miss LOUISA, daughter of Col. J.J. Abert, Topographical Engineers, U.S. Army. (20 NOV 1851)

MARRIAGE. On the 4th inst., in Trinity Church, Pass Christian, Miss., by the Rev. Thomas S. Savage, D.D., Professor RUEL KEITH, U.S. Navy, to Miss MARTHA B. CLEVELAND, daughter of Wm. Cleveland, Esq. (20 NOV 1851)

MARRIAGE. In Richmond, on the 19th inst., ALEXANDER F. TAYLOR, of Culpeper Co., to Mrs. ELVIRA M. HIGGINBOTHAM, daughter of John Henry, of Charlotte Co., Va. (20 NOV 1851)

MARRIAGE. On the 20th inst., by the Rev. Mr. Hill, Mr. WM. G. BROCK, of Norfolk, Va., to Miss MARY F. JAMES, of Rockville, Md. (22 NOV 1851)

MARRIAGE. At Camden, N.J., Tuesday morning, the 18th inst., by Rev. Abel C. Thomas, Lieut. BAYSE NEWCOMB WESTCOTT, U.S. Navy, to MARY, daughter of Sam'l Hart. (22 NOV 1851)

DEATH. At Georgetown, on Thursday, the 20th inst., JOHN PICKRELL, in the 69th year of his age. His funeral will take place this (Saturday) afternoon at 3 o'clock, from his late residence on 1st street, Georgetown. (22 NOV 1851)

DEATH. On the evening of the 20th, after a brief illness, at his father's residence, FRANCIS KING, Esq., eldest son of W.W. King, of this city. His friends and the friends of the family are respectfully invited to attend his funeral this (Saturday) afternoon, at 4 o'clock. (22 NOV 1851)

Daily National Intelligencer, Marriage and Death Notices, 1851-1854

DEATH. On Monday, the 10th inst., at the residence of her husband, in Clarksville, Tenn., Mrs. ELIZABETH JOHNSON, wife of the Hon. Cave Johnson. (22 NOV 1851)

MARRIAGE. On the 19th inst., by the Rev. Jas. P. Donelan, JAS. B. FRENCH to Miss AMANDA JANE DANT, all of this city. (24 NOV 1851)

MARRIAGE. On the 20th inst., by the Rev. W.T. Eva, JOHN LACEY and ELIZA BEAGLE, all of this city. (24 NOV 1851)

MARRIAGE. On Thursday evening, the 20th inst., by the Rev. Mr. Rogers, Mr. JAMES MEDFORD, formerly of Annapolis, Md., to Miss ANN E. SMITH, of Alexandria. (24 NOV 1851)

MARRIAGE. At Aldie, on Tuesday evening, the 18th inst., by the Rev. George Adie, RICHARD S. COX, Esq., of Georgetown, D.C., to Miss MARY L., daughter of Louis Berkley, Esq., of Loudoun Co., Va. (24 NOV 1851)

DEATH. On the 22d inst., Mr. SAMUEL WALKER, of this city, in the 49th year of his age. His funeral will take place at his residence, on 12th street, near F, on this (Monday) evening, at 3 o'clock. His friends and acquaintances are respectfully invited to attend. (24 NOV 1851)

DEATH. In this city, on Wednesday night, the 19th inst., Mr. JOSHUA HUGGINS, machinist, of New York, in the 27th year of his age. (24 NOV 1851)

DEATH. On the 23d inst., after a short illness, Mr. DANA MILLER, in the 34th year of age, formerly of [Dummerston], Ver., and at the time of his decease, and for the last thirteen months, a clerk in the Census Office. He was much respected by those who knew him for intelligence and gentlemanly deportment. (24 NOV 1851)

MARRIAGE. On the 23d inst., by the Rev. Mr. Slattery, Mr. JAMES W. DRANE to Mrs. ELIZABETH A. JONES, all of this city. (25 NOV 1851)

MARRIAGE. On Tuesday, 11th inst., by the Rev. Mr. Pendleton, of Fauquier, G. WOODSON HANSBROUGH to VIRGINIA, the daughter of Samuel Chancellor, Esq., of Rappahannock. (25 NOV 1851)

MARRIAGE. On the 17th inst., by the Rev. Mathias Alig, in St. Mary's Church, Mr. JOSEPH BISHOP to Miss GERTRUDE HERBERT. (26 NOV 1851)

MARRIAGE. On the 22d inst., by the Rev. Mathias Alig, in St. Mary's Church, Mr. FRANCIS ROONEY to Miss ELIZABETH CONNOR, all of this city. (26 NOV 1851)

DEATH. On Monday morning, the 24th inst., at the Navy Yard, in this city, after an illness of six weeks, THOMAS KELLY, of Georgetown, D.C., in the 40th year of his age, leaving a wife and six children to mourn their loss. His friends and those of the family are respectfully invited to the funeral, which takes place this day, at 2 o'clock, from his late residence near Odd Fellows' Hall, Navy Yard. (26 NOV 1851)

DEATH. Yesterday morning [26 NOV 1851], of consumption, MICHAEL J. SHEAHAN, in the 26th year of his age. His friends and acquaintances and those of the family are invited to attend his funeral this afternoon at half-past three o'clock, from the residence of his father on 1st street west, near the corner of Pennsylvania avenue. (26 NOV 1851)

MARRIAGE. In Richmond, Va., on Wednesday, 19th inst., by the Rev. C.H. Read, JAS. D. BULLOCH, U.S. Navy, to LIZZIE E., daughter of John Caskie, of Richmond. (27 NOV 1851)

Daily National Intelligencer, Marriage and Death Notices, 1851-1854

MARRIAGE. On the 25th inst., by the Rev. John C. Smith, Mr. NOBLE D. LARNER to Miss ANN MARGARET KELLER, both of this city. (27 NOV 1851)

DEATH. In this city, on Tuesday, November 25th, Mrs. MARGARET WATKINS, in the 87th year of her age. Her funeral will take place from the residence of B.F. Beers, near the Navy Yard, this day (Thursday) at two o'clock P.M. (27 NOV 1851)

DEATH. In this city, on the 20th inst., Mr. WILFRED SMITH, in the 43d year of his age. (27 NOV 1851)

DEATH. At Harper's Ferry, Va., on Monday, the 24th inst., after a short illness, in the 34th year of his age, JAMES WALTER MEEM, the oldest son of Geo. A. Meem, Esq., of Georgetown. His remains having been brought to town, his funeral will take place this (Thursday) morning, at 10 o'clock, from the residence of his Father-in-law, Mr. James Murray, on High street. The relatives and friends of the family are requested to attend without further notice. (27 NOV 1851)

DEATH. At Lapsley Hall, his residence, near Bowling Green, Ky., on the 20th October, Capt. THOMAS ROGERS, in the 86th year of his age. Capt. Rogers was a native of Caroline Co., Va. He moved to Kentucky in 1811, and has since resided in this county. He was a brother of Capt. John Rogers, of the cavalry, belonging to Gen. Clark's expedition to the Illinois country, and maternal uncle of the Hon. J.R. Underwood, at present of the U.S. Senate from Kentucky. He was a sincere, warm, and enlightened patriot. Though too young to take an active part in the struggle of the Revolution, he was of the right age to receive the impressions of that stirring period. Washington was with him the beau ideal of the man and the patriot. He loved to study his model to the day of his death. The cane, cut from the grove around Washington's tomb, which he carried to sustain his fame, feeble from age, was an emblem of Washington's moral and political principles, which were the guide of his political life. He loved his country, her honor abroad and her integrity at home. He plead for the perpetuity of the Union, the integrity of our constitutional principles and compromises, and full obedience to the law. Through the long period of his political enfranchisement he lost but one or two opportunities of voting. He kept himself, by the regular perusal of several of the best journals of the country, well advised of the current events of the world. He was, in all the relations of life, an example to be contemplated with veneration and respect. He died in the Christian's hope of a blessed immortality. [The *Richmond Whig* and *Louisville Courier* please copy.] (29 NOV 1851)

DEATH. Suddenly, on the 27th inst., JOHN AUGUSTUS, son of Isaac and Johanah Hill, aged six years. (29 NOV 1851)

DEATH. On Sunday, November 30, HANNAH KETTLEWELL, infant child of S.J. and Hannah Ober. Relatives and friends are invited to attend the funeral from F street, between 6th and 7th streets, at 3 o'clock P.M. this day. (1 DEC 1851)

MARRIAGE. In Albemarle Co., Va., on the 27th ult., by the Rev. Charles E. Ambler, Lieut. HENRY H. BELL, U.S. Navy, to MARGARET C. HENDERSON, daughter of the late Major Richard Pollard. (2 DEC 1851)

DEATH. On Sunday evening, 30th ult. [30 NOV 1851], after a short illness, in the 22d year of her age, Mrs. ELIZABETH CHASE wife of Mr. Wm. Chase, of this city. Her funeral will take place this day, at 2 o'clock, from her late residence on 7th street west, between New York avenue and L street north. (2 DEC 1851)

DEATH. On the 24th ult., at Annapolis, Md., Mrs. MARY ANN NELSON, wife of Rev. C.K. Nelson, and daughter of John Marbury, Esq., of Georgetown. (2 DEC 1851)

DEATH. In Griffin, Ga., on the 18th of November, JOHN C. MANGHAM, Jr., aged 28 years, late Second Lieutenant and Adjutant of the 13th Regiment of U.S. Infantry. (2 DEC 1851)

Daily National Intelligencer, Marriage and Death Notices, 1851-1854

DEATH. At Meadow Grove, Fauquier Co., Va., the residence of his sister, Mrs. Carter, on Saturday, the 15th ult., about 8 o'clock, A.M., ALEXANDER B. SCOTT, in the 57th year of his age. (2 DEC 1851)

MARRIAGE. On the 27th ult., by Rev. David Kerr, Rector of Rock Creek Parish, at the residence of George W. Riggs, Esq., Mr. TOBIAS F. TALBERT to Miss ELIZABETH PERRY, all of the District of Columbia. (3 DEC 1851)

MARRIAGE. On the 1st inst., by Rev. David Kerr, Rector of Rock Creek Parish, Mr. HARVEY M. NEWHOUSE to Miss SARAH DAWSON, both of Fauquier Co., Va. (3 DEC 1851)

DEATH. On the 2d inst., WILLIAM QUIGLY, aged twenty months and three days, son of William and Mary Quigly. The relatives and friends of the family are invited to attend the funeral at two o'clock P.M. (3 DEC 1851)

MARRIAGE. In this city, on Monday evening [1 DEC 1851], by the Rev. Mr. Hill, Mr. WILLIAM H. SCOTT to Miss MARTHA E. DAVISON, daughter of Samuel C. Davison, all of this city. (4 DEC 1851)

MARRIAGE. On Tuesday evening [2 DEC 1851], by the Rev. Mr. Wayman, Mr. SAMUEL PROCTER, of Baltimore, to Miss CASSA ANN MARTON, of Rockville, Md. (4 DEC 1851)

MARRIAGE. At the "Grove," near Warrenton, Fauquier Co., Va., on Tuesday, the 25th ult., by the Rev. Geo. Norton, ALFRED B. CARTER, of Mississippi, to BETTIE, daughter of Capt. C.C. Randolph, of Virginia. (4 DEC 1851)

DEATH. On Tuesday evening last, the 2d inst., after a very short illness, FRANCIS BARRY, Sr., in the 70th year of his age. His funeral will take place from his late residence, on 7th street east (Navy Yard,) on this day, at 2 o'clock P.M., and from St. Peter's Church, Capitol Hill, at 3 o'clock P.M., to which the friends and acquaintances of the family are respectfully invited to attend. (4 DEC 1851)

DEATH. On Tuesday evening, the 2d inst., after a short illness, in the 9th year of her age, AMELIA ELENORA LITTLE, daughter of James and Araminta Little. Her funeral will take place this afternoon, at 2 o'clock, from her father's residence, on Virginia avenue, near the Navy Yard, to which the friends of the family are respectfully invited. (4 DEC 1851)

MARRIAGE. On Thursday afternoon [4 DEC 1851], by the Rev. John C. Smith, PETER DAGGY, Esq., to Miss JULIA LUNT, all of this city. (5 DEC 1851)

MARRIAGE. On the 3d inst., at the U.S. Hotel, by the Rev. W.T. Eva, WILLIAM O. JOHNSON and VIRGINIA A. HARPER, all of Louisa Co., Va. (5 DEC 1851)

DEATH. Suddenly, on the 3d inst., PATRICK DOWLING, in the 61st year of his age, a native of the county Farmanagh, Ireland, but for the last 35 years a citizen of the District of Columbia. His funeral will take place from the residence of his brother, William Dowling, on F street, between 13th and 14th streets, tomorrow afternoon, at 3 o'clock, where his friends are respectfully requested to attend. (5 DEC 1851)

DEATH. On Friday morning, the 5th inst., ISAAC S. LAUCK, Esq., in the 59th year of age. Descended from a Revolutionary sire, the son, at an early age, in the war of 1812, marched as a volunteer from the same place (his native town of Winchester, Va.) whence his father had marched in the war of independence, to meet the enemies of his country, and to assist in driving them from the soil of his native State. The funeral of the deceased will take place from his late residence on G street north, between 12th and 13th streets, this (Saturday) afternoon at 3 o'clock. (6 DEC 1851)

Daily National Intelligencer, Marriage and Death Notices, 1851-1854

DEATH. Yesterday [5 DEC 1851], LIZZIE F. GORDON, in the 13th year of her age. Her funeral will take place from the residence of her mother, Mrs. Alfred B. Thruston, at 2 o'clock P.M. this day. The friends of the family are respectfully invited to attend. (6 DEC 1851)

MARRIAGE. In Georgetown, on Thursday, the 4th inst., by the Rev. John Lanahan, Mr. JOHN H. MEREDITY, of this city, to Miss ELLEN G. WILSON. (8 DEC 1851)

DEATH. At Brownville, N.Y., November 27, suddenly, MARGARET LOVEL, wife of John E. Brown, Esq., and daughter of the late Major Gen. Jacob Brown. (8 DEC 1851)

MARRIAGE. At Goodwood, Prince George's Co., Md., on Wednesday, the 3d inst., by the Rev. Mr. Mackenheimer, Col. ODEN BOWIE to ALICE, second daughter of Charles H. Carter, Esq. (9 DEC 1851)

DEATH. In this city, on Sunday last [7 DEC 1851], Mrs. BEULAH STELLE, relict of the late Pontius D. Stelle, aged 84 years. Mrs. Stelle was one of the oldest inhabitants of Washington, having come here from New Jersey with the Government in 1800. She had consequently seen the place rise from field and forest into a city worthy to bear the great name of its immortal founder, and worthy of the high position it holds as the metropolis of the great Republic of the world. Mrs. Stelle was one of the young ladies selected to strew flowers in the path of Washington as he crossed the bridge at Trenton, on the occasion of his visiting New York and the Eastern States, while President of the United States, and to sing an ode of welcome written for the gratifying occasion. With others who, while living, formed connecting links between us and the glorious era of the Revolution, she has now passed away. The friends of the family are invited to attend her funeral at half-past two o'clock this day, from the residence o her son, Mr. E.B. Stelle. (9 DEC 1851)

DEATH. On the 8th inst., in this city, Mrs. MARY DOUGLAS STETSON, formerly of Alexandria, Va., consort of the late Capt. John Stetson, of Massachusetts, in the 51st year of her age. Her funeral will take place from her late residence on Pennsylvania avenue, between 3d and 4½ streets, at 11 o'clock on Wednesday, the 10th inst. Her friends and acquaintances are respectfully invited to attend. (9 DEC 1851)

DEATH. Yesterday morning [8 DEC 1851], CALDWELL, the youngest child of Charles W. and Mary Jane Pairo, aged two years. The friends of the family are invited to attend the funeral services at half-past nine o'clock this (Tuesday) morning, at the residence of the parents on Prospect street, Georgetown. (9 DEC 1851)

MARRIAGE. On the 9th inst., at St. John's Church, Washington, by the Rev. Dr. Pyne, GOOLD HOYT, Esq., of New York, to Miss CAMILLA SCOTT, daughter of Gen. Scott, of the U.S. Army. (10 DEC 1851)

MARRIAGE. On the 4th inst., by the Rev. Jas. B. Donelan, WM. E. DANT to Miss SARAH J. BEARDSLEY, daughter of the late Jos. Beardsley, Sr., all of this city. (10 DEC 1851)

OBITUARY. Departed this life, in Greensboro, Ga., on the 30th ult., Mrs. SIDNEY WINGFIELD, widow of the late Thomas Wingfield, of that place, and mother of the late Mrs. Henrietta Dawson, so well known in this city as the amiable and accomplished consort of the Hon. Wm. C. Dawson, of the U.S. Senate. Mrs. Wingfield had attained the age of 73 years, and was in the enjoyment of usual health until a few days before her death. Her loss will make a void that can never be filled, not only in the domestic circle where she presided so long and with so many affectionate endearments, but in the whole community in which she lived, and in that large and extensive circle of friends and acquaintances who were attached to her by many ties and associations, and which it is the good fortune of but few to possess. For most truly may it be said that in her were united and happily blended all those natural qualities and Christian virtues which eminently adorn the female character, and which, when properly cultivated, give to woman such power and influence in her appropriate sphere. Long will her memory be cherished by all who knew her; and well may they indulge the constant and earnest wish that their "last end may be like hers." (10 DEC 1851)

Daily National Intelligencer, Marriage and Death Notices, 1851-1854

DEATH. On Tuesday evening last [9 DEC 1851], Mrs. MARY M., wife of D.O. Hare. The friends of the family are respectfully invited to attend the funeral this day at 11 o'clock, from her late residence, 10th street, between L and M streets. (11 DEC 1851)

MARRIAGE. At Ft. Snelling, Minnesota Territory, November 19th, T.L. CASTER, First Lieut. U.S. Dragoons, to Mrs. M.C. WHITEHORN, daughter of the Rev. E.G. Gear, Chaplain U.S. Army. (12 DEC 1851)

DEATH. On Thursday morning, the 11th inst., at 2 o'clock, Mrs. DORCAS WALKER, aged 80 years, for sixty years a resident of this city. Her friends and acquaintances are respectfully invited to attend her funeral, from her residence on I street, between 18th and 19th streets, adjoining the Friends' meeting-house, First Ward, at 2 o'clock this afternoon. (12 DEC 1851)

DEATH. On the 11th inst., Mrs. JANE LYON, widow of the late Jacob Lyon, in her 81st year. The friends and relatives of the family are respectfully invited to attend her funeral on Saturday, the 13th inst., at 1 o'clock, from her late residence on New York avenue, between 9th and 10th streets. (12 DEC 1851)

MARRIAGE. On the 11th inst., by the Rev. Mr. Hodges, Mr. SAMUEL E. ARNOLD to Miss SARAH ANN CHAMPION, all of this city. (13 DEC 1851)

MARRIAGE. In this city, on the 5th of November, by the Rev. C.M. Butler, Mr. ALONZO R. FOWLER to Miss FRANCES A.E. DRAPER, third daughter of the late Dr. A.C. Draper, of Philadelphia. (13 DEC 1851)

MARRIAGE. On Thursday evening, 11th inst., by the Rev. N.P. [Tillinghast], Passed Midshipman LEONARD PAULDING, U.S. Navy, to Miss HELEN, daughter of the late John H. Offley, of Georgetown. (13 DEC 1851)

MARRIAGE. In Baltimore, on Thursday, 11th inst., by the Rev. David Kerr, Rector of Rock Creek Parish, D.C., ALBERT TROUP EMORY, Esq., of Queen Anne's Co., to Miss SALLY R. WINDER, of Baltimore, Md. (13 DEC 1851)

MARRIAGE. At Norwich, Conn., on the 8th inst., by the Rev. Wm. F. Morgan, WILLIAM P. WILLIAMS, of New York, to JULIA WOODBRIDGE, second daughter of Charles Jas. Lanman, Esq., of Norwich. (13 DEC 1851)

DEATH. Yesterday morning [12 DEC 1851], after a few days' illness, JOHN A. DONOHOO, Esq., in the 55th year of his age, leaving a large family to mourn their loss. His and the family's friends and acquaintances are respectfully invited to attend his funeral tomorrow (Sunday) afternoon at 1 o'clock, without further notice. (13 DEC 1851)

DEATH. In Georgetown, on the 10th inst., at the late residence of Henry H. Chapman, Miss MARGARET DAVIDSON, formerly of Annapolis, Md., in her 77th year. Her friends and those of the family, are requested to attend the funeral this (Saturday) afternoon at 3 o'clock. (13 DEC 1851)

MARRIAGE. Yesterday evening [14 DEC 1851], at St. Peter's Church, by the Rev. Mr. Lanahan, Mr. THOMAS O. PRIOR, of Saratoga Co., N.Y., to Miss EMILY A. BARRETT, of Washington, D.C. (15 DEC 1851)

MARRIAGE. At St. Louis, on Wednesday evening, the 19th ult. [19 NOV 1851], by the Rev. Mr. Gassoway, Major D.C. BUELL, of the Adjutant General's Department U.S. Army, to Mrs. MARGARET MASON, of St. Louis, Mo. (15 DEC 1851)

DEATH. On the 12th inst., in this city, Miss ANN MARIA DOUGHTY, daughter of Col. William Doughty, of Georgetown, aged 52 years. (15 DEC 1851)

Daily National Intelligencer, Marriage and Death Notices, 1851-1854

DEATH. At Ft. Gates, Tex., on the 13th November last, SALLY H., daughter of Dr. John J. Minge, and wife of Capt. Geo. E. Pickett, U.S. Army. (17 DEC 1851)

DEATH. At Easton, Md., on the 6th inst., in the 87th year of his age, SOLOMON BARROTT, Esq., an aged and esteemed resident of that place. In 1781 he was in the Southern army under Gen. Green, and participated in the battles of the Cowpens, Guilford Court-house, Camden, and Eutaw Springs, courageously fighting for those principles which he cherished to his dying day. (17 DEC 1851)

MARRIAGE. On Wednesday morning, 17th inst., at the Methodist Episcopal Church South, by the Rev. Leonidas Rosser, THOMAS W. JOHNSON to CHARLOTTE PINKNEY, daughter of Rev. C.A. Davis, all of this city. (18 DEC 1851)

MARRIAGE. In Paris, at the Episcopal Church, in October, by the Rev. Mr. Chamier, LORENZO DRAPER, Esq., U.S. Consul at Havre, to Mrs. ANN ALECIA HAWKINS, of Baltimore, Md. (18 DEC 1851)

DEATH. In this city, at 8 o'clock, on the morning of the 17th inst., Lieut. Col. DANIEL RANDALL, Deputy Paymaster General U.S. Army, in the 60th year of his age. Col. Randall was a native of Annapolis, Md., and entered the army in July 1818, as Paymaster to the 1st regiment of infantry. During his military career he was always actively employed in the duties of his responsible position, and ever proved himself an able, efficient, and meritorious officer. In the performance of his duty he shrank from no danger, nor hesitated to incur any necessary responsibility, but always cheerfully bore the fatigues and exposures inseparable from a long service in a Southern climate and on an unhealthy frontier. In his death the Pay Department has sustained a loss which will long continue to be felt. His courteous and gentlemanly deportment and his high moral character endeared him to the army generally, procured for him many and devoted friends, and renders his loss doubly severe to his afflicted relatives. His body will be conveyed to Annapolis for interment. His friends are invited to attend his funeral at 10 o'clock A.M. on Friday, the 19th inst., from the residence of Mrs. Hagner, Pennsylvania avenue. (18 DEC 1851)

DEATH. In this city, yesterday afternoon [18 DEC 1851], JOHN FRANCIS, aged six months and nine days, son of Wm. F. and Mary F.E. Purcell. The funeral will take place this evening at half-past 2 o'clock, on Maryland avenue between 6th and 7th streets. (19 DEC 1851)

MARRIAGE. On Tuesday morning, the 16th inst., in the M.E. Church, Winchester, Va., by Rev. Wm. Krebs, Rev. JOHN S. DEALE, of Cumberland, Md., to Miss SALLIE, daughter of N. Buckmaster, Esq., of Pittsburg, Pa. (20 DEC 1851)

MARRIAGE. On the 20th August 1851, at Salem, Ohio, by the Rev. Mr. Henderson, J. GIDEON CROWLEY, of Washington, D.C., to Miss MARY S. SPROAT, of the former place. (20 DEC 1851)

DEATH. On Friday morning, [19 DEC 1851], at 4 o'clock, JOHN HARRISON JOHNSON, in the 23d year of his age. His friends are invited to attend his funeral, without further notice, at the residence of his uncle, Mr. Wm. Orme, on 11th street, at 10 o'clock this day. (20 DEC 1851)

DEATH. On Friday, the 19th inst., Mrs. M. KIRBY, wife of James Kirby, and daughter of the late Raphael Boarman. Her funeral will take place on Sunday, at two o'clock P.M., on the corner of 16th and I streets west, near St. John's Church, where her friends are invited to attend. (20 DEC 1851)

DEATH. In this city, on the 21st inst., Mrs. ELIZABETH WATERMAN LEADBITTER, daughter of the late Nathan Waterman, Jr., of Providence, R.I., and wife of Lieut. D. Leadbitter, U.S. Corps of Engineers. (22 DEC 1851)

DEATH. On the 19th inst., CHARLES EDWARD, son of William and Elizabeth A. Hoover, aged 5 months and 12 days. (22 DEC 1851)

Daily National Intelligencer, Marriage and Death Notices, 1851-1854

MARRIAGE. On Sabbath evening [21 DEC 1851], by the Rev. John C. Smith, Mr. JOHN W. SPEAKES to Miss SARAH CATHARINE WILSON, all of this city. (23 DEC 1851)

DEATH. On the 22d inst., after a short illness, Mrs. BRIDGET NUGENT, a native of the county of Westmeath, Ireland, aged 58 years. Her funeral will take place this day, (23d inst.) from her son's residence, near the corner of 13th and F streets, at 3 o'clock P.M. The friends of the family are invited to attend. (23 DEC 1851)

DEATH. On Monday, the 22d inst., suddenly, at the residence of Mrs. A. Sweeny, THOMAS O'NEILL, of Philadelphia, in the 39th year of his age. His remains will be taken to the cars this (Tuesday) evening at 4 o'clock. (23 DEC 1851)

DEATH. On the 21st inst., after a brief illness of six days, from typhoid pneumonia, EDMUND BROOKE, Esq., in his 56th year, late a clerk in the Pension Office. His funeral will take place this morning at 10½ o'clock, from his late residence on the Island, opposite the Smithsonian Institute. His friends and relatives are respectfully invited to attend. (23 DEC 1851)

DEATH. In this city, on Sunday night [21 DEC 1851], after a short illness, Miss MARY JOSEPHINE LADD. The angel of death came early to this sweet girl and transplanted her from a world of sorrow and affliction to the calm serenity of Heaven. She possessed an exceedingly pure mind and gentle heart; and the stricken family have the assurances that she was fully prepared for an exchange of worlds. Her death was as calm and placid as an infant's sleep, and her face beamed with a holy expression. Funeral this afternoon, at 3 o'clock, from Mr. Boak's, corner of 4½ street and Pennsylvania avenue, south side; the relatives and friends are invited to attend. (23 DEC 1851)

DEATH. On the 21st inst., ANNA CATHARINE, daughter of Jno. P. and Sarah M. White, aged two years and four months. The friends of the family are invited to attend her funeral this afternoon, at two o'clock, from the residence of her father, New Jersey avenue, near D street south. (23 DEC 1851)

DEATH. At her mother's residence in Rockville, Md., in the 21st year of her age, MARTHA HALE PROUT, daughter of the late Wm. Prout, of this city. (23 DEC 1851)

DEATH. On the morning of the 22d inst., in Georgetown, ELIZABETH A., daughter of the late Henry H. and Mary Chapman, aged 46 years. Her friends and those of the family, are requested to attend the funeral this (Wednesday) afternoon at 3 o'clock. (24 DEC 1851)

DEATH. On the morning of the 23d inst., GEORGE PEYTON, son of Leonidas and Mary Bowen, in the 3d year of his age. His funeral will take place tomorrow (Thursday) at 2 o'clock, to which the friends of the family are invited to attend. (24 DEC 1851)

DEATH. [Communicated.] Departed this life, in the 52d year of his age, after a lingering illness, NATHANIEL HERBERT, long known as a faithful messenger in the Post Office Department. He was appointed by Postmaster General Meigs, in 1812, forty years since, and during that long period was noted for the correct, faithful, and willing discharge of his duties, and valued for his great integrity of character. As a husband, father, neighbor, and friend, he was kind, affectionate, and charitable. His friends and acquaintances are respectfully invited to attend his funeral today (Wednesday) at 2 o'clock. (24 DEC 1851)

MARRIAGE. On the 23d inst., at the E Street Baptist Church, by the Rev. J.D. Anderson, Rev. J. TILSON, of Hingham, Mass., to Miss MARTHA D., daughter of Robt. P. Anderson, Esq., of this city. (25 DEC 1851)

MARRIAGE. On Tuesday, the 23d inst., by the Rev. Mr. Hodges, SAMUEL GEORGE COX to Miss ANNA MARIA GODDARD, of the District of Columbia. (25 DEC 1851)

Daily National Intelligencer, Marriage and Death Notices, 1851-1854

DEATH. In this city, on the 24th inst., Mrs. MARY DOUGHERTY, relict of the late Joseph Dougherty, a native of Ireland, and a resident of this city for more than half a century, aged 86. Her funeral will take place from her residence on 6th street, beyond I, on Friday, at 3 o'clock P.M. Her friends and acquaintances are invited to attend. (25 DEC 1851)

MARRIAGE. On the evening of the 24th inst., by the Rev. Dr. Butler, Dr. WILLIAM H. SAUNDERS to HANNAH S., daughter of Joseph H. Bradley, all of this city. (27 DEC 1851)

MARRIAGE. On the morning of the 25th inst., in Georgetown, D.C., by the Rev. George N. Israel, Rev. SAMUEL CORNELIUS, of the Baltimore Annual Conference, to VIRGINIA C. WOODWARD. (27 DEC 1851)

MARRIAGE. In this city, on Tuesday, the 23d inst., by the Rev. J.W. Newton, Doctor D.N. MAHON, of Carlisle, Pa., to JULIA M., daughter of Capt. J.B. Montgomery, of the U.S. Navy. (27 DEC 1851)

MARRIAGE. On the 18th inst., at Old Point Comfort, by the Rev. M.L. Chevers, Major HENRY J. HUNT, U.S. Army, to Miss EMILY C., daughter of Lieut. Col. R.E. DeRussy, U.S. Corps [of] Engineers. (27 DEC 1851)

MARRIAGE. On the 23d inst., in Anne Arundel Co., Md., by the Rev. Mr. Nelson, THOMAS H. WORTHINGTON, of this city, to ELIZABETH M. WILLIAMS, of the former place. (27 DEC 1851)

DEATH. On the 24th inst., in the 82d year of her age, Mrs. NELLY WILSON, a native of Somerset Co., Md., but for the last 28 years a resident of this city. (27 DEC 1851)

MARRIAGE. On the 23d inst., at the new Trinity Church, in Georgetown, by the Rev. P.B. O'Flanagan, Mr. JOSEPH COLLINS to Miss MARY A. HURDLE. (29 DEC 1851)

DEATH. In this city, on Monday, the 22d inst., at 7 o'clock A.M., Mrs. NANCY KING, consort of William King, Esq., of the Navy Department. Mrs. King was a native of Gettysburg, Pa., and had been only a short time a resident of Washington — long enough, however, to have endeared her to many, especially her fellow-worshippers in F Street Presbyterian Church, who highly appreciated the excellence of her character as a benevolent and a consistent Christian. As her life was that of the Christian, so her death was cheered by the Christian's hope, "*the hope that maketh not ashamed*." (29 DEC 1851)

DEATH. In the city of Raleigh, N.C., on Sunday evening, the 21st inst., Mrs. DELIA HAYWOOD, aged 69 years, relict of the late Stephen Haywood, formerly of that place, and daughter of Col. Philemon Hawkins, late of Warren Co., N.C. (29 DEC 1851)

DEATH. On the 26th inst., at his residence in Baltimore Co., DENNIS A. SMITH, in the 71st year of his age. A native of Calvert Co., he removed to Baltimore in 1795, and at a period as early as the year 1813 had become not only the most prominent banker and shipper of that growing city, but enjoyed a high reputation throughout the country for his financial skill and connexion with the negotiations of the Government loans during the war. The great commercial and financial depression that succeeded the war with England and the fall of Napoleon resulted in his embarrassment and ultimate failure; and although his subsequent career continued to exhibit the same activity and bold enterprise, yet he never succeeded in retrieving his fortune; but he retained, under all circumstances, the devotion of his many friends and the esteem and kind wishes of the whole community. (29 DEC 1851)

DEATH. In this city, on Wednesday evening, December 24, at the residence of his brother, on 9th street, NATHANIEL W. ADAMS, a Clerk in the Treasury Department, formerly a resident of Buffalo, N.Y., and a native of Connecticut, aged 29 years. His remains were interred on Friday in the Congressional Cemetery. (30 DEC 1851)

Daily National Intelligencer, Marriage and Death Notices, 1851-1854

DEATH. In this city, on Sunday night last [28 DEC 1851], REUBEN, son of Mr. Henry and Mrs. Catherine Walker, aged 5 years. Funeral this afternoon at 3 o'clock, from the residence of his parents on 16th, near I street. (30 DEC 1851)

DEATH. In this city, on Monday morning [29 DEC 1851], at one o'clock, MARY ANN, daughter of James and Jane Lynch, aged 3 years and 4 days. The funeral will take place this (Tuesday) afternoon, at 2 o'clock, to which the friends of the family are invited. (30 DEC 1851)

DEATH. At New York, suddenly, in the 96th year of her age, Mrs. JANE KIP. (30 DEC 1851)

DEATH. At Darien, Conn., recently, THADDEUS BELL, aged 93. He was present at the burning of Danbury, during the revolutionary war, and took part in the pursuit of the British. He was one of the congregation who, with their pastor, Dr. Marthen, were seized during Divine worship by a band of Tories, and conveyed to the British headquarters at New York. (30 DEC 1851)

OBITUARY. In the city of Philadelphia, on the 9th inst., Madame ASIGOIGNE, aged 81 years [text continues]. (30 DEC 1851)

MARRIAGE. On the 30th inst., by the Rev. Dr. Laurie, JOHN S. MAXWELL to Miss MARY L. WILSON, all of this city. (31 DEC 1851)

DEATH. On the 30th inst., Mr. JOHN F. SWEENY, aged 25 years. His funeral will take place on Thursday, January 1st, at 3 o'clock P.M. The friends of the deceased will please attend, at his mother's residence, Mrs. A. Sweeny, Capitol Hill. (31 DEC 1851)

DEATH. Suddenly, in Georgetown, D.C., on Sunday evening, the 28th inst., Mrs. ELETHEA BURNETT, aged 70 years, relict of the late Charles A. Burnett. The friends of the family are invited to attend her funeral, from her late residence, on Bridge street, this day, at 3 o'clock. (31 DEC 1851)

Daily National Intelligencer, Marriage and Death Notices, 1851-1854

❋ ❋ ❋ 1852 ❋ ❋ ❋

MARRIAGE. On Tuesday evening, 30th December 1851, by the Rev. Mr. Marks, Mr. JOHN T. LIGHTER, of the District of Columbia, to Miss MARY A. TOWNSAND, of Montgomery Co., Md. On the same evening, by the same, Mr. EDWARD SUMMERS to Miss MARY BOSSELL, of the District of Columbia. (1 JAN 1852)

MARRIAGE. On the 25th December, by Rev. L.F. Morgan, Mr. FRANCIS GERMON to JANE E. COLLIER, all of this city. (1 JAN 1852)

MARRIAGE. On Tuesday evening last [30 DEC 1851], by the Rev. Mr. Morgan, JOSEPH THAW, Esq., to Miss MARY ANN KEARNS, all of Washington. (1 JAN 1852)

MARRIAGE. On the 30th ult. [30 DEC 1851]. by the Rev. Mr. Slattery, Mr. JNO. P. DENNIS, of Baltimore, to Miss JANE E. MILLINGTON, of Montgomery Co., Md. (1 JAN 1852)

DEATH. At the residence of Mr. Edward McCubbin, on 8th street, LOUIS F. JONCHEREZ, aged about forty years. His friends are invited to attend his funeral this day [January 1, 1852], at 3 o'clock P.M. (1 JAN 1852)

DEATH. On the 30th ult. [30 DEC 1851], LAURISTON WARD, Esq., formerly of Saco, Me., late a clerk in the Navy Department. (2 JAN 1852)

DEATH. Yesterday morning, after a short illness, ALICE ANN, adopted daughter of Christopher and Ellen N. Atz. The funeral will take place at 3 o'clock this afternoon, from G street, between 11th and 12th streets. (2 JAN 1852)

MARRIAGE. On Thursday, the 1st inst., by the Rev. Mr. Hodges, JOHN GODDARD to Miss NANCY THOMPSON, both of Prince George's Co., Md. (3 JAN 1852)

MARRIAGE. On the 30th ult. [30 DEC 1851], by the Rev. Mr. Kepler, Dr. WM. P. HEREFORE to Miss LUCY A. SIMPSON, both of Prince William Co., Va. (3 JAN 1852)

MARRIAGE. On the 1st inst., by the Rev. John C. Smith, Mr. GEORGE GIDEON WILSON to Miss MARIAN LOUISA PLOWMAN, all of this city. On the same evening, by the same, Mr. WILLIAM H. FORREST to Miss SARAH JANE MOORE, all of this city. (3 JAN 1852)

MARRIAGE. In Georgetown, on the 23d ult. [23 DEC 1851], by the Rev. J.M.P. Atkinson, JACOB YOUNG to SUSANNAH HOLT. (3 JAN 1852)

MARRIAGE. On Thursday, the 1st inst., by the Rev. Peter Lanahan, Mr. LEMUEL D. WILLIAMS to Miss SARAH M. O'DONNELL, all of this city. (3 JAN 1852)

MARRIAGE. On the 29th ult. [29 DEC 1851], by the Rev. Stephen P. Hill, Mr. JOHN B. QUIRK, of Philadelphia, to Miss MARY ANN SKIRVING, of this city. (3 JAN 1852)

DEATH. Suddenly, in Georgetown, on Thursday morning, 1st inst., SAMUEL WOLLARD, aged 45 years. His funeral will take place on Sunday, 4th inst., from his late residence on Bridge street, Georgetown, at 2½ o'clock. (3 JAN 1852)

DEATH. At Beverly, his late residence, in the county of Worcester, Md., JOHN U. DENNIS, Esq., in the 59th year of his age, after a lingering illness of near twelve months, which he bore with a patience and fortitude which none but a Christian could exhibit; he died, seemingly without a struggle, in the arms of his loving and much loved wife, on Tuesday, the 23d inst. [text continues], (3 JAN 1852)

MARRIAGE. On the 30th December [1851], by the Rev. Mr. Lynch, L.F. CLARK and MARY C. CISSEL, daughter of Mr. Thomas Cissel, all of this city. (5 JAN 1852]

MARRIAGE. On the 1st inst., by the Rev. Mr. Edwards, and on the 2d inst., by the Rev. Mr. Donelan, Miss MARY V. HAY and Mr. CHARLES G. BALL, of this city. (5 JAN 1852)

DEATH. At New York, at one o'clock on Saturday last [3 JAN 1852], JOSEPHINE, wife of Peter Augustus Jay, and daughter of the late Hon. Joseph Pearson, of this city. (5 JAN 1852)

DEATH. In Georgetown, on the 23d ult. [23 DEC 1851], of typhoid fever, WILLIAM T. BURROUGHS, in the 24th year of his age, formerly of St. Mary's Co., Md. Truly may it be said that in the death of this young man society has lost one of its most promising ornaments. (5 JAN 1852)

DEATH. On the 4th inst., Mrs. DOROTHY KOONTZ, in the 89th year of her age. The friends and acquaintances are respectfully invited to attend her funeral, from the residence of her son-in-law, Mr. John L. Anderson, on E, between 11th and 12th streets, this (Monday) afternoon, at half past two o'clock. (5 JAN 1852)

DEATH. On the 21st ult. [21 DEC 1851], MARY ELIZA, wife of John G. Poindexter, of New Orleans, daughter of Carter Braxton Poindexter, deceased, and Eleanor Metcaff, late of Norfolk, Va. (5 JAN 1852)

DEATH. On the 22d ult. [22 DEC 1851], at his residence near Edenton, JOSEPH BLOUNT SKINNER, Esq., in the 71st year of his age. Mr. Skinner was no ordinary man, and his loss will be deeply felt in the community in which he resided. After spending some time at Princeton College, he studied law under Gov. Samuel Johnson. He lived two years under the roof of that eminent man, enjoying not only the benefit of his legal instruction, but the still superior advantages of his accomplished manners and interesting conversation, his varied and extensive learning, and his thorough knowledge of the world. Soon after engaging in the practice of his profession, Mr. Skinner obtained a high and enviable position at the bar. Distinguished for his integrity and close application of his duties, his excellent sense and skill as an advocate, rather than for any brilliant talent of display, he was a leading counsel in every cause of importance within his circuit. So lucrative was his practice that in a few years he found himself possessed of an ample competence. He then exchanged his profession for a pursuit more congenial to his taste, and purchased a farm, on which he had ever since resided, in the neighborhood of Edenton. (6 JAN 1852)

DEATH. At New York, on Wednesday morning, December 21, [1851], CATHARINE MATILDA, wife of Lieut. John Calhoun, U.S. Navy, and daughter of John C. Clarkson. (6 JAN 1852)

DEATH. At Pittsburg, Pa., on the 2d inst., of typhoid fever, Miss LIZZIE HAYES, of New York city, aged 17 years and 4 months. (6 JAN 1852)

MARRIAGE. On the 1st inst., by the Rev. Mr. Finkel, Mr. JOHN CORCORAN to Miss URSULA MOHLER, all of this city. (7 JAN 1852)

MARRIAGE. In Washington, by the Rev. Mr. N.B. Collings, of the Baptist denomination, Mr. JOS. G. VENABLE to Miss CAROLINE C. HUTCHISON, all of the above place. (7 JAN 1852)

DEATH. At Richmond, on Sunday morning, the 4th inst., in the 71st year of his age, PHILIP HARRISON, Sr. (7 JAN 1852)

Daily National Intelligencer, Marriage and Death Notices, 1851-1854

DEATH. At her residence in Upper Marlborough, Prince George's Co., Md., on Monday, the 22d day of December, Mrs. GRACE C. TYLER, relict of the late Trueman Tyler, Esq., in the 75th year of her age, after a short but violent illness, which she bore with great patience and Christian meekness, surrounded by her children and grandchildren, and other near and dear relatives, who witnessed her dissolution with hopes full of assurance that her steadfast faith in the religion of her Redeemer had triumphed over the penalties of death, and transported her sanctified spirit to the never-ending joys of Heaven. In the death of this pious and most excellent lady, the circle of her associations has been deprived of one of its sweetest and most charming attractions. Mrs. Tyler was the oldest inhabitant of Upper Marlborough [text continues]. (7 JAN 1852)

MARRIAGE. On the 6th inst., by the Rev. F.S. Evans, Mr. JOS. FAULKNER to Miss JULIA A. LANHAM. On the same evening, by the same, Mr. THOS. CARDEN to Miss MARGARET MOTHERSHEAD. (9 JAN 1852)

MARRIAGE. In Christ Church, by the Rev. Mr. Hodges, Rector, on the 6th inst., Wm. GUINAND, of Philadelphia, to Miss ELIZABETH JANE ACTON, of this city. (9 JAN 1852)

OBITUARY. Died on the 23d December last [23 DEC 1851], in Worcester Co., Md., JOHN UPSHUR DENNIS, Esq., in the 59th year of his age. To those who knew him nothing can be said in relation to the deceased which would enhance their estimation of his character, or diminish the feeling of their bereavement; but to distant friends and relatives it may be grateful to hear the outpourings of the heart from one who respected and venerated and loved their departed kinsman. Associated in early life with the generation of men whose intellects were disciplined and matured by the events which followed the American Revolution and the adoption of the Constitution of the U.S., his character was that of the man of that era — decided and energetic, but devoid of all pomp and parade; courteous, unselfish, and disinterested. He was educated at Washington Academy, in Somerset Co., Md., and at the University of Pennsylvania, and through life had a fondness for classical literature, and highly valued classical education [text continues]. (9 JAN 1852)

DEATH. At the residence of her son-in-law, Dr. Grafton Tyler, in Georgetown, on the morning of the 8th inst., Mrs. AMELIA M. BOWIE, relict of the late Walter Bowie, Esq., of Prince George's Co., Md., in the 62d year of her age. (10 JAN 1852)

DEATH. On the 9th inst., MARY FRENCH, wife of Thomas French. The friends of the family are requested to attend the funeral from her late residence, on the corner of 9th street and New York avenue, tomorrow (Sunday) afternoon, at 2 o'clock. (10 JAN 1852)

MARRIAGE. On Thursday evening, the 8th inst., by the Rev. Wm. Hamilton, Mr. JOHN E. PORTER to Miss SARAH V. DICK, all of this city. (12 JAN 1852)

MARRIAGE. On the 6th inst., by the Rev. T. Myers, JOHN E. BATES, of this city, to Miss CHARLOTTE J., only daughter of Mr. Geo. Williams, late of Lockport, N.Y. (12 JAN 1852)

MARRIAGE. On Thursday afternoon, the 8th inst., by the Rev. Jas. B. Donelan, Dr. J.B. GARDNER to Miss ROSA M., daughter of the late Nathaniel Manning, of Loudoun Co., Va. (12 JAN 1852)

MARRIAGE. On the 8th inst., by the Rev. Chas. McElfresh, Mr. JOHN BURY and Miss ANNE MARIA CALVERT, all of this city. (12 JAN 1852)

MARRIAGE. On the 7th inst., at Wesley Chapel, by the Rev. Wm. B. Edwards, Dr. J. WILSON WISHART, of Washington, Pa., to Miss ANNIE S. GREEN, daughter of A. Green, of this city. (12 JAN 1852)

MARRIAGE. On the 8th inst., by the Rev. O.B. Brown, Mr. JAMES H. SMITH to Miss ANN E. BROWN, both of this city. (12 JAN 1852)

Daily National Intelligencer, Marriage and Death Notices, 1851-1854

MARRIAGE. At St. Ann's Church, Annapolis, Md., on the 6th inst., by the Rev. Dr. Winslow, of Staten Island, SAMUEL MARCY, of the U.S. Navy, to ELIZA M., daughter of Rev. Dr. Humphreys, President of St. John's College, Annapolis. Also, at the same time and place, by Dr. Winslow, LOUISA, daughter of President Humphreys, to ROBERT RANDOLPH CARTER, of the U.S. Navy. (12 JAN 1852)

MARRIAGE. At Experiment, Saline Co., Mo., on the 13th of December [13 DEC 1851], WM. N. BERKELEY, of Virginia, to CYNTHIA W., daughter of the late Gen. T.A. Smith, U.S. Army. (12 JAN 1852)

DEATH. On Saturday morning, the 10th inst., after a few days' illness, VIRGINIA, the youngest daughter of Commodore Aulick. The friends of the family are invited to attend the funeral on Monday, at 12 o'clock, from the house of Mr. Williams, on the avenue, near 17th street. (12 JAN 1852)

DEATH. On Thursday, 8th inst., at the residence of William H. Fowle, in Alexandria, Mrs. MARGARETTA S., wife of Richard H. Turner, of Woodlawn, King George Co., Va., and daughter of the late James H. Hooe, Esq. (12 JAN 1852)

DEATH. Suddenly, in this city, on Friday night last, of disease of the heart, at the residence of G.R. Adams, on 11th, near F street, Hon. LEMUEL SAWYER, formerly a Representative in Congress, for nearly twenty years, from North Carolina. (12 JAN 1852)

DEATH. On Sunday morning, the 11th inst., GEORGE BEAL, infant son of C.S. and Virginia Whittlesey. (13 JAN 1852)

MARRIAGE. On Monday evening [12 JAN 1852], by the Rev. John C. Smith, Mr. NATHAN E. WORTHINGTON to Miss VIRGINIA C. NOTT, all of this city. (14 JAN 1852)

MARRIAGE. On the 22d of December [1851], in St. Mary's Church, by the Rev. Mathias Alig, Mr. JOHN ANTOINE DAUME to CANIGUNDA SCHNAPPAUF, of this city. (14 JAN 1852)

MARRIAGE. On the 6th inst., by [Rev. Mathias Alig at St. Mary's Church], Mr. JOHN SHAAHY to Miss CATHARINE CASSICK. On the 13th inst., by the same, at their residence, Mr. NICOLAUS MURRAY to REBECCA SMITH, all of this city. (14 JAN 1852)

MARRIAGE. On Tuesday evening, 30th ult. [30 DEC 1851], by the Rev. J.G. Gassaway, at Belmont, the residence of James E. Yeatman, Esq., (near St. Louis,) Mr. RICHARD J. LOCKWOOD, of St. Louis, to Miss ANGELICA P. ROBINSON, of Jefferson Co., Va. (14 JAN 1852)

MARRIAGE. At York, Pa., on Tuesday, the 6th inst., by the Rev. M.F. Martin, Mr. HENRY KUHL, of Washington, to Miss CAROLINE T. ERNEY, of York, Pa., formerly of Baltimore, Md. (14 JAN 1852)

DEATH. On the 6th January [1852], at the residence of John F. Wilson, of Anne Arundel Co., Md., in the 25th year of her age, AMANDA S.D. WILSON, wife of John E. Wilson, of Wakefield, Westmoreland Co., Va., and daughter of George W. Duvall, Esq., of Prince George's Co., Md. (15 JAN 1852)

DEATH. At Memphis, Tenn., on the 5th inst., Mrs. ELIZABETH C. ARMOUR, at the age of 50 years [text continues]. (15 JAN 1852)

DEATH. On the 7th inst., ANNIE CANDACE, daughter of R.W. and C.E. Burgess, aged two years and six months. (15 JAN 1852)

MARRIAGE. On the 15th inst., by Rev. Mr. Myers, JAMES W. ABBOTT to Miss J. REBECCA, eldest daughter of Rev. Samuel S. Briggs, all of Washington. By the same, HENRY N. OBER to Miss CAROLINE, youngest daughter of Mr. William Burdine, all of Washington. (16 JAN 1852)

Daily National Intelligencer, Marriage and Death Notices, 1851-1854

MARRIAGE. On the 15th inst., at St. Paul's Lutheran Church, by the Rev. J.G. Butler, Mr. SAMUEL F.D. OURAND, of Washington, to Miss MARGARET MILLER, formerly of Baltimore. (16 JAN 1852)

DEATH. Yesterday [15 JAN 1852], EUGENIUS EMORY, infant son of Thos. H. and Mary Cornelia Havenner, aged 1 year. The friends of the family are invited to attend the funeral this (Friday) evening, at 3 o'clock. (16 JAN 1852)

DEATH. In Philadelphia, on Saturday, the 10th inst., MARY, wife of James Robertson, in the 77th year of her age. (16 JAN 1852)

MARRIAGE. In this city, on the 15th inst., by the Rev. Mr. Morgan, WILLIAM STICKNEY, formerly of Bangor, Me., to Miss JEANNIE, daughter of Hon. Amos Kendall. (17 JAN 1852)

MARRIAGE. On the 15th inst., by the Rev. J.R. Eckard, Mr. RICHARD H. ABBOT to Miss REBECCA J. HARRIS, of this city, late of Philadelphia. (17 JAN 1852)

DEATH. At Cincinnati, on Sunday, 28th of December [1851], Mrs. JANE FINDLAY, relict of Gen. James Findlay, in the 83d year of her age. (17 JAN 1852)

DEATH. On the 15th inst., in the 61st year of her age, Mrs. ANN GANTT, relict of the late Thomas T. Gantt, and daughter of the late Benjamin Stoddert. Her funeral will take place from the residence of her son-in-law, Jonathan Prout, this day at 12 o'clock M. The friends of the family are invited to attend. (17 JAN 1852)

DEATH. In this city, on Thursday night last, the 15th inst., at the residence of her brother-in-law, Mr. M.P. Callan, Miss MARGARET A. FLANNEGAN, second daughter of the late Edward Flannegan, of the city of New York. (17 JAN 1852)

DEATH. On Sunday evening, 18th inst., Mr. ROBERT LATHAM, of the Treasury Department. His friends and acquaintances are invited to attend his funeral, to take place at 2½ o'clock this evening, from his late residence on 4½ street. (20 JAN 1852)

DEATH. In Charleston, S.C., on the morning of the 14th inst., after a painful and protracted illness, borne with patience and fortitude and terminated with calmness, Mrs. MARY SHUBRICK HORRY, widow of the late Elias Horry, Esq., and sister of Commodore Shubrick, U.S. Navy. (20 JAN 1852)

DEATH. At Orange Springs, Marion Co., Fla., on the 8th of December last [8 DEC 1851], A.G. ANDERSON, Esq., of Pulaski, Tenn., in the 31st year of his age. (20 JAN 1852)

DEATH. On the 13th inst., JAMES THOMAS, aged three months, and on the 19th inst., ALBERT, aged four years, children of E.W. and Mary Ann Forteney. Within one little week, two lovely babes, the joy and hope of the household, passed to that "home not made with hands, eternal in the heavens." One had only tarried with us a few days, when its sweet life slowly departed; the other, in the midst of roseate health, suddenly perished by fire. "Thy will be done!" (21 JAN 1852)

SUDDEN DEATH. — An inquest was held by Coroner Woodward, on Tuesday, over the body of a man by the name of Smith, supposed to have been born in Snow Hill, Md., and late of Baltimore. He died on board the schooner *George Ann*, of Baltimore, and previous to his death stated that he had two children living in Philadelphia. The verdict of the jury was that he came to his death by disease of the heart. Further information may be obtained by addressing H.F. Prichard, in this city. (22 JAN 1852)

MARRIAGE. At St. Patrick's Church, on Wednesday, the 21st inst., by the Rev. Wm. Matthews, Mr. JOHN P. FAHERTY, of Baltimore, to Miss ELIZA J. CATON, of this city. (23 JAN 1852)

Daily National Intelligencer, Marriage and Death Notices, 1851-1854

MARRIAGE. In Dranesville, Va., on Tuesday, the 20th inst., by the Rev. Mr. Blackwell, Mr. J.S. HOLLINGSHEAD, of Washington, to Miss MARY M. DRANE, of Fairfax Co. (23 JAN 1852)

MARRIAGE. On the 22d inst., by the Rev. W.B. Edwards, C.O. WALL, Esq., of Washington, to Miss ELIZABETH A. HOBBS, of Baltimore, Md. (23 JAN 1852)

DEATH. On Wednesday night last [21 JAN 1852], at 12 o'clock, MARY, wife of Jilson Dove, in the 58th year of her age. Her funeral will take place this afternoon, at 2 o'clock, from the residence of her son, Wm. T. Dove, 19th street, between G and H. Her friends, as well as those of the family, are respectfully invited to attend. (23 JAN 1852)

DEATH. On Tuesday evening, 20th inst., Mr. JAMES WATSON, in the 58th year of his age. The friends and acquaintances are respectfully invited to attend his funeral this (Friday) afternoon, at 3 o'clock, from his late residence on M street, between 15th and 16th streets. (23 JAN 1852)

MARRIAGE. In Georgetown, on Thursday, the 22d inst., by the Rev. B.F. Bittinger, Dr. HENRY JACOBS, of Pennsylvania, to Miss MARGARET, daughter of Mr. John Bittinger. (24 JAN 1852)

DEATH. In Philadelphia, on the 16th inst., Mrs. MARY OWNER, wife of Capt. James Owner, of this city, and daughter of the late Hon. Robert McMullen, of the former place. (24 JAN 1852)

DEATH. At Evergreen, Prince William Co., on the 9th inst., Mrs. ELIZABETH C. FITZHUGH, wife of Dr. John P.T. Fitzhugh, and daughter of the late Col. Beall, of Georgetown, D.C. (24 JAN 1852)

DEATH. At St. John's, the residence of the family, near Port Tobacco, Md., on the 8th of January, Mrs. MARY J. BARNES, consort of Judge Richard Barnes, in the 46th year of her age. (24 JAN 1852)

DEATH. At his residence, in Charles Co., Md., on the 26th ult. [26 DEC 1851], SAMUEL BARKLEY, Esq., late Postmaster at Pomonkey, in the 66th year of his age. (24 JAN 1852)

MARRIAGE. On Thursday, 22d inst., at Christ Church, Georgetown, by the Rev. Mr. Caldwell, FRANCIS DODGE to FANNY J., daughter of the late Henry H. Chapman, of Maryland. (26 JAN 1852)

DEATH. On the afternoon of Saturday, 24th inst., in the 37th year of her age, after a few days' illness, ELIZABETH, wife of B.F. Middleton. Her funeral will take place tomorrow (Tuesday) morning, the 27th inst., at half-past 10 o'clock, from the residence of her husband, on Louisiana avenue. The friends of the family are invited to attend. (26 JAN 1852)

DEATH. On yesterday, 25th inst., after a short illness, JOSEPH N. PATTERSON, Esq., clerk in the Post Office Department. His funeral will take place this afternoon at 3 o'clock, from his late residence, north A street, Capitol Hill. The friends of the family are invited to attend. (26 JAN 1852)

DEATH. At Annapolis, on the morning of Wednesday, the 21st inst., WILLIAM WIRT RANDALL, eldest child of Hon. Alexander Randall, aged nine years and three months. (26 JAN 1852)

DEATH. Yesterday morning [26 JAN 1852], at 8 o'clock, THOMAS P. TENCH, in the 27th year of his age. His funeral will take place tomorrow afternoon, at 2 o'clock, from the residence of his mother, near the Navy Yard. The friends of the family are respectfully invited to attend. (27 JAN 1852)

DEATH. In this city, on the 26th inst., Mr. CHRISTIAN H. WEBER, aged 50 years. His friends and acquaintances are respectfully invited to attend his funeral on Wednesday afternoon, at 3 o'clock, from his late residence on G street south (Navy Yard,) two doors east of the Protestant Church. (27 JAN 1852)

Daily National Intelligencer, Marriage and Death Notices, 1851-1854

DEATH. In this city, on the morning of the 17th inst., JOHN PAYNE TODD, Esq., in the 61st year of his age. (27 JAN 1852)

DEATH. At College Hill, D.C., on the 24th inst., after a short illness, WILLIAM TAYLOR WHITE, of [Accomack] Co., Va., aged 17 years. (28 JAN 1852)

DEATH. On Monday night, the 26th inst., CHARLES EDWARD, aged 4 years, youngest son of J.W. DeKraft. The friends of the family are invited to attend the funeral this (Wednesday) morning, at 12 o'clock. (28 JAN 1852)

DEATH. On the 27th inst., JOSIAH HICKS, only child of A.J. and Mary L. Larner, aged 13 months and 27 days. The friends of the family are invited to attend the funeral this afternoon, at 3 o'clock, from the residence of Mr. Goodrich, corner of 5th and H streets. (28 JAN 1852)

MARRIAGE. On Tuesday, 27th inst., by the Rev. J.W. French, JOHN W. HOGG, of Tennessee, to SARAH E., eldest daughter of the late Jesse E. Dow, of this city. (29 JAN 1852)

DEATH. In this city, on Tuesday evening [27 JAN 1852], in the 29th year of her age, Mrs. MARY ANN MEGINLEY, daughter of Mr. Thomas Goodall. The friends of the family are invited to attend her funeral this afternoon, at two o'clock, from the residence of her father. (29 JAN 1852)

MARRIAGE. On Thursday, the 29th inst., at "Leamington," near Washington, by the Rev. Mr. Donelan, Lieut. BOLTON S. PORTER, U.S. Navy, to MARY ANN AUGUSTA, eldest daughter of E. Lindsley, Esq. (30 JAN 1852)

MARRIAGE. By the Rev. Mr. Slattery, Mr. MICHAEL GREEN, of Norfolk, Va., to MARY F. GANNON, daughter of Mr. Owen Leddy, of Washington. (30 JAN 1852)

DEATH. At Meadville, Pa., on the 28th inst., HELEN, wife of Rev. John Barker, D.D., President of Alleghany College, aged 32 years; a lady distinguished for the loveliness of her character in all the relations of life. (30 JAN 1852)

MARRIAGE. In this city, on the 29th inst., at the Church of the Epiphany, by the Rev. Mr. French, S.B. KNOX, U.S. Navy, to MARY FRANCES, daughter of the late James M. Selden, of Virginia. (31 JAN 1852)

MARRIAGE. On the 27th inst., by the Rev. James B. Donelan, Mr. JAMES T. BARNES to Miss HARRIET KING, all of this city. (31 JAN 1852)

DEATH. In Georgetown, D.C., on Friday, January 30th [1852]., of erysipelas, Mr. GEORGE TEMPLEMAN, in the 61st year of his age. His friends and acquaintances are respectfully invited to attend his funeral on Sunday afternoon, February 1st at 3 o'clock. (31 JAN 1852)

DEATH. Friday evening, January 30th, FREDERIC CARLTEN, infant son of Guy C. and A. Rebecca Humphries. (2 FEB 1852)

DEATH. On Friday, the 30th inst., WM. SANFORD, only child of Mary and the late Jonathan Nesbit, aged 4 years and 5 months. (2 FEB 1852)

DEATH. At his residence in Morehouse Parish, La., on the 28th of December last [28 DEC 1851], after a brief illness, ROBERT HENDERSON, Esq., in the 32d year of his age. His friends in Virginia, where he spent the greater part of his life, will remember his kindness, manliness, and stainless integrity. The Christian faith in which he had walked during the last years of his life fully sustained him in its last moments. (2 FEB 1852)

Daily National Intelligencer, Marriage and Death Notices, 1851-1854

DEATH. On Sunday, the 1st inst., at noon, at the residence of her brother, in Washington Co., D.C., Mrs. ANN MARIA ISRAEL, relict of the late Otho Israel, of Anne Arundel Co., Md. The funeral will take place this morning at 11 o'clock, from her late residence on 6th street, near H. The friends and acquaintances of the family are invited to attend. (3 FEB 1852)

DEATH. At Henderson, Ky., on the 24th November last [24 NOV 1851], in the 79th year of his age, Capt. JOHN POSEY, eldest son of the late Major General Thomas Posey, of the Revolutionary Army. John Posey was born in Virginia, and served with credit as an officer of dragoons in the troop commanded by Solomon Van Rensselaer, in Wayne's army, during the celebrated campaign of 1795, in the Northwestern Territory; and by his death the venerable General Van Rensselaer remains the only surviving officer of that army. At the conclusion of that war, Capt. Posey married and settled in Kentucky, where he resided until his decease, beloved and honored by all who knew him. He was a graduate of the University of Pennsylvania, a man of good sense, highly cultivated mind, and refined taste. Gentle, upright, honorable, unsophisticated in heart and manners, he was one of the kindest and most generous of men. He combined the qualities of a brave soldier, a polished gentleman, a devout Christian, and a true-hearted man. Retired from all public duties, he spent a long life in the bosom of a numerous and amiable family, a rare example of an unambitious, disinterested country gentleman, devoting the abilities and acquirements which might have adorned a high public station to the discharge of domestic duties and religious obligations, and the practice of a generous hospitality. Kind and sincere in all his relations, he never wronged a human being nor made an enemy, and closed an exemplary life in the full faith and cheerful hope of a blessed resurrection. (3 FEB 1852)

MARRIAGE. In this city, on the 28th ult. [28 JAN 1852], at the Church of the Epiphany, by the Rev. Mr. French, A. DOUBLEDAY, U.S. Army, to MARY B., daughter of the late R. Hewett, of Baltimore. (4 FEB 1852)

MARRIAGE. On the 1st inst., by the Rev. Mr. Eva, Mr. JOSEPHUS GREEN to Miss ARABELLA WHEELER, all of this city. (4 FEB 1852)

MARRIAGE. On the 1st inst., by the Rev. James B. Donelan, Mr. ALFRED C. SHAW to Miss JULIA E. WALSH, all of this city. (4 FEB 1852)

MARRIAGE. On Tuesday evening, the 3d inst., by the Rev. Dr. Ducachet, of Stephen's Church, Philadelphia, AUGUSTUS S. NICHOLSON and JANE FINDLEY, daughter of Major General Jesup, of the U.S. Army. (4 FEB 1852)

DEATH. In this city, on the 2d inst., RACHEL, wife of Wm. D. Pratt, of New London, Conn., and daughter of the late Daniel Landen, Esq., of Troy, N.Y., aged 28 years and 5 months. The friends and acquaintances of the family are respectfully requested to attend her funeral from the church of the Ascension, corner of H and 9th streets, on Thursday, the 5th inst., at 10 A.M., without further invitation. (4 FEB 1852)

DEATH. In this city, on the 26th ult., EMMA JANE, aged two years four months and twenty-two days, the daughter of George H. and A. Atchison. (4 FEB 1852)

MARRIAGE. On the 1st inst., by the Rev. Mr. Eva, Mr. JOEL C. GREEN to Miss ISABELLA E. WHEELER, all of this city. (6 FEB 1852)

MARRIAGE. On the 3d inst., by the Rev. Mathew Alig, in St. Mary's Church, Mr. JOHN RAGAN to Miss MARY GALLAHER, all of this city. On the same day, by the same, HUGH JONES to ELIZABETH BENNETT. (6 FEB 1852)

MARRIAGE. In the Cherokee Nation, on the 29th of December [1851], by the Rev. Thomas Bertholf, Mr. JAMES BUTLER, of South Carolina, (son of our esteemed Agent, Dr. Butler, and brother of our present

Daily National Intelligencer, Marriage and Death Notices, 1851-1854

worthy Agent, George Butler,) to Miss FRANCES TAYLOR, daughter of Richard Taylor, Second Chief of the Cherokee Nation. *Cherokee Advocate*. (6 FEB 1852)

DEATH. In this city, on the 3d inst., aged 6 years, SELDEN, son of Frances E. and Commander William H. Gardner, U.S. Navy. (6 FEB 1852)

OBITUARY. Died, in Owensboro, Ky., on Saturday, the 24th January 1852, of erysipelas, Mrs. ELIZA H. TRIPLETT, wife of Hon. Philip Triplett, in the 47th year of her age. In the full maturity of her intellectual and physical strength, the destroyer came, gathered her home to the Heaven to Rest and the presence of the God whom she delighted to serve. She had been for many years a most meek and devout Christian; and, having attached herself to the Cumberland Presbyterian Church, her walk and conversation at all times evinced her fitness, not only for that station, but for the society of Heaven [text continues]. (7 FEB 1852)

MARRIAGE. In Christ Church, in this city, by the Rev. Mr. Hodges, JOSEPH HUGH McCAFFERY to Miss MARY JANE KENNEDY, all of this city. (9 FEB 1852)

MARRIAGE. On Wednesday, 4th inst., by the Rev. Mr. Slattery, Mr. JOHN H. ROBY to Miss MARGARET E. KEATING, all of this city. (9 FEB 1852)

DEATH. On Sunday morning, the 8th inst., at 4 o'clock, in the 67th year of his age, Mr. PAUL KINCHEY, a native of Switzerland, and a resident of this city for the last 34 years. The funeral will take place from his late residence on the hill opposite 20th street, on Wednesday next, the 11th inst., at 2 o'clock P.M. His friends and acquaintances are requested to attend the funeral without further notice. Carriages will be in readiness at the St. Paul's Lutheran Church, corner of 11th and H streets, at 1 o'clock, to convey persons who wish to attend the funeral to the residence above named. (9 FEB 1852)

OBITUARY. Died, at Pittsburg, on Thursday, the 29th ult. [29 JAN 1852], HARMAR DENNY, a gentleman well known to this community. Mr. Denny never fully recovered from an almost fatal attack of malarious fever which he contracted in a journey to Philadelphia last summer. After a partial convalescence and return home, he gradually declined under infirmities undoubtedly left by that violent illness, the most painful of which was a neuralgic affection of the breast and neck. He was in his 58th year. Those who had heard of him so long ago as a public man, and were familiar with his name and reputation, which began to be wisely known whilst he was yet very young, and those who have seen him only of late when his prepossessing features had become prematurely venerable, will hardly believe that he was not an older man. He was born in May 1794, whilst his father commanded a military expedition to Presque Isle against the Indians. He was named from a bosom friend and chivalrous brother officer. The name ever sat gracefully upon him; for he, too, was "without fear and without reproach." If he had any trait which, from childhood, predominated over all others in his pure character, it was constitutional courage and personal intrepidity. Mr. Denny graduated at Dickinson College. He married an accomplished and amiable lady -- in goodness, gentleness, and in every Christian virtue a congenial spirit. In the Legislature of this State, in the Congress of the U.S., and the Convention which formed the present constitution of Pennsylvania; in the councils of his native city, and other offices of trust and honor, he maintained a respectable standing by his sound judgment, firmness, tact, and practical abilities [text continues]. *Philadelphia Inquirer*. (9 FEB 1852)

DEATH. At her residence, near Lawrenceville, N.J., on Sunday evening, 1st inst., after a lingering illness, Mrs. MARIA S. INMAN, wife of Capt. Wm. Inman, U.S. Navy. (10 FEB 1852)

DEATH. At the residence of J.F. Wilson, Esq., Anne Arundel Co., Md., January 6, Mrs. AMANDA S. WILSON, wife of J.E. Wilson, of Westmoreland Co., Va. (10 FEB 1852)

DEATH. On Sunday, the 8th inst., GEORGE SUTHERLAND, son of William and Mary Martin, in the 15th year of his age. The friends and acquaintances of the family are respectfully invited to attend his funeral

Daily National Intelligencer, Marriage and Death Notices, 1851-1854

this (Tuesday) afternoon, at 2 o'clock, from the residence of his father, on D street, three doors east of 7th street. (10 FEB 1852)

OBITUARY. Died, in this city, yesterday morning [10 FEB 1852], at half-past one o'clock, after a protracted illness of 19 months, Dr. FREDERICK DAWES, in the 74th year of his age. This distinguished physician, valuable citizen, and amiable and excellent man was a native of the town of Huntingdon, in the county of Huntingdon, England. After enjoying the advantages of a regular medical education, in the course of which he studied under the celebrated Sir Astley Cooper, he commenced the practice of his profession at Wisbeach, in Lincolnshire. Subsequently, he was induced to accept a commission in the service of the Emperor of Russia, acting as surgeon with great acceptance on board a Russian man-of-war in the Mediterranean. After this he returned to his native land, and resumed his profession there, but being a liberal in politics, and having contracted a warm admiration for the Government and policy of the U.S., he in 1819 embarked with his family from Liverpool to New York. Though strong inducements were held out to him, both in New York and Philadelphia, to continue in those cities, his first practice in the U.S. was in Washington. Here he remained several years, and then removed to Illinois, where he purchased and resided on a farm. Not satisfied with the West, he recrossed the mountains, and located himself on a farm in Westmoreland Co., Va., where he continued three years. In 1839, he returned to Washington, where he has remained ever since. Dr. Dawes always maintained a distinguished position in the ranks of the medical profession of this city. His judgment in general was very good, but in the diagnosis of diseases pre-eminent. Towards his medical brethren, as indeed to all with whom he had intercourse, his bearing was ever that of a most benevolent, intelligent, high-toned gentleman; modest, kind, considerate, always delicately mindful of the rights, the welfare, and comfort of others. For the country of his nativity he kept a tender recollection, which by no means interfered with the deep interest he took in the honor, the progress, and dignity of his adopted land. A faithful husband, a tenderly affectionate father, a kind master, he was admired and beloved by all who knew him, and by those most who knew him best. For the week previous to his decease he suffered greatly, but, as throughout his trying illness, with wonderful patience and submission. The funeral will take place from the residence, corner of D and 9th streets, on Thursday afternoon, at half-past three o'clock, to which the friends of the family are, without further notice, invited. (11 FEB 1852)

MARRIAGE. On Monday evening, the 9th inst., by the Rev. Mr. Slattery, Mr. ROBERT T. DAVIS to Miss MARIA JOSEPHINE WELCH, both of this city. (11 FEB 1852)

MARRIAGE. On the 9th inst., by the Rev. Thos. Atkinson, D.D., RICHARD T. ALLISON, U.S. Navy, to MARIA KEY TANEY, daughter of Roger B. Taney, Chief Justice of the U.S. (11 FEB 1852)

MARRIAGE. At Lynn, Mass., on the 3d inst., by the Rev. Mr. Shackford, Mr. JOHN B. KIBBEY, of this city, to Miss HELEN, daughter of Phineas Drew, Esq., of Lynn. (11 FEB 1852)

MARRIAGE. In this city, on the 31st January, by the Rev. Mr. Brown, P.H. HOLMES, of Winthrop, Me., to MARY W. HILLIARD, formerly of Lawrence, Mass. (11 FEB 1852)

DEATH. On Monday morning, the 9th inst., after a serious illness of two weeks, WILLIAM FISCHER, in the 54th years of his age. The friends of the family are respectfully invited to attend his funeral from his late residence, C street, this morning (Wednesday) at 11 o'clock. (11 FEB 1852)

DEATH. At his residence near Columbia, Tenn., the Hon. EDMUND DILLAHUNTY, Judge of State Court for the eighth circuit. Judge D. was one of the most eminent and distinguished citizens, and one of the ablest jurists of Tennessee; his general benevolence, his active philanthropy, his known high morality and winning urbanity of manner, rendering him a great favorite with every body who knew him well. (11 FEB 1852)

DEATH. Suddenly, at Richmond, Va., on the 7th inst., GEORGE PARK CRUMP, Esq. Mr. Crump was one of those rare men, kind and gentle in their natures, for whom a whole community entertain warm feelings

Daily National Intelligencer, Marriage and Death Notices, 1851-1854

of regard. We do not believe he has left behind him in the breast of an individual a feeling of animosity, nor in the mind of an acquaintance any sentiment but regret for his loss and respect for his virtues [text continues]. (11 FEB 1852)

DEATH. On Wednesday morning, the 11th inst., of pulmonary consumption, Mrs. HELEN C., wife of James L. Boyd, of Philadelphia, in the 36th year of her age. Her friends and the friends of the family are respectfully invited to attend her funeral, from the residence of her brother-in-law, Theodore Scheckels, on 7th street, between I and K streets, west side, this (Thursday) afternoon, at 2 o'clock, without further notice. (12 FEB 1852)

DEATH. On Wednesday, the 11th inst., at her residence, in Georgetown, D.C., MALVINA E. ADLER, aged 42 years, wife of Morris Adler, Esq. The relatives and friends of the family are requested to attend the funeral this (Thursday) afternoon, at 3½ o'clock. (12 FEB 1852)

DEATH. At Decatur, Newton Co., Miss., on the 27th of November last [1851], aged 28 years, HENRY L. SCOTT, Esq., a native of Virginia, but for several years past a resident of Mississippi. (12 FEB 1852)

DEATH. On the morning of the 11th inst., CHARLES G., son of Dr. G. and Margaret L. Bailey, aged three months. (13 FEB 1852)

DEATH. On the 11th inst., in the 67th year of her age, after a short illness, Mrs. SARAH WELCH, formerly of Annapolis, Md. Her funeral will take place tomorrow (Sunday) afternoon, at 2½ o'clock, from the residence of her son-in-law. G.W. Robinson. (14 FEB 1852)

DEATH. On the evening of the 11th inst., ELLA, daughter of William and Elizabeth Lord, aged 18 days. (16 FEB 1852)

DEATH. On the 15th inst., Mrs. ELIZABETH E., wife of Perez Packard, in the 63d year of her age. The friends of the family are requested to attend her funeral tomorrow, (Tuesday) at 12 o'clock M., from her late residence near Rock Creek Church. (16 FEB 1852)

MARRIAGE. At Grand Coteau, La., on the 27th January, 1852, by the Rev. Mr. Giles, THOMAS E. GARDINER, Esq., to Miss JOSEPHINE C. McPHERSON, eldest daughter of S.C. McPherson, Esq., both formerly of Charles Co., Md. (17 FEB 1852)

DEATH. Suddenly, on Sunday night, the 15th inst., Mr. JAS. H. BENNETT, formerly of Loudoun Co., Va. His funeral will take place this morning, at 11 o'clock, from the residence of Mr. James Frasier, on G street, between 4th and 5th, to which the friends of the family are respectfully invited. (17 FEB 1852)

DEATH. On Sunday night, the 15th inst., at Elkridge, Md., MARY CAMPBELL, wife of J.T.B. Dorsey, Esq., and eldest daughter of Dr. Thomas Harris, Chief of Bureau of Medicine and Surgery. (17 FEB 1852)

DEATH. On Monday afternoon, the 16th inst., MARY FRANCES McNERHANY, aged two years and ten months. The friends of the family are requested to attend the funeral this afternoon, at 4 o'clock, from the residence of her parents, corner of 14th and L streets. (17 FEB 1852)

OBITUARY. At Savannah, on the morning of the 2d inst. [2 FEB 1852], in the 42d year of her age, ELIZA CECIL, consort of the Hon. John MacPherson Berrien, and daughter of Col. James Hunter, of that city [text continues]. (18 FEB 1852)

DEATH. On the 30th ult., at New Albany, Ind. (where he was universally esteemed as a man and a physician,) Dr. HENRY M. DOWLING, a native of Loudoun Co., Va., in about the 43d year of his age. (18 FEB 1852)

Daily National Intelligencer, Marriage and Death Notices, 1851-1854

DEATH. On the 16th inst., Mrs. MARY TAYLOR, relict of the late Joseph Taylor, Esq., of Saratoga Co., N.Y. Funeral at 11 o'clock this morning, from the Presbyterian Church, 4½ street. (18 FEB 1852)

DEATH. On the 16th inst., MARY LOUISA, daughter of Washington and Caroline Rollings, after a protracted illness of three months, in the 3d year of her age. The friends of the family are invited to attend her funeral, at 4 o'clock this afternoon, from the residence of her parents. (18 FEB 1852)

MARRIAGE. On the 14th inst., by the Rev. Matthew Alig, in St. Mary's Church, Mr. JEREMIAH SULLIVAN to Miss CATHERINE DEASY. (20 FEB 1852)

MARRIAGE. On the 17th inst., at the U.S. Hotel, by the Rev. W.T. Eva, Mr. JOSEPH CREWS and Miss HESTER ANN MARTIN. (20 FEB 1852)

DEATH. In Philadelphia, on the morning of the 14th inst., after a short illness, Mrs. MARY ANN SHIELDS, in her 63d year. She was formerly from Alexandria, Va., but had resided for a number of years in this city until recently. (20 FEB 1852)

DEATH. At New Orleans, on the 8th inst. [8 FEB 1852], WM. P. HORT, assayer of the U.S. Branch Mint of that city. (20 FEB 1852)

OBITUARY. On Friday, the 23d of January [1852], our venerable fellow-citizen, Capt. HENRY AUSTIN, the last of the older portion of the family which colonized Texas, expired at his residence in Galveston [text continues]. (21 FEB 1852)

MARRIAGE. In Georgetown, on Tuesday morning, the 17th inst., by the Rev. Thomas Sewall, the Rev. J.H. HOOVER, of the Baltimore Annual Conference, to EMILY SANDFORD, daughter of Thomas Brown, Esq. (23 FEB 1852)

MARRIAGE. In this city, on Thursday, the 19th inst., by the Rev. Mr. Marks, Mr. JAS. T. SANSBURY to Miss SARAH JANE DULY, both of Prince George's Co., Md. (23 FEB 1852)

DEATH. In this city, on the night of Friday, the 20th inst., in the 67th year of her age, Mrs. SUSAN STANSBURY, wife of Arthur J. Stansbury, and eldest daughter of the late Hon. Benjamin Brown, member of the House of Representatives for the State of Maine. Mrs. S. was in perfect health on the morning of that day, and, while looking at Healy's great picture of Webster before the Senate, was suddenly seized with an apoplectic attack, of which she died. The friends of the family, and of her sons, Capt. Howard and Charles F. Stansbury, are invited to attend her funeral from her late residence, corner of F and 12th streets, at 11 o'clock this (Monday) morning. (23 FEB 1852)

DEATH. On the 21st inst., VINCENT LOUIS, infant son of Joseph R. and Rosalia Massoletti. The friends of the family are respectfully invited to attend his funeral on Tuesday morning, at 11 o'clock. Residence, 10th street, between D and E streets. (23 FEB 1852)

DEATH. Yesterday morning, the 23d inst., at half-past five o'clock, after a painful illness of a few weeks, Mrs. MARY ANN, consort of Samuel Brereton, of this city, aged 53 years. The friends of the family are respectfully invited to attend her funeral on this (Tuesday) afternoon at three o'clock, from the residence of her husband, corner of 7th and F streets. (24 FEB 1852)

DEATH. At Clover Hill, the residence of her brother, Richard Beckett, Esq., in Calvert Co., Md., on the 19th inst., Miss MARY H. BECKETT, in the 63d year of her age. The death of this excellent lady is deeply lamented by a large circle of relatives and friends, who will long cherish in fond remembrance her affectionate disposition and many Christian virtues. "Blessed *are* the dead which die in the Lord from henceforth: Yea, saith the spirit, that they may rest from their labors, and their works do follow them." (24 FEB 1852)

Daily National Intelligencer, Marriage and Death Notices, 1851-1854

MARRIAGE. On Sunday evening, 22d inst., by the Rev. Mr. Lanahan, Mr. RICHARD W. CLARKE to Miss MARY A. BARRETT, all of Washington. (25 FEB 1852)

MARRIAGE. On the 17th inst., by the Rev. D.X. Junkin, D.D., Mr. FRED'K M. DETWEILLER, of Philadelphia, to Miss JANE ELIZABETH TARLTON, of Washington. (25 FEB 1852)

MARRIAGE. In Georgetown, on the 22d inst., by the Rev. J.F. Eaken, RICHARD H. TRUNNELL to Miss MARGARET A. CUNNINGHAM, both of that place. (25 FEB 1852)

DEATH. In Philadelphia, on the morning of the 21st inst., aged 21 years, MARGARET CAMPBELL GRAHAM, daughter of Lieut.-Col. James D. and Charlotte Meade Graham. Her friends are invited to attend her funeral at St. John's Church in this city, this day, the 25th, at half-past 12 o'clock. (25 FEB 1852)

DEATH. On the 5th of February, THOS. MILTON McGILL, aged four months and one week, son of Thos. McGill, deceased. (25 FEB 1852)

DEATH. Yesterday afternoon, of scarlet fever, JOHN SMITH, in his sixth year, youngest child of Michael and Christiana Larner. The friends and acquaintances of the family are invited to attend the funeral this (Wednesday) afternoon at 3 o'clock. Residence F, near 6th street. (25 FEB 1852)

DEATH. On the morning of the 25th inst., JOHN A. YOUNG, in the 70th year of his age. The deceased was a soldier in the American army during the last war with Great Britain, and for many years Assistant Warden in the penitentiary of the District of Columbia. His funeral will take place this (Thursday) afternoon, at 3 o'clock P.M., from his late residence on Louisiana avenue, near 7th street. The friends of the family, members of Central Lodge No. 1, I.O.O.F., and Columbian Encampment No. 1, I.O.O.F., are respectfully invited to attend. (26 FEB 1852)

DEATH. On the morning of the 25th inst., after a painful illness of three months, WM. McCARTHY, in the thirty-third year of his age. His funeral will take place this day at 3 o'clock, from his residence, on the corner of East Capitol and First street. (27 FEB 1852)

DEATH. On the 23d inst., after a severe illness of eight months, Mr. GEORGE DUCKWORTH, aged eighty-five years. Mr. Duckworth came to this city about 1800, and remained here from that day to his death, and may be considered one of the pioneers of the city, respected by all who knew him. (27 FEB 1852)

DEATH. In Alexandria, on the 23d inst., SAMUEL HILTON, an old and highly respected citizen of that place, who was one of those who bore the pall at the funeral of Washington in 1799, and expired on the day celebrated as the anniversary of the birth of Washington in 1852. Mr. Hilton maintained through life the esteem of all who knew him. (27 FEB 1852)

DEATH. On the evening of the 23d inst., WILLIAM HENRY GOULD, in the 3d year of his age, son of Stephen and Anna M. Gould. (27 FEB 1852)

DEATH. On Wednesday, the 25th inst., after a lingering illness, JOSEPH C., youngest son of the late Joseph N. Patterson, in the sixth year of his age. (27 FEB 1852)

MARRIAGE. On the 26th inst., at the English Lutheran Church, by the Rev. Mr. Butler, HARMAN BURNS to Miss JULIA LOUISA DeSAULES, all of this city. (28 FEB 1852)

MARRIAGE. On Thursday evening, by the Rev. John C. Smith, Mr. GEORGE W. FAIRBANKS to Miss JANE CLARKE, all of this city. (28 FEB 1852)

MARRIAGE. In this city, on the 1st inst., by the Rev. W.B. Edwards, Mr. J. ALLANSON STAATS, of New Orleans, La., to Miss ELIZA ANTOINETTE, daughter of Orson King, Esq., of Massachusetts. (2 MAR 1852)

MARRIAGE. At Talcahuano, in Chili, in December last [1851], Passed Midshipman DAWSON PHENIX, of the Navy, to the Senorita Dona ECARNACION INIGUEZ, daughter of the Senor Don Manuel Iniguez, Minister of the Customs of Talcahuano. (2 MAR 1852)

DEATH. On Saturday evening, the 28th ult., ten minutes after six o'clock, CAROLINE EMILY SCHUSSLER, daughter of the late Rev. Mr. Biscamp, a native of Heyne, in the Electorate of Hesse, in Germany, wife of Charles Schussler, in the 52 year of her age. The friends of the family and acquaintance are respectfully invited to attend her funeral today, at two o'clock P.M., from her husband's residence on Seventh street, opposite the *National Intelligencer* office. (2 MAR 1852)

DEATH. On the morning of the 1st inst., in the 39th year of her age, CAROLINE H., wife of Geo. L. Watkins, and daughter of the late Col. Henry Ashton, of this city. Her funeral will take place this day at 3 o'clock, P.M. The friends of the family are invited to attend. (3 MAR 1852)

DEATH. In this city, on Friday, 27th February, suddenly, Mr. JOHN O'HARE, in the 35th year of his age. (3 MAR 1852)

MARRIAGE. In Salisbury, Litchfield Co., Conn., on the 26th ult. [26 FEB 1852], by the Rev. A. Reed, Mr. GRANVILLE WHITTLESEY, of New York city, and Miss ELLEN E. JOSELEN, of the former place. (4 MAR 1852)

MARRIAGE. At Clay Hill, near Marietta, Ga., by the Rev. L.J. Davis, Mr. JAMES R. LOCKHART, formerly of Grantville, S.C., and Miss ELIZA EMILY, daughter of Gen. E.K. Mills. (4 MAR 1852)

DEATH. On the 3d inst., Dr. JOSEPH M. MUNDING, in the 44th year of his age. His friends and acquaintances are respectfully requested to attend his funeral at 2 o'clock on Friday afternoon, from his late residence, on E street, between 11th and 12th streets. (4 MAR 1852)

MARRIAGE. On the 2d inst., by the Rev. S.P. Hill, ALEXANDER FRANK to Miss MARY ELIZABETH WILKERSON, all of King George Co., Va. (5 MAR 1852)

MARRIAGE. On Thursday afternoon [4 MAR 1852], in the Fourth Presbyterian Church, by the Rev. John C. Smith, JAMES HENRY, Esq. to Miss RACHEL AMELIA, daughter of John T. Clements, Esq., all of this city. (5 MAR 1852)

DEATH. On the 3d inst., GEORGE WILLIAM COUMBE, aged 4 years 2 months and 5 days, only son of Ann M. and John T. Coumbe. (5 MAR 1852)

MARRIAGE. On Thursday evening, the 4th inst., at the parsonage of the Methodist Episcopal Church South, by Rev. Leo. Rosser, Mr. JOHN JENNINGS to Miss JULIA ANN STONE, all of this city. (6 MAR 1852)

MARRIAGE. On the 24th ult. [24 FEB 1852], by the Rev. Mr. Gilliss, MADISON GASSAWAY to Miss LUCINDA WHITE, both of this city. (6 MAR 1852)

DEATH. At the residence of his sister, in Exeter, Me., of consumption, on the 24th February, Hon. SAMUEL CARTLAND, aged 58. He was a native of Lee, N.H., a graduate of Dartmouth College, a lawyer by profession, and had been a member of both branches of the Legislature of his native State, President of the Senate, Judge of Probate, and, for a short time, acting Governor. The delicate state of his health compelling him to seek a milder climate, he was subsequently for some years a Clerk in the

Daily National Intelligencer, Marriage and Death Notices, 1851-1854

Treasury Department at Washington, which place he relinquished in October 1850; and in all situations he maintained a character for ability and spotless integrity that placed him high in the esteem of his friends and the public. (6 MAR 1852)

OBITUARY. [Communicated.] Died in this city, on the 8th of February, in the 67th year of his age, Mr. PAUL KINCHY, a native of Switzerland, but for more than thirty years a resident of Washington. By industry, frugality, integrity, and activity in business he was enabled to acquire a handsome estate, and for the last few years had lived in retirement, devoting his time, thoughts, and means to the promotion of the virtue and happiness of his family, friends, and mankind. He was eminently a faithful, kind, and good man, warmly attached to the Lutheran Church, of which he had long been an exemplary member, and which he was always ready to aid by his contributions and prayers. Acts of kindness and generosity on the part of this truly Christian man have come to our knowledge which invest his character with a bright and shining light. His disease was pneumonia, which, notwithstanding the most anxious assiduities of his friends and the best medical advice, gradually increased in power, until it terminated in his departure, which, as well as his whole illness, was attended with the consolation of the religion of which he was a sincere professor. (6 MAR 1852)

MARRIAGE. On the 1st inst., by the Rev. Mr. Edwards, WALTER W. GIBSON to Miss CATHARINE A.G. ROBINSON, all of Washington. (8 MAR 1852)

MARRIAGE. On the 2d inst., in Georgetown, D.C., by the Rev. J.J. Murray, Rev. J.M. SHAPLEY to Miss BETTY S. HUTCHINSON. (8 MAR 1852)

MARRIAGE. On Monday last [8 MAR 1852], at the Episcopal Theological Seminary, Alexandria Co., Va., by the Rev. Dr. Sparrow, Miss ELIZA WESTWOOD W. MACRAE, of Fairfax, to ALEX. C.N. SMETS, Esq., of Marietta, Ga. (9 MAR 1852)

DEATH. In this city, on Sunday, the 7th inst., at 9 o'clock P.M., RICHARD G. ENNIS, eldest son of the late Philip and Jane Ennis, in the 27th year of his age. His funeral will take place from the residence of his father-in-law, Mr. Patrick O'Donnoghue, on G, between 4½ and 5th streets, this (Tuesday) afternoon at 3½ o'clock. (9 MAR 1852)

DEATH. On the 8th inst., GEORGE N. WEBSTER, in the 24th year of his age. The friends of the family are invited to attend his funeral this day at 2 o'clock, from his brother's residence on 11th street, between I and K streets. (9 MAR 1852)

DEATH. On the evening of the 3d inst., of inflammation of the brain, WILLIAM H., youngest son of George Johnson, of this city. (9 MAR 1852)

DEATH. In this city, on the 8th inst., CLOYE ANN STEWART, in the 74th year of her age. Her funeral will take place from the residence of her son, George W. Stewart, at the corner of 12th and H streets, tomorrow afternoon at two o'clock, to which her friends are invited. (9 MAR 1852)

DEATH. In Keokuk, Ia., on 20th of February, Rev. JOHN L. CUMMINS, Pastor of the Second Presbyterian Church, in the 31st year of his age. To his many friends every where this announcement will bring feelings of intense sorrow. Eloquent as a preacher, beloved as a pastor, kind as a companion, and popular as a man, by his friends his memory will be ever cherished fondly, and to them the recollections of his life will be ever dear. A bond to earth is broken, but "*there is one more tie binding them to Heaven.*" (9 MAR 1852)

DEATH. On Tuesday, the 9th inst., EMMA, daughter of the Rev. Newton Heston, of the Philadelphia Conference, aged 4 years 3 months and 20 days. The friends and relatives of the family are respectfully invited to attend her funeral today, (10th inst.,) at 4 o'clock P.M., from the residence of Jos. W. Beck, Esq., Capitol Hill. (10 MAR 1852)

DEATH. At Alta Vista, near Beltsville, Prince George's Co., Md., on the morning of the 9th inst., EMMA O., daughter of John T. and America B. Holtzman, in the 14th year of her age. Funeral on Thursday morning at 11 o'clock from the Railroad Depot, Washington, D.C. The friends of the family are invited to attend. (10 MAR 1852)

DEATH. At Alexandria, on Sunday last [6 MAR 1852], LOUIS A. CAZENOVE, Esq., in the forty-fifth year of his age. (11 MAR 1852)

MARRIAGE. On the 24th ult. [24 FEB 1852], by the Rev. Mr. French, MADISON GASSAWAY to Miss LUCINDA WHITE, both of this city. (12 MAR 1852)

MARRIAGE. On the 9th inst., by the Rev. Hodges, ALFRED RICHARDSON to Miss MALINDA STONE, all of this city. (12 MAR 1852)

MARRIAGE. On the 9th inst., by the Rev. Mr. Henning, THOMAS PHENIX, Jr., of Baltimore, to REBECCA M., daughter of John A. Smith, Esq., of this city. (12 MAR 1852)

MARRIAGE. On the evening of the 9th inst., in the English Lutheran Church, by the Rev. J.G. Butler, LOUIS H. SCHNEIDER to Miss JANE TURTON, all of this city. (12 MAR 1852)

DEATH. At New Orleans, on the 1st inst., in the 80th year of his age, ANDREA DIMITRY, a native of Greece, but for sixty years a resident of New Orleans, and one of its valiant defenders in 1815. (12 MAR 1852)

DEATH. At Enfield, N.C., on the 15th ult., ANNIE MAY, daughter of Lemuel C. and Annie H. Wheat, aged 11 months. (12 MAR 1852)

MARRIAGE. At Fredericksburg, Va., on Tuesday, the 9th inst., by the Rev. E.C. McGuire, Hon. J. BALESTIER, late Envoy to Southeastern Asia, to Mrs. CAROLINE M. THOMSON, of Fredericksburg. (13 MAR 1852)

DEATH. At the house of her daughter, Mrs. Sprigg, Mrs. JANE THORNTON, at the advanced age of 79 years, many of which she had passed in the service of that God, who, early sought and found by her, shed over her couch of pain the comfort and peace of mind that can spring only from Him. The friends of the family are respectfully invited to attend her funeral from her late residence on C street, between 4½ and 3d, this day at 3½ o'clock P.M. (13 MAR 1852)

DEATH. Departed this life on the 11th inst., at half-past nine o'clock A.M., Mrs. SOPHIA H. PERRIE, formerly of Prince George's Co., Md., in the 42d year of her age. The friends and relatives of the family are respectfully invited to attend her funeral tomorrow (Sunday) afternoon at 3½ o'clock, from her late residence on Fifth, between G and H streets. (13 MAR 1852)

DEATH. On the 14th inst., at 3 o'clock A.M., Miss SARAH BIRCKHEAD, in the 70th year of her age. The friends and relatives of the family are respectfully invited to attend her funeral this afternoon, at 3½ o'clock, from her late residence on 4½ street, near Louisiana avenue. (15 MAR 1852)

DEATH. In this city, on Thursday, the 11th inst., CHARLES CARROLL, aged 4 years and 7 months, son of Hon. Isaac P. and Elizabeth H. Walker, of Wisconsin. (15 MAR 1852)

MARRIAGE. On the 10th inst., at Cleveland, King George Co., Va., by the Rev. Wm. Friend, Lieut. DABNEY H. MAURY, U.S. Army, to Miss NANNIE R. MASON, eldest daughter of W.R. Mason, Esq. (16 MAR 1852)

Daily National Intelligencer, Marriage and Death Notices, 1851-1854

DEATH. On Saturday, the 13th inst., LOUISA ELIZABETH, aged six years, three months, and four days, daughter of Andrew and Catharine Noerr, of this city. (16 MAR 1852)

DEATH. On Monday, the 15th inst., at the residence of her son-in-law, Mr. James H. Jones, near the Navy Yard, Mrs. JAMIMA ADAMS, consort of the late George Adams, in the 54th year of her age. The deceased was for upwards of 35 years a consistent member of the Methodist Episcopal Church. The friends of the family are invited to attend her funeral, at 3 o'clock this (Wednesday) afternoon, from the Ebenezer Church. (17 MAR 1852)

DEATH. In this city, on the 6th inst., ELIZABETH MARTHA, daughter of Samuel Sanderson, of Alexandria, Va., aged 7 years and 4 months. (17 MAR 1852)

MARRIAGE. On the 11th of March, in St. Anne's Church, Annapolis, by the Rev. C.K. Nelson, PHILIP G. SCHWRAR, to H. KENT HALL, daughter of the late Col. Wm. J. Hall, all of the above place. (18 MAR 1852)

MARRIAGE. In Christ Church, Washington, on Tuesday, the 16th inst., by the Rev. Mr. Hodges, JAMES N. MILLER to Miss MARY A. MARTIN, all of this city. (19 MAR 1852)

MARRIAGE. On Thursday afternoon, by the Rev. John C. Smith, Mr. WILLIAMSON HARRISON to Miss CATHARINE SOPHIA BRAYFIELD, all of this city. (19 MAR 1852)

DEATH. At her residence in Calvert Co., Md., on Sunday morning, February 29, Mrs. MARGARET M. DARE, in the 73d year of her age. (19 MAR 1852)

MARRIAGE. On the 15th inst., by the Rev. Wm. H. McGuffey, Mr. WM. B. HAMILTON, of West Feliciana, La., to Miss VIRGINIA C. WATSON, of Albemarle Co., Va. [P.S. New Orleans and Bayou Sara papers please copy.] (20 MAR 1852)

MARRIAGE. On Thursday evening, by the Rev. John C. Smith, Mr. RUSSELL P. DAVIS to Miss MARTHA E.B. DePUY, both formerly of New York, now of this city. (20 MAR 1852)

MARRIAGE. In Baltimore, on Thursday, 18th inst., by the Rev. Thos. H. Stockton, SAMUEL W. TUCKER, of Washington, to Miss MARY STILLINGS, of the former place. (20 MAR 1852)

MARRIAGE. On the 16th inst., by the Rev. L.F. Morgan, THOS. F. SAUNDERS, Esq., of Charlottesville, Va., to Miss ELIZABETH E. GOGGIN, of this city. (22 MAR 1852)

MARRIAGE. On the 2d inst., at Alexandria, Va., by the Rev. J.T. Johnston, A.B. FAIRFAX, Esq., U.S. Navy, to Miss E.M. NORRIS, daughter of the late Rev. Oliver Norris, Rector of Christ's Church in that place. (22 MAR 1852)

DEATH. In this city, on the 21st inst., THOMAS DUMPHRIEUS, in the 37th year of his age. His relatives and friends are invited to attend his funeral at 4 o'clock this afternoon, from his late residence, on 10th street east, between C and D north. (22 MAR 1852)

DEATH. On Sunday, the 14th inst., IMOGEN REBECCA, aged nine months, infant daughter of Orlando R. and Ann Rebecca Delphey. (22 MAR 1852)

DEATH. At Poughkeepsie, on the 18th inst., EGBERT B. KELLEY, for 20 years Editor of the *Poughkeepsie Telegraph*, aged 50 years. (22 MAR 1852)

DEATH. At Fayetteville, Onondaga Co., N.Y., on the 11th inst., at the residence of his son, Porter Tremain, the Hon. Judge AUGUSTUS TREMAIN, formerly of Columbia Co., N.Y., aged 76 years. (22 MAR 1852)

Daily National Intelligencer, Marriage and Death Notices, 1851-1854

DEATH. At Watervliet, on the 17th inst., Hon. JAMES BURT, a patriot of the Revolution, aged 90 years. (22 MAR 1852)

DEATH. In Paramaribo, Surinam, (S.A.) January 22, MARTHA ISABELLA, wife of Dr. Francis W. Bragin, U.S. Consul, and daughter of the Rev. B. Fowler, of Stockbridge, Mass. (22 MAR 1852)

DEATH. On the 22d inst., ANADORA, youngest daughter of Geo. H. and Eliza Ann Plant, aged two years six months and eleven days. The friends of the family are respectfully invited to attend the funeral this day at 4 o'clock P.M. (23 MAR 1852)

DEATH. In this city, on Tuesday, the 23d inst., Mrs. ANN REBECCA, wife of Guy C. Humphreys, and daughter of Mason A. Piggot, in the 21st year of her age. The friends of her husband and father's family are respectfully invited to attend her funeral, from the residence of her father, on Pennsylvania avenue, between 4½ and 6th streets, on Thursday, 25th, at 4 o'clock P.M., without further invitation. (24 MAR 1852)

MARRIAGE. Yesterday, at 3 o'clock P.M., at the Methodist Episcopal Church South, by the Rev. Leo. Rosser, Rev. WM. McKENNEY, U.S. Navy, to Miss ANNA MARIA McLEAN RAGSDALE, of this city. (25 MAR 1852)

DEATH. In this city, on Saturday morning, the 20th inst., Mr. JOSEPH DODDS, formerly of Alexandria, Va., in the 85th year of his age. (25 MAR 1852)

DEATH. In this city, on the 24th inst., REBECCA JOHNSON, third daughter of Geo. Johnson. Her funeral will take place on Friday next, at 10 o'clock A.M., to which the friends of the family are invited without further notice. (25 MAR 1852)

DEATH. At his residence, in Philadelphia, on the 9th inst., EDWIN AUGUSTUS ATLEE, M.D., one of the oldest and most respectable physicians of that city. He was in the 76th year of his age. (25 MAR 1852)

MARRIAGE. On Sabbath afternoon [21 MAR 1852], by the Rev. John C. Smith, Mr. GEORGE H. SMITH to Miss MARY OSBORNE, all of this city. (26 MAR 1852)

MARRIAGE. On Wednesday evening, by the Rev. John C. Smith, Mr. EDWARD LEROY PORTER to Miss CLARA ANN McDONALD, both of Massachusetts. (26 MAR 1852)

DEATH. On the 25th inst., in Baltimore, at the residence of Bishop Waugh, KATE, only child of W.B. Waugh, of this city, in her ninth year. The funeral will take place from the Washington Depot, at 11 o'clock this day. (27 MAR 1852)

DEATH. In this city, on Friday, 26th inst., MARY SWEENY, aged 59 years. Her funeral will take place from her late residence, on Capitol Hill, on Sunday next, at 3 o'clock, to which her friends and those of the family are respectfully invited. (27 MAR 1852)

DEATH. On the 26th inst., of croup, JAMES HOWARD, son of Stewart and Lucy A. More, aged six years and one month. His funeral will take place today, (Saturday,) the 27th inst., at 11 o'clock, from the residence of his parents, on L street north, between 8th and Ninth streets. The friends of the family are invited to attend. (27 MAR 1852)

DEATH. On the 25th inst., GEORGE BEVERLY TAYLOR, aged seven months and nineteen days, son of Thomas and Eliza R. Brown. (27 MAR 1852)

DEATH. At the residence of his father in St. Louis, Mo., on Wednesday, the 17th inst., of a sudden and violent bilious attack, JOHN RANDOLPH BENTON, only son of Col. Thomas H. Benton, aged 22 years and four months. It was the brief summons of a youth in the bloom and vigor of life. On Tuesday, the 10th, he was one of the myriad that met Kossuth; on Thursday, the 12th, he was at the St. Louis University, arranging with the President for some branches of study on which he was eager to enter; that night he was taken ill; at sunrise on the morning of the 17th he had breathed his last. Seldom has there been a more impressive example of the shadowy fleetness of this life. *St. Louis Intelligencer.* (27 MAR 1852)

MARRIAGE. On the 25th inst., at the First Presbyterian Church in this city, by the Rev. John Decker, JOHN DECKER, Jr., of Prince George's Co., Md., to HELEN MAR, youngest daughter of the late Dr. Thos. Patterson, of Montgomery Co., Md. (29 MAR 1852)

DEATH. On Saturday afternoon, the 27th inst., ANNA LOUISA, second daughter of Samuel and Anna R. Bull, aged 4 years 7 months and 9 days. The friends of the family, without further notice, are requested to attend the funeral this day, (Monday) at 4 P.M., from the residence of her parents, corner of 12th street and Pennsylvania avenue. (29 MAR 1852)

DEATH. On Monday, the 22d inst., in the 70th year of her age, MARGARET COATS, relict of the late Richard W. Meade. (29 MAR 1852)

DEATH. In Georgetown, on Saturday, 27th inst., Miss ROSANNA McAVOY, formerly of Alexandria, Va., in the twentieth year of her age. Her friends and those of the family are respectfully invited to attend her funeral this (Monday) afternoon at 4 o'clock, from the residence of Mr. T. O'Neale, Fayette street, above the Convent. (29 MAR 1852)

DEATH. At the marine barracks, on the 26th inst., Sergeant DANIEL CUNNINGHAM, of the Marine Corps. He was in the U.S. service 30 years, and always noted for energy and good conduct. He was severely wounded in the Florida war, and was engaged in the battle of Waterloo, belonging at that time to the Enniskelan regiment of dragoons. (29 MAR 1852)

DEATH. At the residence of his uncle, N.M. McGregor, on Capitol Hill, on the morning of the 28th inst., JESSE EWELL, in the 23rd year of his age. His funeral will take place on Monday, at half-past three o'clock P.M. His acquaintances and friends are invited to attend. (29 MAR 1852)

DEATH. On Sunday, the 28th inst., ARTHUR S. VALENTINE, infant son of Mathias and P.J. Valentine, aged eight months and four days. His funeral will take place from the residence of Wm. Greer, on Tenth street, near Pennsylvania avenue, on this (Monday) afternoon at half-past 3 o'clock, at which the friends of the family are respectfully invited to attend without further notice. (29 MAR 1852)

DEATH. On Sunday, the 28th inst., Capt. FURMAN BLACK, in the 55th year of his age. Capt. B. has been a resident not only in our community, but in Philadelphia, Savannah, New York, and Connecticut, and extensively known as a commander of steamboats on several important lines. A paroxysm of grief, caused by the loss of an only son within a year past, brought on the illness that has terminated a life of much active usefulness and of the kindliest nature. He died as he lived, a good man, at the last moment pronouncing his blessing on his wife and daughters, and his hopeful supplication to Divine Grace to receive his departing spirit. His funeral will take place, without further notice, from the National Hotel, at 2 o'clock this afternoon. (29 MAR 1852)

MARRIAGE. On the 25th inst., by the Rev. Dr. Wyatt, GEORGE WASHINGTON LEWIS, of Virginia, to EMILY CONTEE JOHNSON, daughter of Hon. Reverdy Johnson. (30 MAR 1852)

DEATH. On Sunday evening, March 28th, Mrs. REBECCA D. PIGGOTT, in the 52d year of her age. Her friends and acquaintances are respectfully invited to attend her funeral this (Tuesday) afternoon at 4 o'clock. (30 MAR 1852)

DEATH. Yesterday morning, in this city, SARAH HANNAH, infant daughter of John and Mary Ann Mills, aged nine months and ten days. Funeral this afternoon at 2 o'clock, from the residence of her parents on 6th street, between D and E streets. (1 APR 1852)

DEATH. In Charles Co., Md., on Monday, March 23d, Mrs. SARAH A. DIXON, the only daughter of the late John A. Maddox, in the 20th year of her age. (1 APR 1852)

DEATH. At The Cottage, King George, Va., on Friday, 26th March, at 7 o'clock A.M., GEORGE NICHOLAS, eldest son of N. Quisenberry, aged ten years three months and eighteen days. (1 APR 1852)

DEATH. At Philadelphia, 28th ult. [28 MAR 1852], in his 41st year, WILLIAM R. GRANT, M.D., Professor of Anatomy in the Pennsylvania Medical College. (2 APR 1852)

DEATH. At Philadelphia, 28th ult. [28 MAR 1852], of apoplexy, in the 59th year of his age, JOHN HAVILAND, Esq., Architect. (2 APR 1852)

MARRIAGE. In Brooklyn, N.Y., at the residence of her grandfather, T. Craven, Esq., on Wednesday, the 24th ult., by the Rev. Francis Vinton, D.D., the Rev. E.R. CRAVEN, of Somerville, N.J., to HANNAH TINGEY, daughter of the late Francis Sanderson, U.S.N. (3 APR 1852)

MARRIAGE. On the 30th ult. [30 MAR 1852], at Connaconerara, N.C., the residence of Thomas P. Devereux, Esq., by the Rev. Drury Lacy, PETER AUGUSTUS PORTER, Esq., of Niagra Falls, N.Y., to MARY CABELL, daughter of the late John Breckenridge, D.D., of Kentucky. (3 APR 1852)

DEATH. At Snow Hill, Md., on the 28th March, in the 32d year of his age, Col. CHARLES N. HANDY, son of the late James H. Handy, of this city. (3 APR 1852)

DEATH. On the 26th of March, OGDEN, aged 17 months and 3 days, youngest son of Lieut. W.D. Porter, U.S.N. (3 APR 1852)

DEATH. Of consumption, on Saturday night, at 11 o'clock, Mr. BARTLETT W. MORRISON, in the 25th year of his age. His funeral will take place from the residence of his father, Wm. M. Morrison, corner of C and 10th streets, on the Island, this (Monday) afternoon, at one o'clock. The friends and acquaintances of the family are respectfully invited to attend. (5 APR 1852)

DEATH. On the Sabbath morning, April 4, from the effects of scarlet fever, LILLIE, youngest daughter of Charles H. and Ann E. Lane, in the 4th year of her age. The friends of the family are respectfully invited to attend her funeral from the residence of her father, on Indiana avenue, near 2d street, this Monday afternoon, the 5th inst., at 3 o'clock. (5 APR 1852)

DEATH. On the 31st ult. [31 MAR 1852], at Afton, the residence of Col. Wm. H. Spicknall, Calvert Co., Md., JANE SINGLETON GARNER, in the 18th year of her age, daughter of the late Capt. H. Garner, U.S. Army. *Alexandria Gazette* please copy. (6 APR 1852)

DEATH. At the residence of his father, in this city, on the 5th inst., THOMAS St. CLAIR CLARKE, youngest child of A. and Margaret St.C. C. Barnes, aged seven years, eleven months, and twelve days. The friends of the family are invited to attend his funeral, from the residence of his father, corner of F and 20th streets, this afternoon, April 6th, at 2 o'clock. (6 APR 1852)

MARRIAGE. On the 6th inst., by the Rev. Mr. Rosser, DWIGHT R. WATERS, of New York, to Miss MARCELIA EDMONSON, of Washington, D.C. (7 APR 1852)

MARRIAGE. On Tuesday morning [6 APR 1852], at Mt. Pleasant, Md., by the Rev. John C. Smith, Mr. GEORGE H. HOWELL to Miss VIRGINIA T. MAGRUDER, both of Prince George's Co. (8 APR 1852)

Daily National Intelligencer, Marriage and Death Notices, 1851-1854

DEATH. On the 6th inst., CATHERINE S., consort of James W. Johnson. Her funeral will take place today, (Thursday,) the 8th inst., at 3 o'clock, from her late residence on Second, near East Capitol street. The friends of the family are requested to attend. (8 APR 1852)

MARRIAGE. At the McKendree Chapel, on the 7th inst., by the Rev. Mr. Hamilton, JOHN W. SIMMS to Miss ELIZA M. FERGUSON, both of this city. (9 APR 1852)

MARRIAGE. On the 8th inst., by the Rev. Leo. Rosser, Mr. JOHN HANDY THOMAS and Miss EMILY DORDEN, all of this city. (9 APR 1852)

DEATH. In Georgetown, at the residence of her son, John H. King, on the 27th ult. [27 MAR 1852], Mrs. ELEANOR H. KING, at the advanced age of 81 years. Her memory is precious to her numerous surviving friends, and she will be long remembered for her many acts of kindness and benevolence by those who now lament her death. (9 APR 1852)

MARRIAGE. On Thursday, the 8th inst., by the Rev. S. Roszell, WM. R. WOODWARD, of Georgetown, to MARY ANN, daughter of Wm. Redin. (10 APR 1852)

MARRIAGE. On Tuesday, the 6th inst., by the Rev. Mr. Caldwell, of Christ Church, Georgetown, JOHN W. BURROUGHS, of Prince George's Co., to MARY E. POSEY, of Montgomery Co., Md. (10 APR 1852)

DEATH. On the 9th inst., ELIZABETH, consort of the late John Kreamer, in the 62d year of her age. Her friends are requested to attend the funeral at 3 o'clock tomorrow (Sunday) afternoon, at Edward Thomas's, 4½ street, near N street north. (10 APR 1852)

DEATH. Yesterday morning [11 APR 1852], aged fifty years, Mrs. ESTHER WOODWARD, wife of William Woodward, and formerly of Chestnut Hill, near Germantown, Pa., and for the last twenty-six years a resident of this city. Funeral from the residence of her husband, on Massachusetts avenue, this (Monday) afternoon at three o'clock. (12 APR 1852)

DEATH. On Sunday, the 11th inst., Mrs. MARY ANN WILLIAMS, widow of the late James Williams, of St. Mary's Co., Md., aged 68 years. Her funeral will take place on Tuesday morning next, at 10 o'clock, from the residence of her son-in-law, W.L. Newton, on K, between 9th and 10th streets, where his and her friends are respectfully invited to attend. (12 APR 1852)

DEATH. On Friday morning, 9th inst., in Alexandria Co., Va., JOHN REED, the eldest son of the late Isaac Reed, in the 55th year of his age. (12 APR 1852)

DEATH. Suddenly, in Philadelphia, on Friday morning, the 9th inst., WILLIAM P. BLIGHT, in the 45th year of his age. (12 APR 1852)

OBITUARY. It is always with difficulty that the death of a friend is realized. His absence, when the mind is inactive and dormant, is regarded as temporary; and it is only when reason and reflection resume their throne that we feel the magnitude of our loss. Thus we have felt the demise of the late Dr. B.W. MORRISON... on the night of the 3d of April, surrounded by his friends, and with all the consolation of the Christian religion, he breathed his last. (12 APR 1852)

OBITUARY. In Boston, on the 29th of February last, Mrs. SARAH MARIA UPHAM, wife of Henry Upham, Esq. (12 APR 1852)

DEATH. Yesterday, the 12th inst., after an illness of about an hour, SARAH BRETT, wife of Matthew Waite, aged nearly sixty years. This deceased lady has been a consistent and esteemed member of the

Methodist Episcopal Church for more than forty years. The funeral will take place from Wesley Chapel on Wednesday morning next, at 10 o'clock, where the friends of the family are respectfully invited to attend. (13 APR 1852)

DEATH. On the 12th inst., RODOLPHUS, son of Mrs. Elizabeth Clute, aged 19 years and 6 months. His friends and the friends of the family, and the members of Timothy Division, No. 1, Sons of Temperance, of which he was a member, are respectfully invited to attend his funeral from the residence of Mr. Joseph Nardin, 10th and C streets, this day, at 4 o'clock. (13 APR 1852)

DEATH. In this city, on the 10th inst., CALVIN WILLEY, Jr., of Chicago, Ill., in the 57th year of his age. (13 APR 1852)

MARRIAGE. At the city of St. Domingo, on the 27th of January last, by his Grace, the most Rev. Dr. D. Thomas de Portes y Infante, Archbishop of St. Domingo, JONATHAN ELLIOT, Esq., United States Consul, and MARIA MERCED, only daughter of Don Domingo dela Rocha, Ex-Governor of the Province and City of St. Domingo. (14 and 23 APR 1852)

DEATH. On Tuesday, the 13th., inst., GEORGE W., aged nine months, son of George W. and Mary Ann Robinson. The friends of the family are invited to attend the funeral this afternoon at 4 o'clock. (14 APR 1852)

DEATH. Yesterday morning [14 APR 1852], after a lingering illness, THOMAS MUNROE, Esq., in the 81st year of his age, the oldest as well as one of the most respectable of the residence of Washington. Mr. Munroe, was one of the earliest Commissioners of this city during the Administration of President Washington; and after the removal of the seat of Government hitherto, in 1800, he was appointed Postmaster for this city, which office he filled until the year 1829. His funeral will take place this afternoon at 5 o'clock, from his late residence on Pennsylvania avenue west. (15 APR 1852)

DEATH. On Wednesday, the 14th inst., Mrs. AMELIA H. PEABODY, aged 51 years, widow of Capt. Jno. Peabody, and daughter of the late James Leander Cathcart. The funeral will take place on Friday morning, at 10 o'clock, from her late residence, on B street north, Capitol Hill. (15 APR 1852)

DEATH. At the Irving House, in this city, on the 13th inst., after a lingering illness and extreme suffering, commencing with scarlet fever, SALLY, only daughter of Capt. A.W. Reynolds, U.S. Army, aged 8 years and 11 months. (15 APR 1852)

MARRIAGE. At Blandwood, in the vicinity of Greensborough, N.C., on the 6th inst., by the Rev. C.F. Deems, Mr. RUFUS LENOIR PATTERSON, of Caldwell Co., to Miss MARIE LOUISE, daughter of Hon. John M. Morehead. (16 APR 1852)

MARRIAGE. On the 6th inst., by the Rev. Samuel D. Finckel, CHARLES E. DAVIS to CAROLINE A., daughter of the Rev. S.D. Finckel. (16 APR 1852)

MARRIAGE. On the 10th inst., by the Rev. Samuel D. Finckel, GEORGE GITTINGS to Miss MARY CASS. (16 APR 1852)

MARRIAGE. On the 11th inst., by the Rev. Charles A. Davis, Mr. ROBERT HURST to Miss MARY JANE MASSEY, of Fairfax Co., Va. (16 APR 1852)

DEATH. Died, at St. Augustine, Fla., on the 26th ult. [26 MAR 1852], where he had gone for the benefit of his health, Hon. GIDEON BARSTOW, aged 69 years. He had been long and prominently connected with politics of his native State, (Massachusetts,) having been a member of both branches of its Legislature, and a Representative from its second Congressional district in 1821-1822. (16 APR 1852)

Daily National Intelligencer, Marriage and Death Notices, 1851-1854

DEATH. On the 15th inst., at Mt. Pleasant, D.C., Miss MARTHA ELLEN WHITE, daughter of the late Capt. James White. She was an affectionate daughter and sister, a sincere friend, a devout Christian. "None knew her but to love her, None named her but to praise." The friends of the family are invited to attend the funeral on Saturday at 2 o'clock P.M. (16 APR 1852)

DEATH. In Georgetown, on the 14th inst., at 8½ P.M., LIZZIE R., wife of Wm. Clabough, and third daughter of Thos. Cissel, Esq., aged 18 years. The friends of the family are respectfully invited to attend the funeral on this (Friday) afternoon at 3 o'clock, from her late residence on Market street. (16 APR 1852)

DEATH. On Wednesday, the 14th April, CHARLES HENRY, infant son of the Hon. D.J. Bailey, of Georgia, aged about 2 years. "Of such is the Kingdom of Heaven." The funeral will take place on Friday, at 10 A.M. The friends of the family are invited to attend. (16 APR 1852)

DEATH. Yesterday, the 16th inst., Mrs. RACHEL DUNN, aged 79 years, widow of the late Thos. Dunn, formerly Sergeant-at-Arms of the House of Representatives. The friends and acquaintances of the family are respectfully invited to attend her funeral on tomorrow (Sunday) afternoon, at 3½ o'clock, from the First Baptist Church, 10th street. (17 APR 1852)

DEATH. On the 15th inst., WM. BURY, in the fifty-third year of his age. His relatives and friends are respectfully invited to attend his funeral this afternoon at two o'clock, from his late residence near the Navy Yard. (17 APR 1852)

DEATH. Friday morning [16 APR 1852], at 1 o'clock, ANN AMANDA, youngest child of Daniel and Mary Quigley, aged fourteen months and five days. The friends and acquaintances of the family are respectfully requested to attend the funeral from the residence of the family this afternoon, at three o'clock, near the Navy Yard. (17 APR 1852)

MARRIAGE. At Raleigh, N.C., on the morning of the 16th inst., by the Rev. Drury Lacy, ANNIE FORSTER HINTON, of that place, and JOHN R.S. BOND, of Cincinnati, Ohio. (19 APR 1852)

MARRIAGE. On Thursday evening [17 APR 1852], by the Rev. John C. Smith, Mr. JAMES ROBERT CLAYTON to Miss VIRGINIA ELIZABETH WILLIAMSON, all of this city. (19 APR 1852)

DEATH. On Saturday morning, after a lingering illness, which he bore with Christian patience and resignation, PATRICK H. CATON, in the 42d year of his age. His friends are invited to attend his funeral this evening, the 19th, at half-past 4 o'clock, from his late residence on 5th street, near Massachusetts avenue. (19 APR 1852)

DEATH. Suddenly, on Saturday morning, the 17th inst., MARC CLAVAUX, in the 50th year of his age. His friends and acquaintances are invited to attend his funeral on this (Monday) afternoon, at 3 o'clock, from his late residence, 6th street, near East Capitol street. (19 APR 1852)

DEATH. At the residence of Mrs. Ellis, on 8th street, yesterday morning [19 APR 1852], after a few days' illness, CATHERINE FRANCES, youngest daughter of David and the late Sarah E. Little, in the 15th year of her age. Her associates and the friends of the family are invited to attend her funeral this afternoon at 3 o'clock, from the residence of her aunt, as above. (20 APR 1852)

DEATH. Near Brentville, Prince William, Va., in the 77th year of her age, Mrs. ELIZABETH SEXSMITH, a native of Virginia, and for many years a resident of this city. (20 APR 1852)

MARRIAGE. On Tuesday morning [20 APR 1852], by the Rev. John C. Smith, JOHN TODD, Esq., to Miss JOSEPHINE S. CRAIG, all of this city. (21 APR 1852)

Daily National Intelligencer, Marriage and Death Notices, 1851-1854

MARRIAGE. At Montevideo, on the 5th of February, by the Rev. M. Stewart, U.S. Navy, Dr. JOHN WARD, U.S. Navy, to Miss MARY GRACE DALTON, youngest daughter of Robert M. Hamilton, Esq., Consul of the U.S. in that city. (23 APR 1852)

MARRIAGE. On Tuesday, the 20th inst., by the Rev. Mr. Hodges, JOSEPH W. ARNOLD to Miss JANE V. PADGETT, all of Washington. (23 APR 1852)

DEATH. On Wednesday, the 14th inst., at his late residence, in Prince George's Co., Md., after a brief illness, Major IGNATIUS MANNING, aged 76 years. (23 APR 1852)

MARRIAGE. On the 19th inst., by Rev. Mr. Lanahan, Mr. MARTIN MACK to Miss MARY ELIZABETH SMITH, of Virginia. (24 APR 1852)

MARRIAGE. On the 22d inst., by the Rev. Dr. Butler, rector of Trinity Church, SAMUEL B. WAUGH, of Philadelphia, and ELIZA, daughter of the late Rev. Noble Young, of Maryland. (24 APR 1852)

MARRIAGE. On the 22d inst., by the Rev. Mr. Johnston, in Alexandria, Va., Major JAMES A. BLAKE, of Charlotte, N.C., to SARAH F. CONTEE, daughter of the late Gov. Kent, of Maryland. (24 APR 1852)

DEATH. On Friday, the 23d inst., in this city, at the residence of Mr. Rich'd Ricketts, after a lingering illness, Miss SUSAN CONNELL, late of Montgomery Co., Md. (24 APR 1852)

MARRIAGE. On the 22d inst., by the Rev. Mr. Slattery, JAMES McSHERRY, Esq., of Martinsburg, Va., to HELEN MARY, daughter of the late James Carberry, of Washington. (26 APR 1852)

DEATH. Yesterday morning [26 APR 1852], after a short but painful illness, Professor WALTER R. JOHNSON, aged 57 years. The funeral will take place on Wednesday morning, at 10 o'clock, from his late residence on 12th street, near E. The friends of the family are invited to attend. (27 APR 1852)

DEATH. On Sunday, the 25th inst., RACHEL, consort of Samuel T. Drury, and youngest daughter of William and Susan Greer. Her funeral will take place today, (Tuesday, the 27th inst.,) at 4 o'clock P.M., from the residence of her father, on 10th, between D and E streets, to which the friends of the family are invited. (27 APR 1852)

DEATH. In Georgetown, on Sunday, the 25th inst., MATHIAS DUFFEY, in the 49th year of his age. His funeral will take [place] from his residence, at the end of Fayette street, (on the Heights of the town,) tomorrow (Wednesday) morning, at half-past nine o'clock. His friends and acquaintances are invited to attend. (27 APR 1852)

DEATH. On the 26th inst., EMILY, infant daughter of Jane and Robert Farnham, aged 2 years and 8 months. (27 APR 1852)

DEATH. On the 23d inst., aged three months and twenty-one days, JULIAN, son of B.F. and A.H. Isherwood. (27 APR 1852)

MARRIAGE. On the 26th inst., by the Rev. L.F. Morgan, JUSTIN H. HOWARD, Esq., to S. EMMA SERGEANT, daughter of John Sergeant, Esq., all of this city. (28 APR 1852)

MARRIAGE. On Tuesday, the 27th inst., by the Rev. Mr. Hodges, JOHN PADGET to Miss MAHALY CAMPBELL, of Montgomery Co., Md. (28 APR 1852)

DEATH. On the 19th inst., of pulmonary consumption, LUCRETIA, wife of Mr. Wesley Hyatt, of Prince George's Co., Md. (28 APR 1852)

Daily National Intelligencer, Marriage and Death Notices, 1851-1854

DEATH. In this city, on the 20th inst., after a few days' suffering from pneumonia, Mr. RICHARD NUTT, in the 92 year of his age. Mr. Nutt was a native of Virginia, and resided in Fauquier Co. until about the year 1835, when he removed to Missouri and settled in St. Louis Co., from whence he was returning to visit his daughter and numerous descendants in Virginia. It was his good fortune, throughout his long life, to enjoy uninterruptedly the confidence and affectionate regard of those who knew him. Under the influences of Christian experience, he was always cheerful, and awaited with confidence his summons from time as a sure passport to endless felicity. (28 APR 1852)

DEATH. On Friday, the 23d inst., of pulmonary consumption, while on a visit in Prince George's Co., Md., RICH'D M. BEALL, of this city, in the 50th year of his age. (29 APR 1852)

DEATH. On Tuesday, 27th inst., CLARA JANE, infant daughter of Catharine A. and R. Finley Hunt, aged 2 months and 16 days. (29 APR 1852)

DEATH. On Thursday morning, April 29, at half-past six o'clock, Mrs. MARGARET PAYNE, in the 56th year of her age. Her friends and acquaintances are respectfully invited to attend her funeral this (Friday) afternoon, at half-past three o'clock, from her late residence, on Sixth street, south of Pennsylvania avenue. (30 APR 1852)

DEATH. At Pilatka, Fla., on Tuesday, 13th inst., Lieut. A.B. LINCOLN, of the 4th Infantry, U.S. Army, aged 32 years — a native of the State of New York. (30 APR 1852)

DEATH. In Richmond, Va., on the 25th inst., ANNE LOVE, wife of Dr. Carter P. Johnson, and daughter of the late Henry Forrest, of this city. (30 APR 1852)

DEATH. In Montgomery Co., Md., near Darnestown, on the 25th inst., ELIZABETH TRUMAN, wife of Josiah Truman, aged twenty-one years. (30 APR 1852)

MARRIAGE. On Thursday, the 29th ult. [29 APR 1852], by the Rev. Samuel K. Stewart, Dr. WILLIAM STEWART, of Princess Anne, Somerset Co., Md., to Miss MARGARET C., youngest daughter of S.W. Handy, Esq., of this city. (1 MAY 1852)

DEATH. On Thursday, April 29, Miss MARY ANN McCARTHY, aged 25 years and 6 months. Her funeral will take place from her late residence on F between 6th and 7th streets, tomorrow (Sunday) afternoon, at 4½ o'clock. The friends and acquaintances of the family are respectfully invited to attend. (1 MAY 1852)

DEATH. In Georgetown, D.C., EDWARD RHODES, in the 46th year of his age. His funeral will take place tomorrow (Sunday) afternoon, at 4 o'clock, from his late residence, upper end of High street. His friends and acquaintances are respectfully invited to attend. (1 MAY 1852)

DEATH. On the 30th ult. [30 APR 1852], JOHN A. LYNCH, in the 39th year of his age. His friends and acquaintances are respectfully invited to attend his funeral, on Sunday afternoon, the 2d of May, at 3 o'clock, from the residence of the late Mary Sweeny, on Capitol Hill. (1 MAY 1852)

MARRIAGE. On Thursday, the 29th ult. [29 APR 1852], by the Rev. Mr. Hodges, JOHN WOODS to ELIZABETH McKENNEY, all of Washington, D.C. (3 MAY 1852)

DEATH. On Sunday morning, the 2d inst., at half past two o'clock, in the 73d year of his age, the Rev. O.B. BROWN, who was for nearly fifty years the Pastor of the First Baptist Church in this city. The Clergy of the city and friends of the family are invited to attend the funeral at the First Baptist Church, Tenth street, on Tuesday afternoon, at 3 o'clock. (3 MAY 1852)

DEATH. On the 1st inst., GEO. MARTIN PHILLIPS, Esq., of this city, (formerly of Carlisle, Pa.,) aged about 38 years. (4 MAY 1852)

Daily National Intelligencer, Marriage and Death Notices, 1851-1854

DEATH. On the 3d inst., THOMAS HOWARD, son of Samuel and Mary Ann Bacon, aged three years and three months. The friends of the family are respectfully invited to attend his funeral this afternoon, (Tuesday) at three o'clock. (4 MAY 1852)

DEATH. In this city, on the 2d inst., JULIA MONTGOMERY, daughter of ANDREW FOSTER, Esq., of Lawrence, Mass., aged fourteen months and five days. (4 MAY 1852)

MARRIAGE. On the 3d inst., by the Rev. Mathias Alig, in St. Mary's Church, Mr. CHARLES FRANKINBERGER to MARGARET CARL, both of this city. (5 MAY 1852)

MARRIAGE. On the 8th of April, by the Rev. Mathias Alig, in [St. Mary's Church], Mr. PATRICK CRUMMIN to ELLEN MURPHY, of this city. (5 MAY 1852)

DEATH. In this city, on the 4th inst., Rev. D. STEELE, of the Baltimore Annual Conference, in the 60th year of his age. The friends and acquaintances of his family are respectfully invited to attend his funeral on this (Wednesday) evening, at 4 o'clock, from his residence on 6th street, without further notice. (5 MAY 1852)

DEATH. At Pensacola, on the 26th ult. [26 APR 1852], Mrs. MARIA R. HOLLINS, wife of Commander Geo. N. Hollins, U.S. Navy. (5 MAY 1852)

DEATH. On the 4th inst., FELIX, aged one year and ten months, youngest son of Jonas P. and Sarah Keller. The friends of the family are respectfully invited to attend the funeral this afternoon, at half-past 4 o'clock, from the residence of his parents, east front of Lafayette square. (5 MAY 1852)

DEATH. In Georgetown, on the 5th inst., Mrs. D. THOMAS, aged 80 years. The friends of the family are invited to attend her funeral this afternoon, at 3 o'clock, from her late residence on High street. (6 MAY 1852)

MARRIAGE. On the 4th inst., by the Rev. Mathias Alig, in St. Mary's Church, Mr. JOHN SULLIVAN to Miss CATHARINE DRISCOLL, both of this city. (7 MAY 1852)

MARRIAGE. In New York, on the 21st of April, by the Rev. Smith Pyne, W.W. PARKIN, Esq., to FRANCES B., daughter of the late J. Smyth Rogers, M.D. (7 MAY 1852)

MARRIAGE. At St. Bartholomew's Church, New York, on the 28th of April by the Rev. Smith Pyne, JOHN PYNE to ANNE, daughter of Stephen Cambreling, Esq. (7 MAY 1852)

MARRIAGE. At St. Paul's Lutheran Church, on the 4th inst., by Rev. J. Geo. Butler, Mr. JONATHAN EADER, formerly of Frederick city, to Miss CATHARINE P. BRIDWELL, of Washington. (7 MAY 1852)

DEATH. In this city, yesterday [6 MAY 1852], about noon, MATTHEW ST. CLAIR CLARKE, Esq., in the sixty-second year of his age, heretofore for a long time Clerk of the House of Representatives, and in that public capacity widely known. Universally esteemed for his amiable and social qualities, he had others, never ostentatiously displayed, but well known to those who have been in intimacy with him. He was a devout Christian, an affectionate husband and parent, a faithful friend, and an upright and honorable man. Of him it may be said, with entire truth, that he had a soul for pity, and "a hand open as day to melting charity." In lamenting his death, after a long and painful illness, we may well console ourselves with the reflection that he has left us for a better world, "Where the wicked cease from troubling, And the weary are at rest." The funeral of the deceased will take place this (Friday) afternoon, at 4 o'clock, from his late residence at Mr. Willard's, near F and Fourteenth streets. (7 MAY 1852)

DEATH. On Sunday morning, May 2d, at the residence of her son-in-law, Dr. Orlando Fairfax, in Alexandria, Va., Mrs. VIRGINIA CAREY, relict of the late Wilson Jefferson Carey, of Virginia, in the 67th year of her age. Mrs. Carey was the youngest daughter of the late Thomas Mann Randolph, of Tuckahoe,

Daily National Intelligencer, Marriage and Death Notices, 1851-1854

Va., and sister of the late Thomas Mann Randolph, Governor of Virginia. For many of the earlier years of her life she was an inmate of the family of Thomas Jefferson, to whose nephew she was subsequently united in marriage. She was a lady of superior intellect, and many of her productions, both in prose and verse, have had extensive circulation during the last thirty years. Her "Letters on Female Character," "Mutius," "Ruth Churchill," "Christian Parents' Assistant," and other works, have been widely read and are favorably known. She was universally beloved in all the relations of life, and, after a long probation of Christian benevolence and charity, died with a full assurance of immortality beyond the grave. She leaves behind, to admire and imitate her example, besides her own sons and daughters, twenty-seven descendants in the second generation. (7 MAY 1852)

DEATH. Died, on the 31st of January, after a brief illness, in the 47th year of her age, Mrs. OTWAYANNA OWEN, wife of Dr. Wm. Owen, and daughter of Charles Carter and Betty Lewis, the favorite niece of Gen. Washington. This unexpected event imparts a pang to a wide circle of friends and a ramified family connexion. She was deservedly a cherished favorite. A native warmth and kindliness of heart, refined and heightened by Christian principles and the influences of that gospel of which she had long been a professor, endeared her to all who enjoyed her acquaintance [text continues]. (7 MAY 1852)

DEATH. On the 3d inst., in the Forest of Prince George, Md., MARY, only daughter of Benjamin Duvall, and wife of Geo. A. Mitchell, in the 24th year of her age. She died in full triumph of Christian faith, trusting in her blessed Redeemer; and while we deplore her loss, death is her eternal gain. (8 MAY 1852)

MARRIAGE. At New Orleans, on the 1st inst., by Judge Derbes, Mr. MAURICE STRAKOSCH, the pianist, to Miss AMALIA PATTI, of the Parodi troup of singers. (10 MAY 1852)

DEATH. On the morning of the 10th inst., REBECCA, aged 8 years and 3 months, third daughter of John F. and Rebecca Clark. The friends of the family are requested to attend her funeral this (Tuesday,) afternoon, at 4 o'clock. (11 MAY 1852)

MARRIAGE. On the evening of the 11th inst., at McKendree Chapel, by the Rev. Wm. Hamilton, Mr. LOUIS DEMOS TREDWAY, of Baltimore, to Miss FEROLIN AMELIA FALES, formerly of Thomaston, Me. (12 MAY 1852)

MARRIAGE. On Tuesday afternoon [11 MAY 1852], by the Rev. John C. Smith, Mr. JAMES KEMBLE to Miss ANNA E. OGDEN, both of Alexandria, Va. (12 MAY 1852)

MARRIAGE. At Washington, Pa., on Wednesday, the 5th inst., by the Rev. J.J. Brownson, EDWARD B. NEELY, Esq., of [Accomack] Co., E.S., Virginia, to CHARLOTTE, youngest daughter of Jacob Slagle, Esq., of the former place. (12 MAY 1852)

DEATH. On the 11th inst., Mrs. ELEANOR HIBBS, wife of Chas. Hibbs, in her 47th year. Her funeral will take place today, Wednesday, the 12th, from her late residence on Massachusetts avenue, between 4th and 5th streets, at 5 o'clock. The friends of the family are invited to attend. (12 MAY 1852)

DEATH. On the morning of Tuesday, the 11th inst., in the 77th year of her age, Mrs. REBECCA RUSS, a native of England, but for 58 years a resident of the U.S., and for the greater part of that time a resident of this city. Her friends and acquaintances, and those of the family, are respectfully invited to attend her funeral, this (Thursday) afternoon, at 3 o'clock, from the residence of her daughter, Mrs. A. Ober, corner of 10th and K streets, Navy Yard. (13 MAY 1852)

DEATH. On the evening of the 11th inst., Miss MARY MARGARET, youngest daughter of J. Jacob Seufferele, aged 22 years and 2 months. The friends of the family are respectfully requested to attend her funeral, from the residence of her father, corner of 6th and F streets, this (Thursday) afternoon, at 3 o'clock, without further notice. (13 MAY 1852)

Daily National Intelligencer, Marriage and Death Notices, 1851-1854

DEATH. On the 11th inst., CHARLES M. INGERSOLL, Esq., for several years a clerk in the office of the Secretary of Treasury. His friends are respectfully invited to attend his funeral this evening, at 4 o'clock, at his late residence, on F, between 13th and 14th streets. (13 MAY 1852)

DEATH. In this city, on the 11th inst., after a long illness, Mrs. MARY ANN REDDY, aged 43 years, a native of Philadelphia, but for some time a resident of this city. (13 MAY 1852)

MARRIAGE. On the 11th inst., by Rev. J.G. Butler, HENRY INGLE, of this city, to ELIZABETH C. LOYED, of Farmville, Prince Edward Co., Va. (14 MAY 1852)

MARRIAGE. On the 6th inst., by the Rev. Mr. Covington, W. TASKER WEIR to REBECCA M., daughter of the late Samuel Latimer, all of Prince William Co., Va. (14 MAY 1852)

MARRIAGE. At Woodstock, near Washington, on Thursday, the 13th inst., by the Rev. Peter B. Lenaghan, ROBERT S. CHILTON to MARY VIRGINIA, daughter of the late Col. Wm. Brent. (14 MAY 1852)

DEATH. On Friday morning, the 14th inst., at 8 o'clock, MARY, wife of John Sinon, and last surviving daughter of the late James Draine, of this city; a native of the county Antrim, Ireland, but for the last thirty-one years a resident of Washington. The friends and acquaintances of the family are requested, without further notice, to attend the funeral of the deceased from her late residence, corner of Four-and-a-half street and Maryland avenue, tomorrow (Sunday) afternoon at 3 o'clock. (15 MAY 1852)

MARRIAGE. On Thursday, the 13th inst., by the Rev. Mr. Hodges, ALEXANDER MADDOX to Miss JANE GREEN, all of this city. (17 MAY 1852)

MARRIAGE. On Thursday, the 13th inst., at Trinity Church, Georgetown, by the Rev. P.O. Flannigan, Mr. DENNIS O. DONOGHUE to Miss E. THERESA JAMIESON, both of this city. (17 MAY 1852)

MARRIAGE. On Thursday, the 6th inst., in St. Paul's Church, Richmond, Va., by the Rev. Dr. Jones, VIRGINIA CARY, third daughter of John G. Mosby, Esq., to JOHN ADAIR PLEASANTS, of Akron, Ohio. (17 MAY 1852)

DEATH. On Saturday, the 15th inst., at her house, in F street, Mrs. LOUISA C. ADAMS, the venerable relict of the late President John Quincy Adams. The funeral till take place from her late residence, on Tuesday next, at 11 o'clock in the morning. Relatives and friends are requested to attend without further invitation. (17 MAY 1852)

DEATH. On Saturday morning last, WILLIAM S. DERRICK, Chief Clerk in the Department of State. Mr. Derrick was born in Westchester, Pa., on or about the 31st of July 1802. He was appointed a clerk in the Department of State in 1827. He was well acquainted with the French and Spanish languages and with English literature. Throughout the term of his service in the Department he strove to earn promotion, and obtained it, not by courting the acquaintance of those having or likely to have political importance, but by the conscientious and accurate discharge of the duties assigned to him, without any taint of personal servility to his superiors in office, and by employing his leisure in those pursuits which were adapted to inform, expand, and elevate his mind, and to improve his great natural capacity for business. By his death the public has lost a faithful and laborious servant, his immediate family an affectionate husband, father, and friend, his associates in the Department a valuable exemplar, and his friends one whose worth they will always hold in vivid remembrance. The friends of the family are respectfully invited to attend his funeral this (Monday) afternoon, at 4 o'clock, from the Church of the Epiphany, (Rev. Mr. French's,) on G street, between 13th and 14th. (17 MAY 1852)

DEATH. On Saturday evening, 15th inst., Miss AMANDA FRANCE, daughter of James and Margaretta G. France, of this city. Her funeral will take place this (Monday) afternoon, at 4 o'clock, at the residence of her father on 7th street. The friends and acquaintances of the family are invited to attend. (17 MAY 1852)

DEATH. At Carlisle, Pa., on the 12th ult. [12 APR 1852], PATIENCE ELLIOT IRVINE, relict of Gen. Callender Irvine. (17 MAY 1852)

DEATH. At New York, on the 12th inst., in the 53d year of his age, Major JOHN RICHARDSON, formerly of the British army. He was in active service on the Canada frontier in the war of 1812-15, and was taken prisoner during one of the engagements. He resigned his commission a number of years since, and for the last three or four years has resided in this city. He was the author of Wacosta and several other works of considerable merit in their way. *Journal of Commerce.* (17 MAY 1852)

DEATH. On the morning of the 17th inst., at Mt. Pleasant, Prince George's Co., Md., OLIVER B. MAGRUDER, in his 34th year, after a long and painful illness, which he bore with Christian resignation, leaving an affectionate wife and four children to mourn their loss. His funeral will take place on Wednesday, the 19th inst., at 10 o'clock. The friends of the family are invited to attend. (19 MAY 1852)

DEATH. On Tuesday evening, the 18th inst., at the Infirmary, of a few days illness, Dr. THOMAS GLYNN. (19 MAY 1852)

DEATH. On Sabbath, the 18th ult. [18 APR 1852], in Guelph, Mrs. HARRIETT MIDDLETON PETERSON, wife of H.W. Peterson, Esq., Registrar of the united counties of Wellington, Waterloo, and Grey. Her illness was short, but painfully severe. She was born May 6th, 1798, in Sussex Co., Del., U.S., and consequently lacked a few days of completing her 54th year at the time of her death. Her family name was Clayton, which is found honorably mentioned with the earlier history of her native state. She was the third of seven children born to James and Sarah Clayton, of whom the only survivor is the Hon. JOHN M. CLAYTON, ex-Secretary of State of the U.S. In 1813, the subject of this notice was married to Walter Douglas, Esq., who died in 1826, leaving her the mother of three children, two of whom only survive — a son who holds a prominent and responsible commission in the American navy, and a daughter, the wife of a distinguished legal and civic gentleman in Delaware. In 1831, she was married to Mr. Peterson, and with him she leaves a son to mourn their irreparable loss. *Toronto Guardian.* (19 MAY 1852)

OBITUARY. Died, on the 13th of April, in Charleston, S.C., in the 19th year of her age, Miss FRANCES A. POST, youngest daughter of Rev. Dr. Reuben Post, of that city, formerly of Washington [text continues]. (19 MAY 1852)

MARRIAGE. At the U.S. Hotel, on the 19th inst., by the Rev. Mr. Hodges, Mr. L.O. MAGRATH to Miss AGNES M. GROTZ, all of Fredericksburg, Va. (21 MAY 1852)

MARRIAGE. On Wednesday, 19th inst., by Rev. Mr. Kepler, Mr. F. FARISH, of Virginia, to Miss MARCY GOGGIN, of this city. (21 MAY 1852)

MARRIAGE. In Philadelphia, on the 12th inst., by the Rev. Dr. Plummer, Rev. T.V. MOORE to Miss MATILDA C., daughter of H.B. Gwathmey, Esq., of Richmond, Va. (21 MAY 1852)

MARRIAGE. In Wilmington, Del., on the 11th inst., by the Rt. Rev. Bishop Lee, J. ROUSBY PLATER, of Maryland, to MARGARET, daughter of Joseph T. Price, Esq., of that city. (21 MAY 1852)

DEATH. Suddenly, on the afternoon of the 20th inst., Mrs. HARRIET J.C., consort of Robert Wright, and daughter of the late Elias B. Caldwell, Esq., aged about 40 years. The relatives and friends of the family are respectfully invited to attend her funeral on Saturday morning, 22d inst., at 10 o'clock, from her late residence, Bladensburg, to proceed to the Congressional Burial Ground. (22 MAY 1852)

Daily National Intelligencer, Marriage and Death Notices, 1851-1854

DEATH. Departed this life, at Warrenton, Va., on the evening of Wednesday, th 19th inst., EMILY, youngest daughter of Inman Horner, aged 23 years. (22 MAY 1852)

MARRIAGE. On the 20th inst., at Trinity Church, Georgetown, by the Rev. Mr. Aikin, Mr. WM. N. KEEFE, of Washington, to Miss ANNINA MORAN, of Georgetown. (24 MAY 1852)

MARRIAGE. At Montevideo, on the 5th of February, by the Rev. Chas. S. Stewart, Chaplain of the U.S. frigate *Congress*, Dr. JOHN WARD, U.S.N., to Miss MARY GRACE DALTON, youngest daughter of Robert M. Hamilton, Esq., Consul of the U.S. at that city. (24 MAY 1852)

DEATH. On the 24th of this month, at 2 o'clock A.M., Miss AMELIA MARIA WALLER, daughter of James D. Waller, in the 15th year of her age. Her funeral will take place tomorrow from the residence of Mr. I.H. Wailes, at 10 o'clock. The friends and acquaintances of the family are respectfully invited to attend. (25 MAY 1852)

DEATH. In this city yesterday [24 MAY 1852], after a short but severe illness, which she bore with Christian fortitude and resignation, Mrs. LYDIA THOMPSON, in the 74th year of her age. The friends and acquaintances of the deceased are respectfully invited to attend her funeral at her late residence on Second street east, near Maryland avenue, Capitol Hill, this (Tuesday) afternoon at 3 o'clock, P.M. (25 MAY 1852)

MARRIAGE. At Philadelphia, on the 22d inst., by the Rev. James H. Fowles, Dr. ANDREW A. HENDERSON, U.S. Navy, and MARY VIRGINIA, daughter of the late Dr. J.W. Peaco, U.S. Navy. (26 MAY 1852)

DEATH. At Baltimore, on Sunday morning, of pulmonary consumption, in the 24th year of his age, JOHN STRICKER NICHOLSON, son of Commodore J.J. Nicholson, and grandson of the late Gen. John Stricker. (26 MAY 1852)

DEATH. In this city, on the 25th inst., after a short illness, MARY ELIZABETH, daughter of Ignatius F. and Sarah J. Mudd, aged two years and four months. Her funeral will take place on Thursday, at three o'clock P.M., from the residence of her father, on D street, between 7th and 8th streets. The friends of the family are respectfully invited to attend. (26 MAY 1852)

DEATH. On the 23d inst., of consumption, which he bore with Christian fortitude and resignation, Mr. JAMES LAWRENCE, for many years a respectable resident of this city, in the 60th year of his age. (27 MAY 1852)

DEATH. In this city, last evening [26 MAY 1852], EPHRAIM M. CUNNINGHAM, Esq., aged 60 years. (27 MAY 1852)

DEATH. At New York, on Tuesday, 25th inst., MARGARET, wife of Lieut. B.M. Dove, U.S. Navy. (27 MAY 1852)

MARRIAGE. In Louisville, Ky., on the 18th inst., Col. JOHN T. BUNCH, Attorney-at-law of Henderson, Ky., to MARTHA ISABELLA, widow of the late Maj. P.N. Barbour, of the U.S. Army. (28 MAY 1852)

DEATH. At Raleigh, N.C., on Saturday afternoon last [22 MAY 1852], of consumption, Major [JOEL] A. BUCK, in the 34th year of his age. Until within the past year or two, Major Buck had been a resident of Raleigh for several years, and was universally esteemed for the uprightness of his intentions and conduct and the amiability of his character. Maj. B. served with great usefulness in the N.C. regiment during the Mexican war; After the close of which he resided for some time in this city, (Washington,) sustaining here, as elsewhere, a highly estimable character. (28 MAY 1852)

Daily National Intelligencer, Marriage and Death Notices, 1851-1854

MARRIAGE. In this city, on Thursday last [27 MAY 1852], by the Rev. Mr. Gallaher, Hon. JOHN A. WILCOX, Representative in Congress from Mississippi, to Miss MARY E. DONELSON, eldest daughter of Hon. A.J. Donelson, late Minister of the U.S. at Berlin, and more recently Editor of the *Washington Union*. (29 MAY 1852)

DEATH. Departed this life, on the morning of the 28th inst., in this city, after a long and painful illness, Dr. JAMES S. GUNNELL, in the 65th year of his age, formerly of Virginia, but for the last twenty-nine years an esteemed citizen of this place. His funeral will take place this (Saturday) afternoon, at 5 o'clock. (29 MAY 1852)

MARRIAGE. In Charlotte, N.C., on the 18th inst., by the Rev. Cyrus Johnston, Dr. E. NYE HUTCHISON to Miss ADALINE PARKS. (31 MAY 1852)

MARRIAGE. In England, at the Unitarian Chapel, Stoke Newington Green, near London, on the 13th inst., by the Rev. Thomas Madge, CHARLES E. FLOWER, eldest son of Edward Flower, Esq., of Stratford-upon-Avon, to SARAH, youngest daughter of Peter Martineau, Esq., of Highbury Terrace, Islington, in the county of Middlesex. (31 MAY 1852)

DEATH. In this city, on Saturday morning, the 29th inst., after a lingering illness, which he bore with Christian fortitude and resignation, GEO. H. POOR, aged 46 years, son of the late Moses Poor. Funeral from his mother's residence, on F street, this (Monday) morning, at 10 o'clock. The friends of the family are invited to attend. (31 MAY 1852)

DEATH. In Georgetown, on the morning of the 30th inst., JOHN R.P. FORBES, aged 26, son of George Forbes, Esq., and grandson of the late Judge Plater, of Maryland. His funeral will take place this (Monday) afternoon, from the residence of his uncle, Wm. G. Ridgely, on First street, at 5 o'clock. The friends of the family are invited to attend without further notice. (31 MAY 1852)

DEATH. In this city, on Saturday morning, the 29th inst., CHARLES COLLINS, infant son of Horatio and Ann C. King, aged about 7 months. (31 MAY 1852)

MARRIAGE. In Trinity Church, Washington, D.C., on Thursday, 27th ult., by the Rev. Dr. Butler, Dr. CHARLES PAGE, U.S. Army, to EMILY H., daughter of Dr. Edward H. Carmichael, of Virginia. (1 JUN 1852)

DEATH. In this city, on Friday evening, the 21st ult. [21 MAY 1852], Mrs. AGNES E.H. BARTLETT, wife of Wm. O. Bartlett, Esq., of New York, and youngest daughter of the late Dr. Geo. Willard, of Uxbridge, Mass., aged 30 years. (1 JUN 1852)

DEATH. On the 31st ult. [31 MAY 1852], after a painful illness, ALBERT HENRY LAY, son of Richard and Susan Lay, aged nine years and three months. His funeral will take place tomorrow, (Tuesday), from the corner of F and 9th streets, at 5 o'clock P.M., where the friends of the family are respectfully invited to attend. (1 JUN 1852)

MARRIAGE. On Sunday, the 30th May, at New York city, by the Rev. Mr. O'Neill, HENRY MIOTT McGILL, Esq., of Washington, D.C., to Miss MARY ELIZA KELLY, of the former city. (2 JUN 1852)

MARRIAGE. In Baton Rouge, on the 12th of May, by the Rev. J.S. Chadburn, J.M. WAMPLER, U.S. Coast Survey, to Miss KATE N., daughter of the late J.M. Cummings, Esq. (2 JUN 1852)

DEATH. On the 30th ult. [30 MAY 1852], of inflammation of the brain, JENNY LIND MELHAM, aged 1 year, 8 months. (2 JUN 1852)

Daily National Intelligencer, Marriage and Death Notices, 1851-1854

MARRIAGE. In this city, on the 2d of June, at the Church of the Epiphany, by the Rev. John W. French, CAUSTEN BROWNE, Esq., of New York city, to Miss KATE EVELETH, daughter of Capt. Wm. Maynadier, U.S. Army. (3 JUN 1852)

MARRIAGE. On Tuesday, June 1, by the Rev. Mr. Hodges, RICHARD W. BURR and FANNY A., daughter of the late William Radcliffe, Esq. (3 JUN 1852)

MARRIAGE. In Christ Church, on Tuesday morning, 1st inst., by the Rev. Mr. Hodges, BENJAMIN T. HODGES, of Prince George's Co., Md., to Miss ELIZABETH W. RILEY, of Washington. (3 JUN 1852)

DEATH. At Auburn, Culpeper Co., Va., on Thursday evening, the 29th April, Mrs. FRANCES J. BECKHAM, consort of Mr. James A. Beckham, aged 32 years and 11 months [text continues]. (3 JUN 1852)

MARRIAGE. On Thursday afternoon [3 JUN 1852], in the Fourth Presbyterian Church, by the Rev. John C. Smith, JOHN MEILY, Esq., of Jonestown, Pa., to Miss HELEN LUCRETIA, daughter of Nicholas Halter, Esq., of this city. (4 JUN 1852)

DEATH. On Thursday morning, the 3d inst., after a lingering illness, WILLIAM INGMAN, in the 46th year of his age. His friends and those of the family are invited to attend his funeral this evening, at 4 o'clock, from his late residence on 10th street, between G and H. (4 JUN 1852)

DEATH. In Georgetown, on Friday morning, the 4th inst., after a protracted illness, IDA, daughter of Charles E. and Catherine S. Mix, aged 13 months. Her funeral will take place from their residence, on High street, opposite Fourth. The friends of the family are respectfully invited to attend. (5 JUN 1852)

MARRIAGE. On Thursday evening, by the Rev. John C. Smith, Mr. ALEXANDER FURTNER to Miss ELIZA ANN GODDARD, all of this city. (7 JUN 1852)

MARRIAGE. On Thursday evening, the 3d inst., by the Rev. J.W. French, JNO. W. RANKIN, of Vienna, to GERTRUDE C. ANDERSON, daughter of Garret Anderson, of this city. (7 JUN 1852)

MARRIAGE. On Monday, May 31st, at Waterford, Loudoun Co., Va., by the Rev. Mr. Holland, Mr. JNO. SKIRVING, Jr., of this city, to Miss FANNIE E. TOWNER, of the first named place. (7 JUN 1852)

MARRIAGE. On Thursday evening last [3 JUN 1852], by the Rev. Mr. Clark, Dr. MARTIN H. JOHNSON to Miss MARY P. RANDOLPH, eldest daughter of Col. James J. Randolph, of this city. (7 JUN 1852)

MARRIAGE. On the 1st inst., by the Rev. Dr. Wyatt, Dr. JAS. SIMONS, U.S. Army, of South Carolina, to MARY T., daughter of Lambert Gittings, Esq., of Baltimore. (7 JUN 1852)

MARRIAGE. On the 2d inst., at St. Peter's Church, by the Rev. Dr. Atkinson, Major N.S. WALDRON, of U.S. Marine Corps, to VIRGINIA, daughter of George W. Riggs, Esq., of Baltimore. (7 JUN 1852)

DEATH. In this city, on Saturday, the 5th inst., Col. JOHN HENRY SHERBURNE, of New York, formerly a resident of the city of Washington. His friends and acquaintances are respectfully requested to attend his funeral this afternoon, at 4 o'clock, from the residence of Mrs. M. Ward, corner of Missouri avenue and Four-and-a-half street. (7 JUN 1852)

DEATH. On the 31st of May, at Edgewood, his late residence in Greene Co., Va., WILLIAM H. CONWAY, Esq., aged about forty years. (7 JUN 1852)

DEATH. At Baltimore, on Sunday, 6th of June, of a protracted illness of two years, WILLIAM GILMAN LYFORD, aged 68 years, a native of Exeter, N.H., but for the last twenty-four years a resident of Baltimore. (8 JUN 1852)

Daily National Intelligencer, Marriage and Death Notices, 1851-1854

MARRIAGE. In Chestertown, Md., on the 1st inst., by the Rev. Dr. Jones, Dr. LOUIS BURRISS, of Virginia, to Miss CATHARINE J., daughter of the Hon. J.A. Pearce. On the same afternoon, in the Fourth Presbyterian Church, by the Rev. John C. Smith, Hon. S.D. JACOBS, of Tennessee, First Assistant Postmaster General, to Mrs. MATILDA N. JOHNSON, daughter of the Hon. John B. Nevitte, of Mississippi. (9 JUN 1852)

MARRIAGE. On Tuesday afternoon [8 JUN 1852], by the Rev. John C. Smith, JOHN WATERS, Esq. to Miss JULIA E., daughter of the late Robert Tweedy, Esq., all of this city. (9 JUN 1852)

MARRIAGE. On Tuesday morning, the 8th inst., by the Rev. John F. Cook, Mr. JOHN OLIVER, of Boston, Mass., to Miss LOUISA W. DEMORTIA, of Norfolk, Va. (9 JUN 1852)

DEATH. On the 22d inst., at his residence in West Baton Rouge, La., after a lingering illness, Judge THOMAS W. CHINN, for many years a resident of that parish, and formerly a Representative in Congress from Louisiana. (9 JUN 1852)

DEATH. On Tuesday, the 8th inst., after a few days' illness, Capt. PETER JONES. His funeral will take place tomorrow, (Thursday,) from his residence near the steamboat wharf, at 10 o'clock. His friends and acquaintances are respectfully requested to attend. (9 JUN 1852)

MARRIAGE. On the 14th of April last, in Christ's Church, at Grand Coteau, La., by Rev. Mr. Rockerford, Mr. JOHN J. GARDNER to Miss MARY AUGUSTA, second daughter of Mr. Samuel C. McPherson, all of Grand Coteau, La., and formerly of Charles Co., Md. (10 JUN 1852)

MARRIAGE. At San Francisco, Calif., on the 21st of April last, by the Rev. Dr. VerMehr, Mr. HENRY OWNER to Miss MARY ELLEN SIMPTON, eldest daughter of Capt. George Simpton, of San Francisco. (11 JUN 1852)

DEATH. On Thursday, the 10th inst., HARRIET, eldest daughter of John and Harriet Miller, in the 19th year of her age. The friends and acquaintances of the family are invited to attend her funeral this day at 5 o'clock P.M. from the residence of her parents on M street, between 19th and 20th streets. (11 JUN 1852)

DEATH. On the 10th inst., after a long and painful illness, which she bore with the meekness and resignation of a Christian, MARY MELVINA, consort of Henry W. Gray, and daughter of John Waters, Esq., in the 32d year of her age. The friends of the family are requested to attend her funeral this evening (Friday) at 4 o'clock. (11 JUN 1852)

DEATH. At St. Louis, on the 1st inst., R.E. AULD, of the firm of Auld & Brother, aged 32 years. He leaves a wife and two children to mourn his loss. (11 JUN 1852)

DEATH. At Easton, Pa., yesterday morning, June 10, Mr. HENRY B. SAGE, an old and respected citizen of that place, and for many years connected with the Press, as a printer and editor, in the 76th year of his age. (11 JUN 1852)

DEATH. On the 3d inst., GABRIEL WINFIELD, youngest son of Augustin and Catharine Jullien, aged two years and eight months. (11 JUN 1852)

MARRIAGE. On the 8th inst., by the Rev. R.M. Lipscomb, THEODORE SNIFFEN to MARY C. BOHLAYER, of this city. (14 JUN 1852)

MARRIAGE. On Thursday morning, the 10th inst., by the Rev. Mr. Clark, EDWARD TAYLOR, Jr., of Cincinnati, Ohio, to MARY, daughter of Richard Burgess, Esq., of Washington. (14 JUN 1852)

DEATH. At New York, on the 9th inst., MARTHA PYNE, wife of Gerard W. Morris, Esq., and daughter of the late John Pyne, of South Carolina. (14 JUN 1852)

DEATH. At Morristown, N.J., June 10, ELIZABETH, wife of Alfred Vail, and daughter of Catharine and the late James Cummings. (14 JUN 1852)

DEATH. At "Ellerslie," the residence of Enoch Tucker, near Washington, on the morning of Sunday, 13th inst., HIRAM OPIE, aged 17 months, youngest child of S.S. and Maria S. Williams. The friends of the [family] are invited to attend the funeral this (Monday) afternoon, at 4 o'clock. (14 JUN 1852)

DEATH. Died, at the Hotel D'Albion, in the city of Paris, on 6th May last, in the 66th year of his age, JAMES H. FITZGERALD, of Fredericksburg, Va. [text not included here]. A communicant in the presbyterian Church, he died as he had lived, a firm believer in the truths of the Gospel, expressing in his last moments a sure reliance upon the merits of the atoning Saviour. His moral remains were brought across the Atlantic and interred on the 3d inst., in the private burying ground on his "Falls" plantation, near Fredericksburg. (14 JUN 1852)

DEATH. On Sunday morning, the 6th inst., at his residence near Athens, Ga., Major THOMAS MITCHELL, in the 82d year of his age. A native of Virginia, he had resided in Clark county during the last forty-eight years, and enjoyed to a large extent the confidence and respect of his fellow citizens. (15 JUN 1852)

MARRIAGE. In Georgetown, on the 15th inst., by the Rev. Mr. Caldwell, HUGH W. FRY, Jr., Esq., of Richmond, Va., to MARY L., daughter of John Davidson, Esq., of the former place. (16 JUN 1852)

MARRIAGE. On the 9th inst., by the Rev. D.C. Pharr, Mr. C. BIAS, late of Memphis, Tenn., to Miss MARY KATE GATEWOOD, of Bath Co., Va. (16 JUN 1852)

MARRIAGE. In Charlotte, N.C., on the 18th of May, by the Rev. Cyrus Johnston, C. NYE HUTCHISON, M.D. to Miss MARY A., daughter of D. Parks, Esq. (16 JUN 1852)

DEATH. On Tuesday morning, at 11 o'clock, ELKANAH WATERS, aged sixty-one years. The friends of the family are requested to attend his funeral, this afternoon, at 4 o'clock, from the Foundry Church, G and 14th streets. (16 JUN 1852)

MARRIAGE. In the city of Baltimore, on the 15th June, by the Rev. Thomas Atkinson, D.D., Lieut. Col. FRANCIS TAYLOR, U.S.A., to SOPHIA BROOKE, daughter of the Hon. Mr. Chief Justice Tanye. (18 JUN 1852)

MARRIAGE. On Tuesday, the 15th inst., in the Presbyterian Church, Georgetown, D.C., by the Rev. Daniel Motzer, S. HARRISON HOWELL, Esq., to Miss JANE LARNED MACOMB, youngest daughter of the late William Williamson, Esq., all of Georgetown. (18 JUN 1852)

DEATH. At Detroit, Mich., on Saturday, the 12th inst., WILLIAM HENRY, son of Capt. John N. Macomb, U.S.A., aged 17 months. (18 JUN 1852)

DEATH. In this city, on the 18th inst., of diarrhea, MARIA LOUISA, only daughter of William and Frances Dawson, aged 5 months and 10 days. The friends of the family are respectfully requested to attend the funeral on Sunday evening, at 5 o'clock, from their residence on K street, between 11th and 12th. (19 JUN 1852)

DEATH. On the 17th inst., in Piscataway, Prince George's Co., Md., WILLIAM THOMAS, formerly of Alexandria, Va., but for the last ten years a resident of this city. (19 JUN 1852)

Daily National Intelligencer, Marriage and Death Notices, 1851-1854

DEATH. On the 17th inst., after a lingering and distressing illness, EDWARD ALFRED, second son of Edward and Rosina M. Harte, aged 15 months and 8 days. (19 JUN 1852)

DEATH. On Wednesday morning, the 16th, MIRIAM, and on Thursday evening, the 17th inst., ANNE, twin daughters of Thomas and Emily S. Blagden, aged 6 and a half months. The funeral will take place from the residence of their parents, New Jersey avenue, at 5 o'clock this afternoon, which the friends of the family are invited to attend. (19 JUN 1852)

MARRIAGE. On the 17th inst., by the Rev. Mr. Slattery, DENIS O'LEARY to ANN O'LEARY, both of Washington. (21 JUN 1852)

MARRIAGE. In Baltimore, on Thursday evening, June 17, by the Rev. Mr. Wilson, Mr. CHAS. P. WANNALL, of this city, to Miss MARY ANN HOLLINGSHEAD. (21 JUN 1852)

DEATH. Suddenly, in this city, yesterday morning [20 JUN 1852], Senor Don ANTONIO de AYCIENA, late Consul General of Guatemala, and for the last twenty-two years a resident of this country. The funeral will take place tomorrow, (Tuesday, the 22d inst.,) from the Church of St. Mathew, (Rev. Mr. Donelan,) on H and 15th streets. His friends are requested to join the funeral. (21 JUN 1852)

DEATH. On the 16th inst., in the 47th year of her age, after a long and painful illness, Mrs. SARAH A. CORRY. May she rest in peace! (21 JUN 1852)

DEATH. Yesterday morning [21 JUN 1852], after a lingering illness, PETER J. PARENT, a native of New Jersey, and for five years past a resident of this city, aged twenty-six years. His funeral will take place from his late residence on Pennsylvania avenue, between 4½ and 6th streets. The friends and acquaintances of the family are requested to attend without further notice. (22 JUN 1852)

MARRIAGE. At St. John's Church, on the 22d inst., by the Rev. Dr. Pyne, HENRY B. RENWICK to MARGARET, second daughter of the late Jonathan Janney, of Alexandria, Va. (23 JUN 1852)

DEATH. At his residence in Brooklyn, N.Y., on Sunday [20 JUN 1852], aged 57 years, Dr. JOHN S. WILY, a Surgeon in the navy of the U.S. He was born in Virginia, and entered the Navy at an early age, and was last in service, as Fleet Surgeon in the Gulf, during the war with Mexico. (23 JUN 1852)

DEATH. Suddenly, on Monday morning [21 JUN 1852], at the residence of Cornelius W. Lawrence, near New York, Mrs. MONROE, wife of Hon. James Monroe. She had been an invalid for some months previously. The deceased was universally beloved by all who knew here noble qualities, and her death will create a vacancy in the wide circle of her friends which cannot soon be filled. Mrs. Monroe was a Miss Douglass, descended from a Scotch family of wealth and distinction. Her parents took up their residence, however, in this country, we believe, before she was born. *Evening Post*. (23 JUN 1852)

DEATH. At Baltimore, Mr. SAMUEL HOFFMAN, one among the most opulent and respected merchants of that city, in the 70th year of his age. (23 JUN 1852)

DEATH. At his residence in Baltimore, on the 21st inst., JOHN McTAVISH, Esq., the much-esteemed Consul of her Britannic Majesty for the State of Maryland, in the 65th year of his age. He had filled the office of Consul with efficiency and honor for the last 17 years. The deceased married a grand-daughter of the late Charles Carroll of [Carrollton], one of the Maryland signers of the Declaration of Independence. (24 JUN 1852)

DEATH. At Bath, Me., on the 17th inst., Hon. WILLIAM KING, aged 84 years. Mr. King was a member of the Legislature of Massachusetts when Maine formed a portion of it. He was the first Governor of Maine, one of the Board of Commissioners for Spanish claims, and for many years collector of customs for Bath.

Daily National Intelligencer, Marriage and Death Notices, 1851-1854

His discharge of the various and responsible duties was ever characterized by energy, firmness, and integrity. (24 JUN 1852)

DEATH. Yesterday morning [23 JUN 1852], MYRON STANLEY, infant son of James and Elizabeth B. Colegate, aged seven months. His funeral will take place this day, the 24th inst., at the residence of his grandfather, the Rev. Dr. Laurie, at 4½ o'clock. (24 JUN 1852)

MARRIAGE. At New York, on Thursday, the 17th inst., by the Rev. Dr. Parker, his excellency Don MANUEL CARVALLO, Envoy Extraordinary and Minister Plenipotentiary from Chili, to ANNA JUDSON, daughter of John A. Miller, Esq., of that city. (25 JUN 1852)

MARRIAGE. On Tuesday, the 22d inst., at Millersville, Anne Arundel Co., Md., by the Rev. C.K. Nelson, PHILIP J. BUCKLEY, of Wilmington, Del., formerly of Washington, to MARY, daughter of John Miller, Esq., of the former place. (25 JUN 1852)

DEATH. On the 25th inst., JOHN MARTIN, in the fifty-fourth year of his age. The friends of the family are invited to attend his funeral from Greenleaf's Point, on N street, between 4th and 5th streets, tomorrow (Sunday) evening, at 4 o'clock. (26 JUN 1852)

DEATH. In Montreal, June 11, Mrs. MARY SHELTON, wife of E.E. Shelton, Esq., and daughter of the late Rev. Dr. Butler, of Troy. (26 JUN 1852)

OBITUARY. [Communicated.] DIED, on the morning of the 24th inst., in the metropolis of his diocese, the Rt. Rev. C.E. GADSDEN, Bishop of the Protestant Episcopal Church of South Carolina. Bishop Gadsden was born on the 25th November 1785, and was in his 67th year on the day of his decease. A graduate of Yale College, and of the same class with the late John C. Calhoun, he commenced (if we may so say) life in his 19th year, and at that early age became the protector and supporter of a young and numerous family, which the adverse circumstances and sad misfortunes of a beloved parent in a measure cast upon him as the elder born. With what care, devotion, and scarcely paralleled disinterestedness he cherished, supported, and educated them, the recipients of his more than brotherly, aye, fatherly affection, are ready to attest. He received Episcopal orders in 1807; he was elected Rector of the Parish Church in St. John's, Berkley, in 1808; Assistant Minister of St. Philip's Church, Charleston, S.C., in 1810; Rector of the same in 1814, and Bishop of the Diocese in 1840 — 42 years connected with the venerable house of worship of his fathers [text continues]. (26 JUN 1852)

MARRIAGE. At Georgetown, D.C., on the 17th inst., by the Rev. Mr. Flanigan, JOHN MURPHY, of Baltimore, to MARGARET E., daughter of T. O'Donnoghue, Esq. (28 JUN 1852)

DEATH. On the 27th inst., after a short but painful illness, Mrs. SARAH CLARE, in the 57th year of her age. Her funeral will take place on this (Monday) afternoon, from the residence of her father, Mr. Peter Little, Sr., on L street north, near the Navy Yard. The friends of the family are respectfully invited to attend. (28 JUN 1852)

DEATH. On the 27th inst., MARY FRANCES JONES, in the 20th year of her age. Her friends are respectfully invited to attend her funeral at five o'clock this (Monday) afternoon, from the residence of W.A. Griffith, on Ninth street. (28 JUN 1852)

DEATH. On Sunday morning, the 27th inst., MARTHA L., infant daughter of John and Agnes McDermott, aged 11 months. The friends of the family are respectfully invited to attend the funeral this (Monday) afternoon, at four o'clock. (28 JUN 1852)

DEATH. At Alexandria, Va., on the 14th inst., Mr. JOHN McNEMARA, in the 99th year of his age, a native of Queens county, Ireland, and for the last twenty-four years a resident of Alexandria. (28 JUN 1852)

DEATH. On the morning of the 28th inst., of consumption, ARAMINTA, daughter of the late Samuel Bootes. The relatives and friends of the family are respectfully invited to attend her funeral on this (Tuesday) afternoon, at 5 o'clock, from her late residence on Bridge street, Georgetown. (29 JUN 1852)

DEATH. In Philadelphia, on Saturday morning, the 26th inst., SALLY A. NILES, relict of Hazekiah Niles, formerly Editor of *Niles's Register*. She was a daughter of the late John Warner, of Delaware, formerly U.S. Consul at Havana. Her mind had been highly cultivated, and she was endeared to her family and friends by the many estimable qualities of her heart. (29 JUN 1852)

BY TELEGRAPH. Baltimore, June 29. A few minutes subsequent to the melancholy event the telegraph this morning announced the death of Henry Clay [text continues]. (30 JUN 1852, numerous items)

MARRIAGE. On Tuesday afternoon [29 JUN 1852], by the Rev. John C. Smith, Mr. CRAVEN DEVIS to Miss MARY WHELAN, both of Fairfax Co., Va. (30 JUN 1852)

DEATH. On the 29th inst., Dr. DENNIS BURKE, after a short but severe illness, aged about one hundred years, a native of Ireland, and for many years a citizen of the U.S. Dr. B. was well known to the Army, having been assistant surgeon at West Point for many years. His friends and acquaintances are respectfully invited to attend his funeral from St. Patrick's Church, F street, at 5 o'clock P.M. this day. (30 JUN 1852)

DEATH. On the 28th inst., LEWELEN CLOTILDUS, youngest daughter of Benjamin H. and Mary C.L. Clements, aged 15 months and 20 days. Funeral this afternoon at 4 o'clock, from their residence on M street, between 18th and 19th, First Ward. (30 JUN 1852)

DEATH. At her residence in Charleston, S.C., on the 25th ins., CORNELIA W., wife of Wm. C. Breese, and daughter of the late David Edmond, of Vermont. (30 JUN 1852)

MARRIAGE. On the 29th ult. [29 JUN 1852], at the Church of the Epiphany, by the Rev. William J. Clark, J.C. GARDINER, Esq., of Cuba, to Miss INDIANA IRENE, daughter of James McClery, Esq., of this city. (1 JUL 1852)

MARRIAGE. In Fairfax Co., Va., on the 29th ult. [29 JUN 1852], by the Rev. Mr. Blackwell, Mr. JOHN J. CAMMACK, of Georgetown, D.C., to Miss MARGARET C. HUNTER, daughter of Col. J.B. Hunter. (1 JUL 1852)

MARRIAGE. In this city, on Tuesday last [29 JUN 1852], by the Rev. Dr. C.M. Butler, Mr. ROBERT A. MATTHEWS, of Georgia, to Miss MATILDA, eldest daughter of Hon. Richard M. Young, of Illinois. (1 JUL 1852)

DEATH. At Honolulu, Sandwich Islands, on the 30th of April last [1852], JOHN S. OWEN, of Stockton, Calif., a native of this city, where he leaves many friends to lament his early death. (1 JUL 1852)

DEATH. At Ormesby, Yorkshire, England, on the 3d ult. [3 JUN 1852], at the residence of his son, Mr. ROBERT EASBY, formerly of Highfield House, near Stokesley, in the 96th year of his age, much and deservedly respected. (1 JUL 1852)

MARRIAGE. On the 1st inst., by the Rev. Mr. Slattery, WILLIAM MacMANUS PAYNE to Miss MARIA ANN QUIGLEY, both of this city. (2 JUL 1852)

MARRIAGE. On Tuesday afternoon [29 JUN 1852], by the Rev. Mr. Dice, Mr. ANDREW J. WHEATLEY to Miss SARAH ANN BAYLESS, all of this city. (2 JUL 1852)

DEATH. On the 1st inst., after a long and painful illness, MARY MARIA SCRIVENER, consort of John

Scrivener, in the 54th year of her age. Her friends and acquaintances are respectfully invited to attend her funeral from McKendree Chapel, this afternoon, at 4 o'clock P.M. (2 JUL 1852)

DEATH. On the 23d of May [1852], at the residence of Judge Harper, San Francisco, Calif., Dr. MOREAU FORREST, aged 47 years, late U.S. Marshal of Maryland. (5 JUL 1852)

MARRIAGE. At the Church of the Epiphany, in this city, by the Rev. William J. Clark, on Monday, the 5th inst., S. CORNING JUDD, Esq., junior Editor of the *Syracuse (N.Y.) Star*," to Miss LAVINIA J. JAMES, of Washington, daughter of William James, deceased. (7 JUL 1852)

MARRIAGE. In this city, on Thursday last [1 JUL 1852], in the First Presbyterian Church, by the Rev. Wm. McLean, Dr. BEDFORD BROWN, of Virginia, and MARY E. SIMPSON, daughter of the late Joel Simpson, of Montgomery Co., Md. (7 JUL 1852)

MARRIAGE. On the 30th ult. [30 JUN 1852], in Loudoun Co., Va., by the Rev. Mr. Hurst, THOMAS ORME, of Georgetown, D.C., to MARGARET M., daughter of John Burson, Esq., of the former place. (7 JUL 1852)

DEATH. On the 5th inst., Miss ANN ELIZABETH NEALE, of Charles Co., Md., in the 54th year of her age. Her funeral will take place this afternoon, at 4½ o'clock, from the residence of Dr. Eliot, 7th street. (7 JUL 1852)

DEATH. On the 5th inst., WILLIE HOLLAND, son of John E. Holland, aged 2 months and 20 days. (7 JUL 1852)

DEATH. On the 2d inst., at Charlottesville, Albemarle Co., Va., REBECCA JEWETT, aged nine months, daughter of Charles and Adelaide C. Haskins, of this city. (7 JUL 1852)

I.O.O.F. -- The members of Washington Lodge are requested to meet at the Hall this afternoon [7 JUL 1852], at half-past 3 o'clock, to attend the funeral, from the Hall, of our late brother, JOHN LIPPHARDT. Members of sister Lodges are fraternally invited to attend. By order. Jas. A. Brown, Sec. pro tem. (7 JUL 1852)

MARRIAGE. In Alexandria, Va., on the 6th inst., by the Rev. Charles H. Page, THEODORE BROWN, Esq., of Jefferson Co., Ky., to Miss SALLY, youngest daughter of Daniel Bryan, of the former place. (8 JUL 1852)

DEATH. On Wednesday, the 30th June, at his late residence in the city of New York, SILAS WOOD, Esq., in the 66th year of his age. Mr. Wood was for many years an eminent merchant in Fredericksburg, Va., where he has left many friends and connexions to mourn his loss. (8 JUL 1852)

DEATH. In Baltimore, on the 4th inst., Mrs. RACHAEL CULVERWELL, consort of Stephen Culverwell, in the 72d year of her age. (8 JUL 1852)

DEATH. On the morning of the 5th inst., JOHN BLAN, infant son of A.J. and Margaret F. Harvey, aged 8 months. (8 JUL 1852)

MARRIAGE. On Tuesday evening, July 6, by the Rev. James Laurie, D.D., Mr. MARSHALL C. SULLIVAN to Miss ELIZABETH JOHNSTON, all of this city. (9 JUL 1852)

MARRIAGE. At Indianapolis, Ind., on Thursday, June 24th, by the Rev. John A. McClung, Mr. WOOD BROWNING, of Cincinnati, to Miss MARY A. BROWN, daughter of Hon. Wm. J. Brown. (9 JUL 1852)

Daily National Intelligencer, Marriage and Death Notices, 1851-1854

DEATH. On yesterday morning [8 JUL 1852], at 7 o'clock, of [w]hooping cough, ELIZA HELLEN, aged 13 months, infant daughter of Francis and Anna Mohun. Her funeral will take place this (Friday) afternoon, at 5 o'clock, from the residence of her parents on 8th near G street, north of Patent Office. The friends of the family are respectfully invited. (9 JUL 1852)

DEATH. On Monday, July 5th, MARGARETTA GRACE DENT, infant daughter of James and Deborah Mankin, in the third month of her age. (9 JUL 1852)

DEATH. On Friday, the 9th inst., KATE ALBERTA, only daughter of Samuel V. and Grace M. Hurdle, aged 13 months and 9 days. The friends of the family are invited to attend the funeral on Sunday, the 11th inst., from the residence of Mr. Charles Calvert, on 19th street, between I and K, at 4 o'clock P.M. (10 JUL 1852)

DEATH. On Friday, the 9th inst., Mrs. A.M. ECK, at the residence of her son-in-law, Mr. Lenthall. The funeral will take place on Sunday, the 11th inst., at 3 P.M., at St. Patrick's Church, where the body will be deposited. (10 JUL 1852)

DEATH. On the 9th inst., MARY ELIZABETH, infant daughter of George S. and Elizabeth McElfresh, aged eleven months and eleven days. The friends of the family are respectfully requested to attend the funeral on tomorrow (Sunday) afternoon at 4 o'clock. (10 JUL 1852)

DEATH. On Friday morning, July 9th, ELIZABETH PRISCILLA, aged 5 months and 29 days, daughter of George R. and Sarah Jane Ruff. The friends of the family are invited to attend the funeral from the residence of her parents this (Saturday) afternoon at 4 o'clock. (10 JUL 1852)

MARRIAGE. At West Point, N.Y., on the 7th inst., by the Rev. W.T. Sprole, WM. B. FRANKLIN, U.S. Topographical Engineers, to ANNA LOUISA, youngest daughter of the late M. St. Clair Clarke, Esq. (12 JUL 1852)

MARRIAGE. On Tuesday, the 6th inst., at Rochester, N.Y., by Rev. W. O'Reilly, KATE DOUGLAS, daughter of Henry J. Brent, and DANIEL H. FITZHUGH, Jr. (12 JUL 1852)

MARRIAGES. On the 4th inst., by the Rev. Mathias Alig, at St. Mary's Church, Mr. FRIEDERICH THEILICH to MARGARETTA STEFFIN. On the 19th of June, by the same, in St. Mary's church, ERNST ZUNGEL to LOUISA W. THAFT. On the 17th of June, by the same, Mr. JAMES GLORSON to Miss MARGARET BRASNAHAN. On the 14th of June, by the same, Mr. CASPAR RUPPERT to Miss THERESIA ARNOLD. (12 JUL 1852)

DEATH. On the 10th inst., Mr. JACOB BRODBECK, a native of Switzerland, in the 85th year of his age, and for the last fifty years a resident of this city. His friends and acquaintances are requested to attend his funeral this (Monday) afternoon at 5 o'clock, from his residence on Pennsylvania avenue, between 17th and 18th streets. (12 JUL 1852)

DEATH. On the 10th inst., DELILAH, in the 24th year of her age, the beloved wife of P.M. Dubant, and youngest daughter of James Mead. Her friends and acquaintances are respectfully invited to attend her funeral this (Monday) afternoon, at four o'clock, from the residence of her brother-in-law, James Boiseau, near the Navy Yard gate. (12 JUL 1852)

DEATH. On Saturday last, at the Warm Springs in Virginia, Dr. JOHN BROCKENBROUGH, in the 84th year of his age. He was one of the best and purest men and the most enlightened and accomplished gentlemen we have ever known. After a distressing illness, he has died full of years and good works, respected, beloved, and admired by his numerous friends. *Richmond Inquirer*. (12 JUL 1852)

Daily National Intelligencer, Marriage and Death Notices, 1851-1854

DEATH. In this city, on the 11th inst., aged three months, HENRY FORREST, infant son of Dr. Carter P. Johnson, of Richmond, Va. (13 JUL 1852)

DEATH. Yesterday afternoon [12 JUL 1852], at five o'clock, MILLARD, youngest child of Charles W. and Elizabeth R. Fenton, aged one year, one month, and eighteen days. The family are respectfully requested to attend the funeral tomorrow (Wednesday) morning, at 10 o'clock, from his parents' residence, G street south, between 8th and 9th streets. (13 JUL 1852)

MARRIAGE. On the 14th inst., at the residence of Mrs. Wise, by the Rev. Wm. F. Broaddus, of Kentucky, Mr. HENRY T. FANT, of Warrenton, Va., to Miss LOUISE A. MORGAN, of Kentucky, sister of Lieut. Morgan, U.S.N. (15 JUL 1852)

DEATH. At his residence, in Hagerstown, Md., on Sunday evening last [11 JUL 1852], at an advanced age, Gen. OTHO HOLLAND WILLIAMS. The deceased was the nephew of Gen. O.H. Williams, of the Revolutionary army, possessing much of the patriotism of his distinguished uncle, and was, in truth, a gentleman of the old school, dignified in manner, yet courteous in all his intercourse with his fellow citizens, possessing their respect and confidence during his long life. He was appointed Clerk of the County Court for Washington county in April 1800, and continued to hold said office until February 1845, a period of nearly forty-five years; the duties of which office he discharged with great ability, and to the satisfaction of the Court, Bar, and the public generally. He was also subsequently a Judge of the Orphans' Court for Washington county. Born in the heat of the Revolution, it will be no disparagement to his character to say that he was in his political principles an ardent and never-faltering Whig. (16 JUL 1852)

DEATH. In this city, yesterday morning [15 JUL 1852], CHARLES HENRY MARRILAT, of Bern, Switzerland, aged 50 years. The friends of the family are requested to attend his funeral, on Friday, this day, at 4 o'clock, from his late residence, corner of H and 4th streets. (16 JUL 1852)

DEATH. On the Heights of Georgetown, on the 16th inst., at the residence of Mr. Barber, her son-in-law, Mrs. ADLUM, relict of the late Major Adlum, in the 86th year of her age. The friends and acquaintances of the deceased are invited to attend her funeral this afternoon at 5 o'clock. (17 JUL 1852)

DEATH. On Monday, the 12th inst., MARY AGNES, aged eight months, infant daughter of Edward and Elizabeth A. Short. (17 JUL 1852)

DEATH. In this city, on the 15th inst., CHARLES, infant son of Thomas H. and Ellen Lane, aged five months and ten days. (17 JUL 1852)

DEATH. On the 17th inst., MICHAEL BROWN, a native of the county of Longford, Ireland, and for the last four years a resident of the U.S., aged 47 years. His friends are invited to attend his funeral this (Monday) afternoon, at half-past 3 o'clock, from his late residence, on the corner of C and 10th streets. (19 JUL 1852)

MARRIAGE. At Baton Rouge, La., on the 8th inst., by the Rev. John S. Chadbourne, Lieut. HENRY E. MAYNADIER, U.S. Army, to JULIA, eldest daughter of the late Capt. Thos. Barker, 1st Regiment U.S. Infantry. (20 JUL 1852)

DEATH. Suddenly, of congestion of the lungs, on the 8th of July, at the residence of Wm. Duke, Esq., near Paris, Ky., Lieut. NATHANIEL WILSON DUKE, U.S. Navy, in the 48th year of his age. (20 JUL 1852)

DEATH. Suddenly, in Georgetown, in the 70th year of her age, Mrs. DOROTHY GOLDING. Her funeral will take place this day, (Tuesday,) at 2 o'clock, from the late residence of her late son-in-law, Mr. Edward Rhodes, to which the friends of the family are invited. (20 JUL 1852)

MARRIAGE. In Christ Church, the 18th inst., by the Rev. Mr. Hodges, MARSHALL R. ANDERSON to SARAH EMBRY, all of Washington. (21 JUL 1852)

DEATH. In Cincinnati, Ohio, ALLISON C. LOOKER, of cholera. The deceased was a printer, and a man highly esteemed in the community for his many, lofty, and noble traits of character. He leaves an aged mother, wife, and family. The Typographical Society honored his memory by attendance of the remains to the grave. (21 JUL 1852)

DEATH. On Tuesday, the 20th inst., JOHN P., son of Patrick and Margaret Wilson, aged one year and twenty-eight days. The funeral will take place from their residence, on 10th street, near F, on this (Wednesday) afternoon, at 6 o'clock. (21 JUL 1852)

DEATH. On the morning of the 21st inst., SOPHIA, wife of Major Gen. Nathan Towson, U.S. Army. The friends and acquaintances of the family are invited to attend the funeral from their residence, corner of F and 17th streets, on Friday at 6 P.M. (23 JUL 1852)

DEATH. After a few days' illness, VIRGINIA, daughter of Joseph R. and Rebecca Quinter, aged 7 years 5 months and 22 days. The friends of the family are invited to attend her funeral today, 23d inst., from her father's residence, corner of N street north and 20th street, at 5 o'clock P.M. (23 JUL 1852)

DEATH. The friends of WILLIAM S. EVELETH, in Washington, are invited to attend his funeral from his father's house, in Alexandria, this (Friday) morning at 10 o'clock. (23 JUL 1852)

DEATH. On the 22d inst., JOHN, youngest son of Wm. A. and Jane F. Mulloy, aged 8 months and 4 days. The friends of the family are invited to attend the funeral this evening at 4 o'clock. (23 JUL 1852)

MARRIAGE. In Newburgh, N.Y., on the 22d inst., by the Rev. Dr. John Johnson, JOHN R. JONES, Esq., of Vincennes, Ind., to Miss SARAH M., eldest daughter of George Cornwell, Esq., of the former place. (26 JUL 1852)

MARRIAGE. At the Blue Sulphur Springs, Va., on the 14th inst., by the Rev. J. McFarland, Dr. THOS. C. BUFFINGTON, of Guyandotte, Va., to Miss MARY PHENTON HOLDERBY, of the same place. (26 JUL 1852)

DEATH. On Monday, the 26th inst., HENRY THOMPSON, aged 52 years, a resident of Washington. The funeral will take place on Tuesday, the 27th, at 3 o'clock, from his late residence on Virginia avenue, near 3d street east, where his friends will please attend. (27 JUL 1852)

DEATH. Yesterday morning [26 JUL 1852], Mr. HENRY HASLUP, of this city, aged 45 years. His funeral will take place this afternoon, at 4 o'clock, from his residence on 9th street, between I and New York avenue. (27 JUL 1852)

DEATH. In Georgetown, after a protracted illness, on the morning of the 26th inst., REMUS R. OULD, aged 34 years. The friends of the family are requested to attend his funeral at 5 o'clock this (Tuesday) afternoon, from the residence of his mother at the corner of Dunbarton and Montgomery streets. (27 JUL 1852)

DEATH. On the 27th inst., LEAH SUMMERS, infant daughter of John J. and Ellen Willson, aged eight months. The friends and acquaintances of the family are respectfully invited to attend her funeral tomorrow evening, at 5 o'clock, from the residence of her parents, on G, between 4th and 5th streets, without further notice. (28 JUL 1852)

OBITUARY. Died, in this city, on the 21st inst., in the sixty-fifth year of her age, SOPHIA, wife of Major Gen. Nathan Towson, U.S.A.... Mrs. Towson was the daughter of Caleb Bingham, Esq., of Boston, of

Daily National Intelligencer, Marriage and Death Notices, 1851-1854

which city she was a native... More than thirty years ago she became the wife of him who now so deeply mourns her loss; and not long after their marriage they came to this city, which has ever since been their residence... A large concourse attended her remains to the place of sepulture, in that lovely spot the Georgetown Cemetery. Dr. Laurie and the Rev. Messrs. Eckard and Hill participated with Dr. Junkin in the funeral solemnities. A long train of the orphans of the Asylum followed to the grave, and, after the coffin was deposited, strewed its lid with wreathes of fragrant flowers; all seeming to feel that they had lost a friend. "*Be ye also ready.*" "*He mourns the dead who lives as they desired.*" (29 JUL 1852)

OBITUARY. At the residence of Mr. Barber, her son-in-law, on the Heights of Georgetown, on Friday, the 16th inst., Mrs. ADLUM, relict of the late Major Adlum, in the 86th year of her age. Mrs. Adlum was one of the oldest residents in the District of Columbia... For a very large part of her life she had been a consistent member of the Protestant Episcopal communion, worshipping in the venerable church of St. John's, Georgetown [text continues]. (30 JUL 1852)

MARRIAGE. In St. Matthew's Lutheran Church, New street, Philadelphia, on the morning of July 22, 1852, by the Rev. E.W. Hutter, Mr. ANTHONY S. ELY, of Lebanon, Pa., to Miss LIZZIE S. GOSHERT, (niece of the Pastor,) of Philadelphia, formerly of Washington, D.C. (30 JUL 1852)

DEATH. On Thursday morning, 29th inst., Mrs. CHARLOTTE P., consort of T.W. Johnson, Esq., and daughter of the Rev. C.A. and Charlotte Davis. Her funeral will take place on this (Friday) afternoon, at 4½ o'clock, from the Union Chapel. The friends of the family are respectfully invited to attend. (30 JUL 1852)

DEATH. At Baltimore, on Tuesday, the 20th inst., EMILY C. GORDON, wife of John M. Gordon, Esq., of that city, and daughter of N. Chapman, M.D., of Philadelphia. (30 JUL 1852)

DEATH. On the morning of the 27th inst., at nine o'clock, FLODOARDO HOWARD, son of John L. and Rebecca Maria Smith, aged three years, of congestion of the brain. (30 JUL 1852)

DEATH. On the morning of the 29th inst., SAMUEL WHEELER, only child of Richard J. and Julia W. Ryon, aged two years and nineteen days. The funeral will take place this morning, at nine o'clock from the residence of his parents, on 6th street, between G and H streets. (30 JUL 1852)

DEATH. On the 21st inst., AGNES JANE, daughter of William A. and Ann M. Scott, aged six months. (30 JUL 1852)

MARRIAGE. Yesterday evening [1 AUG 1852], by the Rev. Mr. Roszell, Mr. JOHN S. BROWN to Miss HENRIETTA T. BETTS, all of this city. (2 AUG 1852)

MARRIAGE. In Snow Hill, Md., on the 13th ult. [13 JUL 1852], by the Rev. P.G. McPhail, Hon. ISAAC D. JONES, of Somerset Co., to MARY KING, daughter of the late Dr. John S. Martin, of the former place. (2 AUG 1852)

MARRIAGE. At Staunton, Va., on the 7th of July, by the Rev. T.T. Castleman, ROBT. HULL, of Baltimore, to SUSAN R., daughter of Hon. Lucas P. Thompson, of the former place. (2 AUG 1852)

DEATH. Departed this life, on the morning of the 1st inst., aged about 83 years, Mrs. BARBARA REILY, relict of the late Major William Reily, an officer of the Fourth Maryland regiment of the Revolution. This estimable, accomplished, and truly amiable lady, through a long life, was the friend of the friendless. An humble and pious Christian, she was a devout member for more than 30 years of the Methodist Episcopal Church in this city. Sincere in all her professions of love and friendship, she was actuated solely by the desire of doing good. She exhibited throughout life those estimable qualities of the heart that endeared her to all who knew her, and died, as she had lived, in the Christian's hope of immortality. To her bereaved children her loss is irreparable. By her church her death will be piously regretted; and by the poor her

Daily National Intelligencer, Marriage and Death Notices, 1851-1854

memory will be cherished. Her funeral will take place on Tuesday next, at 10 o'clock A.M., from the residence of her son, John H. Reily, on 12th street, to which the friends of the family are respectfully invited. (2 AUG 1852)

DEATH. On the 1st inst., of cholera infantum, CLARENCE CYRILLUS, infant son of John L. and Rebecca M. Smith, aged 5 months and 24 days. The friends of the family are invited to attend its funeral, from the residence of its parents, this afternoon at 5 o'clock. (2 AUG 1852)

DEATH. On Monday morning [2 AUG 1852], of dysentery, WILLIAM SEATON, youngest child of J.B. and Jane Ellis, aged nineteen months and twenty days. The friends of the family are respectfully invited to attend the funeral this (Tuesday) afternoon, at four o'clock. (3 AUG 1852)

DEATH. On the 2d inst., MARY VIRGINIA, daughter of P.A. and Mary J. Byrne, aged six years and four months. The friends of the family are requested to attend the funeral this afternoon, from the residence of her parents, at 5 o'clock. (3 AUG 1852)

MARRIAGE. On the 1st of August, by the Rev. Mr. Eckard, Mr. JOHN H. STEWART to Miss MARY CARR. (4 AUG 1852)

MARRIAGE. On the 2d, by Rev. Mr. Eckard, JOHN S. NELSON to MARTHA ANN C. BELT. (4 AUG 1852)

DEATH. In Georgetown, on Tuesday, 3d inst., Mrs. H. RHOADS, wife of the late Edward Rhoads, of this town, in the 38th year of her age. Her funeral will take place this (Wednesday) evening, at 4½ o'clock, from her late residence on the Heights of Georgetown, when and where her friends are respectfully requested to attend without further notice. (4 AUG 1852)

MARRIAGE. At Annapolis, on the 3d of August, by the Rev. Mr. Nelson, J. VAN NESS PHILIP, U.S. Navy, to LAURA, daughter of Chancellor Johnson, of Maryland. (6 AUG 1852)

DEATH. At Thoroughfare, Prince William Co., Va., on Friday, the 30th ult. [30 JUL 1752], THOMAS WILLIAM, only son of Thomas W. and Helen M. Swann, aged 5 months. (6 AUG 1852)

DEATH. Yesterday, in this city, very suddenly, Mrs. MARIANNA T. THORNTON, the beloved wife of Col. J.B. Thornton, of Memphis, Tenn., aged about 40 years. She was on her way with her husband and daughter to visit their relatives in Virginia, when death so suddenly and distressingly called her from the world, furnishing a most painful and impressive admonition of the uncertainty of life. (6 AUG 1852)

DEATH. In York Co., Pa., on the 26th inst., EMMA ALMIRA, only daughter of Rachel M. and John W. Hauptman, aged 11 months. (6 AUG 1852)

DEATH. On the 4th inst., CATHERINE, daughter of John and Margaret [Shugrue], aged 1 year and 3 months. (6 AUG 1852)

MARRIAGE. On Thursday evening, by the Rev. John C. Smith, Mr. GEO. H. KING to Miss AMANDA McDONALD, all of this city. (7 AUG 1852)

MARRIAGE. On Thursday, the 5th inst., by the Rev. Samuel H. Worcester, Minister of the First New Jerusalem Church of Baltimore, THOS. PASCHALL, Esq. and MARGARET L. COOMBS, both of Philadelphia. (7 AUG 1852)

MARRIAGE. On the 4th inst., at Auburn, Loudoun Co., Va., by the Rev. Mr. Towles, Dr. J.M. BROOKS, of Mississippi, to Miss VIRGINIA L. PRALL, of Virginia. (9 AUG 1852)

Daily National Intelligencer, Marriage and Death Notices, 1851-1854

MARRIAGE. On Monday morning [9 AUG 1852], by the Rev. John C. Smith, Mr. WM. FOX to Miss VIRGINIA THOMPSON, both of Virginia. (10 AUG 1852)

DEATH. On Monday, August 9th, Mrs. JANE LENTHALL, relict of the late John Lenthall, in the 74th year of her age. The friends of the family are invited to attend her funeral from the Church of the Epiphany, Thursday morning, at 10 o'clock. (10 AUG 1852)

DEATH. On the 8th inst., CHARLES BLODGET, aged nineteen months, son of Wm. H. West, of this city. (10 AUG 1852)

DEATH. On Monday night last [9 AUG 1852], at the residence of her father, in this city, MARY, the interesting daughter of the Hon. W.M. Gwin, aged 11 years. (11 AUG 1852)

DEATH. On Monday, the 9th inst., Mrs. HENRIETTA ELZEY, relict of the late Dr. Arnold Elzey, in the 86th year of her age. The friends of the deceased are invited to attend her funeral from her late residence, on G, between 18th and 19th streets, this afternoon, at 5 o'clock. (11 AUG 1852)

DEATH. In the communion of the Protestant Episcopal Church, in the comfort of a religious and holy hope, and in the confidence of a blessed resurrection, died, at Annapolis, on the night of the 7th August 1852, ANN CHASE, second daughter of the late Judge Samuel Chase, of Maryland, in the 82d year of her age. "Those who sleep in Jesus will God bring with him." (11 AUG 1852)

MARRIAGE. At West Hoboken, N.J., August 5th, by the Rev. H. Bruce, BERTRAM HARRISON, Esq., Principal of the Bancroft Institute, N.Y. city, and Cliff Cottage, West Hoboken, to Mademoiselle ALBERTINE MARTIN, of Georgetown, D.C. (12 AUG 1852)

MARRIAGE. At the Spanish Legation, on Tuesday morning, the 10th inst., by the Rt. Rev. Dr. McGill, Bishop of Richmond, JOSE MARIA deMAGELLON y CAMPUZANO, of Madrid, present by his proxy, the Spanish Minister, to AGGRIPINA, third daughter of Alexander Norman MacLeod, late of Harris, Scotland. (13 AUG 1852)

DEATH. On Friday morning, August 6th, in New York, after a brief illness, GEORGE ARCULARIUS, in the 88th year of his age. (13 AUG 1852)

DEATH. At Naugatuck, Conn., August 3d, Col. LEVI WHITING, U.S. Army, aged 62 years. (13 AUG 1852)

DEATH. On the 13th inst., after a lingering and painful illness, in the sixty-ninth year of her age, Mrs. MARY WATKINS, daughter of the late Geo. Simpson, Esq., of Philadelphia, and for more than 50 years the faithful wife of Dr. Tobias Watkins, of this city. She will be buried from the residence of her family, on 9th street, on Monday afternoon, at 4 o'clock. (14 AUG 1852)

DEATH. Departed this life on Monday, 9th inst., at Ingleside, Westmoreland, Va., the residence of her father, Col. Henry F. Garnett, Mrs. GENEVIEVE HAMILTON WELLING, wife of James C. Welling, Esq., of the city of New York. New York, Virginia, and New Jersey papers please copy. (14 AUG 1852)

DEATH. On the evening of Thursday last, 12th inst., at the residence of Mrs. Clare, in this city, ANN MARY, wife of John Wheeler, Esq., and daughter of the late Col. T.F.W. Vinson, of Rockville, Md., in the 28th year of her age. The deceased leaves behind a group of interesting children, devoted husband, and a large circle of attached relatives and friends to mourn her early departure to the untried realities of the spirit land. Thus has passed away, in the bloom of womanhood, a fond parent, affectionate wife, and a sincere and confiding friend. (14 AUG 1852)

Daily National Intelligencer, Marriage and Death Notices, 1851-1854

DEATH. On Friday morning, August 13, after one week's illness, PRISCILLA LOUISA, aged 22 months, daughter of Dr. Charles H. and Amelia C. Van Patten. The friends of the family are respectfully invited to attend the funeral, at their residence, at 10 o'clock this (Saturday) morning. (14 AUG 1852)

MARRIAGE. In Charleston, S.C., on the 3d inst., Lieut. JOHN N. MAFFITT, of the U.S. Navy, to Mrs. CAROLINE LAURENS READ. (16 AUG 1852)

DEATH. On the 14th inst., JOHN P. KLEINDIENST, in the 35th year of his age. His friends and relatives are invited to attend his funeral on this (Monday) afternoon, at 2 o'clock. (16 AUG 1852)

DEATH. At Sing Sing, Wednesday morning, the 11th inst., BENJAMIN DABNEY, only child of Harriet J. and Maj. S. Anderson, U.S. Army. (16 AUG 1852)

DEATH. At Wood's Hole, Mass., on the 8th inst., WM. MAXWELL WOODHULL, youngest son of Ellen F. and Lieut. Maxwell Woodhull, U.S. Navy, aged 2 years. (16 AUG 1852)

DEATH. In this city, on the 15th inst., ROBERT W., son of George W. and Catharine J.H. Hinton, aged 17 months and 15 days. The funeral will take place this afternoon, at 3½ o'clock. (16 AUG 1852)

DEATH. At Salem, N.J., on Saturday last [14 AUG 1852], Mrs. ELIZABETH KEASBY, the amiable consort of A.Q. Keasby, Esq., and eldest daughter of the Hon. Jacob W. Miller, of New Jersey. (17 AUG 1852)

DEATH. Yesterday [16 AUG 1852], of consumption, Mrs. LAVENDER, aged forty. Her funeral will take place today, at four o'clock from her late residence, corner of 5th and N streets. (17 AUG 1852)

DEATH. On the 13th inst., JOHN R., son of John P. and Mary R. Brown, aged 1 month and 2 days. (17 AUG 1852)

MARRIAGE. On Monday, the 16th inst., by the Rev. Mr. Wilson, Mr. B.B. CHAMBERS, of Prince George's Co., Md., to Miss MARY LIZZIE WASHINGTON, of Jefferson Co., Va. (18 AUG 1852)

MARRIAGE. On Monday evening [16 AUG 1852], by the Rev. John C. Smith, Mr. JOHN JAS. BAIRD to Miss EMMA REBECCA CREAMER, all of this city. (18 AUG 1852)

DEATH. At East Pascagoula, Miss., August 14, 1852, Mrs. MARGARET TAYLOR, aged 65, widow of Gen. Zachary Taylor, late President of the U.S. (18 AUG 1852) The Funeral of Mrs. Taylor, widow of the late President Taylor, took place at New Orleans on the 17th inst., from the residence of Col. Bliss. (25 AUG 1852)

DEATH. Drowned, near Marbury's Landing, on the 9th inst., WM. BRYAN, aged 18 years, son of W.J. and Catherine Bryan, of King George Co., Va. (18 AUG 1852)

DEATH. On the 16th inst., JOHN O'LEARY, aged 33 years. His friends and acquaintances are respectfully requested to attend his funeral, which will take place at 4 o'clock this (Wednesday) afternoon, from his mother's residence on Pennsylvania avenue, between 4½ and 6th streets. (18 AUG 1852)

DEATH. In Fairfax Co., Va., on Saturday, 14th inst., SARAH LOUISA, aged 23 years, daughter of the Rev. Norval Wilson. (18 AUG 1852)

DEATH. On the 17th inst., CHARLES S., son of Robert and Georgiana Downing. (18 AUG 1852)

DEATH. On the morning of the 17th inst., MARY LOUISA, second daughter of Mary and Robert Widdicombe. The friends of the family are respectfully invited to attend her funeral this morning at 11 o'clock, at the Church of the Epiphany. (18 AUG 1852)

Daily National Intelligencer, Marriage and Death Notices, 1851-1854

DEATH. On the 15th inst., PHILIP, infant son of James and Martha Riordan, aged 7 months and 15 days. (18 AUG 1852)

DEATH. In this city, on Wednesday morning [18 AUG 1852], of a short and painful illness, ALEXANDER W. BUEL, only child of Mr. and Mrs. Herman H. Heath, aged 20 months and 25 days. The friends and acquaintances of the family are respectfully invited to attend the funeral, at 4 o'clock on Thursday, the 19th inst., from the residence of Mrs. Tilley, corner of 3d street and Missouri avenue. (19 AUG 1852)

DEATH. At Pensacola, Fla., on the 9th inst., ELIZABETH COATES LOVE, only child of Lieut. James W. Watson, U.S. Navy, aged 15 months and 15 days. (19 AUG 1852)

DEATH. Departed this life, on the 9th of August, at the residence of his father, near Colesville, Montgomery Co., Md., WILLIAM CULVER BALDENAR, in the 29th year of his age. It is seldom the privilege of friendship to record the combination of so many admirable traits of character in one so young. Proverbially honest and upright in his principles, a gentleman in thought and feeling, kind and considerate in his deportment to others, tender of their good names, and not a judge of their infirmities or frailties, he died, as he had lived, universally beloved and respected. Many tears bedew his grave and many hearts mourn his early death. (19 AUG 1852)

DEATH. At the residence of Mr. Edwin W. Latimer, near Brentsville, Prince William Co., Va., on the 19th inst., CHARLES RICHARD YOUNG, in the 19th year of his age, son of Richard Young, Esq., of Prince George's Co., Md. Amiable in disposition, uncontaminated by vice, with impulses of a high and noble character, he bid fair to realize the fondest anticipations of his parents and friends. The friends of the family are invited to attend his funeral at the residence of his father, at 10 o'clock this morning, the 21st inst. (21 AUG 1852)

DEATH. In this city, on Friday morning [20 AUG 1852], after a long and painful illness, which she bore with great Christian fortitude and resignation, Mrs. ANN E. NAYLOR, wife of Mr. Francis Y. Naylor, in the 42d year of her age. Her funeral will take place tomorrow (Sunday) afternoon, at three o'clock, from the residence of her husband, near Trinity Church. The friends and acquaintances of the family are respectfully invited to attend. (21 AUG 1852)

DEATH. On Friday, 20th inst., PRESTON, son of Lawrence and Mary Ricker, aged eight years. The friends of the family are requested to attend his funeral on Sunday evening next, from the residence of his father on C street, between 9th and 10th. (21 AUG 1852)

DEATH. On Sunday, the 22d inst., at North Dorset, Ver., in the 52d year of his age, ASA F. WILCOX, Esq., for many years a clerk in the War Department, and a respected member of the E Street Baptist Church of this city. (25 AUG 1852)

DEATH. In this city, on the 24th inst., ELIZABETH ALZERA, youngest daughter of Wm. and Margaret E. Morgan, aged 19 months. (25 AUG 1852)

DEATH. On the 23d inst., EDWARD, eldest son of Patrick and A. Higgins, in the 15th year of his age. The friends of the family are requested to attend his funeral this (Wednesday) afternoon, at 4 o'clock, from the residence of his father on 3d street, near East Capitol street, Capitol Hill. (25 AUG 1852)

DEATH. Yesterday morning [25 AUG 1852], in this city, FREDERICK L. KELLER, son of the late Frederick L. Keller, in the 31st year of his age. His funeral will take place this afternoon, at four o'clock, from the residence of Mrs. Ignatius Mudd, on Maryland avenue. The friends of the family are respectfully invited. (26 AUG 1852)

MARRIAGE. At the Winthrop House, Boston, on the 10th inst., by the Rev. Patrick Henry Greenleaf, Rector of St. Paul's Church, Capt. GEORGE F. LINDSAY, of the U.S. Marine Corps, to Miss MARGARET

Daily National Intelligencer, Marriage and Death Notices, 1851-1854

FRASER, daughter of John Fraser, Esq., of Newfield House, near Glasgow, Scotland. (27 AUG 1852)

MARRIAGE. On Wednesday evening [25 AUG 1852], by the Rev. John C. Smith, Mr. JOHN T. BROOKS, of New Albany, Ind., to Mrs. ELIZABETH A. TSCHIFFELLY, of this city. (27 AUG 1852)

DEATH. On the 7th inst., at Little Rock, Ark., Dr. SHEPHERD LAURIE, son of the Rev. Dr. Laurie, of this city. (28 AUG 1852)

DEATH. In Georgetown, on Thursday, the 26th inst., MARY GOUGH, daughter of the late Stephen Gough, Esq., of St. Mary's Co., Md. The friends of the family are invited to attend her funeral this (Saturday) afternoon, at 4½ o'clock, from the residence of her brother, on Frederick street. (28 AUG 1852)

DEATH. At Rustin Hill, Prince William Co., Va., on the 25th inst., of bilious fever, MARIA ANN QUIGLEY, wife of Wm. McManus Payne, in the 91st year of her age. The funeral will take place in tomorrow evening (Sunday) at three o'clock, from the vault of St. Patrick's Church. Relatives and friends of the family are respectfully invited to attend. (28 AUG 1852)

MARRIAGE. In this city, on the 25th inst., by the Rev. Dr. Butler, Chaplain of the Senate, Capt. THOMAS DUNCAN, U.S. Army, to MARY S., daughter of Joseph S. Wilson, Esq., of Washington. (30 AUG 1852)

DEATH. On the 30th inst., MARY A., consort of B. Mulraney, in the 48th year of her age. The friends and acquaintances of the family are invited to attend her funeral this afternoon (Tuesday) at 4 o'clock, from her late residence on G, between 12th and 13th streets. (31 AUG 1852)

MARRIAGE. On the 30th inst. [30 AUG 1852], by the Rev. Mr. Knight, CHAS. BURDION to LAURA A. BRAWNER, both of this city. (1 SEP 1852)

MARRIAGE. Near Georgetown, D.C., on Tuesday morning last [31 AUG 1852], by Rev. S.R. Cox, WM. D. CLARK, Esq., of Orange Co., Va., to AMANDA, daughter of John Lyons, Esq. (1 SEP 1852)

DEATH. In this city, on yesterday, the 31st of August, after a short illness, Col. JOHN NOLAN, of West Baton Rouge, La., aged 73 years. His friends and acquaintances are invited to attend his funeral, from the National Hotel, at 2 o'clock P.M. this day. (1 SEP 1852)

DEATH. At the residence of his father on the East River, New York, on Thursday, August 16, 1852, LAWSON WHITE JAUDON, youngest son of Samuel and Marguerite Peyton Jaudon, aged 16 years. (1 SEP 1852)

MARRIAGES. On Tuesday morning, the 31st of August, by the Rev. T.C. Teasdale, Mr. CHARLES McKNEW and Miss MARIA ROBINSON; at the same time, by the same, Mr. JAMES F. BYERS and Miss ELEANOR ROBINSON, daughters of John G. Robinson, Esq., of this city. (2 SEP 1852)

DEATH. In this city, on the 31st ult. [30 AUG 1852], ESTELLE, daughter of Thomas and Caroline D. Bartlett, aged four years. (2 SEP 1852)

DEATH. In Montgomery Co., Md., on the 1st inst., at the residence of Osborne Sprigg Wilson, CHARLES HIGGINS, youngest child of the late Franklin Higgins. (3 SEP 1852)

DEATH. In New York, on the 26th of August, Gen. WALTER CUNNINGHAM, aged 62 years. His many friends in this city will hear of his decease with deep regret. (3 SEP 1852)

Daily National Intelligencer, Marriage and Death Notices, 1851-1854

DEATH. Yesterday morning [3 SEP 1852], after an illness of six weeks, THOMAS, son of Thomas and Ellen Lucas, aged 18 months and nine days. Funeral this (Saturday) morning at 10 o'clock, from the residence of his parents, on D street, between 9th and 10th streets. The friends of the family are invited to attend. (4 SEP 1852)

MARRIAGE. In this city, at Brown's Hotel, September 4th, by the Rev. R.W. Cushman, CHARLES E. WHITE to HELEN A., eldest daughter of Wm. S. Lovell, Esq., all of Boston, Mass. (6 SEP 1852)

DEATH. In this city, on the 4th inst., after a protracted illness, Mr. JAMES FRANCE, in the 54th year of his age, formerly of Baltimore. His friends and acquaintances are respectfully invited to attend his funeral on this (Monday) afternoon, at 4 o'clock, at his late residence on Seventh street, between D and E. (6 SEP 1852)

DEATH. Yesterday [7 SEP 1852], at one o'clock P.M., after a protracted illness, Mrs. NANCY C. EDELIN, wife of Major James Edelin, in the 42d year of her age. In the confident hope of a blissful immortality her end was peaceful. The friends of the family are respectfully invited to attend the funeral, without further notice, from the residence of Major Edelin, on B street south, near Pennsylvania avenue, at 10 o'clock tomorrow (Tuesday) morning. (6 SEP 1852)

DEATH. At Albany, N.Y., on Wednesday last [1 SEP 1852], in the 28th year of his age, Mr. JOHN HANCOCK, late a Clerk in one of the bureaus of the Post Office Department in this city. (6 SEP 1852)

DEATH. On the 22d of August, at Ringwood, Fauquier Co., the residence of her son-in-law, Rev. T.B. Balch, Mrs. A.B. MAFFIT, relict of the Rev. Wm. Maffit, of Fairfax Co., in the 85th year of her age. (6 SEP 1852)

DEATH. At Hollywood, Baldwin Co., Ala., on the morning of the 27th ult. [27 AUG 1852], in the 23d year of her age, JANET ELLIOT BRENT, wife of R. Carrere Brent, of Baton Rouge, La. (7 SEP 1852)

DEATH. On the 7th inst., after a brief illness, MARGARET ANN, wife of Eli Davis. The friends and acquaintances of the family are requested to attend her funeral this (Wednesday) afternoon at 4 o'clock, from her late residence on 11th street. (8 SEP 1852)

DEATH. Died, at his residence in St. Paul, Minn., on the 27th ult. [27 AUG 1852], Col. JAMES M. GOODHUE, the Editor of the *Minnesota Pioneer*. He was a native of the state of New Hampshire, and at the time of his death was aged about 41 years. (8 SEP 1852)

MARRIAGE. On Tuesday evening [7 SEP 1852], by the Rev. John C. Smith, Mr. JOHN EARL to Miss MARIA CATON, all of this city. (10 SEP 1852)

MARRIAGE. In this city, on the 7th inst., by the Rev. F. Stanly, Mr. JAMES POOL, of Sante Fe, N.M., to Miss ELIZA JANE HARDING, of Maryland. (10 SEP 1852)

DEATH. Yesterday morning [9 SEP 1852], at Saratoga Springs, in the 56th year of his age, JOSHUA SKINNER, Esq., an estimable man and good citizen, who has long resided near the town of Edenton, N.C. (10 SEP 1852)

MARRIAGE. On the 2d inst., by the Rev. J.T. Peck, Mr. GEO. BELL to Miss MARGARET HARVEY, both of Prince George's Co., Md. (11 SEP 1852)

MARRIAGE. On the 3d inst., by Rev. J.T. Peck, Mr. CHARLES H. MERILL, of this city, to Miss ELIZABETH E. CAMMACK, of Georgetown. (11 SEP 1852)

Daily National Intelligencer, Marriage and Death Notices, 1851-1854

MARRIAGE. On the 5th inst., by Rev. J.T. Peck, Mr. THOMAS W. BELT to Miss MARY C. BRADFORD, both of this city. (11 SEP 1852)

MARRIAGE. On the 9th inst., by Rev. J.T. Peck, Mr. JOHN COOK to Miss HENRIETTA FRIEND, both of this city. (11 SEP 1852)

MARRIAGE. On the 9th inst., by the Rev. Mr. Lanahan, Mr. JOHN McINTOSH, of Virginia, to Miss NORAH ANN BERRY, of Maryland. (11 SEP 1852)

DEATH. In Georgetown, on Thursday night, the 9th inst., Mrs. MARY H. HOWELL, aged 63 years, relict of the late Dr. Samuel L. Howell, of Princeton, N.J. Her funeral will take place from the residence of her son-in-law, A.H. Dodge, this afternoon, at 5 o'clock. (11 SEP 1852)

DEATH. In this city, on the evening of the 7th inst., WILLIAM WINN, son of Col. Wm. Henry and Mary Louisa Daingerfield, aged 11 months. (11 SEP 1852)

MARRIAGE. In this city, on the 8th of September, at St. Matthew's Church, by the Rev. J.E. Paluber, J. FRANCIS MITCHELL to Miss LAURA A. SIMONDS, all of this city. (13 SEP 1852)

MARRIAGE. On the 1st of September, at St. Patrick's Cathedral, by the Rev. Dr. Bailey, CHARLES OLIVER O'DONNELL, of Baltimore, to LUIZINHA IANTHA PEREIRA, daughter of the Chevalier de Sodre, Minister from Brazil. (13 SEP 1852)

MARRIAGE. On Tuesday, September 7th, at Trinity Church, in New York, by the Rev. Dr. Higbee, ALEXANDER WADSWORTH, Esq., of Washington, D.C., to HELEN McMORINE, daughter of the late John McMorine, Esq., of Elizabeth City, N.C. (13 SEP 1852)

DEATH. At the Tuleries, Clarke Co., Va., on Saturday morning, the 11th inst., Mrs. ELIZABETH BROWN, relict of the late Rev. O.B. Brown, of this city. The friends and acquaintances of the family are invited to attend her funeral at the First Baptist Church, 10th street, on Tuesday afternoon, the 14th inst., at 3 o'clock. (13 SEP 1852)

DEATH. Mrs. LOVEDAY PAIRO, relict of the late Thomas W. Pairo, in the 78th year of her age. The friends of the family are respectfully invited to attend her funeral to Rock Creek Church, from her late residence, near the city. (14 and 15 SEP 1852)

MARRIAGE. On Tuesday morning [14 SEP 1852], by the Rev. John C. Smith, Mr. CHAPMAN KERR to Miss CATHARINE JOHNSON, both of Virginia. (15 SEP 1852)

DEATH. At Springfield, Mass., on Thursday, the 8th inst., Mrs. INDIANA H., wife of John Brooks, Esq., of that place, and daughter of the late Robert C. Jennings, of Norfolk, Va. (15 SEP 1852)

MARRIAGE. On Wednesday, September 15th, at Trinity Church, in Washington, by the Rev. Dr. Butler, GRANVILLE S. OLDFIELD, Jr., of Baltimore, Md., to MARY VIRGINIA, daughter of the late Comm. Thos. H. Stevens, of the U.S. Navy. (17 SEP 1852)

MARRIAGE. On the 2d inst., by the Rev. S.S. Roszel, JAMES N. HILL to SARAH ANN WATSON, both of Washington, D.C. (17 SEP 1852)

MARRIAGES. On the 22d ult., at St. Paul's Lutheran Church, by the Rev. J. Geo. Butler, JOSEPH R.B. SCHWARTZE to CAROLINE HEITMULLER, both of Washington. On the 14th inst., at the same place, by the same, EPHRAIM A. FIROR to ANN E.A. BAGGITT, both of Washington. (17 SEP 1852)

Daily National Intelligencer, Marriage and Death Notices, 1851-1854

MARRIAGE. On Tuesday, the 14th inst., by the Rev. Mr. Hodges, THEODORE HURLY to Miss ANN BOND, all of Washington, D.C. (17 SEP 1852)

MARRIAGE. On the 8th September, at Redlands, Albemarle Co., Va., by the Rev. R.K. Meade, Mr. HENRY PRESTON, of Washington Co., Va., to Miss ANN C. CARTER, daughter of Capt. John C. Carter, of Farmington, Va. (17 SEP 1852)

DEATH. In this city, on Tuesday morning, the 15th inst., Mrs. ELIZA M. SENGSTACK, aged 54 years. (17 SEP 1852)

DEATH. On the 27th ult. [27 AUG 1852], at Grand Coteau, La., Mrs. CATHERINE SMITH, wife of Dr. Robert Smith, and youngest daughter of Lewis Carbery, Esq., of Georgetown. (17 SEP 1852)

DEATH. At his residence, in Marlborough, Prince George's Co., Md., September 14th, after a long and painful illness, RICHARD OSBOURN, formerly of Georgetown, D.C., aged sixty years. (17 SEP 1852)

MARRIAGE. On Wednesday, September 15th, at the Methodist Protestant Church in this city, by the Rev. Mr. Reese, Mr. JOHN GOLDIN to Miss CORDELIA STEVENS, both of Washington. (18 SEP 1852)

DEATH. On the 16th inst., in the fourth year of his age, IRVIN AUGUSTUS, son of Jas. A. and Harriet Ann Wise. His funeral will take place today, at 10 o'clock, from his father's residence, on Seventh street, between G and H streets, to which the friends of the family are invited. (18 SEP 1852)

DEATH. Yesterday, at 5 o'clock A.M., after a brief illness, MICHAEL LAPEYRE, a native of Bayoune, France, in the 21st year of his age. His friends and the friends of the family are respectfully invited to attend the funeral on this (Monday) afternoon, at 4 o'clock, from the residence of Charles DeSelding, on Sixth street, near the corner of F street. (20 SEP 1852)

DEATH. In Detroit, Mich., on the evening of the 13th inst., Col. JOHN MASON McCARTY, of Fairfax Co., Va., in the 57th year of his age. (20 SEP 1852)

DEATH. At Galena, Ill., on the 11th inst., in the 50th year of her age, SUSAN WILSON, formerly of Alexandria, Va., and wife of Samuel McLean, U.S. Consul at Trinidad de Cuba. (20 SEP 1852)

DEATH. In Cincinnati, on the 17th inst., of cholera, Mr. THOMAS FINLEY, formerly Postmaster at Baltimore, and for more than fifty years a resident of that city. (20 SEP 1852)

DEATH. On Sunday evening, after a short illness, MICHAEL JOSEPH, infant son of John and Ann Joyce. His funeral will take place this afternoon, at 5 o'clock, from their residence, on 13th street. Their friends and acquaintances are respectfully invited to attend. (20 SEP 1852)

MARRIAGE. On Sabbath evening [19 SEP 1852], by the Rev. John C. Smith, Mr. WILLIAM W. GRANT to Miss LOUISA ANN WAGONER, all of this city. (21 SEP 1852)

MARRIAGE. In this city, on Thursday, September 16th, by the Rev. Henry Stanly, of New York, E.B. CAMP, Esq., of Indiana Co., Pa., to FANNY E., daughter of A.B. Waller, Esq., of Washington. (22 SEP 1852)

DEATH. On the 20th, in this city, Mrs. ELIZABETH BROCKET, consort of the late Robert Brocket, sen., of Alexandria. She died as she had lived, a Christian and an estimable lady. She was long a member of the Baptist Church. Friends and acquaintances are invited to attend the funeral this afternoon, at 4 o'clock, from the residence of Thomas E. France, on C street, near Carusi's Saloon. (22 SEP 1852)

Daily National Intelligencer, Marriage and Death Notices, 1851-1854

DEATH. In Georgetown, on the 20th inst., Mr. WM. R. ABBOT. The friends of the family are respectfully invited to attend his funeral this (Wednesday) afternoon, at 4 o'clock precisely, from Christ Church, Georgetown. (22 SEP 1852)

MARRIAGE. On the 22d inst., in Trinity Church, by the Rev. C.M. Butler, I. EDMONDSON TODHUNTER, of Baltimore, and EMMA, daughter of Robt. Keyworth, Esq., of this city. (25 SEP 1852)

MARRIAGE. On the 20th inst., by the Rev. Mr. Teasdale, SAMUEL C. WROE, of Montgomery Co., Md. (formerly of Washington,) to Miss EMILY A.D. FOWLER, of this city. (25 SEP 1852)

MARRIAGE. On the 16th inst., by the Rev. W. McLain, JOHN A. CAMPBELL to Miss ELIZA BUCKLEY, all of this city. (25 SEP 1852)

MARRIAGE. On the evening of the 22d inst., by the Rev. Jesse T. Peck, RICHARD L. SMALLWOOD and ANNIE C., eldest daughter of the late Geo. McDuell. (25 SEP 1852)

MARRIAGE. At Charleston, Va., on the 22d inst., by the Rev. Dr. Atkinson, THOS. H. KENT, of Jos., of Baltimore, to MARY, daughter of Andrew Hunter, Esq., of the former place. (25 SEP 1852)

DEATH. On Thursday evening, the 23d inst., after a lingering and painful illness, Mrs. ANN MARIA TOPPING, widow of the late Nathan H. Topping, of New York, aged 62 years. (25 SEP 1852)

DEATH. In this city, on the 24th inst., Mr. PETER T. MARCERON, in the 24th year of his age. His friends and acquaintances are invited to attend his funeral, from his late residence on New Jersey avenue, south, Capitol Hill, this (Saturday) evening a 3 o'clock. (25 SEP 1852)

MARRIAGE. On Tuesday last, the 21st inst., at Newport, R.I., M. LeCOUNT deSARTIGES, Minister of France, to Miss ANNA D. THORNDIKE, second daughter of the late Charles Thorndike, Esq., of Boston. (27 SEP 1852)

MARRIAGE. On the 23d inst., at a Meeting of the Society of Friends, FRANCIS MILLER and CAROLINE, daughter of Benjamin H[a]llowell, all of Alexandria, Va. (27 SEP 1852)

DEATH. On Sunday morning, at 3½ o'clock, after a lingering illness, SUSAN B., wife of John T. Towers, in the 36th year of her age. The friends of the family are respectfully invited to attend her funeral, from her late residence, tomorrow (Tuesday) afternoon, at 3 o'clock. (27 SEP 1852)

DEATH. On the evening of the 25th inst., ADAH BLAIR, infant daughter of Oliver and Elizabeth Whittlesey, aged 14 months. The friends of the family are invited to attend the funeral this (Monday) morning, at 11 o'clock. (27 SEP 1852)

DEATH. At Alexandria, on the 24th of the 9th month, in the 57th year of his age, WILLIAM STABLER, eldest son of Edward and Mary Stabler, deceased. (27 SEP 1852)

DEATH. On the 26th inst., MARY ANNIE, aged six months, infant daughter of J. James and Mary F. Greenough. (27 SEP 1852)

MARRIAGE. On the 1st of September, by the Rev. J.W. Shipman, Mr. ZACHARIAH T. MATTINGLY, formerly of Prince George's Co., Md., to Miss MARTHA WHITE, daughter of John Houston, Esq., of Jasper, Tex. (28 SEP 1852)

MARRIAGE. On Thursday morning, the 23d inst., at Fruit Farm, Fauquier Co., Va., by Elder T.D. Herndon, Mr. RALPH WORMLEY, of Memphis, Tenn., to Miss MARY ELOISE, youngest daughter of the late Capt. James S. Pickett. (28 SEP 1852)

DEATH. At Baltimore, on Sunday last [26 SEP 1852], Mrs. CATHERINE DELOUGHERY, relict of the late John Deloughery, in the 86th year of her age. For the last sixty years she was a much respected resident of that city, where she leaves a large circle of friends and acquaintances to lament her decease and imitate her example. (28 SEP 1852)

DEATH. On the 29th inst., WILLIAM HENRY, aged fourteen years and six months, son of Mathias M. and Ellen White. The friends of the family are requested to attend the funeral, at 3 o'clock this afternoon, from the residence of his father, on Pennsylvania avenue, south side, between 3d and 4½ streets. (30 SEP 1852)

MARRIAGE. On Thursday, September 30th, by the Rev. Dr. Laurie, HENRY GIEZE to SARAH N. SCHOLFIELD, both of Washington. (1 OCT 1852)

MARRIAGE. In this city, on Tuesday last, 28th September, by the Rev. D.X. Junkin, D.D., the Rev. NATHAN SHOTWELL, of West Liberty, Va., to Miss MARY L. McCLEERY, of Milton, Pa. (1 OCT 1852)

DEATH. On the 30th September, WM. J., son of Richard W. and Sarah A. Cates, aged 11 years. His funeral will take place from the residence of his father, on 10th street, today at 2½ o'clock P.M. The friends of the family are respectfully invited to attend. (1 OCT 1852)

DEATH. In Williamsburg, N.Y., on the 26th ult. [26 SEP 1852], Mrs. MARY A. IRONSIDE, in the 61st year of her age. The deceased, at the time of her death, was on a visit to her relatives in that city, in the hope that her health, which had been declining for some time previous, might be restored; when her life was suddenly terminated, much to the regret of her friends and relatives there, as also to those residing in this city. Her body has been brought to this city, to be deposited with that of her late husband, Dr. Geo. E. Ironside. (2 OCT 1852)

DEATH. At Castle Pinckney, Charleston Harbor, S.C., on the morning of September 28th, Brevet Major JOHN F. ROLAND, captain in the 2d regiment of U.S. Artillery, aged 35 years. The deceased was a native of Pennsylvania, and entered the service of his country at the early age of fourteen, as a Cadet of the U.S. Military Academy. From thence he was promoted to a commission in the regiment of which he was a member, and served in it to the present time. At the battles of Palo Alto and Resaca de la Palma he was the senior lieutenant of Duncan's celebrated battery, and commanded the section which, under the orders of his captain, did so much towards securing the triumph of American arms on the 8th of May. At Monterey Lieut. Roland commanded and served the howitzer which contributed powerfully to the expulsion of the enemy from Obispado. For gallant and meritorious conduct upon these occasions he was successively breveted to the grades of Captain and Major. By his death his country has lost a gallant and faithful officer, and his comrades in arms an esteemed and beloved companion. (2 OCT 1852)

MARRIAGE. On Saturday morning, October 2, in Trinity Church, by the Rev. C.M. Butler, D.D., ASA WHITNEY, Esq., of New York, to Mrs. CATHERINE M. CAMPBELL, of this city. (4 OCT 1852)

DEATH. In Georgetown, D.C., on the 3d inst., Mrs. ANN WINGERD, widow of the late J.P. Wingerd, in the 51st year of her age. The friends and acquaintances of the family are invited to attend her funeral from her late residence on Beale street, this (Monday) evening at 4 o'clock. (4 OCT 1852)

DEATH. In this city yesterday afternoon [3 OCT 1852], after an illness of about three weeks, from paralysis, Mrs. SARAH KING, widow of the late Vincent King, in the 68th year of her age. Her funeral will take place this afternoon at four o'clock from her late residence on E street, opposite the General Post Office. The friends of the family are respectfully invited to attend. (4 OCT 1852)

DEATH. In Tennessee, on the 7th August last, and on the same day with his brother, Dr. Shepherd Laurie, of Little Rock, Ark., ALEXANDER SHEPHERD LAURIE, son of the Rev. James Laurie, of this city. (4 OCT 1852)

DEATH. At her residence, in McDonough Co., Ill., on the 15th of September last, Mrs. ANGELINA WALKER, wife of John M. Walker, and eldest daughter of the late John Pickrell, of Georgetown, D.C. (5 OCT 1852)

DEATH. On the 4th inst., in this city, MARY, youngest daughter of James King, Esq., in the 6th year of her age. The funeral will take place this evening, at 4 o'clock, from her father's residence on E street. (5 OCT 1852)

MARRIAGE. By the Rev. Mr. Hodges, on the 3d inst., JOSEPH ZADOCK WILLIAMS to Miss MARY HOWELL, all of this city. (6 OCT 1852)

DEATH. On Monday, the 4th inst., at the residence of C.T. Gardner, in this city, Mrs. MARY HUBBARD, aged about 87 years, formerly a resident of Fayetteville, N.C. (6 OCT 1852

MARRIAGE. At Tallahassee, Fla., on Tuesday, 28th September, by the Right Rev. Bishop Rutledge, JAMES CLUNAS, of New Orleans, to ELIZABETH WIRT, daughter of the Hon. Thomas Randall, of Florida. (7 OCT 1852)

DEATH. On the 6th inst., MERRILL H. OBER, in the 22d year of his age, formerly of Monkton, Ver. His friends and acquaintances are respectfully invited to attend his funeral on this (Thursday) afternoon, at 3 o'clock, from the residence of Mrs. Langton, Capitol Hill. (7 OCT 1852)

DEATH. In Alexandria, Va., on the 29th ult. [29 SEP 1852], WILLIAM H. GREEN, in the twenty-second year of his age, formerly of this city. (7 OCT 1852)

MARRIAGE. At Chelsea, on the 21st ult. [21 SEP 1852], by the Rev. Mr. Lambert, U.S.N., Dr. S.R. ADDISON, U.S.N., to JULIA HOWE, daughter of Commodore Charles Morris. (8 OCT 1852)

MARRIAGE. On the 28th of September, by the Rev. Charles A. Davis, CHRISTOPHER H. BRASHEARS, of Washington, D.C., to Mrs. ELLEN HODGES, daughter of Thos. N. Wilson, Esq., of Montgomery Co., Md. (8 OCT 1852)

DEATH. At the residence of her son-in-law, the Rev. B.S. Schneck, on the 11th ult. [11 SEP 1852], Mrs. ARIANA RIDDLE, relict of the late Judge James Riddle, and daughter of the late Dr. John Steuart, of Bladensburg, Md., aged 81 years. During the last six years of life, Mrs. Riddle was constantly confined to her bed by physical debility [text continues]. (8 OCT 1852)

MARRIAGE. In this city, on Thursday evening [7 OCT 1852], by the Rev. A.B. Paterson, WM. PATERSON, of New Jersey, to SALVADORA McLAUGHLIN, daughter of the late Richard W. Meade, of Philadelphia. (9 OCT 1852)

MARRIAGE. At New York, on Thursday, October 7th, by the Rev. Dr. Hutton, ELBERT HERRING VAN KLEECK, Esq., of this city, to R. ISABELLA, daughter of John Mortimer, Jr., Esq., of the city of New York. (9 OCT 1852)

DEATH. In this city, on the 8th inst., after a protracted illness, Sergt. Major VENERANDO PULIZZI, U.S. Marines, aged 57 years. The friends and acquaintances of the family are respectfully invited to attend his funeral tomorrow (Sunday) afternoon at two o'clock, from his late residence, Navy Yard. (9 OCT 1852)

Daily National Intelligencer, Marriage and Death Notices, 1851-1854

MARRIAGE. On the 7th inst., by the Rev. Mr. Hamilton, SAMUEL MURPHY, of this city, to ABIGAIL JANE MEAD, of Baltimore. (11 OCT 1852)

MARRIAGE. On Monday, the 4th inst., by Rev. Mr. Mackenheimer, HENRY WHITE, Esq., of Mobile, Ala., and Miss SOPHIA M. OSBOURN, of Upper Marlboro', Md. (11 OCT 1852)

MARRIAGE. At Woodfield, near Philadelphia, on Tuesday, the 5th inst., by the Rev. Dr. Balch, THOMAS BALCH, Esq., to Miss EMILY, daughter of Mr. Joseph Swift. (11 OCT 1852)

DEATH. On Sunday, the 10th inst., at the residence of his son-in-law, Amos Kendall, near this city, ALEXANDER KYLE, aged eighty-five years. His funeral will take place at the house of Mr. Kendall, on Tuesday next, at 11 o'clock A.M., where the friends of the family are respectfully invited to attend. (11 OCT 1852)

DEATH. On Sunday, 10th inst., in the 66th year of his age, ROBERT BARNARD, Esq. His funeral will take place tomorrow morning, at 9 o'clock, at Normanstone, his late residence. (11 OCT 1852)

DEATH. On Saturday night last [9 OCT 1852], JOHN DAVIS, aged 72, whom many citizens well knew as the obliging and respectful old gardener on 6th street, north of New York avenue. The person of whom he was the freeman, and for thirty years the faithful servant, pays this tribute to his honesty, truth, and goodness. God gave him a colored skin, but as pure a soul as imperfect humanity could ever boast. (11 OCT 1852)

MARRIAGE. On the 10th inst., by the Rev. M.A. Turner, ALFRED BERRY WILKINSON to MARY AMELIA COBEY, all of this city. (13 OCT 1852)

MARRIAGE, At Effingham, the residence of John A. Smith, Esq., on Thursday evening, October 7th, by the Rev. Mr. Tillinghast, JOHN P. McELDERRY, of Baltimore, to ELLEN MARY, youngest daughter of the late Col. John Cox, of Georgetown, D.C. (13 OCT 1852)

MARRIAGE. On Sunday, the 10th inst., by the Rev. John C. Smith, Mr. WILLIAM EDWIN NOTT, of this city, to Miss SARAH SCOTT, of Philadelphia. (15 OCT 1852)

MARRIAGE. In Baltimore, on the 11th inst., by Rev. Mr. McMullen, Mr. ANDREW TATE, of Washington, to Miss HANNAH CHALFANT, of Baltimore. (15 OCT 1852)

MARRIAGE. On the 21st September, at Mrs. Maguire's, near Columbia, Tenn., by the Rev. Mr. Mack, THOMAS W. PRESTON, of Arkansas, to Miss SUE B. MAGUIRE, of Columbia. (15 OCT 1852)

DEATH. On Saturday morning [9 OCT 1852], at 3 o'clock, Mrs. SARAH A. HILL, in the 62d year of her age, from Derbyshire, England, but a resident of the U.S. for the last thirty years. (15 OCT 1852)

MARRIAGE. On Thursday afternoon [14 OCT 1852], by the Rev. John C. Smith, Mr. MATTHEW EAKIN to Miss MARY WILKINSON, all of this city. (18 OCT 1852)

MARRIAGE. At New York, on the 12th inst., by the Rev. Ravaud Kearny Rodgers, EDWARD N. STRONG to SUSAN W., daughter of John Warren. (18 OCT 1852)

MARRIAGE. At Philadelphia, on the 12th inst., by the Rev. H.A. Boardman, D.D., WILLIAM D. LEWIS, Jr., to CLARA, daughter of Thomas S.R. Fassitt, Esq., all of that city. (18 OCT 1852)

DEATH. On Friday evening, October 15th, of congestion of the brain, after an illness of two days, Capt. FREDERICK A. SMITH, of the Corps of Engineers, U.S. Army, in the 41st year of his age. His

Daily National Intelligencer, Marriage and Death Notices, 1851-1854

relatives and friends are invited to attend his funeral this morning, at 11 o'clock, from his late residence, corner of 20th and I streets. (18 OCT 1852)

DEATH. On Saturday afternoon [16 OCT 1852], in the 76th year of his age, JAMES PILLING, Sr., a native of Yorkshire, England, and a resident of this city for the last twenty-four years. His friends and those of the family are respectfully invited to attend his funeral, from his late residence, on Fifteenth street, south of F street, on Tuesday, the 19th inst., at 2 o'clock P.M. (18 OCT 1852)

DEATH. On Saturday morning, September 25th, at the residence of her father, near the U.S. Arsenal, Chattahoochee, Fla., in the 9th year of her age, ALICE MONROE, only daughter of Dr. Samuel and Elizabeth Ann Boar[d]man, and grand-daughter of the late Dr. T.J.C. Monroe, U.S. Army. (18 OCT 1852)

DEATH BY FALLING. An old colored woman, of unsound mind, calling herself Betty, and not otherwise known, threw herself from the roof of a portion of the Columbian College building on Sunday morning [17 OCT 1852], killing herself by the fall. She entered the building unobserved, and so crept her way to the edge of the roof. When discovered in that perilous situation every effort that humanity could devise was made to entice her from it, but to no avail. Her body was much bruised. The verdict of the jury was according to these facts. (19 OCT 1852)

DEATH. On the 18th inst., after a short illness, Mrs. MARY FILL, in the 87th year of her age, a native of Reading, Berkshire, England, and for the last fifteen years a resident of this city. The friends and acquaintances of the family are respectfully invited to attend her funeral on this (Tuesday) afternoon, at 2½ o'clock, from the residence of her daughter, Mrs. Barker, 10th street. (19 OCT 1852)

DEATH. in this city, on the 16th inst., GEORGE OURAND POTTER, aged one year and ten months, son of Thomas L. and Allethia F.F. Potter. *"Suffer little children to come unto me, and forbid them not; for of such is the kingdom of God."* (19 OCT 1852)

MARRIAGE. On Sabbath evening [17 OCT 1852], by the Rev. John C. Smith, Mr. JOHN LOMAX to Miss FRANCES HEAD, all of this city. (20 OCT 1852)

MARRIAGE. On Monday [18 OCT 1852], by the Rev. John C. Smith, SAMUEL GRIDLEY HYDE, Esq., to MARY A. HOPKINS RIDGELY, all of this city. (20 OCT 1852)

MARRIAGE. In Clinton, Miss., on the 4th inst., GEORGE W. HARPER, Editor of the *Hinds County Gazette*, to Miss ANN LITTLE SIMS, all of Hinds Co., Miss. (20 OCT 1852)

MARRIAGE. On Monday, 18th inst., by the Rev. Mr. Hodges, BENJAMIN F. GODDARD, of Prince George's Co., Md., to Miss ROSALIE SHECKELL, of the District of Columbia. (20 OCT 1852)

DEATH. On the 15th inst., at Norfolk, Va., in the 51st year of her age, Mrs. HENRIETTE PIERCY, widow of Commander W.P. Piercy, late of the U.S. Navy, leaving many friends who deeply mourn her loss. *"None knew her but to love her, None named her but to praise."* (20 OCT 1852)

DEATH. On the 19th inst., Mr. WILLIAM DOWLING, a native of county Fermanagh, Ireland, and for upwards of thirty years a resident of this city, aged sixty-seven years. His friends and acquaintances are respectfully invited to attend his funeral, which will take place at four o'clock P.M. on Wednesday, the 20th, from his late residence on F street, between 13th and 14th streets. The members of the Washington Benevolent Society will please also attend. (20 OCT 1852)

DEATH. At Alexandria, on Saturday [16 OCT 1852], ANTHONY C. CAZENOVE, in his 78th year. Mr. Cazenove was a native of Geneva, in Switzerland, but has been a citizen and eminent merchant of

Alexandria more than fifty years. Mr. C's first settlement in this country was at New Geneva, in Western Pennsylvania, in company with Albert Gallatin, and other Swiss, where he put in operation the first flour mill west of the Alleghanies. (20 OCT 1852)

DEATH. It is with much regret that we find the annexed obituary notice in a Panama paper. Mr. WALLACH, whose death it announces, was the youngest son of the late respected Richard Wallach, Esq., of this city, and his early decease will be lamented by a large circle of esteemed relatives and friends: "OBITUARY. — With no common feelings of regret we are called upon to announce the sudden death of Mr. ROBERT R. WALLACH, for some three years past a resident citizen of Panama. Mr. W. was connected by marriage with one of the most respectable native families of this city, and has ever borne an excellent reputation and enjoyed the confidence and esteem of a large circle of both native and foreign residents. He had suffered ill health for some months past, and had been evidently sinking gradually. His death, however, was very sudden; for we remember having exchanged a few words with him in the street on Sunday afternoon, and in rising in the morning we were informed of his decease. Mr. Wallach was generous, capable, and industrious, but he had been singularly unfortunate, and like many others he could not be induced to resuscitate his health by prolonged absence from business. He was attached to the house of Hurtado & Co. at the time of his death." (20 OCT 1852)

OBITUARY. At five minutes before twelve o'clock, on Saturday night [16 OCT 1852], after a short indisposition, of which no fatal result had been apprehended, Dr. SHEPHERD LAURIE, in the meridian of life and in the midst of his usefulness, breathed his last, and before sunrise next morning the melancholy intelligence was heard by every person in town, and received in every house with mourning and tears... As a physician he was deservedly eminent, we had almost said pre-eminent in his profession [text continues]. (20 OCT 1852)

MARRIAGE. By the Rev. Dr. Dashiells, on the 3d of June, ALBERT NOYES, of Georgetown, to Miss JULIA A. CROSS, of this city. (22 OCT 1852)

MARRIAGE. On the 20th inst., by the Rev. J.W. Hodges, Mr. JOHN B. MECARTNEY, of Lancaster, Pa., and VIRGINIA, daughter of Rev. James S. Petty, of Washington. (22 OCT 1852)

MARRIAGE. In Winchester, Va., on Tuesday morning, 19th October, 1852, by the Rev. C.P. Kranth, Dr. RICHARD A. WELLS, of Jefferson City, Mo., and Miss MARY ELLEN, daughter of Tho. B. Campbell, Esq. (22 OCT 1852)

MARRIAGE. On Wednesday morning [20 OCT 1852], by the Rev. John C. Smith, Mr. GEORGE W. McCLELLAND, to Miss MARY ELIZABETH SMITH, all of this city. (22 OCT 1852)

DEATH. On Thursday morning, October 21st, in the 49th year of her age, Miss MARTHA SCHOFIELD, after a lingering illness of fifteen months, which she bore with Christian fortitude and resignation. Her friends are respectfully invited to attend her funeral from the residence of her sister, on Eighth street, between L and M streets, today, at 3 o'clock P.M. (22 OCT 1852)

DEATH. On yesterday morning [22 OCT 1852], Mr. JAMES REGAN, a native of Leuth, in Ireland, but for twenty years past a resident of this city. Funeral tomorrow at one o'clock P.M., from his late residence on F street, between 2d and 3d. (23 OCT 1852)

MARRIAGE. On the 21st inst., by the Rev. Mr. Dashiell, Mr. JOSEPH B. MOORE to Miss AMELIA H. PRETTYMAN, all of this city. (25 OCT 1852)

MARRIAGE. On Thursday evening [21 OCT 1852], by the Rev. John C. Smith, Mr. WILLIAM CAREY to Miss BRIDGET DOOLEY, all of this city. (25 OCT 1852)

Daily National Intelligencer, Marriage and Death Notices, 1851-1854

DEATH. On the 27th inst., Mrs. MARY ANN K. BADEN, wife of John W. Baden, and daughter of the late Robert Wallace, of Montgomery Co., Md. The funeral will take place on Friday next, at nine A.M., from the residence of Mrs. Wallace, on F, between 6th and 7th streets, and proceed to the country for interment. The friends of the family are invited to attend. (28 OCT 1852)

DEATH. Suddenly, on the 23d inst., at Bloomsburg, [Pa.], EMILY NEWMAN, daughter of Dr. James T. Johnston, of Frederick Co., Md. (28 OCT 1852)

MARRIAGE. At Rockville, Md., on the 27th inst., by the Rev. Mr. Russell, Passed Midshipman BADGER, U.S. Navy, to Miss MARGARET M. JOHNSON, daughter of Commander Z.F. Johnston [sic], U.S. Navy. (28 OCT 1852)

MARRIAGE. At Cincinnati, Ohio, on Thursday, the 21st inst., by the Rev. E.W. Peet, JOHN A. ROBINSON, Esq., of New York, to ELLEN J., daughter of the Hon. Wm. Key Bond, of Cincinnati. (28 OCT 1852)

OBITUARY. Died on the 18th inst., in Martinsburgh, Va., Mrs. MARY H. CHRISTIAN, aged 64 years [text continues]. (29 OCT 1852)

MARRIAGE. On the 28th inst., by the Rev. James B. Donelan, Mr. JAMES SUTTON to Miss CATHERINE ISABELLA LOCKE, both of this city. (29 OCT 1852)

MARRIAGE. On Tuesday, the 26th inst., by the Rev. Thomas J. Foley, JOHN F. ELLIS, of Portsmouth, Va., to MARY ANN, youngest daughter of Gregory Ennis, Esq., of this city. (29 OCT 1852)

MARRIAGE. On Tuesday morning, 26th inst., at Pleasantville, Fauquier Co., Va., by the Rev. Mr. Covington, Mr. WILLIAM H. CARLIN to Miss FRANCES ELIZABETH ESKRIDGE, both of Fauquier. (29 OCT 1852)

DEATH. On the morning of the 24th inst., at Morrisville, Bucks Co., Pa., Mrs. MARY WILLING, relict of the late Henry Clymer, in the 83d year of her age. (29 OCT 1852)

DEATH. At the Oaks, in St. Mary's Co., Md., on Sunday morning, 11th inst., JAMES KEECH, in the 74th year of his age, after a protracted and painful illness, which he bore with Christian patience and resignation. Of the deceased it may be truly said that, in the various relations of life which he sustained, he was actuated by elevated principles, and was supported in the dreary hours of adversity, sickness, and death by the confident assurance of a blissful immortality. (29 OCT 1852)

DEATH. In this city, on the 27th inst., at the National Hotel, Dr. WILLIAM LAWSON FAUNTLEROY, of Gloucester Co., Va., in the 23d year of his age. (29 OCT 1852)

DEATH. On the 18th inst., at the residence of her grandfather, S. Lindsay, Esq., Alexandria, Va., MAGGIE MUTTER, only child of Dr. Wm. P. and Martha A. Gunnell, of Fairfax Court-house, Va., aged 11 months and 25 days. (29 OCT 1852)

DEATH. On Wednesday, the 27th inst., JOHN DOUGLAS, Sr., in the 77th year of his age. His friends are invited to attend his funeral on Sunday, the 31st inst., at 1½ o'clock, from his late residence, 20th street north. (30 OCT 1852)

MARRIAGE. At Glen Ord, on the 26th October, by the Rev. Mr. Hargrave, Dr. JOHN C. MACKENZIE, of Baltimore, to ELLA, daughter of Col. Lloyd Noland, of Fauquier Co., Va. (1 NOV 1852)

MARRIAGE. On the 28th of October, at Mt. Vernon Church, Boston, by Rev. Ed. N. Kirk, Lieut. EDWARD B. HUNT, Corps of Engineers U.S. Army, to Miss HELEN M. FISKE, daughter of Professor N.W. Fiske, of Amherst College. (1 NOV 1852)

Daily National Intelligencer, Marriage and Death Notices, 1851-1854

DEATH. At his residence in Chester Co., Pa., on the 25th ult. [25 OCT 1852], in the 83d year of his age, Hon. ISAAC WAYNE, the only son of Maj. Gen. Anthony Wayne, of the Revolutionary War. Col. Wayne was an excellent citizen, and well worthy of the distinguished name he bore. In early times he took a prominent part in the politics of the State, and was a member of the 18th Congress. He was also the candidate for Governor of the Federal party in 1814, in opposition to Gov. Snyder. (2 NOV 1852)

DEATH. At New York city, on the 27th of October, of consumption, EDWARD A. DUNSCOMB, eldest son of the late Daniel Edward and Caroline Dunscomb, of this city. (2 NOV 1852)

MARRIAGE. At Rockville, Md., on the 14th ult. [14 OCT 1852], by the Rev. Bazil Barry, Dr. EDWARD E. STONESTREET to Miss MARTHA R. BARRY, only daughter of the officiating clergyman. (3 NOV 1852)

MARRIAGE. On Tuesday morning the 2d inst., by the Rev. T.C. Teasdale, D.D., Mr. JEREMIAH McKNEW to Miss ROSALIE B. TAYLOR, all of this city. (3 NOV 1852)

DEATH. In this city, on the 2d inst., of consumption, Mrs. JANE LUCINDA BARBER, aged 36 years. Her relatives and friends are requested to attend her funeral tomorrow (Thursday) afternoon, at 2 o'clock P.M., from the residence of her husband, George Barber, near the Navy Yard. (3 NOV 1852)

DEATH. On Tuesday morning, the 2d inst., at half past five o'clock, Mrs. ANN BURGESS, wife of Richard Burgess, formerly of Georgetown, but for the last twelve years a resident of this city, in the 54th year of her age. Her funeral will take place on Thursday morning next, at 11 o'clock, from her late residence on F street, between 13th and 14th, to which her friends and acquaintances are invited. (3 NOV 1852)

DEATH. On Tuesday morning [2 NOV 1852], at the residence of her brother-in-law, Mr. Richard L. Ogle, Mrs. CAROLINE LANSDALE SPRIGG, in the 23d year of her age, wife of Osborn Sprigg, of Prince George's Co., and eldest daughter of the late Robert W. Bowie, leaving an afflicted husband and three small children, with numerous relations and friends, to mourn her untimely death. (4 NOV 1852)

DEATH. On the 2d inst., Mrs. LETETIA KENNEDY, in the 77th year of her age. The friends of the family are respectfully requested to attend her funeral this afternoon at 4 o'clock, from her late residence on Indiana avenue, opposite the City Hall. (4 NOV 1852)

DEATH. On the 3d inst., at the residence of Henry P. Leslie, Annapolis, Md., GEORGE W. GRAY, Esq., formerly of this city, aged 40 years. The subject of this notice has suffered for years with consumption, which he bore with Christian fortitude. "To die with him was gain," as his dying moments were his happiest. He possessed a mind richly stored with literature and science, but the jewel was too rich for the casket, which mouldered away while the jewel itself was in all its brilliancy. Having also devoted some attention to the political affairs of his country, he was nominated by his political friends for Congress in the contest of 1848. The exertions then made for his party no doubt hastened his end. He leaves a wife, sisters, and brother, with numerous friends, to cherish his memory. (5 NOV 1852)

DEATH. Departed this life, in the city of New York, on the morning of Tuesday, the 2d November, after a protracted illness, Brig. Gen. DON CARLOS de ALVEAR, Envoy Extraordinary and Minister Plenipotentiary of the Argentine Confederation near the American Government. The funeral ceremony will take place on Saturday, the 5th inst., at 4 o'clock P.M., at St. Patrick's Cathedral, where the body will be deposited. (5 NOV 1852)

DEATH. On Thursday morning, the 4th inst., at quarter of 10 o'clock, Mrs. SUSAN BAYLISS, in the 30th year of her age. The friends of the family are invited to attend her funeral this (Friday) evening, at 3 o'clock, from the residence of Mr. Germon, on M street, between 7th and 8th streets. (5 NOV 1852)

Daily National Intelligencer, Marriage and Death Notices, 1851-1854

DEATH. At the residence of her father in Montgomery Co., Md., Miss CATHERINE BOUCHER, in the 20th year of her age. Her friends and acquaintances are requested to attend her funeral on this (Friday) morning, at 8½ o'clock, from the new Trinity Church, Georgetown, D.C. (5 NOV 1852)

DEATH. On yesterday morning [5 NOV 1852], at half-past 3 o'clock, of an affection of the heart, with which he had suffered from birth, RICHARD WALLACH, youngest child of William and Mary M.M. Towers, aged eighteen months. The funeral services (at which the friends of the family are respectfully invited) will take place at two o'clock today, when his remains will be conveyed to Virginia for interment. (6 NOV 1852)

DEATH. On the morning of the 5th inst., MARY E., beloved wife of Henry D. Gunnell, in the 40th year of her age. The friends of the family are respectfully invited to attend the funeral, from her late residence, tomorrow (Sunday) at 2 o'clock P.M. (6 NOV 1852)

MARRIAGE. On Wednesday evening, the 3d inst., by the Rev. J.S. Bacon, WILLIAM HENRY PLEASANTS, of Roanoke, Va., to MINTA E., daughter of Samuel Smoot, Esq., of this city. (8 NOV 1852)

MARRIAGE. On Thursday, November 4th, at St. Mathew's Church, by the Rev. Mr. Donelan, JOHN W. BURGESS, of Prince George's Co., Md., to Miss MARTHA CORDELIA TRUCKSON, of Washington Co., D.C. (8 NOV 1852)

MARRIAGE. On Monday morning, the 8th inst., at the Fourth Presbyterian Church, by the Rev. John C. Smith, the Hon. ALEXANDER G. PENN, of Louisiana, to Mrs. ELIZABETH C. SCOTT, of Washington. (9 NOV 1852)

MARRIAGE. At Wesley Chapel, on Tuesday, the 9th inst., by the Rev. Mr. Guest, Mr. ROBERT ISRAEL to Miss ELIZABETH GUEST, second daughter of George McNeir, Esq., all of this city. (10 NOV 1852)

MARRIAGE. On the 2d inst., at Foundry Church, by the Rev. Dr. Peck, Mr. J.S. EWELL, of Virginia, to Miss HELEN, eldest daughter of N.M. McGregor, Esq., of this city. (10 NOV 1852)

MARRIAGE. On the 2d inst., by the Rev. Mr. Hodges, JOSEPH COOK to Miss ELIZA H. BERRY, all of this city. (10 NOV 1852)

DEATH. On the 5th inst., BENJAMIN C., aged 3 years 10 months and 20 days, son of Benjamin C. and Margaret E. Ridgate. (10 NOV 1852)

DEATH. On Tuesday evening last [9 NOV 1852], ANNIE PAYNE, the beloved wife of James H. Causten, Jr., in the 33d year of her age. Funeral services will take place on Saturday morning next, at 11 o'clock, from St. John's Church, in which her friends are requested to participate without further invitation. (11 NOV 1852)

DEATH. In this city, on Wednesday morning, the 10th inst., in the 30th year of his age, DANIEL CONVERS GODDARD, son of Charles B. Goddard, Esq., of Zanesville, Ohio, and late Chief Clerk of the Department of the Interior. The time of the funeral will be hereafter announced. (11 NOV 1852) The funeral service of the late D.C. Goddard, Esq., will take place at St. Patrick's Church on Saturday morning at 10 o'clock. The friends and acquaintances are respectfully invited to attend without further notice. (12 NOV 1852)

MARRIAGE. In Oswego, N.Y., on the 8th inst., by the Rev. Mr. Gallagher, Lieut. J.C. CLARK, 4th U.S. Artillery, to Miss MARY E. GOODELL, of Oswego. (12 NOV 1852)

MARRIAGE. On the 10th inst., by Rev. Mr. Lockwood, Dr. JAMES C. HILL, of Opelousas, La., and Miss FANNY LEMOINE, of Wellington, Fairfax Co., Va. (12 NOV 1852)

Daily National Intelligencer, Marriage and Death Notices, 1851-1854

MARRIAGE. On the 10th inst., by the Rev. Jas. B. Donelan, B.J. HOBSON, of Virginia, to MARY ELIZABETH, daughter of Benj. T. Watson, of Washington. (12 NOV 1852)

MARRIAGE. At Camden, N.J., on the 11th inst., by the Rev. Geo. B. Ide, Mr. FREDERICK KOONES, of Washington, D.C., to Miss JOSEPHINE B. SHEPPARD, daughter of the late Rev. J. Sheppard, of Camden, N.J. (15 NOV 1852)

MARRIAGE. In the Methodist Protestant Church, Georgetown, D.C., on the 10th inst., by the Rev. S.K. Cox, Mr. JOHN KING, of Wm., to Miss AMANDA M. MORGAN, all of said town. (15 NOV 1852)

DEATH. On the 9th inst., at her residence in Prince George's Co., Md., Mrs. ANNE S. HEILEMAN, in the 50th year of her age, widow of the late Col. Julius F. Heileman, of the U.S. Army. (15 NOV 1852)

DEATH. On the 14th inst., after a lingering and painful illness, which she bore with Christian fortitude, Mrs. MARGARET ZIMMERMAN, in the 36th year of her age, wife of Henry F. Zimmerman. Her funeral will take place on this (Tuesday) afternoon, from the Methodist Episcopal church, south 8th street, rear of the Patent Office, at 2½ o'clock, which the friends of the family are invited to attend. (16 NOV 1852)

MARRIAGE. On the 2d inst., by the Rev. Jesse T. Peck, Mr. JOSEPH H. COLLINS, of Washington, to Miss SUSANNAH C. CARR, of Maryland. (17 NOV 1852)

MARRIAGE. On the 11th inst., by the Rev. Jesse T. Peck, Mr. GEORGE MILLER to Miss ELEANOR D. ROGERSON, all of Washington. (17 NOV 1852)

MARRIAGE. On Sunday, 14th inst., at the Foundry Church, by the Rev. Dr. Peck, CHRISTOPHER R. BYRNE to FANNY V. MIDDLETON, daughter of the late Robert Middleton, all of this city. (17 NOV 1852)

MARRIAGE. On the 14th inst., by the Rev. J.G. Butler, ALFRED GAWLER and HENRIETTA TRYER, both of this city. (17 NOV 1852)

DEATH. At New Orleans, on Sunday, the 7th inst., ANDREW L. ADDISON, second son of the late John Addison, Esq., of Maryland, in the 56th year of his age. (17 NOV 1852)

DEATH. On Tuesday evening, the 16th inst., JANE LAWRENCE, aged 5 years, youngest child of Dr. Noble and Adelaide Young. The funeral will take place this (Thursday) morning at 11 o'clock; the friends of the family are invited to attend. (18 NOV 1852)

DEATH. Yesterday morning [17 NOV 1852], JAMES, youngest son of James and Christina Casparis, aged 2 months and 8 days. The friends and acquaintances of the family are respectfully invited to attend the funeral this afternoon at 2 o'clock. (18 NOV 1852)

MARRIAGE. In this city, on the 16th inst., by the Rev. Mr. Pyne, WM. W. YOUNG, of Charleston, S.C., to Miss MARTHA WETHERILL, daughter of the late Samuel M. Wetherill. (19 NOV 1852)

DEATH. On Thursday morning, the 18th inst., EDWARD N., aged 2 years and six days, youngest son of Edward N. and Catharine A. Roach. The friends of the family are respectfully invited to attend the funeral this (Friday) afternoon at 4 o'clock, from the residence of his father on 10th street. (19 NOV 1852)

DEATH. In San Francisco, Calif., on the evening of the 21st of August last, after a brief illness, CLEMENT HUMPHREYS, city and county Surveyor of San Francisco, and recently of Georgetown, D.C. Possessed of fine talents and a cultivated taste, and of those virtues that adorn the manly character; pure in life and of high integrity, he won esteem and confidence wherever known. (20 NOV 1852)

Daily National Intelligencer, Marriage and Death Notices, 1851-1854

DEATH. On the 19th inst., JOHN C. O'DONNELL, aged 20 years and nine months. The friends and acquaintances of the family are respectfully invited to attend his funeral from the residence of his mother, Mrs. Elleanor O'Donnell, 8th street east, near the Navy Yard, on Sunday next at 2 o'clock P.M. (20 NOV 1852)

DEATH. On Thursday night [18 NOV 1852], at 11 o'clock, ALFRED, youngest son of Anthony and Mary Holmead, in the 16th year of his age. The friends of the family are requested to attend the funeral this (Saturday) morning at 11 o'clock, from the residence of his father on F street, between 9th and 10th streets. (20 NOV 1852)

MARRIAGE. At Locust Hill, near Leesburg, on the 16th inst., by the Rev. George Adie, WILLIAM BEVERLY, Esq., to Miss FANNIE W., eldest daughter of Wm. H. Gray, Esq., all of Loudoun Co., Va. (22 NOV 1852)

MARRIAGE. On Thursday evening, the 18th inst., in Georgetown, D.C., by the Rev. Mr. Atkinson, B. EUGENE POITIAUX, Esq., of Richmond, Va., to Miss EMILIE NOYES, youngest daughter of Capt. William Noyes, of the former place. (22 NOV 1852)

DEATH. On Sunday, the 21st inst., in the 41st year of his age, BEN. TRUMAN GREENFIELD, born in St. Mary's Co., Md., but for twelve years past a resident of this city. He lived respected and beloved, and the memory of his virtues will be cherished by all who knew him. His funeral will proceed from the residence of his father-in-law, David Hepburn, corner of 12th and C street, (Island,) at 2 o'clock P.M. this day. (23 NOV 1852)

DEATH. At Aikin, S.C., on the 29th ult. [29 OCT 1852], THOMAS POLLARD, aged 23 years, of King and Queen Co., Va., late Tutor in the Columbian College, in the District of Columbia... In the hope of obtaining relief from a pulmonary disease under which he had been for some time laboring, he journeyed southward, and there, at the house of a friend, formerly a classmate, he met, in the full assurance of the Christian's faith and hope, the summons which called him from the cares and toils, of earth to the joys of the upper and "better world." (23 NOV 1852)

MARRIAGE. On Sabbath evening [21 NOV 1852], by the Rev. John C. Smith, Mr. ALBERT HORBACH to Miss EMILIE SEMENS, all of this city. (24 NOV 1852)

MARRIAGE. In this city, on Monday, the 22d inst., by the Rev. Mr. Butler, Mr. FRANK WOOD DIXSON, of Staunton, Va., to Miss ANNIE ELIZABETH LYLES, of Fairfax Co., Va. (24 NOV 1852)

DEATH. At Stockholm, Sweden, October 12th, after a lingering illness, EVELINA M. ABERG, wife of Ernest Aberg, and daughter of S.D. Heap, late U.S. Consul at Tunis, Barbary. (24 and 25 NOV 1852)

DEATH. On the 24th inst., in the full hope of a blissful immortality, Mrs. CATHARINE BAUM, in the 67th year of her age. Her friends and the friends of the family are respectfully invited to attend her funeral on this (Thursday) afternoon, at 2 o'clock, from the residence of her son-in-law, Mr. James Bowen. (25 NOV 1852)

DEATH. On Thursday last [25 NOV 1852], at 8 o'clock P.M., RICHARD HENRY THOMPSON, in the 36th year of his age. His friends and those of his family are respectfully invited to attend his funeral on tomorrow (Sunday) afternoon, at 3 o'clock, from his late residence on M street north, between 14th and 15th streets. (27 NOV 1852)

DEATH. On the 26th inst., of consumption, JOHN GALT, aged 24 years. His funeral will take place on tomorrow, (Sunday,) 28th inst., at 2 o'clock P.M., from the residence of his mother, 9th street, between D and E streets. The friends of the family are invited to attend. (27 NOV 1852)

Daily National Intelligencer, Marriage and Death Notices, 1851-1854

MARRIAGE. On Wednesday, November 24th, by the Rev. Mr. Hodges, Lieut. JOHN C. CASH, U.S. Marines, to Miss MARY, daughter of John P. Ingle, Esq., of this city. (29 NOV 1852)

MARRIAGE. On the 25th inst., by the Rev. Dr. Laurie, Mr. HENRY ECKARDT and Miss ELLEN FALCONER, all of this city. (29 NOV 1852)

MARRIAGE. On the 15th inst., by the Rev. C.M. Butler, Mr. THOMAS R. BRIGHTWELL to Miss MARY L. MOORE, all of this city. (29 NOV 1852)

MARRIAGE. On Thursday morning [25 NOV 1852], by the Rev. John C. Smith, Mr. SAMUEL MILLER to Miss MARY ANN KOFFMAN, both of Albemarle Co., Va. (29 NOV 1852)

MARRIAGE. On the 23d inst., by the Rev. James B. Donelan, Mr. G. THOMAS STEWART to ANN ELIZA MILLER, all of this city. (29 NOV 1852)

MARRIAGE. On the 18th inst., at the Highlands, by the Rev. A. Ten Broeck, CHARLES CARROLL SIMMS, of the U.S. Navy, and ELIZABETH I., daughter of the late Major Charles J. Nourse. (29 NOV 1852)

MARRIAGE. On the 25th inst., by the Rev. T.G. Jones, Dr. CORNELIUS BOYLE, of this city, to Miss FANNIE R. GREENE, of Portsmouth, Va. (29 NOV 1852)

DEATH. On Friday night [26 NOV 1852], at 9½ o'clock, HENRY GALILEO, eldest child of Henry and Mary Ann Johnson, aged four years and twelve days. (29 NOV 1852)

DEATH. On Monday, the 29th inst., after a long and painful illness, RICHARD J. MORSELL, in the 60th year of his age. The friends of the deceased and family are respectfully invited to attend his funeral, which will take place this afternoon at two o'clock, at the Methodist Foundry Church, on Fourteenth street. (30 NOV 1852)

MARRIAGE. On Tuesday, November 20th, by the Rev. Smith Pyne, Mr. AUGUSTUS SIOUSSA to Miss CATHERINE M. BERRY, all of Washington. (1 DEC 1852)

MARRIAGE. On Tuesday last [30 NOV 1852], at the residence of Col. Robert Lucas, near Shepherdstown, by the Rev. C.W. Andrews, Mr. JOSEPH A. CRAIGHILL to EMELINE LUCAS, all of Jefferson Co., Va. (1 DEC 1852)

DEATH. By a letter from the U.S. Legation at the Hague, the painful information has reached her friends in this city of the decease of Mrs. MARY ELIZABETH LEE, [consort] of Baron de Maltitz, now and many years past Minister of the Emperor of Russia at the Hague. The Baroness was the daughter of William Lee, deceased, formerly U.S. Consul at Bordezux, and afterwards for a number of years a resident of this city and in the public employ. The news of the death of a Lady so distinguished as she was, for her eminent virtues and qualities, cannot but cause a pang in the breast of every relative and friend who survives her. (1 DEC 1852)

DEATH. Mrs. DEBORAH RANDALL, died at the city of Annapolis, Md., on Saturday night last [27 NOV 1852], in the 96th year of her age. She had often danced with Gen. Washington. She had children down to the third generation, and was the mother of several distinguished sons, viz. Judge Randall, of Fla.; Dr. Burton Randall, U.S.A.; Hon. Alexander Randall, formerly member of Congress from Maryland; John Randall, Esq., a prominent planter there; Maj. Daniel Randall, late paymaster of the U.S.A., deceased; and Hon. Richard Randall, deceased, and formerly Governor of Liberia. (1 DEC 1852)

DEATH. On Monday, the 29th ult. [29 NOV 1852], MARY ARMENIA BROWN, aged 18 years, daughter of the late J.G. Brown, of the National Observatory, Washington. (2 DEC 1852)

Daily National Intelligencer, Marriage and Death Notices, 1851-1854

DEATH. On the morning of the 1st inst., SARAH HOWARD, aged 68 years. Her funeral will take place on Friday, the 3d inst., at 11 o'clock A.M., from the residence of her son, Dr. F. Howard, corner of F and 10th streets. The friends of the family are invited to attend. (2 DEC 1852)

MARRIAGE. On the 4th ult. [4 NOV 1852], at New York, by the Rev. Mr. McFarland, at Seventh street M.E. Church, Dr. EBENEZER McFarland to Miss CLEMENIA E., only daughter of John M. and Clemenia Holley, all of Williamsburg, Long Island. (3 DEC 1852)

DEATH. Yesterday morning, the 2d inst., Miss GEORGIANNA THOMPSON, second daughter of Geo. and Estella M. Thompson, of typhoid fever, in her eighteenth year. The friends of the family are respectfully invited to attend her funeral, which will take place this afternoon, at four o'clock, from her father's residence, fourth house, Smith's Row, 1st street, Georgetown. (3 DEC 1852)

DEATH. On Monday evening [29 NOV 1852], ELIZABETH GILMAN, daughter of George J. and Ann T.G. Abbot, aged nine months and twenty-two days. (3 DEC 1852)

OBITUARY. Departed this life, on the 23d ult., at his residence in Norristown, Pa., the Hon. JOSEPH FORNANCE. Entering at an early age the profession of law, he pursued his course steadily onward, surmounting all difficulties, until the time of his death he had acquired a reputation for legal ability and sterling integrity which few men enjoy [text continues]. (3 DEC 1852)

MARRIAGE. On the 2d inst., by the Rev. James B. Donelan, Mr. WILLIAM GILES NEWTON to Miss MARY ELIZABETH LITTLE, both of this city. (6 DEC 1852)

MARRIAGE. On Thursday, the 2d inst., by the Rev. James B. Donelan, Mr. WILLIAM WALLACE KIRBY to Miss VIRGINIA BEERS, all of this city. (6 DEC 1852)

MARRIAGE. On Wednesday evening, 1st inst., by the Rev. Dr. Butler, J. TAYLOR and JANE, daughter of the late Rev. A.T. McCormick, of this city. (6 DEC 1852)

DEATH. On the 3d inst., at Ft. McHenry, Musician HENRY WILLIAMS, of Light Company A., Second Artillery. He went out to Corpus Christi with Duncan's Battery, in 1846, and served in it throughout the entire war. He was engaged in the battles of Palo Alto and Resaca de la Palma, the sieges of Monterey and Vera Cruz, the battles of Cerro Gordo, San Antonio, and Churubusco, the storming of Chepultepec and the Garita of San Cosmo. For his good conduct and gallantry in these actions he received the highest reward a soldier can receive--a certificate of merit from the President of the United States. (6 DEC 1852)

DEATH. In this city, of consumption, on the 2d inst., THOMAS W. HOYE, formerly of Nottingham, Prince George's Co., Md., in the 44th year of his age. (6 DEC 1852)

DEATH. On Tuesday night, the 30th ult. [30 NOV 1852], Mr. JOHN BARNES, of Montgomery Co., Md., aged 74 years. *May he rest in peace.* (9 DEC 1852)

DEATH. At Ft. Towson, on Sunday, the 14th ult. [14 NOV 1852], CLEMENTINA CRAWFORD, infant and only child of Eulalia Emma and Dr. Lewis A. Edwards, U.S. Army. (9 DEC 1852)

MARRIAGE. On Thursday, the 9th inst., by the Rev. C.M. Butler, Mr. WM. DUNKINSON, of Maryland, to Miss ANNIE, daughter of G.C. Grammar, Esq., of this city. (10 DEC 1852)

MARRIAGE. On Wednesday morning [8 DEC 1852], by the Rev. John C. Smith, Mr. STEPHEN HAMILL to Miss JULIA A. GOODWIN, both of Virginia. (10 DEC 1852)

Daily National Intelligencer, Marriage and Death Notices, 1851-1854

DEATH. Yesterday morning [9 DEC 1852], Mr. DAVID MILLER, of this city, in the 41st year of his age. His friends and acquaintances are invited to attend his funeral this (Friday) morning, at 10½ o'clock, from his late residence, Pennsylvania avenue, near 9th street. (10 DEC 1852)

MARRIAGE. At Roseland, near Carlisle, Pa., on Wednesday, the 8th inst., by Rev. James G. Craighead, A.G. EGE, Esq., of Taneytown, Md., to Miss MATILDA H., only daughter of the late Wm. Craighead, of the former place. (11 DEC 1852)

MARRIAGE. On Thursday, the 9th inst., by the Rev. Septimus Tustin, D.D., Mr. JAMES S. WOODS, formerly of Glasgow, Scotland, to Mrs. MARY F. CLAGETT, youngest daughter of the late Hugh W. Minor, of Fairfax Co., Va. (11 DEC 1852)

MARRIAGE. On the 7th inst., by the Rev. C.H. Nourse, CORNELIUS STRIBLING, Esq., of Annapolis, Md., to EMMA J. NOURSE, of this city, eldest daughter of the late Dr. Benjamin F. Nourse, U.S. Army. (11 DEC 1852)

DEATH. On Thursday afternoon, the 9th inst., after a protracted illness, RICHARD PIERCE, in the 56th year of his age. His friends and the friends of the family are invited to attend his funeral on this (Saturday) afternoon, at 3 o'clock, from his late residence on Capitol Hill. (11 DEC 1852)

DEATH. In St. Louis, on the 7th ult. [7 NOV 1852], very peacefully, after a protracted illness, Miss AMELIA S. HOCKADAY, eldest daughter of P.B. Hockaday, Esq., and grand-daughter of Samuel Hanson, Esq., of Kentucky. (11 DEC 1852)

DEATH. On Friday, the 10th inst., of chronic croup, ZULEIMA FORREST, second daughter of the late Chas. G. Wilcox, aged about 5 years. The friends of the family are respectfully invited to attend her funeral on Sunday, at 3 o'clock P.M., from the residence of her mother, corner of 12th and N streets. (11 DEC 1852)

MARRIAGE. On Tuesday, the 23d ult. [23 NOV 1852], in Princess Anne, Somerset Co., Md., Mr. JOHN WOOLFORD to Miss CAROLINE E.G. POLK, formerly of this city. (13 DEC 1852)

DEATH. In Sheffield, England, on the 16th November, Mr. GEO. OATES, Sr., of Charleston, in the 64th year of his age. He had been sojourning in his native country for some months, and was about to embark for his adopted home, when he was taken ill, and died in a few days. (13 DEC 1852)

MARRIAGE. On Thursday, the 9th inst., by the Rev. Mr. Stanley, THOMAS F. PENDLE and SARAH ANN CLEMENTSON, both of Washington. (15 DEC 1852)

MARRIAGE. At Cincinnati, On the 29th ult. [29 NOV 1852], the Hon. EDWARD C. MARSHALL, Representative in Congress from California, to Miss JOSEPHINE, daughter of Robert Chalfrant, Esq. (15 DEC 1852)

MARRIAGE. In Lincolnton, N.C., on the 22d of November, by the Rev. D. Crooks, Mr. LUCIUS Y. LUSK, of New Orleans, La., to Miss MARGARET E., daughter of the late E. Hoyle, Esq., of Gaston Co., N.C. (15 DEC 1852)

DEATH. On Tuesday morning, the 14th inst., of dropsy in the chest, JOHN V. GIBBS, in the 74th year of his age, formerly a resident of Prince George's Co., Md. His friends and those of his son-in-law, J.P. Keller, are respectfully invited to attend his funeral, from the Church of the Epiphany, on Wednesday, (this day,) at half-past 12 o'clock. (15 DEC 1852)

DEATH. At the residence of her son-in-law, D.C. Reed, Mrs. MARY LANSDALE, aged 65 years. (15 DEC 1852)

DEATH. In this city, on Monday, the 6th inst., MARY, eldest daughter of Thos. Synott, of 46 Harding street, Liverpool, in the 18th year of her age. (15 DEC 1852)

DEATH. In this city, on Tuesday, the 14th inst., Mrs. MARTHA D. DICKINSON, in the 25th year of her age. (15 DEC 1852)

DEATH. Yesterday [15 DEC 1852], Mrs. LYDIA EVERETT. Her funeral will be attended at the residence of her son, Dr. Everett, on M street, between 9th and 10th, this day, (Thursday) at eleven o'clock A.M. (16 DEC 1852)

MARRIAGE. On the 16th inst., by the Rev. Mr. Tillinghast, Mr. WM. C. MORRISON, of Washington, to Miss MARY V., daughter of Chas. E. Mix, Esq., of Georgetown. (17 DEC 1852)

MARRIAGE. On Tuesday, the 14th inst., by the Rev. R.L. Dashiell, Mr. ROBERT M. SUTTON to Miss LAURA VIRGINIA DEGGES, all of this city. (17 DEC 1852)

MARRIAGE. On Thursday morning, the 16th, JAS. R. ROCHE to SUSAN E., youngest daughter of the late Dr. Spencer Mitchell. (17 DEC 1852)

MARRIAGE. At Union Chapel, on the 9th inst., by the Rev. R.L. Dashiell, Mr. ELISHA LAZENBY to Mrs. MARY A. ADAMS, of Georgetown, D.C. (17 DEC 1852)

DEATH. On the morning of the 16th inst., after a severe illness, Mrs. ELIZA COSTIGAN, in the 83d year of her age. Her friends are respectfully invited to attend her funeral from the residence of her son, Dr. John Costigan, near the Navy Yard, on Sunday next, at 2 o'clock, P.M. (17 DEC 1852)

OBITUARY. Died, at her residence at Harewood, Culpeper Co., Va., on Monday, the 6th inst., Mrs. MARIA CHAMPE CARTER, relict of the late Wm. Champe Carter, of "Farley," in the 77th year of her age. The deceased was the last of the four children of Jas. Parks Farley, on the Island of Antigua, and Elizabeth Hill Byrd, daughter of Col. Wm. Byrd, of "Westover." She was for near forty years a pious and consistent member of the Protestant Episcopal Church; and, although an heiress of a large fortune, which was considerably increased by her marriage, her tastes and habits were simple and unostentatious. She preferred to dispense it, as long as she was able, with a liberal hand amongst her needy relatives and all who were in want around her. Her house, while at Farley, was always the seat of an open and generous hospitality. She was a lady of great intelligence and wit, of refined and cultivated mind, of great vivacity, and remarkable flow of spirits; of generous disposition, perfectly unselfish and disinterested [text continues]. (17 DEC 1852)

MARRIAGE. On Tuesday evening, 23d ult. [23 NOV 1852], by the Rev. Chas. B. Dana, JOHN W. BURKE to JULIA THOMPSON, both of Alexandria. [20 DEC 1852]

MARRIAGE. On the 9th inst., at Tudor Hall, St. Mary's Co., Md., by the Rev. Mr. Buck, WALTER ROBINSON, Esq., of Charles Co., to Miss SARAH ANN KEY, niece of the Hon. H.G.S. Key. (20 DEC 1852)

DEATH. In Baltimore, on Tuesday last [14 DEC 1852], JAMES KENT, Esq., of Anne Arundel Co., Md., in the 51st year of his age. Mr. K. has frequently represented Calvert and Anne Arundel counties in the Legislature of Maryland. He was a most noble-hearted man, kind and charitable to the poor, and a true friend. His death will be deeply regretted by his numerous friends throughout the State. (20 DEC 1852)

DEATH. On the 20th inst., after a short but painful illness, Mrs. REBECCA BUTT, in the 34th year of her age, wife of Solomon Butt. The friends of the family are invited to attend her funeral tomorrow, at 3 o'clock P.M. (21 DEC 1852)

Daily National Intelligencer, Marriage and Death Notices, 1851-1854

MARRIAGE. At the Foundry Methodist Episcopal Church, on the 16th inst., by the Rev. Jesse T. Peck, Mr. HARVEY J. HUNT to Miss SARAH JANE PETTICORD, all of Washington. (22 DEC 1852)

MARRIAGE. On Sabbath evening [19 DEC 1852], by the Rev. John C. Smith, Mr. JAMES R. THOMPSON to Miss MARY A. COLLIER, and, on Monday evening [20 DEC 1852], Mr. WILLIAM J. BLAKE to Miss MARY ANN SCOTT, all of this city. (22 DEC 1852)

DEATH. On Tuesday morning, the 21st inst., of consumption, Miss ANNA PAULINE WALTER, of Würtemberg, Germany, in the 24th year of her age. Her funeral will take place at St. Mary's Church, Fifth street, this morning, at half-past 9 o'clock. (22 DEC 1852)

MARRIAGE. On the 19th inst., by the Rev. Mr. Hodges, WARREN S. WATERS to MARY KINNEY, all of Washington, D.C. (23 DEC 1852)

MARRIAGE. On Tuesday, the 21st inst., by Rev. Mr. Hodges, A. FRANCIS LUSBY to Miss LUCY ANN GRAY, of Prince George's Co., Md. (23 DEC 1852)

MARRIAGE. In Newburyport, Mass., on Thursday evening, the 16th inst., by the Rev. George Wildes, RICHARD M. HANSON, of this city, to DELIA WALKER, daughter of Hon. Dennis Condry, of the former place. (24 DEC 1852)

DEATH. At his residence in Orange Co., N.C., on the 7th inst., the Hon. JAMES S. SMITH, M.D., in the 66th year of his age. More than 30 years ago Dr. Smith represented for several years the District of his State in which he lived and died. (24 DEC 1852)

DEATH. On the 9th inst., of scarlet fever, JULIA ANNA, aged 1 year and 11 months; and on the 23d inst., CHARLES NEAL, aged 3 weeks and 5 days, children of Patrick H. and Louisa Jane McNantz. The funeral of Charles Neal will take place this (Friday) afternoon, at 3 o'clock. (24 DEC 1852)

MARRIAGE. On Thursday, the 16th, by the Rev. Wm. H. Bebee, J. JEFFERSON, son of Wm. G.W. White, of Washington, to Miss E.C. SMITH, of Monmouth Co., N.Y. [sic] (27 DEC 1852)

DEATH. On Saturday morning last [25 DEC 1852], at the residence of her husband, Mr. Geo. M. Kendall, Mrs. CHARLOTTE S. KENDALL, aged 52 years and seven months. Her funeral will take place from the E Street Baptist Church tomorrow morning at 11 o'clock. (27 DEC 1852)

DEATH. On the 26th inst., of scarlet fever, JACQUELINE P., second daughter of Wm. and Mary Ann McPeak, aged seven years. The friends of the family are invited to attend the funeral without further notice this day, at 2 o'clock P.M. at their residence, on Maryland avenue, between 4½ and 6th streets. (27 DEC 1852)

OBITUARY. The *New York Evening Post* says: The sad intelligence has just reached us of the death of Mr. SAMUEL RIGGS, a prominent merchant and banker of this city. He died at his residence on Sunday evening, about 9 o'clock, after an illness of some days' duration, but which betrayed no alarming symptom until Sunday. Mr. Riggs commenced business in the city of Baltimore about the year 1825, forming one of the firm of Peabody, Riggs & Co. His partners were George Peabody, the eminent banker now doing business in London, and Elisha Riggs, the uncle of the deceased, now a wealthy and influential banker of the city of New York city. About two years since Mr. Riggs removed to New York, and commenced business in company with Mr. Hitchcock and his eldest son, Wm. Riggs, under the firm of Riggs, Hitchcock & Co., and on the first of January next he was to have opened an Banking House in New York, in company with his son, William, and Mr. George Riggs, formerly of the firm of Corcoran & Riggs, of Washington. The latter gentleman is expected to arrive by the steamer *Pacific* from London, where he has been for the past month making preliminary arrangements for the firm. Mr. Riggs was about 52 years of age; possessed a constitution of remarkable vigor, and has enjoyed from his youth upwards almost uninterrupted health.

His loss will be severely felt far beyond the bereaved circle to which he was bound by the ties of blood and kindred. (29 DEC 1852)

MARRIAGE. On the 26th inst., by the Rev. Mr. Hodges, CHAS. EDWARD NELSON to Miss REBECCA JANE BRYAN, all of the District of Columbia. (29 DEC 1852)

MARRIAGE. On the 6th, by the Rev. Simon Watkins, Mr. THOS. POLLEY to Miss ANNIE M. GOLDSMITH, of Annapolis. (29 DEC 1852)

MARRIAGE. In Georgetown, on the 25th, by the Rev. Mr. Bryson, RICHARD ADAMS, of Washington, to Miss LOUISA V. MARTIN, of the same place. (29 DEC 1852)

DEATH. Yesterday, the 29th inst., EDGAR F. WADE, in the 19th year of his age. The friends and acquaintances of the family are invited to attend his funeral from the residence of his mother, on 6th street, at three o'clock today. (30 DEC 1852)

DEATH. On Wednesday, December 29th, Miss JANE E. MURPHY. The friends and acquaintances of the family are respectfully requested to attend her funeral this (Friday) evening, at 3 o'clock, from the residence of her mother, corner of 8th and G streets. (31 DEC 1852)

DEATH. On the 29th inst., GRENVILLE T. WINTHROP, infant son of Geo. R. and Catharine Hooper, aged 14 months. The friends of the family are requested to attend the funeral this (Friday) morning, at 11 o'clock. (31 DEC 1852)

DEATH. On the 26th inst., of scarlet fever, MARGARET LAVINA, in the 7th year of her age, and on the 27th inst., of the same disease, EDWARD ROBERT, aged 23 months, children of William and Mary Jane Douglass. And on the 29th inst., after a brief illness, MARY JANE, consort of William Douglas, in the 37th year of her age. The friends of the family are invited to attend her funeral at 3 o'clock, this day, from the residence of her husband, 18th and P streets north. (31 DEC 1852)

Daily National Intelligencer, Marriage and Death Notices, 1851-1854

❀ ❀ ❀ 1853 ❀ ❀ ❀

DEATH. On Thursday [30 DEC 1852], at her residence in this city, aged 76, Mrs. SALLY STOTT, widow of the late James Stott. She lived a long and exemplary Christian life, and died a peaceful death. Her friends are invited to attend her funeral tomorrow (Sabbath) afternoon, at two o'clock, at her late residence, without further notice. (1 JAN 1853)

DEATH. At San Francisco, Calif., on the 4th ult. [4 DEC 1852], Mrs. WILHELMINA ELLMORE, formerly of this city, and eldest daughter of H.B. Sage, Esq., in the 47th year of her age. (1 JAN 1853)

MARRIAGE. On the 30th ult. [30 DEC 1852], by the Rev. H.I. Denecker, Mr. JOHN H. HOOD to Miss MARGARET A. MILLER, of this city. (3 JAN 1853)

DEATH. On the 2d inst., in Georgetown, MARY M. BRYSON, late consort of Rev. Samuel Bryson, in the 47th year of her age. Her funeral will take place from the Methodist Episcopal Church, on Dunbarton street, on Tuesday morning, at 10 o'clock. (3 JAN 1853)

DEATH. Suddenly, on the 15th ult. [15 DEC 1852], of a disease of the heart, in the city of St. Louis, Mo., Mr. ROBERDEAU ANNAN, in the 48th year of his age. Mr. Annan was a native of Virginia, but for a number of years resided at Hagerstown, from which place he removed about ten years ago to the State of Missouri. (3 JAN 1853)

DEATH. At Alexandria, on Saturday last [1 JAN 1853], JOHN ROBERTS, Esq., in the 87th year of his age. He had been for many years a resident, and formerly an active merchant of Alexandria. His intelligence and probity secured him the high respect of his fellow-citizens, and he had served several years as Mayor. He leaves numerous descendants and friends to lament his lost. *Gazette.* (3 JAN 1853)

DEATH. On the 3d inst., Mrs. ANN ELIZABETH BALDWIN, consort of Gabriel L. Baldwin, in the 25th year of her age. The friends of the family are particularly invited to attend her funeral this (Tuesday) morning at 10 o'clock, at St. Peter's Church, Capitol Hill. (4 JAN 1853)

DEATH. On Sunday evening, the 2d inst., RANDOLPH POMEROY, only child of Wm. H. and Nannie Innes Hull, aged 14 months and 11 days. The friends of the family are respectfully invited to attend his funeral today, (Tuesday,) at 12 o'clock, from the residence of Col. James J. Randolph, on 7th street, between I street and Massachusetts avenue. (4 JAN 1853)

MARRIAGE. On Saturday, 1st January 1853, by the Rev. James Laurie, D.D., Mr. ALEXANDER ANDERSON to Miss MARGARET WHITTAKER, all of this city. (5 JAN 1853)

MARRIAGE. On the 3d inst., by the Rev. Mr. Hodges, HORATIO R. MARYMAN to Miss MARY LOUISA ARTH, all of this city. (5 JAN 1853)

MARRIAGE. In this city, on Monday, the 3d inst., by the Rev. S.B. Sotherland, Mr. JOHN T. STORY, of Baltimore, Md., to Miss LAURA A. WOODDALL, of Washington. (5 JAN 1853)

MARRIAGE. In this city, on Sunday, the 2d inst., by the Rev. G.W. Samson, Mr. JAMES JONES to Miss MARTHA MARMEDUKE, both of Washington. (5 JAN 1853)

DEATH. Suddenly, on the morning of the 4th inst., in the 70th year of his age, PEYTON RANDOLPH, Esq., formerly of Virginia, but for the last twelve years a resident of this city, and an inmate of the family of his son, Col. James Innes Randolph. He had but a few minutes before returned from market, and had just remarked to his son how well he felt. But he had scarcely taken his seat in the parlor, where the corpse of a great-grandchild lay ready for interment, when he fell heavily upon the floor without speech or motion,

Daily National Intelligencer, Marriage and Death Notices, 1851-1854

and breathed his last before the family physician could arrive to see him. He leaves a widow, son, and daughter, and a large family of grandchildren, already bowed down with affliction at the death of another beloved one then unburied. May God in his mercy sanctify to them all this double bereavement! (5 JAN 1853)

DEATH. In Washington, on the 2d of January, ELIZABETH OWENS, in the 72d year of her age, formerly a resident of Calvert Co., Md. (5 JAN 1853)

DEATH. In this city, on the 4th inst., WILLIAM H. LOKER, of St. Mary's Co., Md., aged 52 years. (5 JAN 1853)

DEATH. At her residence in Tazewell Co., Va., on Sunday night, the 12th ult., Mrs. LETITIA PRESTON FLOYD, widow of the late Gov. John Floyd, and daughter of Col. William Preston, of Virginia. She was the last survivor of a large and distinguished generation. A brief illness, closing a long decline, terminated her existence, in the 74th year of her age, without pain and without a struggle. Conscious of her approaching end, and resigned to death, she passed away tranquilly in the bosom of her family, having left no duties in a long and memorable life unperformed, and transmitting the memory of her brilliant qualities and high virtues to sooth the anguish occasioned by this bereavement in the numerous and venerating circle of her relatives and friends. (5 JAN 1853)

DEATH. At Quincy, Ill., on the 17th ult. [17 DEC 1852], CORNELIA, wife of Dr. Daniel Stahl, and eldest daughter of the late F.C. DeKrafft, Esq., of this city. (5 JAN 1853)

OBITUARY. At Medford, Mass., a few days ago, occurred the death of Madame BIGELOW, relict of the late Hon. Timothy Bigelow. Mrs. Bigelow was born in Groton, Mass., on March 13th, 1771. She was the daughter of Hon. Oliver Prescott, an eminent physician, and a patriot of the age and school of Washington. Her father was distinguished for various civil office which he held in public life. He was one of the early associates of the Mass. Medical Society, and also the American Academy of Arts and Sciences; and during many of the latter years of his life was Judge of Probate for the county of Middlesex. Judge Prescott was brother of the famous Col. William Prescott, whose valor and patriotism are identified with the story of Bunker Hill. In September 1791, Miss Lucy Prescott, the subject of this notice, was married to Timothy Bigelow, at that time a young lawyer of rising distinction in Groton [text continues]. (5 JAN 1853)

MARRIAGE. On Thursday, the 6th inst., by the Rev. Smith Pyne, C.G. BAYLOR, Esq., U.S. Consul at Amsterdam, to LOUISA D., eldest daughter of the late Commander Wadsworth. (7 and 12 JAN 1853)

DEATH. On the morning of the 6th inst., after a long and protracted illness, which she bore with Christian fortitude, Mrs. SARAH CLEMENTS, in the 86th year of her age. Her friends and acquaintances and those of the family are respectfully invited to attend her funeral, from the residence of her son-in-law, Thomas Bayne, Esq., on 8th street, Navy Yard, near the Garrison, on Sunday, the 9th inst., at 2 o'clock P.M. (7 JAN 1853)

DEATH. On Wednesday, 5th inst., SIDNEY TRAVERS, aged 73 years, long a resident of this city. Her friends and acquaintances are invited to attend her funeral from her late residence, on Pennsylvania avenue, between 12th and 13th streets, this evening, at 3 o'clock. (7 JAN 1853)

DEATH. In Prince George's Co., Md., on the 29th of December [1852], OLIVIA E., wife of Dr. T.D. Jones, late of Montgomery Co., Md., and daughter of the late Dr. Alexander Edmonston, in the 57th year of her age. (7 JAN 1853)

DEATH. On the 23d of October last [1852], Mrs. ELIZABETH AN HILLEARY, wife of John M. Hilleary, Esq., and daughter of the late James Waring, all of Prince George's Co., Md. (7 JAN 1853)

Daily National Intelligencer, Marriage and Death Notices, 1851-1854

DEATH. Suddenly, on Friday afternoon [7 JAN 1853], MARTHA WASHINGTON, in the fifth year of her age, youngest daughter of H.D. and Susan Cooper. The friends of the family are requested to attend her funeral from the residence of her parents, on H street, below Fifth, at 2½ o'clock, on Sunday afternoon. (8 JAN 1853)

DEATH. On the 6th inst., in the fiftieth year of his age, O.J. PRATHER. His funeral will take place from his late residence, on I street, between 4th and 5th streets, at 2 o'clock, on Sunday next. The friends and acquaintances of the family are respectfully invited to attend. (8 JAN 1853)

DEATH. On the 6th inst., near Colesville, Montgomery Co., Md., ZACHARIAH H. WORTHINGTON, aged 54 years. (8 JAN 1853)

MARRIAGE. On the 6th inst., by the Rev. C.M. Butler, Mr. GEORGE W. BAMBERGER, of this city, to Miss ELIZABETH ANN INGERSOLL, of Somerset Co., Md. (10 JAN 1853)

DEATH. On Sabbath evening, 9th inst., of scarlet fever, MARY NORMA THERESA NYE, in the 5th year of her age, daughter of the late Norman Willard and Mary Ann Nye, and grand-daughter of J.W. and P. Nye. The friends of the family are respectfully invited to attend her funeral this evening at 2 o'clock P.M., from the residence of J.W. Nye, on L, between 6th and 7th streets. (11 JAN 1853)

DEATH. On Sunday night, 9th inst., WILLIAM HENRY LACY, in the 33d year of his age. His friends are requested to attend his funeral, from his residence on the Island, near 6th street, this day at 3 P.M. (11 JAN 1853)

MARRIAGE. On Thursday, the 6th inst., by the Rev. Mr. Alig, Mr. RUDOLPH EICHHORN to Miss ANN ELIZABETH CONLAN, all of this city. (12 JAN 1853)

MARRIAGE. On Thursday, the 6th inst., by the Rev. Smith Pyne, C.G. BAYLOR, Esq., U.S. Consul at Amsterdam, to LOUISA D., eldest daughter of the late Commodore Wadsworth. [Republished to correct an error.] (12 JAN 1853)

MARRIAGE. At Baltimore, on the 6th inst., by the Rev. H.V.D. Johns, REVERDY JOHNSON, Jr., Esq., to CAROLINE PATTERSON, all of Baltimore. (12 JAN 1853)

MARRIAGE. On the 6th inst., by the Rev. Job W. Lambeth, B.D. SPALDING to PRISCILLA, daughter of H.A. Moore, Esq., both of Charles Co., Md. (12 JAN 1853)

MARRIAGE. On Monday afternoon [10 JAN 1853], by the Rev. John C. Smith, Mr. JAMES E. WALD to Miss JANE GRAY, all of this city. (12 JAN 1853)

DEATH. In Baltimore, on Sunday, the 9th inst., Mrs. ANN PHILLIPS, aged eighty-three, relict of the late Capt. Isaac Phillips. (12 JAN 1853)

DEATH. At Benecia, Calif., December 7 [1852], Maj. ALBERT S. MILLER, of the 2d U.S. Infantry. (12 JAN 1853)

DEATH. In Baltimore, on Monday, the 10th inst., at a few minutes past 1 in the afternoon, at the residence of her brother, Dr. Wm. Wirt, in Cathedral street, Mrs. CATHARINE WIRT RANDALL, after months of meekly borne sufferings. (12 and 20 JAN 1853)

DEATH. Recently, on the voyage from Hong Kong, China, to San Francisco, Calif., in the 23d year of his age, HEZEKIAH NILES, son of the late Hezekiah Niles, editor of "*Niles' Register*." Mr. Niles was attached to the commercial house of Messrs. Forbes & Co., of Canton, and was, at the time of his death, the supercargo of the barque *Wilhelmina*. He was a young gentleman of fine talents and great private worth,

Daily National Intelligencer, Marriage and Death Notices, 1851-1854

and, had his life been preserved, would doubtless have become an eminent and prosperous merchant. (13 JAN 1853)

DEATH. On the 12th inst., of a pulmonary disease, CHAS. P. HOOVER, aged 26 years. His friends and acquaintances, and those of the family, are requested to attend his funeral on Friday afternoon at 3 o'clock, from the residence of his father, Mr. Andrew Hoover, First Ward. (13 JAN 1853)

DEATH. On Monday evening, the 9th inst., in the 84th year of her age, Mrs. SARAH RAGAN, a native of Prince George's Co., but a resident of Georgetown for forty years. Her friends, and those of the family, are respectfully invited to attend her funeral this (Thursday) afternoon at 3 o'clock. (13 JAN 1853)

MARRIAGE. On the 6th January [1853], by the Rev. Mr. Watson, Lieut. W.A. NIMMO, of the U.S. Army, to Miss CORA MARBURY, of Prince George's Co., Md. (14 JAN 1853)

MARRIAGE. On the 6th inst., by the Rev. Mr. Cox, JOHN G. DEEBLE to Miss MARY JANE CARROLL, both of this city. (14 JAN 1853)

MARRIAGE. In Richmond, Va., on Wednesday, the 5th inst., by the Right Rev. Bishop Johns, Brevet Major P.V. HAGNER, U.S. Army, and SUSAN S., eldest daughter of Gen. Bernard Peyton, of that city. (14 JAN 1853)

DEATH. In the city of Paris, on the 16th day of December 1852, of pleurisy, in the 24th year of his age, Dr. JULIAN TAYLOR, youngest son of the late Robert J. Taylor, Esq., of Alexandria, Va. (14 and 21 JAN 1853)

MARRIAGE. On the morning of the 13th inst., at St. Matthew's Church, by the Rev. J.B. Donelan, JAMES A. REILEY to REBECCA A., second daughter of Geo. A. Meem, all of Georgetown, D.C. (17 JAN 1853)

MARRIAGE. On the 13th inst., in Baltimore, by the Rev. Henry Tarring, E. FORD SIMPSON, of Washington, to E. ADA, youngest daughter of the late Benj. Shipley, of Baltimore. (17 JAN 1853)

MARRIAGE. In Oregon, on Thursday morning, the 25th November, by the Rev. St. M. Fackler, at the residence of the Hon. J.B. Preston, Surveyor General of Oregon, JOHN P. GAINES, Governor of Oregon, to Miss MARGARET B. WANDS, formerly of Albany, New York. (17 JAN 1853)

DEATH. At Chattahoochee, Fla., November 25 [1852], after a painful and lingering illness, JOHN WILLIAMSON MONROE, aged twelve years and six months, only child of Samuel and Elizabeth Ann Boardman, and grandson of the late Dr. T.L.C. Monroe. (17 JAN 1853)

DEATH. Of scarlet fever, on Friday evening, the 14th inst., MARGARET ELIZABETH LAMBRIGHT, daughter of the late George and Mary Lambright, and grand-daughter of George Crandell, in the 7th year of her age. (17 JAN 1853)

DEATH. On Saturday, January 15, EMMA JANE, only child of George and Ann Jane Sylvester, aged one year and four months. (17 JAN 1853)

DEATH. Died at his residence, Morgansburg, Fauquier Co., Va., October 12th, 1852, of dropsy of the chest, of which disease he lingered many months, Capt. JOSEPH MORGAN, aged seventy years. In the death of this old and estimable citizen the community in which he resided has lost a valued friend. His door was ever open to the houseless and his heart to the wants of the poor. The writer of this humble tribute to his memory knew him well, and can testify to the goodness of his heart and his ardent friendship. He has left a bright example of honesty of purpose and uprightedness of principle for those to imitate who come after him. In a word, his faults were few, his virtues many. *Peace to his ashes!* (18 JAN 1853)

DEATH. Yesterday [17 JAN 1853], at half-past 12 o'clock, Mrs. ELIZABETH TONGE, relict of Mr. Thomas Tonge, in the 33d year of her age. Her funeral will take place on Wednesday, (tomorrow,) the 19th inst., from the residence of her brother-in-law, Mr. J.R. Pollard, on B street south, between 6th and 7th streets west, where the friends and acquaintances of the family are respectfully invited to attend without further notice. (18 JAN 1853) The funeral of Mrs. Elizabeth Tonge will take place today at 2 o'clock from the residence of Mr. R. Pollard, on the Island. (19 JAN 1853)

DEATH. Yesterday morning [18 JAN 1853], THOMAS R. VAN TYNE, son of the late Dr. J.P. Van Tyne, in the 22d year of his age. The friends of the family are respectfully invited to attend his funeral, from the residence of his mother, on F street, near 13th street, tomorrow afternoon, at 3 o'clock. (19 JAN 1853)

DEATH. Suddenly, on the 16th inst., Mrs. ANN EDWARDS, consort of Gen. Samuel M. Edwards, in the 60th year of her age. The friends of the family are respectfully invited to attend her funeral this day, (Wednesday,) at 2 o'clock P.M., from her late residence on 13th street, between B and C streets, (Island). (19 JAN 1853)

DEATH. On the evening of the 15th inst., after an illness of eighteen days, of water on the brain, produced by teething, LELIA McNUTT, aged 21 months, only child of William T. and Martha E. Smithson. (19 JAN 1853)

OBITUARY. Died, in Baltimore, on the 10th inst., Mrs. CATHARINE WIRT RANDALL, wife of Alexander Randall, Esq., of Annapolis, and daughter of the late William Wirt [text continues]. (20 JAN 1853)

DEATH. Departed this life on Wednesday morning, January 19, Mr. GARRET ANDERSON, aged fifty-six years. His friends are invited to attend his funeral, which will take place on Thursday, 20th inst., at 12 o'clock noon, from his late residence on Pennsylvania avenue. (20 JAN 1853)

DEATH. On the 15th January, at the residence of its grandfather, Darius Clagett, after the short illness of forty-eight hours, in the fourth year of his age, CHAS. CLAGETT THOMPSON, eldest son of Smith and Mary Ann Thompson. (20 JAN 1853)

DEATH. On Tuesday morning, the 18th inst., after a short illness, Mrs. CHRISTINA HINES, consort of the late Frederick Hines, in the 58th year of her age. The friends of the family and the public generally are respectfully invited to attend her funeral on this (Thursday) afternoon, the 20th inst., at 3 o'clock P.M., from the Union Chapel, First Ward. (20 JAN 1853)

DEATH. In this city, on Wednesday, 19th inst., Mrs. ELIZABETH NELSON, consort of Samuel Nelson, in the 50th year of her age. Her funeral will take place from Christ Church (Protestant Episcopal,) near the Navy Yard, on Friday, the 21st, at 2 o'clock P.M. Her friends and acquaintances are invited to attend. (20 JAN 1853)

DEATH. At the residence of her husband in this city, on the 19th inst., at 4 o'clock P.M., after a few days' illness, MARTHA, wife of the Hon. Stephen A. Douglas, of Illinois, and only surviving child of the late Col. Martin, of North Carolina. The funeral will take place from her late residence on Saturday next, at 2 o'clock P.M. The friends of the family are invited to attend. (20 JAN 1853) We learn that the funeral of the late Mrs. Martha M. Douglas will take place tomorrow, (Saturday,) at twelve o'clock. (21 and 24 JAN 1853)

OBITUARY. Died, in the city of Paris, on the 16th of December [1852], in the 24th year of his age, JULIAN TAYLOR, youngest son of the late Robert J. Taylor, Esq., of Alexandria, Va. He graduated in the year 1848, at the College of New Jersey, and afterwards took the degree of Doctor of Medicine in Philadelphia. From his earliest boyhood he was preeminently distinguished for all those qualities which have ever attached to each other generous minds. Intelligent, high-spirited, amiable, he made friends wherever he went. One so idolized by his family, so beloved by his friends, it has never been the fortune of the writer of this poor tribute to meet. He was expected soon from Paris, whither he had gone to perfect himself in his professional studies; but, just as the hearts of his family and friends were swelling with hope and expectation, there came to them the heart-rending tidings that, in obedience to other summons, he had already departed "for the undiscovered country from whose bourne no traveler returns." Yet though he died far from his home, devoted friends were about his bedside, who tenderly nursed him during his short and fatal illness, closed his eyes in death, and will bear to his bereaved family his last words and tokens of love. Peaceful be his long rest, whether beneath the sod of sunny France or near those whom in life he loved so well. (21 JAN 1853)

DEATH. In this city, yesterday morning [20 JAN 1853], aged about 48 years, RICHARD CONNOLLY, a clerk in the Census Office. Mr. Connolly was for many years the principal of one of the public grammar schools of Baltimore, where he was highly respected and esteemed, and much valued as a competent and faithful instructor of youth. (21 JAN 1853)

DEATH. In the 8th year of her age, MARY HUMES, the daughter of Dr. Samuel A. and Agnes Houston. The friends of the family are respectfully invited to attend the funeral at 10 o'clock today from the residence on Missouri avenue, between 6th and 4½ streets. (21 JAN 1853)

DEATH. On Tuesday, the 28th of December 1852, at Ft. Snelling, Minnesota Territory, GEORGE SIBLEY LEE, son of Col. F. Lee, U.S. Army, aged 28 years. (22 JAN 1853)

DEATH. At Woodstock, the residence of her sister Mrs. Elizabeth Brent, on the morning of the 20th inst., Miss PRISCILLA NEALE, in the 55th year of her age. The funeral will take place at 2 P.M. this day, (Saturday,) at St. Peter's Catholic Church, Capitol Hill. The friends of the family are respectfully invited to attend. (22 JAN 1853)

DEATH. At Providence, R.I., on the 16th inst., ANN M., wife of William A. Williams, in the 39th year of her age. (22 JAN 1853)

OBITUARY. The past week has taken away from us one of the best and purest of God's creation. Mrs. MARTHA MARTIN DOUGLAS has entered the "ponderous and marble jaws" of the tomb. Insatiate Death demanded the sacrifice, and we are left to mourn over the early fate of a loved one, whose example was a shining light to those who survive her. It was my happiness to know this estimable lady, at her home in Chicago, and deeply does her demise fall upon the heart whose tears almost obliterate the lines endeavored to be traced upon the cold, passionless paper [text continues]. (24 JAN 1853)

MARRIAGE. At Hannibal, Mo., on the 9th ult. [9 DEC 1852], by Rev. Mr. Modisett, Mr. JOSIAH T. HINTON to Miss SARAH E. KEHOE, formerly of Washington. (24 JAN 1853)

MARRIAGE. In Baltimore, on the 20th inst., by the Rev. B.H. Nadall, Mr. JOHN TAYLOR to Miss MARY JANE HALIDAY, both of that city. (24 JAN 1853)

DEATH. On Saturday, the 22d inst., in the 79th year of his age, JOHN DAVIS, of Abel, a native of Newark, Del., but for the last forty-eight years a resident of this city. Mr. Davis has been in the service of the Government during his entire residence in this city, and discharged all his duties skillfully and faithfully; and he lived and died an honest man. His death will be regretted by his many friends. The friends of the family are invited to attend his funeral, from his late residence, near the Marine Barracks, on Tuesday next, the 25th inst., at 2 o'clock P.M. (24 JAN 1853)

DEATH. On Saturday, January 22d, JOSEPHINE PEARSON, only child of Carlile P. and Eliza W. Patterson, aged 14 months and 16 days. The relatives and friends of the family are invited to attend her funeral this day, (Monday,) at one o'clock, without further invitation, from Brentwood, the residence of Mrs. Pearson. (24 JAN 1853)

DEATH. On Thursday, the 20th inst., SARAH, daughter of John P. Wheeler and the late Anna M. Vinson, aged three years, three months and fifteen days. (24 and 25 JAN 1853)

DEATH. Very suddenly, of congestive fever, at the Naval School, Annapolis, Md., on Sunday last [23 JAN 1853], Midshipman ALFRED W. BRODHEAD, aged seventeen, son of John M. Brodhead, Esq., and Mrs. Josephine Brodhead, of this city, and grandson of the late Hon. John Brodhead, of New Hampshire [text continues]... Funeral this day, at two o'clock, from the residence of his father on New Jersey avenue. (25 JAN 1853)

DEATH. On Saturday, the 22d inst., CHARLES McLEAN, son of Capt. G.W. and Rebecca J. McLean. He was drowned, by falling through the ice, whilst skating on a mill-pond near the residence of his parents, at Rahway, N.J. The unfortunate youth was only twelve years of age, and had given evidence of high intellectual and moral excellence. May kind Providence soothe the wound this inscrutable dispensation has given to his numerous connexions and friends! (25 JAN 1853)

DEATH. On the 25th inst., VICTORIA HILL, in the 14th year of her age. Her funeral will take place this (Wednesday) evening at 3 o'clock, from the residence of her mother, on 5th, between G and H streets. (26 JAN 1853)

DEATH. Suddenly, on the 24th inst., Mrs. ELIZABETH NALLEY, relict of the late Aaron Nalley, of this city, in the 66th year of her age. The relatives and friends of the family are invited to attend her funeral this day, (Wednesday,) at 2 o'clock P.M. from her late residence, on Twelfth street, between E and F streets. (26 JAN 1853)

DEATH. In this city, on the 23d inst., JOHN FRANCIS ZAVIERS FORTIER, aged 2 years 3 months and 5 days, son of P.M. and Eugenia V. Fortier. (27 JAN 1853)

MARRIAGE. On the 27th inst., by the Rev. Smith Pyne, D.D., at Mrs. Wainwright's residence, and afterwards at her Britannic Majesty's Legation, WILLIAM WEBB FOLLETT SYNGE, Esq., Attache to the Legation, to HENRIETTA MARY, youngest daughter of the late Col. Wainwright, of the U.S. Marine Corps. (28 JAN 1853)

DEATH. Of apoplexy, at his residence in Barren Co., Ky., on the 21st inst., in the 78th year of his age, Mr. WILLIAM BELL, one of the most respected citizens of that State. Mr. B. was the father of the wife of the Hon. Wm. M. Gwin, of the U.S. Senate, and has left a large circle of friends to mourn over his sudden decease. (28 JAN 1853)

DEATH. On the 26th inst., SARAH, aged 14 years, daughter of Hester A. and the late Gen. T.T. Wheeler. The friends and acquaintances of the family are respectfully invited to attend her funeral on Saturday, the 29th inst., at 3 o'clock, from her mother's residence, on Prospect street, Georgetown, D.C. (28 JAN 1853)

DEATH. At South Bend, Ark., on the 23d of last month [23 DEC 1852], ROBERT R. RICE, Esq., aged 43 years, a merchant and a large landed proprietor; one of the best men in the community in which he lived, whose death is deeply lamented by a large circle of friends as well as by his family. (29 JAN 1853)

MARRIAGE. On Wednesday, the 26th inst., by the Rev. Mr. Hodges, RICHARD S. ROBY to Miss SARAH E. SCOTT, all of this city. (31 JAN 1853)

MARRIAGE. On Thursday, 27th inst., by the Rev. Mr. Hodges, Mr. ALBERT SUMMERS to Miss ELIZABETH STAPLES, of the District of Columbia. (31 JAN 1853)

MARRIAGE. In this city, on Tuesday, the 25th inst., by the Rev. Mr. Eckell, ROBERT S. FLAGG, of Martinsburg, Va., to MARGARET A., daughter of the late Nathaniel Hughes. (31 JAN 1853)

Daily National Intelligencer, Marriage and Death Notices, 1851-1854

MARRIAGE. On the 25th inst., at E Street Baptist Church, by the Rev. Mr. Sampson, L.A. IARDELLA to ANNA M. WALKER, all of Washington. (31 JAN 1853)

DEATH. On the 29th ult. [29 JAN 1853], of paralysis, which she bore with submission and Christian meekness for the last nineteen years, Miss SARAH GRIFFIN, daughter of Lancelot and Ann Griffin, in the 59th year of her age. (1 FEB 1853)

DEATH. On the 29th ult. [29 JAN 1853], after ten days' illness, RICHARD PRICE, aged three months and twenty-nine days, infant son of Richard H. and Mary J. Campbell. (1 FEB 1853)

DEATH. At Mrs. Ennis's, Capitol Hill, on yesterday [31 JAN 1853], JOHN F., infant son of Hon. John F. Darby, of Missouri, aged 10 months and 27 days. (1 FEB 1853)

MARRIAGE. In Georgetown, D.C., on Thursday evening, 27th ult. [27 JAN 1853], by the Rev. Mr. Bryson, Mr. JAMES H. STONE to Miss CATHERINE STEVENS, all of said town. (2 FEB 1853)

DEATH. On Tuesday evening, February 1, Mrs. MARGARET ROWAN, in the 49th year of her age. The friends of the family are respectfully invited to attend her funeral tomorrow (Thursday) afternoon, at 3½ o'clock, from the residence of her son-in-law, Mr. Wm. J. Parham, without further notice. (2 FEB 1853)

DEATH. In Baltimore, Md., on Friday, the 28th ult., of pneumonia, Mr. WILLIAM JOSEPH CLARKE, in the 24th year of his age, son of the late Robert Clarke, Esq., of this city. (2 FEB 1853)

MARRIAGE. At Trinity Church, on the 3d inst., by the Rev. C.M. Butler, THOMAS M. O'BRIEN, of Baltimore, to Miss MARY E. PORTER, of this city. (4 FEB 1853)

MARRIAGE. On Tuesday, 1st inst., by the Rev. Mr. Hodges, NATHAN LOWE, of Bladensburg, Md., to Miss MARY GLADMAN, of this city. (4 FEB 1853)

MARRIAGE. In this city, on the 31st ult. [31 JAN 1853], by the Rev. Mr. Hamilton, JOHN A. OWINGS to Miss CAROLINE RECIDES, both of Baltimore. (4 FEB 1853)

MARRIAGE. On the 1st inst., by the Rev. Mr. Elder, RICHARD E. SIMMS, of California, to Miss FANNY L.G. STEARNS, niece of Alpheus Hyatt, of Baltimore. (4 FEB 1853)

MARRIAGE. In Washington, on Monday, February 1, by the Rev. Mr. Blackwell, Mr. ROBERT DRANE to Miss SALLY ANN ELGIN, all of Fairfax Co., Va. (4 FEB 1853)

MARRIAGE. At the Hermitage, Tenn., on the 25th ult. [25 JAN 1853], by the Rev. J.T. Edgar, D.D., JOHN MARSHALL LAWRENCE, M.D. to Miss RACHAEL, only daughter of Andrew Jackson, Esq. (4 FEB 1853)

MARRIAGE. At Baltimore, on the 1st inst., by the Rev. Henry V.D. Johns, Lieut. WILLIAM MAY, U.S. Navy, to CLINTONIA GUSTAVIA, daughter of W.H.D.C. Wright, of Baltimore. (4 FEB 1853)

MARRIAGE. At Colross, near Alexandria, Va., on Tuesday, February 1st, by the Rev. C.B. Dana, WILLIAM H. DAVIDGE, of New York, to VIRGINIA MASON, daughter of the late Judge Thomson F. Mason, of the above place. (4 FEB 1853)

DEATH. Suddenly, on Wednesday evening last [2 FEB 1853], from hemorrhage of the lungs, Mrs. ROSANNA BROWN, relict of the late Jesse Brown, aged 76 years. The friends of the family are respectfully invited to attend the funeral of the deceased, from the residence of her sons, "Brown's Hotel," on Saturday, the 5th inst., at 12 o'clock M. (4 FEB 1853)

Daily National Intelligencer, Marriage and Death Notices, 1851-1854

MARRIAGES. On the 1st inst., in St. Mary's Church, by the Rev. Mathias Alig, Mr. TIMOTHY SUGHRUE to Miss CATHARINE FLAVAHAR, both of Virginia. On the same day, by the same, Mr. DANIEL CONNER to Miss HONORA SUGHRUE, both of Virginia. On the 3d inst., by the same, Mr. CASPAR MARBEL to Miss CATHARINE RUPPERT, of this city. On the same day, by the same, Mr. MICHAEL BURKE to Miss ELLEN BURKE, of this city. On the 24th of January, by the same, Mr. PATRICK SCANLON to Miss JOHANNA LYNCH. On the 20th of January, by the same, Mr. HENRICK OSTENDORF to Miss ELIZABETH PULSFORT. On the 16th January, by the same, Mr. JOHN JUDGE to Miss MARY FEENY. On the 10th of January, by the same, Mr. DAVID DILLON to Miss HONORA O'CONNOR. On the 6th of January, by the same, Mr. CAROLUS HOHMAN to Miss MARGARET ARNOLD. On the same day, by the same, Mr. MICHAEL GEARNEY to Miss CATHARINE PRENDABLE. On the 3d inst., by the same, Mr. MATHEW MAYERS to Miss BRIDGETT McKEAN. On the same day, by the same, Mr. JEREMIAH HARRINGTON to Miss CATHARINE HARRINGTON. On the 2d inst., by the same, Mr. MATHEW FINN to Miss JANE EAGAN, all of this city. (5 FEB 1853)

DEATH. On the 3d inst., EMMA R., aged two years three months and twenty-six days, daughter of Wm. H. and Wilhelmina Fanning. Her funeral will take place from the residence of her father, on D street, between 13th and 13½ streets, on Saturday, 5th inst., at 3 o'clock. (5 FEB 1853)

MARRIAGE. On the 3d inst., by the Rev. Mr. McManus, Mr. JAMES A. CONWAY to Miss SARAH ELIZABETH MULLOY, both of this city. (9 FEB 1853)

DEATH. On the 6th inst., of scarlet fever, GEORGE MARSH, aged 4 years and 6 months, youngest child of Lieut. J.M. Gilliss, U.S. Navy. (9 FEB 1853)

DEATH. At the residence of Mayor Denny, on the 8th inst., EDWARD HARDING DENNY, in the third year of his age, son of W.C. and Elizabeth O'Harra Denny, of Pittsburgh. (9 FEB 1853)

DEATH. In Annapolis, Md., on the 7th inst., Cadet SAMUEL STANHOPE SWANN, of the U.S. Millitary Academy, eldest child of Richard and Annie H. Swann, aged 16 years and 7 months. (9 FEB 1853)

DEATH. In St. Louis, Mo., on the 28th of last month, GEORGE A. HYDE, a native of Georgetown, D.C., but for the last fifteen years a resident, and at the time of his death Recorder, of the city of St. Louis. (9 and 28 FEB 1853)

DEATH. On the 8th inst., WILHELMINA AUGUSTA, daughter of Henry R. and Eliza Day, aged two years and three months. The friends of the family are invited to attend the funeral today, at one o'clock P.M. on 10th street, above L street. (10 FEB 1853)

MARRIAGE. On the 8th inst., by the Rev. Mr. Samson, WILLIAM H. STONE, Esq., of London, England, to Miss CHARLOTTE V. MINNIX, of this city. (11 FEB 1853)

MARRIAGE. On the 8th inst., by the Rev. George W. Sampson, Mr. JOSEPH FOWLER to Mrs. MARY W. DENHAM, all of this city. (11 FEB 1853)

MARRIAGE. In Georgetown, D.C., on Thursday, the 10th inst., by the Rev. J.M.P. Atkinson, COATES WALTON, of Philadelphia, to MARY R. SHOEMAKER, of the former place; and by the same, DAVID L. SHOEMAKER to ESTELLE E. THOMSON, both of Georgetown. (11 FEB 1853)

DEATH. On the 17th ult. [17 JAN 1853], at St. Louis, Mo., Mr. JOHN J. GOOCH, of London, formerly a resident of Washington, aged 22 years, deeply regretted by all who knew him. (11 FEB 1853)

DEATH. On the 30th ult. [30 JAN 1853], at the residence of her uncle, Mr. Wm. B. Bayne, Prince George's Co., Md., after a brief illness, EMILY, only daughter of Hanson G. and Ellen A. Catlett, in the 19th year of her age. (11 FEB 1853)

Daily National Intelligencer, Marriage and Death Notices, 1851-1854

MARRIAGE. In this city, on Friday, the 11th inst., by Rev. Jas. Gallaher, at the U.S. Hotel, Mr. GEORGE N. TUNSTELL and Miss MARGARET S. CRUMP. (14 FEB 1853)

DEATH. At his residence, in Eutaw, Ala., on the 4th inst., of somewhat protracted illness, Col. JOSEPH PICKENS, youngest son of Gen. Andrew Pickens, of Revolutionary memory in South Carolina. He left a devoted wife and family of children, as well as a numerous circle of relatives and friends who deeply mourn the sand bereavement. Only four days ago a friend called and paid his subscription a year in advance for the National Intelligencer, to which he was during many years a subscriber. (14 FEB 1853)

DEATH. At Oak Lawn, near Piscataway, Prince George's Co., Md., on Saturday, the 5th inst., Mrs. EMILY, wife of Dr. B.J. Semmes. *Resquiescat in pace!* (14 and 18 FEB 1853)

DEATH. In this city, on Saturday, the 12th inst., of pneumonia, SALLIE, infant daughter of Mr. Edward A. Gallaher, of Richmond, aged 8 months and 7 days. (14 FEB 1853)

DEATH. In this city, on Friday morning, the 11th inst., after a short but severe illness, Mr. ROBERT M. LOUCK, formerly of Virginia, but for a number of years past a resident of Georgetown, D.C., leaving a wife and two small children to mourn his loss. (16 FEB 1853)

MARRIAGE. At Baltimore, on the 15th inst., by the Rev. Dr. Atkinson, Lieut. D.R. Jones, U.S. Army, to REBECCA, daughter of Col. J.P. Taylor, U.S. Army. (18 FEB 1853)

MARRIAGE. In Georgetown, on Thursday morning, the 17th inst., by the Rev. Mr. Tillinghast, THOMAS R. EASBY, Esq., of Prince George's Co., Md., and Miss ELIZABETH A. HOPKINS, of Georgetown. (18 FEB 1853)

MARRIAGE. At St. John's Church, in Portsmouth, N.H., on the 10th inst., by the Rev. Charles Burroughs, D.D., RALPH HASKINS, Esq., of this city, to MARIA LOUISA, daughter of the late J.H. Beall, Esq., of Maryland. (18 FEB 1853)

DEATH. In this city, on Wednesday night last [16 FEB 1853], after a lingering illness, Mrs. ANN FITZGERALD COWING, a native of Newfoundland, but for many years a resident of Washington. The friends of the family are invited to attend her funeral at 11 o'clock today, from her residence on I, near 7 street. (18 FEB 1853)

DEATH. At Brooklyn, N.Y., on the 16th inst., Gen. WILLIAM GIBBS McNEILL, in the 52d year of his age. He was educated at West Point, and was formerly connected with the U.S. army, but for some years past had withdrawn from military service to devote himself to private pursuits as an engineer. He was employed in the construction of many of the most important railroads in the U.S., and built the dry dock at Brooklyn. During the Dorr excitement in Rhode Island he commanded the State troops, acting throughout with great prudence and judgment. (18 FEB 1853)

DEATH. At Oak Lawn, Prince George's Co., Md., the family residence, after a long and painful illness, Mrs. EMILY SEMMES, wife of Dr. Benedict I. Semmes, in the 53d year of her age [text continues]. (18 FEB 1853)

DEATH. On the 14th inst., LAMBERT TREE, youngest child of Martha S. and F.J. Bartlett, aged 4 months and 6 days. (18 FEB 1853)

MARRIAGE. In Wesley Chapel, on Thursday, the 17th inst., by Rev. S.S. Roszel, Mr. FIELDER M. MAGRUDER to Miss MARY A. CUMMINGS, all of this city. (19 FEB 1853)

Daily National Intelligencer, Marriage and Death Notices, 1851-1854

DEATH. On Thursday, the 17th inst., after a short but painful illness, Mrs. SARAH RAWLINGS, in the 63d year of her age. The friends of the family are invited to attend her funeral, from her late residence, on 20th street, this day, at 2 o'clock P.M. (19 FEB 1853)

DEATH. On the morning of the 18th, Mr. CLEMENT GRANGER, in the 70th year of his age. His funeral will take place on Sunday afternoon, at 3½ o'clock, from the residence of Michael E. Bright, L street, near the Navy Yard. (19 FEB 1853)

DEATH. On the morning of the 18th inst., BRIDGET RUTHERDALE, aged twenty-one years, consort of Jno. S. Rutherdale. The friends and acquaintances of the family are respectfully invited to attend the funeral on Sunday afternoon at 3 o'clock, from her late residence on First street, near Pennsylvania avenue. (19 FEB 1853)

DEATH. At his residence near Iowa City, (Iowa,) on the 7th inst., Ex-Governor ROBERT LUCAS, in the 73d year of his age. For nearly half a century past he has occupied a large space in the public mind. He served his country with zeal and ability in one of the most trying periods of our military history; was twice elected Governor of the State of Ohio, and was Governor (we believe the first Governor) of the Territory of Iowa. He has left us full of years and full of honor. *Republican.* (19 FEB 1853)

DEATH. On Saturday, 19th February, at 11 o'clock and 40 minutes P.M., JAMES DOUGLASS, third son of Frederic D. Stuart, aged six years six months and twenty-five days. The friends of the family are respectfully invited to attend his funeral from the residence of his parents, H street north, between 7th and 8th streets west, on Monday afternoon at 3 o'clock. (21 FEB 1853)

DEATH. At sea, on board the steamship *Tennessee*, in the Pacific ocean, of yellow fever, on the 8th of January, while on the voyage from Panama to San Francisco, Capt. GEO. CLINTON WESTCOTT, of the second regiment of infantry, U.S. Army. Capt. Westcott was the seventh son of the late Judge Westcott, of New Jersey. He entered the army as a second lieutenant in 1836, and served with credit in Florida for three years. Subsequently he was stationed at Buffalo, Detroit, Saut Ste. Marie, Toldeo, Pottsville, Pennsylvania, and New York, in all of which places he has many friends. He served in Mexico under Gen. Scott with his regiment, commanded by the intrepid Riley, and at the storming of Chepultepec he relinquished his post in the staff, and volunteered with the forlorn hope detailed from his regiment. His conduct secured merited commendation from his commanders, and he was breveted for his gallantry, and was subsequently promoted to a full captaincy. In 1848 he accompanied his regiment to California, under Gen. Riley, and served there two years, and when he died he was again on his way, under orders, to join his regiment. Capt. W. was a brave, honorable, and highly intelligent officer, esteemed and beloved by his friends, and his death will be regretted by all who knew him. (21 FEB 1853)

DEATH. At Lanark, Canada West, on the 8th February, at the residence of her uncle, the Rev. Thomas Fraser, Miss JANE FRASER, aged 32 years, daughter of John Fraser, Esq., of Newfield House, near Glasgow, Scotland. (21 FEB 1853)

DEATH. At Eltham, Westmoreland Co., Va., on the 29th ult. [29 JAN 1853], SARAH P. DITTY, aged seventeen, the eldest daughter of Dr. Thomas R. and Eliza A. Ditty. Consumption was the chosen agent by which, thus early in life, the great Creator reclaimed his gift... (21 FEB 1853)

DEATH. On Saturday, February 19th, MARY ELIZABETH, only daughter of Lewis H. and Elizabeth Poole, aged two years six months and sixteen days. (22 FEB 1853)

DEATH. At Portsmouth, Va., on Wednesday night, Maj. THOMAS A. LINTON, of the U.S. Marine Corps. He was one of the oldest and most accomplished officers in the corps, and a gentleman of much intelligence and of the most honorable character. *Norfolk Beacon.* (22 FEB 1853)

Daily National Intelligencer, Marriage and Death Notices, 1851-1854

DEATH. At the residence of his father, Ambrose Lynch, JOHN LYNCH, in the 45th year of his age. His funeral will take place tomorrow, (Wednesday), February 23d, at St. Patrick's Church, at 9 o'clock A.M. (22 FEB 1853)

DEATH. On Sunday last [19 FEB 1853], Miss CATHERINE MURPHY, aged 23 years, a native of county Carlow, Ireland, but for some years a resident of this city. Her funeral will take place from the residence of her brother on 7th street, near Maryland avenue, today at 3 o'clock. (22 FEB 1853)

DEATH. On the 20th ult. [20 JAN 1853], on his homeward voyage from Port-au-Prince, whither he had gone for the benefit of his health, ROBERT SERRELL WOOD, Esq., of Osmington, Dorset, England, but recently of Mt. Hermon, near Washington, D.C. He was favorably known in our literary circle by his scientific acquirements, illustrated and established by his valuable contributions to the National Institute, and by a very able treatise on the nature of electricity and its intention in the economy of the universe. A considerate and generous friend of the poor, his loss will be long and deeply deplored in the neighborhood of his late residence. (22 FEB 1853)

DEATH. Suddenly yesterday morning, the 22d inst., at 10½ o'clock, Mr. EPHRAIM GILMAN, in the 75th year of his age. His funeral will take place from his late residence on Boundary street, at 3 o'clock P.M. this day, which his friends and those of the family are invited to attend, without further notice. (23 FEB 1853)

DEATH. In Georgetown, on the morning of the 22d inst., in the 50th year of her age, Mrs. MARY MORGAN, wife of Geo. R. Morgan, and second daughter of the late Jas. Norris, of Baltimore. The friends and acquaintances of the family are invited to attend her funeral from her late residence, south Jefferson street, at 3 o'clock P.M. (23 FEB 1853)

DEATH. Suddenly, at Philadelphia, on Sunday morning last [20 FEB 1853], Lieut. GEORGE W. CHAPMAN, of the U.S. Navy. (23 FEB 1853)

DEATH. On the 5th inst., at Carrollton, Mo., EDWIN D. SLYE, Esq., of California, in the 36th year of his age. His family and friends will feel a consolation in knowing that, although comparatively among strangers, he received every tender and affectionate attention from Col. Graham and family, at whose hospitable mansion he was confined, which he could have received from his own immediate family. (23 FEB 1853)

DEATH. On the 22d inst., JOSEPH LEWIS SCHWARTZ, aged one year and three months. (23 FEB 1853)

DEATH. On the 23d inst., of scarlet fever, HANNAH, second daughter of William and Hannah Dixon, in the 5th year of her age. Her funeral will take place this (Thursday) afternoon, at 3 o'clock, from the residence of her father, on 4th street east. The friends of the family are respectfully invited to attend. (24 FEB 1853)

DEATH. At Georgetown, D.C., on the 20th inst., HENRY GODDARD, in the 34th year of his age. (24 FEB 1853)

MARRIAGE. In Georgetown, on Thursday morning last [24 FEB 1853], by the Rev. Mr. Tillinghast, THOMAS R. EARLY, Esq., of Upper Marlboro, and Miss ELIZABETH A. HOSKINS, of Georgetown. (25 FEB 1853)

MARRIAGE. In this city, on Saturday, 19th inst., by the Rev. Mr. Hodges, SYLVESTER D. LANGLEY to MARY MARGARET HOLT, of Charles Co., Md. (25 FEB 1853)

MARRIAGE. On Thursday morning [24 FEB 1853], by the Rev. John C. Smith, Mr. THOMAS MORRISETT to Miss FRANCES, daughter of Mr. John Anderson, all of this city. (25 FEB 1853)

Daily National Intelligencer, Marriage and Death Notices, 1851-1854

DEATH. On the morning of the 24th inst., GEORGE EPHRAIM, youngest child of William H. and Margaret D. Gilman, aged six months and eleven days. His funeral will take place from the residence of his parents on 2d street, near C, this afternoon at 3½ o'clock. The friends of the family are invited to attend. (25 FEB 1853)

DEATH. On the 25th inst., after a protracted illness of scarlet fever, WILLIAM THOMAS, youngest son of Matthew and Hester McNelly, aged 2 years and 5 months. His funeral will take place from the residence of his father on M street south, near the Navy Yard, tomorrow (Sunday) afternoon, at 3 o'clock. (26 FEB 1853)

MARRIAGE. In this city, on Sabbath evening, February 27, at St. Paul's Church, by the Rev. Smith Pyne, Hon. JOHN J. CRITTENDEN, Attorney General of the U.S., to Mrs. ELIZABETH ASHLEY, of St. Louis, Mo. (28 FEB 1853)

MARRIAGE. On the 25th inst., by the Rev. Mr. Marks, Mr. MICHAEL KELLY to Mrs. MARY ANN MURPHY, all of this city. (28 FEB 1853)

DEATH. On Saturday evening, the 26th inst., CATHARINE BRIDGET CLEMENTS, in the 14th year of her age. Her funeral will take place this afternoon from the residence of Mr. Richard Bridget, on Eleventh street, between L and M streets, at which the friends of the family are requested to attend. (28 FEB 1853)

DEATH. On the 17th February, at the residence of the Rev. Charles Fox, Gross Isle, Mich., HENRY, second son of Maj. D. Henry Rucker, Quartermaster U.S. Army, and great-grandson of the late Mrs. J. Macomb of Washington, aged seven years and nine months. [Major R. is at present stationed at Santa Fe, Mexico.] (28 FEB 1853)

DEATH. On Sunday, the 20th inst., at the residence of her father, in Brooklyn, Long Island, JANE, the daughter of Wm. and Sarah Hogan. (28 FEB 1853)

DEATH. At her residence in Prince George's Co., Sunday, the 20th inst., Mrs. MARY R.M. GUNTON, consort of William A. Gunton, Esq., and daughter of John B. Mullikin, in the 27th year of her age. The duty devolved upon us in recording the above is a very melancholy one, for there are few of our readers to whom it will not be the occasion of much heartfelt sorrow [text continues]. (28 FEB 1853)

DEATH. At Richmond, Va., on the night of the 22d inst., SAMUEL TAYLOR, Esq., an eminent and aged lawyer and greatly respected gentleman. The immediate cause of his death was a fall received in passing, on the evening before about 5 o'clock, from the Danville cars to a carriage which was to convey him to his home, after returning from the Powhatan Court, where he had been to argue an important cause. (28 FEB 1853)

The numerous friends of this District of the late GEO. A. HYDE, Esq., formerly of Georgetown, whose lamented death we lately announced, will read with grateful emotion the evidence of the high esteem in which he was held in the city of his adoption, contained in the subjoined obituary from the *St. Louis Republican* of the 29th ult. [29 JAN 1853]: Among the death notices of today is that of GEORGE A. HYDE, Esq., late City Recorder, and very generally known in the city. He died yesterday afternoon, after much suffering. Yesterday the Criminal Court, Recorder's Court, and several Justices' Courts were closed in testimony of respect to the deceased. The funeral will take place tomorrow. The Liberty Fire Company, of which the deceased was a member, propose to attend it in a body. Mr. Hyde came to this city in 1836 or 1837, having removed from the District of Columbia to try his fortune in the West. He practised law for awhile. Subsequently he served under Mr. Gamble as a clerk in the Circuit Court, and was afterwards elected Justice of the Peace in the Fourth Ward, which office he held several years. During that period he was elected two or three times to represent the Ward in the City Council. In 1848, he was elected City

Daily National Intelligencer, Marriage and Death Notices, 1851-1854

Recorder, and again in 1852. The deceased was possessed of many estimable qualities, and leaves an interesting family and a large circle of friends to mourn his death. [Resolution described and adopted.] (28 FEB 1853)

MARRIAGE. On Sabbath evening [27 FEB 1853], by the Rev. John C. Smith, Mr. BENJAMIN POLGLASE to Miss E. CROWN, all of this city. (1 MAR 1853)

DEATH. In Baltimore, on Monday, the 28th ult. [28 FEB 1853], after a protracted illness, Mrs. ANN DANIELS, aged 35 years, formerly of this city. Her funeral will take place at 3 o'clock P.M. this day, March 1st, from the residence of Mr. Daniel S. Harkness, H street, between 11th and 12th streets. The friends of the family are invited to attend. (1 MAR 1853)

DEATH. On the 28th February, JOHN B. JOHNSON, in the 43d year of his age. His funeral will take place from the residence of his brother James Johnson, on Greenleaf's Point, this evening, at 2 o'clock. (1 MAR 1853)

DEATH. On Monday evening, the 28th ult. [28 FEB 1853], Miss MARY E. BIRCKHEAD, in the 77th year of her age. Her funeral will take place from her late residence on 4½ street, this evening at 3 o'clock. The friends of the family are invited to attend. (2 MAR 1853)

DEATH. On Monday evening, 28th ult. [28 FEB 1853], at 8 o'clock, MARY, daughter of the late Greenbury Gaither, after an illness of several months, throughout which she manifested that submissive resignation and experienced those sustaining consolations which only attend the suffering and departure of the truly pious. The church, of which she was a devoted member, feel and lament their loss, and her young associates deeply sympathize in the sorrow of her bereaved relatives. The friends of the family are invited to attend the funeral services this afternoon, at 3½ o'clock, at the E Street Baptist Church. (2 MAR 1853)

DEATH. In this city, on Wednesday, March 2d, JABEZ B. BOOKER, Esq., in the 61st year of his age. The friends of the family are requested to attend the funeral at his late residence, corner of 6th and F streets, this (Thursday) afternoon, at half-past 3 o'clock. (3 MAR 1853)

DEATH. On Wednesday morning, March 2d, VARNUM, second son of Silas H. and Mary B. Hill, aged four years and seven months. The friends of the family are respectfully invited to attend the funeral, at 12 o'clock this day, from the residence of his parents, corner of E and 6th streets. (3 MAR 1853)

DEATH. On the morning of the 27th of February, GEORGE C., son of Mary A. and Geo. C. Jackson. (3 MAR 1853)

DEATH. on the 3d inst., Mrs. JULIET D., wife of Matthew G. Emery. The friends of the family are respectfully invited to attend her funeral on Saturday, the 5th inst., at 10 o'clock, from Wesley Chapel, corner of 5th and F streets. (4 MAR 1853)

DEATH. On the night of the 2d inst., Miss JANE BIRTH. Her funeral will move from Wesley Chapel at 3 o'clock this afternoon. Her friends, and those of the family, are invited. (4 MAR 1853)

DEATH. Departed this life, in this city, on the 1st inst., Mrs. SARAH HAMILTON, in the fortieth year of her age, consort of the late Evan Hamilton, of Baltimore. (4 MAR 1853)

DEATH. In this city, on the 3d inst., WM. P. McKINSTRY, in the 42d year of his age. His friends are respectfully invited to attend his funeral at his late residence on D street, on Sunday morning, the 6th inst., at 10 o'clock A.M. (5 MAR 1853)

DEATH. On the 3d inst., at the residence of his son-in-law, F.G. Skinner, Dr. PHILIP THORNTON, of Montpelier, Rappahannock Co., Va. (5 MAR 1853)

DEATH. On the 3d inst., HENRY THOMAS, youngest son of James R. and Elizabeth C. Ferguson, in the second her of his age. The friends of the family are respectfully invited to attend his funeral from the residence of his father, corner of 3d street east and E street south, today at three o'clock P.M. (5 MAR 1853)

MARRIAGE. On the 3d inst., WILLIAM REILY, U.S. Navy, to Miss ELLEN T. ROCHE, of Washington. (7 MAR 1853)

MARRIAGE. At Oswego, N.Y., on the 2d inst., by the Rev. Robert Condict, WM. EGBERT HARVEY, C.E., of Washington, to Miss HARRIETT M., daughter of Capt. John Eno, of the former place. (7 MAR 1853)

DEATH. On the 4th inst., ANNIE, daughter of Capt. Sutherland, of the Marine Corps, aged 21 months. The funeral will take place this (Monday) afternoon, at 1 o'clock, from the residence of her grandfather, Maj. Nicholson. (7 MAR 1853)

DEATH. In this city, on the 6th inst., after a few days' illness, of scarlet fever, BELL, only daughter of John and Margaret Kelly, aged six years. The friends of the family are invited to attend the funeral on this (Monday) afternoon, at 4 o'clock, from the residence, corner of D and 8th streets. (7 MAR 1853)

DEATH. On Friday morning, the 4th inst., LUCY WADSWORTH, infant daughter of J.B.H. and Henrietta Smith. (7 MAR 1853)

DEATH. At Upperville, Va., on the 1st inst., aged eight years, BROWN, son of Rev. H.W. and Abigail B. Dodge. (7 MAR 1853)

DEATH. At Mt. Hope, Sisters of Charity, Md., on the 5th inst., Mrs. JANE EDGAR, wife of John Edgar, of Washington. (7 MAR 1853)

DEATH. On the 7th inst., at half-past 7 o'clock A.M., after a few hours' illness, WILLIAM, eldest son of Wm. D. and Isabella A. Brackenbridge, aged 3 years and 4 months. The friends of the family are respectfully invited to attend the funeral, from their residence on 6th street, between G and H streets, this afternoon, at three o'clock. (8 MAR 1853)

DEATH. On the morning of the 7th inst., ELIZABETH GARNET, youngest daughter of Richard and Margaret Downer, aged 2 years and 1 month. The friends of the family are invited to attend her funeral, from the residence of her parents, on 11th street, between E and F streets, this afternoon, at three o'clock. (8 MAR 1853)

DEATH. On the morning of the 8th inst., of scarlatina, MARY ELIZABETH, eldest daughter of Jesse B. and Anna A. Wilson, aged two years and eight months. The friends and relatives of the family are invited to attend the funeral this (Wednesday) morning, at 10 o'clock, from her father's residence, on Ninth street, between I street and New York avenue. (9 MAR 1853)

MARRIAGE. In this city, on the 9th inst., at the Unitarian Church, by Rev. Dr. Dewey, EDWARD JONES and MARY REBECCA MOORE, daughter of Jacob B. Moore, Esq., of San Francisco, Calif. (10 MAR 1853)

MARRIAGE. On Tuesday evening [8 MAR 1853], by the Rev. John C. Smith, Mr. JOSIAH TRUMAN to Miss MARTHA LANGFITT, all of this city. (10 MAR 1853)

MARRIAGE. On Wednesday afternoon [9 MAR 1853], by the Rev. John C. Smith, Mr. JOHN PARHAM to Miss MARGARET S. ROWAN, all of this city. (10 MAR 1853)

Daily National Intelligencer, Marriage and Death Notices, 1851-1854

MARRIAGE. At Alexandria, on the 2d inst., by the Rev. J.N. Danforth, Mr. CHARLES A. BALDWIN and Miss MARIA LOUISA McVEIGH, all of Alexandria, Va. (11 MAR 1853)

MARRIAGE. At the Second Presbyterian Church, on the 9th inst., by the Rev. J.R. Eckard, Mr. WM. H. BALDWIN and Miss CORNELIA A. GILMAN, youngest daughter of the late E. Gilman, Esq., all of this city. (11 MAR 1853)

DEATH. In this city, on the 10th inst., FRANCIS CLARK, youngest son of J.J. and M.F. Greenough, aged six years. The funeral will take place this (Thursday) afternoon, at 3 o'clock. (11 MAR 1853)

DEATH. On the 11th inst., at 5 o'clock, A.M. at his residence in Alexandria, Va., Capt. CHARLES McKNIGHT, in the 76th year of his age. Born in Baltimore, he passed the greater part of his long life in Alexandria. He there commanded a volunteer company in active service in the war of 1812. Though a young man at the time of Gen. Washington's death, he was one of his personal friends. Thus is severed another one of the links connecting us with the past. His funeral will take place on Sunday, the 13th inst., at 3 o'clock P.M. (12 MAR 1853)

DEATH. Departed this life, in this city, at 4 o'clock A.M. the 11th inst., after a long and severe affliction of chronic pulmonary consumption, which she bore with Christian resignation to the will of God, Mrs. ELIZABETH F. MADDOX, consort of the late Wm. R. Maddox, formerly of Charles Co., Md., but for many years a resident of this city. She was a kind and affectionate wife, devoted to her children, a warm and sincere friend, and beloved by all who knew her. *May she rest in peace*! Her friends and acquaintances are respectfully invited to attend her funeral on Sunday afternoon, at half-past three o'clock, from her late residence, corner of 3d street east and N street south, near the Eastern Branch. (12 MAR 1853)

MARRIAGE. On Thursday afternoon [10 MAR 1853], by the Rev. John C. Smith, Mr. JAMES W. McDANIEL to Miss ELLEN O. ANDERSON, all of this city. (14 MAR 1853)

MARRIAGE. At St. Louis, Mo., on the 2d inst., by Rev. Mr. Clerc, THOMAS W. OSBODBY, of this city, to Miss SARAH L. DUBBS, of the former place. (14 MAR 1853)

DEATH. On the 12th inst., Mrs. SARAH, consort of F.B. Huggins, in the 63d year of her age. The friends and acquaintances of the family are respectfully requested to attend the funeral this (Monday) afternoon, at 3 o'clock, from her late residence on the corner of 4th street and New York avenue, without further notice. (14 MAR 1853)

DEATH. Near Leesburg, Va., on Friday last [11 MAR 1853], Mr. ELEAZER THOMAS, a revolutionary soldier, in his 96th year. (15 MAR 1853)

DEATH. At his residence in Prince George's Co., Md., on the morning of the 3d inst., after a long and painful illness, which he bore with great fortitude and patience, Mr. HORATIO M. WARD, aged 54 years. (15 MAR 1853)

MARRIAGE. On the 14th inst., in F Street Church, by the Rev. James Laurie, D.D., Mr. JOSEPH HARVEY NOURSE, son of the Rev. James Nourse, and Miss ISABEL LAURIE RITTENHOUSE, daughter of Benjamin F. Rittenhouse, Esq., and grand-daughter of Dr. Laurie. Mr. Nourse goes out a Missionary among the Choctaw Indians, and will be stationed at Spencer. (16 MAR 1853)

MARRIAGE. On the 15th inst., by the Rev. Dr. Junkin, Mr. FRANKLIN BUTTERFIELD, of Illinois, and Miss NANNIE H., daughter of I.H. Wailes, Esq., of this city. (17 MAR 1853)

DEATH. At Neabsco, Prince William Co., Va., on the 4th inst., in the 81st year of her age, Mrs. ARAMINTA MONTGOMERY KANKEY, widow of the late Rev. Zebulon Kankey, of that county. (17 MAR 1853)

DEATH. On the 16th inst., in this city, Mr. THOS. NICHOLSON, in his thirty-fourth year. His friends are requested to attend his funeral tomorrow afternoon, at 3 o'clock, from the corner of F and 26th streets west. (17 MAR 1853)

DEATH. In Georgetown, on the 16th inst., HENRY TRUNNELL, after a short illness, of paralysis, aged 62 years. The friends of the family are respectfully invited to attend his funeral, at half-past ten o'clock this (Thursday) morning, at his residence on Fayette street, Georgetown. (17 MAR 1853)

DEATH. At the residence of Jonathan Seaver, Esq., near this city, on Sunday, the 13th inst., ELIZABETH SEAVER, infant daughter of Hon. George G. and Elizabeth C. King, aged 10 months. (17 MAR 1853)

DEATH. On Monday, the 14th inst., MARION, only child of J.W. and the late M.A.K. Baden, aged six months and one day. (17 MAR 1853)

DEATH. In Claiborne Co., Miss., on the 27th of February, of typhoid fever, JAMES GREEN RAILEY, aged 26, eldest son of Col. James Railey, of Adams Co., Miss. (18 MAR 1853)

DEATH. At the National Hotel yesterday [17 MAR 1853], Mr. GEORGE E. BARTOL, of Boston. (18 and 19 MAR 1853)

MARRIAGE. On the 17th inst., by the Rev. A.W. Wayman, Mr. ROBERT B. GREEN, of Georgetown, to ADDEL JOHNSON, of Washington. (19 MAR 1853)

MARRIAGE. On the 17th inst., by the Rev. A.W. Wayman, Mr. HENRY LEE, of Washington, to Miss JULIA HARRIS, of Baltimore, Md. (19 MAR 1853)

MARRIAGE. In this city, on Tuesday, 15th inst., by the Rev. D.X. Junkin, D.D., Mr. FRANKLIN BUTTERFIELD, of Illinois, to Miss MARY N.H. WAILES, of this city. (19 MAR 1853)

DEATH. In Nashville, on the 7th inst., MORGAN W. BROWN, U.S. District Judge of the district of Tennessee [text continues]. (21 MAR 1853)

DEATH. In this city, on Friday, the 18th inst., WILLIAM CORRIE, aged 5 months and 18 days, son of W.C. and M.J.C. Lipscomb. (21 MAR 1853)

DEATH. Yesterday morning, 20th March 1853, GEORGIANA HILL GREER, infant daughter of James C. and Henrietta Greer. Her funeral will take place from the residence of her grandfather, Wm. Greer, on Eleventh street, between G and H streets, today at 4 P.M., where the friends and acquaintances of the family are respectfully invited to attend without further notice. (21 MAR 1853)

MARRIAGE. At Alexandria, Va., on the 17th inst., by the Rev. C. Dana, LOUIS A. GARNETT, of San Francisco, Calif., to MARIA CHAMPE, daughter of Muscoe Garnett, Esq., of Essex Co., Va. (22 MAR 1853)

MARRIAGE. At the Church of the Epiphany [no date], by the Rev. Mr. French, GEORGE PATTEN to EMMA HAMILTON, daughter of Richard Patten. (22 MAR 1853)

MARRIAGE. At St. Matthew's Church, on the 19th inst., by the Rev. James B. Donelan, GEORGE A. YOUNG, of Nevada, Calif., to MARTHA ROSALIE ANDERSON, of this city. (22 MAR 1853)

DEATH. At Poplar Hill, Prince George's Co., Md., on the 18th inst., ROBERT D. SEWALL, Esq., in the 61st year of his age, a most worthy and esteemed gentleman, and highly respected and beloved by all who knew him. (22 MAR 1853)

DEATH. At New York city, on the 15th inst., ELIZABETH, eldest daughter of the late Elias Kane, for many years a resident of this city. (22 MAR 1853)

DEATH. At Georgetown, on Sunday evening, the 20th inst., Miss ELIZABETH M. COX, in the 25th year of her age. The friends of the family are invited to attend her funeral on this (Tuesday) afternoon, from the residence of W.S. Cox, at four o'clock. The deceased had been for years a prey to the keenest suffering [text continues]. (22 MAR 1853)

DEATH. On the 14th inst., at Portici, Prince William Co., Va., ALFRED BALL, Esq., in the 55th year of his age. This afflictive dispensation will be deeply mourned by a widely extended circle of friends and acquaintances, to whom he was endeared by his many noble qualities and sterling virtues [text continues]. (22 MAR 1853)

DEATH. The latest dates from California bring intelligence of the death of Passed Midshipman E.D. DENNY, of the U.S. Navy, who died at Sonoma, at the residence of his relative, the Hon. Charles P. Wilkins, in the 28th year of his age. It appears from the Naval Register that this young gentleman took a high number in his numerous date, and that his proportion of sea service was unusually large. He served in the Gulf during the war with Mexico, and for the last four years has been on the Pacific coast, attached to the Coast Survey of California and Oregon. He was remarkable for his prepossessing appearance and gentlemanly bearing, and had the reputation of being a young gentleman of fine talents, energy, and courage. (22 MAR 1853)

DEATH. On Friday, the 18th inst., of scarlet fever, LYDIA LUCILLE, youngest daughter of James M. and Elizabeth R. McRea, aged eight years. (22 MAR 1853)

MARRIAGE. On Tuesday, the 22 inst., in F Street Church, city of Washington, by the Rev. James Laurie, D.D., Mr. JAMES C. DELLETT, of Mifflin Co., Pa., to Miss JEANETTE AULD, of Washington. Mr. Dellett goes as a Missionary among the Omaha Indians. (23 MAR 1853)

DEATH. In Baltimore, on the 19th inst., JAMES LAWRENCE, aged four years, second son of Thomas H. and Julia Parsons, of this city. (23 MAR 1853)

MARRIAGE. On Tuesday evening, the 22d inst., by the Rev. Mr. French, Mr. THOMAS HITAFFER to Miss MARGARET HILL, all of this city. (24 MAR 1853)

DEATH. In this city, on the 23d inst., Miss ANN WELSH, after a painful and protracted illness. She was for many years a resident of this city, and was a kind friend and a sincere Christian. May she rest in peace! Her funeral will take place this day, (Thursday,) at half past 3 o'clock P.M., from the residence of Mr. R. Burdine, on H street, near the corner of 7th street, and her friends are invited to attend. (24 MAR 1853)

DEATH. On Tuesday evening [22 MAR 1853], after a brief illness, Mr. GEORGE HENRY McDUELL, aged 28 years. His friends and acquaintances are respectfully invited to attend his funeral from his late residence on L street, between 9th and 10th, this morning at 10 o'clock. (24 MAR 1853)

DEATH. Departed this life, on the 23d inst., at Clermont, Fairfax Co., Va., (the residence of her father,) EMILY C.W. FORREST, consort of A.F. Warley, U.S. Navy, and only daughter of Capt. F. Forrest, U.S.N. Her funeral will take place from St. John's Church on Friday, at 1 o'clock P.M. (24 MAR 1853)

DEATH. On Saturday, 19th February, at 10 o'clock A.M., JAMES D. WALLER, aged 59 years. (24 MAR 1853)

Daily National Intelligencer, Marriage and Death Notices, 1851-1854

MARRIAGE. In this city, on Thursday, the 24th inst., by the Rev. T.W. Sampson, FRANKLIN C. GRAY, Esq., of California, to MATILDA C., daughter of the late James French, of Warrenton, Va. (25 and 26 MAR 1853)

DEATH. On Wednesday morning last [23 MAR 1853], in this city, JOHN, infant son of Robert A. and Anne Sommerville, aged three weeks and four days. (25 MAR 1853)

MARRIAGE. On the 24th March, by the Rev. G.W. Samson, Mr. CHARLES W. HAVENNER to Miss MARGARET T. WAKE, all of this city. (26 MAR 1853)

MARRIAGE. On Thursday evening [24 MAR 1853], by the Rev. John C. Smith, Mr. JAMES LAVENDER to Miss MARY ELLEN ENGLISH, all of this city. (26 MAR 1853)

DEATH. On the 24th inst., Mr. JOHN BORLAND, in the 54th year of his age. His funeral will take place from his late residence on Fifteenth street, between L and M, tomorrow (Sunday) the 27th inst., at 3 o'clock, to which the friends of the family are respectfully invited to attend. (26 MAR 1853)

DEATH. On the 25th inst., JOSEPH W. ECKLOFF, eldest son of Christian and Sarah Eckloff, aged 35 years. (26 MAR 1853)

DEATH. In this city, on the 23d inst., SOPHIA CLAUSS, wife of F.C. Clauss. (26 MAR 1853)

DEATH. On the 26th inst., FRANCIS X. MASTERSON, in the 33d year of his age, late of New Orleans. His funeral will take place this day, 28th inst., at 3 o'clock P.M., from the residence of his mother, Fairfax street, Alexandria, Va. (28 MAR 1853)

DEATH. On the 26th inst., after a brief but painful illness, GEORGE H. WRIGHT, aged 34 years. The friends of the family of the deceased are respectfully requested to attend his funeral from his late residence, this day, the 28th, at 2 o'clock P.M. (28 MAR 1853)

DEATH. In this city, on the 27th inst., Mrs. MARY WHITCOMB, aged thirty-eight years. Her funeral will take place today, at 4 o'clock, at the residence of her sister, Mrs. Emily Dexter, on E street, between 9th and 10th. (28 MAR 1853)

DEATH. In Georgetown, on Thursday morning last, 24th inst., Mrs. ELLEN JEWELL, in the 37th year of her age. (29 MAR 1853)

DEATH. On yesterday, 28th inst., MARY EFFIE, infant daughter of Sidney and Mary Ann Bassett. (29 MAR 1853)

DEATH. In this city, yesterday [28 MAR 1853], AMELIA BERTHA, child of F. and Susan Wingenroth, aged ten months. The friends of the family are invited to attend the funeral on Wednesday afternoon, at 3 o'clock. (29 MAR 1853)

DATH. On Monday night, March 29th, Mrs. MARY C. BRUSH, aged 90 years... Her remains will be placed at St. Patrick's Church at 4 o'clock this afternoon, where her friends are requested to attend. (30 MAR 1853)

DEATH. On March 29th, THOMAS BEVAN, aged 61 years, a native of Llangavellach, South Wales, and a resident of this city for the last ten years. His friends are invited to attend his funeral this afternoon, at 4 o'clock, from his late residence, corner of 13th and D streets, without further notice. (30 MAR 1853)

DEATH. Suddenly, on the 17th inst., at Woodbury, St. Mary's Co., Md., CATHARINE MILLARD, in the 74th year of her age. Few lives present a more constant and untiring practice of the Christian virtues than hers,

Daily National Intelligencer, Marriage and Death Notices, 1851-1854

and none afford better evidences of the promptness and efficacy with which religion is always ready to minister to the pangs of affliction. (30 MAR 1853)

DIED. It is with unaffected sorrow that we announce the death of Mrs. ABIGAIL FILLMORE, the excellent wife of Ex-President Fillmore. She died yesterday morning, at Willard's Hotel, in this city, aged fifty-six years. Mrs. Fillmore was the youngest child of the late Rev. Lemuel and Abigail Powers, of New York. She was attacked on the 6th instant with bronchial inflammation of the lungs, which was soon followed with suffusion of water; a combined disease was thus formed which resisted the most eminent medical skill. All that affection could suggest and a sympathizing community offer was most cordially rendered to the sufferer... She expired at 9 o'clock A.M., without a struggle or a groan, surrounded by her afflicted family, in hope of a blessed immortality. Her remains will be taken to Buffalo for interment. (31 MAR 1853)

DEATH. At 5 o'clock yesterday morning, the 31st of March, after an illness of a few hours, Mrs. MARY ANN RIVES, wife of John C. Rives, Esq., Editor of the "*Glove*," in the 43d year of her age. Mrs. Rives was a lady of the most estimable qualities of head and heart. She was self-educated, but well educated, and she devoted all the means which her energy and talent gave in her early years to bring comforts within her widowed mother's house... Mrs. Rives was religious, and this consoled her amid apprehensions, caused by the state of her health, and which too truly anticipated the sad result. This, too, offers all the consolation that can be given to her afflicted husband and the seven young children she has left to his care. The funeral will take place today, at 4 o'clock, at Mr. Rives's residence, where his friends will attend. (1 APR 1853)

DEATH. At Hedgesville, Berkeley Co., Va., on the 14th ult. [14 MAR 1853], Miss ELIZABETH MOUNTZ, aged 22 years, youngest daughter of the late Jacob Mountz, of Georgetown, D.C. [text continues]. (1 APR 1853)

DEATH. In Philadelphia, on the 22d ult. [22 MAR 1853], Mr. DAVID P. SIMMONS, in the 84th year of his age. Mr. Simmons was a native of Pennsylvania, but lived in this city some time, soon after its being laid out, where he has now residing a number of grand and great grand-children. The deceased lived an exemplary Christian, beloved by his friends and respected by all who knew him, and died in the full hope of a blessed immortality. (1 APR 1853)

DEATH. On the 26th March, at Lucymont, Calvert Co., Md., in the 21st year of her age, LUCY A. SPICKNALL, wife of John W. Spicknall, Esq., and daughter of the late Capt. H. Garner, U.S. Army. (1 APR 1853)

DEATH. On Thursday [31 MAR 1853], at 11 P.M., Mrs. JOAHANNAH ELIZABETH CLAXTON, consort of Mr. A.B. Claxton, in the 34th year of her age. She bore her sufferings, which were great, with the patience and fortitude of a Christian, and left behind the pleasing assurance of having attained to a blessed immortality. Her funeral will take place this afternoon, from her late residence on Ninth street, at 3 o'clock P.M. The relatives and friends of the family are respectfully requested to attend. (2 APR 1853)

DEATH. In New Orleans, March 16th, Mrs. ELLEN W. McCORMICK, wife of Dr. Charles McCormick, U.S. Army, and daughter of the late William Wirt [text continues]. (2 APR 1853)

MARRIAGE. On the 22d of March, at the residence of her father, BEN. EDWARDS GREY, of Kentucky, member of the last Congress, to Mrs. ELIZA FRANCES CARSON, daughter of Col. Thornton B. Goldsby, of Summerfield, Dallas Co., Ark. (4 APR 1853)

DEATH. On Sunday, the 27th ult. [27 MAR 1853], FLAVEL S.M. WOOTTON, of Mt. Pleasant, Henry Co., Iowa, formerly of Rockville, Md., in the 23d year of his age--one of the victims of the melancholy accident on the Baltimore and Ohio railroad above Cumberland. (4 APR 1853)

Daily National Intelligencer, Marriage and Death Notices, 1851-1854

DEATH. At Catonville, Md., on the 24th March, Mrs. RACHEL ROBERTSON, aged 74 years. (4 APR 1853)

DEATH. The last mail from Santa Fe brought intelligence of the death of Lieut. CLARENDON J.L. WILSON, of the 1st regiment of Dragoons, at Albuquerque, on the 21st of February. Lieut. Wilson graduated at West Point in 1846, was breveted 1st lieut. February 4, 1847, for "gallant and meritorious conduct in the conflicts at Embordo and Taos, N.M." In one of the conflicts with the Navajo Indians, a party of four, consisting of Maj. Grier, Lieut. Wilson, Sergeant Price, and a private of Dragoons, becoming separated from the main party and surrounded by a large and formidable body of mounted Navajoes, extricated themselves by an exercise of the most determined bravery and skill, killing two of the Indian chiefs. His death will be deeply mourned by his numerous friends and brother officers, to whom he was endeared by the highest qualities which should distinguish a soldier. (4 APR 1853)

MARRIAGE. On Monday morning [4 APR 1853], by the Rev. John C. Smith, Mr. JOHN W. ANDERSON to Miss ANN ELIZABETH COFFER, both of Virginia. (5 APR 1853)

DEATH. On Monday afternoon, 4th inst., WM. MANN, son of Charles Mann, aged 17 years. His funeral will take place on Wednesday morning, at 10 o'clock, from the residence of his father, opposite the Patent Office, where the friends of the family are requested to attend. (5 APR 1853)

DEATH. On the 1st inst., after a short illness, at her residence on East Capitol street, Mrs. SARAH A.J. PATTERSON, aged 63 years. (5 APR 1853)

DEATH. In this city, on Friday morning last [1 APR 1853], in the 27th year of her age, CYNTHIA S., wife of R.W. Burgess, and youngest daughter of I.I. Baldwin, Esq., of Buffalo, N.Y. Gentle, amiable, and lovely in all the relations of life, her piety and purity of character were fitly and beautifully exemplified in the serenity of her death. (5 APR 1853)

DEATH. On Sunday last, the 3d inst., at the residence of her son, J.R. Dorsey, in this city, HOPEWELL, widow of the late Hon. Walter Dorsey, Chief Judge of the sixth judicial district of Maryland, leaving a large family connexion and circle of friends to mourn the loss of one whose long life was a practical illustration of every social and Christian virtue. (5 APR 1853)

DEATH. Died at Georgetown College, D.C., on Saturday morning last, 26th ult. [26 MAR 1853], THOMAS BELT MAGRUDER, eldest son of Caleb C. Magruder, Esq., of Upper Marlboro, in the 17th year of his age... At the time of his death he had barely commenced his collegiate course, having entered Georgetown College but a few days before sickness overtook him, and soon overthrew an already enfeebled constitution... *Marlborough Advocate.* (5 APR 1853)

MARRIAGE. In Boston, Mass., on the 28th ult. [28 MAR 1853], by the Rev. Dr. Frothingham, CHARLES EDWARD BROWN SEQUARD, M.D., of Paris, to Miss ELLEN FLETCHER, daughter of the late Timothy Fletcher, of Boston. (6 APR 1853)

DEATH. On Monday, the 4th inst., in the 86th year of his age, LUND WASHINGTON. He was born in King George Co., Va., and for 29 years resided in that State. For 56 years he has lived in this city, where, after an illness of near three months, he met his death with Christian resignation and hope. His funeral will take place this (Wednesday) afternoon, at half-past four o'clock, from the Church of the Epiphany, on G street. The friends of the deceased, and of the family, are respectfully invited to attend. (6 APR 1853)

DEATH. At the Hot Springs, Ark., on the 18th ult. [18 MAR 1853], HEBE G., wife of Capt. Thomas R. Gedney, U.S. Navy. In the early part of last winter Mrs. Gedney left her home in this city to accompany her afflicted husband to the springs, with the hope that his sufferings might find alleviation. There she continued during the winter, assiduous in her attention to her suffering companion, until, smitten down by his side with paralysis, she died. By the death of this estimable lady a chasm has been made in the large circle of her friends which in this world cannot be filled; her bereaved relatives have lost one tenderly beloved; her affectionate and afflicted husband has been bereft of the chief solace of his heart, the tender and sympathizing partner of his joys and sorrows; and her church (F Street Presbyterian) mourns one of its brightest ornaments. The gallant heart of her fond husband, which never quailed in the hour of danger, lies bleeding under this blow. But it is his privilege, and that of all her surviving friends, to find consolation in the lovely profs which memory cherishes that she was an heir of immortal glory. (6 APR 1853)

DEATH. On the 5th inst., Mrs. MARGARETTA MECHLIN, widow of the late Jos. Mechlin, of this city. The friends of the family are respectfully invited to attend her funeral from the residence of her son, 19th near I street, this afternoon, at 3½ o'clock. (7 APR 1853)

DEATH. On the 6th inst., WILLIAM, third child of J. Robert and Elizabeth Sutton, aged two years and four months. The friends of the family are invited to attend the funeral this (Friday) afternoon, at 3 o'clock, from the residence on Ninth street, between D and E streets. (8 and 9 APR 1853)

DEATH. On Tuesday night last, the 5th inst., Miss MARY ANN MOUNTZ, daughter of John Mountz. Her funeral will take place from her father's residence, Bridge street, Georgetown, this afternoon, at four o'clock. (9 APR 1853)

DEATH. On the 8th inst., ANNA LILLY, daughter of John Y. Bryant, aged eight months. Funeral from the father's residence this day, at 4 o'clock P.M. (9 APR 1853)

DEATH. On the 6th inst., WILLIAM, aged two years and four months, and on the 8th inst., REBECCA, aged nine months, children of J. Robert and Elizabeth Sutton. The friends of the family are invited to attend the funeral on this (Saturday) afternoon at 3 o'clock, from the residence on Ninth street, between D and E streets. (9 APR 1853)

MARRIAGE. On Thursday evening, the 7th inst., by the Rev. Jas. B. Donelan, A.L. NEWTON to Miss MARY F. NEVINS, all of this city. (11 APR 1853)

DEATH. In this city, on Saturday, the 9th inst., between the hours of 12 and 1 P.M., CHARLES McGARVEY, aged 32 years, a native of the county of Donegal, Ireland, but for the last 14 years a resident of this city. His friends and acquaintances are invited to attend his funeral at 4 o'clock P.M. this day, the 11th from his late residence, on the corner of 27th and K streets north. (11 APR 1853)

DEATH. On Thursday evening, the 7th inst., ANNIE BLANCHE, aged 9 years, daughter of J.B.H. and A.S. Fulton. (11 APR 1853)

MARRIAGE. In this city, on Sunday, 10th inst., by the Rev. G.W. Samson, Mr. WILLIAM P. BROWN to Miss AMANDA A. MITCHELL, both of Washington. (12 APR 1853)

DEATH. On the 11th inst., Mr. WILLIAM GARDENER, aged 53 years. His funeral will take place this afternoon at 3 o'clock, from his residence on C street, between 11th and 12th streets. (12 APR 1853)

OBITUARY. Died, at his residence in Marietta, Ohio, in the morning of the 3d of April. 1853, DUDLEY WOODBRIDGE, Esq., in the 75th year of his age... Many, very many years ago he became a professing member of the Church of God upon earth; and since that eventful period his whole life, to his latest breath, has demonstrated the sincerity of his professions, the fervency of his zeal, and his unwavering faith in the promises of the gospel. (13 APR 1853)

DEATH. After a few days' illness, ALFRED BRYANT, youngest child of Emma and the late Rev. Wm. Bryant, of Virginia. The funeral will take place at the residence of his mother, on G street, south side, between 13th and 14th, at 10 o'clock A.M., this day, the 13th inst. (13 APR 1853)

Daily National Intelligencer, Marriage and Death Notices, 1851-1854

DEATH. In this city, on Sunday morning, the 10th inst., MARGARET ANN, daughter of John and Eliza Ann Marron, aged two years and six months. (13 APR 1853)

DEATH. On the 11th inst., after a short but severe illness of scarlet fever, JOHN MALCOM, aged four years eleven months and eight days, son of John H. and Virginia Cooke. (13 APR 1853)

DEATH. On Wednesday morning, the 13th inst., ROBERT HENDERSON CAFFEE, Esq., formerly of Lancaster, Ohio, in the 38th year of his age. His friends and acquaintances are respectfully invited to attend his funeral, from the residence of Mrs. Weaver, on 15th street, between L and M streets, this (Thursday) afternoon, at 4 o'clock. (14 APR 1853)

DEATH. On Thursday, the 14th inst., of consumption, JOHN F. CRAMPTON, in the 25th year of his age. (15 APR 1853)

DEATH. Capt. THOMAS T. WEBB, of the U.S. Navy, died on the 11th inst., at his residence in Norfolk, Va. He entered the navy in 1808. (15 APR 1853)

MARRIAGE. On the 12th inst., by Rev. N. Schlosser, ROBERT KELLY to MARY MOTHERSHEAD, all of this city. (16 APR 1853)

DEATH. In this city, at 9 o'clock P.M. Thursday, the 14th inst., JOHN B. TEEPLE, formerly of Philadelphia. His funeral will take place, at 2 o'clock P.M. on Sunday, 17th, from the Masonic Hall, corner of 10th and E streets. The members of St. John's Lodge No. 11, and Master Masons generally, are requested to attend at the above place and hour. (16 APR 1853)

OBITUARY. Died, at his residence in Aldie, Loudoun Co., Va., on Wednesday, the 13th day of April, LEWIS BERKELEY, Esq., in the 64th year of his age. Mr. Berkeley was born at "Barn Elms," in the county of Middlesex, and was descended from one among the most ancient and respectable families in Virginia. After he had completed his education at William and Mary College, he took possession of his patrimonial estate, and became a highly respected and successful planter and farmer. Having been brought up in the most exemplary observance of all the rites and ceremonies of the Protestant Episcopal church, he had been for many years a worthy communicant of that church, a member of the vestry, and frequently a lay delegate to the annual Convention of the Protestant Episcopal Church in Virginia. He was a gentleman of courteous manners, and distinguished for a high sense of humor, a sound understanding, a correct judgment, a benevolent heart, and a manly firmness and independence of character. He was a most devoted husband, an affectionate father, a humane and indulgent master, and a kind friend and neighbor [text continues]. (16 APR 1853)

MARRIAGE. On Sunday, 17th inst., by the Rev. Mr. Hodges, WILLIAM G. RICHARDS to Miss MARY R. ADAMS, all of Charles Co., Md. (18 APR 1853)

DEATH. On the 16th inst., Mrs. ELIZABETH O'DRISCOLL, in the 68th year of her age. Her friends and those of the family are respectfully invited to attend her funeral from her late residence on 10th street, between G and H, this (Monday) afternoon at 4 o'clock. (18 APR 1853)

DEATH. On Saturday night, at 12 o'clock, CORDELIA, daughter of W.N. and Ann C. Ball, aged about five years. The friends of the family are requested to attend the funeral on Monday evening, at 3 o'clock, on 13th, near G street. (18 APR 1853)

DEATH. At his residence in this city, yesterday, the 18th inst., after a brief illness, and in the peaceful hope of a happy immortality, the Rev. JAMES LAURIE, D.D., for half a century the Pastor of F Street Presbyterian Church. His funeral will proceed from his late residence, in E street, at 3 o'clock tomorrow (Wednesday) afternoon, to the F Street Presbyterian Church, where the services will commence at 3½ o'clock. The friends of the family are invited to attend without further notice. (19 APR 1853)

Daily National Intelligencer, Marriage and Death Notices, 1851-1854

MARRIAGE. On Saturday morning last [16 APR 1853], by the Rev. Dr. O'Toole, LOUIS F. TASISTRO, of Ireland, to Miss CATHERINE QUIN, of Norfolk, Va. (22 APR 1853)

MARRIAGE. At Baltimore, on the morning of the 21st inst., by the Rev. Mr. Morgan, EDWIN LILLY, of Lexington, Ky., to ANNA JOSEPHINE, daughter of Col. Jas. L. Ridgely, of Baltimore Co. (22 APR 1853)

MARRIAGE. On Thursday afternoon, the 21st inst., by the Rev. Chas. A. Davis, Mr. CHAS. C. TUCKER to Miss MARY VIRGINIA CROSS, all of this city. (23 APR 1853)

DEATH. On Thursday evening [21 APR 1853], after an illness of a few weeks, borne with exemplary calmness, Mrs. JANE AGNES COPPER, as she was extensively known to the society of Washington, and valued and respected in all her associations, so the sorrow for her loss will be deep and universal. The friends of the family are invited to attend her funeral from the residence of Mr. George W. Riggs, this (Saturday) afternoon at 4 o'clock. (23 APR 1853)

DEATH. On Friday morning, 22d inst., WILLIAM J. BARRY, son of the late Francis Barry, Sr., in the 27th year of his age. To a disposition of uncommon cheerfulness the deceased united a kindness of heart and manner which gained for him the esteem of a large number of friends, and his loss will be severely felt in that circle in which he was so great a favorite. He bore his protracted illness with singular calmness, and, consoled by the ministrations of religion, his end was peace. His funeral will take place at his late residence, tomorrow (Sunday) evening, at 3 o'clock. (23 APR 1853)

DEATH. On the 12th inst., at the residence of his brother, in the city of Washington, PATRICK GIVENY, at the advanced age of 73 years. He was a man highly esteemed and beloved by all who knew him. *Requiescat in pace*! His friends and acquaintances are respectfully invited to attend his funeral from the vault of St. Patrick's Church on the evening of Sunday, 24th inst., at four o'clock, without further notice. (23 APR 1853)

DEATH. At his residence in Roxbury, Mass., on the 19th inst., in the 70th year of his age, Capt. EPES SARGENT, father of John O. Sargent, editor of the "*Republic*" of this city, and of Epes Sargent, Jr., of Boston. (23 APR 1853)

MARRIAGE. On the 21st inst., by the Rev. Mr. Hodges, Mr. ALOYSIUS LANGLEY to Miss SARAH WILKINSON, both of this city. (25 APR 1853)

DEATH. On the 22d of April, after a short spell of sickness, which she bore with Christian fortitude, Mrs. ANN TOOMEY, aged 58 years. Born in the county of Cork, Ireland, but for many years a resident of this city. (25 APR 1853)

DEATH. On the 18th inst., PENELOPE BENBURY CREECY, aged eight years and seven months, daughter of James R. and Henrietta B. Creecy. (25 APR 1853)

MARRIAGE. At St. Paul's Church, Troy, N.Y., by the Rev. Dr. Van Kleeck, CICERO PRICE, Esq., of the U.S. Navy, to ELIZABETH H., daughter of the late John Paine, Esq., of Troy. (26 APR 1853)

DEATH. Of apoplexy, on the 17th of January last, after a few hours' illness, on board the U.S. frigate *Congress*, at Montevideo, CHARLES GOLDING, seaman, a native of Washington, D.C. [This is the second death that has occurred on board the frigate since she was put in commission, about three years ago.] (26 APR 1853)

DEATH. On the 25th inst., JAMES WILSON, in the 76th year of his age. The friends of the family are requested to attend his funeral on Wednesday, the 27th, at 12 o'clock, from his residence on Q street, between B and C streets. (26 APR 1853)

Daily National Intelligencer, Marriage and Death Notices, 1851-1854

DEATH. On the 25th inst., after a lingering illness, which he bore with Christian fortitude, Mr. WILLIAM HUGHES, aged 46 years, born in the county of Monohun, Ireland, but for many years a resident of this city. His friends and acquaintances are respectfully invited to attend his funeral on this (Tuesday) evening at 3 o'clock, from his residence on G street, between First and Second streets. (26 APR 1853)

MARRIAGE. In this city, on Tuesday, the 26th inst., by the Rev. Mr. Blackwell, THOMAS A. CROSS and ARABELLA DUVALL, daughter of Dennis Duvall, Esq., all of Prince George's Co., Md. (28 APR 1853)

DEATH. In this city, on the 27th inst., after a few days' illness, Miss ANN E. SIPE, in the 41st year of her age. Her friends, and those of the family, are respectfully invited to attend her funeral this day, 28th inst., at 3 o'clock, from the residence of Mr. Henry Lee, on Maryland avenue, between 4½ and 6th streets. (28 APR 1853)

MARRIAGE. On the 27th inst., by the Rev. George Hildt, J. CARSON WATSON, Publisher of the *Winchester (Va.) Republican*, and Miss ANNIE CORRELL, all of Winchester, Va. (29 APR 1853)

MARRIAGE. On the 28th inst., by the Rev. J.C. Smith, Mr. GIDEON W. LARNER to Miss LAURA A., only daughter of James P. McKean, Esq., all of this city. (29 APR 1853)

MARRIAGE. On Thursday, the 27th inst., by the Rev. D.X. Junkin, D.D., G.W. MORRIS, Esq. to Miss DOROTHY C[L]ECKHARDT, all of this city. (2 MAY 1853)

MARRIAGE. On the 28th ult. [28 APR 1853], by the Rev. J.B. Donelan, Mr. JAMES R. HITAFFER to Miss MARY L. COLUMBUS, second daughter of Mr. Charles Columbus, all of this city. (2 MAY 1853)

MARRIAGE. Near the Navy Yard, on the 28th ult., by the Rev. Edward Knight, GEORGE W. HARRINGTON, of Alexandria, Va., to MARY M. CALLAGHAN, of Washington, D.C. (2 MAY 1853)

DEATH. At San Francisco, Calif., on the 9th of March, Mr. THOMAS H. FISHER, late of the Post Office Department. Mr. F. was a native of New York, but resided in this city for some years, where he leaves a number of friends to mourn his early death. (2 MAY 1853)

DEATH. On Saturday morning last [30 APR 1853], LUCRETIA JANE, youngest daughter of John H. and Emma Gibbs, aged 2 years 6 months and 23 days. (2 MAY 1853)

MARRIAGE. On the 2d inst., by the Rev. Father Knight, Dr. WM. J.C. DUHAMEL to Mrs. ELIZABETH H. AGATE, all of this city. (4 MAY 1853)

MARRIAGE. On the 3d inst., by the Rev. F.S. Evans, WASHINGTON WINDER OWEN, Esq., of Montgomery Co., Md., to Mrs. MARY WINDSOR, of this city. (4 MAY 1853)

MARRIAGE. On the 30th ult. [30 APR 1853], at St. John's Church, by the Rev. Smyth Pyne, Capt. WM. H. GARDENER, U.S. Navy, to Miss VIRGINIA SELDEN, daughter of the late Maj. [Cary] Selden, of this city. (4 MAY 1853)

MARRIAGE. On the 1st of May, by the Rev. J.B. Donelan, JOS. ROSENBERG, of Baltimore, Md., to MARY E. OWENS, of Washington. (4 MAY 1853)

DEATH. In this city, on Tuesday morning, 3d May, at 4 o'clock, after an illness of about four weeks, which he bore with truly Christian fortitude and resignation to the will of God, in the 19th year of his age, EDWARD CHARLES CATON, a native of this city, and eldest son of the late Patrick H. Caton. His funeral will take place from his late residence on Fifth street, between I and K streets, on Wednesday evening, the 4th inst., at 2 o'clock. (4 MAY 1853)

Daily National Intelligencer, Marriage and Death Notices, 1851-1854

MARRIAGE. In this city, at the residence of George S. Gideon, Esq., on Wednesday afternoon, by the Rev. John C. Smith, Col. PHILIP H. RAIFORD, of Alabama, to Miss FANNIE A. JEFFERSON, of Missouri, daughter of the late Hamilton Jefferson, Esq., of Virginia. (5 MAY 1853)

MARRIAGE. In Washington, Ga., on Thursday, 28th April, by the Rev. George F. Pierce, D.D., WM. F. ALEXANDER to MARY LOUISA, daughter of the Hon. Robt. Toombs. (5 MAY 1853)

MARRIAGE. On the 28th ult. [28 APR 1853], by the Rev. D. Evans Reese, Mr. WILLIAM H. LAMBERT, of Alexandria, Va., to Miss LAURA STEER, of this city. (5 MAY 1853)

DEATH. At 9 o'clock last night [4 MAY 1853], Mrs. ISABELLA LEAVITT HOWARD, wife of Mr. Charles S. West, of this city. Mrs. West was grand-daughter to James Howard, who, in 1756, was one of those who founded the now flourishing city of Augusta, Maine. The friends of the family are invited to attend the funeral without further notice this afternoon at 4 P.M. precisely from her late residence in 10th street, between E and F streets. (5 MAY 1853)

DEATH. In this city, on the 30th ult. [30 APR 1853], Miss RACHEL A. SAFFELL, formerly of Montgomery Co., Md. (5 MAY 1853)

DEATH. At Ft. Smith, Ark., on the 19th April last, FRANK ALEXANDER, son of Capt. F. and Mathilde Gardener, U.S. Army, aged one year and eleven months. (5 MAY 1853)

DEATH. In this city, on the morning of the 5th inst., WM. B. STONE, son of the late Wm. B. and Sarah Stone, of Stafford Co., Va. (6 MAY 1853)

DEATH. At the residence of his brother-in-law, Dr. Grafton Tyler, on Thursday, the 5th inst., in the 23d year of his age, Dr. J.W.L.W. BOWIE, of Montgomery Co., Md. His funeral will take place at Locust Grove, in Prince George's Co., Md., on Saturday, the 7th, at 11 o'clock A.M. (6 MAY 1853)

DEATH. In Prince George's Co., Md., on Sunday morning, May 1, Mr. R.J. WALL, in the 27th year of his age, after a long and lingering sickness, which he bore with Christian fortitude. (6 MAY 1853)

MARRIAGE. On Tuesday, the 3d inst., in the Church of the Epiphany, by the Rev. J.W. French, Mr. WM. A. VEIRO, of Florida, to Miss REBECCA T. BIAYS, daughter of the late Philip G. Biays, of Maryland. (7 MAY 1853)

DEATH. In Georgetown, D.C., on the 5th inst., Mr. H.G. KORFF, in the 36th year of his age. His funeral will take place from his late residence on Bridge street tomorrow (Sunday) afternoon, at 4 o'clock P.M. His friends and those of the family are requested to attend, and also the Germania Benevolent Society of Washington and Georgetown, without further notice. (7 MAY 1853)

MARRIAGE. In the city of Raleigh, N.C., on Wednesday evening last [4 MAY 1853], by the Rev. Dr. Mason, JOHN W. CAMERON, Esq., of Washington, to Miss ALTONA F. GALES, daughter of the late Weston R. Gales. (9 MAY 1853)

DEATH. In this city, on the 6th inst., Mrs. LYDIA, wife of Mr. R.P. Anderson, in the 67th year of her age. Her funeral will take place at the residence of her husband, on H street, between 10th and 11th streets, this (Monday) afternoon, at 4 o'clock P.M. Her friends and the friends of the family are requested to attend without further notice. (9 MAY 1853)

DEATH. In this city, on the 6th inst., Mrs. CHARLOTTE GARRATT, in the 47th year of her age. The funeral will take place from the residence of Benj. Williamson, on 11th street, between K and L streets, this (Monday) morning, at 10 o'clock. Her friends and those of the family are requested to attend without further notice. (9 MAY 1853)

Daily National Intelligencer, Marriage and Death Notices, 1851-1854

DEATH. On the 7th inst., after a long and painful illness, which she bore with Christian fortitude, Mrs. BELL JANE ECKHARDT, of this city, formerly of Seaford, Del. (9 MAY 1853)

DEATH. At Bencoolen, Island of Sumatra, on the 30th of December last [1852], of pulmonary consumption, MARY, wife of Edward Ely, Esq., Consul of the U.S. at Bombay, aged 19 years and 10 months. (10 MAY 1853)

DEATH. On the 9th inst., Mr. FRANCIS A. DUNN, in the 33d year of his age. The friends and acquaintances of the deceased are respectfully requested to attend the funeral this evening, at 4 o'clock, from his late residence on Pennsylvania avenue, between 2d and 3d streets. (11 MAY 1853)

DEATH. On board the steamer *Palmetto*, on the morning of the 10th inst., on her passage from Charleston to Baltimore, Lieut. JOSEPH S. TOTEN, of the 2d regiment of artillery. The funeral will take place from his father's residence, Gadsby's Row, this afternoon at 4 o'clock. The friends of the family are invited to attend without further notice. (11 MAY 1853)

DEATH. Yesterday morning [10 MAY 1853], in the third year of her age, MARGARET LOUISE, daughter of Jas. C. and Margaret McGuire, of this city. The friends of the family are respectfully requested to attend her funeral, which will take place this afternoon, at 4 o'clock. (11 MAY 1853)

DEATHS. Suddenly, at Norwalk, on 6th May, from the New Haven Railroad accident, Mrs. ANN TEMPLE GREENE, aged 72 years, widow of John R. Greene, U.S. Navy, and daughter of the late Commodore Samuel Nicholson, of Kent Co., Md. At the same time and place, SAMUEL NICHOLSON HASSARD, aged fourteen years, grandson of Mrs. Ann T. Greene. (11 MAY 1853)

DEATH. At the residence of his brother, Charles Stewart, in this city, of consumption, GEORGE M. STEWART, in the 28th year of his age. (11 MAY 1853)

MELANCHOLY ACCIDENT. An accident of the most distressing nature occurred at the Marine Barracks, in this city, on Tuesday last [10 MAY 1853], by which CHARLES R. TANSIL [sic], an interesting lad of twelve years of age, a son of Serg't G.S. Tansil, of the Marine Corps, came by his death. It seems that by some means a loaded musket was left standing in the doorway of the quarters occupied by Serg't Luskey, when a son of his, a lad of about ten years of age, snapped it, and it was discharged, instantly killing young Tansil. The friends and acquaintances of G.S. Tansil are respectfully invited to attend the funeral of his son this (Thursday) evening, at 3 o'clock, from his residence at the Marine Barracks. (12 MAY 1853) Students at the East Washington Seminary call a meeting after hearing of the unexpected death of one of their number, CHARLES MONTGOMERY TANSILL, son of G.S. Tansill, Orderly Sergeant. (14 MAY 1853)

MARRIAGE. On the 10th inst., by Rev. Jesse T. Peck, Mr. FRANCIS B. HUGGINS to Miss JULIA ANN WROE, all of Washington. (13 MAY 1853)

MARRIAGE. On Thursday morning, April 28th, in Trinity Church, Shepherdstown, Jefferson Co., Va., by the Rev. C.W. Andrews, Dr. V.M. BUTLER to MATILDA W., daughter of Henry Berry, Esq., all of the above place. (13 MAY 1853)

MARRIAGE. At St. Michael's Church, Charleston, on Wednesday morning, April 20, by the Rev. P. Tapier Keith, CHAS. LOCKHART PETTIGREW, of North Carolina, to JANE CAROLINE, eldest daughter of the late John Gough North. (13 MAY 1853)

MARRIAGE. In Christ Church, by the Rev. Mr. Hodges, on the 11th inst., FREDERICK PROSPERI to Miss MARY ELLEN COOK, all of Washington, D.C. (13 MAY 1853)

Daily National Intelligencer, Marriage and Death Notices, 1851-1854

DEATH. In this city, on the night of the 12th inst., Mr. PATRICK WHITE, a native of the county of Cork, Ireland. *May he rest in peace*! His friends and acquaintances are requested to attend his funeral this afternoon at four o'clock, from E street, Capitol Hill. (14 MAY 1853)

MARRIAGE. In Philadelphia, on the 11th inst., by the Rev. Dr. J.C. Clay, Mr. WILLIAM BLANCHARD, of Washington, to Miss ELLA VIRGINIA EMMONS, of Philadelphia. (16 MAY 1853)

MARRIAGE. On the 8th inst., by the Rev. Mr. Alig, Mr. COLUMBUS HALL to Miss MARY F. BAILEY, all of this city. (16 MAY 1853)

DEATH. Near the Navy Yard, on the 15th inst., SAMUEL LINDSAY, youngest son of Dennis and Mary Callaghan, after an illness of 9 days, aged 2 years and 11 days. The funeral will take place this day, at 3 o'clock, from the corner of D and 4th streets east. (16 MAY 1853)

DEATH. On Saturday night, 14th inst., Mrs. MARY HAWKE, in the 34th year of her age. Her funeral will take place on Tuesday morning, from the residence of her brother, Patrick H. Sweeney, on Massachusetts avenue, between 9th and 10th streets, where the friends and acquaintance of the families are respectfully invited to attend. (16 MAY 1853)

DEATH. On Saturday, the 14th inst., BENJ. ODEN, infant son of Benj. Oden and Helen M. West, aged one year and eight months. (16 MAY 1853)

DEATH. On the 16th inst., SARAH ELLEN, daughter of Elisha and Sarah A. Falkoner, in her fourth year. Her funeral will take place today, (Tuesday,) the 17th, at 4 o'clock, from her father's residence on Seventh street, between H and I streets, to which the friends of the family are respectfully invited. (17 MAY 1853)

DEATH. On Friday evening, 13th inst., of disease of the brain, in the 3d year of his age, EDWARD TSCHIFFELY, son of Joseph A. and Elizabeth G. Deeble. (17 MAY 1853)

MARRIAGE. On Tuesday, the 10th inst., at the residence of Mrs. D. Hall, of Lowndes Co., Ala., by the Rev. Wm. H. Platt, Hon. LYMAN GIBBONS, one of the Judges of the Supreme Court of Alabama, to Miss EMMA E., daughter of the late Hon. James Dellet. (18 MAY 1853)

MARRIAGE. On the 16th inst., by the Rev. J.D. Blackwell, Mr. WILLIAM HEIGL and Miss MARY HUMPHREY, all of this city. (18 MAY 1853)

MARRIAGE. On the 15th inst., at St. Mary's Church, by the Rev. Matthias Alig, HAMILTON G. FANT, of Missouri, to JOSEPHINE, only daughter of Johnson Hellen, Esq., of this city. (18 MAY 1853)

MARRIAGE. On the 15th inst., in St. Mary's Church, by Rev. Matthias Alig, Mr. PATRICK HERBERT, to Miss MARY MURNS. (18 MAY 1853)

MARRIAGE. On the 5th inst., by Rev. Matthias Alig, in St. Mary's Church, Mr. HUGH L. REESE to Miss ELIZABETH O'NEALE. (18 MAY 1853)

MARRIAGE. On the 28th of April, by Rev. Matthias Alig, in St. Mary's Church, Mr. JOHN M. FLYNN to Mrs. MARGARET O'CONNEL. On the same day, by the same, Mr. NICHOLAS HAYS to Mrs. MARY FITZGERALD, all of this city. (18 MAY 1853)

MARRIAGE. At Brown's Hotel, on Tuesday evening, May 17, by the Rev. Mr. Stringfellow, Maj. EVERARD FIELD to Miss LOUISA FOX, all of Petersburg, Va. (19 MAY 1853)

MARRIAGE. On Monday evening, May 16th, by the Rev. Mr. DeNecker, EDWARD A. WHIPPLE, U.S. Navy, to CAMILLA, daughter of Elexius Simms, Esq., of this city. (19 MAY 1853)

Daily National Intelligencer, Marriage and Death Notices, 1851-1854

MARRIAGE. On Tuesday, 17th inst., by the Rev. Mr. Hodges, THOMAS M. HANSON to Miss MARY P. BARRY, all of this city. (19 MAY 1853)

DEATH. At the University of Virginia, on the 16th inst., VIRGINIA H. COURTENAY, consort of Prof. E.H. Courtenay, and eldest daughter of Prof. Henry Howard. (19 MAY 1853)

MARRIAGE. On the 17th inst., at the Church of the Ascension, by the Rev. Henry Stanley, JOHN C. KENNEDY to M.A.B. HAMMOND, all of this city. (20 MAY 1853)

MARRIAGE. On the 17th inst., by the Rev. J.R. Eckard, Mr. JOHN H. BUTLER to AGNES B. NORRIS. (20 MAY 1853)

DEATH. On the 18th inst., MAGDALENE WEBER, second daughter of the late Christian H. and Mary Weber, aged 14 years and 3 months. The friends of the family are invited to attend her funeral this (Friday) afternoon, at 3 o'clock, from the residence of Mr. Peter Little, Navy Yard. (20 MAY 1853)

DEATH. On the 19th inst., MARY EMMA, aged 10 months, daughter of William R. and Eliza Jane Simmons. The friends of the family are respectfully invited to attend the funeral from the residence of her parents on 7th, between M and N streets, on Friday at 10 o'clock. (20 MAY 1853)

MARRIAGE. On the 19th inst., by Rev. Jesse T. Peck, Mr. ARCHIBALD R. GREEN to Miss H. PETERS, all of Washington. (21 MAY 1853)

MARRIAGE. On the 17th inst., by Rev. Mason Noble, JOHN F.B. PURSELL to Miss ELIZABETH KNIGHT, all of this city. (21 MAY 1853)

MARRIAGE. On Tuesday, the 17th inst., by the Rev. Father DeNecker, S.J., Dr. JOHN J. DYER to ELIZA FRANCES, daughter of the late Edward Dyer. (21 MAY 1853)

MARRIAGE. In Alexandria, Va., on the 17th inst., by the Rev. J.T. Johnston, J.W. IRWIN, of Kentucky, and AURELIA HERBERT, daughter of the late Thomas Fairfax, of Fairfax Co., Va. (21 MAY 1853)

MARRIAGE. In Brunswick, Va., on the 11th inst., by the Rev. B.R. Duval, JOHN HARDING, Jr., of Davidson, Tenn., to Miss SOPHIA MERRITT, daughter of Wm. H.E. Merritt, of the former place. (21 MAY 1853)

MARRIAGE. In Brunswick, Va., on the 11th inst., Rev. THOMAS WHEELER, of the Virginia Conference, to Miss MARIA L. RIVES, daughter of John G. Rives, deceased. (21 MAY 1853)

DEATH. In Brunswick, Va., on the 3d inst., of paralysis, PASCAL HICKS, aged 68 years. (21 MAY 1853)

DEATH. In Brunswick, Va., on the 16th inst., Capt. WILLIAM GREGG, aged about 78 years. (21 MAY 1853)

DEATH. At her late residence, No. 58 East 34th street, New York, on Sunday night, May 15th, after an illness of two weeks, HANNAH, widow of the late Col. Elisha Jenkins, aged sixty-one. (21 MAY 1853)

DEATH BY DROWNING. On Wednesday [18 MAY 1853] a young man, WILLIAM WOODWARD, son of Mr. Sedley Woodward, some years deceased, and for a long period a resident of Georgetown, was drowned in an effort to swim in the Potomac between Mason's Island and the main land. (21 MAY 1853)

DEATHS. In Georgetown, on Saturday, the 14th inst., HELEN HILDRETH, infant daughter of Dr. Chas. H. and Mary Cragin, aged 4 days, and on Saturday, the 21st inst., MARY, wife of Dr. Chas. H. Cragin. The

Daily National Intelligencer, Marriage and Death Notices, 1851-1854

funeral will take place at the residence of her father, Samuel McKenney, Esq., this (Monday) morning, the 23d inst., at 10 o'clock. Friends of the family are invited to attend. (23 MAY 1853)

DEATH. On the 22d inst., of disease of the heart, Mr. JAMES GRIGSBY, in the 32d year of his age. The friends of the family are respectfully invited to attend his funeral this (Monday) afternoon, at 4 o'clock, from his late residence, on 14th street, near I street. (23 MAY 1853)

DEATH. On the 21st inst., at 11 o'clock A.M., in the 44th year of his age, of disease of the heart, ABNER B. PROCTOR, a native of New Hampshire, but for the last twenty-four years a resident of this city. (23 MAY 1853)

DEATH. On the 23d inst., after a long and protracted illness, which she bore with Christian fortitude, Mrs. SARAH STANLEY, in the 52d year of her age. Her funeral will take place on Tuesday, the 24th inst., from the First Baptist Church, 10th street. (24 MAY 1853)

MARRIAGE. On the 23d inst., by Rev. Chas. A. Davis, WILLIAM HENRY PADGETT to Miss MARGARET DROWNS. On the same day, by the same, CHARLES M. DRISCOLL to ALCINDA J. POWELL. (25 MAY 1853)

MARRIAGE. On the 24th inst., by the Rev. J.W. French, Dr. LOGAN BRANDT, of Charles Co., Md., to Miss BETTIE, daughter of the late Jas. Selden, Esq., of Virginia. (25 MAY 1853)

MARRIAGE. At Ft. Smith, Ark., on the 25th of April 1853, by the Rev. C. Washburn, Capt. T. HENDRICKSON, U.S. Army, and Miss LIZZIE A. GRIFFITH, eldest daughter of the late Capt. Geo. Griffith, of Harford Co., Md. (27 MAY 1853)

MARRIAGES. On Tuesday, the 19th inst., by the Rev. S.D. Finckel, Mr. JACOB SHETLIN to Miss MARGARET HITZ. On the same day, by the same, Mr. GEO. SHUCH to Miss PHILIPINE FREUND, all of this city. (27 MAY 1853)

MARRIAGES. On the 22d inst., at the Wesley Chapel parsonage, by the Rev. Jas. H. Brown, Mr. JOHN NEWELL to Miss CATHARINE JANE BROWN, both of Georgetown. On the 26th inst., by the same. Mr. CALEB STEWART to Miss JOSEPHINE CUVILIER, both of this city. (27 MAY 1853)

DEATH. In this city, on Thursday, the 26th inst., after a short illness, in the blessed hope of a glorious immortality, HENRIETTA EARLE KERR, wife of Rev. David Kerr, Rector of Trinity Church, Marlborough, Md. (27 MAY 1853)

DEATH. On Monday evening, 23d May, at Dunkirk, N.Y., Mrs. MARY WAUGH, wife of M.M. [Waugh?], and daughter of the late Rev. Thomas Smith, of Virginia. She had scarcely bloomed into womanhood ere she was called away. Lovely and beloved in life, she is deeply and sincerely mourned in death, and has left a void long to be felt in the hearts of a large circle of sorrowing friends and relatives. (27 MAY 1853)

MARRIAGE. At Christ's Church, on May 26th, 1853, by the Rev. Mr. Hodges, Mr. J. MARION BRIGGS to Miss MARY ELLEN, youngest daughter of Mrs. Malinda Smith, all of Washington. (28 MAY 1853)

MARRIAGE. In New York city, on the 16th of April, by the Rev. Newton Brown, D.D., GEORGE T. BRADLEY, Esq., of that city, to Miss MARY E. NEELY, daughter of the late Mr. John Neely, of Accomack Co., Va. (28 MAY 1853)

DEATH. Yesterday morning [27 MAY 1853], at 5 o'clock A.M., Mrs. JULIA S. MORGAN, relict of the late Commodore Charles W. Morgan, U.S.N. Her funeral will take place at 4 o'clock this afternoon, from her late residence on the corner of second and Frederick streets, Georgetown. Her friends and acquaintances are invited to attend without further notice. (28 MAY 1853)

Daily National Intelligencer, Marriage and Death Notices, 1851-1854

DEATH. On Friday morning, the 27th inst., at 8 o'clock A.M., MARY A. KING, wife of James D. King, of this city. Her funeral will take place from Mr. Boak's boarding-house, Pennsylvania avenue, this afternoon at 8 o'clock. (28 MAY 1853)

DEATH. In Georgetown, on the 27th inst., in the 10th year of his age, ALEXANDER PETERKIN, second son of George and Estelle M. Thomson. The friends of the family are invited to attend the funeral at 5 o'clock, this (Saturday) evening, from his father's residence on First street. (28 MAY 1853)

DEATH. In this city, on Thursday evening, 26th inst., of scarlet fever, ANN JANET, daughter of A.M. Gangewer, aged three years and three months. (28 MAY 1853)

MARRIAGE. At Elk Hill, Goochland Co., Va., on the 26th inst., by the Rev. F.M. Whittle, ALEXANDER B. HAGNER, of Annapolis, and LOUISA, youngest daughter of the late Randolph Harrison, Esq. (30 MAY 1853)

DEATH. In this city, yesterday [29 MAY 1853], Mr. CORDER BULK, aged 77. His funeral will take place this evening, at 5 o'clock, from his late residence, New York avenue, between 3d and 4th streets. (30 MAY 1853)

MARRIAGE. On the 30th inst., by the Rev. Mr. Lipscomb, RICHARD W. BRUFF, of Baltimore, to Miss JANE C. FRY, of this city. (31 MAY 1853)

MARRIAGE. In this city, on Monday, the 30th inst., by Rev. G.W. Samson, Mr. JAMES E. GODDIN and Miss GEORGIANA B. SUTTON, both of Richmond, Va. (31 MAY 1853)

MARRIAGE. At the Church of the Epiphany, by the Rev. Mr. French, on the 31st ult., PETER F. WILSON, Esq. and Miss CORNELIA M. KELLER, of Washington. (1 JUN 1853)

DEATH. In this city on Tuesday [31 MAY 1853], at noon, after a protracted and painful illness, Miss ELLEN C. CURRAN, the eldest of the then surviving daughters of the late Philip Curran, of Annapolis, Md. She lived a good woman and died as became a Christian. The friends of the family will, without further notice, be pleased to attend the funeral of the deceased on Thursday morning, at 8½ o'clock, from the residence of Wm. W. Curran, on Indiana avenue, nearly opposite the City Hall. (1 JUN 1853)

DEATH. In this city, on the 26th May, HARRIET ANN COX, wife of John Cox, formerly of Charles Co., (near Port Tobacco,) Maryland, in the 36th year of her age, leaving a husband and six young children to mourn her loss. (1 JUN 1853)

DEATH. In Alexandria, Va., on Friday, 28th ult. [28 MAY 1853], of pulmonary consumption, Lieut. SAMUEL WILCOX, U.S. Revenue Marine, in the 30th year of his age. (1 JUN 1853)

DEATH. At her residence, in Frederick Co., Md., on Wednesday, 25th ult. [25 MAY 1853], aged 39 years, CATHARINE, wife of Mr. William P. Allnutt, and eldest daughter of Mr. William Jewell, of Georgetown, D.C. (1 JUN 1853)

MARRIAGE. In the morning of Tuesday, the 10th of May, in the Presbyterian Church in Salem, Va., by the Rev. James E. Hughes, Dr. GEO. S. HAMILTON to Miss MARIANNA T. SCOTT, all of Fauquier Co., Va. (2 JUN 1853)

MARRIAGE. Last evening [1 JUN 1853], at the Fourth Presbyterian Church, by the Rev. John C. Smith, Mr. HENRY CLAY BALDWIN and Miss VIRGINIA BOKEE MOORE, daughter of Mr. Wm. W. Moore, all of this city. (2 JUN 1853)

Daily National Intelligencer, Marriage and Death Notices, 1851-1854

MARRIAGE. On the 25th ult. [25 MAY 1853], by the Rev. C.B. Young, AZEL BEALL, Esq. to Miss ELLEN T. HILLEARY, daughter of Capt. C.T. HILLEARY, all of Prince George's Co., Md. (2 JUN 1853)

DEATH. On the 31st ult. [31 MAY 1853], THOMAS A.M. KIRK. His funeral will take place at 10 o'clock, on the 2d inst., from the residence of his brother, G.E. Kirk, south F street, between 7th and 8th, Island, to which the relatives and friends of the family are invited to attend without further notice. (2 JUN 1853)

MARRIAGE. At Paris, Ky., on the 17th ult. [17 MAY 1853], by the Rev. Dr. Mitchell, Mr. WM. C. McGOWAN, of Montgomery, to Miss CARRIE DAVIS, daughter of the Hon. Garrett Davis. (3 JUN 1853)

DEATH. On Thursday, 2d of June, 1853, Miss HESTER A. IRWIN, daughter of the late Henry Irwin, of Georgetown. Her funeral will take place this day, 3d June, at 3 o'clock P.M., from the residence of J.H. Wheat, where the friends and acquaintances are respectfully invited to attend without further notice. Hacks will be at the residence of Wm. Greer, on 11th street, between G and H streets, Washington, at 2½ o'clock P.M., to convey persons out to Mr. Wheat's. (3 JUN 1853)

DEATH. On the evening of the 1st inst., at her residence on Pennsylvania avenue, ADELIA A., wife of S.L. Cole, aged 36 years. Her friends and acquaintances are respectfully invited to attend her funeral this morning, at 11 o'clock. The subject of the above was truly the embodiment of female excellence, a mother in the most elevated and ennobling sense of the word, and a fond and beloved companion, esteemed and admired by all who moved within the sphere of her acquaintance. Commanding in an enlarged degree those refined attributes of character which dignify and adorn her sex, to those who appreciated the virtues she was a continuous centre of attraction! Endowed by nature with a warm and confiding temperament, secured to her a constant incentive to humane action. She has left an affectionate husband and tender offspring to deplore her early departure. (3 JUN 1853)

DEATH. At No. 23, Oxford street, Laurieston, Glasgow, Scotland, on the 14th of May last, Mr. DAVID MUNRO, for many years a resident of this city. (3 JUN 1853)

MARRIAGE. On the 30th ult. [30 MAY 1853], by the Rev. Mr. Wysong, Mr. RICHARD J. BEALL to Miss CORNELIA EDMONSTON, all of Washington. (4 JUN 1853)

MARRIAGE. On the 1st inst., in the Presbyterian Church at Charlestown, Jefferson Co., Va., by the Rev. T.W. Simpson, JOHN MACFARLAND, Esq. to JANE S., eldest daughter of the late Isaac R. Douglass. (4 JUN 1853)

DEATH. Of consumption, on the 3d inst., Mrs. ELIZABETH COLLISON, in the 47th year of her age. Her friends and acquaintances are invited to attend her funeral, from her late residence on 6th street, on Sunday evening, at 5 o'clock. (4 JUN 1853)

DEATH. At Dewberry, Hanover Co., Va., on Friday, the 27th of May, MARY C. NOLAND, only daughter of Lieut. C. St. Geo. Noland, U.S.N. (4 JUN 1853)

DEATH. In this city, at half-past 11 on Friday night last [3 JUN 1853], MARY, daughter of Mr. Luke and Mrs. Mary Lea, aged eighteen months. (6 JUN 1853)

MARRIAGE. At Newtown, Worcester Co., Md., on the 6th inst., by the Rev. John Crosdale, Mr. O.H. MORRISON, of this city, to Miss EMMA CLARKE, of the former place. (7 JUN 1853)

DEATH. On the 6th inst., after a lingering illness, Mrs. ELIZABETH LANPHIER, aged 79 years. The friends of the family are invited to attend her funeral this afternoon, from her late residence on Pennsylvania avenue, between 9th and 10th streets. (7 JUN 1853)

Daily National Intelligencer, Marriage and Death Notices, 1851-1854

MARRIAGE. On Tuesday, the 7th of June, in Trinity Church, Washington city, by the Rev. Dr. Sparrow, WILLIAM J. BROWN, of New York, to ANNIE L., daughter of James W. McCulloh. (8 JUN 1853)

OBITUARY. The melancholy duty devolves on us of announcing the demise at the City Hotel, Alexandria, on Sunday morning [5 JUN 1853], at 12½ o'clock, of CHARLOTTE AUGUSTA, second youngest daughter of John C. and Ann D. Bowyer, of that city, in the 15th year of her age... Her remains were conveyed by yesterday's mail-boat to Staunton, to be deposited in the family vault where the ashes of her kindred repose. (8 JUN 1853)

DEATH. In this city, on the 3d inst., of disease of the lungs, Mr. GEORGE EDWARDS, in the 42d year of his age, a native of the county Sussex, England, but for 28 years a resident of the U.S., leaving a wife and three children. (9 JUN 1853)

DEATH. At Baltimore, on the 7th inst., FIELDING LUCAS, in the 41st year of his age, second son of Fielding Lucas, Jr. (9 JUN 1853)

MARRIAGE. In Georgetown, D.C., on the 7th inst., by the Rev. Henry Slicer, Rev. WM. HARDEN, of Baltimore Annual Conference, to Miss LIZZIE S., eldest daughter of the officiating minister. (9 JUN 1853)

OBITUARY. Died, of typhoid fever, on the 21st of May, at the residence of her father, in Georgetown, MARY, daughter of Samuel McKenny, Esq., and the beloved consort of Dr. Charles Cragin, of the same place [text continues]. (10 JUN 1853)

MARRIAGE. On Thursday morning, 9th June, at St. Matthew's Church, by the Rev. James B. Donelan, His Excellency the Commander JOZE DE MARCOLETA, Minister Plenipotentiary from Nicaragua, to JULIA AUGUSTA, eldest daughter of A.T. Kieckhoefer, Esq., of this city. (10 JUN 1853)

DEATH. In this city, on the 8th inst., after a severe illness, Mr. WM. P. KING, of Clarksburg district, Montgomery Co., Md., in the 21st year of his age. (11 JUN 1853)

DEATH. On the 9th inst., in the 65th year of her age, Mrs. JANE McGARVEY, a native of Dunneygall, Ireland. Her funeral will take place today (Saturday,) the 11th inst., at 3 o'clock, from her late residence on the corner of L and 27th streets, to which her friends are respectfully invited to attend. (11 JUN 1853)

DEATH. At the residence of her grandfather, Gen. Gratiot, MARY VICTORIA GRATIOT, daughter of Chas. P. and Juliet A. Chouteau, of St. Louis, aged 20 months. (11 JUN 1853)

MARRIAGE. On Thursday, 9th inst., by the Rev. Mr. McMannus, Mr. SAM. SIMMONS, of this city, to Miss HELENA C. MURPHY, of Boston. (13 JUN 1853)

MARRIAGE. On Friday, the 6th inst., at the house of William D. Brackenridge, Esq., by the Rev. D.X. Junkin, D.D., Mr. JOHN SMITH to Miss MARGARET BATCHIN, all of this city. (13 JUN 1853)

DEATH. On Saturday, the 11th inst., at the residence of his father, George Gillis, Esq., in Louisville, Ky., Passed Midshipman WALTER V. GILLIS, U.S.N. (13 JUN 1853)

DEATH. Yesterday morning [12 JUN 1853], at 3 o'clock, after a short illness, from croup, WILLIAM F. BATES, in his sixth year, only son of William and Mary Bates. The funeral will take place this afternoon, at four o'clock. (13 JUN 1853)

MARRIAGE. On the 11th inst., by the Rev. J. George Butler, Mr. WILLIAM LYDDANE to Miss MARY JANE HILL, all of Berkeley Co., Va. (14 JUN 1853)

Daily National Intelligencer, Marriage and Death Notices, 1851-1854

MARRIAGE. At Washington, January 4, 1853, by Rev. J.W. Hedges, Mr. RICHARD GOSNELL to Miss ANN REBECCA HARRYMAN, all of Baltimore. (15 JUN 1853)

DEATH. Yesterday morning [14 JUN 1853], in the sixty-seventh year of his age, JILSON DOVE, a native of Virginia, but for the last thirty-three years a resident of Washington. His funeral will take place this afternoon at 5 o'clock, from the residence of his son-in-law, Thomas B. Entwisle, on 10th street, between E and F streets, to which the friends of the deceased, as well as those of the family, are invited to attend. (15 JUN 1853)

DEATH. On Sunday, the 12th inst., ALEXANDER LEWIS, only son of Charles and Margaret Frankenberger, aged 5 months and 10 days. (15 JUN 1853)

MARRIAGE. In Baltimore, on the 14th inst., by the Rev. John Poisal, JOHN G. MITCHELL, of Prince George's Co., Md., to Miss DEBORAH O. COKEY, of Baltimore city. (16 JUN 1853)

DEATH. In this city, on the evening of 13th inst., aged 20 months and 17 days, GEORGE ST. CLAIR, twin son of Geo. A.D. and Mary V. Clarke, of Cumberland, Md. (16 JUN 1853)

MARRIAGE. On the 30th of March, by the Rev. Mr. Finckel, WM. A. BAIRD to Miss CATHERINE B. DALE, all of Washington. (17 JUN 1853)

MARRIAGE. On Thursday afternoon [16 JUN 1853], by the Rev. John C. Smith, Mr. XAVIER FENDRICH to Miss MARY ESTHER, daughter of Mr. Samuel Cunningham, all of this city. (18 JUN 1853)

DEATH. On Friday, the 17th inst., ANGELINE COOLIDGE HARRIS, infant daughter of Arnold and Susan Harris, and grand-daughter of Gen. Robert Armstrong. The friends of the family are invited to attend the funeral at five o'clock this afternoon, from the residence of Gen. Armstrong. (18 JUN 1853)

DEATH. On Thursday evening, 16th inst., CHARLES, infant son of James and Elizabeth M. Colegate. (18 JUN 1853)

MARRIAGE. On Thursday, June 2, at St. Paul's Church, Paterson, N.J., by the Right Rev. S.A. McCoskey, Bishop of Michigan, Lieut. Col. ANDREW PORTER, U.S. Army to MARGARETTA FALCONER, daughter of John Biddle, of Michigan. (21 JUN 1853)

MARRIAGE. At the Church of the Ascension, on the 20th inst., by the Rev. Mr. Stanley, GRAFTON D. HANSON and MARIA, daughter of John P. Ingle, Esq., all of this city. (21 JUN 1853)

DEATH. In this city, on Monday, the 13th inst., at the residence of C.E. Sherman, Esq., while on a visit to her relatives, in the 81st year of her age, Mrs. MARY FARQUHAR, relict of Amos Farquhar, Esq., of Montgomery Co., Md. The deceased was a well-known and highly esteemed member of the Society of Friends. (21 JUN 1853)

DEATH. In this city, on the 20th inst., in the 45th year of his age, JOSEPH A. GASTON, formerly of Somerville, N.J. *Those who knew him best loved him most.* (21 JUN 1853)

DEATH. On the morning of the 19th inst., Mrs. MARGARET MAGRUDER, in the 81st year of her age. She was a native of Dover, Del., but for 64 years a resident of Alexandria, Va., where she lived and died one of its most respected inhabitants. She was for many years a consistent member of the Episcopal Church, and died trusting in her Saviour, on whom she relied. (21 JUN 1853)

DEATH. On the morning of the 19th inst., at the residence of his father, in Montgomery Co., Md., Mr. JAMES WHITE, in the 30th year of his age. He was a good son, an affectionate brother, and a warm friend. (22 JUN 1853)

Daily National Intelligencer, Marriage and Death Notices, 1851-1854

DEATH. In this city, yesterday evening [21 JUN 1853], Mrs. CHARITY BOONE, in the 78th year of her age, formerly of Charles Co., Md. The friends of the family are respectfully invited to attend her funeral this morning, at 10 o'clock, from her late residence, on East Capitol and Third streets, Capitol Hill. (22 JUN 1853)

DEATH. On the 20th inst., after a short illness, Mrs. ANN C.H., wife of Charles Edmonston, in the 35th year of her age. The friends of the family are respectfully invited to attend her funeral this (Wednesday) afternoon, at 4 o'clock, from the residence of her husband, on I street, between 9th and 10th streets. (22 JUN 1853)

MARRIAGE. In Washington city, at the U.S. Hotel, at 9 o'clock A.M., June 22, 1853, by the Rev. T.T. Wysong, Mr. JOHN P. SMITH to Miss FRANCES M. CLARK, all of Richmond city, Va. On the same morning, at the same time and place, by same, Mr. LEWIS J. HAWLEY to Miss ELIZABETH A. MORRIS, all of Richmond, Va. (23 JUN 1853)

DEATH. On last evening, the 22d inst., in the 59th year of her age, Mrs. CHARLOTTE WILLIAMS, wife of Ezra Williams, Esq., of this city. Mrs. Williams was a native of Massachusetts, but resided for many years in Detroit, Mich. Since 1845 she has been a resident of Washington. She bore her last illness with fortitude, and died in the Christian's hope. In her life were exhibited all the social virtues. She was a crown to her husband and a blessing to her children. The friends of the family are respectfully invited to attend the burial, which will take place on Friday afternoon, at half-past four o'clock, from the residence of John S. Gallaher, Esq., on 9th street, between E and F. (23 JUN 1853)

DEATH. In this city, on the 21st inst., after a lingering illness, Mr. JOHN HAGGARTY, a native of parish of Temple Michael, county Longford, Ireland, and for the last twenty-five years a resident of this city, leaving a wife and six children to mourn his loss. The friends of the family are invited to attend his funeral this afternoon, at 4 o'clock, from his late residence on 9th street, near L. (23 JUN 1853)

DEATH. Departed this life, in Philadelphia, on Sunday, the 19th inst., JULIA, consort of the Rev. Cameron F. McRae. (23 JUN 1853)

MARRIAGE. By the Rev. J.B. Donelan, on the 21st inst., Mr. JOHN R. MORGAN to Miss HARRIET WELCH, both of Washington, D.C. (24 JUN 1853)

DEATH. On Thursday, June 23, 1853, at 1½ A.M., Miss MARY ELIZA, eldest daughter of his Excellency Senor Don Manuel Carvallo, Minister of Chile, aged 17 years and 22 years. Her obsequies will take place today, Friday 24th, at 9 o'clock, at St. Patrick's Church, on F between 9th and 10th streets, from whence she will be conveyed to the Congressional cemetery. (24 JUN 1853)

DEATH. At the residence of Mr. Hitz, in this city, on the 22d inst., Mrs. LUCY MICHEL, a native of Switzerland, and for 17 years a resident of this city. (24 JUN 1853)

DEATH. [Communicated.] Died, at Rose Mont, near Nashville, on the 21st inst., the Hon. Judge BALCH. He was a native of Georgetown, D.C. He was graduated at Nassau Hall in 1805. He read law with John Hanson Thomas, of Frederick, Md. For some time he practiced law in the District Courts, but in 1809 emigrated to Columbia, Tenn. Subsequently he removed to Nashville, where for many years he devoted himself most laboriously to his profession, and appeared in many weighty causes. During the administration of General Jackson, he was appointed Commissioner on Indian Treaties, and afterwards Judge in Florida, and resided two years in Tallahassee. Upon his return to Tennessee he withdrew from the Bar, and spent the residue of his life at his farm near Nashville. Judge Balch was a sound lawyer, clear in argument and rapid in his elocution, remarkably moral in his habits and honorable in all his intercourse with men. His industry was untiring. He was the friend of learning, and remarkable for his acquaintance with the Greek language. In all the details of his profession he never neglected the cultivation of his literary taste. He was a respecter of religion, and always cherished the tenderest feelings towards the poor and distressed. His relatives are deeply afflicted at his decease, but they sorrow not as they who have no hope. (24 JUN 1853)

MARRIAGE. At the residence of Mr. Jno. Moreland, near Washington, on Thursday evening, 23d inst., by the Rev. Mr. Marks, Mr. NEHEMIAH ROBEY, of Portsmouth, Va., to Miss OCTAVIA MORELAND, of the District of Columbia. (25 JUN 1853)

DEATH. On Sunday evening, the 19th inst., in the 57th year of her age, Mrs. JULIA WHITNEY, relict of the late Reuben M. Whitney, and daughter of the late Col. Dulongpre, of Montreal. (25 JUN 1853)

DEATH. At Leesburg, Va., on the 20th inst., WILLIAM B. BENEDICT, Professor of Mathematics in the U.S. Navy. He was for several years connected with the Observatory in this city -- a zealous and efficient co-laborer with his associates in that institution. His loss is deeply deplored by a circle of friends here, but especially by the Corps of which he was a highly esteemed and valued member. (25 JUN 1853)

MARRIAGE. On the 21st of June, at Lexington, Ky., by the Rev. R.G. Brank, Mr. JOSEPH A. HUMPHREYS, of Woodford Co., Ky., to Miss SARAH THOMPSON, daughter of Tobias Gibson, Esq., of the Parish of Terre Bonne, La. (27 JUN 1853)

DEATH. On Saturday, the 25th, MARGARET VIRGINIA, youngest daughter of Walter and Margaret Nicholson, aged one year and nine months. (27 JUN 1853)

DEATH. On the 27th inst., BARNERD MULLRANY, aged 63 years. His funeral will take place at the residence of Hugh Haney, Pennsylvania avenue, near corner of 17th street, this day at 4 o'clock. His friends and acquaintances are invited to attend. (28 JUN 1853)

DEATH. At Baltimore, on Sunday evening, 26th inst., Capt. LOUIS A.B. WALBACH, of the U.S. Ordnance Corps. Capt. W. had command of the U.S. Arsenal at Pikesville, Baltimore Co., and was highly esteemed as an efficient and accomplished officer. He was a son of the veteran Gen. Walbach. (28 JUN 1853)

MARRIAGE. In this city, yesterday, the 28th inst., by the Rev. Smith Pyne, WILLIAM C. JOHNSON, Esq., of Utica, N.Y., to MARY LOUISA, only daughter of the late JOHN ADAMS, of this city, and grand-daughter of Ex-President John Quincy Adams. (29 JUN 1853)

MARRIAGE. At Christ Church, on the 28th inst., by the Rev. Mr. Hodges, J.J.S. HASSLER, Assistant U.S. Coast Survey, and ELIZABETH SOMERVILLE, daughter of the late Col. William Hebb, of this city. (29 JUN 1853)

MARRIAGE. On the 16th inst., by the Rev. Mr. Hittle, HUGH THOMAS DOUGLAS, Esq., of Zanesville, Ohio, and Miss MARIAN J. BRIGGS, daughter of Thomas Briggs, of Air Hill, Clarke Co., Va. (29 JUN 1853)

DEATH. At Selma, near Leesburg, on the 15th of June, J. BRADSHAW BEVERLY, in the 56th year of his age. *"Blessed are the dead who die in the Lord."* (29 JUN 1853)

MARRIAGE. On Tuesday evening, the 28th inst., by the Rev. T.T. Wysong, Mr. JOHN F. MILLER to Miss MARY JANE BARNES. (30 JUN 1853)

DEATH. In this city, on Tuesday, the 28th inst., HARRIET STARR, in the 34th year of her age. (30 JUN 1853)

DEATH. In this;; city, on the 30th ult. [30 JUN 1853], Mrs. HARRIET SIOUSSA, wife of Mr. Frederick Sioussa, aged 31 years. The friends of the family are invited to attend her funeral from her late residence this evening at 5 o'clock. (1 JUL 1853)

DEATH. In Alexandria, Va., on the morning of June the 28th, after a short illness, JAMES W. SEARS, Sr., in [the] 65th year of his age. (2 JUL 1853)

MARRIAGE. On Tuesday morning [5 JUL 1853], in the Fourth Presbyterian Church, by the Rev. John C. Smith, JAMES OSMOND WILSON, Esq., to Miss SARAH A.W., daughter of Henry Hungerford, Esq., all of this city. (6 JUL 1853)

MARRIAGE. In Georgetown, on Tuesday, July 5, at 2 o'clock P.M., by the Rev. Dr. Caldwell, of Christ's Church, JAMES GRAY JEWELL, Esq., of Mississippi, to Miss FANNIE ISADORA, youngest daughter of Maj. William Jewell, of Georgetown, D.C. (6 JUL 1853)

DEATH. On Tuesday evening, the 5th inst., Mrs. MARY ANN, consort of Mr. A.R. Quantrile. The friends of the deceased are requested to attend her funeral, on Thursday, at 10 o'clock A.M., from the residence of her husband, on Vermont avenue, between H and I streets. (6 JUL 1853)

DEATH. In this city, on the 3d inst., Mr. W. VOSS. (6 JUL 1853)

DEATH. In this city yesterday afternoon [5 JUL 1853], after a short and painful illness, ROBERT POWERS, infant son of Robert and Martha Grimes, aged six months. The friends of the family are invited to attend his funeral this (Wednesday) afternoon, at 4 o'clock, from the residence of his parents. (6 JUL 1853)

DEATH. At the Island of Puerto Rico, June 12th, of yellow fever, in the 18th year of his age, FREDERICK T., son of the late Gustavus Harrison, of Georgetown, D.C. (6 JUL 1853)

DEATH. On the morning of the 6th of July, at 7½ A.M., after a few days' illness, HENRY CLAY, son of James L. and Rachel W. White, aged thirteen months. The funeral will proceed from the residence of Mrs. H. Esterly, on Pennsylvania avenue, near Third street, on Thursday, the 7th inst., at 5 o'clock P.M. The friends of the family are respectfully invited to attend. (7 JUL 1853)

DEATH. On Tuesday, July 5th, WILLIAM W., son of A.O. and P.J. Douglas, in the 10th year of his age. The funeral will take place from the residence of his father, on I street, between 6th and 7th streets, this (Thursday) morning, at 10 o'clock, at which time and place the friends and acquaintances of the family are respectfully invited to attend without further notice. (7 JUL 1853)

DEATH. On the 26th of June, in Spotsylvania Co., Va., at the residence of her niece, the wife of the Rev. Mr. Wharton, Miss CATHARINE PEARCE, of Chestertown, Md., in the 77th year of her age. She was the aunt, and mother by adoption, of the Hon. J.A. Pearce. The deceased was a lady of fine literary taste and vigorous and highly cultivated mind. But the best traits in her character were her devotion as a Christian, her sincerity and truth as a friend, and her self-sacrificing practical benevolence. By these here long and most useful life was governed to its last hour. (8 JUL 1853)

DEATH. In Prince Frederick, Calvert Co., Md., July 1st, LOUISA ELLEN, wife of Rev. Edward Dulin, in her 33d year, formerly of this city. (8 JUL 1853)

DEATH. On Friday morning, the 1st inst., at Mt. Herman, near this city, the residence of her mother, LENORE, youngest child of Mrs. Elizabeth and the late Robert Serrell Wood, Esq., aged ten months. (8 JUL 1853)

DEATH. In this city, on Thursday morning, July 7th, HENRY COOLIDGE, son of John and Susan M. Van Santwoord, aged 11 months. (8 JUL 1853)

MARRIAGE. On the 7th inst., by the Rev. Mr. Wysong, JOHN Y. DONN to Miss MARGARET COOPER, all of this city. (9 JUL 1853)

Daily National Intelligencer, Marriage and Death Notices, 1851-1854

DEATH. On the 7th inst., MICHAEL DELANEY, in the 25th year of his age, a native of Queens county, Ireland. His friends and relations are invited to attend his funeral on Saturday, the 9th inst., at 3½ o'clock P.M., from his late residence, corner of 6th and C streets, Island, without further notice. (9 JUL 1853)

DEATH. At Hagerstown, Md., on the 4th inst., after a severe illness of many moths, ELLEN SERENA NESBITT, aged eighteen years, only daughter of Isaac Nesbitt, Clerk of the Circuit Court for that county. She endured her intense sufferings with quiet resignation to the Heavenly will, giving a happy assurance of a glorious immortality. (9 JUL 1853)

DEATH. We are sincerely pained to learn the death, yesterday evening [8 JUL 1853], at his residence near Baltimore, of the Hon. JOHN GLENN, District Judge of the U.S. for the District of Maryland. His loss will be deeply and extensively felt as an able Judge and as a high-minded and estimable man. (9 JUL 1853)

DEATH OF JUDGE TALIAFERRO.--The *Lynchburg Virginian* announces the death of Judge Norbourne M. Taliaferro, of the Bedford Circuit, which occurred at his residence near Franklin Courthouse a few days since. Judge T. was universally esteemed for his virtues as a man and his probity and ability as a public officer. His death will be widely and deeply deplored. *Richmond Enquirer*. (11 JUL 1853)

DEATH. At Lothian, on West River, Md., on the third of July, in the 90th year of her age, Mrs. CORNELIA LANSDALE, relict of Maj. Thomas Lancaster Lansdale, of Smallwood's brigade in the war of the Revolution. (11 JUL 1853)

DEATH. At his residence in Montgomery Co., Md., on the 6th July, CYRUS WATERS, M.D., leaving a wife and three children to lament their early bereavement. His disease was consumption, brought on by over-exertions in the medical profession, to which he was ardently attached. For nearly three years he lingered with a perfect consciousness that his case was irrecoverable. By his death society is deprived of a highly useful and intelligent member, and the sick have to mourn the departure of a benefactor and friend. (11 JUL 1853)

DEATH. At Gordonsdale, of prevailing dysentery, on the 6th inst., WALTER JONES, and on the 7th inst., EDWARD MARSHALL, children of Dr. Robt. E. and Mrs. Nannette Peyton. This heavy two fold blow has fallen on the hearts of fond parents; but, sustained by the holy religion they both profess and practice, they have been enabled, with a Christian fortitude and submission the most exemplary, to commit the bodies of these bright boys to the tomb without a murmur, believing their freed spirits wing their celestial way to the bosom of Him who hath said "*suffer little children to come unto me, for of such is the kingdom of Heaven.*" (11 JUL 1853)

MARRIAGE. On the 16th June, by the Rev. R.L. Dashiell, Mr. JOHN B. HINES to Miss LYDIA A. CUNNINGHAM, all of this place. (12 JUL 1853)

MARRIAGE. On the 8th inst., at the F Street Presbyterian Church, by the Rev. D.X. Junkin, Dr. GEORGE M. DALE to Miss ELLEN L. EVANS, all of this city. (12 JUL 1853)

MARRIAGE. At St. Louis, Mo., on the 30th ult. [30 JUN 1853], by the Rev. Mr. Leclerc, EDWARD GRAHAM ATKINSON to HARRIET L. WALKER, daughter of Maj. B. Walker, U.S. Army. (12 JUL 1853)

MARRIAGE. At Oak Grove, Richmond Co., Va., on the 5th inst., by the Rev. Mr. Ward, Mr. A.F. YERBY, of Washington, to Miss OLIVIA BEALE McCARTY. (12 JUL 1853)

DEATH. At his residence in St. Mary's Co., Md., on Wednesday, the 6th inst., about 5 o'clock P.M., after a severe illness of a few hours, Mr. GEORGE H. SMITH, aged about 50 years, leaving an affectionate wife and five small children to mourn their irreparable loss. Mr. Smith was a good man, universally beloved by a large circle of relations and friends. (12 JUL 1853)

Daily National Intelligencer, Marriage and Death Notices, 1851-1854

MARRIAGE. On Monday, 11th inst., by the Rev. Mr. Hodges, WILLIAM WATSON to ELIZA CURTIN, of Prince George's Co., Md. (13 JUL 1853)

MARRIAGE. On the 15th inst., by the Rev. S.K. Cox, Mr. S.B.B. GOSZLER, of Georgetown, D.C., to Miss SARAH E. CONNOR, of Montgomery Co., Md. (13 JUL 1853)

DEATH. At her residence (Island) in this city, on Thursday last, the 7th inst., Mrs. ELIZABETH E. BARNES, in the 38th year of her age. (13 JUL 1853)

DEATH. At Cazenovia, near Washington, on Saturday night, the 9th inst., DANIEL WEBSTER, son of Col. James R. and Henrietta B. Creecy, aged three years and four months. (13 JUL 1853)

DEATH. In this city, in hopes of a blessed immortality, JOHN GREEVES, Esq., in the 40th year of his age. His friends and acquaintances are respectfully invited to attend his funeral at the residence of his mother, on 10th, between K and L streets, on Friday, the 15th inst., at 10 A.M. (14 JUL 1853)

DEATH. At his residence, in the Catawba, in Mecklenburg Co., N.C., on Tuesday, the 14th ult. [14 JUN 1853], ROBERT DAVIDSON, Esq., in the 85th year of his age. (15 JUL 1853)

DEATH. On the 14th inst., near Beltsville, Prince George's Co., Md., BENEDICT BRASHEAR, aged 65 years. (15 JUL 1853)

MARRIAGE. At Liberty, Tex., on the 30th June last, by [Rev.] J.H. Griffin, Esq., Mr. F.G. WARING to Mrs. H.E. BENOIST, late of St. Louis, Mo. (18 JUL 1853)

MARRIAGE. On Thursday evening, 14th inst., by Rev. Mr. Marks, Mr. JOHN F. TAYLOR to Miss CAROLINE HAZZARD. (18 JUL 1853)

MARRIAGE. On Thursday, the 14th inst., by the Rev. Mr. Hodges, EDWIN C. MORGAN to Miss EVELINE P., daughter of Maj. R.B. Lee, of Washington. (18 JUL 1853)

MARRIAGE. In Cincinnati, Ohio, on the 12th inst., by the Rev. Horace Bushnell, J. THOMAS McDUFFIE, of Washington, D.C., to Miss MARY A. PRICE, only daughter of Gen. Reese E. Price, of the former place. (18 JUL 1853)

MARRIAGE. On Thursday evening, the 14th inst., by the Rev. D. Evans Reese, ROBERT L. BOZZEL to ISABEL A. FOXWELL, all of this city. (18 JUL 1853)

DEATH. At four o'clock on the morning of the 17th inst., Miss LUCY ANN BROOKE, daughter of the late Walter Brooke, of Fairfax Co., Va. The friends of the family are invited to attend her funeral this afternoon at 4 o'clock, from the residence of her brother-in-law, Wm. S. Darrell, on L street, between 9th and 10th streets. (18 JUL and 7 SEP 1853)

DEATH. On the morning of the 16th, after a short and painful illness, Mrs. REBECCA M. SMITH, the beloved wife of J.L. Smith, Esq., in the 37th year of her age. (18 JUL 1853)

DEATH. On Wednesday morning, July 13th, MATHEW H., infant son of R.M. and Elizabeth Farnum, aged ten months. (18 JUL 1853)

MARRIAGE. On the 18th of May, by the Rev. J.W. Brown, Mr. WM. W. RAPLEY to Miss C.S. HARRYMAN, both of Baltimore, Md. (20 JUL 1853)

MARRIAGE. On Sabbath evening, 17th inst., by the Rev. James H. Brown, Mr. STEPHEN R. GOODWIN, of Annapolis, to Miss MARY JANE HOPKINS, of Washington. (20 JUL 1853)

Daily National Intelligencer, Marriage and Death Notices, 1851-1854

MARRIAGE. On the 29th ult. [29 JUN 1853], by the Rev. James H. Brown, Mr. RICHARD F. BOWERS to Miss LOUISA J. GAINES, both of Culpeper, Va. (20 JUL 1853)

DEATH. In this city, on the 16th inst., after a severe illness, Mrs. EDNEY WILLIAMS, wife of Zadock Williams, in the 41st year of her age, leaving her husband and ten children to mourn the loss of a kind wife and affectionate mother. (20 JUL 1853)

DEATH. On the 17th inst., JOHN FRANCIS, infant son of James and Martha Riordan. (20 JUL 1853)

DEATH. On Monday evening, the 18th inst., CORNELIA CLINTON McKNIGHT, youngest daughter of the Rev. Dr. John McKnight, formerly pastor of the Presbyterian Churches, New York. The funeral will take place today at 10 o'clock, from the residence of G.B. McKnight, on Third street. The friends of the family are respectfully invited to attend. (20 JUL 1853)

DEATH. On the 18th inst., at Rockville, Md., JONES, youngest son of Robert W. and Catharine C. Latham, aged one year and eight days. The funeral will take place from the residence of his father at four o'clock P.M. on the 20th inst. The friends of the family are invited to attend. (20 JUL 1853)

DEATHS. On the 16th inst., after a lingering illness, THERESA ELIZABETH, in the 13th year of her age; and on the 19th inst., GEORGE HENRY, after an illness of ten days, in the 6th year of his age, children of W. and C. Hager. The friends and acquaintances of the family are respectfully invited to attend the funeral of the latter on Wednesday, the 20th, at 4 o'clock, from [His] father's residence, on 18th street, between H and I streets. (20 JUL 1853)

DEATH. On the morning of the 14th inst., at Silver Spring, residence of Francis P. Blair, Esq., where it had been carried for change of air, ANNE BEVERLY, infant daughter of Col. Fremont, born at Paris, February 1, 1853. (20 JUL 1853)

DEATH. On the 17th inst., at Spring Park, Alexandria Co., JOHN FRANCIS, infant son of James and Martha Riordan. (20 JUL 1853)

DEATH. On the 10th inst., in Georgetown, in the 68th year of her age, Mrs. L. BLAGROVE, wife of H.B. Blagrove, ater a severe dispensation of Providence of nearly seventeen months, caused by three violent attacks of paralysis, rendering her during that time wholly helpless and speechless. May she rest in peace. *"Within the cold grave her pains now cease, Her sins being all forgiven' Her body calmly lies in peace, Her soul now dwells in Heaven!"* (21 JUL 1853)

DEATH. On the 20th inst., near the Navy Yard, of consumption, CATHERINE E., only daughter of Dennis and Mary Callaghan, after a lingering illness of near four months, aged 7 years 6 months and 20 days. The funeral will take place this (Thursday) evening at 3 o'clock, corner of 4th and D streets east. (21 JUL 1853)

DEATH. On the 10th inst., WILLIAM FRANCIS, youngest son of Wm. P. Elliot. (21 JUL 1853)

MARRIAGE. At Gadsby's Hotel, on the 21st inst., by the Rev. Hugh Harrison, of Maryland, WILLIAM HAZZARD WIGG, Esq., of South Carolina, to Miss EMMA MARIA, daughter of the late Commodore Thomas Holdup Stevens, of the U.S. Navy. (22 JUL 1853)

MARRIAGE. In Baltimore, on Thursday, the 30th ult. [30 JUN 1853], by the Rev. J. Newman Hank, Dr. J.W.F. HANK to Miss ANNA M. KEENER, all of that city. (23 JUL 1853)

MARRIAGE. On the 28th June, by the Rev. Dr. Isaac Cole, WILLIAM McCARTEY MILLS to ELIZABETH REBECCA STALLINGS. On the 20th of July, by the same, MOSES R. SWAIM to LYDIA KNIGHTS, all of this city. (23 JUL 1853)

Daily National Intelligencer, Marriage and Death Notices, 1851-1854

MARRIAGE. At the Cathedral, Baltimore, on the 21st inst., by the Rev. Mr. Coskery, EBEN FAXON to AMBROSIA M. JENKINS, all of Baltimore. (25 JUL 1853)

DEATH. At the residence of his father, Mr. Samuel Cropley, Bridge street, Georgetown, between the hours of 12 and 1 o'clock P.M., on the 23d inst., of tetanus, Mr. SAMUEL BARNARD CROPLEY, eldest son of the above, ater a short illness, which he bore with exemplary patience, at the age of 21 years and 7 months. His funeral will take place from his father's residence on Monday, the 25th inst., at 5 o'clock, P.M., when his friends are kindly invited to attend. (25 JUL 1853)

DEATH. At Savannah, Ga., on the 16th inst., CORNELIA AUGUSTA, wife of Judge Henry R. Jackson, of that place, and only sister of Henry K. Davenport, U.S. Navy. (25 JUL 1853)

DEATH. In this city, on Saturday morning last [23 JUL 1853], SENECA MARSHALL, son of Vincent and Susan Emily Barnes, aged 2 years and 16 days. (25 JUL 1853)

MARRIAGE. On the 21st of June, by the Rev. Alph. Charlier, Mr. WM. KLEMANN to Miss ELENORA HELLER. (26 JUL 1853)

DEATH. On the 23d inst., Mrs. SARAH THOMAS, aged 65 years, the daughter of Maj. Richard Dorsey, of the Old Maryland Line in the war of the Revolution. (26 JUL 1853)

DEATH. At Mt. Calm, the residence of Mr. Charles J. Meriwether, in Albemarle Co., Va., on the 22d inst., JOHN CHRISTIAN, infant son of J.C. and Caroline C. Walker, aged fourteen months and three days. (26 JUL 1853)

MARRIAGE. In this city, on the 23d inst., by the Rev. Mr. Reese, Mr. O.C. HARRIS, of Upper Marlboro, Prince George's Co., Md., to Miss ELIZABETH A. CRACKLIN, of Calvert Co., Md. (27 JUL 1853)

DEATH. On the 25th inst., after a long and protracted illness, which she bore with Christian resignation, Miss MARY E. TANNER, aged 30 years. Her friends and relations are respectfully invited to attend her funeral from the house of Joseph Huggins, her late residence, Pennsylvania avenue, near 13th street, this evening at 4 o'clock. (27 JUL 1853)

DEATH. In this city, on Tuesday, July 21st, Mr. JOSEPH MARKRITER, a native of Georgetown, in the thirty-fifth year of his age. (27 JUL 1853)

DEATHS In Monongahela City, Pa., on Wednesday, the 13th inst., SAMUEL KING, aged 10 months; and on Saturday, the 16th, THOMAS HARLAN, in the 3d year of his age, only children of Thomas H. and Louisa Baird, of this city. (27 JUL 1853)

MARRIAGE. At Ft. Leavenworth, on Tuesday morning, July 5, by the Rev. Leander Ker, Chaplain U.S.A., Adjutant J.H. WHITTLESY, U.S. dragoons, to Miss KATE K. FAUNTLEROY, youngest daughter of Col. Thomas T. Fauntleroy, U.S. dragoons. (28 JUL 1853)

DEATH. In this city, yesterday afternoon [27 JUL 1853], NATHANIEL B. PAGE, Esq., a native of Virginia, but late of Anne Arundel Co., Md. Due notice will be given of the time and place of his funeral. (28 JUL 1853)

DEATH. On Monday, July 25th, of scarlet fever, EDWARD St. PIERRE, aged one year, infant son of George M. and Ellen GROUARD. (28 JUL 1853)

DEATH. On the evening of the 26th inst., VIRGINIA, aged seventeen months, the youngest daughter of Wm. P. and Eliza J. Ferguson. The relatives and friends of the family are respectfully invited to attend her

Daily National Intelligencer, Marriage and Death Notices, 1851-1854

funeral on this (Thursday) afternoon at half-past two o'clock, from the residence of her parents, on Georgia avenue, between Third and Fourth streets east. (28 JUL 1853)

DEATH. In Washington, on the 26th inst., MARGARETTA, aged 11 months and 18 days, second child of William B. and Mary E. Dobbins. (28 JUL 1853)

MARRIAGE. On the 26th inst., by the Rev. Jas. H. Brown, Mr. JOHN COX to Miss ELIZABETH E. KNIGHTON, both of this city. (29 JUL 1853)

DEATH. On Monday, the 25th inst., at his residence in Emmittsburg, Md., of the epidemic diarrhea, after an illness of six days, Dr. AUGUSTINE TANEY, aged 56 years 5 months and 6 days. A gentleman of accomplished manners, kind and amiable in his disposition, and energetic in the performance of duty, the deceased exerted a deservedly great influence in the circle of his friends. Having been highly esteemed in life, his unexpected death has produced deep lamentation; but to his sorrowing relatives and friends he has left the high consolation that he died in the full confidence of the Christian faith which he professed, and was attended to the last hour of his earthly existence by the prayers and pious ministrations of his sympathizing friends and pastors. (29 JUL 1853)

MARRIAGE. In this city, on Wednesday, the 27th inst., by Rev. Charles H. Nourse, of Montgomery Co., Md., Rev. JACOB W. WINANS, of Elizabethtown, N.J., and Miss SUSAN S. NOURSE, daughter of the late Dr. Benjamin P. Nourse, U.S. Army. (30 JUL 1853)

DEATH. On the 28th inst., JOSEPH JAMES BORROWS, aged 19 months and 16 days, only child of J. William and Julia A. Plant. The friends and acquaintances of the family are requested to attend the funeral from the residence of his grandfather on D street, between 9th and 10th streets, on Sunday afternoon at 3 o'clock. (30 JUL 1853)

DEATH. On the 30th July, in the full triumphs of the Christian faith, after a protracted consumption of two years and three months duration, which she bore without a murmur or a groan, ELLEN JOSEPHINE NYE, in the 22d year of her age, daughter of J.W. and P. Nye. She was for a number of years a pious and exemplary member of the Methodist Episcopal Church and a Sabbath School teacher at McKendree station. Her friends are respectfully requested to attend her funeral, at the residence of her parents, on L street, between 6th and 7th, this (Monday) afternoon at three o'clock. (1 AUG 1853)

MARRIAGE. In this city, on the 28th ult. [28 JUL 1853], by the Rev. D.X. Junkin, D.C., Mr. ROBERT CLARKSON to Miss CAROLINA SEIFERT, all of Washington. (2 AUG 1853)

DEATH. On Sunday night, the 31st of July, in the 76th year of her age, Mrs. TERESE RITTER, relict of the late Peter Ritter, of Georgetown. Her funeral will take place on Tuesday afternoon, at 4 o'clock, from her late residence in Georgetown. (2 AUG 1853)

DEATH. On Monday morning, August 1st, CHARLES RICHARD, aged 3 years and 6 months, only son of Charles H. and Maria Tavenner. The relations and friends of the family are invited to attend his funeral on this Tuesday afternoon, at 3 o'clock, from the residence of his grandfather, Philip Otterback, near the Navy Yard. (2 AUG 1853)

DEATH. On the 2d inst., after a short illness, WILLIAM COX, Sr., in the 85th year of his age. His funeral will take place this (Wednesday) afternoon, at 5 o'clock, from the residence of his son, W.W. Cox, on I, between 9th and 10th streets. The friends of the family are respectfully invited to attend. (3 AUG 1853)

DEATH. On the 2d inst., after a few days' illness, JESSE WEBSTER, only son of Jesse B. and Anna A. Wilson, aged ten months. The friends and relatives of the family are respectfully invited to attend the funeral this (Wednesday) evening at 4 o'clock, from the residence of his parents on 9th street, between New York avenue and I street. (3 AUG 1853)

Daily National Intelligencer, Marriage and Death Notices, 1851-1854

MARRIAGE. On the 26th ult. [26 JUL 1853], by the Rev. Mr. Finkel, Mr. A. EICHSTADT to Miss METTA SCHUARZKOPF, all of this place. (4 AUG 1853)

MARRIAGE. On Thursday morning, August 4th, in the Church of the Ascension, by the Rev. L.I. Gilliss, R.B. IRONSIDE, M.D., of Yreka, Calif., and MARY WHARTENBY, second daughter of John Hood, Esq., of this city. (5 AUG 1853)

DEATH. In February last, at his residence near Fishing Creek, Calvert Co., Md., Mr. RICHARD B. DARNALL, aged 35 years. (5 AUG 1853)

DEATH. On the 24th ult. [24 JUL 1853], at Annapolis, Mr. NICHOLAS L. DARNALL, in the 24th year of his age. (5 AUG 1853)

MARRIAGE. Near Charlestown, Cecil Co., Md., on the 2d inst., by Rev. A.A. Hodge, JOHN T. CROW, of Baltimore, formerly of Georgetown, and MARY E. OWENS, of Cecil Co., Md. (6 AUG 1853)

DEATH. At noon, on Friday, the 5th inst., in the 62d year of her age, Mrs. MARY GIDEON, wife of Jacob Gideon. Her funeral will take place this (Saturday) afternoon, at 5 o'clock, from her late residence, on Seventh street, opposite the Post Office. The friends of the family are invited to attend without further notice. (6 and 15 AUG 1853)

DEATH. Yesterday [6 AUG 1853], at noon, after a long and painful illness, which she bore with Christian patience and fortitude, Mrs. MARGARET Y. HARKNESS, consort of John C. Harkness. Her funeral will take place from her late residence, on New York avenue, this (Saturday) afternoon at 4 o'clock. Her friends and acquaintances are respectfully requested to attend without further notice. (6 AUG 1853)

OBITUARY. Mr. ELISHA RIGGS, whose decease we announced yesterday, was one of the oldest and wealthiest bankers in the U.S. He was born in Montgomery Co., Md., in 1779, and first entered into business for himself at Georgetown, in the District of Columbia, where he resided for several years, during which period George Peabody, the wealthy London banker, then under age, was taken into partnership with him. They afterwards together established the house of Riggs, Peabody & Co., of Baltimore. In the course of time, Mr. Riggs retired from that firm and removed to New York, where he resided for many years previous to his death, and where he always took an active part in all the leading enterprises of his time requiring large means and commercial experience. He was one of the most active friends of the New York and Liverpool line of steamships, and contributed largely towards its establishment. One of his sons is a partner with Mr. Collins in the agency of that line. Mr. Riggs died on the evening of the 3d inst., in the 75th year of his age, after an illness of several weeks. He was a man of strong domestic affections, and leaves a widow and six children, five of them sons, to mourn his loss. One of his sons, Elisha, is a member of the firm of Corcoran & Riggs; and his son George retired from the same firm a few years since with a large fortune. *New York Evening Post*. (8 AUG and 4 NOV 1853)

DEATH. In Baltimore, on the 6th inst., after a short but severe illness, ANNA ROSETTA, eldest daughter of Marion B. and the late James Hoban, of this city, aged 19 years. (9 AUG 1853)

DEATH. In Georgetown, on Sunday night, the 7th inst., LIZZIE B., wife of the Rev. D. Motzer, and eldest daughter of the late William Williamson. Her friends and the friends of the family are invited to attend her funeral, from the residence of Mrs. Hepburn, on West street, at 5 o'clock this afternoon. (9 and 10 AUG 1853)

DEATH. On the 4th inst., at her residence, West River, Mrs. ELIZA L. GIBBS, wife of A. Chisholm Gibbs, and daughter of the late Dr. H.H. Hayden, of Baltimore. (9 AUG 1853)

OBITUARY. Died, on Sabbath evening, the 7th inst., in Georgetown, D.C., in the 29th year of her age, Mrs. ELIZABETH B. MOTZER, wife of the Rev. Daniel Motzer, eldest daughter of the late

Daily National Intelligencer, Marriage and Death Notices, 1851-1854

William Williamson, Esq., and granddaughter of the late Rev. Stephen B. Balch, D.D. [text continues]. (10 AUG 1853)

DEATH. Died, on the 7th inst., MEDORA, eldest daughter of Louisa and Col. James Kearney, U.S. Army. The deceased suffered under a long and painful illness, which she bore to the last with that resignation which marks the "children of God" [text continues]. (10 AUG 1853)

MARRIAGE. In this city, on Sunday, the 7th inst., by the Rev. G.W. Samson, Mr. WILLIAM HUMPHREY to Miss SUSAN HUMPHREY, of Alexandria, Va. (10 AUG 1853)

DEATH. On Tuesday evening, 9th inst., MARIA LOUISA, infant daughter of Edward and Maria Louisa Swann. The funeral will take place from Mr. Swann's residence, on Louisiana avenue, on Thursday morning next, at 10 o'clock. (10 AUG 1853)

DEATH. Yesterday [9 AUG 1853], MARY ANN, daughter of Wm. R. Woodward, aged 22 months. Funeral this afternoon at 4 o'clock, from the residence of her father, corner of O street north and Fifth street west. (10 AUG 1853)

MARRIAGE. On the 9th of August, by the Rev. Stephen P. Hill, THOMAS L. COCHRANE to MARY E. DOWNEY, both of this city. (11 AUG 1853)

MARRIAGE. On Wednesday, 10th inst., by the Rev. J.C. Smith, JOHN E. LATHAM to Miss VIRGINIA, daughter of Jas. and Margaret Withers, all of this city. (11 AUG 1853)

DEATH. On the 6th inst., near Port Tobacco, Charles Co., Md., after a short illness, Miss SUSAN B. FRYERS, formerly of Newport, R.I.; a zealous, conscientious, and benevolent Christian. (11 AUG 1853)

OBITUARY. An aged Loyalist, named JAMES BURWELL, one of the remnant of the United Empire Loyalists, died on the 18th of June, at the advanced age of 93 years and 5 months, in Canada. He was born at Rockaway, N.J., on the 18th day of January 1754. One of his ancestors was of Virginia deputation in the year 1646 to invite the fallen monarch, Charles the first, to come to America for protection against the rebellious Puritan subjects. The subject of this obituary enlisted in his Majesty's service in the year 1776, at the age of twenty-two, was present at the battle of Yorktown, when Lord Cornwallis surrendered to General Washington, and was there slightly wounded. After the war of 1783 he moved to Nova Scotia, where he remained four years; he then returned to New Jersey, to take care of his aged mother, where he married. He removed to the Talbot settlement in the year 1810. Some few years since he had a renewed head of youthful hair, and could see to read without glasses. (11 AUG 1853)

DEATH. On Thursday, August 11th, of consumption, JOSEPHINE WATSON, fourth daughter of John B. and Camilla Coddington. The friends and acquaintances of the family are respectfully invited to attend her funeral from the residence of her mother, on B street, between 2d and 3d streets, this (Friday) afternoon, at 4 o'clock. (12 AUG 1853)

DEATH. On Wednesday, August 11th, at noon, MARY ANN, beloved wife of Jas. A. Clark, in the 26th year of her age. *"None knew her but to love her."* The relatives and friends of the family are invited to attend her funeral from her late residence on I street, between 9th and 10th streets, this (Friday) afternoon, at 5 o'clock. (12 AUG 1853)

MARRIAGE. In Venecia, Calif., July 5th, 1853, by the Rev. Mr. Gallagher, Bvt. Capt. CHARLES P. STONE, Ordnance Corps U.S. Army, to Miss MARIA L. CLARY, daughter of Capt. R.E. Clary, U.S. Army. (13 AUG 1853)

𝔇𝔞𝔦𝔩𝔶 𝔑𝔞𝔱𝔦𝔬𝔫𝔞𝔩 𝔍𝔫𝔱𝔢𝔩𝔩𝔦𝔤𝔢𝔫𝔠𝔢𝔯, Marriage and Death Notices, 1851-1854

DEATH. On Sunday morning, the 7th inst., at the residence of E. Bashaw, Esq., Fauquier Co., Va., Miss MARGARET M. HUME, aged sixty-three years. Deeply will her death be felt by those to whose comfort and happiness she devoted her life; but their loss is her eternal gain. (13 AUG 1853)

DEATH. In Georgetown, on the evening of the 11th inst., JULIA C., wife of Mr. Jas. A. Simpson. Her funeral will take place this (Saturday) evening, at 5 o'clock, from her late residence on Market street. (13 AUG 1853)

DEATH. On the 4th inst., after a few days' illness, at the Rectory, Anne Arundel Co., Md., in the full assurance of Christian faith, Mrs. FRANCES CORLIS YOUNG, wife of the Rev. Jas. Young, of the parish of All-Hallows. (13 AUG 1853)

DEATH. On the 12th inst., JANE, only daughter of Hugh and Jane Lochrey, aged 5 months. The friends of the family are invited to attend the funeral on Saturday, 13th, at 4 o'clock P.M. (13 AUG 1853)

DEATH OF MRS. GIDEON. From the *Philadelphia Observer*, Letter to one of the Editors, Washington, Monday, August 8, 1853. Mrs. MARY GIDEON, wife of our Elder, Jacob Gideon, Esq., was lying seriously and as many thought dangerously ill. I could not think so, nor was my confidence shaken until last Thursday evening when a change occurred that roused my most painful apprehensions. She died at noon on Friday. She was identified with the Fourth Church, was one of the little band that organized it in 1828, and always had a large place in the confidence and affections of all up to the hour of her departure... The funeral services were conducted by Rev. Messrs. J.N. Danforth, Mason Noble, Byron Sunderland, and myself [John C. Smith]... A large concourse of mourning friends gathered around her coffin. Of these, I must make particular mention of one, the President of these United States. His pew is immediately in front of Mr. Gideon's. When a Senator, he always sat with Mr. and Mrs. Gideon. Thus he came to know, and to know was to love her. The President was in the Navy Yard on Saturday, and when the booming of the cannon had ceased was about to embark on a short excursion in a U.S. steamer. At this moment he was incidentally informed of the death. He expressed regret that he had not heard of it before, and said he would have postponed the excursion, but now it was too late. He, however, communicated his wishes for an early return. He was gratified and came at the appointed hour as one of the congregation, without invitation, other than that which all received... John C. Smith. (15 AUG 1853)

DEATH. On Wednesday evening, the 10th inst., of bilious dysentery, Mrs. ELIZA M.D. CLEARY, wife of Nicholas Cleary, Esq., of this city, and only daughter of the late Thos. Reilly, Esq., of Norfolk, Va. *Requiescat in pace!* (15 AUG 1853)

DEATH. In this city, on the 14th inst., at half-past 10 o'clock P.M., after a short illness, Mrs. MARY R. SHREVE, the beloved wife of John Shreve, Esq., of this city, in the 41st year of her age. (16 AUG 1853)

DEATH. On Monday morning, the 15th inst., Mrs. CAROLINE SKELLY, in the 54th year of her age. The friends of the deceased are respectfully requested to attend her funeral, at the residence of her son, North Capitol street, Capitol Hill, at 9 o'clock this (Tuesday) morning. (16 AUG 1853)

DEATH. In this city, on Monday, the 8th inst., at the house of Mr. L. Coyle, CORNELIUS LAVERGNE, infant son of William C. Breese, Esq., of Charleston, S.C. (16 AUG 1853)

DEATHS AT EMMITSBURG. A letter in the *Chambersburg Compiler* gives a list of deaths from the epidemic at Emmitsburg, Md. [lists 27 persons, including Rev. Thomas A. McCaffrey, D.D.]. (16 AUG 1853)

DEATH. At the residence of his brother, James A. Bowen, in Prince George's Co., Md., on Sunday night, the 14th inst., after a lingering and painful illness, which he bore with Christian resignation, JOHN F. BOWEN, in the 22d year of his age. (17 AUG 1853)

DEATH. At New Orleans, La., on the 11th of August inst., of typhoid yellow fever, after an illness of eight days, CHARLES C. SNETHEN, aged forty-four years, second son of the late Rev. Nicholas Snethen. (17 AUG 1853)

DEATH. At her residence, Mt. Pleasant, Charles Co., Md., on the 18th ult. [18 JUL 1853], Miss ELIZA JAMESON, in the 68th year of her age [text continues]. (17 AUG 1853)

MARRIAGE. At Boonesboro, Md., on the 3d inst., by the Rev. William Prettyman, JOHN W. McKIM, Esq., of this city, to Miss MARGARETTA F. PRETTYMAN. (18 AUG 1853)

FATAL OCCURRENCE.--The *Leesburg Washingtonian* states that SAMUEL GIBSON and PHINEAS GIBSON, two brothers, in Fauquier Co., Va., got into a fight a few days ago, while at work, which resulted in the death of Samuel. He was afflicted with a disease of the heart, and the excitement, it is supposed, caused death to ensue. (18 AUG 1853)

MARRIAGE. ON the 18th inst., by the Rev. Mr. Hill, GEORGE W. PAYNE to Miss ELIZA JANE BIRNEY, all of this city. (19 AUG 1853)

MARRIAGE. In St. Paul's Church, Norfolk, Va., on the 16th August, by the Rev. M.R. Talbot, Dr. CHARLES EVERSFIELD, of the U.S. Navy, and Miss JOS. TRUXTUN TALBOT, daughter of the Rev. M. Talbot, U.S.N. (19 and 22 AUG 1853)

DEATH. Suddenly, in Richmond, on the 10th inst., Mrs. ELIZABETH S. WICKHAM, relict of the late John Wickham, Esq., a lady of great worth and universally respected. (22 AUG 1853)

DEATH. At New Orleans, on the 4th inst., of the prevailing epidemic, MURRAY MASON, aged about twenty-one years, son of Maynadier Mason, Esq., of Rose Hill, Va. Descended from a distinguished Revolutionary family, there have been none who have borne the name possessed of nobler qualities or more elevated principles. Scarcely twenty-one years of age, and but a few months in the country, he was employed in a responsible situation on the Ponchartrain Railroad, and had made many friends among the young men of New Orleans, who will long lament his untimely death, and cherish the recollection of his gentlemanly manners, generous qualities, and honorable bearing. If the highest medical skill, the assiduity of friends, or the prayers of relatives could have arrested the fell destroyer "who loves a shining mark," poor Murray had not died. *Piscayne*. (22 AUG 1853)

DIED. At Bladensburg, Md., on the 19th inst., of cholera infantum, THOMAS GASTON, youngest son of Capt. W.J. Newton, U.S. Army, and Cornelia S. Newton, aged two years and nine months. (22 AUG 1853)

MARRIAGE. On Sabbath evening [21 AUG 1853], by the Rev. John C. Smith, Mr. FRANCIS LaBARRE to Miss MARY A. BURKHARDT, all of this city. (23 AUG 1853)

DEATH. At Mt. Vernon, Ohio, on the 19th inst., Mrs. MARY ELLIOTT, wife of Mr. Alexander Elliott, of this city, aged about 50 years. (23 AUG 1853)

OBITUARY. From the *Union* of Yesterday [23 AUG 1853]. Died as sea, on board the U.S. ship *Preble*, on the 5th ult. [5 JUL 1853], EDMUND MARCY, youngest son of Hon. Wm. L. Marcy, Secretary of State, in the 22d year of his age. The melancholy intelligence of the premature death of this amiable and highly-accomplished young gentleman will be received with the deepest sensibility by a numerous circle of friends who knew the noble qualities of his nature, and who looked with high anticipations upon the opening promise of his life. A year or two since he graduated at Trinity College, Hartford, Conn., with a high reputation for ability and success in the studies to which his attention had been devoted, and, returning to his home at Albany, entered with ardor upon the pursuits connected with civil engineering, the profession which he had chosen, and in which his rare aptitude and ability as a mathematician seemed to ensure his success and distinction. It is probable that the zeal and assiduity with which he gave himself to these labors and studies contributed still more to undermine his already precarious health. Alarming symptoms of consumption soon developed themselves; and early in the last autumn he was compelled, under the watchful care of his father, to seek, in a journey to the Southern States, and afterwards to the West Indies, the alleviation and aid which a milder climate might bring to his condition. Returning to the North with his health still unrestored, he determined, under the advice of his physicians, to try the effect of a sea voyage, and with that view took passage in the company and under the affectionate care of his brother, Lieut. Marcy, on the Preble, bound to the coast of Spain. He left Norfolk on the 30th of June last, and breathed his last five days afterwards [text continues]. (24 AUG 1853)

MARRIAGE. On the 16th inst., by the Rev. Mr. Davis, J. CLAYTON BRASHEAR and Miss LAURA VAN LEAR, daughter of the late Dr. Watson, of Bedford, Pa. (24 AUG 1853)

DEATH. On the 22d inst., at 3½ o'clock P.M., MARTHA REBECCA, in the 23d year of her age, wife of John C. Sprigg, of this city, and only daughter of Thomas and the late Rebecca Stansbury, of Baltimore. The friends of the family are respectfully invited to attend her funeral, on this (Wednesday) morning, at 10 o'clock, without further notice. (24 AUG 1853)

DEATH. Yesterday [24 AUG 1853], of consumption, ALICE KAVENAUGH, aged 14 years. Her funeral will take place this morning at 11 o'clock from the residence of Mrs. Jeffers, Missouri avenue. The friends of the family are invited to attend. (25 AUG 1853)

MARRIAGE. At the house of Col. Wm. Hunter, in this city, on Thursday, 25th inst., by the Rev. D.X. Junkin, D.D., ROBERT C. MURPHY, Esq., American Consul for the port of Shanghai, China, to Miss LAVINIA H. LYNE, of this city. (26 AUG 1853)

MARRIAGE. On the 23d inst., at St. John's Church, Elkridge, by the Rev. Hugh T. Harrison, EDWARD SIMPSON, U.S. Navy, to MARY A., daughter of the late Charles Sterett Ridgely, of Howard Co., Md. (26 AUG 1853)

DEATH. On the 24th inst., EMMA BLANCHE, aged seven months, daughter of Dr. W. Brooke and Emma Jones. The funeral will take place at 10 o'clock this (Friday) morning from St. Patrick's Church. (26 AUG 1853)

DEATH. On Friday morning, the 26th inst., after a short and painful illness, CHARLES EDWARD THOMAS, in the 27th year of his age, only child of the late John W. and Mary Ann Thomas, of Petersburg, Va. His friends and those of the family are invited to attend his funeral from the residence of his uncle, Capt. Thos. J. Williams, on H street, on Sunday afternoon, at half-past 4 o'clock. (27 AUG 1853)

DEATH. On the 22d of August, at "Glencoe," King George Co., Va., Miss JANE S. PARK, in the 57th year of her age. She has left a large circle of relatives and friends, to whom she was greatly endeared, to mourn her loss. (27 AUG 1853)

OBITUARY. HUGH ROGERS died at his residence, near Middleburg, Loudoun Co., Va., on Monday morning, 15th inst., in the 86th year of his age. He died loved, respected, and lamented, alike by the friends whose affection had lasted for more than three-quarters of a century and by those of more recent date, leaving a widow, with whom he had lived in unclouded harmony for threescore years, and a family of ten children, fifty grandchildren, and twenty-eight great-grandchildren, all living within a few hours' ride. His was a most patriarchal character; till lately his snow white hair was almost the only mark of age about him; time seemed loath to lay his hand on so goodly and vigorous a frame, and the destroyer left his heart wholly untouched, and as young as ever. Up to a short time before his death his practice was to visit his children regularly, the most distant thirty miles off, on horseback, and he was daily in the saddle or on foot, with a keen and sagacious interest in all that was going on about him. His health and elastic spirits never failed him until a few months ago, when he was prostrated by paralysis [text continues]. (29 AUG 1853)

Daily National Intelligencer, Marriage and Death Notices, 1851-1854

MARRIAGE. On the 25th inst., at St. Patrick's Church, by the Rev. Mr. O'Toole, WILLIAM C. HARVEY to Miss CATHARINE COCKRELL, both of this city. (29 AUG 1853)

MARRIAGE. On Thursday, 25th inst., by the Rev. Mr. Hodges, NOBLE ANDERSON, of the District of Columbia, to Miss ANNE WEAVER, of Prince George's Co., Md. (29 AUG 1853)

MARRIAGE. In Owensboro, Ky., by the Rev. H.H. Hopkins, on the 18th inst., DAVID S. WATERS, Esq., of this city, to Miss ADA PAYNE, of Louisville, Ky. (29 AUG 1853)

DEATH. In the city of New Orleans, on the morning of August 11th, of the prevailing epidemic, Mrs. CATHERINE F. WINDLE, consort of Mr. George Windle, and daughter of the Rev. William Ashmead, of Charleston, S.C., and granddaughter of the late Dr. Forrester, of Wilmington, Del., aged 28 years. (29 AUG 1853)

DEATH. At Rochfort, France, on the 7th of August, in the 35th year of his age, GEORGE WASHINGTON CAMPBELL, son of the late George W. Campbell, of Nashville, Tenn., and grandson of the late Benjamin Stoddert. (30 AUG 1853)

DEATH. At his residence, on the 24th inst., at Morris, Otsego Co., N.Y., LEWIS LEE MORRIS, Esq., eldest son of the late Gen. Jacob Morris. (30 AUG 1853)

DEATH. At Harper's Ferry, on the 18th inst., the Rev. JOHN DAVIS, a well known Minister of the Methodist Episcopal Church, lately belonging to the Baltimore Conference. (31 AUG 1853)

DEATH. At Portland, on the 25th inst., at the U.S. Hotel, BENJAMIN F. WEST, of Alexandria, Va., assistant in the U.S. Coast Survey, aged 21. (31 AUG 1853)

DEATH. Yesterday morning, August 31st, at 4 o'clock, of hemorrhage of the lungs, Mr. ROBERT MAXWELL, printer, in the 23d year of his age, leaving an aged mother and several sisters and brothers to mourn their irreparable loss. The friends and acquaintances of the family, and the members of the Columbia Typographical Society, are respectfully invited to attend his funeral from his late residence, on Massachusetts avenue, north side, between Sixth and Seventh streets, this (Thursday) afternoon, at 3½ o'clock. (1 SEP 1853)

DEATH. On the 31st of August, in this city, Mrs. RACHAEL HODGKINS, in the 78th year of her age. Her funeral will take place this (Thursday) morning, at 10 o'clock, from the residence of Wm. C. Greenleaf, corner of 9th and L streets. (1 SEP 1853)

DEATH. On Wednesday, the 31st inst. [31 AUG 1853], JOHN S. CHANCEY, in the 63d year of his age. His funeral will take place this evening, at half-past 3 o'clock, from his late residence, on I street, between 4th and 5th. The friends and acquaintances of the family are respectfully invited to attend. (1 SEP 1853)

DEATH. In Northampton Co., Va., on the 17th of August, SUSAN UPSHUR, eldest child of Capt. T.L. Ringgold, U.S. Army, aged five years and eight months. (2 SEP 1853)

DEATH. In Northampton Co., Va., on the 21st of August, ABEL UPSHUR, son of Capt. T.L. Ringgold, U.S. Army, aged four years and two months. (2 SEP 1853)

DEATH. On Tuesday, the 23d of August, of the prevailing epidemic, at her residence in Calvert Co., Md., after a lingering and painful illness, which she bore with Christian fortitude and resignation, in the communion of the Protestant Episcopal church, in the confidence of a certain faith, in the comfort of a reasonable religious and holy hope, in favor with God, and in perfect charity with the world, Mrs. ELIZABETH STANFORTH, wife of Levin Stanforth, Esq., in the 58th year of her age. A dutiful wife, a devoted and affectionate mother, a humane and faithful mistress, a kind and benevolent neighbor, and an exemplary Christian, her labors of love, for a series of years, in the community where she resided, will long be remembered. (2 SEP 1853)

MARRIAGE. On the 1st inst., by the Rev. Mr. O'Toole, PHILLIP S. PILES to Miss LUCINDA DORSEY, all of this city. (3 SEP 1853)

DEATH. In this city, on Thursday evening last, in the 64th year of his age, Mr. JAMES R. MAY, a native of Maryland, and for many years a resident of this city. His friends and relatives are requested to attend his funeral today, at 10 o'clock, from Mr. Townley's, on Ohio avenue. (3 SEP 1853)

DEATH. At North View, Georgetown Heights, the 2d inst., CORNELIUS BARBER, in the 51st year of his age. The funeral procession will move from his late residence, this afternoon at 4 o'clock, to St. John's Church, Georgetown, when the services will commence at half past four. The friends of the family are respectfully invited to attend at the church. (3 and 14 SEP 1853)

DEATH. At his residence near Belleville, N.J., on the 31st August, JOHN BURLEY HILL, in the 78th year of his age, father of Silas H. Hill, of this city. (3 SEP 1853)

DEATH. In Alexandria, on Thursday, 25th ult. [25 AUG 1853], Mrs. SARAH N. GIBSON, wife of Professor Wm. Gibson, of the University of Pennsylvania. (3 SEP 1853)

DEATH. In this city, on the 31st ult., of consumption, JAMES KNOXVEILLE, in the 42d year of his age. (3 SEP 1853)

DEATH. In Warrenton, Va., on Wednesday, the 31st ult. [31 AUG 1853], BARBARA LUCINDA, daughter of Inman Horner, Esq. (5 SEP 1853)

DEATH. Yesterday morning [4 SEP 1853], at 5 o'clock, ELIZABETH, relict of the late Chas. McGarvey, in the 27th year of her age. Her funeral will take place from St. Patrick's Church, at 4 o'clock this afternoon. (5 SEP 1853)

DEATH. On Saturday last [3 SEP 1853], WALLACE EUGENE, infant son of Aaron and Sarah Dawson, aged one year and three months. (5 SEP 1853)

MARRIAGE. On the 1st inst., by the Rev. Mr. Alig, Mr. JOHN WAHL to Miss BRIDGET HERITY, all of this city. (6 SEP 1853)

DEATH. On Sunday, September 4th, MARY, only child of Thos. F. and Maria Marr, aged 13 months and 3 days. (6 SEP 1853)

OBITUARY. Departed this life in Georgetown, D.C., on the evening of the 11th ult. [11 AUG 1853], JULIA C., the fond and affectionate wife of James A. Simpson... She was the fourth daughter of Guiseppe Franzoni, Esq., who was an eminent sculptor, a native of Florence, Italy, and was the first artist whom this Government invited to adorn the Capitol. (7 SEP 1853)

DEATH. In New Orleans, on the 27th ult., of yellow fever, ADAM AUGUSTUS CUNNINGHAM, second son of Mr. Arch. Cunningham, of Georgetown, D.C., in the 26th year of his age. (7 SEP 1853)

DEATH. At Pensacola, Fla., on the 15th of August, of consumption, JOHN HENRY, only son of Col. Jno. L. Gardener, U.S. Army. (7 SEP 1853)

DEATH. At Pensacola, Fla., on the 26th of August, of yellow fever, CATHERINE FRANCES, youngest daughter of Col. Jno. L. Gardener, U.S. Army. (7 SEP 1853)

Daily National Intelligencer, Marriage and Death Notices, 1851-1854

DEATH. In this city, on the 6th inst., Mr. THOS. A. HAWKE, in the 49th year of his age. His funeral will take place this evening (Wednesday) at 3 o'clock. The friends and acquaintances of the family are most respectfully invited to attend, from his late residence, corner of 3d street and Virginia avenue. (7 SEP 1853)

DEATH. On Tuesday evening, the 6th inst., Mrs. HARRIET R. EVANS, aged 60 years and 3 months. Her funeral will take place this (Thursday) afternoon, at 3 o'clock, from the residence of her son-in-law, Mr. Hugh Dougherty, on New Jersey avenue. The friends and acquaintances are respectfully invited to attend. (8 SEP 1853)

DEATH. On the 6th inst., after a lingering and painful illness, MARY ANN, in the 26th year of her age, wife of Southey S. Parker. The funeral will take place this day, (Thursday,) the 8th inst., at four o'clock, from her late residence on H street, between 21st and 22d streets, where the friends of the family are invited to attend. (8 SEP 1853)

DEATH. Yesterday [7 SEP 1853], after a short illness, Miss JULIA HAWKE, aged sixty years, sister of the late Thomas A. Hawke. Thus, in twenty-four hours, has brother and sister been suddenly called from this life. (8 SEP 1853)

DEATH. On Wednesday morning, the 7th inst., at Giesboro, Washington Co., ANNA BARBARA, infant daughter of [I]. Fenwick and Nora C. Young. (8 SEP 1853)

MARRIAGE. On Wednesday morning, the 7th inst., in Trinity Church, by the Rev. Mr. Ashwand, Mr. MARCELLUS GALLAHER, of Washington, to Miss VIRGINIA BROOKS, daughter of Mr. Lewis Brooks, of Georgetown. (9 SEP 1853)

DEATH. In August last, at New Port, Fla., Capt. JOHN PRATT HUNGERFORD, in the 48th year of his age, an estimable and highly esteemed citizen of that place. Mr. H. was a native of King George Co., Va., and leaves numerous relatives and friends in that state. (9 SEP 1853)

DEATH. In Baltimore, September 8, at the residence of R.C. Bowie, MARY ANNA, third daughter of G.W. and Mary Bowie, in the 19th year of her age. (9 SEP 1853)

DEATH. At 4 A.M., on 3d September, at the residence of his grandmother, Mrs. Commodore Rodgers, in this city, CHARLES D. MEIGS, aged 8 years, son of Capt. M.C. Meigs, U.S. Corps of Engineers. (9 SEP 1853)

DEATH. On the 8th inst., in Prince George's Co., Md., Mr. WALLACE KIRKWOOD, in the 43d year of his age. The deceased was formerly an active citizen of Washington. His funeral will take place from his late residence on Saturday, the 10th inst., at 12 o'clock. His friends and acquaintances are invited to attend. (10 SEP 1853)

DEATH. At the residence of her uncle, Geo. A.W. Randall, in this city, Miss LUCINDA RANDALL, of Baltimore, aged 31 years. (10 SEP 1853)

MARRIAGE. On the 6th inst., by the Rev. Dr. Humphreys, at Annapolis, Md., Passed Midshipman WILSON McGUNNEGLE, U.S. Navy, to GABELLA, eldest daughter of the late Dr. Hyde Ray, U.S. Navy. (12 SEP 1853)

DEATH. In this city, on Sunday morning [11 SEP 1853], at two o'clock, GEORGE COVER, Esq., in the 61st year of his age, after an extremely painful illness of several months' duration, which he bore with great fortitude and resignation. His funeral will take place this afternoon, at 3½ o'clock, from the residence of

Daily National Intelligencer, Marriage and Death Notices, 1851-1854

B.B. Curran, on 6th street, Navy Yard. Carriages will be in attendance at the residence of Mr. George Parker, at the corner of 4½ and C streets, to convey such of the friends of the family as desire to attend the funeral. (12 SEP 1853)

DEATH. In this city, on Saturday evening, 10th inst., after a painful illness of three months' duration, Miss CATHARINE A. CURRAN, daughter of the late Philip Curran, Esq., of Annapolis, Md. She died as she had lived, a pious Christian. The funeral of the deceased will take place this (Monday) morning, at 9 o'clock, from the residence of her brother, W.W. Curran, Esq., and proceed to St. Patrick's Church. (12 SEP 1853)

DEATH. On Saturday, the 10th inst., MARIA EUGENIA, daughter of Samuel and Adelaide Carusi, of this city. (12 SEP 1853)

MARRIAGE. On the 12th inst., by the Rev. Dr. Cole, MOSES THOMAS to SOPHRONIA BOSWELL, all of this city. (14 SEP 1853)

DEATH. On Friday, September 9, at Warrenton, Va., Commander ALBERT G. SLAUGHTER, U.S. Navy, in the 54th year of his age. (14 SEP 1853)

DEATH. At North View, Georgetown Heights, on the 2d inst., CORNELIUS BARBER, in the 51st year of his age. By his decease the community has lost a valuable citizen and the church a consistent communicant... A communicant in the church of St. John's, Georgetown... (14 SEP 1853)

MARRIAGE. In Indianola, Tex., on the 23d ult., Lieut. GEORGE C. BARBER, U.S. Army, to Miss FANNY, eldest daughter of Brevet Major Babbitt, U.S. Army. (15 SEP 1853)

DEATH. On Staten Island, August 29, Capt. ANSELM HATCH, in the 61st year of his age. (15 SEP 1853)

DEATH. In the City of Mexico, June 23d, Mrs. MORIA ISABEL BENFIELD, consort of Wm. Benfield, aged 49 years and 7 months. (15 SEP 1853)

DEATH. On the 6th inst., at the residence of Mr. Wilkins, in Oldham Co., Ky., MARY A., daughter of WILLIAM D. GALLAGHER, in the 19th year of her age. This young lady was one of those who are known only to be beloved. Her affectionate disposition endeared her to every one who had the pleasure of being acquainted with her. About three years ago, while playing in the grounds of the Capitol, in Washington, she fell and injured her spine; since that time she has been in almost constant suffering. The writer of this notice remembers her as she was a few years ago, rosy with health, and bounding along the hills like the deer. He can hardly think of her as she lay prostrated by disease, her active limbs paralyzed and her bright mind in an eclipse. It has pleased her Heavenly Father to remove her from this scene of suffering, and to call her to her home, where the cloud that rested upon her is now dissipated by the beams of eternal love. (15 SEP 1853)

DEATH. At the Cottage, King George, Va., on the 10th inst., GEORGE FORREST, infant son of E.R. and Nicholas Quesenbury, aged 5 months and 20 days. (15 SEP 1853)

MARRIAGE. On Tuesday, the 13th inst., by the Rev. James P. Donelan, Mr. WILLIAM LEWIS CHISM to Miss RUTH ELLEN REMINGTON, eldest daughter of the late Jas. Remington, of this city. (16 SEP 1853)

MARRIAGE. On the morning of the 13th inst., at Trinity Church, Shepherdstown, Va., by the Rev. John H. Kehler, S. BULOW ERWIN, Esq., of North Carolina, to S. ELLA, fourth daughter of the officiating clergyman. (16 SEP 1853)

MARRIAGE. On the 14th inst., by the Rev. F.S. Evans, G.C. HUMPHRIES to MARY E. HARRIS. (16 SEP 1853)

Daily National Intelligencer, Marriage and Death Notices, 1851-1854

DEATH. In this city, on the 14th inst., IDA, aged 5 years 11 months and 14 days, daughter of Thomas and Eliza R. Brown. (16 SEP 1853)

DEATH. At Louisville, Ky., on the 10th inst., Mrs. HANNAH M. MOXLEY, in the 38th year of her age, wife of Richard Moxley, Esq., and second daughter of George Gilliss, Esq., late of this city. (16 SEP 1853)

DEATH. After a few hours' illness, on the morning of the 16th inst., of congestive fever, MARY ELLEN PETTIBONE, youngest daughter of William and Jane E. Pettibone, in the 9th year of her age. Her funeral will take place from her father's residence this afternoon at 3 o'clock. The friends of the family are requested to attend without further notice. (17 SEP 1853)

DEATH. In Terre Haute, Ind., on the morning of the 10th inst., greatly regretted, Mrs. HETTY JANE, wife of Col. Thomas Dowling, of that place, and a native of this city. Although for some time in bad health, the immediate cause of Mrs. D.'s death, as detailed in a letter from a friend, is a singular as it was unexpected. On Sunday preceding, "She was walking about the grounds around the house, and when in the act of pulling a peach, one fell from a top branch and struck her on the cheek bone just under the left eye. The slight bruise soon became swollen, and by Tuesday, in spite of poultices and every kind of outward application, rapidly took the shape of erysipelas; spasmodic affections of the stomach, severe pains in the side, and great difficulty in breathing followed, and she suffered most intensely until relieved by death." (17 SEP 1853)

MARRIAGE. On the 25th of June, by the Rev. James Brown, BENJAMIN L. OTTERBACK to Miss CHARLOTTE MILLER, daughter of Mr. Chas. Miller, all of this city. (19 SEP 1853)

DEATH. On the morning of the 17th of September, at the residence of his grandmother, Mrs. Riddall, in this city, ROBERT J. WALKER, twin child of Wm. and Ann P. Handy, aged nine months and sixteen days. (19 SEP 1853)

DEATH. At Louisville, Ky., on the 15th inst., WILLIAM P. GREER, son of Wm. Greer, and brother-in-law of Jos. H. Wheat, of this city, in the 40th year of his age. (19 SEP 1853)

OBITUARY. Died, on Wednesday, the 7th inst., in the 71st year of her age, Mrs. MARGARET F. SMITH [text continues]. Forty years a member of the Baptist Church... (19 SEP 1853)

MARRIAGE. On the 15th inst., by the Rev. Jas. H. Brown, Mr. GEORGE MILLER to Miss CATHARINE ELMORE. (20 SEP 1853)

MARRIAGE. On the 12th inst., by the Rev. Stephen P. Hill, VILLASQUIZ H. FLINN to JULIA H. ROBINSON, of Virginia. (20 SEP 1853)

DEATH. Last Sunday evening [18 SEP 1853], at his residence in Montgomery Co., Md., where he had resided for the last thirty-five years, CHARLES BUNTING, in the sixty-ninth year of his age. His funeral will take place this (Tuesday) morning at 10 o'clock, from his late residence, to which his friends are invited. (20 SEP 1853)

DEATH. At the Warm Springs, Bath Co., Va., on the morning of the 8th inst., ELIZABETH SELDEN MACLURG WICKHAM, daughter of the late John Wickham, of Richmond, Va. [text continues]. (20 SEP 1853)

DEATH. On the 19th inst., in the 58th year of her age, Mrs. ELIZA HARROVER, relict of the late Hiram Harrover, of Fairfax Co., Va. Her funeral will take place from the residence of W.H. Harrover, Seventh street, this afternoon, at half-past three o'clock. (21 SEP 1853)

DEATH. Of croup, on the 20th inst., THOMAS FAUNTLEROY ROANE, son of John J. and Mary A. Roane, aged 4 years and 7 months. The friends of the family are invited to attend his funeral on Wednesday, the 21st inst., at 4 o'clock P.M., at the residence of his parents, on Maryland avenue, between 2d and 3d streets, Capitol Hill. (21 SEP 1853)

DEATH. In this city, on the 18th inst., at 9 o'clock P.M., LUCY ELLEN, youngest child of Capt. P.M. and Susanna J. Henry, aged three years and three months. (21 SEP 1853)

MARRIAGE. On the 20th inst., by the Rev. James H. Brown, Mr. CHARLES G. GASS to Miss LOUISA ASHCRAFT. (23 SEP 1853)

MARRIAGE. On the 21st inst., by the Rev. R.D. Woodley, Mr. JAMES O. WHITNEY, of Washington city, and Miss SALLIE M. MOORE, youngest daughter of Warren Moore, late of St. Mary's Co., Md. (23 SEP 1853)

MARRIAGE. On the 15th inst., at Cold Spring, N.Y., Lieut. HENRY F. WITTER, U.S. Army, to Miss IDA W. MORRIS, eldest daughter of Gen. George P. Morris. (23 SEP 1853)

DEATH. On the 20th inst., ANNIE, infant daughter of Dr. Alex. Y.P. and Mary W. Garnett, aged 18 days. (23 SEP 1853)

DEATH. At Burlington, Ver., on the 2d inst., Mrs. LYDIA SAWYER, aged 81 years, relict of Col. James Sawyer, of the revolutionary army. Mrs. Sawyer was for more than half a century a resident of Burlington, and greatly endeared to a wide circle of friends by her many excellent qualities of mind and heart. She was a Christian in heart and practice. Descended herself from the revolutionary stock, she gave to her country four sons, two in the Army and two in the Navy, of whom one along survives. (24 SEP 1853)

DEATH. In St. Petersburgh, on the 28th of August, after an illness of sixteen days, at the residence of Mrs. Bodisco, her sister, Miss VIRGINIA WILLIAMS, of Georgetown, D.C. (26 SEP 1853)

DEATH. Yesterday [25 SEP 1853], MARTHA MARTIN, infant daughter of the Hon. S.A. Douglas, aged 8 months. The friends of the family are invited to attend the funeral services this afternoon at half-past three o'clock, at the residence of Mr. Douglas. (26 SEP 1853)

MARRIAGE. On Monday morning [26 SEP 1853], by the Rev. John C. Smith, Mr. WILLIAM R. RIDGELY to Miss SALLIE R. STONE, all of this city. (27 SEP 1853)

DEATH. On last Sabbath morning [25 SEP 1853], Mr. JAMES MOORE, one of our oldest and most worthy citizens. Mr. Moore was of the number of those, now reduced to a very few, who saw our city in its infancy, having come to reside among us more than half a century ago. Being a printer by profession, he was employed in days long gone by in the office of the *National Intelligencer*, even before this ancient journal came into the hands of its present venerable and respected editors. For many years past he discharged with scrupulous fidelity the duties of a place of trust in the office of the Treasurer of the U.S. For a period of about thirty years he was a ruling elder of the First Presbyterian Church of this city, and at the time of his death was the oldest elder in the church. How conscientiously he performed the duties of that sacred office is well known to his brethren in the eldership and members of the church. His bereaved widow and children have by this dispensation been deprived of an affectionate husband and father. He has descended to the grave full of years, and having long lived the "life of the righteous, so his last end was like His." The news of his death fell sadly on many hearts; and numerous friends and the church he served, and with whom he so long worshipped, will cherish the memory of their departed Elder Moore. The funeral will take place from the First Presbyterian Church, on 4½ street, this afternoon at 3 o'clock. (27 SEP 1853)

Daily National Intelligencer, Marriage and Death Notices, 1851-1854

DEATH. On the 10th inst., at Woodlands, Charles Co., Md., in the 42d year of her age, MARY E., wife of Charles S. Williams, and daughter of the late Col. Wm. Hamilton, of the above county. Few persons have lived more generally beloved, and few have died more sincerely regretted by all who came within the scope of her influence. (27 SEP 1853)

OBITUARY. Departed this life, in the animating prospect of a better, at the residence of her father, in Washington, on Monday evening, the 26th inst., in the 25th year of her age, Mrs. MATILDA S. CROSBY, wife of Lieut. Peirce Crosby, U.S. Navy, and eldest daughter of John C. Bowyer, Esq. [text continues]. (28 SEP 1853)

MARRIAGE. At St. Paul's English Lutheran Church, on the 27th inst., by the Rev. J.G. Butler, Mr. JOHN RHEEM and Miss CATHARINE G. SCHNEIDER, all of this city. (29 SEP 1853)

MARRIAGE. On Wednesday afternoon [28 SEP 1853], by the Rev. Mr. Clarkson, Mr. A. STEWART LUM, of California, to Miss HELEN C. SHERWOOD, of this city. (30 SEP and 1 OCT 1853)

MARRIAGE. At Ajax, Fauquier Co., Va., on the 20th September, by the Rev. D. Motzer, FRANCIS A. CHILDS, Esq., of Virginia, to Miss SARAH A.E., daughter of Capt. E. Strother, of Missouri. (30 SEP 1853)

DEATH. On the 29th inst., in the 43d year of his age, Mr. SAMUEL LEWIS. The friends of the family are invited to attend his funeral, from his late residence, on Pennsylvania avenue, near the corner of Third street, this (Friday) afternoon, at 4 o'clock. (30 SEP 1853)

DEATH. At Lafayette Station, Memphis and Charleston Railroad, on the 14th inst., J. BROOKE HUNTER, Civil Engineer, of injuries received by a fall from the cars. Mr. Hunter was a native of Virginia. He entered the service of the Memphis and Charleston Railroad Company three years ago, during the preliminary surveys, and has been engaged for the past two years on the Western division of the road. A severe illness compelled him, a few months ago, to leave the scene of his duties, and he had but just returned with restored health when his life was cut short by the accident of Wednesday. He lived but a few hours after the occurrence, and bore his great sufferings with calm fortitude [text continues]. (30 SEP 1853)

DEATHS. At the U.S. Navy Yard, Pensacola, August 31st ult. [31 AUG 1853], of the yellow fever, Purser D. FAUNTLEROY, of the U.S. Navy. On the 12th inst., ANNIE; and on the 14th inst., VIRGINIA D., both daughters of the late Purser Fauntleroy, of the same disease. (30 SEP 1853)

DEATHS. Of scarlet fever, at the residence of her father, in Warrenton, Va., on the 5th of September, MAUD, youngest child of Rice W. and America Payne, aged twenty months. Also, of the same disease, on the 25th inst., CHARLES BORROMEO PAYNE, the eldest child, aged four years and ten months. (30 SEP 1853)

MARRIAGE. In Philadelphia, on Monday, 26th of September, by the Rev. Richard DeCharms, Mr. GEORGE W. BRADFORD, of Washington, Ind., to Miss CASSIE CLARK, of Washington, D.C. (1 OCT 1853)

MARRIAGE. On the 29th ult. [29 SEP 1853], by the Rev. Smith Pyne, Mr. JOHN H. GERMAN, of Allentown, Pa., to Miss MARY S. FRERE, of this city. (3 OCT 1853)

DEATH. On the 1st inst., at 7½ o'clock P.M., WILLIE G., son of Prudence E. and William H. Frazure, aged 2 years and 11 months. The friends of the family are requested to attend the funeral, which will take place this (Monday) afternoon, at 2 o'clock, from the residence of his father, on Eighth street, between M and N streets. (3 OCT 1853)

DEATH. On Friday night last, the 30th ult. [30 SEP 1853], Mr. JOHN MYERS, quietly and peacefully expired at his residence, in Georgetown, D.C., in the 75th year of his age. He became a citizen of

Georgetown in 1809, and since then has uniformly and consistently adorned the relations of a good citizen, a sincere friend, just business man, affectionate husband, kind parent, and for nearly forty years an exemplary citizen. For the past forty years, with an interim of only some three, he has been a subscriber to your excellent periodical. None read it more attentively nor subscribed more cordially to your sound opinions on the various subjects connected with the history of our country than he. A widow, seven children, thirty grandchildren, and three great-grandchildren mourn his irreparable loss, to whom he has left the priceless legacy of an untarnished name and most worthy example. "*Mark the perfect man, and behold the upright; for the end of that man is peace.*" (4 OCT 1853)

DEATH. On the 24th September, at New Orleans, of pneumonia, ELIZA, wife of Henry Siebrecht, and daughter of the late Joseph Etter, of this city, aged 38 years. (4 OCT 1853)

MARRIAGE. On the 3d inst., at the Church of the Epiphany, by the Rev. Mr. French, S. LEDYARD PHELPS, U.S.N., to Miss ELIZA, daughter of Capt. William Maynadier, U.S. Army. (5 OCT 1853)

DEATH. In Richmond, Va., on the 3d inst., ROBERT V. SIMMES, of this city, in the 23d year of his age. His friends and the friends of his father's family are respectfully requested to attend his funeral this morning, at 10 o'clock, from the residence of his father, on L street, between 10th and 11th streets. (5 OCT 1853)

DEATH. On Thursday morning, 29th ult., ISABELLA, daughter of the late Archibald Keightley, of Liverpool, and wife of Hugh C. Smith, of Alexandria, Va. (5 OCT 1853)

OBITUARY. Among the valuable lives which have lately fallen in the South by that horrid scourge, the yellow fever, we are deeply pained to record the name of Lieut. JOHN J. HANSON, of the U.S. Navy. This promising and gallant young officer was a son of Mr. Isaac K. Hanson, of Washington, and is the third and last son whom that venerable gentleman has given to his country, and who has perished in the performance of his duty. Capt. Weightman K.F. Hanson, the eldest died in consequence of disease contracted in the Florida war, where he was distinguished by his gallantry, talents, and devotion to the service and the flag. Capt. Charles Hanson, the second brother, served with great distinction in the Mexican war, was one of the first who scaled the heights of Cerro Gordo, and fell gallantly fighting at the battle of Contreras. And now the last of the brave brotherhood has gone, having fallen before a more destructive enemy than the cannon, and in a manner worthy of the hero. While young Hanson was at Pensacola, on his return from a southern cruise, the U.S. schooner *Vixen*, to which he had been attached, came into port with all her officers down with the fever. Young Hanson, voluntarily and from a sense of duty to the service, went on board the plague-ship and took command, devoting his whole energies to the welfare of the unfortunate vessel and of her sick and dying crew. He has fallen victim to the loyalty and courage of a noble nature, and in his death the navy has lost one of its best officers, and the last spark of earthly hope of an old man's hearth has gone out, to be rekindled, we trust, in brighter skies. Peace to the ashes of the brave! *Richmond Dispatch*. (5 OCT 1853)

MARRIAGE. On Thursday, 29th September, at Easton, Md., by the Rev. Henry M. Mason, D.D., Capt. EDMUND L.F. HARDCASTLE, U.S. Army, to SALLIE D., daughter of the late Col. Wm. Hughlett. (6 OCT 1853)

DEATH. On Wednesday morning, the 5th inst., BIANCA, only daughter of Titus and Mary Bastianelli, in the fourth year of her age. The friends and acquaintance of the family are requested to attend her funeral this morning, at 10 o'clock, from the residence of her father, on Pennsylvania avenue, between 4½ and 6th streets. (6 OCT 1853)

DEATH. In New Orleans, of yellow fever, on the 22d of August, Mr. CHARLES D. MOREHEAD, a brother of ex-Governor Morehead, of Kentucky. On the 26th of August, Mrs. ELIZA, consort of Charles D. Morehead. On the 19th of August, CHARLES EDWIN MOREHEAD, son, and on the 22d, Miss EMMA A. MOREHEAD, daughter of the above, all of Bowling Green, Ky. (6 OCT 1853)

MARRIAGE. On Tuesday, the 4th inst., by the Rev. Mr. Hodges, JOSEPH H. PADGETT to Miss MARY ANN E. SMITH, all of this city. (7 OCT 1853)

MARRIAGES. On Tuesday evening last [4 OCT 1853], at Boydville, near Martinsburg, Va., by the Rev. A.H.H. Boyd, GERRIT V. LOTT, Esq., of the city of New York, to Miss SALLIE PENDLETON FAULKNER, eldest daughter of the Hon. Chas. Jas. Faulkner. On the same evening, at the same place, by the Rev. A.H.H. Boyd, the Hon. THOMAS S. BOCOCK, of Virginia, to Miss ANNIE HOLMES FAULKNER, second daughter of the Hon. Chas. Jas. Faulkner. (7 OCT 1853)

MARRIAGE. On Tuesday evening, the 4th inst., by the Rev. Mr. Marks, Mr. WM. L. GRIGGS, of this city, to Miss REBECCA WATERS, of Alexandria, Va. (7 OCT 1853)

MARRIAGE. On Thursday morning, 6th inst., by Rev. Mr. Marks, Mr. THOMAS KING to Miss ELIZABETH TALBERT, both of Prince George's Co., Md. (7 OCT 1853)

DEATH. At Wanesborough [Waynesboro], Augusta, Va., on the 5th inst., in the 75th year of her age, Mrs. LUCY ROSE, relict of Thomas Rose, Esq., late of Richmond, and sister of the junior Editor of this paper. She was for fifty years an exemplary member of the Methodist Episcopal Church, and died with the calmness and confidence of a sincere and consistent Christian. (7 OCT 1853)

DEATH. At Springfield, La., on the 23d ult. [23 SEP 1853[, of yellow fever, Mr. PETER F. MOORE, aged about 48 years. He was of the firm of Moore, Edwards & Co., contractors on the New Orleans and Jackson railroad, and leaves a wife and family residing in this city. (7 OCT 1853)

DEATH. At Oatland, Fauquier Co., Va., on the 9th ult. [9 SEP 1853], Col. GEORGE LOVE, in the 73d year of his age. (7 OCT 1853)

DEATH. At Montebello, Fauquier Co., Va., on the 17th ult. [17 SEP 1853], Miss MARTHA LOVE, in the 70th year of her age. (7 OCT 1853)

MARRIAGE. In St. Matthew's Church, on Thursday, the 6th inst., by the Rev. Mr. McLaughlin, Mr. JOHN YOUNG, of Alexandria, Va., to Mrs. SARAH WELLS, of this city. (8 OCT 1853)

MARRIAGE. On Tuesday, the 4th inst., by the Rev. Mr. Blackwell, CHARLES W. COLEMAN, Esq., to Miss LAVINIA V. FARR, all of Virginia. (8 OCT 1853)

DEATH. At London, on the 6th of August last, fell overboard from the ship *Ocean Queen*, of New York, and was drowned, JAMES HENRY, aged 17 years and 4 months, eldest son of James and Henrietta Tucker, of Washington city. (8 OCT 1853)

DEATH. At Rockville, Md., on Wednesday, the 28th ult. [28 SEP 1853], in the 34th year of her age, after a protracted and painful illness, and in the well-grounded hope of a blissful immortality, Mrs. SERENA S. YOUNG, wife of Mr. Alex. H. Young, of this city [text continues]. Member of the Church of the Ascension. (8 OCT 1853)

DEATH. On the 4th inst., ANDREW G.C., child of James and Mary Maxwell. (8 OCT 1853)

DEATH. On the 3d inst., MARY MARIA LEANER, in the twenty-third month of her age, daughter of Louisa and William Leaner. (8 OCT 1853)

MARRIAGE. On the 6th inst., by the Rev. J. Thos. Ward, of Philadelphia, RICHARD B. NORMENT, Esq., formerly of Arkansas, to Miss MARGARET ANNA, youngest daughter of Rev. Ulysses Ward, of this city. (10 OCT 1853)

Daily National Intelligencer, Marriage and Death Notices, 1851-1854

DEATH. On the 5th inst., of consumption, WM. FURGERSON. The deceased was a man of irreproachable character, possessing the confidence of all who knew him, and died, as he had lived, a true Christian. (10 OCT 1853)

DEATH. On Saturday morning, October 8, VINCENT TROWBRIDGE, aged two years, son of Capt. Montgomery C. Meigs, U.S. Corps of Engineers. (10 OCT 1853)

DEATH. On the 10th inst., in Georgetown, Mrs. MARGARET BROOKS, wife of Lewis Brooks, Esq., in the fiftieth year of her age. The friends of the family are requested to attend her funeral on Wednesday, 12th inst., at 10 o'clock A.M., from her late residence on High street, Georgetown. (11 OCT 1853)

MARRIAGE. On the 4th inst., in Wake Co., N.C., by Rev. James S. Purify, Mr. JOHN R. WILLIAMS, of Arkansas, to Miss REBECCA T. MANGUM, of Wake Forest. (12 OCT 1853)

MARRIAGE. On Tuesday morning [11 OCT 1853], by the Rev. John C. Smith, Mr. ROBERT H. NASH, Jr., to Miss JOSEPHINE SMITH. (12 OCT 1853)

MARRIAGE. In San Francisco, September 13th, by the Rev. C.C. Wyatt, Mr. HARVEY LEE to Miss MARY FERGUSON, daughter of John Ferguson, formerly of this city. (12 OCT 1853)

DEATH. On the 11th inst., at the residence of his uncle, Samuel Lundstreet, Esq., Baltimore, in the 17th year of his age, GEORGE M., only son of Thomas T. Barnes, of this city. His friends and acquaintances are invited to attend the funeral from his uncle's residence this day at 3 o'clock P.M. (12 OCT 1853)

DEATH. On the 17th ult. [17 SEP 1853], at his residence in the county of Stafford, after a short but violent attack of bilious fever, DANIEL W. FORD, in the 32d year of his age. The deceased possessed in an eminent degree those social and urbane qualities which attached him warmly to his friends and acquaintances, and them to him. Few who have trod so retired a path of life have left behind them friends who more sincerely regret their loss. (12 OCT 1853)

DEATH. Of scarlet fever, at the residence of her father, in Warrenton, Va., MAUD, youngest child of Rice W. and America Payne, aged twenty months. Also, of the same disease, on the 25th September, CHARLES BORROMEO PAYNE, the eldest child, aged four years and ten months. (12 OCT 1853)

DEATH. In this city, on Monday, the 10th inst., HARRIET, infant daughter of Theodore and Mary Mosher, aged six weeks. (12 OCT 1853)

DEATH. By accidental drowning, on the 12th September, in the 22d year of his age, J. LOUIS PETIGRU, only son of Commander Thomas Petigru. The early fate of this most estimable young man has filled many hearts with grief that the outwardly semblance of mourning but inadequately expresses. (13 OCT 1853)

DEATH. In Georgetown, D.C., on Tuesday, the 11th inst., at 9½ o'clock, Col. WILLIAM STEWART, in the 76th year of his age. The funeral of the deceased will take place at St. John's Church, previous to interment at Rock Creek, on Thursday, the 13th inst., at 10 o'clock, where the friends and acquaintances of the family are respectfully invited to attend. (13 OCT 1853)

DEATH. On Wednesday evening, October 12th, EDMUND F., youngest child of Edmund F. and Margaret A. French, aged sixteen months. The friends of the family are invited to attend the funeral at 3 o'clock Friday afternoon. (13 OCT 1853)

MARRIAGE. At Bordentown, N.J., on the 3d inst., by the Rev. H.M. Goodwin, J.C. WALSH, Lieut. U.S. Navy, to SARAH W., daughter of the late Capt. E.R. McCall, U.S. Navy. (14 OCT 1853)

Daily National Intelligencer, Marriage and Death Notices, 1851-1854

DEATH. In this city, yesterday morning, the 13th inst., WILLIAM H. PEACO, formerly of Annapolis, Md. His friends and acquaintances are invited to attend the funeral at the residence of Mr. Lemuel Etchison, on Sixth street, between G and H streets, this (Friday) afternoon, at 2 o'clock. (14 OCT 1853)

DEATH. In this city, on the 12th inst., after a long and painful illness, ROBERT B. BOYD, in the 82d year of his age, a native of Pennsylvania, but a resident of this place for the last thirty-four years. (14 OCT 1853)

DEATH. In Philadelphia, on Sunday morning, the 9th inst., in the 51st year of his age, EMERSON McILVAINE, son of the late Hon. Joseph McIlvaine, of Burlington, N.J. (14 OCT 1853)

MARRIAGE. On Tuesday afternoon [11 OCT 1853], by the Rev. John C. Smith, Mr. ALEXANDER HUMES to Miss MARY M. TIPPETT, all of this city. (15 OCT 1853)

MARRIAGE. On the evening of the 13th inst., by the Rev. Mr. Huegez, JAMES T. CARROLL to MARIA C. WALKER, all of this city. (15 OCT 1853)

DEATH. On the 12th inst., in the 4th year of his age, JAMES HENRY BISSELL, son of Lieut. S.B. and Sarah Bissell. His funeral will take place on Sunday, the 16th inst., at 2 o'clock P.M., from the residence of his parents, corner Pennsylvania avenue and 21st street, which the friends of the family are respectfully invited to attend. (15 OCT 1853)

DEATH. On the 12th October, at the residence of Professor Holcombe, in Charlottesville, Va., in the 17th year of his age, GEORGE P. CHAPMAN, third son of Gen. John G. Chapman, of Md. This young gentleman left home with the intention of pursuing his studies during the ensuing year at the University of Virginia, but he had scarcely reached his place of destination when he was stricken down by a congestive fever, which, after a brief but violent course, terminated in his death. Surrounded by every thing to make life attractive, and possessed of all the virtues that could endear a son, a brother, or a friend, His premature fate will spread deep affliction over a wide circle of relatives and friends. He has left to this bereaved and mourning circle the precious consolation that his last hours were cheered by Christian faith, and the enduring memory of a bright example. (15 OCT 1853)

DEATH OF REV. SAMUEL BRISON. Resolutions of the Washington Preachers' Meeting. Meeting assembled at the usual time in the Foundry Parsonage, on Friday, the 14th inst. The Rev. James H. Brown was called to the chair, and the decease of Rev. S. BRISON was announced. Whereupon, on motion of Rev. Jesse T. Peck, it was unanimously resolved-- 1st. That we have just received with profound sorrow intelligence of the decease of our highly respected and beloved President, Rev. Samuel Brison, preacher in charge of Georgetown Station [text continues]. (17 OCT 1853)

MARRIAGE. On the 13th inst., by the Rev. Mr. McElfresh, of Baltimore, STEPHEN C. WALES, of this city, to LEAH ANN STANFORD, of the former place. (17 OCT 1853)

DEATH. In this city, on Sunday morning, the 16th inst., aged 48 years, Dr. JOHN M. THOMAS, for many years well and extensively known as a highly prominent and respectable physician in this place. His friends and acquaintances are requested to attend at his late residence, on 15th street, on Tuesday morning, the 18th inst., at a quarter past 9 o'clock, from whence the remains will be removed to St. Patrick's (Rev. Mr. Matthew's) Church, where the funeral services will be performed. (17 OCT 1853)

MARRIAGES. In this city, on Monday morning, the 17th inst., by the Rev. John C. Smith, Mr. WILLIAM GEORGE MOORE to Miss MARY GIDEON ROSE, and Mr. ALEXANDER THOMAS LANGTON to Miss REBECCA ELIZABETH ROSE, grand-daughters of Jacob Gideon, Esq. (18 OCT 1853)

Daily National Intelligencer, Marriage and Death Notices, 1851-1854

MARRIAGE. At Hazlewood, on the 12th inst., by the Rev. Mr. Waters, GEORGE C. OGLE, of Prince George's Co., Md., to ANNA MARIA, daughter of the late George Cooke, of Howard county. (18 OCT 1853)

MARRIAGE. On the 17th inst., by the Rev. C.M. Butler, WM. R. LOVEGROVE to Miss ANNA E. MORRISON, of New York. (18 OCT 1853)

DEATH. On Sunday evening, October 16th, JULIA BRADLEY, eldest daughter of Louis F. Whitney, of this city, aged fourteen years. The funeral will take place on Tuesday afternoon, at 3 o'clock, from St. John's Church. (18 OCT 1853)

DEATH. On the 17th October, WILLIAM CISSIL, in the thirty-ninth year of his age. (18 OCT 1853)

DEATH. In this city, on Sunday morning, the 16th inst., JOHN DOUGLAS, in the 77th year of his age. His funeral will take place this (Tuesday) afternoon, at 3 o'clock, from his late residence on Fifteenth street, between K and L streets. His friends and acquaintances are invited to attend without further notice. (18 OCT 1853)

DEATH. In this city, yesterday morning [17 OCT 1853], at the residence of her uncle, Thomas Conner, OCEANA HUNTER, aged 7 years 11 months and 5 days. The friends of the family and the congregation and Sabbath School of the [McKendree] M.E. Church are respectfully requested to attend the funeral, from her uncle's residence on the corner of 7th and K streets, this afternoon at three o'clock. (18 OCT 1853)

DEATH. In Annapolis, Md., on the night of the 13th inst., Mrs. ELIZABETH WEEMS, in the 77th year of her age, eldest daughter of the late Absolom Ridgely, of that city. (18 OCT 1853)

MARRIAGE. On Tuesday morning, the 18th inst., by the Rev. C.M. Butler, JOHN T. PICKETT, of Kentucky, and KATE, youngest daughter of Robert Keyworth, Esq., of this city. (19 OCT 1853)

DEATH. In Greensboro, N.C., on the morning of the 13th inst., Mrs. CHARLOTTE P., consort of the late Charles E. Eckel, of Georgetown, D.C. (19 OCT 1853)

MARRIAGE. On Tuesday evening, the 18th inst., by Rev. L.J. Gilliss, Mr. MATTHIAS HARRIS, of Baltimore, Md., to Miss REBECCA V. SHERWOOD, of this city. (20 OCT 1853)

MARRIAGE. At the Commandant's mansion, in the Navy Yard, Brooklyn, on Tuesday, the 18th October, by the Most Rev. Archbishop Hughes, WILLIAM H. BROOME, Esq., to Miss MARY JANE, daughter of Capt. Chas. Boarman, of the U.S. Navy, and commandant of the navy yard and station at New York. (20 OCT 1853)

MARRIAGE. At Mountain View, in Fairfax Co., Va., on Tuesday morning last, the Hon. JAMES H. BIRCH, of Missouri, to Mrs. ELIZABETH C. FROST, daughter of the late Wm. Fitzhugh Carter. (20 OCT 1853)

MARRIAGE. At Christ Church, Raleigh, on the 11th inst., by the Rev. Mr. Smedes, the Hon. ROBERT STRANGE, of Fayetteville, to Mrs. MARGARET NELSON, of Raleigh. (20 OCT 1853)

OBITUARY. Died, in Opelousas, on the 21st ult. [21 SEP 1853], Dr. WILLIAM J. DIGGES, late from Port Tobacco, Md., aged 34 years. One of those deplorable events which, from time to time, indicate all the perils which surround the medical man in the exercise of his daily avocations, has suddenly carried off an estimable physician in the outset of a career full of usefulness and honor. Dr. Digges attended on his brother-in-law, Dr. Heard, then sick with yellow fever, and since dead, and but a few days afterwards he himself shared the like fate [text continues]. (20 OCT 1853)

Daily National Intelligencer, Marriage and Death Notices, 1851-1854

MARRIAGE. In this city, on the 18th inst., by the Rev. Dr. Pyne, NICHOLAS H. VAN ZANDT, U.S. Navy, to Miss JANE H.M. CABELL, daughter of Edward A. Cabell, Esq. (21 OCT 1853)

DEATH. On Wednesday evening, the 19th inst., ARTHUR LIVERMORE, infant child of Edmund F. and Margaret A. French. (21 OCT 1853)

MARRIAGE. In this city, on the 20th inst., by the Rev. Dr. Butler, the Hon. PETER V. DANIEL, of Virginia, to ELIZABETH, daughter of Dr. Thos. Harris, U.S. Navy. (22 OCT 1853)

MARRIAGE. In Alexandria, on Tuesday evening, October 18th, by the Rev. C.B. Dana, ALFRED POOR to MARION NOBLE, only daughter of the late Benj. P., of Loudoun Co., Va. (22 OCT 1853)

DEATH. On the 15th inst., at Wood Grove, King George Co., Va., the residence of his father, after a protracted and painful illness, which he bore with Christian firmness and resignation, YELVERTON D. BAKER, aged 31 years. "*Blessed are the dead who die in the Lord.*" (22 OCT 1853)

DEATH. In Warner, N.H., on the 12th inst., of consumption, JOSEPH WARREN CHENEY, in the 29th year of his age, a native of Warner, but for the last seven years a resident of Washington. (24 OCT 1853)

DEATH. At Annapolis, Md., in the full assurance of a blessed immortality, MARGARET S., wife of Prof. A.N. Girault, U.S. Navy. (24 OCT 1853)

DEATH. In Worcester Co., Md., on the 14th inst., SARAH SELBY, wife of the Rev. J.W.K. Handy, and daughter of the late Dr. John S. Martin, of Snow Hill, Md. (24 OCT 1853)

MARRIAGE. On Monday, the 24th inst., by the Rev. Father Matthews, Mr. SILAS KIRK to Miss MARTHA VIRGINIA HANDLEY, all of this city. (25 OCT 1853)

DEATH. On Saturday, the 22d inst., at the residence of Jonathan Seaver, near Washington, Mrs. ELIZABETH C. KING, wife of Hon. George G. King, of Newport, R.I., aged 27 years. (25 OCT 1853)

OBITUARY. Gen. THOMAS CHILDS, of the army, died at Tampa Bay, of yellow fever, on Saturday, the 8th inst. Gen. Childs was a native of Massachusetts. He entered the army as third lieutenant March 11, 1814; was breveted colonel May 9th, 1846, raised to the full rank of major February 16th, 1847, and soon after to the rank of colonel. He greatly distinguished himself at Palo Alto, and on the following day; and at Monterey led one of the storming parties in Gen. Worth's division. The General mentioned him in his official report with high approbation; and he was at the same time recommended by Gen. Taylor to the favorable consideration of the Department. He fought side by side at Cerro Gordo with the intrepid Harney, and like him received the highest commendations of the commander-in-chief. After the capture of Jalapa he was appointed military commander of that place, and in about a month after military governor of Puebla. During the absence of the main army from that place, on the 13th of September, 1847, he was attacked by a large Mexican force, and a siege commenced which lasted nearly a month, conducted part of the time by Santa Anna himself, but the post was so ably defended that Santa Anna had to raise the siege and retire to Atlixco. The whole career, indeed, of Gen. Childs in the Mexican war was brilliant, and the country in his death has lost a gallant soldier. (26 OCT 1853)

MARRIAGE. On the 11th inst., in Todd Co., Ky., FRANCIS G. IRWIN, Esq., of Clarksville, Tenn., to Miss LETITIA SNOWDEN, daughter of George Snowden, Esq. (26 OCT 1853)

MARRIAGE. In Staunton, Va., on Thursday, the 20th inst., by the Rev. Thomas T. Castleman, WILLIAM B. TELFAIR, Esq., of Ohio, to Miss ELIZABETH PEYTON, daughter of the late John Howe Peyton. (26 OCT 1853)

Daily National Intelligencer, Marriage and Death Notices, 1851-1854

MARRIAGE. On the 20th inst., by the Rev. Jas. H. Brown, Mr. SHELDON J. HOAG to Miss ANN WILCOX, both of Fairfax Co., Va. (26 OCT 1853)

DEATH. Of scarlet fever, on Thursday, the 25th inst., FANNIE LANDON, aged 3 years, daughter of Z.M.P. and Henrietta Landon King. Her funeral will take place this afternoon at 2 o'clock, from the residence of her father, corner of Vermont avenue and I street. (27 OCT 1853)

MARRIAGE. On the 28th [sic] inst., by the Rev. Mr. Hodges, MARK L. CAMERON to Miss LAURENTIA CAMERON, all of this city. (28 OCT 1853)

DEATH. On the 25th inst., at the residence of her niece, in this city, Miss MARY ANN POTTS, formerly of Prince William Co., Va., aged seventy-five years. (28 OCT 1853)

MARRIAGE. On Thursday evening, 27th inst., by the Rev. Mr. Marks, Mr. JONATHAN HAYES to Miss MARY EMILY ROBINSON, all of this city. (29 OCT 1853)

MARRIAGE. On the 27th October, at the residence of Gen. John H. Eaton, by the Rev. R.L. Dashiells, Mr. WILLIAM T. EVANS, of Washington city, to Miss JOSEPHINE T. ANDERSON, of Montgomery Co., Md. (29 OCT 1853)

MARRIAGE. On Wednesday morning, 26th inst., at Farley, Culpeper Co., Va., by the Rev. O.A. Kinsolving, JOHN D. ROGERS, of Loudoun Co., and PARKE FARLEY, eldest daughter of Dr. Wm. N. Wellford, of Culpeper Co. (29 OCT 1853)

MARRIAGE. On the 25th inst., by the Right Rev. Archbishop Kenrick, WILLIAM G. WROTH to MARY, daughter of the late Dr. William Poits, all of Baltimore city. (31 OCT 1853)

DEATH. On the 27th inst., at his residence in Prince William Co., Va., Dr. JAMES M.A. MUSCHETT, in the 33d year of his age. (31 OCT 1853)

MARRIAGE. At Grace Church, Prattsville, Greene Co., N.Y., on the 26th ult. [26 OCT 1853], by the Rev. Mr. Wright, Hon. COLIN M. INGERSOLL, M.C., of New Haven, Conn., to JULIA HELEN, only daughter of Hon. Zadoc Pratt, of Prattsville. The parties were accompanied at the altar by Miss Townsend, of New York city, and his Excellency Gov. Seymour, of Connecticut, our new Minister to Russia. (1 NOV 1853)

DEATH. At his residence in this city, on Sunday night [30 OCT 1853], WILLIAM M. PERRY, aged 35 years. His funeral will take place this (Tuesday) afternoon at 2 o'clock. His friends are respectfully invited to attend without further notice. (1 NOV 1853)

MARRIAGE. On Tuesday evening [1 NOV 1853], by the Rev. John C. Smith, Mr. AUGUSTUS R. STEVENS to Miss MARIA H. STONE. (2 NOV 1853)

MARRIAGE. On Monday evening [31 OCT 1853], by the Rev. Mr. Holladay, WILLIAM COLLINS, Esq., of Charlotte C.H., to Miss MARY LOUISE, daughter of Albert G. Green, Esq., of Prince Edward Co., Va. (2 NOV 1853)

DEATH. On the 29th of October, after a lingering illness, which she bore with Christian fortitude, MARY LOUISA ROSS, in the 23d year of her age. (2 NOV 1853)

DEATH. Of chronic croup, on the 1st inst., OWEN THOMAS McGEE, son of Owen and Catherine McGee, aged 3 years. The friends of the family are invited to attend his funeral this day at 2 o'clock P.M., from his father's residence, on Maryland avenue, between 3d and 4th streets, Capitol Hill. (3 NOV 1853)

Daily National Intelligencer, Marriage and Death Notices, 1851-1854

DEATH. In Georgetown, D.C., on the morning of the 2d inst., in the 72d year of her age, Mrs. MARY MORAN, a native of Wexford, Ire., but for the last twenty-five years a resident of the District of Columbia. Her funeral will take place from the residence of her daughter-in-law, Mrs. Alice Moran, on Water street, Georgetown, this afternoon, at 2½ o'clock. (3 NOV 1853)

MARRIAGE. On the morning of the 1st inst., by the Rev. S. Pyne, MARY B., daughter of the late Col. T. Cross, U.S. Army, to J.L. RENO, Bvt. Capt. U.S. Army. (4 NOV 1853)

MARRIAGE. On the 31st ult. [31 OCT 1853], by Rev. J. George Butler, Mr. BARNEY WARDER to Miss MARY BERRY, all of this city. (4 NOV 1853)

MARRIAGE. On Thursday evening, November 4th, at the F Street Presbyterian Church, by the Rev. James Nourse, JOHN W. NAIRN to Miss ELIZABETH R. NOURSE. (5 NOV 1853)

MARRIAGE. On the 3d inst., in this city, at the First Baptist Church, by the Rev. Edward Kingsford, D.D., GEORGE H. BAYNE, Esq., of Alexandria, Va., to MARIAN ELIZA, daughter of Purser William Speiden, U.S. Navy. (5 NOV 1853)

DEATH. Of yellow fever, on the 25th of October, WILLIAM H. McDOWELL, eldest son of A.M. and N.H. McDowell, of Demopolis, Ala. (5 NOV 1853)

DEATH. In this city, at 4 o'clock P.M., on the 4th inst., after a lingering illness, in the 29th year of her age, E. LOUISA SMITH, wife of Major J.R. Hagner, U.S. Army. Her funeral will take place at 3½ o'clock P.M. on Sunday, from the family residence. The friends of the family are respectfully invited to attend. (5 NOV 1853)

OBITUARY. Died, on Tuesday, the 18th of October, Dr. MATTHEW PAGE, formerly of Virginia, but for many years a resident of Edenton, N.C. The death of such a man is a public calamity, for his life was one of usefulness to the community and honor to the church of which he was a member. He first established himself in Richmond, Va., and as he possessed a mind of great original strength, thoroughly cultivated by education, he early distinguished himself both as a skillful physician and as a clear and forcible writer. His contributions to the literature of his profession were characterized by such vigor of thought, depth of research, and elegance of style as to command universal admiration, and to secure for their author several prizes in the contest for which some of the first minds of the country participated. Having been compelled by ill health to abandon a career which opened before him a future of so much usefulness and success, he settled in Edenton, N.C., and devoted the remainder of his days to agricultural pursuits [text continues]. (5 NOV 1853)

OBITUARY. At Washington, Parish of St. Landry, Louisiana, on the 16th of September, 1853, of yellow fever, Dr. EDW'D J. HEARD, at the early age of thirty-four. Dr. Heard was born in Charles Co., Md., was graduated as a doctor of medicine at the University of Maryland in March, 1844, and commenced the practice of his profession in July of the same year in the town in which he died... The bereavement is most melancholy to an old and devoted father, to brothers and sisters who can know no more on earth his kind and gentle sympathy and attentions, and especially to the wife of his bosom and his orphaned children [text continues]. (5 NOV 1853)

OBITUARY. In Staunton, Va., on Friday morning, the 21st October, Mrs. SUSAN CAROLINE THOMPSON, wife of Judge L.P. Thompson, in the 52d year of her ate. In the death of Mrs. Thompson, the society of Staunton has lost one of its brightest ornaments [text continues]. (5 NOV 1853)

MARRIAGE. In this city, on the 3d inst., by the Rev. R.L. Dashiell, MARY J., daughter of the late Jos. Smoot, to Lieut. J. DEMENT, U.S. Army. (7 NOV 1853)

MARRIAGE. At Brooklyn, on Tuesday morning, November 1, at the First Presbyterian Church, by the Rev. Dr. Cox, WM. A. POOR, of Baltimore, to HARRIET M., daughter of Dr. Jos. Lovell, late Surgeon General of the U.S. Army. (7 NOV 1853)

DEATH. On Sunday morning, at 2 o'clock, ELIZA JOSEPHINE WALKER, in the 15th year of her age, third daughter of John and Hannah M. Walker. To use her own words, let me rest in peace. The friends and acquaintances of the family are respectfully invited, without further notice, to attend the funeral this morning at 10 o'clock, from the residence of her father, corner of Third street and New York avenue. (7 and 8 NOV 1853)

DEATH. On Sabbath morning, November 6th, in the full hope of a happy immortality, EMILY SILLIMAN, wife of Thomas Blagden, of this city, and daughter of Gold S. Silliman, Esq., of Brooklyn, N.Y. The friends of the family are invited to attend the funeral from her late residence on New Jersey avenue, on Tuesday afternoon at three o'clock, without further notice. (7 and 18 NOV 1853)

DEATH. On Sunday, the 6th inst., of pulmonary consumption, in the 37th year of her age, MARY ANNA, wife of Samuel Yorke AtLee, of this city. The funeral will take place from the residence of her husband, on south P street, on Tuesday afternoon, at 2 o'clock, to which the friends of the family are respectfully invited. (7 NOV 1853)

DEATH. On the 7th inst., JOSEPH A. THOMPSON, aged 27 years. His friends and acquaintances are respectfully invited to attend his funeral this afternoon at 3½ o'clock, from his late residence at Miss Harvey's, on 8th street east, between C and D streets north. (8 NOV 1853)

DEATH. On Friday, the 27th of October, after a few days' illness, ANN MAGEE, in the 76th year of her age. (8 NOV 1853)

MARRIAGE. In Kentucky, on Saturday, the 29th ult. [29 OCT 1853], the Hon. ARCHIBALD DIXON, U.S. Senator, to Miss SUSAN BULLITT, daughter of William C. Bullitt, Esq., of Jefferson Co., Ky. (9 NOV 1853)

DEATH. On the 3d inst., of consumption, ISAAC N.I. CROGGON, in the 44th year of his age. (9 NOV 1853)

MARRIAGE. In F Street Church, Washington, on the 8th inst., by the Rev. J.M. Henry, Mr. HARRY BAILEY to Miss SARAH E. JENKS, of Virginia. On the same day, and by the same, Mr. WILLIAM H.F. TURNER, of Baltimore, to Miss SARAH ELLEN SCOTT, of this city. (10 NOV 1853)

MARRIAGE. On Tuesday, the 8th inst., at the Fifth Presbyterian Church, by the Rev. A.G. Carothers, Mr. ROBERT W. DOVE to Miss SARAH ANN CLEMENTS, all of this city. (10 NOV 1853)

MARRIAGE. On the 1st inst., by the Rev. J.B. Donelan, Mr. WILLIAM HAYES to Miss ABBE SULLIVAN, all of this city. (10 NOV 1853)

DEATH. At Tuscaloosa, Ala., on the 27th ult. [27 OCT 1853], WASHINGTON J. WHITING, merchant of that place. The deceased was a native of Fauquier Co., Va., and a young man of energy and enterprise, cut down in the full vigor of life. His loss is greatly lamented by his surviving friends and relatives. (10 NOV 1853)

MARRIAGE. On the 9th inst., at the 2d Presbyterian Church, by the Rev. J.R. Eckard, F. WILLIAM BRANDENBURY, of Prussia, to Miss MARTHA J. SIMS, of Fredericksburg, Va. (11 NOV 1853)

MARRIAGE. On Thursday evening, October 27th, by the Rev. Mr. Goodfellow, Mr. WM. WARD ORME to Miss NANNIE L. McCULLOUGH, daughter of Wm. McCullough, Esq., all of Bloomington, Ill. (11 NOV 1853)

Daily National Intelligencer, Marriage and Death Notices, 1851-1854

DEATH. In this city, on the morning of the 10th inst., about 7 o'clock, ALEXANDER TALBURT, in the 76th year of his age. The friends of the deceased are invited to attend his funeral from his late residence on 7th street, between G and H streets, on Saturday morning at 10 o'clock. (11 NOV 1853)

DEATH. At Lisbon, Howard Co., Md., on the 9th inst., Mr. CHARLES McKNEW, aged 30 years, late of the firm of Byers & McKnew, of this city. (11 NOV 1853)

DEATH. Of scarlet fever, on the 4th inst., at the residence of her grandfather, J. Hume, Esq., Fauquier Co., Va., ANNA PAYNE, only child of Richard P. Stewart, deceased, and of Sally M. Stewart, aged two years and eleven months. (11 NOV 1853)

MARRIAGE. On the 10th inst., by Rev. R.L. Dashiell, Mr. PHILIP H. HAUPTMAN to MARGARET M., daughter of Mr. John Fister, all of this city. (12 NOV 1853)

MARRIAGE. In the F Street Presbyterian Church, Washington, on the 10th inst., by the Rev. J.M. Henry, Mr. JOHN M. McFARLAND, of East Washington, to Miss LOUISA M. STEWART, of Granville, N.J. (12 NOV 1853)

DEATH. On the 7th inst., at the residence of her father, in Prince George's Co., Md., LOUISA, infant daughter of Charles F. Dement, Esq. (12 NOV 1853)

DEATH. At Newport, Fla., of yellow fever, JOHN PRATT, eldest son of the late Capt. John P. Hungerford, of this city. (14 NOV 1853)

DEATH. On Saturday evening, the 12th inst., of bilious fever, after an illness of nearly three weeks, MARY CLARE, daughter of Smith and Mary C. Thompson, aged 6 years and 10 months. The friends of the family are respectfully invited to attend her funeral from the residence of her father, near the city, this day at 12 o'clock. (14 NOV 1853)

MARRIAGE. On Thursday evening, 10th inst., by the Rev. John C. Smith, JOHN W. CLARKE to KATE, daughter of Col. Wm. P. Young, all of this city. (15 NOV 1853)

DEATH. In Georgetown, on the morning of the 5th inst., of consumption, MARY, wife of Charles Wilson, and daughter of the late Judge Shriver, of Frederick, Md. (15 NOV 1853)

DEATH. At Pawtuxet, R.I., on the afternoon of the 11th inst., ELIZA ALLEN BARTLETT, wife of John R. Bartlett, and daughter of Christopher Rhodes. (15 NOV 1853)

MARRIAGE. On the 2d inst., at Natchez, Miss., by the Rev. Jas. B. Stratton, LAFAYETTE CALDWELL, C.E., to Miss FRANCES CONSTANCE BABIN, daughter of the late P.P. Babin, Esq., all of the parish of West Baton Rouge, La. (16 NOV 1853)

DEATH. On Wednesday, the 9th inst., at her residence in Culpeper Co., Va., Mrs. MARY H. WINSTON, in the 58th year of her age. (16 NOV 1853)

DEATH. Near Pensacola, Fla., of yellow fever, on the 17th October 1853, EMMA, wife of David P. Smith; and on the 3d November inst., at the same place, and of the same disease, DAVID P. SMITH, a native of Georgetown, D.C., and recently of Calvert Co., Md., in the 37th year of his age. (16 NOV 1853)

DEATH. In this city, on Monday night [14 NOV 1853], Mr. CHARLES FRANCIS KING, in the 19th year of his age, from injuries received by the bursting of a boiler of a steam engine in the Navy Yard on Saturday last. The deceased was a most worthy young man; and from his education and studious habits promised fair to be an ornament to the profession of engineer, which he had selected and was studying theoretically and practically the past three years. He was piously upright in all his ways, and his amiability of manner

Daily National Intelligencer, Marriage and Death Notices, 1851-1854

and gentle kindness of disposition made him a favorite of all who knew him. Truly might it be said, "*None knew him but to love him, None named him but to praise.*" His funeral will take place from the residence of his father, Mr. Martin King, on Wednesday, the 16th, at 2 o'clock, to which the friends of the family are invited without further notice. (16 NOV 1853)

MARRIAGE. On the evening of the 15th inst., at St. Paul's English Lutheran Church, by the Rev. J. George Butler, Mr. GEORGE J. SEUFFERLE and HELEN CORNELIA, eldest daughter of Capt. Walter Warder, all of this city. (17 NOV 1853)

MARRIAGE. On the 15th inst., at St. John's Church, Georgetown, by Rev. Mr. Tillinghast, Lieut. EDMUND H. CUMMINS, U.S.R.S., to JOSEPHINE V., daughter of Maj. James P. Heath, of Baltimore. (17 NOV 1853)

MARRIAGE. In the Fifth Presbyterian Church, on Tuesday, the 15th inst., by the Pastor, Rev. A.G. Carothers, Mr. WM. M. MOORE to Miss MARY CHARLOTTE POWELL, all of this city. (17 NOV 1853)

OBITUARY. Died, suddenly, on Tuesday, the 8th inst., at Mt. Lubentia, Prince George's Co., Md., OTHO B. BELL, Esq., in the 63d year of his age [text continues]. (17 NOV 1853)

DEATH. In the city of New Orleans, of dysentery, on the 11th inst., FLOYD WAGGAMAN, in the 28th year of his age. (17 NOV 1853)

DEATH. On the 9th inst., near Newport, Charles Co., Md., after a short and painful illness, EDWARD R., second son of Alexius and Letitia Lancaster, in the 29th year of his age [text continues]. (18 NOV 1853)

DEATH. On the 17th inst., after a lingering illness, JOHN J. STEWART, formerly of Baltimore, in the 30th year of his age. The friends and acquaintances of the family are requested to attend his funeral tomorrow (Sunday) afternoon, at 2½ o'clock, from his brother's residence on 5th street, between I and K. (19 NOV 1853)

MARRIAGE. At the Exchange Hotel, on the 19th inst., by the Rev. J.M. Henry, Mr. SAMUEL BERLIN to Miss LOUISA V. MARSH, all of Virginia. (21 NOV 1853)

DEATH. Of consumption, on Monday, the 14th inst., at his residence in Georgetown, D.C., EVAN EDWARDS, aged thirty-four years. (21 NOV 1853)

MARRIAGE. On the 16th October, by the Rev. Mr. Wysong, Mr. HENRY C. SMITH to Miss MARIA R.M. RAWLINGS, both of this city. (22 NOV 1853)

MARRIAGE. On the 20th inst., by the Rev. Mr. Evans, Mr. WILLIAM LYNCH to Miss MARY RAWLINGS, both of Prince George's Co. (22 NOV 1853)

DEATH. At his residence in Philadelphia, on Sabbath, 20th inst., Capt. ALEXANDER CAMPBELL, in the 59th year of his age, brother of William H. Campbell, hardware merchant, of this city. Capt. Campbell, in early life, commanded a ship in the merchant service. Since he retired from the sea he has been actively engaged in business, always sustaining a high character for capacity and integrity, and was esteemed by all who knew him; above all, he was a Christian. (22 NOV 1853)

MARRIAGE. On the 13th inst., at the Church of the Epiphany, Washington, by the Rev. Mr. French, Mr. LEONARD VESSEY to Miss MARY ISABELLA SMYTH, all of Washington. (23 NOV 1853)

DEATH. In this city, on the evening of the 21st inst., Miss MARY ELIZABETH, eldest daughter of Mr. Charles and Eliza Pettit. The friends and acquaintances of the family are invited to attend her funeral this (Wednesday) afternoon at three o'clock, from the residence of her father, on E near 6th street. (23 NOV 1853)

DEATH. On yesterday, the 23d inst., Miss SARAH BRUMLEY, in the 57th year of her age. The funeral will take place this afternoon, at 3 o'clock, from the residence of Mr. Claxton, on Ninth street, where the friends of the family are respectfully invited to attend. (24 NOV 1853)

MARRIAGE. On Tuesday, 22d inst., by the Rev. Mr. Hodges, JAS. R. SMITH to Miss MARGARET NOKES, all of this city. (24 NOV 1853)

MARRIAGE. On Wednesday evening, the 23d inst., by the very Rev. Father Matthews, JAMES ENGLISH to Miss MARY ISABELLA ELLSWORTH, all of this city. (26 NOV 1853)

MARRIAGE. On Wednesday, the 23d inst., by the Rev. Mr. Hodges, Lieut. EDWARD JONES to Miss ELIZA G., daughter of Gen. Archibald Henderson, all of this city. (26 NOV 1853)

DEATH. In this city, on the 23d inst., in the 26th year of her age, Mrs. MARTHA W., wife of A.H. Gatton, and daughter of the late Robert A. Lewis, of Alexandria, Va. (28 NOV 1853)

DEATH. In this city, on Thursday, the 24th inst., Mrs. ANN ELEANOR BROOKE, consort of the late Clement Brooke, of "Perry Wood," Prince George's Co., Md., in the 72 year of her age. (28 NOV 1853)

DEATH. Departed this life on Sunday, the 27th inst., ELIZABETH, second daughter of the late Hon. Walter Dorsey, former Chief Judge of the Sixth Judicial District of Maryland. Retired in her habits, it was reserved for those alone who were acquainted with the uncommon intelligence, refined delicacy of sentiment, and exalted moral tone of this estimable lady [text continues]. (28 NOV 1853)

DEATH. On Friday evening [25 NOV 1853], MARY, infant child of C.F.E. and Charlotte Richardson, aged sixteen months. (28 NOV 1853)

DEATH. In Leesburg, Va., on Monday night, the 21st inst., of scarlet fever, WILLIE GRAYSON, only son of John M. and Orra L. Orr, in the 4th year of his age. (28 NOV 1853)

MARRIAGE. At the Wesley Chapel parsonage, on Sabbath evening, the 27th inst., by the Rev. Jas. H. Brown, Mr. JOSEPH L. HEISE to Miss MARY FRANCES BEAGLE, both of Washington. (29 NOV 1853)

MARRIAGE. On the 28th inst., by Rev. R.M. Lipscomb, Mr. GEORGE BARBER and Miss ELIZABETH BUTLER, both of Washington, D.C. (29 NOV 1853)

DEATH. On the 28th inst., JOHN J.C. BIBB, aged 33 years. The friends of the family are respectfully invited to attend his funeral from the residence of Mr. Burnley, on F street, at a quarter before 3 o'clock, this day. (29 NOV 1853)

MARRIAGE. On the 20th inst., by the Rev. French S. Evans, Mr. JOSEPH MATTINGLY to Miss HANNAH M. REEVES, both of this city. (30 NOV 1853)

MARRIAGE. At St. Matthew's Church, in this city, on Sunday, the 27th inst., by the Rev. J.B. Donelan, A. STORRS, of Albany, N.Y., to ANNIE ISABELLA, daughter of T.M. Blount, of Florida. (30 NOV 1853)

MARRIAGE. In this city, on Thursday evening, the 24th inst., by the Rev. James A. Duncan, Mr. EDWARD WINGATE, of Baltimore, and MARY JANE MILLIS, of Georgetown, D.C. (30 NOV 1853)

OBITUARY. Maj. THOMAS M. NELSON, died at his residence, near Columbus, Ga., on the 10th inst., in the 72d year of his age. Thus another gallant soldier of the war of 1812, and a Christian gentleman, honored and beloved, has been gathered to his fathers. Major Nelson was the grandson of Secretary Nelson, of Virginia; a man of renown in the Revolutionary annals of this country. His father, Major John Nelson, was also a gallant soldier of the Revolution, having served with honor as major of cavalry during that eventful period. The subject of this notice entered the army of the U.S. as a captain of infantry at an early period of the war of 1812, and served with high distinction upon the frontier during its entire continuance. Virginia, His native State, testified her sense of his merit by presenting him a splendid sword. On the reduction of the army to the peace establishment he was retained in the service with the rank of Major. In 1815 he resigned his commission, and shortly afterwards was elected to Congress from the Mecklenburg district, in which he resided. In 1817 he was re-elected, and in 1819 he declined a re-election. He thenceforth devoted himself to his family and private affairs, living in Virginia until 1838, when he removed to the State of Georgia. In the 1816 he united himself to the Episcopal Church, and ever after filled the office of warden in the several parishes to which he was attached. As a soldier in the cause of his God and of his country he was alike faithful and fearless, and the memory of his virtues may well serve as a beacon-light to guide his descendants in the path of honor, of piety, and peace. (30 NOV 1853)

MARRIAGE. At the Empire Hotel, on the 29th ult. [29 NOV 1853], by the Rev. Jas. H. Brown, Mr. MATTHIAS B. TOWNSEND to Miss ELIZABETH A. ROBEY, both of Baltimore. (1 DEC 1853)

MARRIAGE. On the 30th ult. [30 NOV 1853], by the Rev. Mr. Aiken, Mr. JOHN THEODORE QUEEN, of this city, to Miss LOUISA M. HALLER, of Frederick, Md. (1 DEC 1853)

OBITUARY. Died, on the 28th ult. [28 NOV 1853], at the house of his brother-in-law, in this city, JOHN J. CRITTENDEN BIBB, aged thirty-three years. He was the son of Chancellor Bibb, of Kentucky. It is the writer's lot to have passed with him the severe and novel ordeal of cadetship at West Point, in 1844; to have been his fellow-officer up to his resignation in '46, and to have seen him, through long and trying sickness, daily yielding his mortality, with the peaceful calmness of a Christian gentleman [text continues]. (1 DEC 1853)

MARRIAGE. On Tuesday evening, November 29th, by the Right Rev. Bishop Johns, of Virginia, JOHN S. GITTINGS, of Baltimore, to CHARLOTTE C. RITCHIE, daughter of Thos. Ritchie, of this city. (2 DEC 1853)

MARRIAGE. In New Castle, on Thursday evening, 10th of November last, by Rev. Mr. Billop, Dr. MARIUS DUVALL, U.S. Navy, to ELIZABETH, daughter of the Hon. Jas. Booth, Chief Justice of Delaware. (5 DEC 1853)

DEATH. In Georgetown, on Saturday evening last [3 DEC 1853], LEWIS McKENDREE DIVINE, in the 32d year of his age. The funeral will take place from the residence of his mother-in-law, Mrs. Shaw, on Bridge street, Georgetown, on this (Monday) afternoon, at 3 o'clock; at which time the friends of the family are respectfully invited to attend. (5 DEC 1853)

DEATH. At Ft. Brooke, Tampa, Fla., on the 1st ult. [1 NOV 1853], of yellow fever, Lieut. C.R.P. BUTLER, of the 2d Artillery, a native of South Carolina, and a young officer highly esteemed and of great promise. Upon the death of Gen. Childs and Lieut. Cook at Tampa the headquarters of the troops in Florida was left without an officer, and Lieut. Butler was ordered to repair to that post and take charge of the public property there. Followed by much solicitude, on the 19th of October he left Charleston. A high sense of duty constrained him to devote himself with diligence to his task, looking after the effects of the two officers who had preceded him, as well as the public property, removing the soldiers from the garrison into camp, and visiting the hospital to see that the sick received proper attention, thus exposing himself to the contagion. On the 22d of October he received a long-looked-for and well-deserved leave of absence, and on the 26th an officer relieved him. The next day he was to take the stage for Pilatka, and in a week would have been with those he dearly loved. Man proposes, but God disposes. During the night he was seized, and, notwithstanding the skill and attention of his two physicians, he struggled in vain. (6 DEC 1853)

Daily National Intelligencer, Marriage and Death Notices, 1851-1854

OBITUARY. Departed this life, on the evening of Tuesday, the 29th day of November, 1853, at half-past 8 o'clock, ELIZABETH ELLICOTT, relict of George Ellicott, Sen'r, in the 92d year of her age. Married to one of that noble and venerable band whose lives were connected with the existence of Ellicott's Mills, whose bands planted its first corner-stones, and whose name it bears, she survived them all. She was in fact the last living Ellicott of Ellicott's Mills. Of her coeval relatives all have died; of their descendants comparatively few survive, and these are scattered over the land. Ellicott's Mills has ceased to be as it was in the olden time, their rallying point; the meeting house on Quaker Hill no longer concentrates their worshippers; its doors are closed, and she, whose noble form once presided in its galleries, has now joined the church triumphant... Mrs. Ellicott was the daughter of James Brooke, Jr., of Montgomery Co., Md., a wealthy citizen, and a distinguished member of the Society of Friends. On her marriage with George Ellicott, Sen., which was in 1789, she came to Ellicott's Mills, and took up her residence in the house where she always lived, and where she died. At the time of her arrival this large town was not even a village. The whole space around was covered with forests of huge trees, inhabited by wolves, wild-cats, and deer. Mrs. Ellicott shared fully in the anxieties, the toils, and the successes of the founders of Ellicott's Mills. For sixty-three years she has uninterruptedly resided here; during all that time a blessing to her fellow-creatures... In her domestic relations, as wife, mother, relative, and friend, she was most happy and exemplary. Her husband, too, was one of the best of man -- a Christian gentleman. Most of us remember well his manly form, His sincere, gentle, and polished manners, His instructive conversation, His kindness, and nobleness of soul. The two were most happy in each other, and lived together forty-two years. She survived him twenty-one years. It is curious in imagination to look back upon the multitudinous scenes, the great and various changes immediately around her and in the world at large, the many remarkable individuals such as one so aged must have seen. The events and chiefs of our Revolution were familiar to her. She had exulted in the peace of 1782; she had been in the presence of Washington, Franklin, Jefferson, Adams, Madison and Rush. Her vigorous mind, improved by careful and continual reading, made her fit company even for them... She was particularly fond of the *National Intelligencer*. Her husband had subscribed to its first number. It was the firm supporter of Thomas Jefferson and his administration, and Mr. Ellicott was his ardent admirer. From that day to the present this journal has been a constant inmate of the house. Her last receipt for subscription is dated November 20th, 1853 [text continues]. [It is due to the memory of this venerable lady to add that, in a letter signed with her own hand, a fortnight ago, she remitted her fifty-fourth year's subscription to the *National Intelligencer* in advance.] (8 DEC 1853)

MARRIAGE. On the 4th inst., by the Rev. J.R. Eckard, Mr. FERDINAND BUTLER to Miss ELIZABETH C., daughter of Jos. Abbott, Esq., all of this city. (8 DEC 1853)

MARRIAGE. On the 1st inst., by the Rev. Jas. Brown, CHAS. MILLER, Jr. to Miss ELIZABETH A.L. MARSHALL. (8 DEC 1853)

MARRIAGE. On Saturday, September 3d, Lieut. GEO. W. DOTY, U.S. Navy, to JULIA, daughter of the late Henry Lynch, of New York. (9 DEC 1853)

MARRIAGE. On Thursday evening, the 8th inst., by Rev. A.G. Carothers, Mr. ROBERT THOMPSON to Miss MARY A. KEMP, all of this city. (10 DEC 1853)

MARRIAGE. By the Rev. J.G. Butler, on the 4th inst., Mr. WILLIAM WARDER and Miss MARY J. DAVIS, both of this city. (10 DEC 1853)

MARRIAGE. At West Springfield, Mass., on the 24th ult. [24 NOV 1853], by Rev. Henry Field, J.M. BAGGE and MARY S., eldest daughter of Nathan Loomis, of Virginia. (10 DEC 1853)

DEATH. At New Orleans, of cholera, on the 28th ult. [28 NOV 1853], Mrs. JANE J. HODGSON. (10 DEC 1853)

Daily National Intelligencer, Marriage and Death Notices, 1851-1854

MARRIAGE. In Philadelphia, on the 7th inst., at the residence of Thomas Robins, Esq., by Rev. Dr. Stephens, ROBERT S. COSTIN, Esq., to KATE P., daughter of the late Gen. S.E. Parker, all of Northampton Co., Va. (12 DEC 1853)

MARRIAGE. On Thursday, the 8th inst., by the Rev. Josiah Varden, Mr. AUGUSTUS GLASGOW, of Baltimore, to Miss ANN E. GRANT, of this city. (13 DEC 1853)

MARRIAGE. On Tuesday, the 29th of November, at Bolton, Somerset Co., Md., the residence of her brother, George R. Dennis, Esq., by the Rev. James Moore, JAMES MURRAY RUSH, Esq., of Philadelphia, to ELIZABETH UPSHUR DENNIS, of Essex, Somerset Co., Md. (14 DEC 1853)

MARRIAGE. In Alexandria, on Tuesday, the 6th inst., by Rev. J.T. Johnston, J. BOWEN SMITH, of Baltimore, and ELIZABETH T. WATTLES, daughter of the late Nathaniel Wattles. (14 DEC 1853)

MARRIAGE. On Tuesday morning, by the Rev. John C. Smith, THOMAS TALBOT, Esq., to Miss RACHAEL L. WALL, both of Prince George's Co., Md. (14 DEC 1853)

DEATH. On the 13th inst., JOHN JACOB, son of John Jacob and Sophia Aigler, aged 4 years and 3 months. The relatives and friends of the family are requested to attend his funeral on Thursday afternoon at 3 o'clock, from the residence of his parents on D, between 11th and 12th streets. (14 DEC 1853)

DEATH. In Hancocktown, Md., December 9th, ALVIN, son of Rev. James P. and Caroline C. Fugitt, aged one year, lately of this city. (14 DEC 1853)

MARRIAGE. On Tuesday evening [13 DEC 1853], by the Rev. John C. Smith, Mr. JOHN KERR to Miss SUSAN SAUNDERS, all of this city. (15 DEC 1853)

MARRIAGE. On the 13th inst., by the Very Rev. Wm. Matthews, Mr. WALTER M. PUMPHREY to Miss ANN ELIZABETH REED, all of this city. (15 DEC 1853)

MARRIAGE. On the 14th inst., by the Rev. Dr. Peck, BENJ. F. GUY to MAGGIE J. MORSELL, all of this city. (15 DEC 1853)

DEATH. At Alexandria, on Tuesday, the 13th inst., in the 38th year of her age, Mrs. MARIA S. ENGLISH, wife of Mr. James A. English, and daughter of Almon and Malinda Baldwin, of this city. The funeral of the deceased will take place from her late residence, at the corner of King and Patrick streets, in Alexandria, this (Thursday) morning, at half-past 10 o'clock, to which the friends of the families are invited. (15 DEC 1853)

DEATH. At Oakdale, Harrison Co., Va., on the morning of the 7th inst., Mrs. SARAH JOHNSON, wife of the Hon. Joseph Johnson, Governor of the State of Virginia. (15 DEC 1853)

OBITUARY. For the *National Intelligencer*, Staunton, Va., December 10. On the 14th of August, of a bright and lovely Sabbath morning, when every thing was calm and serene around, when the church bells were admonishing the citizens of Staunton that it was time to turn their footsteps towards the house of God, attention was called to the fact that the house of WM. COLEMAN had been closed for several days, during which time he had been seen by no one. Suspicion being excited by so unusual a circumstance, the doors were opened, and there was exposed to the astonished and horrified beholders a scene which beggars descriptions. There lay the mangled body of the old man. His frail and dilapidated house had been broken open, robbed, and its inmate most foully and brutally murdered, and left to rot as the carcass of the best of the field. Mr. Coleman had led a secluded life for many years. Death had deprived him of his sister, to whom he was devotedly attached, and the nearest blood relation he had on earth. After he had followed the corps to its last resting place he retired to an old and dilapidated building to pass the rest of his days, with no one to comfort him in his hours of affliction. But there he poured out his heart in prayer to the God who compassionates the cast-down and depressed. Perhaps at that time, indulging in pleasing meditation on that good and aged mother and that devoted sister, or in fancied security that the laws of the land rendered his retail tenement secure, His house was forcibly entered and pillaged and its owner cruelly murdered. Every one was anxious to ferret out the authors of so awful a crime, when suspicion was turned upon two men by the names of Trayer and Wilson, who had sustained previous to the murder very bad characters. Soon suspicion ripened into confidence, and they were arrested, tried, and found guilty. During the trial the courthouse was thronged by both sexes to hear the able pleadings of counsel. The culprits were sentenced to death by Judge Thomson, accompanied by an impressive and pathetic address worthy of that good and able magistrate. January the 6th is appointed for their execution. (16 DEC 1853)

FROM THE *EDGEFIELD, (S.C.) ADVERTISER*. Death of Mrs. Behethland Foote Butler. On the 2d inst. this aged matron and remarkable woman breathed her last at the residence of her son and only surviving child, the Hon. Ap. Butler. Mrs. Behethland Foote Butler was the relict of Gen. Wm. Butler, of the Revolution. She had lived through the dark and perilous days of her country's history, had witnessed the career of that country's greatness in all its mutations, had come down to the fourth generation of American freemen full of those honors which ever cluster around the brow of fearless integrity, and fell asleep at last with a calmness and confidence characteristic only of one who has led a long life of probity and usefulness. She was born in Virginia in the year 1764, but had lived from early youth in this section of South Carolina. She had nearly reached the advanced age of eighty-nine when the decree went forth that the measure of her duties was full, and the servant was called to her reward [text continues]. (16 DEC 1853)

DEATH. On the 16th inst., Mr. PHILIP C. DAVIS, in the 47th year of his age. His funeral will take place tomorrow (Sunday) at 2 o'clock, from his late residence on 14th, between S and T streets, to which his friends are respectfully invited to attend. (17 DEC 1853)

DEATH. Died, in Philadelphia, on the 16th inst., at the residence of his son-in-law, Mr. James Furness, WILLIAM G. ELIOT, Esq., late of this city, in the 73d year of his age. Such a man should not pass from our circle without the record of a written word in this city, where he so long resided and was so highly esteemed. He was, from the foundation of the church of his faith here, (the Unitarian,) a member of it; and no one has in his whole life more beautifully illustrated its high and holy teaching [text continues]. (17 DEC 1853)

DEATH. On the 16th inst., after a lingering illness, THOMAS JOHNS, aged 62 years, formerly of Prince George's Co., Md., but for the last twenty years a resident of this city. (19 DEC 1853)

DEATH. On the morning of the 19th inst., SARAH AMANDA, consort of Thomas A. Lazenby, aged about 35 years, after a protracted illness, which she bore with patience and Christian resignation. The relatives and friends of the family are requested to attend her funeral this afternoon at 2 o'clock, from her late residence on Bridge near Congress street, Georgetown. (20 DEC 1853)

DEATH. In this city, yesterday morning [20 DEC 1853], CATHERINE, wife of Patrick Corbett. The friends of the family are respectfully invited to attend the funeral this (Wednesday) afternoon, at two o'clock, from their residence, on B street, between 10th and 11th streets, Island. (21 DEC 1853)

MARRIAGE. On the 15th inst., by the Rev. French S. Evans, SIDNEY EASTON to CORDELIA DIGGES, eldest daughter of Judson Digges, all of this city. (21 DEC 1853)

DEATH. In this ;city, on the 20th inst., Mrs. ELIZABETH COURTS WATSON, widow of the late James Watson, Esq., in the 75th year of her age. The friends of the family are requested to attend her funeral this day (Thursday) at 2 o'clock, from her late residence, corner of G and 19th streets. (22 DEC 1853)

DEATH. Suddenly, on the 20th inst., Mrs. ANN C. MORGAN, formerly of Long Island, N.Y., but for the last thirty-seven years a resident of this city, aged 62 years. The friends and acquaintances of the deceased

Daily National Intelligencer, Marriage and Death Notices, 1851-1854

are invited to attend her funeral on Thursday (this day) at 11 o'clock A.M., from the residence of her son-in-law, S.L. Cole, on Pennsylvania avenue, between 10th and 11th streets. (22 DEC 1853)

DEATH. On the 20th inst., AUGUST FREDERICK, eldest son of Frederick and Elizabeth Lakemeyer, in the 7th year of his age. The friends and acquaintances of the family are invited to attend the funeral, from the residence of his grandfather, John C. Roemmele, corner of 18th and K streets, this afternoon, the 22d inst., at 3 o'clock. (22 DEC 1853)

DEATH. Yesterday morning [22 DEC 1853], JOHN P., infant son of Peter and Virginia Hevner. His funeral will take place this day at 12 M., from the residence of his parents, on 6th, near H street, to which the friends of the family are respectfully invited. (23 DEC 1853)

MARRIAGE. On Thursday, the 22d inst., by the Rev. Mr. Hodges, RICHARD HENRY TARMAN to Miss MATILDA A. GODARD, of Prince George's Co., Md. On the same day, by the same, Mr. ZACHARIAH H.G. WALKER to Miss SARAH E. LOCKER, all of this city. (26 DEC 1853)

DEATH. On the 25th December, THOMAS GUNTON, aged 70 years, a native of England, and for the last thirty-seven years a resident of this city. His friends and the friends of his brother are respectfully invited to attend his funeral, from the residence of Dr. Gunton, tomorrow (Tuesday) at 2 o'clock. (26 DEC 1853)

DEATH. On the 25th inst., F.F. WINGENROTH, aged 31 years, a native of Nassau, Germany, but for the last five years a resident of this city. The friends of the family are invited to attend the funeral from his late residence, corner of 8th and E streets, Tuesday afternoon, at 2 o'clock. (26 DEC 1853)

DEATH. At St. Louis, on the 14th inst., Mr. JOHN QUIGLEY, aged 41 years, a native of Washington. He came to St. Louis about sixteen years ago, and has been the foreman of our press room, with a few intervals, for the greater portion of that time. He was a kind and honest man and most excellent workman. *St. Louis Rep.* (26 DEC 1853)

DEATH. In this city, yesterday evening [25 DEC 1853], at the house of her daughter, on Capitol Hill, AMELIA BROGDEN, colored, aged one hundred and ten years. (26 DEC 1853)

MARRIAGE. On the 26th inst., by the Rev. Jno. W. Hedges, Mr. FREDERICK T. WILSON to Miss MARY E. BORLAND, both of this city. (29 DEC 1853)

MARRIAGE. On Tuesday morning [27 DEC 1853], by Rev. John C. Smith, Mr. GEORGE HENRY DOVE to Miss ELIZABETH V. DAVIS, of Virginia. (29 DEC 1853)

DEATH. On the 25th inst., at the residence of his brother, in Montgomery Co., Md., WILLIAM G. DAVIDSON, in the 24th year of his age. (29 DEC 1853)

MARRIAGE. On the 29th inst., in Wesley Chapel, by the Rev. James H. Brown, Mr. HENRY B. McELFRESH to Miss VIRGINIA J. PRENAL, both of Washington. (30 DEC 1853)

MARRIAGE. On the 21st inst., by the Rev. Wm. H. Kinkle, of the city of Lynchburg, Va., CHARLES C. OTEY, Esq., to SALLIE P., daughter of the Hon. Wm. L. Goggin, at Peakland, his residence, Bedford Co., Va. (31 DEC 1853)

MARRIAGE. In Philadelphia, on the 26th inst., by the Rev. E.J. Sourin, of St. John's Church, JOHN V. CRAWFORD, Esq., of Havana, eldest son of Joseph T. Crawford, Esq., H.B.M.'s Consul General in Cuba, to MARY VIRGINIA, daughter of Col. Augustus J. Pleasanton, of Philadelphia. (31 DEC 1853)

Daily National Intelligencer, Marriage and Death Notices, 1851-1854

DEATH. In this city, on the 30th inst., MARY MILES, of Somerset Co., Md., in the 73d year of her age. The funeral will take place tomorrow afternoon at three o'clock, from the residence of A.K. Hewitt, Esq. (31 DEC 1853)

Daily National Intelligencer, Marriage and Death Notices, 1851-1854

❋ ❋ ❋ 1854 ❋ ❋ ❋

DEATH. On Sunday afternoon, January 1st, JOHN BRADDOCK PORTER, infant son of John E. and Sarah Porter, aged eleven months and sixteen days. The friends of the family are respectfully invited to the funeral, which will take place on this evening at 3 P.M., from the residence of his uncle, Mr. D.S. Porter. (2 JAN 1854)

MARRIAGE. On the 28th ult. [28 DEC 1853], in the Parish Church of Chestertown, Md., by the Rev. Clement F. Jones, D.D., SAMUEL M. SHOEMAKER, of Baltimore, and AUGUSTA C., eldest daughter of the Hon. John B. Eccleston, of the former place. (3 JAN 1854)_

DEATH. In this city, on the morning of the 3d inst., Mrs. JANE KENNEY, in the 41st year of her age. Her funeral will take place from St. Peter's Church, Capitol Hill, on Thursday morning next, at 10 o'clock, where solemn high mass will be said, to which the friends of the family are respectfully invited to attend. (4 JAN 1854)

MARRIAGE. On the 4th inst., by the Rev. Dr. Butler, CHAS. W. BEATTY, Esq., of Baltimore, to AUGUSTA M., daughter of Dr. A.J. Schwartze, of Washington. (5 JAN 1854)

DEATH. At her residence, in Georgetown, on the 3d inst., Mrs. MARTHA J. WAGGAMAN, the sister of Ex-President Tyler, in her 70th year. Her funeral will take place from her late residence, on 1st street, near High street, and proceed to St. Matthew's Church, this day (Thursday) at 1 o'clock. The acquaintances and friends of the family will attend without further notice. (5 JAN 1854)

DEATH. On Tuesday, the 3d inst., on the Navy Yard, MARY ANN, wife of Merrit Sheckels, in the 32d year of her age. (5 JAN 1854)

MARRIAGE. In this city, on the 4th inst., by the Rev. Geo. W. Samson, JOS. D. GREEN, of Philadelphia, to Mrs. MARY A. GOLD, daughter of Hon. A. Kendall. (6 JAN 1854)

MARRIAGE. On the 2d inst., at Grace Church, by the Rev. Alfred Holmead, SAMUEL C. PENINGTON to ANNA E. DORSEY, daughter of E.J. Dorsey, all of this city. (6 JAN 1854)

DEATH. On the 26th of August, 1853, on board the clipper ship *Antelope*, in the Pacific ocean, RAPHAEL, son of the late Raphael Semmes, of Georgetown, D.C., in the 18th year of his age. (6 JAN 1854)

MARRIAGE. On Thursday, the 5th inst., at Trinity Church, by the Rev. Mr. Hodges, THOMAS W. BRODHEAD, U.S.N., to ELIZA R., daughter of the late James D. Barry, of this city. (7 JAN 1854)

MARRIAGE. On the morning of the 5th, in St. Thomas's Church, by the Rev. S.R. Gordon, Col. WM. D. BOWIE to Miss MARY ODEN, daughter of the late Benj. Oden, all of Prince George's Co., Md. (7 JAN 1854)

MARRIAGE. On Thursday, the 5th inst., by the Rev. John C. Smith, Mr. A.B. CLAXTON to Miss E. JENNIE FISHER, all of this city. (7 JAN 1854)

DEATH. On Friday morning, the 6th inst., at five minutes past one o'clock, HENRY ASHTON BIBB, in his 15th year, youngest son of Hon. Geo. M. Bibb. "*Resquiescat in pace!*" His funeral will take place at St. Patrick's Church this morning at 10 o'clock, to which the friends and acquaintances are invited. (7 and 10 JAN 1854)

Daily National Intelligencer, Marriage and Death Notices, 1851-1854

DEATH. In this city, on the 5th inst., HENRY R., infant son of Fanny and C.R. Byrne. The friends and acquaintances of the family are invited to attend the funeral this (Saturday) afternoon at 2 o'clock, from the residence of Mrs. Middleton, Garrison street, Navy Yard, near Virginia avenue. (7 JAN 1854)

MARRIAGE. On the 22d ult. [22 DEC 1853], by the Rev. J.F. Hoff, PHILIP NELSON to EMMA PAGE, all of Clarke Co., Va. (9 JAN 1854)

DEATH. On the 5th inst., at his residence in Prince George's Co., Md., Mr. RICHARD HYATT, in the 70th year of his age, formerly a merchant of Baltimore. (10 JAN 1854)

MARRIAGE. On Tuesday, January 10, by the Rev. C.M. Butler, JAS. K. SMITH, of Philadelphia, to GEORGIE, daughter of Wm. G.W. White, Esq., of this city. (11 JAN 1854)

MARRIAGE. At Trinity Church, on the 10th inst., by Rev. Dr. Butler, WM. BOWIE BURFORD, of Montgomery Co., Md., and ELIZABETH ANN, eldest daughter of Wm. Thompson, Esq., of this city. (11 JAN 1854)

MARRIAGE. At St. Stephen's Church, Baltimore, on the 10th inst., by Rev. Mr. Reed, NORMAN S. BESTOR, of New Almaden, Calif., to WILLIE J. CHILDS, of Baltimore. (11 JAN 1854)

DEATH. On the morning of the 10th inst., KATE, youngest child of B.F. and E.E. Dyer, aged 2 years and 9 months. The friends of the family are invited to attend the funeral this (Wednesday) afternoon at 3 o'clock. (11 JAN 1854)

MARRIAGE. On the 10thi nst., by the Rev. James B. Donelan, WILLIAM S. DAVIS to SARAH E., eldest daughter of John T. Cassell, Esq. (12 JAN 1854)

MARRIAGE. On Thursday, 12th inst., by Rev. D.X. Junkin, Mr. E. WOOD FOGG, of Philadelphia, to Miss MATTIE A. WILSON, of this city. (13 JAN 1854)

DEATH. On Wednesday evening, the 11th inst., EPHRAIM W. HALL, second son of the late Dr. Jos. Hall, of Anne Arundel Co., Md., and for the last four years a resident of this city. The friends and acquaintances of the family are respectfully requested to attend his funeral, on Friday morning at 10 o'clock, from the residence of his mother, on 11th street, between G and H streets. (13 JAN 1854)

DEATH. In this city, on the morning of the 12th inst., A. CLINTON McLEAN, of New York city. His funeral till take place this (Friday) afternoon at 4 o'clock, from the residence of Col. C.K. Gardner, Capitol Hill. (13 JAN 1854)

DEATH. On Thursday morning, the 12th inst., after a brief illness, AUGUSTUS LOT, aged three years five months and two days, son of John T. and Elizabeth Costin. The relatives and friends of the familoy are requested to attend his funeral on this (Friday) afternoon at 3 o'clock, from the residence of his parents, on the Island. (13 JAN 1854)

DEATH. At Ft. Snelling, Minn., on the 30th of November, ELIZA, wife of Col. Francis Lee, U.S. Army. The death of this devoted wife and mother of the anniversary of the day that saw her a happy bride has cast an impenetrable gloom over the home which for twenty-eight years she has brightened with her presence, and filled with unutterable sorrow the hearts of her widowed husband and orphan children; and not in the home circle alone will her loss be felt, but in every part of the Union hearts will be saddened by the news of her death, and the church, of which she has so long been a useful member, will mourn with them her irreparable loss. (13 JAN 1854)

MARRIAGE. On the 5th inst., by the Rev. Jas. H. Brown, Mr. JOS. H. WRIGHT to Miss HENRIETTA RITTENHOUSE, both of Prince George's Co., Md. (14 JAN 1854)

Daily National Intelligencer, Marriage and Death Notices, 1851-1854

MARRIAGES. On Thursday evening, 12th inst., by Rev. Mr. Marks, Mr. WM. W. BRADLEY to Miss SARAH F. SIMMONS. On the same evening, by the same, Mr. JOHN PULLIN to Miss SUSANNA G. CARDEN. On the 27th December 1853, by the same, Mr. JAMES L. BOSWELL to Miss MARY ANN KING. (14 JAN 1854)

OBITUARY. Died, at his residence on Wye river, in Queen Anne's Co., Md., on the 16th of November last [1853], WILLIAM CARMICHAEL, Esq., in his 79th year. He was born on the 25th of September 1775, at Chestertown, in Kent Co., and educated at Washington College, near that place. His family were Whigs of the Revolution. His father was a volunteer under Gen. Smallwood, and fought at Brandywine and Germantown, remaining in the service more than two years, and holding the rank of captain. His uncle was employed in the diplomatic service of his country, being Secretary of Legation to Mr. Jay while the latter was the Minister of the U.S. near the Court of Madrid, to which he was afterwards commissioned as Charge d'Affairs by Gen. Washington. The subject of this notice was himself a man of marked character and lofty virtues. He studied law at Annapolis, then the seat of the General Court, the great resort of the Maryland Bar, and the best school for lawyers in the U.S. Among his fellow-students were the late Judges Stephen and Magruder, of the Court of Appeals, and the present Chief Justice of the U.S., who was, however, several years his junior. As a man may be known by his companions, so it may serve to indicate his early character to say that he was at this time the intimate associate of the future Chief Justice. The friendship thus formed in early manhood was never interrupted or diminished, and continued to be warm and intimate through life. They were not students in the same office, but were room-mates, and were in the habit of discussing at night the reading of the day which they had pursued apart. Thus was Mr. Carmichael's character formed, by temperance, study, and habits of inquiry, by associations and friendship which could not fail to confirm and invigorate the native qualities of his head and heart. He came to the bar in Queen Anne's Co., and soon acquired large practice and reputation. In the conflicts of the forum he had to contend with the late Richard Tilghman Earle, a sound and able lawyer, afterwards distinguished on the bench of the Court of Appeals; with Thomas Bullit and Nicholas Hammond, Esqs., of Talbot Co.; and Joseph Bailey, of Dorchester, subsequently Attorney General of Maryland; all of whom held high rank in the General Court. The Hon. E.F. Chambers, now the senior member of the Eastern Shore bar, at one time a distinguished Senator of the U.S., and afterwards a judge of the Court of Appeals, though his junior, was for many years his most frequent and perhaps his most formidable antagonist at the bar. In competition with such minds his faculties were trained and disciplined. From 1816 to 1821 he held a seat in the Senate of Maryland, a small but distinguished body, composed of the first men in the State, and numbering among its members, Gen. William H. Winder, Gen. Robert Goodloe Harper, his early friend Mr. Taney, and others of high talent and influence.... More than fifteen years before his death he withdrew from the practice of his profession and devoted his attention to the cultivation and improvement of a large landed estate on the Wye river [text continues]. (16 JAN 1854)

DEATH OF LIEUT. DAVIS. It is our painful duty to announce the death of Lieut. JOHN A. DAVIS, U.S. Navy, which took place at 4 o'clock on Saturday afternoon [14 JAN 1854]. Although the accident was of so sever a nature as at first to preclude almost any hope hof his recovery, yet he rallied so much under the kind, assiduous, and skilful treatment of the professional gentlemen at the Infirmary that his friends were flattered with the belief that he might be restored to health. It proved, however, to be a vain delusion. At 3 o'clock A.M. on Saturday a change for the worse took place; he rapidly sunk, and at 4 o'clock in the afternoon death terminated his sufferings [resolution follows]. His friends are respectfully invited to attend his funeral this morhning, at half past 10 o'clock, from St. Patrick's Church, F street. (16 JAN 1854)

MARRIAGE. On Thursday evening, 12th inst., by Rev. S.A.H. Marks, Mr. W. WALLACE BRADLEY and Miss SARAH F. SIMMONS, all of this city. (16 JAN 1854)

DEATH. On the 15th inst., ELIZABETH JANE, wife of Jas. Miller, and eldest daughter of Alexander and Mary Borland. Her funeral will take place today at 3 o'clock, from the residence of her father, on L street, between 15th and 16th streets, which her friends are respectfully invited to attend. (16 JAN 1854)

Daily National Intelligencer, Marriage and Death Notices, 1851-1854

MARRIAGE. On Sunday afternoon, the 15th inst., by Rev. S.A.H. Marks, Mr. JOHN STAMP to Miss MARTHA WHITE, both of Prince George's Co., Md. (17 JAN 1854)

MARRIAGE. In this city, on Thursday evening, the 12th inst., by the Rev. W. McLain, ROBERT C. FARISH, Esq., and Miss MARY E. YATES. (17 JAN 1854)

MARRIAGE. On the 14th inst., by the Rev. Jas. H. Brown, Mr. CHARLES W. ALCOTT to Miss ADELAIDE J. COCHRAN, both of New York city. (17 JAN 1854)

DEATH. Yesterday morning [16 JAN 1854], Mr. ALEXANDER WITTENAUER, in the 30th year of his age, a native of Baltimore, but for the last two years a resident of this city. (17 JAN 1854)

DEATH. On the 16th inst., PETER LITTLE, Jr., in the 51st year of his age, of disease of the lungs. The friends and acquaintances of the family are respectfully requested to attend his funeral on Thursday afternoon, at 2 o'clock, at his late residence on Virginia avenue, between 4½ and 6th streets, Navy Yard. (18 JAN 1854)

DEATH. On Monday afternoon, 16th inst., MANDEVILLE, second son of James Mandeville Carlisle, aged four years and eleven days. The funeral will take place at 12 o'clock M. today. (18 JAN 1854)

MARRIAGE. On the 16th inst., in the city of New York, by the Rev. C.C. Pise, D.D., WALTER LENOX, Esq., of this city, to RACHEL S. LUDLOW, daughter of Ezra Ludlow, of the former place. (19 JAN 1854)

MARRIAGE. ON the 17th inst., by the Rev. E. Knight, of Washington, at the residence of Mr. Edward Fenwick, RICHARD T. HILL, of Prince George's Co., Md., to Miss ELIZA A. FENWICK, of the District of Columbia. (19 JAN 1854)

MARRIAGE. On Tuesday, the 17th inst., by the Rev. Mr. Caldwell, Rector of Christ Church, Georgetown, D.C., ZACHARIAH BERRY, Esq., of Belmont, Prince George's Co., Md., to ELIZABETH CLAGETT, daughter of Henry Addison, Esq., Mayor of Georgetown. (19 JAN 1854)

MARRIAGE. At Georgetown, on Tuesday, the 17th inst., by the Rev. Mr. Tillinghast, WM. HENRY DENNY, Esq., of Pittsburgh, to Miss MARIA POE, daughter of George Poe, Jr., of the former place. (19 JAN 1854)

OBITUARY. From the *New York Times*. Major and Brev. Lieut. Col. JOHN MARSHALL WASHINGTON, of the U.S. Army, who was swept from the deck of the *San Francisco* soon after her troubles commenced, was one of the most useful, as he had made himself one of the most distinguished, artillery officers belonging to the service. He was a native of Virginia, and must have attained the age of fifty-eight or sixty years. He graduated as a cadet at West Point in the class of 1813, was commissioned 3d lieut. in the artillery in 1817, and rose rank by rank to his majority in the 3d artillery in 1847, February 16. In a week from his promotion he won his brevet as lieutenant colonel by gallant and meritorious conduct on the hotly-contested field of Buena Vista. He was a thorough tactician in the artillery service, and as early as 1824 was made instructor in the artillery school for practice at Ft. Monroe. After the battle of Buena Vista, and at the close of the Mexican War in 1848, Maj. Washington was appointed to command an expedition across the plains of Mexico, via El Paso, to the Pacific Ocean, which he accomplished amidst the greatest physical difficulties and the rigors of the climate. His command was the ninth military deportment, and from October 1848 to October 1849 he acted as the Military Governor of New Mexico. He has since, we believe, been chiefly attached to the service on the Pacific, and it was while in charge of an additional artillery force destined for that distant region that he lost his life, on an element and by a calamity so different from the scenes of danger in which it had been his pride as a soldier to risk it.

    Maj. GEORGE TAYLOR was a cadet of the class of 1833. He won his first brevet, that of captain, in the Florida war, in 1840, and was commissioned captain in February 1847. In 1842 he served as assistant professor of mathematics at West Point. In October 1847, he won his brevet of major by gallant and meritorious conduct at the battle of Huamantla, in Mexico; and in July 1848, distinguished himself in action at Atlixco. He was a native of Georgia. Mrs. Taylor was lost with him from the wreck of the *San Francisco*.

Capt. HORACE D. FIELD was of New York; a graduate of West Point of the class of 1836. He was made brevet captain for gallant and meritorious conduct in the battle of Huamantla, in Mexico, In October 1847. He first entered the 3d artillery in July 1840, as a second lieutenant.

Lieut. RICHARD H. SMITH was of Tennessee, appointed to one of the additional infantry regiments authorized in 1847 (the 14th) as a second lieutenant, and was transferred to the 3d artillery in June 1848. (20 JAN 1854)

MARRIAGE. On the 19th inst., by the Rev. C.M. Butler, NATHAN REEVE, Esq., of Newburgh, N.Y., to MARY, daughter of Hon. Selah R. Hobbie, of this city. (20 JAN 1854)

DEATH. On the evening of the 18th inst., Mrs. ANNA CUNNINGHAM, in the 89th year of her age, at the residence of her son, A.F. Cunningham, Massachusetts avenue. (20 JAN 1854)

MARRIAGE. On Thursday, 19th inst., by Rev. S.A.H. Marks, Mr. GEO. W. DURITY to Miss JANE ELIZABETH WISE, all of Washington. (21 JAN 1854)

MARRIAGE. On the 19th inst., by Rev. James H. Brown, Mr. JOSEPH T. BELL to Miss HARRIET F. BECKETT. Also by the same, Mr. JAMES BROWN to MARY A. WRIGHT, all of Prince George's Co., Md. (21 JAN 1854)

DEATH. In this city, on the 20th inst., of a pulmonary affection from which he had been a patient sufferer for many years, Mr. JAMES S. TURPIN, in the 39th year of his age. He was a devoted husband, in the 39th year of his age. He was a devoted husband, an affectionate father, and a friend in whom there was no guile; combining in his disposition kindness, moral worth, and every virtue that should endear his memory. The friends and acquaintances of the family are requested to attend his funeral tomorrow afternoon, at 2½ o'clock, from his residence on D, near 13th street. (21 JAN 1854)

OBITUARY. We have news of the death, on the 10th inst., of Col. T.H. PERKINS, aged eighty-nine years, at his country residence in Brookline, near Boston. The death of a man so conspicuous not only in enterprises of a commercial nature, but also, in former times, to some extent in the field of politics, demands something more than a passing mention. THOMAS HANDYSYDE PERKINS, was born in Boston, December 15, 1764. His activity and talent soon placed him in prosperous circumstances, and when he died he is supposed to have left property of some two millions, to be divided among his numerous heirs. He began commercial life in partnership with his elder brother, James, constituting the first American firm engaged in the China trade. They embarked extensively in the Northwest Coast, Canton, and Calcutta trade, in which they acquired great wealth. During the war of 1812 he was distinguished, in connexion with Otis and Sullivan, as a strenuous opponent of Mr. Madison's Administration, and was elevated by the Federalists to several important posts in the State and National Government. He was a man of public spirit and great liberality in money matters, and several of the most splendid charitable institutions are monuments of his munificence. He was not, however, without the hobbies which often accompany such generous attributes. Col. Perkins enjoyed an iron constitution, which held out nobly against the gout and other infirmities of his old age, to which he has at length yielded. His death will be sincerely mourned by the public as well as his immediate acquaintances. *New York Evening Post*. (23 JAN 1854)

MARRIAGE. In New York, on the 19th inst., at the residence of Dr. Bern W. Budd, by the Rev. Thomas Gallaudet, JOHN C. HUNTER, Purser of the U.S. Navy, to SOPHIA, daughter of the late Rev. Thomas H. Gallaudet, L.L.D., of Hartford, Conn. (24 JAN 1854)

MARRIAGE. On the 23d inst., in Trinity Church, Georgetown, by the Rev. J.E. Pallhuber, J.C. BERRY, Esq., of Howard Co., Md., to Miss SUSAN CLOUD, of Georgetown. (24 JAN 1854)

Daily National Intelligencer, Marriage and Death Notices, 1851-1854

MARRIAGE. On Sunday evening last [22 JAN 1854], by the Rev. Dr. Butler, Mr. LEVI PUMPHREY to Mrs. ELLEN SWEETING, all of this city. (25 JAN 1854)

MARRIAGE. On the 20th inst., by the Rev. Jas. H. Brown, Mr. JAMES B. ENROUGHTY to Miss HENRIETTA C. HARDAWAY, both of Virginia. (25 JAN 1854)

DEATH. Yesterday morning [24 JAN 1854], Miss ANNE BROOKE, of this city. Her funeral will take place this day, at 10 o'clock A.M., from her late residence, on 13th street west, between G and H, to which her friends are invited. (25 JAN 1854)

MARRIAGE. In Georgetown, on Tuesday, the 24th inst., by the Rev. Jos. Aschwanden, Mr. FRANCIS L. BOARMAN, of Charles Co., Md., to CECILIA, daughter of Capt. Wm. Peters, of the former place. (26 JAN 1854)

DEATH. On Monday evening, January 23d, at the residence of her daughter, Mrs. Farquhar, Mrs. MARY ANNA OSTERLOH, wife of the late Rev. John F. Osterloh, in the 80th year of her age. (26 JAN 1854)

DEATH. At San Francisco, Calif., on the 28th ult. [28 DEC 1853], Judge N.C. READ, formerly of Ohio. Mr. R. had occupied various public offices in the latter State, and was considered one of the ablest lawyers of his age in the West. Soon after he attained majority he was elected Prosecuting Attorney in Hamilton County. From this he was promoted to the office of President Judge of the Court of Common Pleas. From this he was advanced to the Supreme Bench of the State, and discharged the duties of this office with great ability during the period of six years. Last spring he emigrated to California, and was at the time of his death extensively engaged in the practice of his profession as the law-partner of Senator Weller, frm that state. As a lawyer he ranked among the first; as a man he was universally beloved by those who knew him. He was a man of kind, generous, and noble impulses, which, united with a high order of genius, made him felt in any society into which he was thrown. Although he had his faults, he will long live in the memories of his friends and associates. (26 JAN 1854)

DEATH. On Saturday last [21 JAN 1854], ROBT. W.S. YEATMAN, son of Mr. J.H. Yeatman, aged three years, three months, and twenty-seven days. (26 JAN 1854)

DEATH. On the morning of the 26th inst., after a short but painful illness, which he bore with christian fortitude, WILLIAM KEEFE, Sr., in the fifty-fourth year of his age. May he rest in Peace! The friends and acquaintances of the family are respectfully invited to attend his funeral on Saturday morning, at 9 o'clock, from his late resience, on H street, between 17th and 18th, without further notice. (27 JAN 1854)

DEATH. On Thursday morning [26 JAN 1854], at the residence of Mr. S. Worthington, 13th street, Mr. ROGER W. WILCOX, in the 21st year of his age. Though he has been long declining, yet his death was sudden. Having made personal religion a matter of deep concern for some years past, his death was marked with the triumph of christian hope. The funeral will be attended at the E Street Baptist Church on Saturday, 28th inst., at 3 o'clock P.M. His friends and acquaintances are specially invited to attend. (27 JAN 1854)

DEATH. At Marysville, Calif., on the 16th ult. [16 DEC 1853], JOHN HOLMES MAGRUDER, formerly of Montgomery Co., Md., aged 26 years. (27 JAN 1854)

MARRIAGE. At Trinity Church, Boston, on the 17th inst., by the Rt. Rev. Bishop Eastburn, JOHN OSBORNE SARGENT, Esq., of Washington, to GEORGIANA, daughter of Benjamin Welles, Esq., of Boston. (28 JAN 1854)

MARRIAGE. On Thursday evening last [26 JAN 1854], at the Navy Yard, by the Rev. Jas. H. Brown, Mr. JOHN M. MITCHELL to Miss MARY ANN GOODRICH, all of this city. (28 JAN 1854)

Daily National Intelligencer, Marriage and Death Notices, 1851-1854

MARRIAGE. In the Church of the Nativity, Huntsville, Ala., on the 12th inst., ELLEN, daughter of Geo. P. Beirne, and GEORGE A. GORDON, Esq., of Savannah, Ga. (28 JAN 1854)

MARRIAGE. On Thursday afternoon [26 JAN 1854], by the Rev. Jas. H. Brown, JOHN E. EVANS (son of the Rev. French S. Evans), to SOPHIA SMILEY, daughter of James Lawrenson, all of this city. (28 JAN 1854)

MARRIAGE. In Tallahassee, Fla., on Wednesday, January 11th, by Rev. Jesse W. Hume, Col. ALLAN MACFARLAN, of Cheraw, S.C., and Miss JULIA GAMBLE, youngest daughter of the late Col. John G. Gamble, of Florida. (28 JAN 1854)

DEATH. On the 20th inst., after a long and painful illness, in Salisbury, Md., Mrs. ANNA C.J. BRIGGS, in the 40th year of her age, and for the last ten years a resident of this city. (28 JAN 1854)

DEATH. On the 27th of December last [1853], Miss COURTNEY WATERS, of Montgomery Co., in the 65th year of her age. In the death of this estimable lady her relatives and companions have lost one remarkable for many good qualities. Devoted in her kind offices to others, she apeared to lose sight of self to promote the comfort and welfare of those around her. That meekness of character which attended her through life supported her with resignation to the will of her Heavenly Father. (30 JAN 1854)

MARRIAGE. In Georgetown, on Monday, 30th inst., by the Rev. J.R. Eckard, W.H.F. GURLEY, of New York, to Miss ELIZABETH S., daughter of Benj. F. Rittenhouse, Esq., of the former place. (31 JAN 1854)

MARRIAGE. On the 29th ult. [29 JAN 1854], by the Rev. J.S. Smith, Mr. NICHOLAS O. McCUBBIN to Miss MARY E. McDONALD, both of this city. (1 FEB 1854)

DEATH. Yesterday morning [1 FEB 1854], after a long and severe illness, HENRY HOFFMAN, aged 38 years, a native of Germany, but for many years a resident of this city. His friends and acquaintances are respectfully invited to attend his funeral, without further notice, on Sunday next, at 2 o'clock P.M. (2 FEB 1854)

DEATH. On Saturday last, the 28th of January, at his residence, in the city of Philadelphia, JAMES ROBERTSON, Esq., having on the day of his death attained his 82d year. This worthy man died, as he had lived, calmly and peacefully--peacefully with the world, peacefully with his God, of whom he had been the faithful, unpretending, and unostentatious servant; scrupulously fulfilling, whether in the relations of private and domestic life or with regard to the public, every duty incident to the position assigned him by his great Master. Mr. Robertson had formerly, as Cashier of the Branch Bank of the U.S., resided many years in the city of Richmond, Va., and in that community has left numerous friends, by whom his memory will be long and warmly cherished. (2 FEB 1854)

DEATH. At her residence in New Albany, Ind., Mrs. ISABELLA SENGSTACK, consort of Henry E. Sengstack, of Washington, D.C., in the 22d year of her age. (2 FEB 1854)

MARRIAGE. In this city, on Thursday, the 2d inst., at Trinity Church, by the Rev. Dr. Butler, Lieut. JOHN J. ALMY, U.S. Navy, to SARAH McLEAN, daughter of Col. Chas. K. Gardner. (3 FEB 1854)

MARRIAGE. On Tuesday, 21st ult. [21 JAN 1854], by the Rev. Mr. Hodges, JAMES HENRY MOORE to Miss MARGARET ANN FARR, both of Prince George's Co., Md. (3 FEB 1854)

DEATH. In the Washington Infirmary, on Thursday, the 2d inst., Mr. JOHN A. KING, in the 52d year of his age. His funeral will take place this (Friday) evening at Trinity Church, Georgetown, at 3 o'clock. His friends and those of his family are respectfully requested to attend without further notice. (3 FEB 1854)

Daily National Intelligencer, Marriage and Death Notices, 1851-1854

DEATH. Departed this life, on the evening of the 31st January, in the city of Washington, THOMAS J. BOYLE, in the 42d year of his age, only son of the late Capt. Thomas Boyle, of Baltimore. (3 FEB 1854)

DEATH. In this city, after a painful and protracted illness, which she bore with christian fortitude, Mrs. SINIA GRIFFIN, consort of Jas. L. Griffin, aged 47 years. *Requiescat in Pace*! Her funeral will take place at her late residence, on 9th street, between M and N streets, on Sunday afternoon at 2 o'clock. Her friends and acquaintances are respectfully invited to attend. (4 FEB 1854)

DEATH. In this city, on Friday, the 3d of February, ROBERT JOHN, son of D.R. and Anna Lindsay, aged 3 years and 11 months. The friends of D.R. Lindsay, of Tuscumbia, Ala., are invited to attend the funeral at 10 o'clock tomorrow, from Mrs. Taylor's, Pennsylvania avenue, between 4½ and 6th streets, south side. (4 FEB 1854)

MARRIAGE. On the 2d inst., by the Rev. Mr. Holmead, HENRY D. GUNNELL, Esq., to MARY ANN HINTON, daughter of the late George Milburn, all of this city. (6 FEB 1854)

DEATH. On Saturday morning last [4 FEB 1854], at his residence on Capitol Hill, GEORGE WATTERSTON, Esq., one of the oldest and most esteemed citizens of Washington. A witness in early childhood to the laying of the corner-stone of the Capitol, he manifested throughout his life a constant devotion to the interests of the *National Metropolis*. To his early and untiring labors, pursued through all vicissitudes, may be mainly ascribed the success of the great enterprise of erecting in this city the Monument to the memory of the Father of his Country by the contributions of the People; and with that proud memorial of a Nation's gratidude his name is indissolubly associated. Honored by various public trusts, he discharged them all with ability, and in all displayed the same strict integrity, diligence, and loyalty to duty which marked his character in private life. He was also distinguished for his love of letters, as manifested by his frequent compositions on moral, political, and literary subjects. Though ardent in temperament, he was modest and unobtrusive in manner. His sterling merits were most highly estimated by those who had longest known him; and during his mortal illness, protracted for nearly six weeks, the universal and deep anxiety of his neighbors was a tribute to his character which cannot be mistaken. The funeral will take place this afternoon, from his late residence on Capitol Hill, at 3 o'clock. The friends of th family are requested to attend, without further notice. (6 FEB 1854)

DEATH. On the 25th of January last [1854], near Bladensburg, Md., Dr. WILLIAM HENRY DECKER, in the 22d year of his age, son of Rev. John Decker. (6 FEB 1854)

DEATH. On the 7th inst., after a brief illness, Maj. THOMAS FITZPATRICK, U.S. Agent for the Indians on the Upper Platte and Arkansas. His friends and acquaintances are invited to attend his funeral from Brown's Hotel this morning at 10 o'clock. (8 FEB 1854)

DEATH. On the 2d inst., at his residence in Leesburg, Va., THOS. S. DORRELL, in the 49th year of his age. (8 FEB 1854)

DEATH. GEORGE HORACE ELLICOTT, son of Fanny A. and James P. Ellicott, aged two years and eight months. The friends of the family are respectfully invited to attend his funeral from his father's residence, on D street, between 6th and 7th streets, on Wednesday afternoon at 2 o'clock. (8 FEB 1854)

MARRIAGE. On the 7th inst., at Ryland Chapel, by Rev. Mr. Hodges, JOHN R. ELVANS to GEORGIANNA THOMPSON, all of this city. (9 FEB 1854)

MARRIAGE. In this city, on Tuesday, 7th inst., by Rev. G.W. Samson, Mr. WM. HENRY WEST to Miss CATHERINE MILLER, both of this city. (9 FEB 1854)

DEATH. In this city, on Wednesday morning, Mr. JOHN SERGEANT, in the 53d year of his age. As a kind husband and father, the deceased was endeared to a large family circle, and as a citizen, residing amongst us many years, he sustained the reputation of an upright man, faithful in all the relations of life. (9 FEB 1854)

DEATH. On the 8th inst., RICHARD COXE, son of Alexander and Mary G. Mahon, aged 5 years and 6 months. His funeral will take place from the residence of his father, near Washington, this day (Thursday) at 2 o'clock P.M. (9 FEB 1854)

MARRIAGE. On the 9th inst., by the Rev. A.G. Marlatt, WM. Y. ROBINSON, of Baltimore, Md., to MATILDA F. WAYSON, of this city. (10 FEB 1854)

MARRIAGE. On the 9th inst., by Rev. Jesse T. Peck, Mr. PETER F. KESSLER, of Pennsylvania, to Miss SYLVIA PECK, of Washington. (10 FEB 1854)

MARRIAGE. On the 7th inst., at the F Street Presbyterian Church, by the Rev. Jas. R. Eckard, CLIFFORD EVANS to Miss MARY JANE, daughter of George M. Dale, Esq., all of this city. (10 FEB 1854)

DEATH. On Thursday morning, the 9th inst., at 1½ o'clock, Mr. CHARLES F. ADAMS, of the National Theatre. His friends and the theatrical profession are invited to attend his funeral this (Friday) afternoon, at 3 o'clock, from the Washington Infirmary. (10 FEB 1854)

MARRIAGE. In Georgetown, on the 8th inst., by the Rev. J.M.P. Atkinson, BOUDINOT S. LOUEY, Esq., of Baltimore, Md., to Miss NANNIE, daughter of the late Geo. French, Esq., of the District of Columbia. (11 FEB 1854)

DEATH. On Wednesday morning, the 8th inst., in the hope of a blissful immortality, ELEXIUS SIMMS, Esq., in the 58th year of his age. His remains will be conveyed from his late residence, corner of F and 13th streets, to St. Patrick's Church, on Saturday morning, the 11th inst., at 10 o'clock, when mass of requiem will be sung. His friends and those of the family are respectfully invited to attend. (11 FEB 1854)

DEATH. On Thursday night [9 FEB 1854], at 8 o'clock, after a lingering illness, Mrs. ELIZA TREGO, trusting in her Saviour, aged 62 years. Her funeral will take place on Saturday (today), at 2 o'clock P.M., from the residence of Mr. Henry Weaver, on the Heights of, Georgetown, D.C. She will be interred in the family graveyard on the farm. Her friends are respectfully invited to attend without further notice. (11 FEB 1854)

DEATH. On Monday, the 6th inst., FANNY, second daughter of L.B. and Augusta L. Hardin, aged one year nine months and sixteen days. (11 FEB 1854)

DEATH. In New York, February 8th, GEORGEANN, aged fourteen years, eldest child of Lieut. D.D. and Georgeann Porter. (11 FEB 1854)

DEATH. On Friday, the 10th inst., JAMES A. LENMAN, in the 34th year of his age. His remains will be conveyed from his late residence, on 11th street, between G and H streets, to St. Matthew's Church, this morning, the 13th inst., at 10 o'clock, when mass of requiem will be sung. His friends and those of the family are respectfully invited to attend. (13 FEB 1854)

DEATH. On the 11th inst., in this city, Mrs. MARGARET JOHNSTON, aged 77 years. Her funeral will take place on this (Monday) morning, at 11 o'clock, from the residence of her son-in-law, Samuel Kirby, on 8th street, between D and E. The friends of the deceased and those of the family are respectfully invited to attend. (13 FEB 1854)

DEATH. On the 11th inst., after a long and painful illness, RICHARD AYTON, in the 39th year of his age. The friends and acquaintances of the family are invited to attend his funeral, from his late residence on Eighth street, between D and E, (Island,) on Tuesday afternoon at half-past two o'clock. (13 FEB 1854)

DEATH. At New Orleans, on Wednesday, the 8th inst., in the 30th year of his age, PHINEAS JANNEY, Esq., third son of the late Jonathan Janney, of Alexandria, Va. (13 FEB 1854)

DAETH. On the 11th inst., GEORGE HENRY, infant son of John H. and Adelaide Buthmann. (13 FEB 1854)

DEATH. In Baltimore, on the 11th inst., of inflammation of the brain, JOSEPH ANTHONY PECK, youngest son of John T. and Sarah A. Mitchell, aged three years and three months. (14 FEB 1854)

MARRIAGES. On the 14th inst., by the Rev. Jas. H. Brown, Mr. JAMES H. SHREVE to Miss FRANCES ANN SEWELL, both of Washington. On the same day, by the same, Mr. HENRY HAMMOND to Miss REBECCA STALLIONS, all of Annapolis. (15 FEB 1854)

MARRIAGE. On the 14th inst., by the Rev. Rufus Dawes, R.B. DONALDSON to ANNA MARIA, daughter of G.W. Hall, Esq., of Washington. (15 FEB 1854)

DEATH. On the 13th inst., Miss JANE CLARK, after a short illness. Her funeral will take place on Wednesday, the 15th, at 12 o'clock, from the residence of her father, Mr. Robert Clark, Prince George's Co., Md. The friends of the family are respectfully invited to attend without further notice. (15 FEB 1854)

MARRIAGE. On Tuesday evening, the 14th inst., by the Rev. Mr. Pyne, HENRY D. JOHNSON to MARY, youngest daughter of Col. J.J. Abert. (17 FEB 1854)

DEATH. At her residence, in Georgetown, on the evening of the 15th inst., Mrs. EMILY CORCORAN, relict of the late Col. Thos. Corcoran, aged 44 years. Her funeral will take place today at four o'clock P.M. (17 FEB 1854)

DEATH. On Thursday, the 16th inst., CHARLES GILBERT, youngest son of Johanna and Isaac [Hill]. His funeral will take place this afternoon, at 4 o'clock, from the residence of his father, Ninth street, where the friends of the family are respectfully invited to attend without further notice. (17 FEB 1854)

MARRIAGE. In Philadelphia, on the 16th inst., by the Rev. P.F. Mayer, WILLIAM CLABAUGH, of Georgetown, D.C., to MARY A., daughter of John Buddy, Esq., of the former city. (18 FEB 1854)

MARRIAGE. In the Church of the Epiphany, on Thursday, the 16th inst., by the Rev. J.W. French, Dr. WM. B. MAGRUDER to SARAH, eldest daughter of the late Abraham Van Wyck, of this city. (18 FEB 1854)

MARRIAGE. In this city, on the 16th inst., by the Rev. Mr. Hodges, JOHN A. THOMPSON to Miss ELIZABETH M. TURTIN, both of Prince George's Co., Md. (18 FEB 1854)

DEATH. On yesterday morning, the 17th inst., Mr. ROBERT CAMMACK, in the 23d year of his age, son of Mr. Wm. Cammack. The friends of the family are invited to attend his funeral tomorrow afternoon at 3 o'clock, from his father's residence, above Georgetown. (18 FEB 1854)

MARRIAGE. On the 16th inst., by the Rev. Charles A. Davis, Mr. JOHN F. RITTER to Miss ALICE WELCH, all of this city. (20 FEB 1854)

DEATH. On the 20th inst., at the residence of J.S. Rives, Esq., near Washington city, of chronic inflammation of the brain, L. HUNTINGTON YOUNG, in his 49th year, eldest son of the late Col. Guilford D. Young, of Troy, N.Y. (21 FEB 1854)

DEATH. On Wednesday evening, 15th inst., at West River Landing, Md., ANDREW COYLE GIBBS. (21 FEB 1854)

Daily National Intelligencer, Marriage and Death Notices, 1851-1854

MARRIAGE. On the 14th inst., by the Rev. Edmund H. Waring, the Rev. J. WESLEY BOTELER, of the Baltimore Annual Conference, to Miss SUSAN H. PRINTZ, daughter of Mr. Cornelius Printz, of Alleghany Co., Va. (22 FEB 1854)

MARRIAGE. On the 21st, by the Rev. Mr. [Wysong], Mr. R.W. BARNACLO to Miss CATHERINE J. TURNER, both of this city. (23 FEB 1854)

DEATH. On the 21st inst., Mrs. JULIA C. FOWLER, in the 74th year of her age. The relatives and friends of the family are invited to attend her funeral today at 11 o'clock, from the residence of her daughter, Mrs. Wainright, on 2d street, between B and C streets. (23 FEB 1854)

DEATH. Last evening [23 FEB 1854], at his residence in this city, General ROBERT ARMSTRONG, Proprietor of the *Washington Union*, aged about 64 years. He died of congestion of the brain, and had been confined at home some ten or twelve days. He leaves a large family of six or seven children and a wide circle of attached friends to mourn his loss. (24 FEB 1854)

DEATH. On the 22d inst., after a long illness, Mr. FREDERICK GOLDSBOROUGH, in the 50th year of his age. His funeral will take place this day, 24th inst., from his late residence, at the corner of I and 18th streets, at one o'clock. His friends and the friends of the family are respectfully invited to attend. (24 FEB 1854)

DEATH. At Georgetown, on Tuesday, the 21st inst., Mrs. SARAH COOPER, aged seventy-eight years, a native of England, but for the last forty years a resident of Maryland and this District. (24 FEB 1854)

DEATH. On Friday morning, February 17, 1854, ANN CATHERINE, youngest child of F.W. and Margaret E. Eckloff, aged thirteen months and sixteen days. (24 FEB 1854)

DAETH. In Colebrook, N.H., on the 16th inst., Miss MARY JANE ADAMS, of Washington, aged 23 years. (24 FEB 1854)

MARRIAGE. On the 23d inst., by Rev. Jas. H. Brown, Mr. WM. R. JEFFERS to Miss BETTIE M. HUNT, both of Virginia. (25 FEB 1854)

DEATH. On the 17th inst., at Farley, Culpeper Co., Va., REBECCA PARKE FARLEY, wife of Dr. Wm. N. Wellford, and daughter of the late Richard Corbin, of Laneville. (25 FEB 1854)

MARRIAGE. On the 21st inst., at Trinity Church, Georgetown, D.C., by the Rev. Mr. Pallhuben, FRANCIS HARPER to Miss MARY A., only daughter of the late Dennis O'Donnoghue, of that place. (27 FEB 1854)

MARRIAGE. On Thursday, the 23d inst., at Elmwood, Prince George's Co., Md., by the Rev. J.N. Watson, GEORGE R.H. MARSHALL, Esq., of Montgomery Co., Md., to Miss ELEANOR F. MARSHALL, of Prince George's Co., Md. (27 FEB 1854)

DEATH. On Sunday afternoon, at 3 o'clock, after a short but severe illness, Mrs. JANE FREEMAN HOWARD, in the fifty-seventh year of her age. The friends and acquaintances of the family are respectfully invited to attend her funeral from the residence of her son, Wm. E. Morcoe, on 8th street, between G and H, tomorrow (Tuesday) morning at 11 o'clock. (27 FEB 1854)

DEATH. On the 25th inst., Mr. JOSEPH THOMAS, in the 41st year of his age. The relatives and friends of the family are invited to attend his funeral this day, at 3 o'clock, from his residence, corner of 11th and Water streets, Island. (27 FEB 1854)

DEATH. In this city, on Saturday morning, 25th inst., ADOLPHUS HENRY, infant son of J.H.B. Nowland, of Indiana. (27 FEB 1854)

Daily National Intelligencer, Marriage and Death Notices, 1851-1854

MARRIAGE. On Sunday, the 26th inst., by the Rev. J.B. Donelan, ALMERICUS ZAPPONE to Miss MARGARET A. JOYCE, both of this city. (28 FEB 1854, see 25 APR 1854)

DEATH. On Monday, the 27th inst., WILLIAM THOMAS, son of Jno. F. and Annie Havenner, aged 18 months. The friends of the family are requested to attend the funeral from the residence of his parents, on 11th street, near Maryland avenue, Island, this (Tuesday) afternoon at 4 o'clock. (28 FEB 1854)

MARRIAGE. On the 27th ult. [27 FEB 1854], by the Rev. J.C. Smith, D.D., ROBERT H., eldest son of Rev. A.A. Marcellus, of New York, to Miss E. KATE GLOVER, of Washington. (1 MAR 1854)

MARRIAGE. In this city, on the 28th of February, by the Rev. Smith Pyne, Capt. LORENZO SITGREAVES, of the U.S. Army, to LUCY ANN, daughter of Gen. Thomas S. Jesup. (2 MAR 1854)

MARRIAGE. At Trinity Church, in this city, on Tuesday, the 28th ult. [28 FEB 1853], by the Rev. C.M. Butler, Dr. RICHARD H. COOLIDGE, U.S. Army, to HARRIET B. RINGGOLD, daughter of Charles Morris, U.S. Navy. (2 MAR 1854)

DEATH. On the 28th ult. [28 FEB 1854], at his residence in this city, MICHAEL KELLER, in the 58th year of his age. The friends of the family are respectfully invited to attend his funeral, from his late residence on G, between 2d and 3d streets, this afternoon, at 2 o'clock. (2 MAR 1854)

DEATH. On Saturday evening, February 25th, 1854, at his late residence in Washington Co., D.C., LEVI SHERIFF, aged 76 years. (2 MAR 1854)

DEATH. On the 1st inst., AGNES C., aged 6 months, daughter of Thomas F. and Margaret Stewart. (2 MAR 1854)

THE LATE THOMAS G. MOWER, M.D. [From an obituary notice in the *New York Sealpel*.] On the 7th of December [1853], THOMAS G. MOWER, senior surgeon of the U.S. Army, died in this city [New York], after a protracted illness, surrounded by a devoted family and those attached friends that a marked and distinctive character had drawn near him during those latter years of his life that were passed in this city. Thomas Gardner Mower was born in Worcester, Mass., February 18th, 1790; graduated at Harvard University, 1810; studied medicine with Thomas Babbit, an eminent surgeon of Brookfield, Mass., and formerly a surgeon in the U.S. Navy [text continues]. (3 MAR 1854)

MARRIAGE. On the 28th ult. [28 FEB 1854], by the Rev. Dr. Cole, Mr. THOMAS B. TURNER to Miss ELIZABETH E. LUSBY, both of this city. (3 MAR 1854)

DEATH. At Austin, Tex., January 17th, Miss ELIZABETH SCOTT, daughter of the late Alexander Scott, Esq., formerly of Maryland. (3 MAR 1854)

MARRIAGE. On Thursday evening, the 2d inst., by the Rev. J.S. Petty, Mr. ROBERT A. PAYNE to Miss MARTHA ELIZABETH BALDWIN, all of this city. (4 MAR 1854)

MARRIAGE. On Wednesday, the 1st inst., by the Rev. D.E. Reese, THOMAS J. MILLER, of this city, to Miss MARTHA VIRGINIA REED, of Winchester, Va. (4 MAR 1854)

DEATH. On Thursday night, the 2d inst., JAMES MITCHELL, only son of Silas H. and Mary B. Hill, aged fourteen years. The friends and acquaintances are respectfully invited to attend the funeral this day, (Saturday,) the 4th inst., at half-past three o'clock, from the residence of his father, corner of E and Sixth streets. (4 MAR 1854)

DAETH. Yesterday morning, March 3d, CHARLES G. McKNEW, aged six months, infant son of the late Charles and Maria McKnew. (4 MAR 1854)

Daily National Intelligencer, Marriage and Death Notices, 1851-1854

DEATH. On Saturday morning, the 4th inst., in the 77th year of her age, Mrs. ISABELLA ELLSWORTH, a native of Chester, Pa., but for more than 50 years a resident of this city. The deceased passed a life of exemplary piety, and was greatly beloved by a large circle of relatives and friends. May she rest in peace! Her funeral will take place this (Monday) morning, at ten o'clock, from the dwelling of Ferdinand Jefferson, Eleventh street, between L and M streets, at which the friends of the deceased and family are requested to attend. (6 MAR 1854)

DEATH. On Saturday morning, the 4th inst., JAMES A. McLAUGHLIN, (late a clerk in the office of the Auditor for the Post Office Department,) in the 33d year of his age, leaving a disconsolate wife and child to mourn their sad bereavement. He was an affectionate husband, a fond parent, a firm friend, and an honest man. His friends are requested to attend his funeral on Monday, at 10½ o'clock, from his late residence on 11th street, between G and H streets. (6 MAR 1854)

DEATH. ON the 7th inst., LILIAN LONGFELLOW, infant daughter of Samuel L. and Auba C. Harris. (8 MAR 1854)

MARRIAGE. On Wednesday afternoon [8 MAR 1854], by Rev. John C. Smith, Mr. HENRY BOYER to Miss MARY JANE HERBERT, both of Virginia. (9 MAR 1854)

DEATH. On Thursday morning, MATTIE, daughter of Dr. Alexander McD. and Martha Davis, aged eight years. The friends of the family are invited to attend the funeral this day, from the residence of Dr. Davis, on E, between 6th and 7th streets, at 3 o'clock P.M. (10 MAR 1854)

MARRIAGE. On Thursday evening [9 MAR 1854], by the Rev. John C. Smith, Mr. JAMES TAYLOR to Miss BRIDGET MOORE, all of this city. (11 MAR 1854)

DEATH. In this city, on the morning of the 12th inst., of pneumonia, Mrs. MARY LAZENBY, aged about 78 years, of short illness, which she bore with Christian fortitude. The friends of the family are respectfully requested to attend the funeral, from her late residence, on 12th street, between M street and Massachusetts avenue, at half-past 2 o'clock this (Monday) afternoon. (13 MAR 1854)

DEATH. Suddenly, on Thursday evening, the 9th inst., WILLIAM J., infant son of A.L. and Mary Newton, aged eight days. (13 MAR 1854)

DEATH. At [Poolesville], Md., on the 9th inst., in the 76th year of his age, EDWARD FALLON, a native of Ireland, and formerly a resident of this city. (14 MAR 1854)

DEATH. In Tennessee, at her residence in Bedford Co., on the 3d inst., Mrs. GENTRY, wife of the Hon. Meredith P. Gentry, a lady greatly esteemed for the excellence and amiability of her character. (14 MAR 1854)

MARRIAGE. On the 11th inst., by the Rev. Stephen P. Hill, JOHN T. GOLDSMITH to SARAH VAN VASSEL. (15 MAR 1854)

DEATH. On Monday last [13 MAR 1854], MEETA DASHIELL, daughter of Lemuel and Caroline Williams, aged 11 months. (15 MAR 1854)

MARRIAGE. On Tuesday, the 14th inst., at the Church of the Ascension, by the Rev. Mr. Stanley, Mr. WM. NALLEY to Miss VIRGINIA A. KERSEY, both of this city. (16 and 17 MAR 1854)

DEATH. At the residence of her mother, in Georgetown, ANNIE, daughter of H.A. and the late Gen. T.T. Wheeler, of Maryland, in the 18th year of her age. (16 MAR 1854)

Daily National Intelligencer, Marriage and Death Notices, 1851-1854

DEATH. In Camptonville, Calif., on Sunday morning, the 5th of February, after a long and painful illness, Mrs. NANCY A., wife of G.P. Sanders, aged 39 years. The deceased was a daughter of the Hon. Henry Dodge, of Wisconsin, and in her death our society has lost one of its brightest ornaments. Intelligent and affable, she delighted in contributing to the happiness of all with whom she associated, while her deep sympathy was always extended toward the unfortunate; and, while we sympathize with the family and friends for this their sad bereavement, we also hope for her that happy spiritual existence that never ceased. *Marysville Herald*. (16 MAR 1854)

DEATH. Departed this life, on Thursday morning [16 MAR 1854], after a short but severe illness, SAMUEL BRERETON, Esq., in the 80th year of his age. His friends and acquaintances are invited to attend the funeral, without further notice, from his late residence, corner of 7th and F streets, this (Friday) afternoon, at 4 o'clock. (17 MAR 1854)

DEATH. Yesterday morning [16 MAR 1854], Mr. THOMAS MOORE, in the 58th year of his age. His friends are respectfully invited to attend his funeral this evening at 3 o'clock. (17 MAR 1854)

DEATH. On the 15th inst., Mrs. JULIA R. POSEY, aged 46 years. The friends of the family are invited to attend her funeral today, at 2 P.M., from her residence, I street, between 12th and 13th streets. (17 MAR 1854)

MARRIAGE. At Doylestown, Pa., on the 16th inst., by the Rev. S.M. Andrews, Col. T. BIGELOW LAWRENCE, of the U.S. Legation, London, to ELIZABETH, eldest daughter of Hon. Henry Chapman. (18 MAR 1854)

SUDDEN DEATH. We learn that a young gentleman named SCOTT died suddenly at Georgetown College on Thursday [16 MAR 1854], just as he had sat down to dinner. He was afflicted by a disease of the heart. (18 MAR 1854)

DEATH. At Engfield, N.C., LEMUEL C. WHEAT, in the 36th year of his age, son of the late John Wheat. He will be buried from his mother's residence, on Greenleaf's Point, today, at 11 A.M. The friends and acquaintances of the family are invited to attend without further notice. (18 MAR 1854)

DEATH. On the 17th inst., after a short illness, HARRY T., son of Harry C. and Anna Benner, aged 18 years. The friends of the family are respectfully requested to attend his funeral tomorrow (Sunday,) 19th inst., at 3 o'clock P.M., from the residence of his parents, 2d street East and Pennsylvania avenue. (18 MAR 1854)

MARRIAGE. At Laurel, Prince George's Co., on the 16th inst., by the Rev. Mr. Waylen, RICHARD S. EUBANKS, of Essex Co., Va., to SUSAN McKENZIE, third daughter of Thomas J. Talbot, Esq., of Laurel Farm. (20 MAR 1854)

MARRIAGE. On the 14th inst., by the Rev. C.M. Butler, of the Trinity Episcopal Church, Mr. THEODORE L. LAMB, of New York city, to Miss EMELINE R. WATSON, of this city. (20 MAR 1854)

DEATH. On the 19th inst., JOHN SINON, aged 17 years; may he rest in peace. His funeral will take place this (Monday) afternoon at 4 o'clock. (20 MAR 1854)

DEATH. In this city, on Saturday afternoon, Mr. FRANCIS N. SHAW, a native of Massachusetts, aged about twenty-six years. He was an intelligent and amiable young gentleman, a reported by profession, and, previous to his being stricken down by disease, a telegraphic correspondent for the New York associated press. His funeral will take place this afternoon from the Fifth Presbyterian (Rev. Dr. Carothers's) church. Services will commence at 3 o'clock precisely. The Young Men's Christian Association, the reporters of the press, and his friends generally are invited to attend his funeral. (20 MAR 1854)

Daily National Intelligencer, Marriage and Death Notices, 1851-1854

DEATH. On the 2d inst., after a short but painful illness, Mrs. MARTHA PLATER, wife of Dr. Nicholas Brewer, and daughter of Elisha W. Williams, Esq., of Montgomery Co., Md., aged 23 years and 6 months, leaving a devoted husband and four children, together with fond parents, to mourn her early departure. Of her devotedness as a wife, a mother, a daughter, a sister, a friend, the writer could speak in terms of unmeasured eulogy; but it is enough that her record in this respect is engraven indelibly upon many hearts. Her heart's earliest and best affections had been consecrated to her Saviour, and her life was a beautiful exemplification of the christian graces--faith, patience, hope and charity. (20 MAR 1854)

DEATH. On Friday, the 17th inst., of scarlet fever, in his fourth year, HENRY BOCOCK LEWIS, eldest son of Col. Samuel L. Lewis and Catharine E., his wife. If extraordinary intelligence for one of his years, and the most affectionate disposition, especially towards his mother, could have saved this noble little boy from the shafts of death, then he would never have died nor this sad tribute paid to his memory. (20 MAR 1854)

DEATH. In this city, on the 20th inst., Mrs. FRANCES M. GREENE, in the 53d year of her age. Her funeral will take place on Wednesday morning next, at 11 o'clock, from Mrs. Gulager's boarding house, on 4½ street, the residence of her son-in-law, Dr. C. Boyle. The friends and acquaintances of the family are respectfully invited to attend. (21 MAR 1854)

DEATH. On Sunday, 19th March, of typhoid fever, ROBERT S. REID, late of Fairfax Co., aged 28 years. The friends of the family are invited to attend the funeral, from his late residence, on Seventh street, near the corner of South F street, tomorrow (Tuesday) evening, at 3 o'clock P.M. (21 MAR 1854)

DEATH. On the 21st inst., Mrs. LYDIA CRUIT, wife of Richard Cruit, in the 48th year of her age. The funeral will take place this day, (Wednesday,) the 22d inst., from her late residence, on Bridge street, Georgetown. The friends and acquaintances of the family are invited to attend. (22 MAR 1854)

DEATH. On the 21st inst., WILLIAM, son of Andrew D. and Mary J. Melcher, aged nine years. The friends and acquaintances of the family are requested to attend his funeral, from his father's residence, on New York avenue, at half-past two o'clock this day. (22 MAR 1854)

DEATH. Yesterday [21 MAR 1854], at St. Vincent de Paul Female Academy, MARY ELIZABETH CORBET, aged four years. (22 MAR 1854)

DEATH. In St. Louis, Mo., on Saturday, the 11th inst., in the 45th year of his age, PETER BROOKS. The deceased was formerly and for many years a respected citizen of this city, where he has left a large number of friends and relatives, who sincerely mourn and sympathize with his family. (22 MAR 1854)

MARRIAGE. On Tuesday morning [21 MAR 1854], by the Rev. John C. Smith, GEORGE E. HOUSE, Esq., of Mt. Gilead, Ohio, to Miss ELLEN W., daughter of Alexander Elliot, Esq., of this city. (23 MAR 1854)

MARRIAGE. On the 21st inst., at the Foundry Church, in this city, by the Rev. Job Guest, of Alexandria, SAMUEL RIDGELY, of Howard Co., Md., to ANN ELIZA, only daughter of John Robb, Esq., of Washington. (23 MAR 1854)

MARRIAGES. On the 8th inst., near Oxford, Talbot Co., Md., by the Rev. J.H. Alday, ALEXANDER E. BEALL, of Montgomery Co., Md., and NELLIE M. WILLISS; and at the same time, Rev. J.H. LIGHTBOURN and LIZZIE S. WILLISS, daughters of Wm. B. Williss, Esq., of the above place. (23 MAR 1854)

DEATH. On the 22d, CHRISTINER MOELLOR, wife of Charles Schussler, in the 36th year of her age, a native of Eschwege Kurhessen. The funeral will take place at half-past 3 o'clock, at his residence, on the corner of 7th street and New York avenue. (23 MAR 1854)

DEATH. We regret to state that Miss ELIZABETH WESTCOTT, of Florida, an amiable and accomplished daughter of the Hon. J.D. Westcott, ex-Senator from Florida, having been on a visit to this city for a few weeks past, died at the National Hotel yesterday morning [23 MAR 1854], of pneumonia, after an illness of two weeks. Her funeral will take place this afternoon at 3 o'clock from the National Hotel. (24 MAR 1854)

DEATH. In this city, yesterday [23 MAR 1854], of a pulmonary complaint which had long afflicted him, the Hon. SELAH R. HOBBIE, the distinguished First Assistant Postmaster General. His death is truly a national loss. He was born at Newburgh, N.Y., on the 10th of March 1797, and died at the age of fifty-seven. An an early day he established himself at Delhi, Delaware Co., in the practice of the law, where he married a daughter of the distinguished Gen. Root, with whom he was connected in business [text continues]. (24 and 25 MAR 1854)

DEATH. In this city, on the morning of the 19th inst., Gov. WILLIAM P. DUVAL, of Texas, aged about seventy years. Gov. Duvall was a native of Virginia, went to Kentucky in his boyhood, where he studied law and entered on its practice, and attained considerable eminence in early life. In 1812 he was elected a member of Congress from the Bardstown district, and served as such during the sessions of 1813-'14, and was an energetic and influential member in the prosecution of the war then being carried on. In 1822 he was appointed Governor of Florida by President Monroe, and was reappointed by Mr. Adams and by Gen. Jackson. By his administrative acts in that Territory he gave entire satisfaction to those to whom he was officially responsible at Washington, and to the people whose interests were confided to his management. In 1848 he removed to and settled in the State of Texas, where most of his children now reside. Professional business brought him to Washington some months ago, and it has been the will of Providence that his mortal career should terminate at a distance from his home, but yet not among strangers [text continues]. (24 MAR 1854)

DEATH. In this city, on the 23d inst., Maj. SELAH R. HOBBIE, First Assistant Postmaster General, aged 57 years. The friends of his family are invited to attend his funeral this afternoon, at 4 o'clock, at his late residence, on 14th, near F street. (25 MAR 1854)

DEATH. On the morning of the 24th inst., in the 62d year of his age, HENRY AYLMER, a native of Ireland, and for thirty-two years a resident of Petersburg, Va. The funeral will take place on Sunday afternoon at 4 o'clock, from his late residence, corner of Pennsylvania avenue and 17th street, and proceed to St. Matthew's Church. The friends of the family are requested to attend without further notice. (25 MAR 1854)

MARRIAGE. On the 27th inst., at St. Patrick's Church, by the Rev. Father Denecker, Mr. LOUIS MARCERON to Mrs. ROSE L. O'BRYON, both of this city. (29 MAR 1854)

DEATH. At Sydenham, near Philadelphia, on Friday, the 24th inst., Mrs. CATHERINE ELIZA RUSH, wife of the Hon. Richard Rush, in the 71st year of her age. (29 MAR 1854)

DEATH. On the morning of the 28th inst., Mrs. ANN ELIZABETH LANE, consort of Charles H. Lane, of this city, and daughter of the late Jabez B. Rooker. The friends of the family are respectfully invited to attend the funeral on Wednesday afternoon at half past 3 o'clock, from her late residence, on E street, between 6th and 7th. (29 MAR 1854)

DEATH. On the 28th inst., Doct. DANIEL KING, in the 51st year of his age. The funeral will take place today (29th) at four o'clock, from the residence of his father, William King, on Congress street, Georgetown. (29 MAR 1854)

DEATH. On the 27th inst., after a short and severe illness, SARAH A., relict of the late Thomas Cross, in the 78th year of her age. Her funeral will take place this (Wednesday) afternoon at 3 o'clock, from the residence of her son, on Georgia avenue, Navy Yard. (29 MAR 1854)

DEATH. At Lochbie, East Florida, on the 26th ult. [26 FEB 1854], of consumption, EDWARD H. OATES, third and youngest son of the late George Oates, of Charleston, S.C., aged 29 years. In all the various

Daily National Intelligencer, Marriage and Death Notices, 1851-1854

relations of life he exemplified a consistent and symmetrical piety, and died in the full hope of a blissful immortality. Affection will cherish his memory, and his family and friends, while deploring their loss, will rejoice in his eternal gain. (29 MAR 1854)

MARRIAGE. On the 29th inst., by the Rev. George Sampson, Dr. E.M. CHAPIN to HELAN M. WEAVER, all of this city. (30 MAR 1854)

MARRIAGE. In Baltimore, on the 19th inst., by the Rev. Dr. Johns, JAMES L. SMITH to Mrs. LUCINDA L. HOUGH, all of Washington. (30 MAR 1854)

DEATH. On Friday morning, the 31st ult. [31 MAR 1854], after an illness of a few days, WILLIAM CLYNE, aged four years four months and seventeen days, only child of the late Geo. W. and Isabella C. Frazier. The friends and relatives of the family are invited to attend his funeral from the residence of his grandmother, Mrs. Idabella Sutherland, East Capitol street, between First and Second streets, Capitol Hill, on Sunday afternoon, April 2d, at 3 o'clock. (1 APR 1854)

DEATH. On the 1st inst., WILLIAM A. GUNTON, in the 28th year of his age. The friends of the family are respectfully invited to attend his funeral from the residence of his father, Dr. Wm. Gunton, on this (Monday) afternoon at 3½ o'clock, without further notice. (3 and 24 APR 1854)

MARRAIGE. At Keokuk, Iowa, on March 23d, by the Rev. George Denison, WILLIAM W. BELKNAP, formerly of Georgetown, D.C., to Miss CORA LEROY, daughter of the late Alexis LeRoy, of Vincennes, Ind. (4 APR 1854)

DEATH. At Woodbury, Md., on the 4th inst., Dr. JOS. M. TASTET, eldest son of Nicholas Tastet, of this city, aged thirty-one years. The subject of the above obituary lost his life by injuries incurred from being thrown from his horse, and the horse falling upon him, on Monday last [2 APR 1854], in the city of Baltimore. His funeral will take place this afternoon, at half-past 3 o'clock, from the residence of his father-in-law, Mr. Thos. Mustin, on G, between 13th and 14th streets [additional text]. (6 and 10 APR 1854)

MARRIAGE. At Pembroke, N.H., April 3d, by the Rev. Wm. Hewes, M.G. EMERY, Esq., of Washington, to MARY K., youngest daughter of Wm. Haseltine, Esq., of the former place. (8 APR 1854)

MARRIAGE. On Thursday evening [6 APR 1854], by the Rev. John C. Smith, Mr. ROBERT H. GRAHAM to Miss ANN S. HILLER, all of this city. (8 APR 1854)

DEATH. On Thursday afternoon, the 6th inst., after a lingering illness, REBECCA, consort of A. Dixon, in the 31st year of her age. The friends and acquaintances of the family are respectfully invited to attend her funeral, from her late residence, on 8th street, between D and E streets, tomorrow (Sunday) afternoon, at 3 o'clock. (8 APR 1854)

DEATH. In this city, on the 7th inst., CHARLES W. COX, aged two years nine months and fifteen days, son of C.A. and Elizabeth Cox. The friends of the family are requested to attend the funeral this afternoon, at 2 o'clock, from the corner of Fourth street and Pennsylvania avenue east. (8 APR 1854)

DEATH. At Annapolis, on the 5th inst., after an illness of twelve hours, MARIA, youngest daughter of Prof. J.E. and Sarah W. Nourse. (8 APR 1854)

DEATH. JAMES TICER, 18 years of age, son of Mr. Lewis Ticer, of Alexandria, on Saturday morning [8 APR 1854], fell into the hold amongst the machinery of the steamboat *Thomas Collier*, whilst it was in motion, and was almost instantly crushed to death. (10 APR 1854)

Daily National Intelligencer, Marriage and Death Notices, 1851-1854

MARRIAGE. At Locust Hill, the residence of the bride's father, on the 6th inst., by the Rev. Mr. Pinkney, WILLIAM F. HOLTZMAN and MARY M., daughter of Richard Patten, Esq., all of Prince George's Co., Md. (10 APR 1854)

DEATH. At his residence in this city, on Saturday morning last, the 8th inst., JOHN STEVENS, of the Treasury Department, second son of the late William Stevens, Esq., No. 3 Bedford row, John street, London. Mr. Stevens came to the U.S. in 1817, and for the last four years he has resided in this city. The immediate friends of the family are requested to attend the funeral, at the Church of the Ascension, on H street, at 3½ o'clock this afternoon. (10 APR 1854)

DEATH. On the 23d ult. [23 MAR 1854], in Dummerston, Ver., Mr. SUMNER RUST, aged 42 years. He was employed not long since as a Clerk in the Census Bureau, where, by his dilligence and efficiency, added to his blandness of deportment, he endeared himself to all with whom he was associated. (12 APR 1854)

DEATH. At St. Michael's, Talbot Co., Md., where he had gone for the fruitless effort to regain his lost health, CHRISTOPHER R. BYRNE, of this city. He died on Sunday last [9 APR 1854], in the twenty-fourth year of his age. He leaves a large number of attached friends to condole with his widow and immediate relatives in his demise in the prime of early manhood. (13 APR 1854)

DEATH. On yesterday morning, the 12th inst., about 5 o'clock, Mrs. HARRIET McHANNEY, wife of Mr. Jacob McHanney, in the 44th year of her age. The deceased was a native of Baltimore Co., Md., but for the last sixteen years a resident of this city. Her funeral will take place this afternoon at 4 o'clock, from the residence of her husband, corner of F and 5th streets, where the friends and acquaintances of the family are invited to attend. (13 APR 1854)

DEATH. At Harrisburg, on the 10th inst., REBECCA, wife of Judge E. Herrick, of Athens, Pa., daughter of the late Andrew Ross, Esq., of Georgetown, D.C. (13 APR 1854)

DEATH. On the 13th inst., Mr. HANSON [BARNES], of this city. His friends and acquaintances are requested to attend his funeral, at 4 o'clock this afternoon, from his residence, corner of Sixth and D streets, on the Island. (14 APR 1854)

DEATH. In Charleston, S.C., March 22d, of smallpox, Capt. SAMUEL J. DUNCAN, a native of Bath, Me., aged forty-five years. (14 APR 1854)

MARRIAGE. On the 8th inst., by the Rev. Charles A. Davis, STEPHEN Y. McNAIR, of Norristown, Pa., to Miss MARTHA E. KNOWLES, of this city. (15 APR 1854)

MARRIAGE. On the 13th inst., by the Rev. J.E. Eckard, ANDREW MARTINE, of White Plains, N.Y., to Mrs. ELIZABETH A. COOLIDGE, of this city. (15 APR 1854)

DEATH. In Washington, Pa., on the 3d inst., CHARLES MASON, son of the Rev. Dr. E.C. and Emma S. Wines, in the 15th year of his age. The deceased at the time of his death was a member of the preparatory department of Washington College. The disease of which he died was inflammation of the brain, brought on as it is believed by a too close and severe application to his studies. He died in Christian hope. (15 APR 1854)

MARRIAGE. At Portsmouth, N.Y., on the 11th inst., by Rev. Dr. Burroughs, Capt. W.H. TREADWELL to ELLEN, daughter of Comm. G.F. Pearson, U.S. Navy. (17 APR 1854)

DEATH. At New Brunswick, N.J., on the 11th inst., Mrs. CHARLOTTE M. FRELINGHUYSEN, wife of the Hon. Theodore Frelinghuysen. (17 APR 1854)

Daily National Intelligencer, Marriage and Death Notices, 1851-1854

DEATH. On the 14th inst., after a short illness, in the 10th year of his age, CLARENCE P., youngest son of Walter H. and Eliza Fennall. His funeral will take place this (Monday) afternoon, the 17th inst., at 3 o'clock, from his father's residence, on Pennsylvania avenue, opposite Willard's Hotel. The friends and acquaintances of the family are most respectfully invited to attend, without further notice. (17 APR 1854)

DEATH. On the 17th of April, at the residence of her son, Hon. W.S. Ashe, in this city, Mrs. ELIZABETH H. ASHE, of North Carolina, in the 72d year of her age. Mrs. Ashe had survived for many years her husband, Col. Samuel Ashe, who when quite a youth performed distinguished services in the war of the Revolution, and contributed much to embalm the "Ashe" family of the Cape Fear river in the grateful memory of North Carolinians. Mrs. Ashe was the mother of a large and interesting family. She was full of anecdote of the olden time; always cheerful; the favorite of the young, and indeed beloved by all who knew the rare qualities so sweetly blended in her character. (19 APR 1854)

DEATH. At DuPont's Mills, near Wilmington, on Friday, April 14th, in the seventy-sixth year of her age, MARY ALLETTA BELIN, relict of the late Augustus Belin. (19 APR 1854)

DEATH. On the 7th of April 1854, at his residence, Oakleigh, near Greensborough, Ala., Dr. ROBERT C. RANDOLPH, aged 61 years. In the decease of this amiable, accomplished, and useful gentleman his family and society have sustained an irreparable loss. Of the distinguished Randolph family of Virginia, Dr. Randolph served creditably in the navy during the last war with Great Britain, became afterwards eminent as a physician at New Orleans, and, on establishing his valuable plantation in Alabama, endeared as he was to the large circle of his numerous friends, being held in the highest esteem by all for his rare virtues and attractive manners, his residence became extensively known for its liveral hospitality, refinement, elegance, and comforts, suich as are rarely combined in any State of our Union. The death of such a man is to be deplored as a loss to society, to his State, and to the country. Dr. Randolph's memory is embalmed in the hearts of his friends. (19 APR 1854)

MARRIAGE. On the 13th inst., by the Right Rev. Bishop Potter, Mr. CAMPBELL MORFIT to Miss MARIE C. CHANCELLOR, daughter of Mr. Henry Chancellor, of Germantown, Pa. (20 APR 1854)

DEATH. On the 15th inst., in the valley of the Kishacoquillas, Mifflin Co., Pa., of typhoid pneumonia, the Rev. JOSHUA MOORE, in the 54th year of his age. The deceased was formerly of this city, and son of the late Joshua J. Moore, who was Chief Clerk of the Land Office during the administration of Mr. Jefferson. He was of the Presbyterian denomination, (old school,) and had been laboring in the pastoral office in the above named locality for about twenty years. Ever faithful, anxious, and self-sacrificing in the discharge of the functions of his sacred calling, he died as he had desired, "with his harness on." (20 APR 1854)

MARRIAGE. On Tuesday, 18th inst., by the Rev. Wm. Hodges, JOHN T. BURCH to MARY G. HATTON, all of this city. (21 APR 1854)

DEATH. On the 19th inst., AGNES M. EDES, daughter of the late Col. Benjamin Edes, of Baltimore. The friends of the family are invited to attend her funeral from the residence of her brother-in-law, Charles W. Pairo, on Prospect street, Georgetown, this (Friday) afternoon, at 4 o'clock, without further notice. (21 APR 1854)

MARRIAGE. On the 20th inst., by the Rev. Mr. Henry, BENJAMIN F. GETTENER, of Baltimore, to Miss MARY O. FORD, of Washington. (22 APR 1854)

MARRIAGE. At Salem, N.J., on the 18th inst., by the Rev. J.J. Helm, of Philadelphia, Mr. J. HACKETT, of this city, to EMELINE, youngest daughter of Calvin Belden, Esq., of the former place. (22 APR 1854)

MARRIAGE. On the 19th inst., by the Rev. Mr. Vincinanza, THOMAS F. DARNOLD, of Prince George's Co., Md., to Miss HARRIET A. SHEIRBURN. (22 APR 1854)

Daily National Intelligencer, Marriage and Death Notices, 1851-1854

DEATH. On Friday, the 21st inst., GRAYSON PAGE, eldest child of M.W. and Mary Jane Galt, aged 3 years. The funeral will take place from the residence of his parents, 8th street, between E and F, on this (Saturday) afternoon, at half-past 3 o'clock. The friends of the family are invited to attend. (22 APR 1854)

MARRIAGE. In this city, on Thursday evening, April 20th, by the Rev. D. Pyne, of St. John's Church, Rev. C.K. NELSON, of Annapolis, Md., to MARY M., youngest daughter of the late Peter Hagner, Esq., of this city. (24 APR 1854)

MARRIAGE. In Columbia, S.C., on the 18th inst., by the Rev. Mr. Shand, the Hon. CHARLES J. JENKINS, of Augusta, Ga., to EMILY GERTRUDE, daughter of the late Judge Barnes, of Philadelphia. (24 APR 1854)

MARRIAGE. On the 17th inst., in the First Presbyterian Church, Lancaster, Pa., by the Rev. Abeel Baldwin, Mr. Z.D. GILMAN, of Washington, and Miss EMMA H., daughter of the late Robert M. Bare, Esq., of Pennsylvania. (24 APR 1854)

MARRIAGE. At Christ Church, Detroit, Mich., on the evening of the 18th inst., by the Rev. Charles Aldis, Lieut. HENRY RODGERS, U.S. Navy, to KATE S., daughter of Charles C. Trowbridge, Esq., of Detroit. (24 APR 1854)

DEATH. Yesterday morning, the 23d inst., Mr. THOMAS HALL, in the 29th year of his age. The funeral will take place from his late residence on B street south, between Sixth and Seventh streets west, tomorrow, the 25th, at 2 o'clock P.M., where the friends and relations of the family are requested to attend, without further notice. (24 APR 1854)

DEATH. In this city, on the evening of the 22d, of consumption, JAMES EMMETT, only son of William and Laurantine Ryan, aged two years and six months. The friends of the family are respectfully invited to attend the funeral this evening, at 4½ o'clock, from the residence of his parents, 11th street west, between F and G streets. (24 APR 1854)

DEATH. On Sunday evening, the 23d inst., MARY CATHERINE BARRETT, the eldest daughter of Thomas J. and Susan Barrett, aged eight years. The relatives and friends of the family are respectfully invited to attend her funeral this (Monday) evening, at 3 o'clock, from the residence of her father on D street north, between Fifth and Sixth streets east, Capitol Hill. (24 APR 1854)

MARRIAGE. On the 12th day of September 1853, by the [Rev.] Jas. Crandell, Justice of the Peace, A. ZAPPONE to Miss MARGARET A. JOYCE, both of this city. (25 APR 1854)

DEATH. Yesterday morning, the 25th inst., Mrs. ANN ESPEY, in the 60th year of her age. The funeral will take place this afternoon, at 4 o'clock, from the residence of her son-in-law, Jno. H. Thorn, on 5th street, between G and H, where the relatives and friends of the family are requested to attend without further notice. (26 APR 1854)

DEATH. On the 25th inst., of cramp colic, in the 2[9]th year of his age, JOHN McLEAN ADDISON, late of the U.S. Army. His funeral will take place this (Wednesday) afternoon, at 4 o'clock, from the residence of his father, Thos. B. Addison, on the Heights of Georgetown. (26 APR 1854)

DEATH. In this city, on the 24th inst., Dr. EDWARD H. CARMICHAEL, late of Fredericksburg, Va., in the 58th year of his age. Dr. C. has been extensively known as an eminent practitioner of medicine and surgery. He leaves a disconsolate family and numerous friends to deplore his loss. (26 APR 1854)

OBITUARY. Died, on the 20th ult. [20 MAR 1854], Miss ELIZABETH BICKLEY, in the ninety-third year of her age. The death of this venerable lady, which took place at the residence of Lloyd W. Bickley, Esq., at Taconey, is worthy of more than a passing notice [extensive information given in this reprint from the *Philadelphia Evening Bulletin*]. (28 APR 1854)

MARRIAGE. On Tuesday, 25th inst., at St. Rose's Chapel, Montgomery Co., Md., by Rev. John Dougherty, Dr. GEORGE ALEXANDER DYER, of Washington, D.C., to MARY ROBERTA, third daughter of the late George Ashton, of King George Co., Va. (28 APR 1854)

MARRIAGE. At Trinity Church, the 25th inst., by the Right Rev. Bishop Wainwright, WILLIAM SEWELL, late Chief Engineer U.S.N., to Miss CAROLINE M., daughter of the late Col. D.E. Dunscomb, of this city. (28 APR 1854)

MARRIAGE. On Tuesday, April 25th, at Locust Hill, near Washington, by the Rev. Dr. O'Toole, JAMES E. HARVEY, Esq., of Philadelphia, to Miss SELINA M. MOORE, of this city. (28 APR 1854)

MARRIAGE. In this city, on Thursday, the 27th inst., by the Rev. Smith Pyne, GEORGE P. FRICK, Esq., of Baltimore, to Miss KATE TURNBULL, eldest daughter of Col. Wm. Turnbull, U.S. Army. (29 APR 1854)

MARRIAGE. On Tuesday, the 25th inst., at Luray, Page Co., Va., by the Rev. A.C. Booton, Gen. THOMAS L. PRICE to Miss CAROLINE V. LONG, of the former place. (29 APR 1854)

DEATH. On the 15th inst., at Buena Vista, Del., in the 24th year of her age, ELLEN SINCLAIR, wife of James C. Douglass, Esq. A lovely and gentle spirit, so hopeful, so pure, called away from the ties clinging round her of wife, mother and home, there is but left for those who mourn her to cherish the bright confidence that their sad loss is her infinite gain. (29 APR 1854)

MARRIAGE. On the 29th ult. [29 APR 1854], by the Rev. James B. Donelan, Lieut. R.A. MORSELL, U.S. Revenue Service, to ROSA, only daughter of S. Calvert Ford, Esq., all of this city. (1 MAY 1854)

MARRIAGE. On the 29th ult. [20 APR 1854], by the Rev. Jas. H. Brown, Mr. MICHAEL HENRY CARLISLE to Miss LOUISA ODEN. (1 MAY 1854)

MARRIAGE. On the 27th ult., at Cambridge, Md., by the Rev. Mr. Barber, in the Episcopal Church of that place, Dr. N.S. JARVIS, Surgeon, U.S. Army, to Mrs. J.B. MUMFORD, niece of Col. T. Staniford, U.S. Army. (1 MAY 1854)

MARRIAGE. In New York, April 20, by the Rev. J.W. Alexander, JOHN WILKES, Jr., U.S. Navy, to JANE R. SMEDBERG, of that city. (1 MAY 1854)

DEATH. On the 29th ult. [29 APR 1854], Mrs. SARAH ANN WILLIAMS, in the 45th year of her age, after an illness of three weeks, which she bore with Christian fortitude and resignation. Her funeral will take place this (Monday) afternoon, at two o'clock, from her late residence on F street, between 2d and 3d streets. (1 MAY 1854)

DEATH. On Sunday, April 30th, ANNA M. FENWICK, only daughter of R.M.A. and Lavinia L. Fenwick, aged 3 years and 9 months. The friends and acquaintances of the family are invited to attend her funeral this (Monday) afternoon, at 4 o'clock, without further notice. (1 MAY 1854)

DEATH. On Thursday last [27 APR 1854], ELIOT DICKINSON CONDICT, aged nine years and two months. His funeral will take place this day at 12 o'clock, from the residence of his father, Dr. H.F. Condict, on 11th street, between G and H. The friends of the family are invited to attend. (1 MAY 1854)

Daily National Intelligencer, Marriage and Death Notices, 1851-1854

DEATH. On the 28th inst. [28 APR 1854], in Fairfax Co., Va., HARRIET W. SHELDON, wife of Israel Sheldon, Esq., of Gaston, Ala., in the 40th year of her age. (1 MAY 1854)

DEATH. At Baltimore, on Thursday, the 27th April, after a short illness, Lieut. SIMON FRASER BLUNT, of the U.S. Navy, in the 35th year of his age. Lieut. Blunt entered the Navy in 1831, at a very early age, an appointment as midshipman having been tendered him by President Jackson, in consequence of the great gallantry he had displayed and the highly important services he had rendered in the suppression of the Negro insurrection of that year in the southern counties of Virginia. For a great part of his career Lieut. Blunt was engaged in the active duties of his profession, which he discharged always with so much ability and self-devotion as to win the commendation of his superior officers, and to secure the warmest esteem of his associates. To his bereaved family we would offer the deep-felt sorrow of many hearts, but in such affliction how unavailing is human sympathy! Religion, we know, offers them all her best consolations. Time along can bring them healing. (1 MAY 1854)

MARRIAGE. On Thursday evening last, 27th ult. [27 APR 1854], by the Rev. James B. Donelan, Mr. WILLIAM NASH to Miss JANE VIRGINIA CHISM, all of this city. (2 MAY 1854)

DEATH. On the 30th of April, Mrs. ANN SALONY, wife of Mr. Henry Thomas, a native of Prince George's Co., Md., but for the last 29 years a resident of Washington, aged 53 years. The friends and relatives of the family are requested to attend the funeral from her late residence, on L, between 6th and 7th \, without further notice, on this (Tuesday) morning, at 9 o'clock. (2 MAY 1854)

MARRIAGE. On the morning of the 2d inst., at the Fourth Presbyterian Church, 9th street, by the Rev. Dr. John C. Smith, J.M. STANLEY to ALICE, daughter of the late John C. English, all of the city of Washington. (3 MAY 1854)

MARRIAGE. On Tuesday evening, May 2d, by Rev. Chas. A. Davis, Mr. DANIEL L. WEBSTER, of New York, to Miss LYDIA B. CROSS, of this city. (3 MAY 1854)

DEATH. In Baltimore, on Saturday afternoon, 29th ult. [29 APR 1854], ANNA M., wife of Robert Leslie, in the 58th year of her age. (3 MAY 1854)

DEATH. Yesterday morning, the 2d of May, JANET B. PHILIPS, in the 74th year of her age. The funeral will take place from her late residence, on east Capitol street, between 1st and 2d streets east, on Thursday afternoon, May 4th, at three o'clock. The friends of the family are respectfully invited to attend without further notice. (3 MAY 1854)

DEATH. At Hong Kong, China, February 12, Surgeon AMO G. GAMBRILL, U.S. Navy, aged forty-eight. (3 MAY 1854)

DEATH. In Prince George's Co., Md., May 2d, MARY ANN WALL, wife of J.H.D. Wall, in the 55th year of her age. Her funeral will take place from Wesley Chapel this (Thursday) afternoon at 3 o'clock. The friends of the family are respectfully invited to attend her funeral, without further notice. (4 MAY 1854)

DEATH. At Brooklyn, N.Y., on the morning of the 3d inst., CATHARINE H., wife of Rosewell Woodward, Esq. (4 MAY 1854)

MARRIAGE. On Tuesday, the 2d inst., by the Rev. Father Birns, at St. Matthew's Church, DANIEL W. SLYE, Esq., of St. Mary's Co., Md., to Miss GENEVIEVE AGNES, elder daughter of James D. King, Esq., of this city. (5 MAY 1854)

MARRIAGE. In Union Chapel, on the morning of the 4th inst., by the Rev. J.H. Dashiell, the Rev. ROBT. L. DASHIELL, of the Baltimore Annual Conference, to MARY JANE, only daughter of the late Edmund Hanly, of this city. (5 MAY 1854)

Daily National Intelligencer, Marriage and Death Notices, 1851-1854

DEATH. On the 3d inst., in the 64th year of her age, Mrs. MARGARET LUCEY, formerly of Philadelphia. (5 MAY 1854)

RECOVERY OF A BODY. On Thursday afternoon a human body was entangled in his net by a fisherman engaged in his occupation near the Potomac Aqueduct at Georgetown. On being brought ashore it was supposed to be the body of DANIEL MACNAMARA, who was struck down by the falling of the new iron bridge at the Little Falls. The body was subsequently identified by the widow and friends of the poor man, but chiefly by the remnant of clothes on his person. A severe contusion, that must have instantaneously killed him, appears on his forehead. A jury was gathered to sit on the body, whose verdict was in accordance with these facts. We hardly know of a case in which the mercy of the benevolent would be more fitly exercised than in the case of MacNamara's widow, who is left with a large family of quite small children. (6 MAY 1854)

MARRIAGE. On the 27th ult. [27 APR 1854], at Collington Meadows, by the Rev. Mr. Byrne, RICHARD S. HILL to ELIZABETH S., daughter of the late Francis M. Hall, all of Prince George's Co. (8 MAY 1854)

MARRIAGE. On Friday evening [5 MAY 1854], by the Rev. John C. Smith, Mr. WILLIAM C. KEYES to Miss SELMA V. SIMMS, of Virginia. (8 MAY 1854)

DEATH. On the 7th inst., MARY MALVINA, youngest child of John T.C. and Jane E. Clark, aged fifteen months. The friends of the family are invited to attend the funeral this afternoon, at 3½ o'clock, from the residence of her parents, corner of H and 10th streets. (8 MAY 1854)

DEATH. At a meeting of the Medical Society of the District of Columbia, held May 6th, at the Washington Infirmary, it was, unanimously--Resolved, That this Society hears with the most profound regret the recent dispensation of Providence in the removal from his sphere of usefulness of our beloved and distinguished associated, Dr. ALEXANDER S. WOTHERSPOON, of the U.S. Army... (8 MAY 1854)

MARRIAGE. On the 8th inst., at Trinity Church, by Rev. C.M. Butler, JACOB CARTER GIBSON to Miss MARY ARKANSAS McCUTCHEN, both of this city. (9 MAY 1854)

DEATH. On Sunday afternoon, the 7th inst., Mrs. ANN WHITE, in the 62d year of her age. (9 MAY 1854)

DEATH. At Lexington, Mass., on the 4th inst., Lieut. HENRY T. WINGATE, of the U.S. Navy. He was a native of Maine, and entered the naval service in 1831. His strict attention to duty, probity of character, and amenity of manners commanded the universal esteem of his brother officers and a large circle of acquaintances. (9 MAY 1854)

MARRIAGE. On the 9th inst., by the Rev. James H. Brown, Mr. THOMAS J. HARDISTY to Miss MARY ELIZABETH JONES, both of Montgomery Co., Md. (10 MAY 1854)

DEATH. In this city yesterday (Tuesday) morning [9 MAY 1854], PATRICK H. BROOKS, of this city, in the 37th year of his age. (10 MAY 1854)

DEATH. In Cincinnati, on the 4th inst., in the 86th year of her age, Mrs. KATHERINE BROWNE, a native of Massachusetts, but for the last six years a resident of Ohio. Mrs. Browne resided in the District of Columbia thirty-five years, and will be remembered by the elder inhabitants personally as a lady of [illegible] mind, exemplary piety, and fascinating manners. She was for a long time a member of the family of the late Dr. Sewall, and enjoyed the confidence and friendship of John Quincy Adams, Daniel Webster, Rufus Choate, Senator Pearce, Judge McLean, and other distinguished men. Her life was blameless and her end was peaceful. (10 MAY 1854)

MARRIAGE. On Tuesday, the 9th inst., by the Rev. Mr. Hodges, LEWIS WILLIAMS to Mrs. ELIZABETH PRUDEROSKI, all of Washington. (11 MAY 1854)

Daily National Intelligencer, Marriage and Death Notices, 1851-1854

MARRIAGE. On Tuesday, 9th inst., by the Rev. S.A.H. Marks, Mr. WM. W. DULEY to Miss SUSAN SANSBURY, both of Prince George's Co., Md. (11 MAY 1854)

DEATH. On the morning of the 10th inst., JANE HEYER, in the 85th year of her age, a native of the city of New York, but for the last 43 years a resident of this city. The deceased leaves to her family and friends a memory honored and endeared by the exercise of meek piety, active kindness, and warm affection [text continues]. The friends of the deceased, as well as those of her sister, Mrs. Louisa F. Zantzinger, are respectfully invited to attend her funeral, from her late residence, corner of New York avenue and 8th street, on this (Thursday) afternoon, at 4 o'clock, without further notice. (11 MAY 1854)

DEATH. On the 30th April, at his residence in the county of Charlotte, Va., Hon. JAMES W. BOULDIN, who was for several years a member of the Virginia legislature, and after the decease of his brother, Judge Bouldin, was elected from the Charlotte district a member of Congress, in which capacity he served for many years with ability and satisfaction to the district. (11 MAY 1854)

DEATH. At Gibsonville, Calif., on the 27th of March, EDWARD DeKRAFFT, aged 36 years, son of the late F.C. DeKrafft, Esq., of this city. (11 MAY 1854)

MARRIAGE. On the 11th of April, by the Rev. Mr. Dubois, in Putnam, Ohio, Mr. H. SAFFORD, of that place, to Mrs. FRANCES L. BOWERS, formerly Miss Wilson, of Petersburg, Va. (12 MAY 1854)

DEATH. At his residence in this city, on Thursday, the 11th inst., Capt. THOMAS L. RINGGOLD, Ordnance Corps, U.S. Army. His relatives and friends, the officers of the Army and Navy, are respectfully invited to attend his funeral at the Church of the Epiphany (Rev. Mr. French's, on G street,) this (Friday) afternoon, at 5 o'clock. (12 MAY 1854)

DEATH. In this city, on the 11th inst., of pneumonia, Mrs. JANE STAFFORD ELY, wife of Albert Welles Ely, M.D., formerly of New Orleans. Her funeral will take place this afternoon, at 3 o'clock. The friends of the family are invited to attend without further notice. (12 MAY 1854)

DEATH. At his residence in Michigan, on the 8th inst., in the 50th year of his age, the Hon. ISAAC E. CRARY, formerly a Representative in Congress from Michigan for several years immediately succeeding the admission of that State into the Union. (12 MAY 1854)

MARRIAGE. On Thursday evening, the 11th inst., by the Rev. A.G. Carothers, Mr. ARTHUR G. PUMPHREY to Miss LAVINIA F. CHILDRESS, both of this city. (13 MAY 1854)

MARRIAGE. At Castle Hill, Va., on the 10th of May, HENRY SIGOURNEY, Esq., of Boston, to Miss AMELIE LOUISE, daughter of the Hon. William C. Rives. (13 MAY 1854)

MARRIAGE. Near Selma, Ala., on Thursday, the 20th of April last, F. HENRY QUITMAN, son of Gen. Quitman, of Mississippi, to MARY, only daughter of Col. Virgil H. Gardner, of Dallas Co., Ala. (15 MAY 1854)

DEATH. On the morning of the 14th inst., ANTONIO CATALANO, a native of Pelermo, Sicily, a resident of this city for the last 37 years. His friends and acquaintances are invited to attend his funeral from his late residence, near the Navy Yard, on Monday (this day) at 2 o'clock P.M. (15 MAY 1854)

DEATH. Yesterday morning [14 MAY 1854], at half-past 2 o'clock A.M., Miss MARY ELIZABETH REMINGTON, youngest daughter of the late Mr. James Remington, in the 18th year of her age. The funeral will take place from the residence of her uncle, Mr. Richard W. Clarke, on 10th street, between New York avenue and K street, at 4 o'clock P.M. this day. (15 MAY 1854)

Daily National Intelligencer, Marriage and Death Notices, 1851-1854

DEATH. On Sunday afternoon [14 MAY 1854], after a long and severe illness, which he bore with fortitude, Mr. JABEZ YOUNG, in the twenty-fourth year of his age. The friends and acquaintances of the family are invited to attend his funeral from the residence of his sister, Mrs. Peddicord, on E, between Sixth and Seventh streets, at 4 o'clock this day. (15 MAY 1854)

DEATH. At Richmond, Va., on the 12th inst., in the 83d year of her age, Mrs. SUSANNA PLEASANTS, relict of the late Gov. James. (15 MAY 1854)

DEATH. On the 13th inst., GEORGE WILLIAM, youngest child of Andrew J. and Frances M. Joyce, aged 17 months and 16 days. (15 MAY 1854)

MARRIAGE. At Georgetown, D.C., on the 11th inst., by the Rev. J.M.P. Atkinson, GEORGE ARNOLD, of Baltimore, to Miss E.M. TILLEY, of the former place. (16 MAY 1854)

DEATH. In this city, on the 15th inst., JOHN W. SIMONTON, aged about 65 years, formerly a citizen of Key West, Fla., and recently a resident here. His funeral will take place on this (Tuesday) afternoon at half-past four o'clock, from Mrs. Wallingsford's Boarding-house, on Four-and-a-half street, at which his friends and acquaintances are invited to attend. (16 MAY 1854)

MARRIAGE. On the 11th inst., by the Rev. Mr. Finkel, CHARLES WERNER to SOPHIA MARIA BOGUSCH, all of this city. (17 MAY 1854)

MARRIAGE. On Tuesday morning [16 MAY 1854], by the Rev. John C. Smith, ZECHARIAH L. WINSLOW, Esq., of Montgomery Co., to Miss MARY JANE STONE, of Georgetown, D.C. (17 MAY 1854)

DEATH. In this city, after a short illness of pneumonia, at five o'clock on the morning of the 16th inst., SUSAN BORROWS, aged 67 years. The deceased came with her father, the late Joseph Borrows, on the removal of the offices of the National Government from Philadelphia, to this city, and has resided ever since among us. She lived to see what was then a mere wilderness converted into a large city. She was for many years a professor of religion, and at the time of her death a member of the Shiloh Baptist Church. She died in the midst of her family, for whom she had lived and sacrificed with noble generosity the prime of her life, in the full possession of all her mental faculties, strong in faith, and full of confidence of a blessed immortality. Her friends are respectfully invited to attend her funeral, without further notice, on Thursday next, at four o'clock P.M., from her late residence on E street north, between 9th and 10th streets west. (17 MAY 1854)

MARRIAGE. On Wednesday, the 17th inst., by the Rev. Mr. Sunderland, Lieut. JOHN E. WILSON, of the U.S.R. Service, to Miss SUSAN H. OSBOURN, of this city. (18 MAY 1854)

MARRIAGE. On the 18th inst., in Foundry Church, by the Rev. E.P. Phelps, Mr. NATHAN WALKER and Miss ANNA R. SCOTT, of Georgetown. (19 MAY 1854)

MARRIAGE. In Washington city, on the 17th inst., at the residence of Mr. A.G. Southall, by the Rev. Mr. Wingfield, Mrs. ANNA COCKE and Col. SIMEON WHEELER, all of Portsmouth, Va. (19 MAY 1854)

MARRIAGE. At Baltimore, on Tuesday evening, the 16th inst., by the Rev. Mr. Ridout, Mr. BELT S. NORWOOD to Miss ISABELLA McELRAY, both of that place. (19 MAY 1854)

DEATH. On the 17th inst., by sudden visitation of Divine Providence, by lightening, Mrs. ELLEN, wife of Mr. John C. Roemmelle. Mrs. R. was a very worthy member of St. Paul's Lutheran Church, in all things adorning her profession. Her family in this painful bereavement may well be sustained by the blessed hopes of the religion which was her hope and joy through life. "Precious in the sight of the Lord is the death of his saints." Her funeral will take place this evening (Friday) at 3½ o'clock, from St. Paul's Church, corner of H and 11th streets. Her friends are invited to attend. (19 MAY 1854)

Daily National Intelligencer, Marriage and Death Notices, 1851-1854

DEATH. In Georgetown, on Friday morning, the 19th inst., Mrs. MARY A.O. GANNON, aged about 65 years. Her funeral will take place on Sunday next, the 21st, at 2 o'clock, from the Wash-house of Georgetown College, when and where her friends are respectfully requested to attend without further notice. (20 MAY 1854)

MARRIAGE. On the 16th inst., in Union Methodist Episcopal Church, by the Rev. F. Israel, CHARLES CARROLL to SUSANNA P. MILLSON, all of this city. (23 MAY 1854)

MARRIAGE. On the 20th inst., at St. Patrick's Church, by the Rev. Dr. O'Toole, THOMAS P. WATSON, Esq., of Detroit, to Miss MARY ANN BURGEVIN, of Newbern, N.C. (23 MAY 1854)

MARRIAGE. On the 21st inst., by the Rev. Mr. Hodges, GABRIEL CROSS to Miss MARGARET E. LANGLEY, of the District of Columbia. (23 MAY 1854)

DEATH. On Sunday evening last [21 MAY 1854], aged 78 years, Mrs. MARTHA SESSFORD, wife of Mr. John Sessford, Sr., a resident of this city for the last 54 years. Her funeral will take place this (Tuesday) afternoon, at 3 o'clock. The friends of the family are invited to attend. (23 MAY 1854)

DEATH. At 4½ o'clock, on Sunday morning, the 21st inst., JOHN T. FROST, Esq., in his 89th year. His funeral will take place at Mrs. Sprigg's boarding house, on C, between 3d and 4½ streets west, at 10 o'clock, on this (Tuesday) morning, the 23d inst. The friends and acquaintances of the family are respectfully invited to attend. (23 MAY 1854)

DEATH. At Richmond, Va., on the morning of the 22d inst., in the 36th year of his age, THOMAS RITCHIE, Jr., one of the Editors of the *Enquirer*, and third son of Thomas Ritchie, Esq., of this place. (23 MAY 1854)

DEATH. Yesterday [23 MAY 1854], at his residence on N, between 12th and 13th streets, in the 68th year of his age, ALEXANDER MORISON. His funeral will take place this evening at 5 o'clock. (24 MAY 1854)

MARRIAGE. On the 23d inst., by the Rev. James B. Donelan, THOMAS G. CLINTON and L. REBECCA, second daughter of the late Thomas Johns, Esq. (25 MAY 1854)

MARRIAGE. At Boston, on the 17th inst., by Rev. J.C. Stockbridge, Mr. EDWARD TUCKERMAN to Miss SARAH E.S. CUSHING, daughter of Thos. P. Cushing, Esq. (25 MAY 1854)

MARRIAGE. On Tuesday, the 23d inst., at St. Peter's Church, in this city, by the Rev. John F. Hickey, EDWARD M. HAMILTON to HENRIETTA R., eldest daughter of John C. Fitzpatrick, Esq. (25 MAY 1854)

DEATH. Suddenly, on the 24th inst., ANNA DOUGLASS, infant daughter of Samuel E. and Elizabeth A. Douglass, aged 2 years 2 months and 7 days. Her funeral will take place from the residence of her parents, on 20th street west, near E street, this (Thursday) afternoon at 4 o'clock. (25 MAY 1854)

MARRIAGE. On Thursday morning [25 MAY 1854], by the Rev. John C. Smith, WM. H.B. BUTLER, Esq., of Fauquier Co., Va., to Miss MARY A. THOMAS, of this city. (26 MAY 1854)

MARRIAGE. At Ellerslie, near the city, on the 25th inst., by the Rev. T.B. Sargent, WM. T. LANDSTREET, of Baltimore, to M. VIRGINIA, daughter of Enoch Tucker. (26 MAY 1854)

OBITUARY. Died, on the 8th of May, at Horn's Point, Dorchester Co., Md., the residence of her son-in-law, Wm. Goldsborough, Esq., in the 79th year of her age, Mrs. SALLY SCOTT LLOYD, relict of the Hon. Edward Lloyd, formerly Governor of Maryland and Senator of the U.S. from that State. It was but a few weeks ago, Messrs. Editors, that you recorded under your obituary head, the death, also at an advanced age, of Mrs. Catherine Eliza Rush, wife of the Hon. Rush, which occurred at Sydenham, near Philadelphia, the residence of her distinguished husband. These venerable ladies were sisters, and the death of each, occurring within a few weeks of that of the other, has been received with sorrowful interest by a wide circle of admiring acquaintances and attached friends... Companions of the Carrolls, and Catons, and Wellesleys, and Carmarthens, and other equally distinguished woman of that period in Annapolis, where they were born and grew up, then the centre of high fashion and refinement in Maryland, and as now the seat of its government, Mrs. Lloyd and Mrs. Rush, at that time two of the three beautiful Miss Murrays, are remembered as among the most attractive young ladies of the day. The third still lives, relict of the late Gen. John Mason and mother of the present distinguished Senator of Virginia. Charming memories cluster equally around and about her name. Long may her living presence be hallowed by them! Who that has ever shared the delightful hospitalities of Analostan Island can forget the accomplished and high-bred woman who added to the dignified and cordial reception of the honored Virginia gentleman, whose house and home she graced, so many grateful influences of wife and mother! [text continues]. (27 MAY 1854)

MARRIAGE. At St. Patrick's Church, in New York, on Wednesday, May 24th, by his Grace Archbishop Hughes, Hon. JOHN McKEON to JEANNETTE E. WHITTEMORE, daughter of Commodore John D. Sloat, U.S. Navy. (29 MAY 1854)

MARRIAGE. On the 25th inst., in Foundry Church, by Rev. E.P. Phelps, Mr. JOHN HENRY STINCHCOMB and Miss EMMA ELIZABETH WRIGHT, all of this city. (29 MAY 1854)

DEATH. Suddenly, on Friday morning, the 26th inst., Sergeant LEWIS MEINZESHEIMER, of the U.S. Marine Corps, aged 38 years. (29 MAY 1854)

DEATH. At Ft. McHenry, on the 20th inst., FRANCIS HARWOOD TAYLOR, in the 24th year of his age, son of Lieut. Col. Francis Taylor, U.S. Army. (29 MAY 1854)

DEATH. At his late residence, near Warrenton, N.C., on the 16th inst., JAMES SOMERVELL, Esq., in the 71st year of his age. The social qualities and intellectual attainments of Mr. Somervell gave him in the early period of his life an extensive acquaintance... A kind father, his children entertained for him the affection which generosity such as his never fails to secure [text continues]. (29 MAY 1854)

DEATH. At his residence, near Port Tobacco, on the 4th inst., Gen. JOHN MATTHEWS, in the 71st year of his age. The large concourse of persons who attended his interment testified the regard and esteem in which he was held. In early life he entered the office of the Clerk of Charles county, and soon familiarized himself with all its details and duties. It was placed under control, and in its management and direction he showed that industry and vigor of intellect for which he was so remarkable. From youth to old age he discharged with fidelity and honesty the labors which it imposed upon him. During the war of 1812-15, he promptly threw aside the garb of the private citizen for that of the soldier, and entered the field, ready and prepared to defend his country. Gifted by nature with the most determined resolution, he was always found at the post of duty [text continues]. (29 MAY 1854)

DEATH. At Meadville, Pa., of apoplexy, in the 75th year of his age, HARM JAHN HUIDEKOPER, Esq. Descended from an ancient and respectable family in Holland, the subject of the above notice came to this country when a young man, and early entered into the service of the Holland Company, which was possessed of large landed estates in this country, and took charge of the company's office at Meadville, Pa., which he superintended until he became the purchaser of the company's interests in that portion of the State... The flourishing theological institute and Unitarian church of Meadville are the results of his efforts, while to the religious literature of that denomination he was an extensive contributor. In a social point of view his character presented many beauties, and in his domestic relations he was a model of excellence. (29 MAY 1854)

MARRIAGE. On Sunday, the 28th inst., by the Rev. Mr. Hodges, BENJAMIN F. McCATHRAN to Miss SARAH ELLEN MITCHELL, all of Washington. (30 MAY 1854)

Daily National Intelligencer, Marriage and Death Notices, 1851-1854

DEATH. On the 6th inst., at Glasgow, Scotland, of which he was a native, ANDREW SMITH, Esq., aged 85 years, formerly for many years a respected resident of the city of Washington. (30 MAY 1854)

MARRIAGE. On the evening of the 30th, by the Rev. Alfred Holmead, ANTHONY BUCHLY to Miss ELIZABETH J. MARTIN, all of this city. (1 JUN 1854)

MARRIAGE. On Thursday morning, June 1st, in the Fourth Presbyterian Church, by the Rev. J.C. Smith, D.D., THOMAS P. McGILL, to Miss MARY OSBORN, only daughter of WM. DOUGLAS, Esq., all of Washington. (2 JUN 1854)

MARRIAGE. At Sydenham, Philadelphia, on Thursday morning the 1st June, by the Rev. Dr. Hare, Rector of St. Matthew's Church, JOHN CALVERT, Esq., of Mt. Airy, Prince George's Co., Md., to JULIA, daughter of the Hon. Richard Rush. (3 JUN 1854)

DEATH. On Saturday morning, the 3d inst., after 24 hours' illness, MARY, in the 23d year of her age, wife of Wm. H. Heyl and daughter of John and Elizabeth Humphreys. The deceased was from Devonshire, England. (6 JUN 1854)

DEATH. In this city, on the 4th inst., at the Washington Infirmary, JOHN ROCHE, in the 26th year of his age. His friends and acquaintances are invited to attend his funeral from the above place at ten o'clock this morning. (6 JUN 1854)

MARRIAGE. On the 1st inst., by the Rev. Jas. [H.] Brown, Mr. THOMAS DOUGLAS WALKER to Miss ELLEN VIRGINIA WARWICK, both of Washington. (7 JUN 1854)

MARRIAGE. On the 4th inst., by the Rev. Jas. H. Brown, Mr. CHARLES KELLER to Miss ANN REBECCA WALKER, both of Washington. (7 JUN 1854)

MARRIAGE. At Leeds, Fauquier Co., Va., on the 1st inst., by the Rev. Wm. H. Pendleton, the Rev. GEO. NORTON to Miss NANNIE BURWELL, daughter of Jas. K. Marshall. (7 JUN 1854)

MARRIAGE. On Thursday, the 1st inst., at Christ Church, Baltimore, by the Rev. Dr. Johns, DANIEL P. BEDINGER, Esq., of Nicholas Co., Ky., to ANN ELIZABETH, daughter of the late Matthew Ranson, of Jefferson Co., Va. (7 JUN 1854)

MARRIAGE. On the 6th inst., by the Rev. James B. Donelan, J. DEBARTH LITTELE to COLUMBIA, youngest daughter of the late Joseph Thaw, all of Washington. (8 JUN 1854)

MARRIAGE. On the 6th inst., by the Rev. James H. Brown, Mr. JOHN H. ALISON to Miss ANNA MAY, both of Alexandria, Va. (9 JUN 1854)

MARRIAGE. In the Foundry Church, on the 7th inst., by the Rev. E.P. Phelps, Mr. CHARLES W. SHERWOOD and Miss MARGARET M. DIGGES, all of this city. (9 JUN 1854)

MARRIAGE. On Thursday, the 1st inst., at Christ's church, Winchester, Va., by the Rev. C. Walker, ARTHUR M. ALLEN, Esq., of Clarke Co., to JANE SCOTT, eldest daughter of the late Alexander S. Tidball. On the same day, by the same, BEVERLEY R. JONES, Esq., of Frederick Co., to REBECCA J., second daughter of the late ALEXANDER S. TIDBALL. (9 JUN 1854)

DEATH. Yesterday morning, after a painful and protracted illness, which she bore with Christian patience and resignation, Mrs. ANN TALIAFERRO MILLER, wife of James J. Miller, Esq., of this city, and daughter of the late Dr. Taliaferro Stribling, of Clarke Co., Va. The funeral will take place this evening at 5 o'clock. The friends of the family are invited to attend without further notice. (9 and 10 JUN 1854)

Daily National Intelligencer, Marriage and Death Notices, 1851-1854

MARRIAGE. On the 8th inst., by the Rev. F. Israel, Wm. H. CALVERT to FRANCES ANNA JAMES, all of this city. (10 JUN 1854, see 12 JUN 1854)

MARRIAGES. On the 8th inst., by Rev. S.D. Finkel, Mr. HUBERT SCHUTTER to Miss M. ESTHER McCONNELL. Also, on the 6th, by the same, Mr. CHAS. A. SCHOTT to Miss THERESE GILDERMEISTER, all of this city. (12 JUN 1854)

MARRIAGE. On the 8th inst., by Rev. Mr. Israel, Mr. WM. CALVERT to Miss FRANCES R. JAMES, all of this city. (12 JUN 1854)

MARRIAGE. In this city, on the 25th of August last, by the Rev. Mr. Williams, of New York, and on the 7th inst., by the Rev. Mr. Boyle, of this city, Mr. THOMAS GROSVENOR KING, of New York, to Miss CATHARINE McNERHANY, of Washington. (12 JUN 1854)

DEATH. At his father's residence, of consumption, at 6 o'clock, on Saturday evening, Dr. SAMUEL J. ANDERSON, in the 29th year of his age. His friends and the friends of the family are respectfully invited to attend his funeral at five o'clock on Monday evening, without further notice. (12 JUN 1854)

DEATH. On the 5th inst., near Rockville, Montgomery Co., Md., Mr. THOS. READ, aged 60 years. (12 JUN 1854)

MARRIAGE. On the 13th inst., at Green Hill, by the Rev. Mr. Knight, Prof. J.E. MORGAN, of Washington, to NORAH, daughter of the late Wm. Dudley Digges, of Prince George's Co., Md. (14 JUN 1854)

MARRIAGE. At Durhamville, Tenn., at the residence of Mrs. Mary J. Lee, by the Right Rev. Bishop Otey, JAMES B. THORNTON, Esq., of Memphis, to Miss SUSAN STUART, daughter of Col. John S. Thornton, formerly of Virginia, and lately of Georgetown, D.C., and granddaughter of Mrs. Lee. (14 JUN 1854)

MARRIAGE. On the 13th inst., by the Rev. Wm. Hanks, WILLIAM CAMPBELL to Miss RACHEL GRAHAM, all of Washington. (14 JUN 1854)

MARRIAGE. On Monday evening [12 JUN 1854], by the Rev. John C. Smith, Mr. GEORGE SMALL to Miss ELIZA GROVES, all of this city. (14 JUN 1854)

DEATH. In this city, on Friday, the 9th inst., at the residence of A.B. Waller, Esq., Mrs. HELEN M. NOYES, wife of the Hon. Jos. C. Noyes, of Portland, Me. [text continues]. (14 JUN 1854)

DEATH. At Summerfield, the residence of James Carroll, Jr., Esq., near Baltimore, on the morning of the 7th of June inst., Miss SARAH J. WETHERED, daughter of the late John Wethered, Esq., of Kent Co., Md. The death of this venerable and truly estimable lady has cast a gloom over a large circle of attached and admiring relatives and friends. (14 JUN 1854)

MARRIAGE. On Tuesday, the 13th inst., by the Rev. G.W. Sampson, Mr. JAMES A. KING to Miss M.D. VIRGINIA, daughter of Joseph Peck, all of Washington. (15 JUN 1854)

MARRIAGE. In Wesley Chapel, on the 13th inst., by the Rev. James H. Brown, Mr. JOHN R. McGREGOR to Miss MARY McGREGOR, both of Washington. (15 JUN 1854)

MARRIAGE. At St. Patrick's Church, on the 13th inst., by the Rev. T. O'Toole, Mr. THOMAS F. MAGUIRE to Miss MARTHA M. REEVES, all of this city. (15 JUN 1854)

DEATH. On Tuesday evening, the 13th inst., at 5 o'clock, SAMUEL EMORY, only child of Hon. Jefferson Davis, aged 22 months and 14 days. The funeral will take place at the residence of his parents, on Thursday, the 15th inst., at 4 P.M. (15 JUN 1854)

Daily National Intelligencer, Marriage and Death Notices, 1851-1854

MARRIAGE. On Wednesday, the 14th inst., by the Rev. Mr. Hodges, the Hon. WILLIAM R. SMITH, of Alabama, to Miss WILHELMINA, daughter of Capt. Wm. Easby, of Washington, D.C. (16 JUN 1854)

MARRIAGE. On Thursday, the 15th inst., by the Rev. Mr. Donelan, JOHN A. MIDDLETON, of New York, to ANNIE MARIA BERRY, daughter of Washington Berry, Esq. (16 JUN 1854)

DEATH. On the 15th inst., R.H. CROZIER, in the 29th year of his age. His friends are requested to attend his funeral on this (Friday) morning, at 10 o'clock, from the residence of his mother-in-law, Mrs. R. Sears, on 12th streets, between I and K streets. (16 JUN 1854)

MARRIAGE. On Wednesday, the 7th of June, by the Rev. Mr. Todd, HENRY STARR WATTLES, of Alexandria, Va., and CAROLINE, daughter of Richard H. Clagett, Esq., of Swan Point, Md. (17 JUN 1854)

MARRIAGE. On Thursday afternoon [15 JUN 1854], by the Rev. John C. Smith, BARTHOLOMEW OERTLY, Esq., to Miss ELIZABETH ANN, daughter of Samuel Cunningham, Esq., of Georgetown. (17 JUN 1854)

DEATH. At the Washington Infirmary, on the 16th inst., DANIEL ETTIENNE, aged 4 years, 10 months and 12 days, son of Jane E. and the late Daniel Dunscomb. The funeral will take place this (Saturday) morning at 10 o'clock from the Washington Infirmary. The friends of the family are invited to attend without further notice. (17 JUN 1854)

MARRIAGE. June 16th, by the Rev. J.W. Shackelford, Rector of St. Mary's, Brooklyn, the Rev. E.A. WASHBURN, Rector of St. John's, Hartford, to FANNY H., daughter of Dr. Harvey Lindsly, of Washington. (19 JUN 1854)

MARRIAGE. At Rome, on the 21st of May, the Hon. LEWIS CASS, Jr., American Charge d'Affaires, to Miss MARY LUDLAM, daughter of Nicholas Ludlam, Esq., of New York. (19 JUN 1854)

DEATH. On Thursday, the 8th inst., at Indian Springs, Ga., Lieut. Col. GEORGE H. TALCOTT, U.S. Army, in the 43d year of his age. (19 JUN 1854)

DEATH. In New York, on Friday, the 16th inst., of bilious remittent fever, SAMUEL HUMES HOUSTON, U.S. Navy, in the 24th year of his age. His friends and acquaintances, and officers of the navy at present in the city, are respectfully requested to attend his funeral this morning, at 9 o'clock, from the residence of his parents, on Missouri avenue, between 4½ and 6th streets. (19 JUN 1854)

DEATH. On the 17th inst., HENRY MacGILL, in the 22d year of his age. His friends and acquaintances are respectfully invited to attend his funeral on this (Monday) afternoon, at five o'clock, from his late residence, between G and H, on 8th street. (19 JUN 1854)

MARRIAGE. At the University of Virginia, by the Rev. Wm. H. McGuffey, June 15th, WM. WALKER STEWART, M.D., of Colerain Forges, Pa., to Miss MARY H. McGUFFEY, eldest daughter of the officiating clergyman. (20 JUN 1854)

DEATH. In this city, on the night of the 18th, JOSEPH J. MERRICK, formerly of Maryland, in the 64th year of his age. The funeral will take place on Wednesday, the 21st inst., from his late residence, on F street, between 6th and 7th, at 11½ o'clock A.M. (20 JUN 1854)

DEATH. On the 18th of June, 1854, of dysentery, LINA, the infant daughter of Wm. H. and Selina Haslam, of Washington, aged seven months and sixteen days. (20 JUN 1854)

DEATH. In this city, yesterday morning [19 JUN 1854], JOSEPH ELGAR, Esq., formerly Commissioner of Public Buildings, in the 81st year of his age. Mr. Elgar died at a ripe and golden age, venerated and beloved for his integrity and intelligence. In the full possession of his mind and all its affections, he fell gently asleep. His funeral will take place on Tuesday, (this day), at 4½ o'clock, from the residence of his son-in-law, Chas. E. Sherman, Esq., on Third street. His friends and those of the family are invited to attend. (20 JUN 1854)

MARRIAGE. On Tuesday, the 20th inst., by the Rev. Mr. Hodges, WILLIAM L. NELSON to Miss ANN R. DUNCAN, of Prince Edward Co., Va. (21 JUN 1854)

DEATH. In Georgetown, D.C., on the 18th inst., in the 71st year of his age, Mr. JOSEPH CHICK, a native of Cecil Co., Md., and for 52 years a resident of Georgetown. (21 JUN 1854)

DEATH. In Baltimore, on the 18th inst., EDWARD FERRY, aged 44 years. (21 JUN 1854)

DEATH. In this city, on Wednesday, the 21st inst., in the 60th year of her age, JOANNA, wife of Major Parke G. Howle, of the Marine Corps. Her funeral will take place at St. Patrick's Church on Friday morning, the 23d inst., at 9½ o'clock. The friends and relatives of the deceased are requested to meet at the residence of the family at 9 o'clock. (22 and 24 JUN 1854)

DEATH. On the 21st, NATHAN H. TOPPING, infant son of Mary E. and Nathan H. Topping, aged 8 months. The friends and acquaintances of the family are requested to attend his funeral this (Thursday) evening at five o'clock, without further notice. (22 JUN 1854)

DEATH. In Washington, on the 18th inst., GEORGE DUNCAN, aged 36 years, a native of Scotland, but for the last sixteen years a citizen of the U.S. (22 JUN 1854)

DEATH. On the morning of the 22d inst., JOHN W. GIBBONS, of Mississippi, (late a clerk in the Treasury Department,) in the 40th year of his age. His funeral will take place from his late residence on Indiana avenue, between 2d and 3d streets north, on Friday, the 23d inst., at 10 o'clock A.M. His friends and the friends of his family are respectfully invited to attend. (23 JUN 1854)

DEATH. At the residence of her brother, Dr. W.S. Keech, Charles Co., Md., on the 18th inst., Miss CATHARINE A. KEECH, leaving a large circle of devoted friends to mourn her sudden death. Being the oldest of her family, her loss will be severely felt by her two brothers and several surviving sisters. She was not only by her own family beloved, but a favorite with all who knew her. (23 JUN 1854)

DEATH. At his residence, in Prince George's Co., Md., on the 20th of May, THOMAS WOOD, Esq., in the sixtieth year of his age. Protracted disease had long since shattered his health and forbidden his engaging in the duties or pleasures of life, yet, with the consciousness always before him of approaching dissolution, he was ever a bright example to those around him of Christian contentment and resignation [text continues]. (23 JUN 1854)

MARRIAGE. On Thursday evening [22 JUN 1854], by the Rev. John C. Smith, Mr. DANIEL McRAE to Miss MARGARET CUNNINGHAM, all of this city. (24 JUN 1854)

DEATH. At the residence of her father, in this city, on Thursday, the 22d inst., Mrs. EULALIA CRAWFORD EDWARDS, wife of Dr. Lewis A. Edwards, U.S. Army, and daughter of Hon. T. Hartley Crawford. Her funeral will take place on Saturday (this) afternoon, at 4 o'clock, which the friends and acquaintances of the family are respectfully invited to attend. (24 JUN 1854)

DEATH. On the 22d inst., EDWIN CECIL, only child of Edwin C. and Evelyn P. Morgan, aged 1 month and 8 days. (24 JUN 1854)

MARRIAGE. At Princeton, on the 22d inst., by the Rev. Mr. Peterkin, Lieut. JOHN C. HOWELL, U.S. Navy, to MARY, daughter of Hon. Robert F. Stockton. (26 JUN 1854)

Daily National Intelligencer, Marriage and Death Notices, 1851-1854

MARRIAGE. In this city, on Saturday morning [24 JUN 1854], by Rev. Mr. Sunderland, F. COSBY to ANNA SMITH, daughter of Robert Mills, Architect. (26 JUN 1854)

DEATH. In this city, on Sunday morning [25 JUN 1854], at the residence of Dr. Green, of consumption, WILLIAM B. NORTH, late of Newark, N.J., and son of the late Stephen North, of Philadelphia. (26 JUN 1854)

MARRIAGES. On Monday, the 26th inst., by the Rev. Mr. Hodges, JEDSON BUTLER to Miss MARY GARNER, of Prince George's Co., Md. On the same, by the same, WM. VENSION, to JULIA ANN CURTIN, of Prince George's Co., Md. (27 JUN 1854)

MARRIAGE. On the 24th inst., by the Rev. Mr. Finckel, Mr. JOSEPH REESE to ISABELLA C. BROWN. (27 JUN 1854)

DEATH. On March 30th, at sea, OLIVER HENRY MELVILLE, a native of Edinburgh, in the 39th year of his age. Four years ago, Mr. Melville left this place for the gold regions of California, where he worked assiduously for nearly two years without success. Thence he went to Australia and engaged in the mines' disappointment again met him, and he lost his health. Finally, he resolved to rejoin his family in the U.S., and took shipping for America. But he was destined never to revisit his adopted country and his waiting friends. Before the voyage was half completed his broken constitution gave way, and he breathed his last among strangers. (28 JUN 1854)

DEATH. At his residence, in Prince George's Co., Md., on the 14th inst., JOHN H. MARBURY, in the 51st year of his age. (28 JUN 1854)

MARRIAGE. At Lancaster, Pa., on the 15th inst., by the Rev. H.A. Shultz, Dr. J.M. FOLTZ, Surgeon, U.S.N., to Miss REBECCA STEINMAN, daughter of John F. Steinman, Esq. (29 JUN 1854)

DEATH. On the 27th inst., at her residence in Montgomery Co., Md., MARIA A. WATERMAN, wife of Edwin Waterman. The friends and acquaintances of the deceased are respectfully invited to attend her funeral at the residence of her brother, Adam L. Rose, 7th street east, at 3 o'clock this (Thursday) afternoon. (29 JUN 1854)

DEATH. At the residence of her brother, on the 27th inst., after a long and painful illness, which she bore with Christian fortitude, Miss MARY COLCLAZER, in the 74th year of her age. (29 JUN 1854)

MARRIAGE. In Philadelphia, on the 27th inst., by the Rev. Henry J. Morton, D.D., FERDINAND COXE to FANNY TRAVIS COCHRAN, daughter of Wm. G. Cochran, Esq., of Philadelphia. (30 JUN 1854)

MARRIAGE. On the 28th inst., by the Rev. Jas. H. Brown, Mr. JAMES R. HARROVER to Miss VIRGINIA LARKER, both of Washington. (30 JUN 1854)

MARRIAGE. On Thursday, the 29th inst., by the Rev. A.G. Cheniworth, Mr. WM. W. McCATHRAN to Miss MARIA V. BRADLEY, all of this city. (30 JUN 1854)

DEATH. On Thursday, the 29th, Dr. ALEXANDER SPEER, of the 5th Auditor's office. Funeral services at the 1st Presbyterian Church, 4½ street, on Saturday morning, at 8½ o'clock. (30 JUN 1854)

MARRIAGE. On Thursday evening [29 JUN 1854], by the Rev. John C. Smith, Mr. JOHN P. HURLEY to Miss AMANDA JOHNSON, all of this city. (1 JUL 1854)

MARRIAGE. June 27th, by the Rev. W.C. Steel, Mr. ABNER PARROT, of Georgetown, to Miss ELIZA A. COLLINS, of Washington, D.C. (1 JUL 1854)

DEATH. On Friday, the 30th June, at 1 o'clock P.M., in Georgetown, D.C., Mrs. SARAH CRUIKSHANK, in the 83d year of her age. Her friends and those of the family are invited to attend her funeral from her late residence on Potomac street, near St. John's Episcopal Church, at 5½ o'clock. (1 JUL 1854)

MARRIAGE. On Tuesday, the 20th June, at the residence of his father, by the Rev. L. Campbell, of Vicksburg, B.G. WYCHE, M.D., to Miss SALLIE E. GORDON, all of Hinds Co., Miss. (3 JUL 1854)

DEATH. In this city, on Sunday, the 2d inst., LOUTHER TAYLOR, Esq., of Maryland, in the 79th year of his age. His friends and those of his son-in-law, Col. Charles Thomas, are respectfully invited to attend his funeral, at the residence of the latter on New York avenue, at 4½ o'clock this (Monday) afternoon. (3 JUL 1854)

DEATH. Near Woodville, Sandusky Co., Ohio, on the 2d day of June ult. [2 JUN 1854], Capt. JOHN D. HART, a citizen of Hancock, Md. He left his home on the 25th of April last to visit the scenes in which he took so conspicuous a part in the war of 1812 and 1814. He was at that time a captain of cavalry under Gen. Thomas, of Pennsylvania, and from his efficient services received the highest encomiums from his superiors in command. He nobly sustained his character as a man and soldier. His prudence, his genius and benevolence had a bearing which could not but exalt him high in the estimation of all who knew him. He, with others, represented Washington county in the Legislature of Maryland in the memorable contest of 1844, when his State was dishonored by a refusal to discharge liabilities, &c., but he nobly sustained the Executive in all his measures proposed to redeem the fallen and degraded character of the State. He has left a large number of relations and friends to mourn his loss. Capt. Hart died from cholera, supposed to have been contracted on the railroad. He was in his 88th year, and was for thirty years a punctual subscriber to the *National Intelligencer*. (3 JUL 1854)

DEATH. On the 30th of June, after a few hours' illness, JULIA MAY WISE, aged 5 years and 5 months, youngest daughter of Geo. D. Wise, of the U.S. Coast Survey. (3 JUL 1854)

MARRIAGE. On Monday, July 3d, by the Rev. Stephen P. Hill, HENRY HAGAN to LOUISA JANE PATTERSON. (4 JUL 1854)

DEATH. In this city, yesterday, July 3d, at a quarter past 12 o'clock, THOMAS RITCHIE, in the 76th year of his age. Funeral services will take place at his residence tomorrow (Wednesday) afternoon, at 5 o'clock, which his friends are invited to attend. His remains will afterwards be conveyed to Richmond. (4 JUL 1854)

DEATH. Suddenly, at Port Tobacco, Charles Co., Md., on the 29th ult. [29 JUN 1854], Mr. JAMES McCORMICK, formerly of this city, aged 54 years. (4 JUL 1854)

DEATH. On the 30th of June, JULIA-MAY GAITHER, third daughter of the late Greenbury Gaither, of this city. (4 JUL 1854)

DEATH. At St. Paul's, Minnesota Territory, on the 17th of June, ALBERT N. SERGEANT, M.D., of Meadville, Pa., in the 45th year of his age. Dr. S. had gone to St. Louis on account of the illness of his daughter, who was visiting there, and, thinking to improve the time taken in her convalescence by a trip to the Upper Mississippi, he was seized with cholera, after a short time illness died as above stated. Accomplished as a physician, and possessed of great energy of character, his loss will be sensibly felt by that community of which he was recently a member. (4 JUL 1854)

MARRIAGE. On the 4th inst., in Union Methodist Episcopal Church, by Rev. F. Israel, JOHN E. DeVAUGHAN to MARY S. WILSON, all of Washington. (6 JUL 1854)

MARRIAGE. On the 3d inst., at Foundry Parsonage, by Rev. E.P. Phelps, Mr. RICHARD A. HYDE and Miss ELIZABETH A. TUCKER, of this city. (6 JUL 1854)

MARRIAGE. At the woodyard, Prince George's Co., Md., on the 5th inst., J.W.T. GARDINER, First U.S. Dragoons, to ANNIE E. WEST, daughter of the late John Hays, Esq., of Carlisle, Pa. (6 JUL 1854)

DEATH. On Tuesday, the 4th inst., HANSON GASSAWAY, formerly and for many years a merchant in this city. (6 JUL 1854)

DEATHS. On Saturday, the 10th of June, 1854, EMILY REBECCA, aged 5 years, the youngest child of Hamilton and Louisa Loughborough. And on Monday, the 3d of July, DAVID AUGUSTINE, youngest son of the same, in the 9th year of his age. (6 JUL 1854)

DEATH. On Sunday, the 2d inst., at Vineyard Farm, Charles Co., Md., GEORGE W., aged 17 months, only son of Thomas and Pamela Milburn, of this city. (6 JUL 1854)

DEATH. In this city, on the 6th inst., at 2½ o'clock P.M., after a lingering illness, MARY ANN, the wife of JOHN B. FLOYD. The friends of the family are requested to attend her funeral, from the residence of her father, Isaac Beers, on 3d street, near Pennsylvania avenue, on Saturday, July 8th, at 4 o'clock P.M. (7 JUL 1854)

DEATH. At his residence in this city, at 2½ o'clock A.M., on the 5th inst., in the 47th year of his age, Dr. A.J. SCHWARTZE, son of the late Dr. A.J. Schwartze, of Baltimore Co., Md. (7 JUL 1854)

DEATH. In this city, on the 6th inst., ELIZABETH JANE, youngest child of Wm. E. and Teresa Ann Morcoe, aged six months. The friends of the family are requested to attend the funeral this morning at 9 o'clock. (7 JUL 1854)

DEATH. At one o'clock A.M., on the 7th inst., WILLIAM KING, in the 83d year of his age. His funeral will take place at 3½ o'clock P.M., on the 8th inst., from his late residence on Congress street, Georgetown, of which place he was a resident for nearly 60 years. (8 JUL 1854)

DEATH. In Georgetown, on the morning of the 6th inst., in the 12th year of his age, NELSON W., son of the late Thomas J. Davis. (8 JUL 1854)

DEATH. On the 5th inst., JOSEPH, infant son of J.E. and Emma Todhunter. (8 JUL 1854)

DEATH. In this city, on the 6th inst., JANE SEABROOK, only daughter of John D. and Rosannah Brandt, aged seven months and eight days. (8 JUL 1854)

DEATH. On the evening of the 8th inst., in the 74th year of his age, SAMUEL SMOOT, Esq. The friends of his family are invited to attend his funeral from the residence of his son, L.R. SMOOT, on K street, between 26th and 27th, this morning, (Monday,) at 10 o'clock, without further notice. (10 JUL 1854)

DEATH. On the 29th June, near Logan, Hocking Co., Ohio, of a lingering illness of five months, which she bore with Christian fortitude and resignation, SOPHIA AURAND, wife of Jacob Aurand, aged fifty-six years three months and seventeen days. "*Blessed are the dead who die in the Lord.*" (10 JUL 1854)

DEATH. In this city, on Sunday, the 9th inst., at 9½ o'clock A.M., JAMES McCARTHY, in the 57th year of his age. The friends of the family are respectfully requested to attend his funeral, from his late residence, on E, near Sixth street, on tomorrow, (Tuesday,) at 8½ o'clock A.M. (10 JUL 1854)

DEATH. On the 7th inst., at the residence of her son-in-law, Mr. John R. Magruder, in Baltimore, after a short illness, Mrs. ELIZABETH WARING, in the 75th year of her age. She was the only surviving child of the late Gov. Bowie, of Maryland, and was especially dear to her relations and friends from her affectionate disposition and winning character of manner. No one ever more faithfully discharged the duties of life, or left the world more sincerely lamented. (10 JUL 1854)

MARRIAGE. On Wednesday, the 5th inst., at Christ Church, by the Rev. Mr. Hodges, GEO. G. BUTLER, Esq. to ADELINE, daughter of the late Edward Ingle, of this city. (11 JUL 1854)

DEATH. On Monday, the 10th inst., at 9 o'clock A.M., Mrs. ANNE SMOOT, in the 60th year of her age. Her funeral will take place this (Tuesday) afternoon, at 4 o'clock, from her late residence, Pennsylvania avenue, between 3d and 4th streets east. Her friends and acquaintances are respectfully invited to attend without further notice. (11 JUL 1854)

DEATH. In this city, on Monday morning, the 10th inst., of dysentery, GEORGE W., aged 9 years, only son of Julius A. and Mary A. Peters. The friends and acquaintances of the family are respectfully invited to attend his funeral this day, (Tuesday,) 11th inst., at 5 o'clock P.M., from his father's residence, corner of D and 22d streets west. (11 JUL 1854)

MARRIAGE. At Sacramento, Calif., May 31, by the Rev. B.T. Crouch, Jr., Mr. ELLIOTT AUBURY to Miss EMILY J., daughter of C.A. Tweed, both of Sacramento. (12 JUL 1854)

MARRIAGE. On the 9th inst., by the Rev. F.S. Evans, GEORGE W. STROTHER to ANN THOMAS. (12 JUL 1854)

DEATH. On the 11th inst., at half-past 9 o'clock A.M., after a long and painful illness, Mr. HENRY HINES, aged about 76 years, and for the last 54 years a resident of this city. His friends and the friends of the family are respectfully invited to attend his funeral today at 4 o'clock P.M., from his late residence on H, between 18th and 19th streets, in the First Ward. (12 JUL 1854)

DEATH. In this city, on the 10th inst., Mr. EDWARD ADDISON, in the 32d year of his age, leaving a wife and one child, a native of [Accomack] Co., Va., and a resident of this city for the last two years. His funeral will take place from his late residence on K street east, near the Navy Yard, the 12th inst., at 4 o'clock P.M. His friends and acquaintances are invited to attend. (12 JUL 1854)

DEATH. At the residence of her husband, near this city, on Thursday evening, the 6th inst., ELIZABETH GODFREY AGG, wife of John Agg, Esq., and daughter of the late Edward Blackford. Gifted with every quality of mind and person to win the admiration of the most casual observer, she occupied in the hearts of many friends a place which can never more be filled. (13 JUL 1854)

DEATH. On the 9th inst., at his residence, Mr. WILFRED VAN RESWICK, in the 73d year of his age, a native of St. Mary's Co., Md., but for the last thirty-nine years a resident of Washington. (13 JUL 1854)

MARRIAGE. On Wednesday, the 12th inst., at St. John's Church, Georgetown, D.C., by the Rev. Mr. Tillinghast, Mr. W.D. STUART to Miss FRANCES A., daughter of the late S.B. Harris, of Hagerstown, Md. (14 JUL 1854)

DEATH. At the residence of her son, Dr. A.H. Buchanan, in the city of Nashville, on Sunday evening, the 2d inst., after a brief illness, Mrs. SARAH BUCHANAN, widow of the late Alex. Pitt Buchanan, and youngest daughter of the late John Hite, of Berkeley Co., Va. (14 JUL 1854)

DEATH. At Lacton, Cedar Co., Iowa, on the 1st inst., after a short illness, NANCY H., wife of Franklin Butterfield, aged 25 years and 4 months, daughter of Isaac H. Wailes, of this city. (14 JUL 1854)

DEATH. In this city, on the 13th inst., WILLIAM A., son of Wm. P.S. and Martha N. Sanger, in the 20th year of his age. His funeral will take place at the residence of his father on I, between 17th and 18th streets, at 5 P.M., this day. The friends of the family are invited to be present without further notice. (14 JUL 1854)

DEATH. On the 13th inst., JOHN E. VAN RISWICK, aged one year, only son of John and Mary Van Riswick. The funeral will take place this (Friday) evening, at 3 o'clock. (14 JUL 1854)

Daily National Intelligencer, Marriage and Death Notices, 1851-1854

MARRIAGE. At Columbus, Georgia, on the evening of the 5th inst., at the residence of her brother-in-law, Joseph B. Hill, Esq., by the Rev. F. Bowman, D.D., Miss EMMA C. DAWSON, daughter of the Hon. Wm. C. Dawson, and EDWARD W. SEABROOK, Esq., of Edisto Island, S.C. (15 JUL 1854)

MARRIAGE. In Emanuel Church, Warrenton, N.C., on Tuesday morning last [11 JUL 1854], by the Rev. Dr. Smith, Lieut. THOMAS M. CROSSAN, U.S. Navy, to REBECCA, only child of the late Dr. James G. Brehon, of North Carolina. (15 JUL 1854)

MARRIAGE. On the 13th inst., in Union Methodist Episcopal Church, by the Rev. F. Israel, WILLIAM W. HOUGH to SARAH JANE ROBERTSON, all of Washington. (15 JUL 1854)

DEATH. On Thursday evening, the 13th inst., at Tudor Place, Georgetown Heights, D.C., after a short illness, MARTHA CUSTIS PETER, relict of the late Thomas Peter, Esq., in the 77th year of her age. Mrs. Peter was the last survivor but one of the family of the wife of Washington. We learn that her remains will be conveyed early this morning to the family grave yard near Seneca Mills, Montgomery Co., Md. (15 JUL 1854)

DEATH. On Thursday, the 13th inst., AGNES, wife of James Harmon, in the 20th year of her age. Her funeral will take place today, at 10 o'clock A.M., from her late residence, on H street, between 6th and 7th. The friends of the family are invited to attend. (15 JUL 1854)

DEATH. At Saratoga Springs, on the 13th inst., Mr. TIMOTHY O'NEALE. The friends of the deceased are requested to attend his funeral at 10 o'clock this morning, (17th,) from his late residence in Georgetown, D.C. (17 JUL 1854)

DEATH. On Monday morning, July 17th, at 8½ o'clock, Col. GEORGE C. WASHINGTON, in the 65th year of his age. The friends of the deceased are requested to attend his funeral this day, the 18th, at 5 o'clock P.M., from his late residence on the Heights of Georgetown. First president of the Washington Club. (17 and 19 JUL 1854)

DEATH. At the close of Sunday night, July 16th, HARRIOT, daughter of Wm. C. and H.A. Zantzinger, aged four years five months and eighteen days. The friends of the family are respectfully invited to attend the funeral at 4½ o'clock this (Tuesday) afternoon.

DEATH. At Mobile, Ala., on the 29th ult. [29 JUN 1854], LEMUEL R. TOWNSEND, formerly of this city, in the 40th year of his age. (19 JUL 1854)

DEATH. On the 18th inst., JOHN THOMAS, son of James and Rachel Henry, aged 11 months. The friends of the family are invited to attend his funeral this (Thursday) morning, at 9 o'clock, from the residence of his parents, I street between 4th and 5th. (20 JUL 1854)

DEATH. In the city of New York, on the 11th inst., suddenly, of congestion of the brain, Mrs. SARAH ABORN, wife of the Hon. Henry B. Anthony, of Providence, R.I., and daughter of Christopher Rhodes, of Pawtuxet. (20 JUL 1854)

MARRIAGE. In Georgetown, on the evening of the 18th, by the Rev. Mr. Cooper, GEORGE C. COLEMAN, Esq., of Pilot Grove, Md., to Miss MARY A. RUSH, of Washington Co., Md. (21 JUL 1854)

SUDDEN DEATH. Extract of a Letter dated, St. Paul, Minn., July 10, 1854. "It is my sad duty to announce to you the sudden decease of D.H. DUSTIN, Esq..." Mr. Dustin was the District Attorney of Minnesota, and but eleven months ago had a child and its nurse killed by the side of himself and wife on the Amboy railroad, the rest of the family miraculously escaping the same fate. (21 JUL 1854)

Daily National Intelligencer, Marriage and Death Notices, 1851-1854

DEATH. Yesterday morning [20 JUL 1854], Maj. Gen. NATHAN TOWSON, Paymaster General U.S. Army. His friends are respectfully invited to attend his funeral from his late residence, at the corner of F and 17th streets, on Saturday afternoon, the 22d inst. (21 JUL 1854)

DEATH. Yesterday evening [20 JUL 1854], at the residence of Hon. John H. Eaton, in this city, Lieut. JOHN BROCKENBROUGH RANDOLPH, of the U.S. Navy. He had just returned to his family from Japan, after an absence of more than three years. But his return was only to die, for in ten days after reaching home he sank a victim to chronic dysentery, under which he had been laboring for a considerable time. His funeral will take place this (Friday) afternoon, at half past 5 o'clock, from the residence of Mr. Eaton, where the friends of his family are invited to attend. (21 JUL 1854)

DEATH. Yesterday [20 JUL 1854], in this city, Mrs. AGNES WILSON, relict of the late David Wilson, aged about 89 years. Her funeral will take place from the Infirmary at 6 o'clock this evening. (21 JUL 1854)

DEATH. On Wednesday evening, the 19th inst., at 8 o'clock, Mrs. SARAH CHAPIN, relict of the late Rev. Stephen Chapin, D.D., aged 70 years. Funeral this (Friday) morning, at 9½ o'clock, from the residence of Rev. G.W. Samson, on 6th street, between D and E. Friends and acquaintances are invited to attend without further notice. (21 JUL 1854)

DEATH. On Thursday afternoon [20 JUL 1854], Mrs. MARGARET D. LITTLE, wife of Samuel I. Little. The friends and acquaintances are respectfully invited to attend her funeral on Saturday afternoon at two o'clock, from the residence of her husband, near the Navy Yard, without further notice. (21 JUL 1854)

DEATH. In this city, at the residence of Wm. Aiken, of South Carolina, on the 15th inst., Mrs. AMANDA SIEBELS, wife of Edwin W. Siebels, Esq., of Edgefield district, S.C., aged 28 years. (21 JUL 1854)

DEATH. At Salem, Iowa, of cholera, on the 5th inst., the Rev. JAMES NOURSE, of this city, in the 50th year of his age. He was returning to his family after a short absence. (21 and 25 JUL 1854)

MARRIAGE. On the 20th inst., by the Rev. Mr. Gross, Mr. SYLVESTER MUDD to Miss JOANNAH PEAKE, both of this city. (22 JUL 1854)

DEATH. On the 21st inst., JOHN M. FARRAR, aged 64 years. His funeral will take place from his late residence, on Missouri avenue, on Sunday afternoon, at 3 o'clock. His friends are invited to attend. (22 JUL 1854)

DEATH. In this city, on the 19th inst., WILLIAM DENT, infant son of Maj. James Longstreet, U.S. Army. (22 JUL 1854)

DEATH. At Cincinnati, Ohio, on the 13th inst., ANDREW JACKSON PORTER, late of Lancaster, Pa., youngest son of Geo. B. Porter, dec., Gov. of Michigan Territory. Born at Detroit on the 23d June 1832. (22 JUL 1854)

MARRIAGE. On the 22d ult. [24 JUN 1854], in Philadelphia, by Rev. Jno. Dowling, D.D., Mr. ISRAEL E. JAMES to Mrs. MARY S. WALTER, eldest daughter of the late John Struthers, Esq., all of this city. (24 JUL 1854)

MARRIAGE. Near Warrenton, on the 11th inst., by Rev. Josiah Solomon, Mr. WILLIAM P. ROSE to Miss ANN WINIFRED COLLINS, eldest daughter of the late David Collins, all of Warren Co., N.C. (24 JUL 1854)

Daily National Intelligencer, Marriage and Death Notices, 1851-1854

DEATH. In this city, on the 21st inst., WILLIAM BENTER, after a short illness, in the 51st year of his age. The deceased was a native of Alexandria, Va., but for the last twenty years a resident of this city. (24 JUL 1854)

DEATH. On Sunday morning [23 JUL 1854], at 2 o'clock, MICHAEL McGINNALL, in the 22d year of his age. His funeral will take place from his residence this evening, at 4 o'clock, from the corner of 15th and M streets. (24 JUL 1854)

OBITUARY. The late Capt. J. MASON SCARRITT, U.S. Engineers, who died of yellow fever at Key West on the 22d ult. [22 JUN 1854], graduated at the West Point Academy in 1838; served in Florida under Gen. Taylor; was afterwards assistant Professor of Mathematics at West Point; and in 1841 was ordered to Pensacola as assistant to Major W.H. Chase, where he remained until ordered to join the army of observation at Corpus Christi. He was in the battles of Palo Alto and Resaca de la Palma, where his gallant conduct received the notice and commendation of Gen. Taylor, and rendered important services in the siege and capture of Monterey, for which the brevet of captain was conferred on him by the President, and the Legislature of his native State (Illinois) presented him with a sword. (24 JUL 1854)

OBITUARY. Died, in Salem, Henry Co., Iowa, on the 5th of July, the Rev. JAMES NOURSE, of this city, in the fiftieth year of his age. This announcement has filled many hearts with sadness and many eyes with weeping. Mr. Nourse possessed those excellent qualities of mind and heart which greatly endeared him to a large circle of relatives and friends. His history is the history of an accurate and laborious scholar, an humble and devoted Christian, and a faithful preacher of the everlasting gospel. He received the rudiments of his classical and mathematical education under the instruction of the Rev. James Carnahan, D.D., in Georgetown, D.C. He pursued and consummated his college course under the paternal care of the late Dr. Brown, of Cannonsburgh, Pa., and shortly afterwards, for further instruction, attended during one year at Dickinson College, when Dr. John M. Mason was President of that institution. There he made a profession of religion, united with the church under the pastoral care of the Rev. Dr. Duffield, and determined to devote himself to the service of God in the ministry of reconciliation. He pursued his theological studies at Princeton, was licensed to preach the gospel by the Presbytery of the District of Columbia, and after engaging for a few months in the service of the colonization cause in the Southern States, accepted an invitation to preach as a supply to the Presbyterian church in Georgetown, Pa. He preached about eighteen months in Germantown, and then received and accepted a call from the Presbyterian church of Perryville, Pa. To that congregation he continued to preach the gospel, with the exception of a few months, for nineteen years; during which time seal of God's gracious benediction was upon his labors, and many precious souls, through his instrumentality, were brought to the Saviour. Besides attending to the duties belonging to his pastoral charge, he edited the Paragraph Bible with great care and labor, wrote several valuable Tracts, prepared for the press a Critical Commentary upon the Epistle to the Galations, and also an Abridgment of Lowth's Lectures on Hebrew Poetry. In 1849 he was compelled from ill health to relinquish his position as a pastor, and in 1850 he became the Principal of the Central Academy in Washington, in which capacity he continued to labor with great earnestness and fidelity till near the time of his death. For the last few months he had felt that his health was sufficiently restored to justify him in seeking another pastoral charge. His heart longed for the work of a pastor and for the privilege of again preaching Christ; and his eyes were turned to the great valley of the Mississippi as the field of his future labors in the ministry. Towards the close of June he left his family and friends in Washington to visit the southeastern part of Iowa, expecting, if Providence should favor his plans and hopes, to remove there in the fall. But God had not so determined. He went to Iowa to die. He reached Salem on the evening of the 4th of July, and complained of feeling very unwell. The next morning a physician was called, who informed him that his disease was cholera. Prompt and appropriate remedies were administered, but to no purpose. Through the kindness of the Rev. Mr. Cooper, pastor of the Congregational Church of Salem, he received every attention that was possible under the circumstances; but the dreadful malady was not to be arrested; he continued to sink under it; and at six o'clock in the evening life was extinguished and his spirit passed away. His sudden and unexpected departure is a severe blow to all his relatives, but especially to his infirm and aged parents; and as to his bereaved widow and her nine fatherless children, no pen can describe their agony; no human sympathy can do them the good they need. May the Good Shepherd of Israel strengthen them, as He alone can strengthen the weak, and comfort them as He alone can comfort the sorrowing. "*Servant of God, well done!, Rest from thy loved employ; The battle o'er, the victory won, Enter thy Master's joy.*" (25 JUL 1854)

MARRIAGE. On Tuesday, the 18th inst., at the chapel of the Theological Seminary, Va., by the Rev. Dr. Sparrow, Rev. T. GRASON DASHIELL, of the diocese of Virginia, to WILHELMINA, daughter of the officiating clergyman. (25 JUL 1854)

DEATH. At Oak Hill, Montgomery Co., Md., on the 22d inst., ELIZABETH GRAHAM, daughter of Edmund H. and Emily Brooks, aged 18 months. (25 JUL 1854)

MARRIAGE. On the 25th inst., by the Rev. Danl. Motzer, JOHN S. GULICH, Esq., Purser U.S.N., to Miss ELIZABETH MILLIGAN, of Waverley, Va. (26 JUL 1854)

OBITUARY. Died, at the residence of his son-in-law, Gen. Waddy Thompson, in Greenville, on the 21st ult. [21 JUN 1854], Col. JOHN D. JONES, of Wilmington, N.C. The deceased was the son of Maj. David Jones, who served with distinction in the war of the Revolution [text continues]. (28 JUL 1854)

DEATH. At Opelousas, La., on the 14th inst., after a lingering illness, Judge JOHN McLEAN, of New York. (28 JUL 1854)

DEATH. At Warrenton Springs, on Wednesday, the 26th inst., NEAL, infant son of Dr. C. and Fannie R. Boyle, aged 10 months and 13 days. (28 JUL 1854)

DEATH. In this city, on the 28th inst., of bronchitis, Rev. EDWARD L. DULIN, of the Baltimore Annual Conference of the Methodist Episcopal Church. His friends are invited to attend the funeral from his late residence on 6th street west, between D and E streets south, this (Saturday) morning, at 11 o'clock. (29 JUL 1854)

DEATH. At Columbus, Ohio, on the 23d inst., of cholera, JONATHAN PHILLIPS, formerly a resident of this city. (29 JUL 1854)

DEATH. On Friday, the 21st inst., ELIZABETH, daughter of Jeremiah and Mary Deasy, aged 14 months and 4 days. (29 JUL 1854)

OBITUARY. Died, suddenly, on the 11th inst., of cholera, at LaPointe, on Lake Superior, the Hon. WM. GRIFFITH EWING, of Ft. Wayne, Ind. The deceased was on a business tour of Fond du Lac, at the head of Lake Superior, where he had a trading post. On that line of high latitude and pure air most suddenly was he arrested and cut down by this mysterious and appalling scourge. The deceased was the son of Col. Alex. Ewing, a tried soldier of the revolution, and who belonged also to Capt. Wm. Griffith's company of spies that piloted the American army to the battle of the Thames in October, 1813. Wm. Griffith Ewing was born at the town of Monroe, on the River Rasin, in the Territory of Michigan, in October 1800, and was consequently in his fifty-fourth year [text continues]. (31 JUL 1854)

DEATH. On Saturday afternoon last [29 JUL 1854], in the 64th year of his age, Capt. WILLIAM EASBY. His friends and those of his family are respectfully invited to attend his funeral from his late residence on Pennsylvania avenue and 8th street east, at 4½ this (Monday) afternoon. (31 JUL and (obituary) 1 AUG 1854)

DEATH. On Friday morning, the 28th inst., MARY TERESA, infant daughter of Michael R. and Catharine Shyne, aged eight months and fifteen days. (31 JUL 1854)

DEATH. Near Baltimore, on the evening of the 28th of July, ELLEN C., wife of Thomas J. Carson, of New York, and daughter of the late Col. Benjamin Edes, of Baltimore. (31 JUL 1854)

Daily National Intelligencer, Marriage and Death Notices, 1851-1854

DEATH. On Saturday afternoon [29 JUL 1854], RICHARD GRAFTON HYATT, infant son of Richard G. and Margaret Ann Hyatt, aged one year and eleven days. (31 JUL 1854)

DEATH. At "The Cave," Jefferson Co., Va., on Friday, the 14th July, Mrs. ANNE R. SELDEN, wife of John Selden, and daughter of Andrew Kennedy, in the 29th year of her age. (31 JUL 1854)

MARRIAGE. On the 30th ult. [30 JUL 1854], in Foundry Church, by Rev. E.P. Phelps, Mr. WILLIAM H. GOODGER and Miss SARAH E. WOOD, all of this city. (1 AUG 1854)

DEATH. On the 28th inst. [28 JUL 1854], WILLIAM IRVING, Esq., in the 41st year of his age, formerly a citizen of New York, but for the last three or four years a resident of this city. Mr. Irving was an accomplished clerk, intelligent and prompt in the dispatch of business. He had filled in the most acceptable manner the post of Chief Clerk in the Census Bureau, and at the period of his death held a responsible clerkship in the office of the 4th Auditor of the Treasury. Richly endowed by nature, his mind had been stored with much useful information, acquired by extensive travel in his own country and in Europe, and by varied and instructive reading. He was a gentleman of high-toned feelings and greatly esteemed by his friends for the many admirable qualities both of his head and heart. (1 AUG 1854)

DEATH. On Saturday last, the 29th July, aged one year, ELLEN AUGUSTA, infant daughter of Dr. Wm. P. Johnston, of this city. (1 AUG 1854)

DEATH. On Tuesday, August 1st, Mr. JOHN W. FERGUSON, in the 42d year of his age. The funeral will take place tomorrow, (Thursday,) at 3 o'clock, from the Methodist Protestant Church, on Virginia avenue, near the Navy Yard. (2 AUG 1854)

DEATH. Yesterday morning, the 1st inst., in the fourth year of his age, FRANCK PINCKNEY, son of R.W. Latham, Esq., of this city. The friends of the family are invited to attend the funeral at 5 o'clock this evening. (2 AUG 1854)

DEATH. At Georgetown, Ga., July 20th, ROBERT LOWRY MOORE, a native of Washington, and eldest son of the late James Moore, of this city, aged 42 years. (2 AUG 1854)

DEATH. At Petersburg, Va., on the 20th ult., Mrs. SARAH MELLEVILLE BOLLING, aged 41 years, consort of Robt. B. Bolling, Esq. In the death of this truly estimable lady her bereaved husband and family, with her numerous relatives and friends, have indeed sustained an irreparable loss. She was one of the loveliest and purest beings we have ever known. In every womanly grace and in all the relations of life, whether as wife, mother, or friend, she had few equals and no superior. She adorned her elevated position in society by the possession of a highly refined and cultivated intellect, and by becoming dignity yet unaffected modesty of deportment, which secured the love and esteem of all who approached her. (2 AUG 1854)

DEATH. On the 22nd ult. [22 JUL 1854], at Buchanan, Botetourt Co., Va., SAMUEL R.G. OULD, son of Robert and Sarah A. Ould, aged 18 months. (2 AUG 1854)

DEATH. In this city, on the 2d inst., in the 75th year of her age, Mrs. MARGARET STEWART, consort of the late Samuel Stewart. Her funeral will take place on Friday morning next, at 10 o'clock, from her late residence, on Eleventh street, and proceed from thence to St. Patrick's Church, on F street, where mass will be said and other funeral services performed. The relatives and friends of the family are respectfully requested to attend without further notice. (3 AUG 1854)

DEATH. At sea, on his passage from the Sandwich Islands to New York, on the 4th July 1854, PHINEAS BRADLEY SANDERS, in the 23d year of his age, son of B.C. Sanders, Esq., late Collector of the port of San Francisco, Calif. [text continues]. (3 AUG 1854)

Daily National Intelligencer, Marriage and Death Notices, 1851-1854

DEATH. On the morning of the 2d inst., DORA, aged 3 months and 15 days, daughter of Metta and Adolphus Ei[r]hstedt. (3 AUG 1854)

MARRIAGE. On Thursday evening [3 AUG 1854], by the Rev. John C. Smith, Mr. WILLIAM H. GOODMAN to Miss SARAH ANN INGRAHAM, all of this city. (4 AUG 1854)

MARRIAGE. On the 3d, by the Rev. J.W. French, SAMUEL W. OWEN, of Virginia, to KATE E. EVANS, of this city. (4 AUG 1854)

DEATH. In this city, on the 3d inst., Miss ELIZABETH CATHARINE CRAWFORD, daughter of the Hon. T. Hartley Crawford. The funeral will take place from the house of her father, corner of F and 7th streets, on this (Friday) afternoon, at 5 o'clock, which the friends and acquaintance of the family are requested to attend without a more particular invitation. (4 AUG 1854)

DEATH. On Thursday afternoon [3 AUG 1854], of whooping cough, CATHARINE HARRIET, youngest daughter of Mary W. and Moses Kelly, aged 20 months. Her funeral will take place from the residence of her grandmother, Mrs. [Walker], Missouri avenue, this afternoon at 5 o'clock. The friends of the family are respectfully invited to attend. (4 AUG 1854)

DEATH. At his residence on Prince George's Co., Md., on Thursday, July 27th, HENRY H. WARING, in the 58th year of his age. (4 AUG 1854)

DEATH. At Dunham, Conn., July 31, WM. M.W. SMITH, only child of E. Goodrich and Mrs. Susan W. Smith, of this city, aged fourteen years. (4 AUG 1854)

MARRIAGE. On Thursday, the 3d inst., by the Rev. Byron Sunderland, JOHN C. PEDRICK, of New York, to Mrs. AMERICA FATIO, only daughter of the late Col. Samuel Burche, of this city. (5 AUG 1854)

MARRIAGE. On Thursday evening, the 3d inst., by the Rev. Andrew G. Carothers, Mr. JOHN ROBERTS to Miss MARY ELIZABETH PETERS, both of this city. (5 AUG 1854)

OBITUARY. Died, at his residence in this city, yesterday morning [4 AUG 1854], after a brief illness, which he bore with Christian resignation, Dr. BAILEY WASHINGTON, honored as an officer and beloved as a man wherever he was known. Dr. Washington was born in Westmoreland Co., Va., on the 12th of May 1787, and connected by blood and birthright with the illustrious man whose name he bore. At the time of his death he was one of the senior surgeons in the U.S. Navy, having entered it in 1810, and served with fidelity to the country in this department with a devotion seldom surpassed. He was the surgeon of the *Enterprize* when she captured the *Boxer* during the last war, and afterwards served with efficiency on Lake Ontario under Comm. Chauncey, and was selected by that high officer as his fleet surgeon, though a junior. He was successively fleet-surgeon under Comms. Rodgers, Elliott, and Patterson, in the Mediterranean; and closed his active sea-service during the Mexican war. At the time of his death he was consulting and visiting surgeon of the navy yard and marine barracks in this city, securing from the first and maintaining to the last the high esteem and regard of his brother officers and the Government. As a physician few surpassed him in the soundness of his judgment and the calm reflections which a long medical practice had afforded. But as a man the simplicity and force of his character gave tone to its crowning virtues, integrity and truth; while his social affections in the spheres of husband, father, and brother will always associate his memory with those to be beloved and remembered. The death of his gallant brother on board the ill-fated *San Francisco* had clouded his spirits and for the past few months affected his health, not of late years such as it had been. His closing hours of life were soothed by the intense love of his now bereaved widow and children, and he breathed his last under the cheering influence of Christian faith and hope. He died without fear and without reproach. The friends of the family of the late Dr. Washington are requested to attend his funeral this evening at five o'clock P.M., from his late residence. (5 AUG 1854)

Daily National Intelligencer, Marriage and Death Notices, 1851-1854

MARRIAGE. On Thursday, the 3d inst., in St. Ame's Church, at Annapolis, by the Rev. C.K. Nelson, JAMES K. HOWISON to SALLY, daughter of James Murray, Esq. (7 AUG 1854)

DEATH. On the evening of the 5th inst., EDWARD FRANCIS, second and only son of I. Andria and M.A. Iardella, aged three months. His funeral will take place on this (Monday) evening, the 7th inst., at 5 o'clock, from the residence of his father, corner of New Jersey avenue and B street, south Capitol Hill. (7 AUG 1854)

DEATH. On the 6th inst., THOMAS, aged sixteen months, only child of Thomas and Mary Duffy. The friends and acquaintances of the family are respectfully invited to attend the funeral on this (Monday) evening at 5 o'clock. (7 AUG 1854)

DEATH. On the 6th August, MARGARET ANNE, youngest daughter of Charles F. and Catharine McCarthy, aged 22 months. Her funeral will take place on this (Monday) afternoon, at 4 o'clock, from their residence. The friends and acquaintances of the family are invited to attend. (7 AUG 1854)

DEATH. At Edge Hill, Caroline Co, Va., on Wednesday, August 2d, WILLIAM C. NELSON, in the 48th year of his age. At the same place, on Thursday, the 3d of August, WILLIAM D. SCHOOLER, in the 24th year of his age. "*They rest from their labors, and their works do follow them.*" (7 AUG 1854)

MARRIAGE. On the 5th inst., by the Rev. C.M. Butler, D.D., J.D.B. DeBOW, of Louisiana, to CAROLINE, daughter of George Poe, Esq., of Georgetown, D.C. (8 AUG 1854)

DEATHS BY LIGHTNING. Miss CORDELIA GATHRIGHT was killed by lightning a few days ago in Goochland Co., Va.
    On Monday last [7 AUG 1854?], Mr. WILLIAM RICHARDS, overseer of Mr. J.W. George, about 5 miles east of Culpeper Courthouse, Va., was struck by lightning and instantly killed.
    On Wednesday [2 AUG 1854], two Negroes belonging to Mr. William Palmer, of Mecklenburg Co., Va., were killed by lightning while engaged with nine others in a barn assorting tobacco. The balance of the party were severely stunned.
    On Thursday evening [3 AUG 1854], about 5 miles from Petersburg, Va., a Negro girl, while engaged in stacking wheat, was killed by lightning.
    Las week the dead bodies of two boys, aged respectively 17 and 18 years, sons of Mr. Wyatt Brown, of Bedford Co., Va., were found in the Staunton river, a short distance from their father's residence. The boys had left home, the day before their bodies were discovered, to go on an errand a short distance across the river, which was not more than knee deep where they were to cross. Soon after they started a storm of rain, accompanied with thunder and lightning, occurred; and the supposition of the jury of the inquest was that the boys were struck by lightning while wading across the river. (8 AUG 1854)

MARRIAGE. On the 8th inst., by the Rev. J.G. Butler, UPTON H. RIDENOUR to LIZZIE MILLER, both of this city. (9 AUG 1854)

DEATH. At Auvergne plantation, Talahatchie Co., Miss., on the 20th of June last, Col. GEO. W. MARTIN, aged 65 years. He was in the late war, and accompanied Gen. Jackson throughout his campaigns in 1813, 1814 and 1815 and in the Creek war. In the last campaign of Gen. Jackson, Col. Martin served as an aid of Gen. Coffee. In this capacity he rendered efficient service in the defence of New Orleans. (9 AUG 1854)

DEATH. In this city, on the 8th inst., Mr. FREDERICK SPEISCHER, in the 56th year of his age, a native of Germany, but for the last thirty-four years a resident of Washington, leaving a wife and seven children to mourn their irreparable loss. The friends and acquaintances of the family are invited to attend his funeral from his residence, on 11th street east, between K and L, on Thursday, 10th inst., at 4 o'clock P.M. (10 AUG 1854)

Daily National Intelligencer, Marriage and Death Notices, 1851-1854

DEATH. In this city, on the 9th inst., after a lingering illness, Mrs. ELIZABETH E. PAGE, relict of the late Daniel Page, formerly of Prince George's Co., Md., in the 77th year of his age, in the joyful hope of a blessed immortality. Relatives and friends of the family are invited to attend her funeral from the residence of her son-in-law, Jno. L. Chubb, Esq., on I street north, between 6th and 7th streets west, this (Friday) afternoon at 3 o'clock. (11 AUG 1854)

DEATH. On the 31st of July, at "The Grove," the residence of Mrs. Samuel Latimer Barron, Prince William Co., Va., Mrs. REBECCA A. BARRON, wife of Henry A. Barron, Esq., late of said county. (11 AUG 1854)

DEATH. On the 10th inst., after a few days' illness, KATE M., youngest daughter of Wm. T. and Elizabeth T. Duvall, in the 4th year of her age. The relatives and friends of the family are requested to attend the funeral from the residence of her parents, on Pennsylvania avenue, opposite Brown's Hotel, this morning at 9 o'clock. (11 AUG 1854)

MARRIAGE. On Thursday evening, 10th inst., by Rev. S.A.H. Marks, Mr. CHARLES LUSKY to Miss MATILDA A. NALLEY, all of this city. (12 AUG 1854)

DEATH. At Miss Nancy Carroll's, Montgomery Co., Md., on the 11th inst., Mrs. CAROLINE M. HALL, in the 65th year of her age. Her funeral will take place at 10 o'clock this morning, and her friends are invited to attend without further notice. (12 AUG 1854)

DEATH. At Niagara Falls, a few days ago, Mrs. MARY C. PORTER, wife of Peter A. Porter. She was the eldest daughter of the late Rev. Dr. John Breckenridge, of New Orleans, one of the sons of Mr. John Breckenridge, of Kentucky, Attorney General of the U.S. under the Administration of President Jefferson [text continues]. *Buffalo Commercial Advertiser.* (12 AUG 1854)

DEATH. In Georgetown, on the morning of the 11th inst., after a protracted illness, MIRANDA M. GUY, in the 54th year of her age. Her friends and those of the family are respectfully invited to attend her funeral this afternoon at 3 o'clock, from the residence of her son-in-law, Levi Davis, Market street, above 3d street, Georgetown. (12 AUG 1854)

DEATH. On yesterday morning, FRANK, aged fourteen months, infant son of Wm. E. and Hannah Howard. The friends of the family are respectfully invited to attend the funeral this afternoon at 5 o'clock. (12 AUG 1854)

DEATH. On Thursday night [9 AUG 1854], of dysentery, WILLIAM STANHOPE, third son of Benjamin A. and Margaret B. Janvier, of this city, formerly of Delaware, aged four years five months and fifteen days. Friends and acquaintances of the family are requested to attend the funeral from his father's residence, (Philadelphia place, H street), at 4 o'clock this afternoon. (12 AUG 1854)

DEATH. On the 11th inst., ANDREW, aged one year and eleven days, youngest son of Jas. B. and Eugenie Orem. The friends of the family are invited to attend his funeral on this (Saturday) morning at 10 o'clock, on 6th street, between F and G. (12 AUG 1854)

MARRIAGE. August 10th, by the Rev. W.C. Steel, WILLIAM VANSCRIVER to Miss ANN MATILDA LIGHTFORD, both of Georgetown, D.C. (14 AUG 1854)

DEATH. In this city, on the 13th inst., of bilious dysentery, Mrs. MARY E. GATES, wife of the late James Gates, in the 66th year of her age. The friends and acquaintances of the family are respectfully invited to attend her funeral this (Monday) evening, the 14th inst., at 3 o'clock, from her late residence, near the Navy Yard. (14 AUG 1854)

DEATH. On yesterday [13 AUG 1854], about 1 o'clock P.M., in the 7th year of her age, KATE M., daughter of George H. Holtzman, Esq. The friends and acquaintances of the family are invited to attend her funeral, without further notice, at their residence on 11th, between H and I streets, this morning at 10 o'clock. (14 AUG 1854)

DEATH. On Sunday, the 13th inst., HERBERT REGINALD, infant son of Edward and Isabella J. Myers, aged fourteen months. The friends of the family are invited to attend the funeral this morning, at 10 o'clock, from Mrs. Farquhar's, on Twelfth street, east side, three doors above G street. (14 AUG 1854)

DEATH. On the 10th inst., GEORGE WASHINGTON, son of David E. and Sarah A. Irving, aged two years one month and fifteen days. (14 AUG 1854)

MARRIAGE. On the 10th inst., at Foundry Parsonage, by Rev. E.P. Phelps, Mr. WILLIAM JUDGE to Miss MARGARET FASNAUGHT. (15 AUG 1854)

DEATH. In Wilkesbarre, Pa., on the 1st inst., Mrs. SARAH HOLLENBACK BUTLER, wife of the late Hon. Chester Butler. Mrs. Butler spent much of her time in Washington when her husband was in Congress, and greatly endeared herself to a large circle of acquaintances who will deeply mourn her decease. (15 AUG 1854)

MARRIAGE. On Tuesday evening, the 15th inst., by the Rev. Mr. Griffith, Mr. ROBERT JONES, of Boston, Mass., to Miss ELLEN C. NOBLE, of Loudoun Co., Va. (16 AUG 1854)

DEATH. On the 11th inst., at the residence of his son-in-law, Col. Francis H. Smith, at the Virginia Military Institute, Dr. THOMAS HENDERSON, U.S. Army, aged 65 years. A life of active Christian usefulness has thus been brought to a peaceful close, in the confidence of all the promises of the religion of the Saviour. Dr. Henderson was widely known as a practitioner of medicine in Washington and Georgetown prior to his entrance into the army in 1838 [text continues]. (16 AUG 1854)

DEATH. At Leesburg, Va., on Thursday morning, the 10th August, in the 70th year of her age, Mrs. JANE BYRD ROBERTSON, widow of Thomas Robertson, and daughter of the late Robert Beverly, of Blandfield. (16 AUG 1854)

MARRIAGE. At "Hermitage," near Baltimore, on the 15th inst., by Rev. Dr. Wyatt, BENJAMIN HOMANS, Jr., of Cincinnati, to FANNY ELLEN, daughter of Nathaniel F. Williams, Jr., of the former place. (18 AUG 1854)

DEATH. Departed this life, on the evening of the 14th inst., in her 79th year, AMELIA, consort of Bryant Johnson, deceased, of Fairfax Co., Va., but for the last forty-three years a resident of the District of Columbia. She died, as she lived, in great peace and an abiding hope of a blissful eternity. (19 AUG 1854)

DEATH. At Norfolk, Va., on Sunday, the 13th inst., in the 38th year of her age, Mr. ENOCH L. REYNOLDS, of this city, and late clerk in the office of the Secretary of the Treasury. His kind and generous disposition had won for him the esteem of a large circle of acquaintance, by whom his memory will be cherished with grateful affection. His funeral will take place from Odd Fellows' Hall, 7th street, on Monday afternoon, at 4 o'clock. (19 AUG 1854)

DEATH. In Georgetown, on the evening of the 19th inst., JOHN AUSTIN, only son of Chas. and Sarah Abbot, aged one year. The friends of the family are invited to attend the funeral this afternoon at 5 o'clock from the residence of his father on Gay street. (21 AUG 1854)

DEATH. On Saturday morning, 19th inst., JOS. GREGORY, aged four months and nineteen days, only child of John F. and Mary Ann Ellis. (21 AUG 1854)

DEATH. On Friday, the 18th inst., after two days' illness, WM. CLARANCE, infant son of Jas. and Deborah Mankin, aged nine months. (21 AUG 1854)

MARRIAGE. On the 20th inst., by the Rev. Mr. Hodges, LUKE ANDERSON to Miss FANNY CLARKE, all of the District of Columbia. (23 AUG 1854)

DEATH. Departed this life, on the 21st inst., at her residence in this city, Mrs. LOUISA SAVARY PREUSS, aged 67 years. Her remains will be taken to the family burial ground, Montazile, Prince George's Co., on Wednesday morning at 6 o'clock. (23 AUG 1854)

MARRIAGE. At the residence of Absalom B. Woodruff, Esq., Paterson, N.J., by the Rev. Wm. B. Hornblower, Miss CHARLOTTE G., daughter of Gen. George DeWolfe, deceased, of the Island of Cuba, to EDWARD P. GOODE, Esq., of this city. (24 AUG 1854)

DEATH. Yesterday, the 23d inst., from the accidental discharge of his gun, JOHN THOMAS CRANDELL, in the 18th year of his age. His funeral will take place this (Tuesday) afternoon, at half past 4 o'clock, from the residence of his father, Dr. R. Finley Hunt, to which the friends and acquaintances of the family are respectfully invited. (24 AUG 1854)

DEATH. In this city, on the evening of the 22d, KENDALL, youngest son of Wm. and Jennie Stickney. (24 AUG 1854)

DEATH. On Tuesday, the 22d inst., KATHARINE THEODOSIA, infant daughter of Robt. W. and Katharine T.F. Barnard, aged 2 months and 22 days. (24 AUG 1854)

DEATH. In Georgetown, on the 23d inst., after a week's illness, J. ANDERSON JONES, third son of Capt. John C. Jones, of Clean Drinking, Montgomery Co., Md. By his sudden death his family have been deprived of a most affectionate and devoted son and brother. (26 AUG 1854)

DEATH. On Monday night, the 21st inst., in Harrisburg, Pa., after a short illness, SARAH EMMA, the beloved wife of Wm. H. Marquis, of this city, in the 28th year of her age. (26 AUG 1854)

DEATH. Departed this life, yesterday noon [25 AUG 1854], THOMAS JORDAN, Esq., in the 84th year of his age. His friends and acquaintances are invited to attend his funeral this afternoon, at 4½ o'clock, from his late residence on L street, between 8th and 9th streets. (26 AUG 1854)

DEATH. In this city, on the 26th inst., in the 59th year of her age, Mrs. ELIZABETH PULIZZI, widow of the late Serg. Maj. Venerando Pulizzi, U.S.M.C. The friends and acquaintances of the family are requested to attend her funeral from her late residence on I street east, near the Navy Yard, this afternoon at 3 o'clock. (28 AUG 1854)

DEATH. On Sunday noon [27 AUG 1854], JOHN SOMERFIELD HUGHES, youngest child of Robt. B. and Eliza Frances Hughes, aged five years. The friends of the family are requested to attend his funeral from his father's residence, on 12th street, Island, this day at four o'clock. (28 AUG 1854)

DEATH. On Thursday afternoon [24 AUG 1854], ROBT. LATIMER, infant son of John and Cordelia Goldin, aged thirteen months. (28 AUG 1854)

DEATH. At Edinburgh, Saratoga Co., N.Y., where he was on a visit with his mother and two little sisters, on Thursday, the 24th inst., CHAS. AMOS HUNT, aged five years and ten months, an amiable and intelligent scholar of the E Street Baptist Sabbath School, and youngest son of Amos Hunt, Esq., of Capitol Hill, in this city. (28 AUG 1854)

Daily National Intelligencer, Marriage and Death Notices, 1851-1854

MARRIAGE. In this city, on the 21st inst., by the Rev. Mr. Hill, AUREN KNAPP, of New York, to Miss MARY E. NORFLET, of Norfolk, Va. (29 AUG 1854)

DEATH. At Wood Cot, Prince George's Co., Md., yesterday morning, the 28th, Mrs. MARY LOUISA DANGERFIELD, wife of Col. Wm. Henry Dangerfield, and daughter of Mrs. Rebecca Winn, of this city. The friends and acquaintances are respectfully invited to attend the funeral at the Congregational [Congressional?] burying ground on 29th, (this day,), at 4 o'clock P.M. (29 AUG 1854)

DEATH. In this city, of dysentery, on the 28th inst., JOSEPH BORROWS, second son of Josiah R. and Anna E. Bailey, aged two years. The funeral will take place from the residence of his father, on North D street, near 7th, on Wednesday afternoon at 4 o'clock. (28 AUG 1854)

DEATH. On the 28th inst., THOS. DEVLIN BERRY, only son of Thos. B. and Fannie L. Berry, aged one year and two months. Relatives and friends of the family are respectfully invited to attend his funeral tomorrow at 10 A.M., from Mrs. E. Ferguson's, East Capitol street, Capitol Hill, without further notice. (29 AUG 1854)

DEATH. On Saturday, the 26th inst., JOHN MASSEY MOORE, youngest son of Daniel D. and Margaret Davidson, aged one year four months and five days. (29 AUG 1854)

MARRIAGE. On Tuesday, the 29th, by the Rev. S.C. Clarkson, Lieut. EGBERT THOMPSON, U.S. Navy, of New York, and Miss EMILY B., only daughter of the late Ignatius Mudd, of Washington. (30 AUG 1854)

MARRIAGE. On the 25th, by the Rev. Mr. Hodges, JOS. HODGES to Miss ELIZABETH I. JETT, both of Prince George's Co., Md. (30 AUG 1854)

MARRIAGE. On the 12th inst., by the Rev. Stephen Merrick, Mr. NICHOLAS BECK to Miss MATILDA HARRISON, both of Washington. (31 AUG 1854)

DEATH. On the 30th inst., at the residence of her father, Mrs. HARRIET VALINDA FARQUHAR, widow of the late T.C. Farquhar, and daughter of the Rev. John Scrivener, leaving three orphan children. The friends of the family are respectfully requested to attend her funeral this afternoon (Thursday, August 21st,) at 4 o'clock, from the Methodist Episcopal Church South, on 8th, between H and I streets. (31 AUG 1854)

DEATH. On July 19th, on board the ship *Francis P. Sage*, 12 degrees south of the equator, Atlantic, on his passage home, FREDERICK W. DeKRAFFT, of Georgetown, D.C. (31 AUG 1854)

DEATH. On the 29th inst. [21 JUL 1854], at 11½ o'clock P.M., IDA, aged seventeen months and four days, only daughter of Ambrose and Lucina H. Carter. Funeral will take place at 10 o'clock on this (Thursday) morning, 31st inst., at their residence, B street, Capitol Hill. (31 AUG 1854)

MARRIAGE. On the 24th August, by the Rev. Mr. Boyle, Mr. JAS. M. WOODWARD to Mrs. MARY E. BATES, both of Washington. (1 SEP 1854)

DEATH. In Baltimore, on the 31st August, Mrs. CAROLINE HARRINGTON, wife of George Harrington, Esq., of this city. Her funeral services will be performed at the Cathedral, in Baltimore, this morning at 7 o'clock, and her remains will be deposited at 11 o'clock A.M. in the vaults of St. Patrick's Church in this city. (1 SEP 1854)

DEATH. On Wednesday evening, 30th ult. [30 AUG 1854], SAMUEL, third son of Chas. A. and Eliza Anderson, aged two years and six months. (1 SEP 1854)

DEATH. On the 26th August, at the residence of Dr. P.B. Bowen, in the county of Culpeper, Va., WILLIAM FILLISON, son of Woodville and Sarah M. Latham, of this city, aged 10 months and 7 days. (2 SEP 1854)

Daily National Intelligencer, Marriage and Death Notices, 1851-1854

DEATH. On the evening of the 2d inst., Mrs. ANN BIRTH, widow of the late James Birth, in the 73d year of her age. The friends of the family are respectfully requested to attend her funeral from her late residence this morning at 9½ o'clock. (4 SEP 1854)

MARRIAGE. At Ft. Union, N.M., July 13th, 1854, by the Rev. Mr. Smith, Miss EMILY VIRGINIA MACRAE to Capt. GEORGE SYKES, U.S.A. (5 SEP 1854)

DEATH. In this city, on the 4th inst., Mrs. MATILDA M., consort of Wm. Jos. Smith, in the 39th year of her age. (5 SEP 1854)

DEATH. Very suddenly, in Rockville, Md., on Friday, the 1st inst., Mr. DAVID LITTLE, for more than twenty years a resident of this city. (5 SEP 1854)

DEATH. On Sunday evening, the 3d inst., SUSAN, youngest child of J.R. and Mary M. Zimmerman. The friends of the family are invited to attend the funeral this morning at 10 o'clock, from the residence of the parents, on 9th street, between D and E. (5 SEP 1854)

DEATH. On the 1st inst., JESSE F. PLOWMAN, aged seventeen years and three months, youngest son of Jesse and Elizabeth Plowman. (6 SEP 1854)

DEATH. On the 18th of August, JESSE PLOWMAN, aged ten months and eleven days, son of Wm. R. and Elizabeth A. Plowman. (6 SEP 1854)

DEATH. At the Marine Barracks, Washington, on Sunday evening, 3d inst., Corp. JOHN GILCHRIST, formerly of New York. (6 SEP 1854)

DEATH. On the 5th inst., GEORGE, son of Prudence E. and Wm. H. Frazier, aged 1 year 2 months and 2 weeks. Funeral this (Wednesday) morning, at 9 o'clock, from the residence of his father, on 8th street, between M and N streets. (6 SEP 1854)

MARRIAGE. In this city, on Wednesday, 6th inst., by the Rev. Dr. Cole, GEO. P. KRAFFT to Mrs. SARAH WARD, all of this city. (7 SEP 1854)

MARRIAGE. On the 5th inst., by the Rev. F. Israel, DURBIN TUCKER to SARAH ANN DOVE, all of this city. (7 SEP 1854)

DEATH. Yesterday morning [6 SEP 1854], after a long illness, Mr. JAMES Y. FREEMAN, in the 66th year of his age. Mr. F. was a native of Guernsey, but has been a resident of this city for the last thirty years, and was highly esteemed by all who knew him. His funeral will take place from his late residence, on D street, between 9th and 10th streets, this (Thursday) afternoon, at 4 o'clock, where the friends of the family are respectfully requested to attend. (7 SEP 1854)

OBITUARY. From the *Mobile Evening News* of August 21. Died, on Friday morning last [18 AUG 1854], at about half-past six o'clock, in this city, after a short illness, Mrs. SARAH ELIZABETH KETCHUM, wife of Capt. Wm. H. Ketchum, and daughter of Wm. C. and Mary Stoddart Easton, of Mobile. Mrs. Ketchum was born in the city of Washington on the 22d of July, 1829, and she was consequently a few days over twenty-five years old. She was the delight of a large circle of friends, and an accomplished and highly educated lady. Affectionate, friendly, hospitable, her house was the centre of most delightful social and intellectual intercourse. Her decease, it may with the utmost truth be said, took our city by surprise, and many tears and many a moan have testified to the strong feelings of attachment existing amongst us for this lovely and esteemed woman. (7 SEP 1854)

OBITUARY. From the *Union*. We are called upon to record the close of the useful career of a citizen devoted from his youth to the service of his country, and in that service crowding a brief career with distinguished actions. It is that of Brevet Lieut. Col. JOHN McCLELLAN, of the Corps of Topographical Engineers of the Army of the U.S. Born in Franklin Co., Pa., he entered the Military Academy of the U.S. in the year 1822 [text continues]. (8 SEP 1854)

MARRIAGE. On Tuesday, the 5th inst., in New York, by Rev. Spencer H. Cone, D.D., ROBERT B. MORRELL, of Philadelphia, to Miss SALLIE C. McCORKLE, daughter of the late Joseph P. McCorkle, of this city. (8 SEP 1854)

DEATH. On Thursday morning, the 7th inst., at the residence of her son-in-law, Thos. Cookendorfer, Mrs. SUSAN BURNES, in the 82d year of her age, after a protracted illness. The relatives and friends of the family are invited to attend her funeral this (Friday) afternoon, at 4 o'clock, without further notice, from Mr. Cookendorfer's residence, on E street, near Sixth. (8 SEP 1854)

DEATH. In York, Ill., on the 22d ult. [22 AUG 1854], STEPHEN J. OBER, in the 34th year of his age, late of this city. (8 SEP 1854)

DEATH. On Friday, the 8th inst., at the 8th inst., at the residence of her father, MARY E., wife of William H. Falconer, and eldest daughter of Joseph and Octavia Bryan, in the 30th year of her age, after a long and protracted illness. The relatives and friends of the family are requested to attend her funeral on Sunday, the 10th inst., at 8 o'clock P.M., from the residence of her father, on New York avenue. (9 SEP 1854)

DEATH. On the 8th inst., MARY, consort of Jas. Maxwell. Her funeral will take place this morning, at 9 o'clock, from her late residence, on 4th street, between I and K streets. (9 SEP 1854)

DEATH. In this city, on the 8th inst., CHARLES C. BEVERIDGE, in the 44th year of his age. The friends and acquaintances of the family are respectfully invited to attend his funeral from his late residence, on Pennsylvania avenue, at 4 o'clock this afternoon. (9 SEP 1854)

DEATH. On Thursday evening, 7th inst., Mrs. SUSAN C. KLINEHANSE, wife of Geo. D. Klinehanse, in the 41st year of her age. The friends of the family are invited to attend her funeral this (Saturday) afternoon, at 4 o'clock, from the residence of her husband, on Seventh street east, Navy Yard. (9 SEP 1854)

DEATH. On Friday morning, September 8th, MARY HAMMOND, in the sixth year of her age, youngest daughter of William B. and Elizabeth G. Todd. The funeral will take place at 5 o'clock this (Saturday) afternoon, from the residence of her father, corner of C and Third streets. The friends of the family are invited to attend without further notice. (9 SEP 1854)

MARRIAGE. On board U.S. frigate *Cumberland*, lying in the harbor of Spezzia, Sardinia, on the 12th ult. [12 AUG 1854], Lieut. JOHNSTON B. CREIGHTON, U.S. Navy, to EDWINA H., daughter of Comm. S.H. Stringham, commanding U.S. squadron in the Mediterranean. (11 SEP 1854)

MARRIAGE. On the 7th inst., by the Rev. Mr. Hodges, WILLIAM A. SCOTT to Miss ANN REBECCA SCOTT, all of this city. (11 SEP 1854)

MARRIAGE. In Germantown, Pa., on the 7th inst., by the Rev. Luther Albert, HARRISON P. LEWIS, of this city, to LIZZIE B., daughter of Charles Lewis, Esq., of Philadelphia. (11 SEP 1854)

DEATH. On the 10th inst., ROBERT A. CARTER, a clerk in the office of the Sixth Auditor of the Treasury. His friends and acquaintances are respectfully invited to attend his funeral, from his late residence, (Mrs. Preston's,) on 12th street, between E and F streets, at half-past 3 o'clock this afternoon. (11 SEP 1854)

Daily National Intelligencer, Marriage and Death Notices, 1851-1854

DEATH. On Friday, the 8th inst., at noon, ANNE MANDEVILLE, infant daughter of J.M. Carlisle, in the fourteenth month of her age. (11 SEP 1854)

DEATH. At Longwood, Montgomery Co., Md., on the 1st inst., ELISHA W. WILLIAMS, in the 76th year of his age, after a protracted illness of twelve months, which he bore with unexampled patience, Christian meekness, and resignation, under the firm belief his end was approaching... He had for twelve years been a member of the Episcopal Church... (11 SEP 1854)

MARRIAGE. In this city, on the 11th of September, by the Rev. Dr. Eliot, of St. Louis, Mo., FRANK A. ELIOT, of Philadelphia, and MARY J. WHIPPLE, adopted daughter of the late Prof. W.R. Johnson, of Washington. (12 SEP 1854)

OBITUARY. Died, in this city, at 8 o'clock P.M., Sunday, 10th inst., Mrs. ELIZABETH BENTON, wife of the Hon. Thomas H. Benton, aged sixty years... Nurtured in her father's house and among the Virginia Puritans of Rockbridge... [text continues]. Her funeral will take place this afternoon at four o'clock, from the residence of Col. Benton, on C street. (12 SEP 1854)

MARRIAGE. In Baltimore, by the Rev. John A. Gere, JOHN REESE, of this city, to VIRGINIA BOWEN, of Baltimore. (13 SEP 1854)

DEATH. On Sunday, 10th inst., at the residence of her son-in-law, Rev. H.W. Dodge, Upperville, Va., Mrs. PHEBE BROWN, aged 73 years, widow of the late Daniel Brown, of this city. (13 SEP 1854)

DEATH. On the 2d inst., at St. Paul, Minn., WILLIAM FLETCHER, infant son of the late Daniel H. Dustin, Esq., and grandson of Judge Sargent, of this city. (13 SEP 1854)

DEATH. Yesterday [13 SEP 1854], in this city, WM. KAHOE. His friends and acquaintances are requested to attend his funeral, which will take place this day at 4 o'clock from his late residence, Capitol Hill, Second street, between Massachusetts and Maryland avenues. (14 SEP 1854)

MARRIAGE. On Tuesday, the 12th inst., by the Rev. Mr. Hodges, FRANCIS OSBORN to Miss ISABELLA REED, of this city. (15 SEP 1854)

MARRIAGE. On the 12th inst., in Foundry parsonage, by Rev. E.P. Phelps, Mr. JAMES A. MOORE and Miss RACHEL ELLA DEPUTY, both of Baltimore city. (15 SEP 1854)

MARRIAGE. At Baltimore, on the 12th inst., in Grace Church, by the Rev. Dr. Wyatt, LUCIUS CAMPBELL DUNCAN, Esq., Counselor-at-Law, of New Orleans, to Miss MARY REBECCA SMITH, daughter of the late Dennis A. Smith, Esq., of Baltimore. (15 SEP 1854)

DEATH. Yesterday [14 SEP 1854], CHARLES T. KIRBY, printer, aged thirty-five years. His funeral will take place this afternoon, at 3½ o'clock, from his late residence, No. 334 Fifth street, above Massachusetts avenue, which his friends and the members of the Columbia Typographical Society are invited to attend. (15 SEP 1854)

DEATH. On the 14th inst., RICHARD GORMLY, son of Joseph F. and Mary Isabel Hodgson, aged seven months and ten days. The funeral will take place on this (Friday) morning at ten o'clock, from the residence of the parents, on K street north, between Sixth and Seventh streets, where the friends of the family are respectfully invited to attend. (15 SEP 1854)

MARRIAGE. On the 6th inst., at Morven, the residence of her father, by the Rev. Charles E. Ambler, JAMES K. MARSHALL, Jr., to FANNIE L., daughter of Maj. Thos. M. Ambler, of Fauquier Co., Va. (16 SEP 1854)

𝔇𝔞𝔦𝔩𝔶 𝔑𝔞𝔱𝔦𝔬𝔫𝔞𝔩 𝔍𝔫𝔱𝔢𝔩𝔩𝔦𝔤𝔢𝔫𝔠𝔢𝔯, Marriage and Death Notices, 1851-1854

MARRIAGE. On the 14th inst., by the Rev. Mr. Hodges, SYLVESTER CARROLL to Miss MARY DIAMOND, of Prince George's Co., Md. (16 SEP 1854)

MARRIAGE. On the 12th inst., by the Rev. Edward Ells, at Forest Home, Boone Co., Ky., GEORGE WM. RANSON, Esq., of Jefferson Co., Va., to OLIVIA M. TODD, daughter of Dr. B.F. Bedinger. (18 SEP 1854)

MARRIAGE. At Willard's Hotel, in this city, on Thursday, September 14th, by the Rev. A.F.N. Rolfe, of North Carolina, Mr. BUSHROD W. VICK to Miss EUDORA HIGGINS, all of Baltimore, Md. (18 SEP 1854)

DEATH. In this city yesterday [17 SEP 1854], in the 28th year of his age, JOSEPH A. KEENAN, M.D., late of this city, but formerly of Baltimore, where his funeral service will be performed, on Tuesday, 19th inst., in St. Peter's Church, Poppleton street, at 8 o'clock A.M. (18 SEP 1854)

DEATH. On the 7th inst., at Barrytown, Dutchess Co., N.Y., Mrs. HARRIET LEAVENWORTH, widow of the late Gen. Henry Leavenworth, U.S. Army [text continues]. (18 SEP 1854)

FUNERAL HONORS. If the Masons and Odd Fellows desired to present a striking illustration of the humanizing and truly philanthropic influences of their associates, they might point with no small degree of pride to the scenes of Sunday last [17 SEP 1854]. An humble member died on Saturday [16 SEP 1854--a very unpretending member, JAMES JACK — a man without rank, but one who was known to almost every body and whom every body respected... One hundred and sixty of his brethren of the Masonic Order and one hundred and fifty Odd Fellows assembled at the late residence of the deceased and attend his remains to Alexandria, where he formerly resided [text continues]. (19 SEP 1854)

MARRIAGE. On Monday, the 18th inst., by the Rev. Wentworth L. Childs, of St. Alban's Parish, D.C., OGDEN W. BLACKFAN, of Trenton, N.J., and MARY AGNES, daughter of Dr. T. Watkins, of this city. (19 SEP 1854)

MARRIAGE. On the 31st of July, by the Rev. Wm. Norwood, Pastor of Christ Church, Georgetown, JOSEPH T. COLDWELL, Esq., of Petersburg, Va., to VIRGINIA JOSEPHINE, youngest daughter of the late Wm. A. Williams, of this city. (19 SEP 1854)

MARRIAGE. At St. James Church, Richmond, Va., by the Rev. Dr. Empie, on the 14th inst., at 5 o'clock P.M., POLLARD WEBB, Esq., of Washington city, to Miss MILDRED C. CHRISTIAN, daughter of the late John H. Christian, of Richmond. (19 SEP 1854)

MARRIAGE. In Gardiner, Me., Wednesday, September 13th, by the Right Rev. George Burgess, Dr. W. McKENDREE TUCKER, of this city, to CAROLINE A., daughter of the late Capt. James Blish, of Hallowell. (19 SEP 1854)

DEATH. On the 13th inst., after twelve hours' illness, MARY ADELAIDE, the beloved daughter of Wm. A. and Frances E. Griffith. (19 SEP 1854)

DEATH. Suddenly, in this city, yesterday morning [18 SEP 1854], Mr. BENJAMIN HADLEY, aged 42, formerly of Boston. (19 SEP 1854)

DEATH. Departed this life, on the 9th of August, 1854, at his residence near Boonville, Mo., Col. THOMAS RUSSELL, late of Berkeley Co., Va., aged 56 years. (19 SEP 1854)

DEATH. On Saturday morning, 16th inst., FRANK, aged two years, son of J.P. and S.A. Keller, of this city. (19 SEP 1854)

MARRIAGE. On the 18th, by the Rev. James H. Brown, Mr. JOHN RUTHERFORD to Miss SARAH ANN RICHARDSON, all of Virginia. (20 SEP 1854)

Daily National Intelligencer, Marriage and Death Notices, 1851-1854

MARRIAGE. On the 19th inst., by the Rev. James H. Brown, Mr. JAMES H. POSEY to Miss MARY E. JEFFERSON, both of Alexandria, Va. (20 SEP 1854)

DEATH. In this city, on the 19th inst., after a lingering illness, of consumption, Mr. JOHN KERBY, in the 26th year of his age. The friends of the deceased are requested to attend his funeral from the Infirmary, on E street, between 4th and 5th, this afternoon at 4 o'clock. (20 SEP 1854)

DEATH. On the evening of the 8th inst., after a long and painful illness, of dropsy, Mr. FRANCIS H. DARNULL, aged 37 years. (20 SEP 1854)

DEATH OF A VALUABLE PUBLIC OFFICER. We are pained to announce the sudden death of Mr. JOHN L. BARNHILL, one of the principal accountants of the General Land Office, which took place about one o'clock on Monday night [18 SEP 1854], at his residence on the Island, in this city. He returned on Monday morning from a flying visit to the Saut Ste. Marie, Mich., and other points in the Northwest... He leaves a large circle of mourning friends... He was unmarried. (20 SEP 1854)

DEATH. On the morning of the 20th inst., near Davidsonville, Anne Arundel Co., Md., MARCELLUS GALLAHER, of this city, youngest son of John S. Gallaher, Esq., aged 23 years and 3 months, leaving a wife and one child, and numerous relatives and friends to mourn his early death. (21 and 22 SEP 1854)

DEATH. On the 5th of September, CATHARINE CHAUNCEY HAND, eldest daughter of the late Joseph W. Hand, of this city, aged 24 years [text continues]. (22 SEP 1854)

DEATH. At his late residence, Hermitage, Montgomery Co., Md., on the 20th inst., Mr. SAMUEL FITZHUGH, in the 68th year of his age. His friends and those of his family are requested to attend his funeral from the Church of the Ascension, H street, on Friday afternoon at 4 o'clock. (22 SEP 1854)

DEATH. On the 21st inst., JOHN IRVIN MILLER, of Missouri, in the 19th year of his age. His funeral will take place tomorrow morning at eight o'clock, from Mrs. Mary Harrod's, Fourth street, between New York avenue and K street, which his friends are invited to attend. (22 SEP 1854)

DEATH. At Edge Hill, Prince William Co., Va., on the evening of the 19th inst., HELEN, wife of John S. Ewell, and eldest daughter of N.M. McGregor, of this city, aged 25 years. (22 and 27 SEP 1854)

DEATH. Yesterday morning, 21st inst., JOHN SANDS, youngest child of Jas. S. and Elizabeth J. Holland, in his fourth hear. Funeral this afternoon, at three o'clock, from his parents' residence, No. 412 9th street, between H and I streets. Friends and acquaintances are respectfully invited to attend. (22 SEP 1854)

DEATH. At Leesburg, Va., on Thursday morning, September 14, in her second year, SALLY MOORE ORR, daughter of John M. and Orra L. Orr. (22 SEP 1854)

MARRIAGE. On the 21st inst., by the Rev. James H. Brown, Mr. ALFRED W. ANDREWS to Miss ANN VIRGINIA MOORE, both of Virginia. (23 SEP 1854)

MARRIAGE. On the 19th inst., by the Rev. T.B. Dooley, Mr. JOHN T. WEAVER, of California, to Miss VIRGINIA MACDANIEL, daughter of the late Ezekiel Macdaniel of Mason Co., Va. (23 SEP 1854)

DEATH. In this city, on the 21st inst., TIMOTHY J. TUOMY. *Requiescat in pace!* (23 SEP 1854)

DEATH. In this city, on the 21st inst., DORSEY BROWN, only child of James and Ann E. Smith, aged 22 months and 11 days. (23 SEP 1854)

Daily National Intelligencer, Marriage and Death Notices, 1851-1854

DEATH OF JOHN W. TAYLOR. We record in our paper today the death of the Hon. JOHN W. TAYLOR, for many years a leading and prominent statesman of New York. Mr. Taylor was born in Saratoga county in 1784 [text continues]. *Cleveland Herald.* (23 SEP 1854)

MARRIAGE. On Thursday, September 21, in St. Alban's Parish, by the Rev. Mr. Childs, ZACHARIAH COLLINS and NANCY BARBER, all of the District. (25 SEP 1854)

DEATH. On Sunday morning, at 1 o'clock, after a lingering illness, WINIFRED S., youngest daughter of Leonard and W.S. Harbaugh, aged two years and three months. Her funeral will take place from the residence of her parents, on F street, this (Monday) afternoon, at 3½ o'clock. The friends of the family are invited to attend. (25 SEP 1854)

DEATH. In Middleburg, Loudoun Co., Va., on Friday, the 15th inst., RICHARD HENRY, youngest child of Lieut. Daniel F. and Margaret A. Dulany, aged 13 months. (25 SEP 1854)

DEATH. On the 23d inst., after a lingering illness, MARY ELIZABETH, aged five years four months and twenty-eight days, daughter of Thos. F. and Margaret Stewart. (25 SEP 1854)

OBITUARY. The Hon. WILLIAM PLUMER, a distinguished statesman of New Hampshire, died at his residence in Epping, on the 18th inst., after an illness of about a week [text continues]. (25 SEP 1854)

OBITUARY. The Right Rev. FRANCIS XAVIER GARTLAND, Roman Catholic Bishop of the Diocese of Georgia, died at the residence of M. Prendergast, in Savannah, on the 20th inst., of yellow fever [text continues]. (25 SEP 1854)

OBITUARY. The New York papers announce the death of the Rt. Rev. JONATHAN MAYHEW WAINWRIGHT, D.D., Provisional Bishop for the Diocese of New York of the Protestant Episcopal Church [text continues]. (25 SEP 1854)

DEATH. In this city, during the night of the 22d inst., after a protracted illness, MARY ELLEN, consort of George Burns, in the 25th year of her age, with a bright hope of a blissful immortality. (26 SEP 1854)

DEATH. In this city, on the 23d inst., of consumption, VIRGINIA JOSEPHINE, wife of H.A. Hayden, and daughter of the Hon. Henry Dodge, aged 25 years and 5 months. (26 SEP 1854)

DEATH. In this city, on Thursday last, the 21st inst., JOHN IRVING MILLER, in the 19th year of his age, late of Nebraska Territory. It may be consoling to the parents and friends of this young man to know that during his illness every attention was paid him which the best medical attendance and nursing could effect. (26 SEP 1854)

DEATH. In Baltimore, on Friday evening last, the 22d inst., Mr. JOSHUA COLE, Jr., Printer, late of this city, in the 19th year of his age. Three weeks ago both of the young men whose deaths are above recorded [Miller and Cole], left Washington in fine health and spirits for a pleasure trip to Charleston, S.C., where they contracted the fever of which they died after their return. (26 SEP 1854)

DEATH. On Thursday, 21st inst., Mrs. JOHANNA O'REGAN, a native of Bantry, county of Cork, Ireland, aged sixty-three years. (26 SEP 1854)

DEATH. On Sunday, the 24th inst., KATE K., aged fourteen months, youngest child of James and Margaret Selden. The friends of the family are invited to attend her funeral on this (Tuesday) morning at 9 o'clock, from the residence of her parents, on I street, betwen 19th and 20th streets. (26 SEP 1854)

MARRIAGE. On Tuesday, September 26th, by the Rev. Mr. Dashiel, Mr. WARREN LOWE, of Prince George's Co., Md., to Mrs. LOUISA C. ALLEN, of this city. (27 SEP 1854)

Daily National Intelligencer, Marriage and Death Notices, 1851-1854

MARRIAGE. On the 18th inst., by the Rev. Mr. Alig, JAMES R. MAY to Miss MARY A. CHILDRESS, both of this city. (27 SEP 1854)

DEATH. In Georgetown, on Tuesday morning, 26th inst., Mrs. CHRISTINA HOBBS, in the 76th year of her age. Her funeral will take place this (Wednesday) afternoon, at 3½ o'clock, from her late residence, on the corner of Third and Warren streets, where her friends and relatives are requested to attend without further notice. (27 SEP 1854)

DEATH. In this city, on the 25th inst., in the 60th year of her age, Mrs. ANN, the wife of Mr. Jacob Kleiber. The friends of the family are respectfully invited to attend her funeral from the residence of her parents, on East Capitol street, Capitol Hill, at 4 o'clock this afternoon. (27 SEP 1854)

DEATH. Departed this life on Tuesday, the 19th of September, 1854, at Edge Hill, Prince William Co., Va., HELEN WOODS, wife of John S. Ewell, and daughter of N.M. McGregor, of Washington, D.C., aged 25 years and 17 days [text continues]. (27 SEP 1854)

MARRIAGE. At St. Matthew's Church, September 26th, by the Rev. Mr. Donelan, W.E. GREENWELL to MARGARET, youngest daughter of the late Nathaniel Manning, of Virginia. (28 SEP 1854)

DEATH. On the 30th of August last, in Berryville, Clarke Co., Va., Mr. B.H. SINNOTT, formerly of Washington, but for the last eight years a resident of Clarke Co., Va. (28 SEP 1854)

OBITUARY. Among other victims of the direful pestilence that is now scourging the South, we are called upon to chronicle the Right Rev. EDWARD BARRON, D.D., Missionary Bishop (Roman Catholic) of the West Coast of Africa, who died at Savannah on the 12th inst. [text continues]. (28 SEP 1854)

MARRIAGE. At the Wesley Chapel parsonage, on the 28th inst., by the Rev. James H. Brown, Mr. ROBERT COLE to Miss MARTHA SHERBERTT, both of Maryland. (29 SEP 1854)

MARRIAGE. On Thursday afternoon [28 SEP 1854], by the Rev. John C. Smith, Mr. JOHN SMITH to Mrs. PHOEBE ANN VIBBER, of New York. (29 SEP 1854)

DEATH. At "The Bower," Jefferson Co., Va., on Tuesday, the 12th of September, in the 78th year of her age, Mrs. NANCY CLAYTON KENNEDY, widow of the late John Kennedy. Mrs. Kennedy was a lady of very strong intellect, of varied accomplishments, and exalted character. For many years she resided in Baltimore, but for the last 35 years past has lived in Virginia. She leaves four sons: John P. and Anthony Kennedy, of Baltimore, and Andrew and Pendleton Kennedy, ov Virginia. (29 SEP 1854)

MARRIAGE. On the 28th inst., by the Rev. Jas. H. Brown, Mr. JAMES H. GRANGER to Miss MARGARET YOUNG, both of Washington, D.C. (30 SEP 1854)

MARRIAGE. At Colebrook, N.H., on the 26th September, by Rev. J.B. Hill, CORNELIUS B. ADAMS, Esq., of this city, to Miss MARTHA B. LOOMIS, daughter of Gen. L. Loomis, of Colebrook. (30 SEP 1854)

MARRIAGE. On the 28th inst., in the F Street Presbyterian Church of this city, by the Rev. P.D. Gurley, D.D., Rev. NATHAN C. CHAPIN, of Wisconsin, to Miss MARY A. FOUNTAIN. (30 SEP 1854)

MARRIAGE. In this city, on Thursday, the 28th inst., by the Rev. G.W. Samson, Mr. WILLIAM BEAGLE and Miss HENRIETTA BYER, both of Washington. (30 SEP 1854)

MARRIAGE. In Boston, September 13, 1854, by the Rev. R.W. Cushman, D.D., Mr. HIRAM CORSON, Jr., of Washington, to Mademoiselle CAROLINE ROLLIN, of Paris, France. (30 SEP 1854)

Daily National Intelligencer, Marriage and Death Notices, 1851-1854

DEATH. At Waco Village, McClellan Co., Tex., on the 29th July last, after a few days' illness of congestion of the brain, Dr. JONATHAN EDWARDS JACKSON, formerly of this city, youngest son of Mrs. Colonel Tuley, of Clarke Co., Va., and grandson of the late Rev. O.B. Brown, of this city. (30 SEP and 13 OCT 1854)

DEATH. On the 29th inst., Mrs. MARGARET DUCKWORTH, aged eighty-three years--a resident of this city for the last fifty years. Her friends and the friends of W.H. Gunnell are respectfully invited to attend her funeral Sunday, October 1st, at 4 o'clock P.M., without further notice, from C street, between 3d and 4½ streets. (30 SEP 1854)

DEATH. Yesterday morning, the 1st inst., Mrs. ANN BOYALL, at a very advanced age. Her funeral will take place this afternoon, at 3 o'clock, from her late residence, on B street north, Capitol Hill, where her friends and acquaintances are respectfully invited to attend without further notice. (2 OCT 1854)

DEATH. In this city, on the 1st inst., WILLIAM CASH, a native of the county of Wexford, Ireland, and for many years a resident of this city. His funeral will take place from St. Peter's Church, Capitol Hill, this evening, at 3 o'clock, where his friends are respectfully invited to attend. (2 OCT 1854)

MARRIAGES. On the 6th September, 1854, by the Rev. S.A.H. Marks, Mr. JAMES M. LARCOMB to Miss JANE CATHARINE WINDSOR, all of this city. On the 26th September, by the same, Mr. WM. CARRINGTON to SOPHIA E. WATSON. On the 3d inst., by the same, Mr. THOMAS PIERCE to Miss CHARITY ANN ALLEN, both of Prince George's Co., Md. (4 OCT 1854)

MARRIAGE. On the 3d inst., by the Rev. Andrew G. Carothers, Mr. CHARLES SCHUSSLER to Mrs. MARY HUDAL, all of this city. (4 OCT 1854)

MARRIAGE. In the Fourth Presbyterian Church, on Tuesday afternoon [3 OCT 1854], by the Rev. John C. Smith, JOHN T. MOSS, Esq., to ANN VIRGINIA, daughter of John G. Schott, all of this city. (4 OCT 1854)

MARRIAGE. In Baltimore, on the 3d inst., by the Rev. Mr. Morrison, at Christ Church, WILLIAM B. WALWORTH, of Plattsburg, N.Y., and JENNIE GRAY, daughter of the late Col. Henry W. Gray, of Baltimore. (5 OCT 1854)

MARRIAGE. At Wilmington, Del., on the 3d inst., by the Rev. A.D. Pollock, Mr. CHAMPION BISSELL, of New York city, to Miss MARY JOSEPHINE, youngest daughter of Hon. John Wales. (5 OCT 1854)

DEATH. On the 4th inst., Mrs. CATHARINE GIBSON, in her 85th year, a native of St. Mary's Co., Md., but for the last 50 years a resident of this District. Her funeral will take place from the residence of her son, R. Gibson, on the corner of D and 12th streets, at 10 o'clock this morning, which her friends are respectfully invited to attend. (5 OCT 1854)

DEATH. In this city, on the 4th inst., JAMES DAVIS, in the 71st year of his age. The funeral will take place from his late residence, on Seventh, between L and M streets. The friends and acquaintances are invited to attend. (5 OCT 1854)

DEATH. On Tuesday evening, the 3d inst., JOSEPH FREDERICK, only son of Joseph A. and Elizabeth G. Deeble, aged 21 months. The friends of the family are invited to attend his funeral, from his father's residence, on I, between Ninth and Tenth streets, this (Thursday) afternoon, at 4 o'clock. (5 OCT 1854)

MARRIAGE. At the National Hotel, on the 4th inst., by the Rev. James H. Brown, Mr. HENRY A. WARE to Miss JANE G. STARLING, both of Virginia. (6 OCT 1854)

Daily National Intelligencer, Marriage and Death Notices, 1851-1854

MARRIAGES. On the 3d inst., by the Rev. E.P. Phelps, Mr. WILLIAM W. HOLLINGSWORTH and Miss LAVINIA D., daughter of John M. Donn, Esq. On the 5th inst., by the same, at Foundry parsonage, Mr. JOHN W. CAMPBELL and Miss ALCINDA MOSS, both of Alexandria, Va. (6 OCT 1854)

MARRIAGE. On the 5th inst., by the Rev. Dr. Butler, of Trinity Church, Dr. DAVID PORTER HEAP to LIZZIE, daughter of John C. Bowyer, of this city. (6 OCT 1854)

DEATH. In this city yesterday, Mrs. CATHERINE FLINN, in the 89th year of her age, a native of Ireland, country of Wexford. The funeral will take place this afternoon, at 4 o'clock, from her residence on F street, near 11th. (6 OCT 1854)

DEATH. On the 5th inst., GEORGE NELSON, infant son of John A. and Dolly Ann Ruff, aged two years. The friends of the family are invited to attend the funeral this afternoon at 4 o'clock, from his parents' residence, on E, between 5th and 6th streets. (6 OCT 1854)

MARRIAGE. On the 4th inst., by the Rev. Mr. Gurley, Mr. JOHN G. CLARKE to BERTHA, youngest daughter of William Mechlin, Esq., all of this city. (7 and 9 OCT 1854)

THE LATE JOSIAH HOLBROOK. To the Editors of the *National Intelligencer*: Gentlemen: A few months ago I read in the columns of your excellent journal a record of the death of Mr. JOSIAH HOLBROOK. He had been missed from his lodgings at Lynchburg, Va. [text continues]. (7 OCT 1854)

MARRIAGE. On the 11th of September last, near McConnellsville, Ohio, HENRY C. DERRICK, son of the late William S. Derrick, Esq., of this city, to EMMA, daughter of Gen. B.W. Conklin, of that State. (9 OCT 1854)

MARRIAGE. At St. John's Church, in Georgetown, on Wednesday, the 4th inst., by the Rev. Mr. Tillinghast, Rev. JOHN D. POWELL, of Virginia, to ANNIE LEAKE, daughter of the late John M. Hepburn, Esq. (9 OCT 1854)

DEATH. On Friday, October 6th, ANN ELIZABETH, infant daughter of Charles H. Lane, aged six months. "*For of such is the Kingdom of Heaven.*" (9 OCT 1854)

MARRIAGE. On Tuesday, 3d October, in Trinity Church, New York, by the Rev. Smith Pyne, of Washington, Capt. CHARLES WILKES, U.S.N., to MARY H. BOLTON, daughter of the late Henry Lynch, Esq., of New York. (10 OCT 1854)

MARRIAGE. On Friday, the 6th inst., by the Rev. F. Israel, THOMAS BROWN to Mrs. NANCY WYMAN, all of this city. (10 OCT 1854)

DEATH. On the 9th inst., SARAH ANN WHITNEY, aged 21 years. Her friends and acquaintances are respectfully requested to attend her funeral from the residence of her father, Joseph Whitney, on C between 12th and 13th streets, on Wednesday, at 3 o'clock P.M., without further notice. (10 OCT 1854)

DEATH. On the 9th inst., Mr. CHARLES STEWART, in the 60th year of his age, a native of Charles Co., Md., but for many years a resident of Georgetown, D.C., and for the last five years a resident of this city. His funeral will take place this afternoon at 3 o'clock, from his late residence on the corner of 11th and R streets northwest, to which his friends are respectfully invited to attend. (10 OCT 1854)

DEATH. In the county of Fauquier, Va., on the 5th inst., aged three years, MARY SELDEN, daughter of Richard M. and Edmonia Heath. (10 OCT 1854)

OBITUARY. Died, yesterday, in this city, WILLIAM DARBY, Esq., in the 80th year of his age. Mr. D. was a native of Pennsylvania, but in his infancy removed with his parents to the Ohio, when the whole trans-

Daily National Intelligencer, Marriage and Death Notices, 1851-1854

Alleghany country was a wilderness, inhabited only by fierce and savage tribes of Indians [text continues]. His funeral will take place this afternoon, at four o'clock, from Mrs. Clare's boarding-house, which his friends are invited to attend without further notice. (10 OCT 1854)

MARRIAGE. In Groton, Mass., by the Rev. Edwin Bulkley, JOHN KENDALL, of this city, to ELIZABETH LAWRENCE, daughter of Joshua Green, M.D. (11 OCT 1854)

MARRIAGE. On Sunday, July 30th, by Rev. Dr. Scott, Mr. CHAS. WHEATLEIGH, of London, Eng., to Miss SALLY J. ANSEL, of Baltimore, Md. (11 OCT 1854)

DEATH. WM. JAQUELINE TAYLOR, Esq., local editor of the Richmond "Penny Post," died on the 9th inst., after a brief illness. (11 OCT 1854)

MARRIAGE. In St. John's Church, Georgetown, on the 10th inst., by the Rev. N.P. Tillinghast, CHARLES R. SHERMAN, Esq., of Washington, to SALLY, daughter of the late Peyton R. Page, of Virginia. (12 OCT 1854)

MARRIAGE. On the 5th inst., by the Rev. James H. Brown, Mr. JOHN T. DANIEL to Miss OPHELIA E. FAULKNER, both of Virginia. (12 OCT 1854)

MARRIAGE. Also, on the 8th inst., by the Rev. James H. Brown, Mr. GEORGE J. LYNCH to Miss ELIZABETH ANN OSBORNE, all of this city. (12 OCT 1854)

DEATH. On the 11th inst., JAMES EDMONSTON, in the 35th year of his age. His funeral will take place from his late residence, on Massachusetts avenue, this afternoon, at 3 o'clock, to which his friends are respectfully invited to attend. (12 OCT 1854)

DEATH. In this city, on the morning of the 10th inst., Dr. LOUIS R. FECHTIG, in the 31st year of his age, leaving an afflicted wife and two infant children to mourn their great bereavement. Dr. Fechtig had but recently removed to this city and settled himself in the practice of medicine, where his many noble qualities, both of head and heart, had already won him warm and admiring friends. (12 OCT 1854)

DEATH. In Mobile, on the 9th inst., of yellow fever, CHARLES H. CARMICHAEL, son of Dr. E.H. and Sarah Carmichael, aged 22 years. (12 OCT 1854)

DEATH. At Lafayette, Ind., on Tuesday, October 3d, ALBERT HEBARD, the only son of Roswell C. and Annie Ellsworth Smith. (12 OCT 1854)

DEATH. On Tuesday evening, the 10th inst., at 9 o'clock, of typhoid fever, Mr. JNO. S. MARLL, in the 39th year of his age. The friends and acquaintances of the family are requested to attend his funeral tomorrow at 2 o'clock P.M. from his late residence on K, between 3d and 4th streets. (12 OCT 1854)

MARRIAGE. On the 12th inst., at Foundry parsonage, by Rev. E.P. Phelps, Mr. FRANCIS W. ASHLEY and Miss MARGARET D. GREGORY, both of Alexandria, Va. (13 OCT 1854)

DEATH. On the 11th October, WILLIAM FRUSH, of apoplexy, in his 77th year, a native of Baltimore county, but for the last fifty-odd years a resident of Georgetown, D.C. His friends and acquaintances are requested to attend his funeral from his late residence, Green street, this afternoon at 3½ o'clock. (13 OCT 1854)

OBITUARY. Dr. JONATHAN E. JACKSON, of Millwood, Va., died at Waco Village, McClellan Co., Tex., on the 29th July last, after a few days' illness, of congestion of the brain. Dr. Jackson graduated at Princeton College in the year 1849, and received his medical degree at the University of Pennsylvania in 1852 [text continues]. (13 OCT 1854)

Daily National Intelligencer, Marriage and Death Notices, 1851-1854

MARRIAGE. On the 10th inst., at the Church of the Epiphany, by the Rev. J.W. French, Dr. T.C. McINTIRE to SARAH E., daughter of Col. John S. Williams. (14 OCT 1854)

MARRIAGE. At Oakwood, on the 11th inst., by the Rev. Wm. M. Nelson, JOHN R. MITCHELL, of Washington, to FANNIE PERKINS, daughter of Dr. John W. Gantt, of Albemarle Co., Va. (14 OCT 1854)

MARRIAGE. On Thursday, the 11th inst., by the Rev. G.W. Samson, Mr. GEO. W. MITCHELL, of Annapolis, Md., to Miss MARTHA A. BRAYFIELD, niece of Mr. Samuel [Devaughn], of Washington, D.C. (14 OCT 1854)

MARRIAGE. On Tuesday evening, 10th inst., at St. James Church, Richmond, Va., by the Rev. George Cummins, Lieut. JAMES P. ROY, U.S. Army, to Miss KATE S., eldest daughter of David Bridges, Esq. (16 OCT 1854)

MARRIAGE. On the 4th inst., at Rosemont, by the Rev. F.N. Whitele, ISAAC TYSON, Esq., of Baltimore, and Miss FANNIE H., eldest daughter of Howard F. Thornton, Esq., of Clarke Co., Va. (16 OCT 1854)

DEATH. In this city, on the 13th inst., VIRGINIA, wife of William Collins, in the 27th year of her age. (16 OCT 1854)

DEATH. On the 14th inst., ESTELLE, youngest child of P. Louis and Louisa M. Rodier, aged 10 months. (16 OCT 1854)

DEATH. In Bennington, Ver., on the 7th inst., Gen. HENRY ROBINSON, in the 56th year of his age. Gen. Robinson was extensively and favorably known, and leaves many sincere friends in this city to sympathize with his relatives in their loss. (16 OCT 1854)

MARRIAGE. In this city, on Sunday, October 15th, by Rev. G.W. Samson, Mr. WILLIAM JAMES and Miss MARGARET BALLENTINE. (17 OCT 1854)

MARRIAGE. At Beverly, Va., October 12th, Miss E.B. FRAME to Mr. A.R.H. RANSON, both of Jefferson Co., Va. (17 OCT 1854)

DEATH. On the 16th inst., GEO. W. THOMPSON, in the 43d year of his age. The friends of the family are respectfully invited to attend his funeral from his late residence, corner of L street south and 3d street west, this day at 3 P.P. (17 OCT 1854)

MARRIAGE. In this city, October 17th, by the Rev. Stephen P. Hill, at the 10th Street Baptist Church, Mr. JOSEPH KNOWLES LEWIS and Miss VIRGINIA CLARKE, all of Washington. (18 OCT 1854)

DEATH. On the 17th inst., MARY, consort of Edward Cowling, in the 58th year of her age, a native of Cornwall, England, but for the last 22 years a resident of this District. Her funeral will take place this afternoon at 3 o'clock from her late residence, on G, between 13th and 14th streets, which her friends are respectfully invited to attend. (18 OCT 1854)

DEATH. On Tuesday, the 17th inst., MARY JANE, wife of A.H. Brown, of this city, and eldest daughter of the late A.B. Murrey, of Baltimore. (18 OCT 1854)

DEATH. On Wednesday, October 18th, Miss VIRGINIA A. HOWELL, in the 16th year of her age. Her funeral will take place this (Thursday) afternoon at 3 o'clock, from the residence of her mother, on 9th, between G and H streets. The friends of the family will attend without further notice. (19 OCT 1854)

Daily National Intelligencer, Marriage and Death Notices, 1851-1854

DEATH. At Thomaston, Me., on the 12th inst., Mrs. LUCY F.K. THATCHER, in the 87th year of her age. Mrs. Thatcher was the daughter of Maj. Gen. Henry Knox, of the Revolutionary army, and mother of Lieut. H.K. Thatcher, of the U.S. Navy. She was a lady of many and rare accomplishments and of great excellence of character. Her taste and intellect, though highly cultivated, had not been educated to the neglect of her heart, for she was eminently a religious woman. She died where, of all places, she would have chosen to die--in her own house; the noble old mansion erected by her venerable parent, Gen. Knox, the friend and intimate associate of Washington. That elegant old house, with all its revolutionary treasures, in which her parents breathed their last, was her home during the latter years of her widowhood; and to her, as the last surviving child of Gen. Knox, were all its treasures entrusted. Her circle of friends was large, and embraced in it some of the best and most distinguished men and women of our country. *Boston Traveller*. (19 OCT 1854)

DEATH. On the 12th inst., at Brooklyn, HENRY WALLER, Esq., civil engineer, at Baton Rouge, La., eldest son of the late Henry Waller, of Sing Sing, N.Y. (19 OCT 1854)

DEATH. Of typhoid fever, at Salem, the residence of his father, on Tuesday, the 11th inst., ABNER FLOWEREE, in the 27th year of his age. Intelligent, enterprising, and public-spirited, he was widely known and largely esteemed in the county. Agreeable and gentlemanly in his deportment, warm and true in his friendships, he had attached to him many devoted friends, while his domestic virtues and generous traits of character made him the admired centre of the family circle, the much-loved son and brother. (20 OCT 1854)

MARRIAGE. On Thursday, the 19th inst., by the Rev. Mr. Stanley, NORVAL WILSON BURCHEL, of Alexandria, Va., and Miss SARAH F. LANDON, of this city. (21 OCT 1854)

MARRIAGE. On the 9th July, by the Rev. Mr. Doll, Mr. J.W. ROWAN to Mrs. AGNES McGILL, both of this city. (21 OCT 1854)

MARRIAGE. In New York city, on the 12th inst., by the Rev. Edwin Harwood, Rector of the Church of the Incarnation, LEWIS JOHNSON DAVIS, of Washington, D.C., and MARGARET JANE, daughter of Charles M. Keller, Esq., of New York. (21 OCT 1854)

DEATH. On Friday, October 13, at the residence of her son, Dr. R.W. Wheat, near Dumfries, Va., Mrs. RACHEL WHEAT, aged 84 years. She was for many years a resident of this city, and for more than half a century a worthy and devoted member of the Methodist Church. (21 OCT 1854)

MARRIAGE. At Georgetown, D.C., on Tuesday, the 17th inst., by the Rev. B.F. Brooke, Mr. D.W. EDMONSTON, Jr., and Miss MARION J. DAW, of the above place. (23 OCT 1854)

DEATH. On the 14th inst., at the residence of Dr. Bayne, in Prince George's Co., T.S. HOXTON, M.D., in the 25th year of his age. Dr. H. graduated at the University of Maryland, in the session of 1851, with the highest honors. He returned home, full of hope and professional aspirations, and entered upon the duties of the practice. During the brief period that his health permitted him to be engaged in this pursuit he made a most favorable impression in the community in which he was located. His sound judgment, superiority of mind, with an instinctive perception, would have led to high professional distinction; and his courteous deportment, sincerity of character, and refinement of manners, with the sympathies of a benevolent heart, bestowing attention upon all, could not fail to win a secure place in the affections of those who came within the range of his influence. Society will long deplore his loss. None knew him but to love him. (23 OCT 1854)

DEATH. Death of the Rev. Dr. Jennings. The REV. SAMUEL K. JENNINGS, M.D., died at Baltimore on Thursday at the age of 84 years. Few men were more generally known in the Methodist Church than the deceased. He was one of the founders of the Methodist Protestant Church, and for a number of years held a professorship in the Philadelphia Medical College. (23 OCT 1854)

Daily National Intelligencer, Marriage and Death Notices, 1851-1854

DEATH. On Sunday, the 22d inst., WILLIAM HUNTER, Esq., of this city, in the 87th year of his age. The subject of the above notice was born at Brunswick, N.J. His youth was mainly spent in England, after having been captured by a French man-[of]-war, and, with his parents, carried into France. Being left an orphan at an early age in a foreign land, he was placed in a printing office, where he served the usual period and acquired a knowledge of the printing art. In 1793 he returned to the U.S. and established a French and American paper in Philadelphia, and became associated in business with Matthew Carey, with whom his intimacy and friendship continued uninterrupted to the dying hour of that useful man. In 1795, Mr. Hunter removed to Washington, Pa., and established the "*Telegraph*." In 1797 he married Anne Morrison, of Bedford, Pa., (who lives to mourn his loss,) and removed to Washington, Ky., where he established the "*Mirror*." Removing subsequently to Frankfort, in the same State, he published the "*Palladium*," and for ten consecutive years was elected State Printer. Early in Gen. Jackson's administration, Col. Hunter removed to this city, and (in 1829) received an appointment in the Fourth Auditor's office, which he retained to the time of his death. Although for several years previous to his decease the subject of this notice confined his attention to those official duties which were congenial to his declining days, the talents and energy which characterized him early in life found occupation in a much wider field of action, and acquired for him extensive influence in the earlier days of the Republic. Having lived an irreproachable life, and employed the greater portion of a century in honorable and useful pursuits, he has ceased from his labors with the respect and esteem of all who knew his worth. The funeral will take place this afternoon, from his late residence on Twelfth, between H and I streets, which his friends are invited to attend. (24 OCT 1854)

DEATH. In this city, on the 23d inst., SPENCER, the only child of Archibald and Ruth Roane, aged 23 months. The friends of the family are respectfully invited to attend his funeral from Mrs. Gassaway's, D street, this day at 3 o'clock P.M. (24 OCT 1854)

DEATH. On the 23d inst., Dr. RICHARD O. COCHRANE, only surviving brother of Jno. T. Cochrane, Esq., of this city, in the 31st year of his age. His friends and acquaintances and those of the family are respectfully invited to attend his funeral from the residence of his brother-in-law, Mr. James A. Magruder, West street, Georgetown, at 3½ o'clock P.M., this day. (25 OCT 1854)

DEATH. On the 23d inst., after a lingering illness of four months, AGRICOL FAVIER, in the 57th year of his age. The friends and acquaintances of the family are respectfully invited to attend his funeral from his late residence, on this day, at 10 A.M., without further notice. (25 OCT 1854)

DEATH. In Georgetown, October 6th, after a brief but painful illness, in the 63d year of his age, FRANCIS LOWE DARNALL, of Prince George's Co., formerly of Anne Arundel Co., Md., leaving a wife and large family to deplore his death, and all who lived as neighbors to him sympathizing deeply with them. (26 OCT 1854)

DEATH. On Wednesday, October 25th, after a lingering illness, JAMES QUINN, in the 16th year of his age. The friends of the family are invited to attend his funeral, from the house of Mr. Thomas Gallagher, on 4th, between G and H streets, this afternoon at 3½ o'clock. (26 OCT 1854)

DEATH. In this city yesterday [26 OCT 1854], after fifteen days of intense suffering, REBECCA JANE, aged two years and nearly two months, daughter of Joseph L. and Melinda Williams. (26 OCT 1854)

MARRIAGES. At Chantilly, Fairfax Co., Va., on the 19th inst., by the Rev. R. Post, D.D., of Charleston, S.C., WILLIAM M. POST, M.D., of S.C., to MARY C. STUART. At the same time and place, by the Rev. R.T. Brown, the Rev. ADDISON B. ATKINS, of Philadelphia, to ELLEN C. STUART, both daughters of the late Chas. Calvert Stuart, Esq. (27 OCT 1854)

Daily National Intelligencer, Marriage and Death Notices, 1851-1854

DEATH. Yesterday afternoon, the 26th inst., after a long and painful illness, Mrs. SARAH JANE HAMMOND, in the 38th year of her age. The friends and acquaintances of the family are requested to attend her funeral this afternoon at 3 o'clock, from the residence of her mother, Mrs. Tate, on D, between 6th and 7th streets. (27 OCT 1854)

DEATHS. In Georgetown, on Wednesday, the 25th inst., Mrs. ISABELLA H. BEMIS, wife of Mr. N.P. Bemis; and on the 26th inst., Mrs. FRANCES ANNETTE TYLER, wife of Mr. Wm. W. Tyler, both daughters of the late Carter L. Stevenson, of Fredericksburg, Va. The funeral of Mrs. Bemis and Mrs. Tyler will take place this morning at 11 o'clock, from the residence of Mr. Tyler, on Frederick street, near the corner of First street, Georgetown. (27 OCT 1854)

DEATH. At Baltimore, on the 25th inst., WILLIAM SCHROEDER, Esq., well known as among the oldest and most estimable citizens of that city. He was for many years engaged in mercantile pursuits, but was recently, and until a short time since, Secretary of the National Fire Insurance Company. (27 OCT 1854)

DEATH. At Oak Hill, Montgomery Co., Md., on the 24th inst., MARY LOUISA, daughter of Edmund H. and Emily Brooke, aged 7 years and 7 months. (27 OCT 1854)

MARRIAGE. On Thursday, 26th inst., by the Rev. Mr. Hodges, SAMUEL CROSS to Miss VICTORIA J. MILLER, all of this city. (28 OCT 1854)

DEATH. In this city, on Friday, the 27th inst., Mrs. MARY MARGARET JULLIEN, aged 77 years, a native of France, but for the last 52 years a resident of this city. Her friends and acquaintances are invited to attend her funeral from her late residence on Thirteenth street, on Sunday next, the 29th inst., at 2 o'clock. (28 OCT 1854)

DEATH. On Thursday night, October 26, NELLIE L., eldest daughter of Dr. J.L. Fox, U.S.N., aged six years and seven months. The friends of the family are invited to attend her funeral on Saturday, at 3½ o'clock, from the residence of her grandfather, Commodore Morris. (28 OCT 1854)

DEATH. On the 27th inst., AMELIA R., daughter of Dwight R. and Marceila Waters, aged 22 months. The friends and acquaintances are respectfully invited to attend the funeral this afternoon, at 3 o'clock, on 8th, between M and N streets. (28 OCT 1854)

MARRIAGE. At Honeywood, Va., on the evening of the 24th inst., by the Rev. D. Francis Sprigg, WILLIAM LEIGH to MARY WHITE COLSTON, daughter of the late Edw. Colston, Esq. (30 OCT 1854)

MARRIAGE. On Thursday, the 26th inst., at Frederick, Md., by the Rev. Mr. Atkins, JOSEPH C. ISAAC, of Washington, D.C., to Miss MARIA L.B. MACGILL, of Frederick, Md. (30 OCT 1854)

DEATH. On Saturday, the 28th inst., Mr. MICHAEL P. MOHUN, aged 30 years and seven months. The friends and acquaintances are respectfully invited to attend his funeral this afternoon at 2 o'clock, from his late residence on 11th street east, near the Navy Yard bridge, without further notice. (30 OCT 1854)

DEATH. At three o'clock, yesterday morning [29 OCT 1854], after a long and painful illness, LAWRENCE O'BRIEN, a native of Ireland, county Wexford, aged thirty-three years. His funeral will take place today, (Monday,) at three o'clock P.M., from his late residence on Maryland avenue, near 7th street. (30 OCT 1854)

DEATH. At his residence in Woodsfield, Ohio, on the 23d inst., after a lingering illness, Hon. JOSEPH MORRIS, aged fifty-nine years. The deceased was a native of [Greene] Co., Pa., but emigrated to Ohio at an early period in her history. He represented his district in the 28th and 29th Congresses with much honor to himself and to the entire satisfaction of his constituents. He was a man of integrity, ability, and spotless purity of character. In both public and private life he enjoyed in an eminent degree the esteem and confidence of the people [prose continues]. (30 OCT 1854)

MARRIAGE. On the morning of the 26th of October, by the Rev. J.A. Russell, JOHN TAYLOR [sic], of Chatterton, to MARY WILLIS LEWIS, daughter of Daingerfield Lewis, Esq., of "Marmion," all of the county of King George [Co.], Va. (31 OCT and 9 DEC 1854)

MARRIAGE. At Norwich, N.Y., on the 24th inst., Dr. S.A.H. McKIM, of Washington, to Miss CAROLINE L. GIBBS, of the former place. (31 OCT 1854)

DEATH. Yesterday morning, the 30th inst., Mrs. M.D.V. KING, wife of James A. King, of a brief illness, in the 18th year of her age. The friends of the family will please attend her funeral on Tuesday, the 31st inst., at 3 o'clock, from the residence of her father, Joseph Peck, No. 527 H street, between 6th and 7th streets. (31 OCT 1854)

DEATH. In this city yesterday morning, the 30th inst., at 3 o'clock, FRANK STAKELY, aged eight months, son of P.R. and Cornelia M. Wilson. The friends of the family are respectfully invited to attend the funeral, from the residence of his parents, 426 11th street, between H and I streets, this afternoon at 3½ o'clock. (31 OCT 1854)

DEATH. On the 23d inst., at St. Augustine, Fla., after a short illness, Mrs. RACHEL PARKER MILLER, aged 25 years, wife of Andrew J. Miller, Esq., of that city, and only daughter of Dr. John Westcott, Surveyor General of Florida. Mrs. M. spent the past fall with her friends in this city, and left here some four weeks since in good health. Her sudden decease will be severely felt by her numerous friends and relatives in this city and in the States of Pennsylvania, New York and New Jersey, her native State; but they have the consolation that she was an exemplary Christian, and left this world with full faith of going to a better and happier sphere. (31 OCT 1854)

MARRIAGE. Yesterday afternoon [31 OCT 1854], in this city, by Elder R.C. Leachman, Mr. WYATT S. BERRY, of Vandalia, Ill., and Miss MARY ELIZABETH MOORE, of Washington. (1 NOV 1854)

DEATH. In this city, of typhoid fever, THOMAS BOOTH ROBERTS, in the 44th year of his age. His remains were taken to Philadelphia and interred on the 28th October ult., in Laural Hill cemetery. (2 NOV 1854)

DEATH. On the 30th ult. [30 OCT 1854], at the residence of Mr. John Mellor, Maryland avenue and Tenth street east, in the 19th year of his age, EMILY MARY DUNNE, of disease of the heart. (2 NOV 1954)

DEATH. Died, on the 6th of October, of cholera, at St. Paul, Minn., WASHINGTON TERRETT, in the 83d year of his age, after an illness of four days. At the time of his death Mr. Terrett was engaged on duty in the Pay Department of the U.S. Army. Mr. Terrett was one of four brothers who, within the last nine years, have been in the military service of the U.S., the sons of the late Capt. Geo. Hunter Terrett, of Fairfax Co., Va. They were all distinguished for soldierly bearing and manly qualities. Three of this gallant band met death in early manhood. Capt. Burdett A. Terrett, of the 1st dragoons, accidentally shot himself with a pistol at Ft. Scott, Mo., while dismounting from his horse, in the spring of 1845. Lieut. John Chapman Terrett, Adjutant 1st infantry, was killed on the 21st September, 1846, while gallantly fighting at the battle of Monterey. The sole survivor is Brvt. Maj. George Terrett, of the marines, now stationed at the Washington Navy Yard.

Upon the increase of the army during the war in Mexico, Washington Terrett, was appointed 2d Lieut. of the Voltigeur Regiment. He served for some months as quartermaster till appointed adjutant, in which capacity he served till the disbandment of his regiment at the close of the war. He was engaged in four of the decisive battles in the valley of Mexico. He was wounded at Molino del Rey, and highly distinguished in the report of his Colonel for courage and good conduct in the storming of Chepultepec. His brother, Maj. Terrett, won his laurels at the same battle on the opposite side of the Fort.

As a soldier he gained the respect of all by his faithful and devoted attention to every duty, not only on the battle-field, but on guard and at drill. Brave, modest, patient, and humane, he was both beloved and respected by his men.

As a man, he was honorable, upright, sincere, simple, and unobtrusive in tastes and conduct. He had no enemies and many friends.

As a comrade and friend, he was constant and true, generous and considerate, as forgiving to others as he was slow to take offence himself. His virtues were sterling and manly, now showy, not striking at the first glance, but, winning their way slowly and surely, he grappled the hearts of his friends and "hooks of steel."

Under the recent loss of a comrade, knit to the heart by the closest ties of friendship and esteem, linked to the memory with proud associations of common danger and common victory, it is easy to indulge in the extravagant expression of regret or praise; but all who knew the man will recognize in this tribute the strict and simple truth. (2 NOV 1854)

MARRIAGE. At the Church of the Advent, in the city of Boston, on the 1st inst., by the Right Rev. Bishop Southgate, EZRA WILLIAMS, Esq., of this city, to Miss SARAH TOWNSEND, of Medfield, Norfolk Co., Mass. (3 NOV 1854)

MARRIAGE. In F Street Church, on the 31st ult. [31 OCT 1854], by the Rev. J.M. Henry, Miss ESTHER A. NUGENT, formerly of Harrisburg, Pa., to Mr. CHARLES STOTT, of this city. (3 NOV 1854)

MARRIAGE. On the 2d inst., by the Rev. Mr. Reese, Mr. CHAS. TEMPLE WOOD to Miss SARAH AMANDA RATCLIFFE, daughter of Mr. Joseph Ratcliffe, all of this city. (3 NOV 1854)

MARRIAGE. On the 31st October, at Trinity Church, by the Rev. Mr. Clarke, Mr. JOHN S. GUYTHER to Miss SARAH M. HOLTON, both of St. Mary's Co., Md. (3 NOV 1854)

DEATH. In this city, on the morning of the 30th of October, Mrs. LOUISA M., wife of Mr. John M. McFarland, of this city, in the 26th year of her age. Her end was peace. (3 NOV 1854)

DEATH. Died, at the residence of his son-in-law, Dr. John H. Thomas, in the Parish of St. Martin, La., on the 5th ult. [5 OCT 1854], Mr. EDWARD J. HEARD, at the age of seventy-two years. Mr. Heard was born in Charles Co., Md. In the year 1837 he removed to Attakapas, and in 1838 commenced establishing his plantation on Lake Catahoula. Mr. Heard was a man of exceedingly frail constitution, but possessed of indomitable energy and persevering and untiring industry [text continues]. (3 NOV 1854)

MARRIAGE. On the 2d inst., by the Rev. W.F. Speaks, WM. C. HARPER and ANN ELIZA SPEAKS, all of Washington. (4 NOV 1854)

DEATH. On the 3d inst., SARAH J. KEITH, youngest daughter of the late John and Margaret Keith, in the 17th year of her age. Her friends are respectfully invited to attend her funeral this (Saturday) afternoon at 3 o'clock, from the residence of her Uncle, John Tretler, on 9th street, between G and H. (4 NOV 1854)

DEATH. At Byron, Ogle Co., Ill., on the 21st of October, after a brief illness, Mr. DAVID ROWLAND, of this city, in the 36th year of his age. (4 NOV 1854)

MARRIAGE. In Norfolk, by the Rev. Mr. O'Keefe, Mr. RICHARD G. BROUGHTON, Jr., to Miss EMILY R., daughter of Wm. Ward, Esq. (6 NOV 1854)

DEATH. After a few hours' illness, at his late residence on Capitol Hill, in this city, on Friday last [3 NOV 1854], WM. PARKER ELLIOT, Esq., Architect, leaving a wife and six children and a large circle of relations and friends to lament his sudden and premature death in the meridian of life and usefulness. Mr. Elliot was in the 46th year of his age, and, although a native of New Jersey, had been a resident of this city nearly all his life. In the relations of husband, father, friend, and citizen his character was most exemplary and

Daily National Intelligencer, Marriage and Death Notices, 1851-1854

without reproach. He was during several years surveyor of the city of Washington, in which trust he gave evidence of his talents as a civil engineer and of his official integrity. His funeral will take place, from his late residence on Capitol Hill to St. Peter's Church, this morning at nine o'clock. The friends of the family are respectfully invited to attend. (6 NOV 1854) The funeral of the late Wm. P. Elliot, which was yesterday postponed at the suggestion of some of his numerous friends, will, after a full consultation with his attending physicians and several medical and other friends take place from the late residence of the deceased, at 9 o'clock this day, (Tuesday,) on which melancholy occasion the friends of the family are invited to attend. (7 NOV 1854)

DEATH. On Sunday, the 5th inst., LOUIS VIVANS DRURY, aged eighteen months. His funeral will take place from St. Matthew's Church this day (Monday), at 2½ o'clock P.M. (6 NOV 1854)

DEATH. Saturday morning [4 NOV 1854], in this city, after brief but excessive suffering, KATE DOUGLAS, aged three years and six months, daughter of Joseph L. and Melinda Williams. This is the second victim of scarlet fever in this household within nine days. Rebecca Jane is scarcely cold in her grave when the sister, Katy, follows to the gloom of earth and glory of Heaven; "Katy darling," (as the bright and joyous little creature sportively called herself.) Friends are invited to attend the funeral this day, at 12 o'clock, from Mr. Williams's residence, 367 C street. (6 NOV 1854)

DEATH. On Saturday, the 4th inst., ALICE, only daughter of George and Mary E. Emmerich, aged 5 years 1 month and 19 days. (6 NOV 1854)

MARRIAGE. On the 31st ult. [31 OCT 1854], by the Rev. Charles A. Davis, Mr. SOUTHEY S. PARKER to Miss ISABELLA WATERS, all of this city. (7 NOV 1854)

DEATH. At Alexandria, Va., Friday last, 3d inst., CAROLINE HUNTINGTON, aged one year, only daughter of J.H. and Mariana B. Lathrop. (7 NOV 1854)

MARRIAGE. On Tuesday afternoon [7 NOV 1854], by Rev. J.C. Smith, Dr. THOS. R. CHEW, of New Orleans, to Miss MARY CAROLINE, daughter of E.B. Grayson, Esq., of this city. (8 NOV 1854)

MARRIAGE. On Tuesday, the 7th inst., in the Fourth Presbyterian Church, by the Rev. John C. Smith, W. BLAIR LORD, of Baltimore, to LOUISA L. WILLIS, of Washington. (8 NOV 1854)

DEATH. On the 6th inst., at his late residence, near Bladensburg, Mr. JOHN BRERETON, in the 42d year of his age. His funeral will take place this afternoon, at two o'clock. His friends and those of the family are respectfully invited to meet at J.F. Harvey's, (Undertaker,) No. 410 Seventh street, at one o'clock, where hacks will be in readiness to convey them to his late residence. (8 NOV 1854)

DEATH. In Alexandria, Va., on the 3d inst., HORACE HOLMES MOSS, youngest son of John M. Johnson, Postmaster of the House of Representatives U.S., aged two years and six months. (8 NOV 1854)

MARRIAGE. At Trinity Church, on the 7th inst., by the Rev. Mr. Clark, HENRY D. HATTON, Esq., of Prince George's Co., Md., to Miss SARAH C. WILSON, of this city. (9 NOV 1854)

MARRIAGE. At Keokuk, Iowa, October 19th, by Rev. J.T. Umstead, ARTHUR WOLCOTT, Esq., to CLARA, daughter of the late Brigadier General Belknap, U.S. Army. (9 NOV 1854)

DEATH. At St. Augustine, Fla., on the 22d of October, Mr. BURWELL STARK RANDOLPH, in the 54th year of his age. (9 NOV 1854)

DEATH. On Monday, the 6th inst., of consumption, ADDISON CONWAY, in the 46th year of his age. (10 NOV 1854)

Daily National Intelligencer, Marriage and Death Notices, 1851-1854

MARRIAGE. In Boston, on the 30th of October, by the Rt. Rev. Bishop Fitzpatrick, EDW'D GASSETT, Esq., to MARIA W. PERCIVAL, adopted daughter of Capt. John Percival, of the U.S. Navy. (11 NOV 1854)

DEATH. In this city, on the 9th inst., GEO. JOHNSON, Esq., aged 71 years. His funeral will take place from his late residence on K street, this day, the 11th inst., at 10 o'clock A.M. His friends and acquaintances are invited to attend. (11 NOV 1854)

DEATH. In Georgetown, on Friday morning, the 10th inst., Capt. CHARLES CRUIKSHANK, in the 61st year of his age. His friends and those of the family are invited to attend his funeral, from his late dwelling near St. John's Church, Georgetown, at three o'clock P.M. this day, the 11th inst. (11 NOV 1854)

DEATH. At his residence in this city, on the 2d inst., of dropsy of the chest, WILLIAM LEE BOAK, Esq., formerly of Berkeley Co., Va., aged 49 years. Mr. Boak had been for three years a highly respectable and useful delegate in the Legislature of Virginia, and at the time of his death was a clerk in the General Land Office. He was deservedly popular, as well for his known integrity as for the gentleness and kindness of his demeanor. (11 NOV 1854)

DEATH. At Galveston, Tex., on the 7th of October, of yellow fever, JAMES PERCIVAL, aged twenty-one, nephew and adopted son of Capt. John Percival, of U.S. Navy--a young man of much promise. (11 NOV 1854)

MARRIAGE. On the 31st ult. [31 OCT 1854], at Woodlawn, Montgomery Co., Md., by Rev. Mr. Hutton, JOHN T. TOWERS, Mayor of Washington, D.C., and Miss ELIZA, daughter of Dr. Wm. P. Palmer, of the former place. (13 NOV 1854)

MARRIAGE. On the 9th inst., by Rev. F. Israel, THOS. HERBERT to Miss MARGARET LUCAS, all of this city. (13 NOV 1854)

MARRIAGE. On Thursday, the 9th inst., by Rev. G.W. Samson, Mr. JAMES A. HALL to Miss EMMA ROBY, both of this city. (13 NOV 1854)

MARRIAGE. In San Francisco, Calif., on the 14th of October, at the residence of Judge Thompson, by Rt. Rev. Bishop Kip, Capt. E.O.C. ORD, U.S. Army, to Miss MARY MERCER THOMPSON. (13 NOV 1854)

DEATH. On the morning of the 12th inst., after a very brief illness, CATHARINE VIRGINIA, daughter of William C. and Mary Virginia Morrison, aged 14 months. Her funeral will take place this (Monday) afternoon, at 3½ o'clock, from the residence of her grandfather, Chas. E. Mix, Esq., on High, opposite 4th street, Georgetown. The friends of the family are respectfully invited to attend. (13 NOV 1854)

MARRIAGE. In the Church of the Epiphany, by the Rev. Mr. French, Mr. ELASAH MORAN to Miss C. ANGELINE MORAN, both of this city. (14 NOV 1854)

DEATH. On the evening of the 12th inst., suddenly, CHARLES W. STEWART, for many years an officer of the House of Representatives of the U.S. His funeral will take place this (Tuesday) at 11 o'clock A.M. from his late residence, on Missouri avenue, between Third and Four-and-a-half streets. The friends of the family are respectfully invited to attend. (14 NOV 1854)

DEATH. In this city, on Tuesday morning [14 NOV 1854], RICHARD HANSON WEIGHTMAN, son of R.H. and Susan B. Weightman, aged six years and two months. His funeral will take place from the residence of his grandfather, R.S. Coxe, Esq., 4½ street, between C street and Louisiana avenue. (15 NOV 1854)

MARRIAGE. On the 15th inst., by the Rev. John C. Smith, Mr. BERNARD M. CAMPBELL, of Baltimore, to Miss EMILY JANE MOORE, daughter of Mr. Wm. M. Moore, of this city. (16 NOV 1854)

Daily National Intelligencer, Marriage and Death Notices, 1851-1854

MARRIAGE. On the 14th inst., by the Rev. James R. Eckard, Mr. H.W. Blunt, of Georgetown, to Miss MARION A. COOLIDGE, daughter of the late Edmond Coolidge, Esq., of Washington. (17 NOV 1854)

DEATH. On the 15th inst., JAMES E. WALL, in the 26th year of his age. The deceased was endeared by many estimable qualities, and by the conscientious discharge of every duty, to a large circle of friends and acquaintances. His funeral will take place at 2½ o'clock today, (17th,) from his late residence on 11th street west, near Maryland avenue. (17 NOV 1854) FUNERAL PROCESSIONS. Perhaps there is no trait more striking in the character of our citizens than that of a disposition to pay proper honors to the dead and kind solace to the afflicted. Every week almost affords one or more exhibitions of this sort of fraternal regard. Yesterday the Perseverence Fire Company attended to the grave the remains of their companion, JOHN WATSON; and the Odd Fellows followed to his last resting-place the body of their brother, JAMES E. WALL. "*After life's fitful fever, they sleep well.*" (18 NOV 1854)

DEATH. At Scotland, Concordia Parish, La., October 30th, WILLIAM, only son of Field and Mary W. Dunbar, aged 1 year. "*Our God to call us homeward, His only Son sent down, And now, still more to tempt our hearts, Has taken up our own.*" (17 NOV 1854)

MARRIAGE. In Lynchburg, Va., by the Rev. J.D. Mitchell, on the 16th inst., LEONARD H. LYNE, Esq., of the U.S. Navy, and Miss MARY BOOTHROYED, daughter of Mr. Thomas Ferguson, of Lynchburg. (20 NOV 1854)

DEATH. Yesterday morning [19 NOV 1854], in great peace, JOHN N. LOVEJOY, Sr., at the advanced age of 85 years. The deceased was perhaps one of the oldest residents of our city, and none enjoyed more fully the love and respect of all who were favored with his acquaintance. His funeral will take place from the Foundry Church, corner of G and 14th streets, tomorrow, (Tuesday,) at 2 o'clock P.M. (20 NOV 1854)

DEATH. At Williamstown, Mass., on Monday, the 13th inst., Mr. JESSE SABIN, the father-in-law of the Hon. Robert McClelland. (20 NOV 1854)

MARRIAGE. On Thursday, 16th inst., by the Rev. Mr. Hodges, ZADOCK WILLIAMS, of this city, to Miss MARY MORTON, of Baltimore. (22 NOV 1854)

MARRIAGE. On 21st November, by the Rev. R.L. Dashiel, Mr. JOSEPHUS PERRY to Miss CATHERINE MILES, all of this city. (22 NOV 1854)

MARRIAGE. At St. Louis, Mo., on the 16th inst., by the Right Rev. Bishop Hawks, JOHN R. TRIPLETT, Esq., to SALLIE A., daughter of Maj. Benjamin Walker, U.S. Army. (23 NOV 1854)

MARRIAGE. At Alexandria, Va., on the 22d inst., by the Rev. Mr. Johnstone, Rev. CHARLES H. HALL, of Fayetteville, N.C., to Miss ANNIE S., youngest daughter of the late Geo. H. Duffey, of Alexandria. (23 NOV 1854)

DEATH. In this city, yesterday afternoon [27 NOV 1854], Mrs. CATHARINE F. ALEXANDER, relict of the late Walter Stoddard Alexander, of Alexandria Co., Va., in the 70th year of her age. This most excellent and exemplary lady was the second child of the late Col. Baldwin Dade, of Virginia, and was born at Lochobar, near the city of Alexandria. Her illness, though short, was severe, and was borne by her with pious resignation to the Divine Will. A large circle of relatives and friends are left to deplore the loss of one who had, in a protracted life, few superiors in the virtues and graces which adorn and enoble her sex. Her funeral will take place at 2 o'clock today from the residence of her son, Oscar Alexander, on I street, between 6th and 7th, where the friends of her family and of her sister, Mrs. Julia Terrett, are respectfully invited to attend. (28 NOV 1854)

Daily National Intelligencer, Marriage and Death Notices, 1851-1854

MARRIAGES. On the 14th inst., at the Wesley Chapel parsonage, by the Rev. James H. Brown, Mr. CALEB B. RICARD to Miss MARGARET ANN REED, both of Montgomery Co., Md. (1 DEC 1854)

MARRIAGE. On the 28th inst., by the Rev. James H. Brown, MICHAEL SHAY to Mrs. REBECCA FAGE. (1 DEC 1854)

MARRIAGE. In this city, on the 29th inst., by the Rev. P.D. Gurley, WARNER P. JONES, Esq., of Lynchburg, Va., to Miss REBECCA L. PAXTON, of New Orleans. (1 DEC 1854)

MARRIAGE. In Baltimore, on the 16th inst., by the Rev. Myer Levin, JOHN A. HUNNICUTT, Esq., of Washington, to MARY C.B., eldest daughter of Samuel C. Moran, Esq., of Charles Co., Md. (1 DEC 1854)

MARRIAGE. On Wednesday afternoon [29 NOV 1854], by Rev. John C. Smith, Rev. J. EAMES RANKIN, Pastor First Presbyterian Church, Pottsdam, N.Y., to Miss MARY H., daughter of Cyrus Birge, Esq., of this city. (1 DEC 1854)

DEATH. In this city, November 28th, at the residence of her Uncle, Jas. Nokes, Esq., after a severe illness of twenty-four days, of typhoid fever, SUSAN B. CURTIS, of Philadelphia, aged 20 years, daughter of Asa Curtis, U.S. Navy. (1 DEC 1854)

DEATH. At Port Tobacco, Charles Co., Md., JAMES A. BERRY, in the 30th year of his age. (1 DEC 1854)

DEATH. At Baltimore, on the 23d of NOVEMBER, in the forty-sixth year of his age, Lieut. SAMUEL E. MUNN, of the U.S. Navy. He was one of the oldest officers of his grade, but had not been in active service for a number of years. (1 DEC 1854)

DEATH. On the 22d inst., at Malvern, near Theological Seminary, Fairfax Co., MARGARETTA JANE JOHNS, wife of Bishop Johns, and eldest daughter of Dr. J.T. Shaaff, deceased. (1 DEC 1854)

MARRIAGE. On Thursday evening [30 NOV 1854], by the Rev. John C. Smith, Mr. GEORGE H. WALKER to Miss MARY O. ANDERSON, all of this city. (2 DEC 1854)

DEATH. In this city, on the 1st inst., HELEN, infant daughter of Hamilton G. and Josephine Fant. The funeral will take place on Sunday next, at 4 o'clock P.M., from the residence of Mrs. Smith, No. 233 F street. The friends of the parents are invited to attend without further notice. (2 DEC 1854)

OBITUARY. The *Madison (Indiana) Banner* contains the following well-deserved eulogy on the Hon. Williamson Dunn, recently deceased: "In our paper of Monday we announced in brief terms the decease of Hon. Williamson Dunn, in the seventy-third year of his age, at his late residence in this county. The most of his long and useful life having been spent in this county, Judge Dunn was too well known to render any eulogy from us either proper or necessary. In 1809 or '10 he moved from near Danville, Ky., to this county..." [text continues]. (2 DEC 1854)

MARRIAGE. On the 29th ult. [29 NOV 1854], by the Rev. Mr. Leavel, at "Ellerslie," Dr. BUSHROD TAYLOR, of Clarke Co., Va., to Miss ELVIRA LANE, daughter of James Jett, Esq., of Rappahannock Co., Va. (4 DEC 1854)

DEATH. On Sunday, the 3d inst., at one o'clock, ELIZABETH C., the beloved wife of Ferdinand Butler, Esq., and daughter of Joseph Abbott, Esq. The funeral will take place on Tuesday evening, at 2 o'clock, from the residence of her husband, corner of 14th street and Pennsylvania avenue. The friends of her husband's and father's family are respectfully invited to attend. (4 DEC 1854)

DEATH. On the 9th of October, in Thibodaux, La., of yellow fever, Dr. WALTER B. YOUNG. (4 DEC 1854)

DEATH. On the 17th October, in Houma, La., JOHN Y. YOUNG, for many years a resident of Georgetown, D.C. (4 DEC 1854)

DEATH. On the 9th November, near Thibodaux, La., of yellow fever, Dr. THOMAS H. YOUNG. (4 DEC 1854)

MARRIAGE. On the 23d inst., by the Rev. J. McKim Duncan, C.K. GREEN, of Detroit, and SARAH, daughter of Jotham Lawrence, of Exeter, N.H. (5 DEC 1854)

MARRIAGE. At Zanesville, Ohio, on the 28th November, by the Rev. J.M. Platt, Maj. J. VAN HORNE, U.S. Army, to Miss MARY S. GILBERT, daughter of the late Chas. C. Gilbert, of that place. (5 DEC 1854)

DEATH. On the 4th inst., Mrs. ANNA M. MOHUN, consort of Mr. Francis Mohun, in the 43d year of her age. Grief for the unexpected death of this lady extends beyond the family circle, for to neighbors and friends she presented the example of a good and useful life, and well deserved their esteem and affection. The friends and acquaintances of the family are respectfully invited to attend the funeral of the deceased from her late residence on 6th street, between E and F streets, at half-past nine o'clock on Wednesday morning. The funeral service will be held at St. Patrick's Church at ten o'clock the same morning. (5 DEC 1854)

MARRIAGE. In this city, on the 3d inst., by the Rev. Mr. Hodges, Mr. WILLIAM LAWSON to Miss REBECCA HULSE, all of Washington. (6 DEC 1854)

MARRIAGE. On the 30th ult. [30 NOV 1854], at the Foundry parsonage, by Rev. E.P. Phelps, Mr. THOMAS J. ADAMS and Miss ANNIE WRIGHT, both of this city. (6 DEC 1854)

MARRIAGE. On the 5th inst., by Rev. E.P. Phelps, Mr. JAMES W. ST. CLAIR and Miss MARY E. BURCHE, both of this city. (6 DEC 1854)

MARRIAGE. At the residence of Capt. John Edrington, Stafford Co., Va., on the 30th of November, by the Rev. J.M. Henry, of Washington, Col. SAMUEL SIMPSON, late U.S. Consul at Bombay, British India, to Miss ELLA A. EDRINGTON. (6 DEC 1854)

DEATH. At Rockville, Md., on the 2d inst., SARAH S. PROUT, eldest daughter of the late Wm. Prout, of this city. A warm and affectionate heart endeared her to many friends. The adorning trait of her character was a tender and faithful devotion to her remaining parent. She bore with cheerfulness and patience a lingering and painful illness, and departed in full faith of a happy immortality. (6 DEC 1854)

DEATH. Suddenly, but in great peace, on the 3d inst., at Lewisburg, Va., Mrs. LIZZIE S., wife of Rev. Wm. Harden, of the Baltimore Annual Conference, and eldest daughter of the Rev. Henry Slicer, aged 24 years and 6 months. "*Not Lost; only gone before.*" (7 DEC 1854)

DEATH. At 4½ o'clock P.M., December 2d, Mrs. ELIZABETH ELLEN, consort of C.G. Wildman, in the 38th year of her age. (7 DEC 1854)

DEATH. On the 19th of October, ROBERT R. GATTON, Esq., Consul of the U.S. at Mazatlan. (8 DEC 1854)

DEATH. In this city, on the 6th inst., THOMAS HODSON, aged 73, a native of Lincolnshire, Eng., but for several years past a resident of Prince George's Co., Md. (8 DEC 1854)

DEATH. On Wednesday last [6 DEC 1854], Mr. GEORGE W. MOUNTS. His funeral will take place from his Father's residence, Bridge street, Georgetown, this afternoon at 3 o'clock. (8 DEC 1854)

Daily National Intelligencer, Marriage and Death Notices, 1851-1854

DEATH. In Montgomery Co., on the 7th inst., in the 76th year of her age, Mrs. MARGARET CULVER, consort of the late Burgess Culver, and sister to the late Michael Connelly. *May she rest in peace!* (9 DEC 1854)

MARRIAGE. At Marmion, county of King George, Va., on the 26th October, by the Rev. Mr. Russell, JOHN TAYLOE, Esq., to MARY WILLIS LEWIS, daughter of Daingerfield Lewis, Esq., all of the same county and State. (9 DEC 1854)

DEATH. On the 8th inst., WILLIAM DOWLING, a native of Washington. His funeral will take place this morning, at 10 o'clock, from the Infirmary. His friends and acquaintances are invited to attend. (9 DEC 1854)

DEATH. Yesterday morning [8 DEC 1854], after a long and painful illness, in the 50th year of her age, MARY ELIZABETH MAGUIRE, wife of James Maguire, formerly of the U.S. Marine Corps. Her funeral will take place on tomorrow, from the residence of the family, on H street, two doors from 14th street. The friends and acquaintances of the family are invited to attend without further notice. (9 DEC 1854)

MARRIAGE. In this city, on Thursday, December 7th, at St. John's Church, by the Rev. Smith Pyne, STEPHEN B. LUCE, U.S. Navy, to ELIZA, youngest daughter of the late Comm. J.D. Henley. (11 DEC 1854)

MARRIAGE. On the 11th inst., by Rev. F. Israel, JOHN H. HURST, to ANN V. BICKSLER, both of Fairfax Co., Va. (12 DEC 1854)

MARRIAGE. In this city, on Thursday afternoon, the 7th inst., at Trinity Church, by the Rev. William J. Clarke, J. BARTRAM NORTH to ADDIE W., daughter of the late William Lippincott, of Philadelphia. (13 DEC 1854)

DEATH. On the 5th of September, 1854, at sea, aboard the U.S. frigate *Susquehanna*, and buried at Simoda, Japan, Dr. JAMES HAMILTON, U.S. Navy. In the death of Dr. Hamilton his family have met an irreparable loss and the navy deprived of an efficient officer, as his scientific attainments, which were of the first order, gave a promise of much future usefulness. Possessing the most noble and generous qualities, he was beloved by all who knew him, and on a foreign shore was wept for and lamented. (13 DEC 1854)

OBITUARY. Under our obituary head, says the *Baltimore American* of December 11th, will be found notice of the demise of our respected townsman, EDMUND DIDIER, Esq., President of the Mutual Fire and Marine Insurance Company of Baltimore. Mr. Didier was highly esteemed for his uniformly kind and courteous deportment, and his sudden departure from our midst will be deplored by a large circle of friends. (14 DEC 1854)

DEATH OF MAJOR LOWD. We observe the announcement of the death of this gallant officer and estimable man at St. Augustine, Fla. Major (then Captain) Lowd was stationed in this city [Rochester] between 1837 and 1840, in command of a company of the 2d artillery, who were fresh from the Indian wars in Florida. Capt. Lowd was here with his family for a long time, and formed the acquaintance and gained the friendship and esteem of many of our citizens. He and his command served in the Mexican war. He was breveted for gallantry in one of the first battles, under Gen. Taylor, on the Rio Grande. He remained in that line during the war. *Rochester Amer.* (14 DEC 1854)

DEATH. On Thursday morning, the 14th inst., after a few days' illness, Mrs. MARY QUINN, in the 74th year of her age. The deceased was a native of the county of Wexford, Ireland, but for a number of years a resident of Norfolk, Va., and late of this city. Her funeral will take place this evening at three o'clock, from the residence of her son-in-law, John J. Joyce, corner of Thirteenth and F streets, where her friends and acquaintances are respectfully invited to attend. (15 DEC 1854)

MARRIAGE. At Memphis, Tenn., on the 27th ult. [27 NOV 1854], by the Rev. Dr. Page, the Hon. WILLIAM C. DAWSON, of Georgia, to Mrs. ELIZA M. WILLIAMS, of Memphis. (16 DEC 1854)

MARRIAGE. On the 14th inst., in Christ Church, by the Rev. W. Hodges, the Rev. EDMUND ROBERTS, Rector of St. Peter's Parish, Peekskill, N.Y., and HELEN L., daughter of Maj. A.A. Nicholson, of the U.S. Marine Corps, Washington. (16 DEC 1854)

MARRIAGE. In this city, on the 14th inst., by the Rev. Mr. Cheneworth, Mr. THOS. P. WHITE to Miss ESTHER ANN MARSHE, eldest daughter of Thos. Marshe, all of this city. (16 DEC 1854)

MARRIAGE. On the 13th inst., by the Rev. Mr. Cheneworth, ENOCH M. NORRIS, of St. Mary's Co., Md., to Miss SARAH, daughter of Zadock Williams, of Washington. (16 DEC 1854)

MARRIAGE. On Thursday morning, 7th inst., by the Rev. S.A.H. Marks, Mr. BASIL W. DUCKET to Miss CAROLINE ECKTON, both of Prince George's Co., Md. Also, on Thursday evening, 7th inst., by the same, Mr. WASHINGTON BERRY to Miss COLUMBIA SKIDMORE, of the District of Columbia. (16 DEC 1854)

DEATH. On the 22d ult. [22 NOV 1854], at St. Augustine, Fla., where he was temporarily residing, JOHN BLISS, late a Lieut. Colonel in the U.S. army... He was a native of New Hampshire [text continues]. (16 DEC 1854)

MARRIAGE. On Sunday, the 17th inst., by the Rev. H.B. Closkery, in the Cathedral, Baltimore, WM. GRAHAM SCOTT, Esq., of Washington, to Miss ANNA VIRGINIA DEVLIN, of the same place, daughter of Lieut. Devlin, late of the Marine Corps. (18 DEC 1854)

DEATH. On the 2d October last, at his residence in Bryantown, [Md.], Dr. WALTER F. BOARMAN, in the 57th year of his age. (18 DEC 1854)

MARRIAGES. On Thursday, December 14, by the Rev. S.A.H. Marks, MALACKI FARR, Esq., to Miss AMELIA E. OWENS, of the District of Columbia. Also, on Monday morning, December 18, by the same, Mr. LEVI G. KING to Miss REBECCA JONES, of the same place. (19 DEC 1854)

MARRIAGE. At Elm Grove, near Jacksonville, Ill., the residence of Mrs. E.C. Duncan, on December 9th, by Rev. L.M. Glover, CHARLES E. PUTNAM, Esq., of Davenport, Iowa, to Miss MARY L., daughter of the late Gov. Jos. Duncan, of Illinois. (20 DEC 1854)

MARRIAGE. In the First Presbyterian Church, in this city, on the 19th inst., by the Rev. Wm. McLain, EDWARD B. WHEELOCK, Esq., of New Orleans, to MARY LOUISA CLACK, daughter of the late Capt. John H. Clack. (21 DEC 1854)

DEATH. On the 19th inst., JOSEPH W. BECK, Esq., in the 61st year of his age. The friends and acquaintances of the family are respectfully invited to attend his funeral, from his late residence, Capitol Hill, on Friday, at 2 o'clock P.M. (21 DEC 1854)

OBITUARY. Among the notable deaths of the last week was that of Mrs. ANN BAYARD, widow of James A. Bayard, of Delaware. She died in the city of Philadelphia on Sunday evening, the 10th inst., in the 77th year of her age. Few ladies have ever lived or died in the U.S. more honorably connected with its political history. Her father, Richard Bassett, was the first U.S. Senator elected by the State of Delaware. He held his seat from the year 1789 to 1793. Her husband, James A. Bayard, was elected to represent the State of Delaware in the lower House of congress from 1797 to 1803; in 1801 he was appointed Minister Plenipotentiary of the U.S. at the Court of France; in 1804 he was elected U.S. Senator from Delaware. He was re-elected in 1810; in 1815 President Madison appointed him, in connexion with John Quincy Adams and Albert Gallatin, Envoy Extraordinary and Minister Plenipotentiary to negotiate a treaty of peace

Daily National Intelligencer, Marriage and Death Notices, 1851-1854

with Great Britain, under the mediation of the Emperor of Russia. Henry Clay and Jonathan Russell were afterwards added to the commission, and together they negotiated the treaty of Ghent in 1814. In 1815, Mr. Bayard was appointed Envoy Extraordinary and Minister Plenipotentiary to the Court of Russia. He died the same year, in the 48th year of his age, leaving Mrs. Bayard a widow for nearly thirty years. Richard Bayard, one of her sons, has been twice elected to represent the State of Delaware in the U.S. Senate, between the years 1836 and 1845, and represented the U.S. Government as Charge at Belgium under the Administration of President Fillmore; and, finally, James A. Bayard, another son, represents the same seat in the U.S. Senate heretofore occupied so creditably and so long by his grandfather, his father, and his brother. (21 DEC 1854)

DEATH. In his native place, Norfolk, Va., on the morning of the 10th December, Dr. JOEL MARTIN, of the army [text continues]. (22 DEC 1854)

DEATH. In Nottingham District, on Saturday last [16 DEC 1854], Mr. JAMES N. BADEN, an old and highly respected citizen. (22 DEC 1854)

DEATH. Yesterday morning, the 21st inst., Mrs. ANN ELIZA WOOD, wife of Edward Wood, Sr., aged 68 years. The friends and acquaintances of the family are requested to attend her funeral, from her late residence, on 13th street, near B, Island, this afternoon at 2 o'clock. (22 DEC 1854)

MARRIAGE. On Thursday evening [21 DEC 1854], by the Rev. John C. Smith, Mr. JOHN H. GARDNER to Miss ANNA E.J. HARVEY, all of this ;city. (23 DEC 1854)

DEATH. On the 19th inst., after a protracted illness, Miss MARTHA A. BADEN, in the 20th year of her age, formerly of Prince George's Co., Md. (23 DEC 1854)

DEATH. On Sabbath morning, the 24th inst., at about ten o'clock, LIZZIE LIVINGSTON, daughter of Dr. Wm. Gunton, and wife of Rev. Wm. Ives Budington, recently of Charlestown, Mass., but now Philadelphia [text continues]. The friends of the family are respectfully invited to attend the funeral, without further notice, from the residence of her father, tomorrow (Tuesday) morning at 11 o'clock. (25 DEC 1854)

MARRIAGE. On Sabbath, 24th inst., by Rev. Andrew G. Carothers, Mr. CHARLES EDMONDS, of Albany, to Miss SARAH ANN DOUGHERTY, of this city. (27 DEC 1854)

MARRIAGE. On the 23d inst., by the Rev. James H. Brown, Mr. SAMUEL JOHNSTON to Miss ELIZABETH E. YOST, both of Prince George's Co., Md. (27 DEC 1854)

MARRIAGE. On the 14th inst., by the Rev. J. Stratton, at "Hollywood," Adams Co., Miss., Mr. DUDLEY M. HAYDON, of Kentucky, to Miss ANNA, daughter of Jas. A. Gillespie, Esq. (27 DEC 1854)

MARRIAGE. On Wednesday afternoon [27 DEC 1854], by the Rev. John C. Smith, JASPER S. LLOYD, Esq., of Cincinnati, Ohio, to Miss JANE RANDALL, of this city. (28 DEC 1854)

MARRIAGE. In this city, on Tuesday, the 26th inst., by the Rev. W. Hodges, JOHN ROWLAND to Miss ANNA LOCKOR, of Prince George's Co., Md. (28 DEC 1854)

DEATH. On Wednesday, the 27th inst., Mrs. SARAH PILLING, in the 77th year of her age. Her funeral will take place on Friday, the 29th inst., at 2 o'clock, from her late residence on Fifteenth street, which the friends and acquaintances of the family are respectfully invited to attend. (28 DEC 1854)

MARRIAGE. In this city, on the 26th inst., at the E Street Baptist Church, by Rev. G.W. Samson, assisted by Rev. Prof. Huntington, Prof. R.P. LATHAM, of Richmond, Va., to Miss IDA BACON, daughter of J.S. Bacon, D.D., President of Columbian College. (29 DEC 1854)

DEATH. On the 16th inst., suddenly, at his residence in Charles Co., Md., Mr. E. RUDHALL PYE. The deceased was greatly endeared to an extensive circle of friends and relatives by his many amiable qualities. *May he rest in peace!* (29 DEC 1854)

DEATH OF THOMAS W. DORR. The death of Thomas W. Dorr, of Rhode Island, is announced as having occurred at Providence on Wednesday last [27 DEC 1854]. He will be remembered by many of our readers as the leader and hero of a party which, twelve or thirteen years ago, attempted to overthrow the Government of Rhode Island by revolutionary and violent means, in which purpose he was defeated by the People of the State, who resorted to arms in defence of Law and Order of their own State Constitution [text continues]. (29 DEC 1854)

OBITUARY. Died, on the 31st of October last, in the 74th year of his age, at Clifton, his residence, in Clarke Co., Va., DAVID H. ALLEN, Esq. For several years past his health had been declining, and for the last six months he was unable to leave his chamber. He viewed with Christian composure the gradual approach of death, and at last, without apparent pain, passed calmly from life. Mr. Allen was one of the comparatively few survivors of a class of men once numerous in Virginia, who, to fine talents and liberal education, added the advantage of hereditary wealth; an advantage so favorable, when properly used, to mental culture and embellishment. He graduated at Princeton College in 1802, during the Presidency of the celebrated Dr. Smith [text continues]. (29 DEC 1854)

MARRIAGES. In this city, on Thursday, the 28th inst., by the Rev. W. Hodges, ROBERT V. HENRY to Miss MARGARET K. STANFIELD, all of Washington. And, on the 13th inst., by the same, ENOCH M. NORRIS, of Charles Co., Md., to Miss SARAH WILLIAMS, of Washington. (30 DEC 1854)

MARRIAGE. On the 23d inst., by the Rev. F. Israel, WILLIAM HAWLEY to Miss ELIZABETH PARKIN, all of this city. (30 DEC 1854)

MARRIAGE. On the 28th inst., at Foundry parsonage, by Rev. E.P. Phelps, Mr. ARMSTEAD T. MILLS, of Fairfax Co., Va., and Miss ELIZABETH E. GERMON, of this city. (30 DEC 1854)

MARRIAGE. At the Navy Yard, Washington, on the 28th inst., by the Rev. Mr. Hodges, JOHN W. LYNN, Esq., to Miss EMILY BELL, both of Prince George's Co., Md. (30 DEC 1854)

MARRIAGE. At Georgetown, D.C., on the 21st inst., by the Rev. Mr. Sutherland, MORRIS ADLER to CATHARINE, daughter of the late Daniel Kurtz, of that place. (30 DEC 1854)

DEATH. On the evening of the 28th inst., Mr. JOHN D. BROWN, of this city, in the thirty-ninth year of his age. His remains will be taken to Norfolk, Va., for interment, leaving this morning by the train of cars at half-past 8 o'clock. The subject of the above notice came to this city a few years since with nothing to rely upon but his own unaided exertions. By energy and untiring industry he soon succeeded in establishing himself in a prosperous business; and those who have had dealings with him will bear testimony to his integrity and uprightness of character. He was a devoted and affectionate husband, and in his death his bereaved and afflicted wife and children have sustained an irreparable loss. (30 DEC 1854)

Index

A

Abbot
  Ann T.G. 126
  Charles 246
  Elizabeth Gilman 126
  George J. 126
  John Austin 246
  Richard H. 68
  Sarah 246
  William R. 114
Abbott
  Elizabeth C. 198, 268
  James W. 67
  Joseph 198, 268
Abert
  Ernest 124
  Evelina M. 124
  J.J., Col. 54, 212
  Louisa 54
  Mary 212
Abingdon, Va. 49
Accomack Co., Va. 70, 90, 160, 237
Accountant 253
Acton
  Elizabeth Jane 66
Adams
  Anna M. 6
  C.B. 6
  Catharine 15
  Charles F. 211
  Cornelius B. 255
  Ellen 2
  G.R. 67
  George 80
  Jamima 80
  John 166, 198, 218
  John Quincy 91, 166, 225, 271
  Leonard 15
  Louisa C. 91
  Mary A., Mrs. 128
  Mary Jane 213
  Mary Louisa 166
  Mary R. 153
  Mr. 37
  Mrs. 5, 39
  Nathaniel W. 62
  Richard 130
  Thomas 51
  Thomas J. 269
Adams Co., Miss. 147, 272
Adams Co., Pa. 9
Addison
  Andrew L. 123
  Edward 237
  Elizabeth Clagett 206
  Henry 206
  John 123
  John McLean 222
  S.R., Dr. 116
  Thomas B. 222
Adellvig
  Louis, Mrs. 37
Adie
  George, Rev. 55, 124
Adjutant 56
Adler
  M. Virginia 27
  Malvina E. 74
  Morris 27, 74, 273
Adlum
  Maj. 103, 105
  Mrs. 103, 105
Africa 255
Afton, Md. 83
Agate
  Elizabeth H. 155
Agent 48, 71, 210
Agg
  Elizabeth Godfrey 237
  John 237
Aigler
  John Jacob 199
  Sophia 199
Aiken
  Rev. 197
  William 239
Aikin
  Rev. 93
Aikin, S.C. 124
Aintab, Syria 35
Air Hill, Va. 166
Ajax, Va. 184
Akron, Ohio 91
Alabama 156, 158, 232
Albany, N.Y. 111, 134, 176, 196, 272
Albemarle Co., Va. 9, 56, 80, 101, 113, 125, 171, 259
Albert
  Luther, Rev. 250
Albuquerque, N.M. 151
Alcott
  Charles W. 206
Alday
  J.H., Rev. 217
Aldie, Va. 55, 153
Aldis
  Charles, Rev. 222
Alexander
  Archibald, Rev.* 50
  Caroline 53
  Catharine F. 267
  J.W., Rev. 223
  Oscar 267
  Walter Stoddard 267
  William F. 156
Alexandria Co., Va. 20, 78, 84, 170, 267
Alexandria Gazette 83

Alexandria, Va. 5, 7, 8, 12, 16, 19, 23, 29, 34, 35, 40, 46, 47, 52, 54, 55, 58, 67, 75, 76, 79-82, 87, 89, 90, 97-99, 101, 104, 113, 114, 116, 118, 120, 128, 131, 134, 135, 138, 146, 147, 149, 155, 156, 159, 161, 163, 164, 167, 174, 178, 179, 185, 186, 190, 192, 196, 199, 212, 217, 219, 230, 232, 240, 252, 253, 257, 260, 265, 267
Alig
  Mat(t)hew, Rev. 71, 75
  Mat(t)hias, Rev. 8, 19, 22, 36, 37, 42, 45, 49, 53, 55, 67, 89, 102, 133, 139, 158, 179, 255
Alison
  John H. 230
All-Hallows parish, Md. 175
Alleghanies 119
Alleghany Co., Va. 213
Alleghany/Allegheny College 48, 70
Allen
  Arthur M. 230
  Charity Ann 256
  Charles 17
  David H. 273
  Edward S. 18
  Louisa C. 254
Allentown, Pa. 184
Allison
  Richard T. 73
Allnutt
  Catharine 161
  William P. 161
Almy
  John J., Lieut. 209
Alsop
  Richard 7
Alta Vista, Md. 79
Alta Vista, Va. 9
Ambler
  Charles E., Rev. 56, 251
  Fannie L. 251
  Thomas M., Maj. 251
Amboy railroad 238
American Academy of Arts and Sciences 132
American Board of Foreign Missions 32
Amherst College 120
Ammen
  D., Lieut. 29
Amsterdam 132, 133
Analostan Island 229

Anderson
   A.G. 68
   Alexander 131
   Benjamin Dabney 108
   Charles A. 248
   Eliza 248
   Ellen O. 146
   Frances 142
   Garret 95, 135
   Gertrude C. 95
   Harriet J. 108
   J.D., Rev. 61
   John 142
   John L. 65
   John W. 151
   Josephine T. 191
   Luke 247
   Lydia 156
   Marshall R. 104
   Martha D. 61
   Martha Rosalie 147
   Mary O. 268
   Noble 178
   R.P. 156
   Robert P. 61
   S., Maj. 108
   Samuel 248
   Samuel J., Dr. 231
Andrews
   Alfred W. 253
   C.W., Rev. 125, 157
   S.M., Rev. 216
Angel
   Mary Ellen 48
Annan
   Roberdeau 131
Annapolis, Md. 12, 14, 33, 37, 55, 56, 59, 60, 67, 69, 74, 80, 106, 107, 121, 125, 127, 130, 135, 137, 139, 161, 169, 173, 180, 181, 188-190, 205, 212, 219, 222, 229, 244, 259
Anne Arundel Co., Md. 7, 33, 35, 62, 67, 71, 72, 99, 128, 171, 175, 204, 253, 261
Ansel
   Sally J. 258
Anthony
   Henry B., Hon. 238
   Sarah Aborn 238
Antigua 128
Antrim, Ire. 91
Appleby, Md. 40
Archbishop 85
Architect 83, 234, 264
Arcularius
   George 107
Argentine Confederation 121
Arkansas 117, 186, 187
Arkansas river 210
Armenians 35
Armour
   Elizabeth C. 67

Armstrong
   Robert, Gen. 164, 213
Army 2, 14, 15, 17, 18, 20, 23, 29, 30, 32, 36, 38, 40-44, 46, 49, 50, 53, 54, 58-60, 62, 67, 71, 76, 79, 83, 85, 88, 92-95, 97, 100, 103, 104, 107, 108, 110, 117, 118, 120, 123, 125
Arnold
   George 227
   Joseph W. 87
   Margaret 139
   Samuel E. 59
   Theresia 102
Arny
   Caroline C. 5
Arsenal 118
Arth
   Mary Louisa 131
Arthur
   Augusta J. 29
   John A., Gen. 29
Aschwanden
   Joseph, Rev. 208
Ash Grove, Va. 14
Ashcraft
   Louisa 183
Ashe
   Elizabeth H. 221
   Samuel, Col. 221
   W.S., Hon. 221
Ashley
   Elizabeth 143
Ashmead
   Catherine F. 178
   William, Rev.* 178
Ashton
   Caroline H. 77
   George 223
   Henry, Col. 77
   Margaret E. 1
   Mary Roberta 223
Ashwand
   Rev. 180
Asigoigne
   Mme. 63
Atchison
   A. 71
   Emma Jane 71
   George H. 71
Athens, Ga. 97
Athens, Pa. 220
Atkins
   Addison B., Rev.* 261
   Rev. 262
Atkinson
   Edward Graham 168
   George S. 24
   J.M.P., Rev. 64, 139, 211, 227
   Rev. 11, 95, 114, 124, 140
   Thomas, Rev. 73, 97
Atlantic ocean 248

Atlee
   Edwin Augustus, M.D. 81
   Mary Anna 193
   Samuel Yorke 193
Atlixco 190, 207
Attakapas 264
Attorney 93, 238
Attorney General 143, 205, 245
Auburn, Va. 95, 106
Aubury
   Elliott 237
Auditor 18, 29, 52
Augusta, Ga. 222
Augusta, Me. 156
Augusta, Va. 186
Auld
   Jeanette 148
   R.E. 96
Auld & Brother Co. 96
Aulick
   Comm. 67
   Virginia 67
Aurand
   Jacob 236
   Sophia 236
Austin
   Henry, Capt. 75
Austin, Tex. 214
Australia 234
Author 92
Auvergne plantation, Miss. 244
Avondale, Mo. 52
Avoyelles, La. 51
Aylmer
   Henry 218
Ayton
   Richard 211

B

Babbit(t)
   Bvt. Maj., 181
   Fanny, 181
   Thomas, Dr. 214
Babin
   Francis Constance 194
   P.P. 194
Bache
   Maria C. 30
   Richard 30
Bacon
   Ida 272
   J.S. 272
   J.S., Rev. 122
   Joel S., Rev.* 25
   Lemuel P. 25
   Mary Ann 89
   P.F. 41
   Samuel 89
   Thomas Howard 89
Baden
   Clement 16
   J.W. 147

James N. 272
John W. 12, 120
M.A.K. 147
Marion 147
Martha A. 272
Mary Ann K. 120
Badger
   Emily L.H. 33
   Mr. 120
Bagge
   J.M. 198
Baggett/Baggitt
   Ann E.A. 112
   Mary E. 17
Bailey
   Anna E. 248
   Charles G. 74
   Charles Henry 86
   D.J., Hon. 86
   G., Dr. 74
   Harry 193
   Joseph 205
   Josiah R. 248
   Margaret L. 74
   Mary F. 158
   Rev. 112
Baird
   John James 108
   Louisa 171
   Samuel King 171
   Thomas H. 171
   Thomas Harlan 171
   William A. 164
Baker
   Yelverton D. 190
Balch
   Mr., Hon. 165
   Rev. 117
   Stephen B., Rev. 174
   T.B., Rev. 111
   Thomas 117
Baldenar
   William Culver 109
Balderston
   Drucilla 2
Baldwin
   Abeel, Rev. 222
   Almon 199
   Ann Elizabeth 131
   Catharine 5
   Charles A. 146
   Cynthia S. 151
   Gabriel L. 131
   Henry Clay 161
   I.I. 151
   James J. 5
   Malinda 199
   Maria S. 199
   Martha Elizabeth 214
   William H. 146
Baldwin Co., Ala. 111
Balestier
   J., Hon. 79

Ball
   Alfred 148
   Ann C. 153
   Charles G. 65
   Cordelia 153
   W.N. 153
Ballard
   Garland 33
Ballentine
   Margaret 259
Balme
   Mary Ann 49
   Paul 49
Baltimore American 270
Baltimore and Ohio railroad 150
Baltimore Annual Conference 49, 62, 75, 89, 163, 178, 213, 224, 241, 269
Baltimore Argus 46
Baltimore Co., Md. 23, 28, 62, 154, 166, 220, 236
Baltimore Patriot 48
Baltimore, Md. 1, 6, 9-11, 16, 18-21, 23, 24, 26-30, 32, 33, 36, 38-41, 47, 48, 50, 52, 57, 59, 60, 62, 64, 67-69, 71, 79-81, 90, 93, 95, 97-101, 105, 106, 111-115, 117, 128, 129, 131, 133-136, 138, 140, 142, 144, 146-148, 154, 155, 157, 161, 163, 164, 166, 168-171, 173, 177, 180, 187-189, 191, 193, 195-197, 199, 203, 204, 206, 210-212, 219, 221, 223, 224, 227, 228, 230, 231, 233, 236, 241, 246, 248, 251, 252, 254-256, 258-260, 262, 265-268, 271
Bamberger
   George W. 133
Bancroft Institute 107
Bangs
   Cassandra Virginia 32
Bank of Washington 18
Banker 62, 129, 173
Bantry, Ire. 254
Banuelos
   Chevalier 31
Barber
   Ann M. 8
   Cornelius 179, 181
   George 121, 196
   George C. 181
   Jane Lucinda 121
   Mr. 103, 105
   Nancy 254
   Rev. 223
Barbour
   B.J. 3
   James 3
   James, Gov. 3
   Martha Isabella 93

   P.N., Maj. 93
Bare
   Emma H. 222
   Robert M. 222
Barker
   Atharia 1
   Helen 70
   John, Rev. 48
   John, Rev.* 70
   Julia 103
   Mrs. 118
   Thomas, Capt. 103
Barkley
   Samuel 69
Barn Elms, Va. 153
Barnaclo
   R.W. 213
Barnard
   Katharine T.F. 247
   Katharine Theodosia 247
   Robert 117
   Robert W. 247
Barnes
   A. 83
   Bettie M. 2
   Elizabeth E. 169
   Emily Gertrude 222
   George M. 187
   Hanson 220
   Hon. 222
   James T. 70
   John 126
   Joseph K., Dr. 36
   Margaret St.C. C. 83
   Mary J. 69
   Mary Jane 166
   Mary T. 36
   Noble 2
   Richard 69
   Seneca Marshall 171
   Susan Emily 171
   Thomas F. 36
   Thomas St.C. C. 83
   Thomas T. 187
   Vincent 171
Barnhill
   John L. 253
Barnhouse
   Alcuzera 44
Barques
   Wilhelmina 133
Barren Co., Ky. 137
Barrett
   Ellen Ann 33
   Emily A. 59
   Mary A. 76
   Mary Catherine 222
   Nancy 6
   Susan 222
   Thomas J. 222
Barron
   Edward, Rev. 255
   Henry A. 245
   Rebecca A. 245

Samuel Latimer 245
Virginia C.M. 21
Barrott
   Solomon 60
Barry
   Basil/Bazil, Rev. 28, 121
   Eliza R. 203
   Francis 154
   Francis, Sr. 57
   James D. 203
   Martha R. 121
   Mary P. 159
   William J. 154
Barrytown, N.Y. 252
Barstow
   Gideon, Hon. 85
Bartlett
   Agnes E.H. 94
   Caroline D. 110
   Eliza Allen 194
   Estelle 110
   F.J. 140
   John R. 194
   Lambert Tree 140
   Martha S. 140
   Thomas 110
   William O. 94
Bartol
   George E. 147
Bashaw
   E. 175
Bassett
   Ann 271
   Effie Kate 42
   Elenore O'Neil 51
   Mary Ann 149
   Mary Effie 149
   Mary Jane 52
   Richard 271
   Robert T. 42
   Sidney 149
   Susan 42
   William H., Capt. 51
Bastianelli
   Bianca 185
   Mary 185
   Titus 185
Batchin
   Margaret 163
Bates
   John E. 66
   Mary 163
   Mary E. 248
   William 163
   William F. 163
Bath 98
Bath Co., Va. 97, 182
Bath, Me. 98, 220
Batman
   Isabel C. 12
   Jane C. 12
   John H. 12
Baton Rouge, La. 30, 94, 103, 111, 260

Baum
   Catharine 124
Baxter
   William, Rev. 26
Bayard
   Ann 271
   James A. 271
   Richard 272
Bayless/Bayliss
   Sarah Ann 100
   Susan 121
Baylor
   C.G. 132, 133
Bayne
   Dr. 260
   George H. 192
   Kate 9
   Matilda 9
   Thomas 9, 132
   William B. 139
   William H., Capt. 42
Bayou Sara, La. 80
Bayoune, France 113
Beagle
   Eliza 55
   Mary Frances 196
   William 255
Beale
   E.A. 36
   George N. 27
   George, Sr. 36
Beall
   Alexander E. 217
   Alexander Gordon 38
   Azell 162
   Benjamin L., Col. 38
   Col. 69
   Elizabeth C. 69
   J.H. 140
   Maria Louisa 140
   Richard J. 162
   Richard M. 88
   Robert L. 52
Bean
   George 28
Beardsley
   Joseph, Sr. 58
   Sarah J. 58
   Susan 8
Beatley
   C. 40
   Margaret 40
Beatty
   Charles A., Dr. 12
   Charles W. 203
   James 48
   Rosanna A. 12
Bebee
   William H., Rev. 129
Beck
   Joseph W. 78, 271
   Nicholas 248

Beckett
   Harriet F. 207
   Mary H. 75
   Richard 75
Beckham
   Frances J. 95
   James A. 95
Bedford Co., Tenn. 215
Bedford Co., Va. 168, 201, 244
Bedford, Pa. 177, 261
Bedinger
   B.F., Dr. 252
   Daniel P. 230
   Olivia M. Todd 252
Beedle
   Andrew F. 8
Beeler
   L.F. 6
Beers
   B.F. 56
   Isaac 236
   Mary Ann 9
   Virginia 126
Begman
   Catharine 29
   William 29
Beirne
   Ellen 209
   George P. 209
Belden
   Calvin 221
   Emeline 221
Belgium 272
Belin
   Augustus 221
   Mary Alletta 221
Belknap
   Brig. Gen. 265
   Clara 265
   William W. 219
Bell
   Emily 273
   George 111
   Henry H., Lieut. 56
   Joseph T. 207
   Otho B. 195
   Thaddeus 63
   William 137
Belleville, N.J. 179
Belmont, Md. 206
Belmont, Mo. 67
Belt
   Bettie Elton 34
   Martha Ann C. 106
   Thomas W. 112
Beltsville, Md. 79, 169
Bemis
   Isabella H. 262
   N.P. 262
Bencoolen, Sum. 157
Bender
   Harriet 38
   Jacob A. 38
Benecia, Calif. 133

Benedict
  William B. 166
Benfield
  Moria Isabel 181
  William 181
Benner
  Anna 216
  Harry C. 216
  Harry T. 216
Bennett
  A. 4
  Elizabeth 71
  James H. 74
Bennington, Ver. 259
Benoist
  H.E., Mrs. 169
Benson
  Cephas W. 19
  Susan Harriet 19
Benter
  William 240
Bentley
  Caleb 35
Benton
  Col. 251
  Elizabeth 251
  John Randolph 81
  Thomas H., Col. 81
  Thomas H., Hon. 251
Berkeley
  Lewis 153
  William N. 67
Berkeley Co., Va. 11, 150, 163, 237, 252, 266
Berkley
  Louis 55
  Mary L. 55
Berkshire, Eng. 118
Berlin
  Samuel 195
Berlin, Ger. 94
Bern, Switz. 103
Bernard
  Ann 39
Berrien
  Eliza Cecil 74
  John MacPherson, Hon. 74
Berry
  Anna 33
  Annie Maria 232
  Catherine M. 125
  Eliza H. 122
  Fannie L. 248
  Henry 157
  J.C. 207
  James A. 268
  Mary 192
  Matilda W. 157
  Norah Ann 112
  Peter 30
  Rev. 19
  Thomas B. 248
  Thomas Devlin 248
  Washington 232, 271

Washington O. 37
Wyatt S. 263
Zachariah 206
Berryman
  O.H., Capt. 41
Berryville, Va. 255
Bertholf
  Thomas, Rev. 71
Bestor
  Norman S. 204
Bethune
  Rev. 23
Betts
  Henrietta T. 105
Bevan
  Thomas 149
Beveridge
  Charles C. 250
  Hannah Melville 50
Beverly
  J. Bradshaw 166
  Jane Byrd 246
  Robert 246
  William 124
Beverly, Md. 65
Beverly, Va. 259
Beyer
  Samuel B. 23
Bias
  C. 97
Biays
  Philip G. 156
  Rebecca T. 156
Bibb
  Chancellor 197
  George M., Hon. 203
  Henry Ashton 203
  John J. Crittenden 197
  John J.C. 196
Bickley
  Elizabeth 223
  Lloyd W. 223
Bicksler
  Ann V. 270
Biddle
  John 164
  Margaretta Falconer 164
Bigelow
  Lucy Prescott 132
  Mme. 132
  Timothy, Hon. 132
Billing
  William W. 23
Billop
  Rev. 197
Bingham
  Caleb 104
  Emma Jane 9
  Sophia 104
Binney
  F.G., Rev. 17
Birch
  B. 39
  James H., Hon. 189

Mary Frances 39
Birckhead
  Mary E. 144
  Sarah 79
Birge
  Cyrus 268
  Mary H. 268
Birney
  Eliza Jane 176
Birns
  Rev. 224
Birth
  Ann 249
  James 249
  Jane 144
Biscamp
  Rev. 77
Bishop (occupation) 99, 107, 116, 164, 254, 255
Bishop
  Joseph 55
  William G. 2
Bissell
  Champion 256
  James Henry 188
  S.B., Lieut. 188
  Sarah 188
Bittinger
  B.F., Rev. 69
  Edmund C., Rev. 14
  John 69
  Margaret 69
Black
  Furman 29
  Furman, Capt. 82
  Mrs. 82
  Sarah A. 29
Blackfan
  Ogden W. 252
Blackford
  Edward 237
  Elizabeth Godfrey 237
Blackiston
  Ann 39
  Bernard 39
Blackwell
  J.D., Rev. 158
  Rev. 69, 100, 138, 155, 186
Bladensburg, Md. 13, 17, 40, 92, 116, 138, 176, 210, 265
Blagden
  Anne 98
  Emily G. 28
  Emily S. 98
  Emily Silliman 193
  Miriam 98
  Miriam Phillips 28
  Thomas 28, 98, 193
Blagrove
  H.B. 170
  L., Mrs. 170
Blair
  Francis P. 170

Blake
    James A., Maj. 87
    John A., Capt. 46
    William J. 129
Blanchard
    William 158
Blandfield, Va. 246
Blandwood, N.C. 85
Blau
    Joseph A. 40
Blight
    William P. 84
Blish
    Caroline A. 252
    James, Capt. 252
Bliss
    Col. 108
    John, Lieut. 271
Blockley Hospital 3
Bloomington, Ill. 193
Bloomsburg, [Pa.] 120
Blount
    Annie Isabella 196
    T.M. 196
Blue Sulphur Springs, Va. 104
Blunt
    H.W. 267
    Simon Fraser, Lieut. 224
Boak
    Mr. 61, 161
    William Lee 266
Boak's boarding-house 161
Boardman
    Alice Monroe 118
    Elizabeth Ann 118, 134
    H.A., Rev. 117
    John Williamson Monroe 134
    Samuel 134
    Samuel, Dr. 118
Boarman
    Charles, Capt. 11, 189
    Francis L. 208
    M. 60
    Mary Jane 189
    Raphael 60
    Susan Martha 11
    Walter F., Dr. 271
Boatswain 43
Bocock
    Thomas S., Hon. 186
Bodisco
    Mrs. 183
Bogusch
    Sophia Maria 227
Bohlayer
    Mary C. 96
Bohn
    John 19
Boiseau
    James 102
Bolling
    Robert B. 242
    Sarah Melleville 242

Bolton
    Mary H. 257
Bolton, Md. 199
Bombay, British India 157, 269
Bonce
    Mary L. 10
    Thos., Maj. 10
Bond
    Ann 113
    Ellen J. 120
    John R.S. 86
    William Key, Hon. 120
Booker
    Jabez B. 144
Boone
    Charity 165
    John F. 21
Boone Co., Ky. 252
Boonesboro, Md. 176
Boonville, Mo. 252
Bootes
    Araminta 100
    Maria 19
    Samuel 19, 100
Booth
    Elizabeth 197
    James, Hon. 197
Booton
    A.C., Rev. 223
Bordentown, N.J. 187
Bordezux 125
Borland
    Alexander 205
    Elizabeth Jane 205
    John 149
    Mary 205
    Mary E. 201
Borrows
    Joseph 227
    Susan 227
Bossell
    Mary 64
Boston Traveller 260
Boston, Mass. 11, 31, 48, 51, 52,
    84, 96, 104, 109, 111, 114,
    120, 147, 151, 154, 163,
    207, 208, 226, 228, 246,
    252, 255, 264, 266
Boswell
    James L. 205
    Sophronia 181
Boteler
    J. Wesley, Rev.* 213
    William, Dr. 33
Botetourt Co., Va. 242
Bott
    Margaret 45
Botts
    Lawson 9
Boucher
    Catherine 122
    Orford 38
Bouldin
    Hon. 226

James W., Hon. 226
Bowen
    George Peyton 61
    James 124
    James A. 175
    John F. 175
    Leonidas 61
    Mary 61
    P.B., Dr. 248
    Virginia 251
Bower, The 255
Bowers
    Frances L. 226
    Richard F. 170
Bowie
    Amelia M. 66
    Caroline L. 121
    Elizabeth 236
    G.W. 180
    Gov. 236
    J.W.L.W., Dr. 156
    Margaret D. 1
    Mary 180
    Mary Anna 180
    Oden, Col. 58
    R.C. 180
    R.J., Hon. 1
    Robert 1
    Robert W. 121
    Walter 66
    William D., Col. 203
Bowling Green, Ky. 49, 53, 56, 185
Bowman
    F., Rev. 238
Bowyer
    Ann D. 163
    Charlotte Augusta 163
    John C. 163, 184, 257
    Lizzie 257
    Matilda S. 184
Boyall
    Ann 256
Boyd
    A.H.H., Rev. 186
    Amand 3
    Helen C. 74
    James L. 74
    Joseph Knox 17, 18
    Robert 3
    Robert B. 188
Boydville, Va. 186
Boyer
    Henry 215
Boyle
    C., Dr. 217, 241
    Cornelius, Dr. 125
    Fannie R. 241
    Neal 241
    Patrick 1
    Rev. 231, 248
    Thomas J. 210
    Thomas, Capt. 210
Bozzel
    Robert L. 169

Brackenbridge/Brackenridge
　Isabella A. 145
　William 145
　William D. 145, 163
Bradford
　Charles, Capt. 16
　George W. 184
　Mary C. 112
Bradley
　George T. 160
　Hannah S. 62
　Joseph H. 62
　Maria V. 234
　W. Wallace 205
　William W. 205
Bragin
　Francis W., Dr. 81
　Martha Isabella 81
Brandenbury
　F. William 193
Brandt
　Jane Seabrook 236
　John D. 236
　Logan, Dr. 160
　Rosannah 236
Brandywine, Pa. 205
Brank
　R.G., Rev. 166
Brashear
　Benedict 169
　J. Clayton 177
Brashears
　Christopher H. 116
Brasnahan
　Margaret 102
Brawner
　Hezekiah 46
　James T. 46
　Laura A. 110
　Mary Jane 46
　Rosella A. 2
Brayfield
　Catharine Sophia 80
　Martha A. 259
Brazil 112
Breckenridge
　John 83
　John, Rev.* 245
　Mary C. 245
　Mary Cabell 83
Breese
　Cornelia W. 100
　Cornelius Lavergne 175
　William C. 100, 175
Brehon
　James G., Dr. 238
　Rebecca 238
Brent
　Elizabeth 136
　Henry J. 102
　James R. 11
　Janet Elliot 111
　John Carroll 53
　Kate Douglas 102

Mary Virginia 91
　R. Carrere 111
　R. Carrese 39
　William, Col. 91
Brent(s)ville, Va. 86, 109
Brentwood, D.C. 4, 136
Brereton
　John 265
　Mary Ann 75
　Samuel 75, 216
Brewer
　Lucinda J. 23
　Martha Plater 217
　Nicholas, Dr. 217
Brewster
　Joshua, Capt. 26
　William 26
Brick
　Michael 19
Bridges
　David 259
　Kate S. 259
Bridget
　Richard 143
Bridwell
　Catharine P. 89
　Timothy 2
　Virginia 2
Briggs
　Anna C.J. 209
　J. Marion 160
　J. Rebecca 67
　Marian J. 166
　Samuel S., Rev.* 67
　Thomas 166
Bright
　Michael E. 141
Brightwell
　Elizabeth 41
　Thomas R. 125
Briscoe
　Miss 15
Brison
　Samuel, Rev.* 188
Britannic Majesty's Legation 137
Britt
　George R.P. 16
Broad Creek House, Md. 46
Broaddus
　William F., Rev. 103
Brock
　William G. 54
Brockenbrough
　John, Dr. 102
Brocket
　Elizabeth 113
　Robert, Sr. 113
Brodbeck
　Jacob 102
Brodhead
　Alfred W. 137
　John M. 137
　John, Hon. 137
　Josephine 137

Thomas W. 203
Brogden
　Amelia 201
Bronaugh
　John W. 44
　Virginia M. 44
Brooke
　Ann Eleanor 196
　Anne 208
　B.F., Rev. 260
　Clement 196
　Edmund 61
　Edmund H. 262
　Elizabeth 198
　Emily 262
　James, Jr. 198
　Lucy Ann 169
　Mary Louisa 262
　Walter 169
Brookeville, Md. 1
Brookfield, Mass. 214
Brookline, Mass. 207
Brooklyn, (L.I.) N.Y. 23, 39, 47, 83,
　　98, 140, 143, 189, 193,
　　224, 232, 260
Brooks
　Edmund H. 241
　Elizabeth A. 4
　Elizabeth Graham 241
　Emily 241
　Indiana H. 112
　J., Col. 4
　J.M., Dr. 106
　James 30
　John 112
　John T. 110
　Lewis 180, 187
　Margaret 187
　Patrick H. 225
　Peter 217
　Virginia 180
Broom
　Robert H. 4
Broome
　William H. 189
Broughton
　Richard G., Jr. 264
Brown
　A.C. 13
　A.H. 259
　Alexander H. 6
　Ann E. 66
　Bedford, Dr. 101
　Benjamin, Hon. 75
　Catharine Jane 160
　Charlotte L. 43
　Daniel 251
　Dr. 240
　Eliza R. 81, 182
　Elizabeth 112
　Emily F. 19
　Emily Sandford 75
　Emma 43
　Fanny Peyton 25

George B.T. 81
Ida 182
Isabella C. 234
J.G. 125
J.W., Rev. 169
Jacob, Maj. Gen. 58
James 207
James A. 101
James H., Rev. 160, 169, 172, 182, 183, 188, 191, 196, 197, 201, 204, 206-208, 212, 213, 223, 225, 230, 231, 234, 252, 253, 255, 256, 258, 268, 272
James, Rev. 182, 198
Jesse 138
John D. 273
John E. 58
John P. 47, 108
John R. 108
John S. 105
John, Gen. 25
Margaret Lovel 58
Mary A. 101
Mary Ann Virginia 33
Mary Armenia 125
Mary Jane 259
Mary R. 108
Michael 103
Morgan W. 147
Newton, Rev. 160
O.B., Rev. 8, 24, 25, 49, 66
O.B., Rev.* 88, 112, 256
Phebe 251
Philip T. 40
R.T., Rev. 261
Rev. 73
Robert T. 13
Rosanna 138
Theodore 101
Thomas 75, 81, 182, 257
William J. 163
William J., Hon. 101
William P. 152
Wyatt 244
Brown's Hotel 111, 138, 158, 210, 245
Browne
	Causten 95
	Katherine 225
	Lucian Carter 10
	T. Egerton 30
Browning
	Wood 101
Brownson
	J.J., Rev. 90
Brownville, N.Y. 58
Bruce
	H., Rev. 107
Bruff
	Richard W. 161
Brumley
	Sarah 196
Brunswick, N.J. 261

Brunswick, Va. 159
Brush
	Mary C. 149
Bryan
	Catherine 108
	Daniel 101
	Joseph 250
	Mary E. 250
	Octavia 250
	Rebecca Jane 130
	Sally 101
	W.J. 108
	William 108
Bryant
	Alfred 152
	Anna Lilly 152
	Emma 152
	John Y. 152
	William, Rev.* 152
Bryantown, Md. 271
Bryson
	Mary M. 131
	Rev. 130, 138
	Samuel, Rev.* 131
Buchanan
	A.H., Dr. 237
	Alex. Pitt 237
	Sarah 237
	Sarah B. 3
Buchanan, Va. 242
Buchly
	Anthony 230
Buck
	Charles N. 31
	Joel A., Maj. 93
	Rev. 128
Buckington
	John E. 1
Buckler
	Ann Elizabeth 21
	John, Dr. 21
Buckley
	Dennis 32
	Eliza 114
	Hannah 32
	Philip J. 99
Buckmaster
	N. 60
	Sallie 60
Bucks Co., Pa. 120
Budd
	Bern W., Dr. 207
Buddy
	John 212
	Mary A. 212
Budington
	Lizzie Livingston 272
	William Ives, Rev.* 272
Buel
	John McLane 45
Buell
	D.C., Maj. 59
Buena Vista 206
Buena Vista, Del. 12, 223

Buffalo Commercial Advertiser 245
Buffalo, N.Y. 5, 24, 62, 141, 150, 151
Buffington
	Thomas C., Dr. 104
Bulger
	Margaret A. 2
Bulk
	Corder 161
Bulkley
	Edwin, Rev. 258
Bull
	Anna Louisa 82
	Anna R. 82
	Samuel 82
Bullit
	Thomas 205
Bullitt
	Alexander C. 26
	Susan 193
	William C. 193
Bulloch
	James D. 55
Bunch
	John T., Col. 93
Bunker Hill, Mass. 132
Bunting
	Charles 182
	Rev. 39
Burch
	John T. 221
	Remigius 39
Burche
	America Fatio 243
	Mary E. 269
	Samuel, Col. 243
Burchel
	Norval Wilson 260
Burdine
	Caroline 67
	R. 148
	William 67
Burdion
	Charles 110
Bureau of Medicine and Surgery 74
Burford
	Elizabeth 13
	William Bowie 204
Burgess
	Ann 121
	Annie Candace 67
	C.E. 67
	Cynthia S. 151
	George, Rev. 252
	John W. 122
	Mary 96
	R.W. 67, 151
	Richard 96, 121
Burgevin
	Mary Ann 228
burials 211, 238, 247, 248, 252, 263, 270, 273

Burke
- Dennis, Dr. 100
- Ellen 139
- John W. 128
- Michael 139

Burkhardt
- Mary A. 176

Burlington, N.J. 188
Burlington, Ver. 29, 47, 183

Burnap
- George W., Rev. 21

Burnes
- Susan 250

Burnett
- Charles A. 63
- Elethea 63

Burnley
- Mr. 196

Burns
- George 254
- Harman 76
- Mary Ellen 254
- William 47

Burnside, N.C. 40

Burr
- Richard W. 95

Burriss
- Louis, Dr. 96

Burroughs
- Charles, Rev. 140
- John W. 84
- Rev. 220
- William T. 65

Burson
- John 101
- Margaret M. 101

Burt
- James, Hon. 81

Burwell
- James 174

Bury
- John 66
- William 86

Bushnell
- Horace, Rev. 169

Buthmann
- Adelaide 212
- George Henry 212
- John H. 212

Butler
- Ap., Hon. 200
- Behethland Foote 200
- Benjamin F. 39
- C.M., Rev. 19, 53, 59, 100, 114, 115, 125, 126, 133, 138, 189, 204, 207, 214, 216, 225, 244
- C.R.P., Lieut. 197
- Charles 39
- Chester, Hon. 246
- Dr. 257
- Elizabeth 196
- Elizabeth C. 268
- Ferdinand 198, 268
- George 72
- George G. 237
- J. George, Rev. 42, 45, 68, 79, 89, 91, 112, 123, 163, 184, 192, 195, 198, 244
- J. George, Rev.* 49
- James 71
- Jedson 234
- John H. 159
- Rev. 6, 23, 62, 76, 94, 99, 110, 112, 124, 126, 190, 203, 204, 208, 209
- Sarah Hollenback 246
- V.M., Dr. 157
- Walter 39
- William H.B. 228
- William, Gen. 200

Butrick
- Daniel S. 32

Butt
- Rebecca 128
- Solomon 128

Butterfield
- Franklin 146, 147, 237
- Nancy H. 237

Byer/Byers
- Henrietta 255
- James F. 110

Byers & McKnew 194

Byrd
- Elizabeth Hill 128
- William, Col. 128

Byrne
- Barnard M., Dr. 54
- C.R. 204
- Christopher R. 123, 220
- Fanny 204
- Henry R. 204
- Mary J. 106
- Mary Virginia 106
- P.A. 106
- Rev. 225

Byron, Ill. 264

C

Cabell
- Edward A. 190
- Jane H.M. 190

Caffee
- Robert Henderson 153

Cairo, Egypt 35
Calcutta 207

Caldwell
- Elias B. 92
- Harriet J. 92
- James 18
- Lafayette 194
- Rev. 69, 84, 97, 167, 206

Caldwell Co., N.C. 85

Calhoun
- Catharine Matilda 65
- John C. 99
- John, Lieut. 65

California 30, 32, 127, 138, 141, 142, 148, 149, 184, 208, 234, 253

Callaghan
- Catherine E. 170
- Dennis 158, 170
- Mary 158, 170
- Mary M. 155
- Samuel Lindsay 158

Callahan
- Rev. 27

Callan
- M.P. 68

Callaway
- C.M., Rev. 41

Calvary Church 43

Calvert
- Anne Maria 66
- Charles 102
- John 230
- William H. 231

Calvert Co., Md. 20, 26, 62, 75, 80, 83, 128, 132, 150, 167, 171, 173, 178, 194

Calwell
- Columbia 46
- William B. 46

Cambreling
- Anne 89
- Stephen 89

Cambridge, Mass. 2
Cambridge, Md. 5, 223
Camden 60
Camden, N.J. 54, 123

Cameron
- John W. 156
- Laurentia 191
- Mark L. 191
- Thomas Nash, Dr. 31

Cammack
- Elizabeth E. 111
- John J. 100
- Martha 18
- Robert 212
- William 18, 212
- William, Jr. 3

Camp
- E.B. 113

Campbell
- Alexander, Capt. 195
- Bernard M. 266
- Catherine M. 115
- George W. 178
- George Washington 178
- John A. 114
- John W. 257
- L., Rev. 235
- Mahaly 87
- Martha F. 42
- Mary Ellen 119
- Mary J. 138
- Richard H. 138
- Richard Price 138

Samuel 42
Thomas B. 119
William 231
William H. 195
William Thompson 42
Camptonville, Calif. 216
Campuzano
    Jose Maria deMagellon 107
Canada 92, 174
Canada West 141
Cannonsburgh, Pa. 240
Canton, China 133, 207
Cape Fear river 221
Cape Island, N.J. 4
Capitol Hill 1-3, 8, 20, 29, 37, 45,
    52, 53, 57, 63, 69, 72, 78,
    82, 85, 88, 93, 109, 114,
    116, 127, 131, 136, 138,
    158, 165, 175, 183, 191,
    201, 203-204, 210, 219,
    222, 244, 247-248, 251,
    255-256, 264-265, 271
Capron
    E.A., Capt. 27
    H.R.F. 27
Carberry/Carbery
    Catherine 113
    Helen Mary 87
    James 17, 87
    Lewis 113
Carden
    Susanna G. 205
    Thomas 66
Carder
    Rev. 15
Carey
    Matthew 261
    Virginia 89
    William 33, 119
    Wilson Jefferson 89
Carl
    Margaret 89
Carlin
    William H. 120
Carlisle
    Anne Mandeville 251
    J.M. 251
    James Mandeville 206
    Mandeville 206
    Michael Henry 223
Carlisle, Pa. 62, 88, 92, 127, 236
Carlow Co., Ire. 142
Carmarthen
    Family of 229
Carmichael
    Charles H. 258
    E.H., Dr. 258
    Edward H., Dr. 94, 222
    Emily H. 94
    Sarah 258
    William 205
Carnahan
    James, Rev. 240
Caroline Co., Va. 41, 56, 244

Carothers
    A.G., Rev. 193, 195, 198, 226
    Andrew G., Rev. 243, 256, 272
    Rev. 216
Carr
    Mary 106
    Susannah C. 123
Carrington
    William 256
Carroll
    Charles 98, 228
    Family of 229
    James T. 188
    James, Jr. 231
    Mary Jane 134
    Michael B. 43
    Nancy 245
    Sylvester 252
    Virginia Elizabeth 53
Carroll Co., Md. 43
Carrollton, Md. 98
Carrollton, Mo. 142
Carson
    Eliza Frances 150
    Elizabeth 19
    Ellen C. 241
    Thomas J. 241
Carter
    Alfred B. 57
    Alice 58
    Ambrose 248
    Ann C. 113
    Charles H. 27, 58
    Elizabeth 189
    Ida 248
    John C., Capt. 113
    Lucina H. 248
    Maria Champe 128
    Mrs. 57
    Otwayanna 90
    Robert A. 250
    Robert Randolph 67
    Rosalie Eugenia 27
    S. Powhatan 36
    William Champe 128
    William Fitzhugh 189
Cartland
    Samuel, Hon. 77
Carusi
    Adelaide 181
    Maria Eugenia 181
    Nathaniel 44
    Phillippa 44
    Samuel 181
Carusi's Saloon 113
Carvallo
    Don Manuel 14, 99, 165
    Mary Eliza 165
    Mme. 14
Casey
    John 45
Cash
    John C., Lieut. 125
    William 256

Cashier 209
Caskie
    John 55
    Lizzie E. 55
Casparis
    Christina 123
    James 123
Cass
    Lewis, Jr., Hon. 232
    Mary 85
Cassell
    John T. 204
    Sarah E. 204
Cassick
    Catharine 67
Caster
    T.L., Lieut. 59
Castle Hill, Va. 226
Castle Pinckney, S.C. 115
Castleman
    T.T., Rev. 105
    Thomas T., Rev. 190
Catalano
    Antonio 226
Catawba, N.C. 169
Cates
    Richard W. 115
    Sarah A. 115
    William J. 115
Cathcart
    Amelia H. 85
    James Leander 85
Cathedral 171, 248, 271
Catholic Chapel 31
Catlett
    Ellen A. 139
    Emily 139
    Hanson G. 139
Caton
    Edward Charles 155
    Eliza J. 68
    Family of 229
    Maria 111
    Patrick H. 86, 155
Catonville, Md. 151
Causten
    Annie Payne 122
    James H. 122
Cave, The 242
Cazenove
    Anthony C. 118
    Louis A. 79
Cazenovia, D.C. 169
Cecil Co., Md. 173, 233
Cedar Co., Ia. 237
Cedar Hill, Ky. 26
Cedar Hill, Md. 1
Census Bureau 220, 242
Census Office 55
Centre Market 41
Cerro Gordo 126, 185, 190
Chadbourne
    John S., Rev. 103

Chadburn
    J.S., Rev. 94
Chalfant/Chalfrant
    Hannah 117
    Josephine 127
    Robert 127
Chambers
    B.B. 108
    E.F., Hon. 205
Chamier
    Rev. 60
Champion
    Sarah Ann 59
Chancellor 25
    Henry 221
    Marie C. 221
    Samuel 55
    Virginia 55
Chancey
    John S. 178
Chantilly, Va. 261
Chapel of Grace 50
Chapin
    E.M., Dr. 219
    Nathan C., Rev.* 255
    Sarah 239
    Stephen, Rev.* 239
Chaplain 45, 59, 93, 110, 171
Chapman
    Elizabeth 216
    Elizabeth A. 61
    Emily C. 105
    Fanny J. 69
    George 49
    George P. 188
    George W., Lieut. 142
    Henry H. 59, 61, 69
    Henry, Hon. 216
    John G., Gen. 188
    Louisa 49
    Mary 61
    N. 105
Chappell
    E.T. 14
Chaptico, Md. 48
Charles
    Albert 52
Charles Co., Md. 2, 4, 6, 8, 11, 46, 69, 74, 83, 96, 101, 128, 133, 142, 146, 153, 160, 161, 165, 174, 176, 184, 192, 195, 208, 229, 233, 235, 236, 257, 264, 268, 273
Charles I 174
Charleston 127
Charleston Harbor, S.C. 115
Charleston, S.C. 68, 92, 99, 100, 108, 123, 157, 175, 178, 197, 218, 220, 254, 261
Charleston, Va. 114
Charlestown, Mass. 272
Charlestown, Md. 173
Charlestown, Va. 8, 162

Charlier
    Alph., Rev. 171
Charlotte Co., Va. 54, 226
Charlotte Courthouse, Va. 191
Charlotte Hall, Md. 47
Charlotte, N.C. 87, 94, 97
Charlottesville, Va. 80, 101, 188
Chase
    Ann 107
    C.H., Maj. 240
    Carleton, Rev. 54
    Elizabeth 56
    Samuel, Hon. 107
    William 56
Chattahoochee, Fla. 118, 134
Chattanooga, Tenn. 38
Chatterton, Va. 263
Chauncey
    Comm. 243
    Elizabeth 46
    John S. 18
    Maria Graham 18
Cheatham
    E.S., Col. 31
    Jane Ellen 31
Chelsea 116
Cheneworth/Cheniworth
    A.G., Rev. 234
    Rev. 1, 271
Cheney
    Joseph Warren 190
Chepultepec 126, 141, 263
Cheraw, S.C. 209
Cherokee Advocate 72
Cherokee Indians 32
Cherokee Nation 32, 71, 72
Chester Co., Pa. 121
Chester, Pa. 215
Chestertown, Md. 96, 167, 203, 205
Chestnut Hill, Pa. 84
Chevers
    M.L., Rev. 62
Chew
    Thomas R., Dr. 265
Chicago, Ill. 39, 85, 136
Chick
    Joseph 233
Childress
    Lavinia F. 226
    Mary A. 255
Childs
    E.L., Rev. 2
    Francis A. 184
    Gen. 197
    Rev. 254
    Thomas, Gen. 190
    Wentworth L., Rev. 252
Chile (Chili) 9, 14, 16, 99, 165
Chilton
    Robert S. 91
China 7, 21, 35, 207
Chinn
    Thomas W. 96

Chism
    Jane Virginia 224
    William Lewis 181
Choate
    Rufus 225
Choctaw Indians 146
Chouteau
    Charles P. 163
    Juliet A. 163
Christ Church 2, 4, 6, 8, 9, 37, 66, 69, 72, 80, 84, 95, 96, 104, 114, 135, 157, 160, 166, 167, 189, 206, 222, 230, 237, 252, 256, 271
Christian
    Caroline C. 19
    John H. 252
    Mary H. 120
    Mildred C. 252
Chubb
    J. Munroe 50
    John L. 245
Church
    J.M., Rev. 4
Church of God 152
Church of Salem 240
Church of St. Mathew 98
Church of the Advent 264
Church of the Ascension 8, 19, 22, 159, 164, 173, 186, 215, 220, 253
Church of the Epiphany 6, 32, 53, 70, 71, 91, 95, 100, 101, 107, 108, 127, 147, 151, 156, 161, 185, 195, 212, 226, 259, 266
Church of the Incarnation 260
Church of the Nativity 209
Churubusco, Ind. 126
Cincinnati, Ohio 5, 7, 23, 68, 86, 96, 101, 104, 113, 120, 127, 169, 225, 239, 246, 272
Cissel/Cissil
    Elizabeth 3
    Lizzie R. 86
    Mary C. 65
    Thomas 3, 65, 86
    William 189
City Hall 2, 121, 161
City Hotel 163
Civil Engineer (see Engineer) 184
Civita Vecchia 49
Clabaugh
    William 3, 212
Clabough
    Lizzie R. 86
    William 86
Clack
    John H., Capt. 271
    Mary Louisa 271
Clagett
    Caroline 232
    Darius 135

Mary F. 127
Richard H. 232
Richard H., Dr. 7
Claiborne Co., Miss. 26, 147
Clapham
   John 8
Clare
   Mrs. 31, 107
   Sarah 99
Clare's boarding-house 31, 258
Clark
   Cassie 184
   Ellen 12
   Frances M. 165
   Gen. 56
   J.C., Lieut. 122
   James A. 174
   Jane 212
   Jane E. 225
   John F. 90
   John T.C. 225
   L.F. 65
   Mary Ann 174
   Mary Malvina 225
   Milton 8
   Miss 54
   Rebecca 90
   Rev. 95, 96, 265
   Robert 212
   William D. 110
   William J., Rev. 100, 101
Clarke
   Anna Louisa 102
   Emma 162
   Fanny 247
   Frances L. 30
   George A.D. 20, 164
   George St. Clair 164
   Gustavus A. 2
   Jane 76
   Jeanet St. Clair 20
   John G. 257
   John W. 194
   M. St. Clair 102
   Mary V. 20, 164
   Matthew St. Clair 89
   Rev. 264
   Richard W. 76, 226
   Robert 30, 138
   Virginia 259
   William J., Rev. 270
   William Joseph 138
Clarke Co., Va. 97, 112, 166, 204, 230, 255, 256, 259, 268, 273
Clarkson
   Catharine Matilda 65
   John C. 65
   Rev. 184
   Robert 172
   S.S., Rev. 248
Clarksville, Tenn. 55, 190
Clary
   Amanda J. 20

Maria L. 174
R.E., Capt. 20, 174
Clauss
   F.C. 149
   Sophia 149
Clavaux
   Marc 86
Claxton
   A.B. 150, 203
   Johannah Elizabeth 150
   John 15
   Mr. 196
Clay
   Henry 100, 272
   J.C., Dr. 158
Clay Hill, Ga. 77
Clayton
   Harriett Middleton 92
   James 92
   James F. 12
   James Robert 86
   John M., Hon. 12, 92
   Sarah 92
Clean Drinking, Md. 247
Cleary
   Eliza M.D. 175
   Nicholas 175
Cleckhardt
   Dorothy 155
Clements
   Benjamin H. 100
   Catharine Bridget 143
   John T. 77
   Lewelen Clotildus 100
   Mary C.L. 100
   Rachel Amelia 77
   Sarah 132
   Sarah Ann 193
Clementson
   Sarah Ann 127
Clerc
   Rev. 146
Clerk (occupation) 2, 6, 8, 10, 21, 55, 62, 64, 77, 89, 91, 103, 109, 111, 122, 215, 220, 221, 229, 233, 242, 246, 250, 266
Clerk of the Circuit Court 168
Clermont, Va. 148
Cleveland
   Martha B. 54
   William 54
Cleveland Herald 254
Cleveland, Va. 79
Cliff Cottage, N.J. 107
Clifton, Va. 273
Clinton
   Thomas G. 228
Clinton, Miss. 118
Close
   James T. 17
Closkery
   H.B., Rev. 271

Cloud
   Susan 207
Clough
   May Ann 52
   William 52
Clover
   Rev. 17
Clover Hill, Md. 75
Clubb
   Elizabeth 4
   John L. 4
Clunas
   James 116
Clute
   Elizabeth 85
   Rodolphus 85
Clymer
   Henry 120
   Mary Willing 120
Clyne
   William 219
Coast Survey 52, 94, 148, 166, 235
Cobey
   Mary Amelia 117
Cochran
   Adelaide J. 206
   Fanny Travis 234
   William G. 234
Cochrane
   John T. 261
   Richard O., Dr. 261
   Thomas L. 174
Cocke
   Anna 227
Cockrell
   Catharine 178
Coddington
   Camilla 174
   John B. 174
   Josephine Watson 174
Coffee
   Gen. 244
Coffer
   Ann Elizabeth 151
Cokey
   Deborah O. 164
Colchester 52
Colclazer
   Mary 234
Cold Spring, N.Y. 183
Coldwell
   Joseph T. 252
Cole
   Adelia A. 162
   Isaac, Rev. 170
   Joshua, Jr. 254
   Rev. 181, 214, 249
   Robert 255
   S.L. 162, 201
Cole Co., Mo. 13
Colebrook, N.H. 213, 255

Colegate
- Charles 164
- Elizabeth B. 99
- Elizabeth M. 164
- James 99, 164
- Myron Stanley 99

Coleman
- Charles W. 186
- George C. 238
- Margaret 1
- William 199

Colerain Forges, Pa. 232
Colesville, Md. 109, 133
Collector 23, 242
College Chapel 25
College Hill, D.C. 25, 70
College of New Jersey 135

Collier
- Jane E. 64
- Mary A. 129

Collings
- N.B., Rev. 65

Collington Meadows 225

Collins
- Ann Winifred 239
- David 239
- Eliza A. 234
- Ellen 8
- Erastus T., Maj. 18
- Joseph 62
- Joseph H. 123
- Joseph Henry 7
- Joseph S., Rev. 38, 47
- Mr. 173
- Sarah Rebecca 7
- Virginia 259
- William 191, 259
- Zachariah 254

Collinsville, Ill. 37

Collison
- Elizabeth 162

Colross, Va. 138

Colston
- Edw. 262
- Mary White 262

Coltman
- Charles L. 41
- Mary F. 41

Columbia Co., N.Y. 80
Columbia College 25
Columbia Typographical Society 178, 251
Columbia, Pa. 13
Columbia, S.C. 222
Columbia, Tenn. 73, 117, 165
Columbia, Va. 17
Columbian College 118, 124, 272

Columbus
- Charles 155
- Mary L. 155

Columbus, Ga. 196, 238
Commandant's mansion 189
Commissioner 6, 11, 13, 49, 85, 98, 232

Commissioner on Indian Treaties 165

Compton
- A., Rev. 41
- John W. 50

Concord Biblical Institute 24
Concord, N.H. 36
Concordia Parish, La. 267

Condict
- Eliot Dickinson 223
- H.F., Dr. 223
- Robert, Rev. 145

Condry
- Delia Walker 129
- Dennis, Hon. 129

Cone
- Spencer H., Rev. 250

Congress, U.S. 15, 24, 28, 47, 67, 72, 94, 96, 121, 125, 127, 150, 197, 218, 226, 246, 262, 271

Congressional cemetery 46, 62, 92, 165, 248

Conklin
- B.W., Gen. 257
- Emma 257

Conlan
- Ann Elizabeth 133

Connaconerara, N.C. 83
Connecticut 62, 82, 191

Connell
- John W. 49
- Julia 53
- Susan 87

Connelly
- Michael 270
- Thomas 34

Conner
- Daniel 139
- Thomas 189

Connolly
- Richard 136

Connor
- Elizabeth 55
- Sarah E. 169

Conrad
- David Holmes 28, 51
- Rebecca Holmes 28
- Robert Y. 51

Consul (occupation) 49, 60, 81, 85, 87, 93, 98, 100, 113, 124, 125, 157, 177, 201, 269

Consul at Tangiers 22
Consul-General 31

Contee
- Sarah F. 87

Contreras 185
Convent 48, 82

Conway
- Addison 265
- James A. 139
- William H. 95

Cook
- Cecelia Maria 25
- J.C. 25
- John 112
- John F., Rev. 96
- Joseph 122
- Lieut. 197
- Lucinda Alberter 25
- Mary Ellen 157

Cooke
- Anna Maria 189
- George 189
- John H. 153
- John Malcom 153
- Virginia 153

Cookendorfer
- Thomas 250

Coolidge
- Edmond 267
- Elizabeth A. 220
- Marion A. 267
- Richard H., Dr. 214

Coombs
- Margaret L. 106

Cooper
- Astley, Sir 73
- H.D. 133
- Isaac 50
- Margaret 50, 167
- Martha Washington 133
- Rev. 238
- Rev.* 240
- Sarah 213
- Susan 133

Copper
- Jane Agnes 154

Corbet
- Mary Elizabeth 217

Corbett
- Catherine 200
- Patrick 200

Corbin
- Richard 213

Corcoran
- Emily 212
- John 45, 65
- Mary 45
- Thomas, Col. 212

Corcoran & Riggs 129, 173

Cord
- William 36

Cork Co., Ire. 154, 158, 254
Cork, Ire. 32, 53

Cornelius
- Samuel, Rev.* 62
- Thomas, Rev. 49

Cornwall, Eng. 259

Cornwallis
- Lord 174

Cornwell
- George 104
- Sarah M. 104

Coroner 68
Corps of Engineers 60, 62, 117,

120, 187
Corps of Topographical Engineers 20
Corpus Christi, Tex. 53, 126, 240
Correll
   Annie 155
Corridan
   Edward 8
Corry
   Sarah A. 98
Corson
   Hiram, Jr. 255
Cosby
   F. 234
Coskery
   Rev. 171
Costigan
   Eliza 128
   John, Dr. 128
Costin
   Augustus Lot 204
   Elizabeth 204
   John T. 204
   Robert S. 199
Coston
   Benjamin Franklin 22
   Martha Jane 22
Cottage, The, Va. 83
Cottage, Va. 181
Cottringer
   B., Mrs. 39
   Garrett 39
Coumbe
   Ann M. 77
   George William 77
   John T. 77
Counsellor 46
Counsellor at Law 21
counting-house 7
Courtenay
   E.F., Prof. 159
   Virginia H. 159
Courtney
   M., Col. 44
   Mary 44
Cover
   George 180
Covington
   Rev. 91, 120
Cowing
   Ann 140
   Fitzgerald 140
Cowling
   Edward 259
   Mary 259
Cowpens 60
Cox
   C.A. 219
   Charles W. 219
   Charlotte 2
   Elizabeth 219
   Elizabeth M. 148
   Harriet Ann 161
   John 161, 172
   John, Col. 117
   Rev. 134, 193
   Richard S. 55
   S.K., Rev. 123, 169
   S.R., Rev. 110
   Samuel George 61
   W.S. 148
   W.W. 172
   William, Sr. 172
   Wm., Sr. 2
Coxe
   Ferdinand 234
   R.S. 266
Coyle
   L., Mr. 175
Cracklin
   Elizabeth A. 171
Cragin
   Charles H. 159
   Charles, Dr. 163
   Helen Hildreth 159
   Mary 159
Craig
   Josephine S. 86
Craighead
   James G., Rev. 127
   Matilda H. 127
   Wm. 127
Craighill
   Joseph A. 125
Crampton
   John F. 153
Crandell
   George 134
   James, Rev. 222
   John Thomas 247
Crary
   Isaac E., Hon. 226
Craven
   E.R., Rev.* 83
   T. 83
Crawford
   Elizabeth Catharine 243
   Eulalia 233
   John V. 201
   Joseph T. 201
   T. Hartley, Hon. 233, 243
Cray
   Margaret 19
Creamer
   Emma Rebecca 108
Creecy
   Daniel Webster 169
   Henrietta B. 154, 169
   James R. 154, 169
   Penelope Benbury 154
Creighton
   Johnston B., Lieut. 250
Crews
   Joseph 75
Crittenden
   J.J., Mrs. 26
   John J., Hon. 143
Croggon
   Isaac N.I. 193
Croghan
   Rev. 32
Crooks
   D., Rev. 127
Cropley
   Richard E. 5
   Samuel 171
   Samuel Barnard 171
Crosby
   Matilda S. 184
   Peirce, Lieut. 184
Crosdale
   John, Rev. 24, 162
Cross
   Gabriel 228
   Julia A. 119
   Lydia B. 224
   Mary B. 192
   Mary Virginia 154
   Samuel 262
   Sarah A. 218
   T., Col. 192
   Thomas 218
   Thomas A. 155
Crossan
   Thomas M., Lieut. 238
Croswell
   Rev. 47
Crouch
   B.T., Rev. 237
Crow
   John T. 173
Crowley
   J. Gideon 60
Crown
   E. 144
Crozier
   R.H. 232
Cruikshank
   Charles, Capt. 266
   Sarah 235
Cruit
   Lydia 217
   Richard 7, 217
Crummin
   Patrick 89
Crump
   George Park 73
   Margaret S. 140
Crutchett
   J. 24
Cuba 100, 201, 247
Culpeper Co., Va. 54, 95, 128, 191, 194, 213
Culpeper Courthouse, Va. 244
Culpeper, Va. 170, 248
Culver
   Adela 25
   Burgess 270
   F.B., Dr. 25
   Margaret 270

Culverwell
    Rachael 101
    Richard J.A. 27
    Stephen 101
Cumberland
    Sarah A. 52
Cumberland Co., Va. 28, 51
Cumberland Presbyterian Church 72
Cumberland, Md. 6, 60, 150, 164
Cummings
    C.J. 49
    Catharine 97
    J.M. 94
    James 97
    Kate N. 94
    Mary A. 140
Cummins
    Edmund H., Lieut. 195
    George, Rev. 259
    John L., Rev.* 78
Cunningham
    A.F. 207
    Adam Augustus 179
    Anna 207
    Arch. 179
    Daniel, Serg. 82
    Elizabeth Ann 232
    Ephraim M. 93
    Lydia A. 168
    Margaret 233
    Margaret A. 76
    Margaret Allen 53
    Mary Elizabeth 24
    Mary Esther 164
    Samuel 53, 164, 232
    Walter, Gen. 24, 110
Curran
    B.B. 180
    Catharine A. 181
    Philip 181
    W.W. 181
    William W. 161
Curren
    Ellen C. 161
    Philip 161
Curry
    Mr. 53
Curtin
    Eliza 169
    Julia Ann 234
Curtis
    Asa 268
    Susan B. 268
Cushing
    Sarah E.S. 228
    Thomas P. 228
Cushman
    R.W., Rev. 111, 255
    Rev. 30
Cuvilier
    Josephine 160

D

Dade
    Baldwin, Col. 267
    Catharine F. 267
Daggy
    Peter 57
Dahlgren
    John 32
    Lawrence Smith 32
    Mary C. 32
Daingerfield/Dangerfield
    Mary Louisa 112, 248
    William Henry, Col. 112, 248
    William Winn 112
Dale
    Catherine B. 164
    George M. 211
    George M., Dr. 168
    Mary Jane 211
Dallas Co., Ala. 226
Dallas Co., Ark. 150
Dana
    C., Rev. 147
    Charles B., Rev. 34, 128, 138, 190
Danbury, Conn. 63
Danforth
    J.N., Rev. 146, 175
    Rev. 5
Daniel
    John T. 258
    Mary Grace 11
    Peter V., Hon. 190
Daniels
    Ann 144
Dant
    Amanda Jane 55
    Mary Ann 44
    Susan 44
    William 44
    William E. 58
Danville, Ky. 268
Danville, Va. 143
Darby
    John F. 138
    John F., Hon. 138
    William 257
Dare
    Margaret M. 80
Darien, Conn. 63
Darnall
    Edmund B. 40
    Francis L. 40
    Francis Lowe 261
    Mary 40
    Nicholas L. 173
    Richard B. 173
Darnes
    Washington F. 36
Darnestown, Md. 88
Darnold
    Thomas F. 221

Darnull
    Francis H. 253
Darrell
    William S. 169
Dartmouth College 77
Dashiel
    R.L., Rev. 267
    Rev. 254
Dashiell
    Hester E. 40
    J.H., Rev. 224
    R.L., Rev. 128, 168, 192, 194
    Rev. 119
    Robert L., Rev.* 224
    T. Grayson, Rev. 241
Dashiells
    R.L., Rev. 191
    Rev. 119
Daume
    John Antoine 67
Davenport
    Cornelia A. 171
    Henry K. 171
Davenport, Ia. 271
David
    E.W. 21
    Louisa P. 21
Davidge
    William H. 138
Davidson
    Daniel D. 248
    John 97
    John Massey Moore 248
    John W., Lieut. 32
    Margaret 59, 248
    Mary L. 97
    Robert 169
    William G. 201
Davidson, Tenn. 159
Davidsonville, Md. 35, 253
Davis
    Abel 136
    Alexander McD., Dr. 215
    Barnabas 3
    C.A., Rev.* 60
    Carrie 162
    Charles A., Rev. 8, 24, 85, 105, 116, 154, 160, 212, 220, 224, 265
    Charles E. 85
    Charlotte 105
    Charlotte Pinkney 60
    Daniel W. 3
    Eli 111
    Elizabeth 29
    Elizabeth V. 201
    Frances 24
    Garrett, Hon. 162
    Henrietta W.W. 48
    James 256
    Jefferson, Hon. 231
    John 117, 136
    John A., Lieut. 205
    John, Rev.* 178

L.J., Rev. 77
Levi 14, 245
Lewis Johnson 260
M.A. 45
Margaret Ann 111
Mary Alice 45
Mary J. 198
Mattie 215
Nelson W. 236
Philip C. 200
Rev. 31, 177
Robert T. 73
Russell P. 80
Samuel Emory 231
T.M., Col. 48
Thomas J. 236
William S. 204
Davison
    Hannah 47
    Martha E. 57
    Samuel C. 57
Daw
    Marion J. 260
Dawes
    Frederick, Dr. 73
    Rufus, Rev. 212
Dawson
    Aaron 179
    Emma C. 238
    Frances 97
    Henrietta 58
    Maria Louisa 97
    Sarah 57, 179
    Wallace Eugene 179
    William 97
    William C., Hon. 58, 238, 271
    William P. 12
Day
    Catharine V. 23
    Elijah W. 22
    Eliza 139
    Henry R. 139
    Wilhelmina Augusta 139
Dayly
    Margaret 35
de Ayciena
    Don Antonio 98
Deale
    John S., Rev.* 60
deAlvear
    Don Carlos 121
Deasy
    Catherine 75
    Elizabeth 241
    Jeremiah 241
    Mary 241
DeBorboulon
    Alphonse 21
DeBow
    J.D.B. 244
DeCamp
    Abraham 26
DeCarvallo
    James Causten 16

    Manuel 16
    Mary 16
Decatur, Ala. 6
Decatur, Miss. 74
DeCharms
    Richard, Rev. 184
Decker
    John, Jr. 82
    John, Rev. 82
    John, Rev.* 210
    William Henry, Dr. 210
Declaration of Independence 98
Deeble
    Edward Tschiffely 158
    Elizabeth G. 158, 256
    Frances 38
    John G. 38, 134
    Joseph A. 158, 256
    Joseph Frederick 256
Deems
    C.F., Rev. 85
Deep Falls 48
Degges
    Laura Virginia 128
DeKrafft/DeKraft
    Charles Edward 70
    Cornelia 132
    Edward 226
    F.C. 132, 226
    Frederick W. 12, 248
    J.W. 70
    Rosanna A. 12
dela Rocha
    Don Domingo 85
    Maria Merced 85
Delaney
    Michael 168
Delany
    Louisa 21
Delaware 92, 100, 197, 245, 271
Delaware Co., N.Y. 52, 218
Delhi, N.Y. 218
Dellet(t)
    Emma E. 158
    James 148
    James, Hon. 158
Deloughery
    Catherine 115
    John 115
Delphey
    Ann Rebecca 80
    Imogen Rebecca 80
    Orlando R. 80
deMaltitz
    Baron 125
DeMarcoleta
    Joze, Comm. 163
Dement
    Charles F. 194
    J., Lieut. 192
    Louisa 194
Demopolis, Ala. 192
Demortia
    Louisa W. 96

Denecker
    H.I., Rev. 131
    Rev. 158, 159, 218
Denham
    Mary W. 139
Denison
    George, Rev. 219
Dennis
    Elizabeth Upshur 199
    George R. 199
    John P. 64
    John U. 65
    John Upshur 66
Denny
    E.D. 148
    Edward Harding 139
    Elizabeth O'Harra 139
    Harmar 72
    Maj. 139
    W.C. 139
    William Henry 206
Department of the Interior 122
dePortes y Infante
    D. Thomas, Rev. 85
Deputy
    Rachel Ella 251
DePuy
    Martha E.B. 80
Derbes
    Hon. 90
Derbyshire, Eng. 117
Derrick
    Henry C. 257
    William S. 91, 257
DeRussey/DeRussy
    Emily C. 62
    R.E., Lt. Col. 2, 62
deSartiges
    M. LeCount 114
DeSaules
    Julia Louisa 76
DeSelding
    Charles 113
Detroit, Mich. 29, 97, 113, 141,
    165, 222, 228, 239, 269
Detweiller
    Frederick M. 76
Devaughan
    John E. 235
Devaughn
    Samuel 259
Devereux
    Thomas P. 83
Devis
    Craven 100
Devlin
    Anna Virginia 271
    Lieut. 271
Devonshire, Eng. 230
Dewberry, Va. 162
Dewey
    Rev. 145
DeWolfe
    Charlotte G. 247

George, Gen. 247
Dexter
   Emily 149
Diamond
   Mary 252
Dice
   Rev. 100
Dick
   Sarah V. 66
Dickerson
   A.C., Rev. 49
Dickinson
   Martha D. 128
Dickinson College 72, 240
Didier
   Edmund 270
Dietz
   William H. 1
Digges
   Cordelia 200
   Judson 200
   Margaret M. 230
   Norah 231
   William Dudley 231
   William J., Dr. 189
Dillahunty
   Edmund, Hon. 73
Dillon
   David 139
Dimitry
   Andrea 79
Ditty
   Eliza A. 141
   Sarah P. 141
   Thomas R., Dr. 141
Divine
   Lewis McKendree 197
Dixon
   A. 219
   Archibald, Hon. 193
   Hannah 142
   Rebecca 219
   Sarah A. 83
   William 142
Dixson
   Frank Wood 124
Dobbins
   Margaretta 172
   Mary E. 172
   William B. 172
Doctor 135
Dodd
   Thomas A. 9
Dodds
   Joseph 81
Dodge
   A.H. 112
   Abigail B. 145
   Brown 145
   Francis 48, 69
   H.W., Rev.* 145
   Henry W., Rev. 30, 251
   Henry, Col. 254
   Henry, Hon. 216

Mary Elizabeth 30
Nancy A. 216
Virginia Josephine 254
Dodson
   Joseph, Capt. 5
   Priscilla 5
   Rev. 1
Doll
   Rev. 260
Donaldson
   R.B. 212
Donan
   P., Rev. 50
Donegal Co., Ire. 152
Donegaltown, Ire. 47
Donelan
   James B., Rev. 9, 11, 19, 31,
     33, 51, 52, 58, 66, 70, 71,
     120, 123, 125, 126, 134,
     147, 152, 155, 163, 165,
     193, 196, 204, 214, 223,
     224, 228, 230, 232, 255
   James P., Rev. 33, 55, 181
   Rev. 2, 12, 40, 65, 70, 98, 122
Donelson
   A.J., Hon. 94
   Mary E. 94
Donn
   John M. 257
   John Y. 167
   Lavinia D. 257
Donnelly
   Elizabeth 1
   James 1
Donoghue
   Dennis O. 91
Donoho/Donohoo
   John A. 59
   Thomas 22
Donohough
   Mary 53
Donohue
   Margaret 42
Dooley
   Bridget 119
   T.B., Rev. 253
Doorkeeper 26
Dorchester Co., Md. 19, 43, 205,
   228
Dorden
   Emily 84
Dorman
   Albert, Dr. 11
   Charles Albert 11
Dorr
   Thomas W. 273
Dorrell
   Thomas S. 210
Dorset, Eng. 142
Dorsey
   Allen J. 27
   Anna E. 203
   E.J. 203
   Elizabeth 196

J.R. 151
J.T.B. 74
Lucinda 179
Mary Campbell 74
Richard, Maj. 171
Sarah 171
Walter, Hon. 196
Doty
   George W., Lieut. 198
Doubleday
   A. 71
Dougal
   W.H. 27
Dougherty
   Hugh 180
   John, Rev. 223
   Joseph 62
   Mary 62
   Sarah Ann 272
Doughty
   Ann Maria 59
   James W. 16
   William, Col. 59
Douglas
   A.O. 167
   Charles, Dr. 49
   Hugh Thomas 166
   John 189
   John, Sr. 120
   Martha 135
   Martha M. 136
   Martha Martin 183
   Mary Osborn 230
   P.J. 167
   S.A., Hon. 183
   Stephen A., Hon. 135
   Walter 92
   William 230
   William W. 167
Douglass
   Anna 228
   Edward Robert 130
   Elizabeth A. 228
   Ellen Sinclair 223
   Isaac R. 162
   James C. 223
   Jane S. 162
   Margaret Lavina 130
   Mary Jane 130
   Miss 98
   Samuel E. 228
   William 130
Dove
   Ann W. 13
   B.M., Lieut. 93
   George Henry 201
   Jilson 69, 164
   Margaret 93
   Mary 69
   Robert W. 193
   Sarah 19
   Sarah Ann 249
   William T. 69
   William Thomas 13

Wm. S. 13
Dover, Del. 164
Dovilliers
    Leopold, Dr. 44
Dow
    Jesse E. 70
    Sarah E. 70
Dowling
    Henry M., Dr. 74
    Hetty Jane 182
    John, Rev. 239
    Patrick 57
    Thomas, Col. 182
    William 57, 118, 270
Downer
    Elizabeth Garnet 145
    Margaret 145
    Richard 145
Downey
    Mary 50
    Mary E. 174
Downing
    Charles S. 108
    Georgiana 108
    Robert 108
Doylestown, Pa. 216
Dragoons 15, 32, 44, 50, 59, 82,
    151, 171, 236, 263
Draine
    James 91
    Mary 91
Drane
    James W. 55
    Mary M. 69
    Robert 138
Dranesville, Va. 69
Draper
    A.C., Dr. 59
    Frances A.E. 59
    Lorenzo 60
Drew
    Helen 73
    Phineas 73
Driscoll
    Catharine 89
    Charles M. 160
Drowns
    Margaret 160
Drury
    Louis Vivans 265
    Rachel 87
    Samuel T. 87
Dubant
    Delilah 102
    Ellen Elizabeth 28
    P.M. 102
Dubbs
    Sarah L. 146
Dublin, Ire. 53
Dubois
    Rev. 226
Ducachet
    H.W., Rev. 44
    Rev. 42, 71

Ducket
    Basil W. 271
Duckett
    Benjamin M. 16
Duckwall
    Joseph S. 44
Duckworth
    George 76
    Margaret 256
Duffey
    Annie S. 267
    George H. 267
    Mathias 87
Duffield
    Rev.* 240
Duffy
    Mary 244
    Thomas 244
Duhamel
    William J.C., Dr. 155
Duke
    Nathaniel Wilson, Lieut. 103
    William 103
Dulaney
    Elizabeth A.M. 49
Dulany
    Daniel F., Lieut. 254
    Margaret A. 254
    Richard Henry 254
Duley
    William W. 226
Dulin
    Edward L., Rev.* 241
    Edward, Rev.* 167
    Louisa Ellen 167
Dulongpre
    Col. 166
    Julia 166
Duly
    Sarah Jane 75
Dumfries, Va. 260
Dummerston, Ver. 55, 220
Dumphrieus
    Thomas 80
Dunbar
    Field 267
    Mary W. 267
    William 267
Duncan
    Ann R. 233
    E.C., Mrs. 271
    George 233
    J. McKim, Rev. 269
    James A., Rev. 196
    Joseph, Gov. 271
    Lucius Campbell 251
    Mary L. 271
    Mr. 115
    Samuel J., Capt. 220
    Thomas, Capt. 110
Duncan's Battery 126
Dundas
    Harriet 14
    William H. 14

Dunham, Conn. 243
Dunkinson
    William 126
Dunkirk, N.Y. 160
Dunn
    Amelia 18
    Francis A. 157
    J. Irwin, Dr. 4
    Rachel 86
    Rev. 41
    Thomas 86
    Williamson, Hon. 268
Dunne
    Emily Mary 263
Dunneygall, Ire. 163
Dunscomb
    Caroline 121
    Caroline M. 223
    D.E., Col. 223
    Daniel 232
    Daniel Edward 121
    Daniel Ettienne 232
    Edward A. 121
    Jane E. 232
DuPont's Mills, Del. 221
Durham
    James H. 37
    Mrs. 37
    Nancy W. 37
Durhamville, Tenn. 231
Durity
    George W. 207
Dustin
    D.H. 238
    Daniel H. 251
    William Fletcher 251
Dutchess Co., N.Y. 252
Duval
    B.R., Rev. 159
    William P., Gov. 218
Duvall
    Amanda S. 67
    Arabella 155
    Benjamin 90
    Daniel, Col. 9
    Dennis 155
    Elizabeth T. 245
    George W. 67
    Julia 9
    Kate M. 245
    Margaret E. 12
    Marius, Dr. 197
    Marshur 12
    Mary 90
    William T. 245
    William, Col. 38
Duxbury, Mass. 16, 26
Dwight Mission 32
Dyer
    B.F. 204
    E.E. 204
    Edward 159
    Edward C. 34
    Eliza Frances 159

George Alexander, Dr. 223
Henrietta H. 21
John J., Dr. 159
Kate 204

E

E Street Baptist Church 27, 43, 61,
    109, 129, 138, 144, 208,
    272
E Street Baptist Sabbath School
    247
Eader
    Jonathan 89
Eagan
    Jane 139
Eagleson
    Josiah 15
    Margaret A. 15
Eaken
    J.F., Rev. 76
Eakin
    Matthew 117
Earl
    John 111
    Richard 47
Earle
    Caleb, Hon. 35
    Richard Tilghman 205
Early
    Thomas R. 142
Earp
    John William 37
Easby
    Robert 100
    Thomas R. 140
    Wilhelmina 232
    William, Capt. 232, 241
East New Market Parish 19
East Pascagoula, Miss. 108
East River, N.Y. 110
East Washington Seminary 157
Eastburn
    Rev. 208
Eastern Branch 42, 52, 146
Eastern Hill, D.C. 26
Eastern Shore, Md. 5, 45
Eastern Shore, Va. 90
Easton
    Mary Stoddart 249
    Sidney 200
    William C. 249
Easton, Md. 60, 185
Easton, Pa. 96
Eaton
    Bettie Blaney 38
    J.H., Lieut. Col. 38
    John H., Gen. 191
    John H., Hon. 239
Ebenezer Church 80
Eccleston
    Augusta C. 203
    John B., Hon. 203

Eck
    A.M., Mrs. 102
Eckard
    J.E., Rev. 220
    James R., Rev. 42, 68, 146,
        159, 193, 198, 209, 211,
        267
    Rev. 105, 106
Eckardt
    Henry 125
Eckel/Eckell/Eckle
    Charles E. 1, 189
    Charlotte P. 189
    Rev. 137
Eckloff
    Ann Catherine 213
    Christian 149
    F.W. 213
    Joseph W. 149
    Margaret E. 213
    Sarah 149
Eckton
    Caroline 271
Edelen
    Raphael C. 27, 40
    Sarah Ann 40
Edelin
    James, Maj. 111
    Mary 8
    Nancy C. 111
Edenton 65
Edenton, N.C. 111, 192
Edes
    Agnes M. 221
    Benjamin, Col. 221, 241
Edgar
    J.T., Rev. 138
    Jane 145
    John 145
    Rev. 44
Edge Hill, Va. 244, 253, 255
Edgefield district, S.C. 239
Edgewood, Va. 95
Edinburgh, N.Y. 247
Edinburgh, Scot. 234
Edisto Island, S.C. 238
Editor (occupation) 22, 26, 38, 42,
    52, 80, 94, 96, 100, 101,
    111, 118, 154, 183, 186,
    258
Edkhardt
    Bell Jane 157
Edmond
    Cornelia W. 100
    David 100
Edmonds
    Charles 272
Edmonson
    Marcelia 83
Edmonston
    Alexander, Dr. 132
    Ann C.H. 165
    Charles 165
    Cornelia 162

D.W., Jr. 260
James 258
Edrington
    Ella A. 269
    John, Capt. 269
Edwards
    Alpheus L. 38
    Ann 135
    Clementina Crawford 126
    Elizabeth A. 28
    Eulalia Crawford 233
    Eulalia Emma 126
    Evan 195
    George 163
    Howard S. 38
    J.C., Rev. 24
    Lewis A., Dr. 126, 233
    Margaret Mariah 28
    Rev. 5, 6, 32, 37, 65, 78
    Samuel M., Gen. 135
    W.B., Rev. 69, 77
    William B., Rev. 12, 25, 41, 46,
        66
    William B., Rev.* 28
    William, Rev. 34
Effingham 117
Ege
    A.G. 127
Eichhorn
    Elizabeth E. 49
    Rudolph 133
Eichstadt
    A., Mr. 173
Eirhstedt
    Adolphus 243
    Dora 243
    Metta 243
El Paso 206
Elder 175, 183
    Mary Agnes 45
    Rev. 138
Elgar
    Joseph 232
Elgin
    Sally Ann 138
Eliot
    Dr. 101
    Frank A. 251
    Rev. 251
    William G. 200
Eliza 185
Elizabeth City, N.C. 112
Elizabethtown, N.J. 172
Elk Hill, Va. 161
Elkora, Va. 28
Elkridge, Md. 74, 177
Ellerslie 97, 228, 268
Ellicott
    Elizabeth 198
    Fanny A. 210
    George Horace 210
    George, Sr. 198
    James P. 210
Ellicott's Mills 198

Elliot
    Alexander 217
    Ellen W. 217
    Jonathan 85
    William Francis 170
    William P. 170
    William Parker 264
Elliott
    Alexander 176
    Comm. 243
    Mary 176
Ellis
    J.B. 106
    Jane 106
    John F. 120, 246
    Joseph Gregory 246
    Mary Ann 246
    Mrs. 86
    William Seaton 106
Ellmore
    Wilhelmina 131
Ells
    Edward, Rev. 252
Ellsworth
    Isabella 215
    Mary Isabella 196
Elm Grove, Ill. 271
Elmore
    Catharine 182
Elmwood, Md. 24, 213
Eltham, Va. 141
Elvans
    John R. 210
Ely
    Albert Welles 226
    Anthony S. 105
    Edward 157
    Jane Stafford 226
    Mary 157
Elzey
    Arnold, Dr. 107
    Henrietta 107
Emanuel Church 238
Embordo 151
Embry
    Sarah 104
Emery
    Juliet D. 144
    M.G. 219
    Matthew G. 144
Emmerich
    Alice 265
    George 265
    Mary E. 265
Emmit(t)sburg, Md. 2, 172, 175
Emmons
    Ella Virginia 158
Emory
    Albert Troup 59
Emperor of Russia 73, 125, 272
Empie
    Rev. 252
Empire Hotel 197
Enfield, N.C. 79

Engfield, N.C. 216
Engineer (occupation) 5, 140, 194, 223, 260, 265
England 15-17, 20, 21, 38, 62, 90, 94, 98, 201, 213, 261
English
    Alice 224
    James 196
    James A. 199
    John C. 224
    Maria S. 199
    Mary Ellen 149
English Lutheran Church 76, 79
Ennis
    Gregory 120
    Jane 78
    Mary Ann 120
    Mrs. 138
    Philip 45, 78
    Richard G. 78
Eno
    Harriett M. 145
    John, Capt. 145
Enroughty
    James B. 208
Entwisle
    Thomas B. 164
Envoy (occupation) 79, 121, 271
Episcopal Theological Seminary 78
Epping, N.H. 254
Erie 48
Erney
    Caroline T. 67
    V.L. 9
Erwin
    S. Bulow 181
Eschwege Kurhessen 217
Eskridge
    Frances Elizabeth 120
Eslin
    James C. 19
Esperance Plantation, La. 1
Espey
    Ann 222
    Lydia A. 34
    Sallie Ellis 34
    Samuel C. 34
Essex Co., Va. 33, 147, 216
Essex, Eng. 49
Essex, Md. 199
Esterly
    H., Mrs. 167
Estes
    James M. 17
Etchison
    E. Dorsey 40
    Lemuel 188
Etter
    Joseph 185
Eubanks
    Richard S. 216
Europe 242
Eustace
    William W., Dr. 31

Eutaw Springs 60
Eutaw, Ala. 140
Eva
    Rev. 71
    W.T., Rev. 41, 50, 55, 57, 75
Evans
    Ann W. 14
    Clifford 211
    Ellen L. 168
    F.S., Rev. 48, 66, 155, 181, 237
    French S., Rev. 196, 200
    French S., Rev.* 209
    Harriet R. 180
    John E. 209
    Kate E. 243
    Rev. 195
    Richard, Hon. 14
    William T. 191
Eveleth
    William S. 104
Evening Post 98
Everett
    Charles, Jr. 14
    Dr. 128
    Horace 41
    John S. 33
    Lydia 128
    T.S. 46
Evergreen, Va. 69
Evermay, Miss. 26
Eversfield
    Charles, Dr. 176
Ewell
    Fenton Mercer 41
    Helen 253
    Helen Woods 255
    J.S. 122
    Jesse 82
    John S. 253, 255
Ewing
    Alex., Col. 241
    William Griffith, Hon. 241
Exchange Hotel 195
Exeter, Me. 77
Exeter, N.H. 95, 269
Experiment, Mo. 67

F

F Street Church 146, 148, 193, 264
F Street Presbyterian Church 62, 152, 153, 168, 192, 194, 211, 255
Fackler
    St. M., Rev. 134
Fage
    Rebecca 268
Faherty
    John P. 68
Fairbanks
    George W. 76

Fairfax
- A.B. 80
- A.B., Lieut. 39
- Aurelia Herbert 159
- Lucy 39
- Orlando, Dr. 89
- Sarah C. 39
- Thomas 159

Fairfax Co., Va. 14, 17, 22, 23, 38, 53, 54, 69, 78, 85, 100, 108, 111, 113, 122, 124, 127, 138, 148, 159, 169, 182, 189, 191, 217, 224, 246, 261, 263, 268, 270, 273

Fairfax Courthouse, Va. 5, 38, 120

Fairfax News 38

Fairfax, Va. 47

Fairfield, Me. 50

Falconer
- Eleanor 17
- Elisha 17
- Ellen 125
- Mary E. 250
- R.J. 17
- William H. 250

Fales
- Ferolin Amelia 90

Falkoner
- Elisha 158
- Sarah A. 158
- Sarah Ellen 158

Fallon
- Edward 215

Falls plantation 97

Fanning
- Emma R. 139
- Wilhelmina 139
- William H. 139

Fant
- Hamilton G. 158, 268
- Helen 268
- Henry T. 103
- Josephine 268

Farish
- F. 92
- Robert C. 206

Farley 128
- James Parks 128

Farley, Va. 191, 213

Farmanagh, Ire. 57

Farmer 153

Farmington, Va. 113

Farmville, Va. 91

Farnham
- Emily 87
- Jane 87
- Robert 87

Farnum
- Elizabeth 169
- Mathew H. 169
- R.M. 169

Farquhar
- Amos 164
- Harriet Valinda 248
- Mary 164
- Mrs. 208, 246
- T.C. 248
- Thomas C. 18

Farr
- Lavinia V. 186
- Malacki 271
- Margaret Ann 209

Farrar
- John M. 239

Farrell
- Ellen O. 47

Farrelly
- P.A., Lieut. 43

Fasnaught
- Margaret 246

Fassitt
- Clara 117
- Thomas S.R. 117

Faulkner
- Annie Holmes 186
- Charles J., Hon. 186
- Joseph 66
- Ophelia E. 258
- Sallie Pendleton 186

Fauntleroy
- Annie 184
- D. 184
- Kate K. 171
- Thomas T., Col. 171
- Virginia D. 184
- William Lawson, Dr. 120

Fauquier Co., Va. 8, 35, 41, 47, 55, 57, 88, 111, 114, 120, 134, 161, 175, 176, 184, 186, 193, 194, 228, 230, 251, 257

Favier
- Agricol(a) 34, 261

Faxon
- Eben 171

Fay
- Anna Virginia 52

Fayette, Mo. 41

Fayetteville, N.C. 31, 42, 116, 189, 267

Fayetteville, N.Y. 80

Fechtig
- Louis R., Dr. 258

Feeny
- Mary 139

Female Academy 39

Fendrich
- Xavier 164

Fennall
- Clarence P. 221
- Eliza 221
- Walter H. 221

Fenton
- Charles W. 103
- Elizabeth R. 103
- Millard 103

Fenwick
- Anna M. 223
- Edward 206
- Eliza A. 206
- Lavinia L. 223
- R.M.A. 223

Ferguson
- E. 248
- Eliza J. 171
- Eliza M. 84
- Elizabeth C. 145
- Henry Thomas 145
- James R. 145
- John 187
- John W. 242
- Mary 187
- Mary Boothroyed 267
- Thomas 267
- Virginia 171
- William P. 171

Fermanagh, Ire. 118

Ferry
- Edward 233

Fickett
- Sarah A. 29

Field
- Everard, Maj. 158
- Henry, Rev. 198
- Horace D., Capt. 207

Fifth Presbyterian Church 193, 195, 216

Fill
- Mary 118

Fillins
- Amanda 6

Fillmore
- Abigail 150
- Millard, Mrs. 11
- President 150, 272

Finckel/Finkel
- Caroline A. 85
- Rev. 65, 164, 173, 227, 234
- S.D., Rev. 160, 231
- Samuel D., Rev. 85

Findlay
- James, Gen. 68
- Jane 68

Finley
- Thomas 113

Finn
- Mathew 139

Firor
- Ephraim A. 112

First Baptist Church 86, 88, 112, 160, 192

First New Jerusalem Church 106

First Presbyterian Church 3, 82, 101, 183, 193, 222, 234, 268, 271

Fischer
- William 73

Fisher
   E. Jennie 203
   Henry 33
   Thomas H. 155
Fishing Creek, Md. 173
Fiske
   Helen M. 120
   N.W., Prof. 120
Fister
   John 194
   Margaret M. 194
Fitch
   C.W., Rev.* 8
   Catherine B. 8
Fitton
   James, Rev. 31
Fitzgerald
   James H. 97
   Mary 158
   Patrick 8
   Thomas 53
Fitzhugh
   Daniel H., Jr. 102
   Elizabeth C. 69
   John P.T., Dr. 69
   Samuel 253
   William H. 14
   William, Col. 14
Fitzpatrick
   Emma 36
   Henrietta R. 228
   John C. 228
   Rev. 51, 266
   Thomas, Maj. 210
Fitzugh
   Robert Rose 11
   Samuel 11
Flagg
   Edward O., Rev.* 47
   Robert S. 137
Flanagan
   William 49
Flanigan
   Rev. 99
Flannegan
   Edward 68
   Margaret A. 68
   Mary Ann 45
Flannigan
   P.O., Rev. 91
Flavahar
   Catharine 139
Fletcher
   Ellen 151
   Timothy 151
Fleury
   Augustus 29
   Caroline 29
   L.A. 29
Flinn
   Catherine 257
   Villasquiz H. 182
Florence, Italy 179

Florida 30, 44, 82, 116, 125, 141, 156, 165, 185, 196, 209, 217, 218, 240, 263
flour mill 119
Flower
   Charles E. 94
   Edward 94
Floweree
   Abner 260
Floyd
   John B. 236
   John, Gov. 132
   Letitia Preston 132
   Mary Ann 236
Floyd Courthouse, Va. 45
Fluvanna Co., Va. 17
Flynn
   John M. 158
Fogg
   E. Wood 204
Foley
   Rev. 29
   Thomas J., Rev. 120
Follansbee
   Joshua A. 3
Foltz
   J.M., Dr. 234
Fond du Lac 241
Foote
   Eleanor Maria 24
   Thomas 24
   W.H., Rev. 49
Forbes
   George 94
   John R.P. 94
Forbes & Co. 133
Force
   Elizabeth A. 32
   William Marion 32
   William Q. 32
Ford
   Daniel W. 187
   James 19
   Mary O. 221
   Mrs. 22
   Rosa 223
   S. Calvert 223
Foreign Burial Ground 30
Foreman 201
Forest Home, Ky. 252
Fornance
   Joseph, Hon. 126
Fornaro
   Adolph 52
Forrest
   Anne Love 88
   Charles W. 28
   Emily C.W. 148
   F., Capt. 148
   Henry 88
   Louisa Pemberton 28
   Moreau, Dr. 101
   William H. 64

Forrester
   Dr. 178
Forteney
   Albert 68
   E.W. 68
   James Thomas 68
   Mary Ann 68
Fortier
   Eugenia V. 137
   John F.Z. 137
   P.M. 137
Foster
   Andrew 89
   E.H., Hon. 31
   Jane Ellen 31
   Julia Montgomery 89
Foundry Church 10, 24, 33, 48, 97, 122, 123, 125, 129, 188, 217, 227, 229, 230, 235, 242, 246, 251, 257, 267, 269, 273
Fountain
   Mary A. 255
Fourth Presbyterian Church 26, 32, 77, 95, 96, 122, 161, 167, 224, 230, 256, 265
Foutz
   David W. 37
Fowle
   Carolyn Dennis 29
   Esther D. 46
   George D. 29
   George Dashiel 29
   Sarah Ellen 29
   William 46
   William H. 67
Fowler
   Alonzo R. 59
   B., Rev. 81
   Emily A.D. 114
   Joseph 33, 44, 139
   Julia C. 213
Fowles
   James H., Rev. 93
Fox
   Charles, Rev.* 143
   J.L., Dr. 262
   Louisa 158
   Nellie L. 262
   William 107
Foxwell
   Isabel A. 169
Foy
   Peter 38
Frame
   E.B. 259
France 21, 114, 136, 261, 262, 271
France
   Amanda 91
   James 91, 111
   Margaretta G. 91
   Thomas E. 113
Frank
   Alexander 77

Frankenberger
    Alexander Lewis 164
    Charles 164
    Margaret 164
Frankfort, Ky. 26, 261
Frankfort, Mo. 11
Frankinberger
    Charles 89
Franklin
    Benjamin 198
    William B. 102
Franklin Co., Pa. 250
Franklin Co., Va. 168
Franzoni
    Guiseppe 179
    Julia C. 179
Fraser
    Jane 141
    John 110, 141
    Margaret 110
    Priscilla 42
    Thomas, Rev.* 141
Frasier
    James 54, 74
    James Thomas 54
    Mary E. 54
Frazier
    Benjamin W., Jr. 1
    George 249
    George W. 219
    Isabella C. 219
    Prudence E. 249
    William Clyne 219
    William H. 249
Frazure
    Prudence E. 184
    William H. 184
    Willie G. 184
Frederick Co., Md. 9, 13, 17, 18, 27, 33, 38, 120, 161
Frederick Co., Va. 230
Frederick, Md. 2, 11, 36, 89, 165, 194, 197, 262
Fredericksburg News 42
Fredericksburg, Va. 33, 42, 79, 97, 101, 193, 222
Free Masons 252
Freedley
    Catharine V. 23
    George W. 23
Freeman
    James Y. 249
    John 22
    John D., Mrs. 4
    Laura V. 40
    Rebecca 33
Frelinghuysen
    Charlotte M. 220
    Theodore, Hon. 220
Fremont
    Anne Beverly 170
    Col. 170
French
    Arthur Livermore 190
    Edmund F. 187, 190
    Ephraim 19
    George 211
    J.W., Rev. 42, 53, 70, 95, 156, 160, 212, 243, 259
    James 149
    James B. 55
    Jane Elizabeth 19
    John W., Rev. 6, 36, 95
    Margaret A. 187, 190
    Mary 66
    Matilda C. 149
    Nannie 211
    Rev. 15, 22, 32, 53, 70, 71, 79, 91, 147, 148, 161, 185, 195, 226, 266
    Thomas 66
Frere
    Mary S. 184
Freund
    Philipine 160
Frick
    George P. 223
Friend
    Henrietta 112
    William, Rev. 79
Friends' meeting-house 59
frigates
    Congress 93, 154
    Cumberland 250
    Philadelphia 18
    Susquehanna 270
Frost
    Elizabeth C. 189
    John T. 228
Frothingham
    Rev. 151
Fruit Farm, Va. 114
Fry
    Hugh W., Jr. 97
    Jane C. 161
Fryers
    Susan B. 174
Ft. Brooke, Fla. 197
Ft. Gates, Tex. 60
Ft. Hamilton, N.Y. 38
Ft. Leavenworth, Mo. 29, 36, 171
Ft. McHenry 126, 229
Ft. Monroe 206
Ft. Scott 30
Ft. Scott, Mo. 263
Ft. Smith, Ark. 38, 156, 160
Ft. Snelling, Minn. 41, 59, 136, 204
Ft. Towson 126
Ft. Union, N.M. 249
Ft. Washita 43
Ft. Wayne, Ind. 241
Fugitt
    Alvin 199
    Caroline C. 199
    James P., Rev.* 199
Fuller
    Hiram 38
Fulton
    A.S. 152
    Annie Blanche 152
    J.B.H. 152
Furgerson
    William 187
Furness
    Jame 200
Furtner
    Alexander 95

G

Gadsby's Hotel 170
Gadsby's Row 157
Gadsden
    C.E., Rev. 99
Gaines
    John P. 134
    Louisa J. 170
Gainesville, Ala. 41
Gaither
    Eliza 30
    Greenbury 144, 235
    Henry C. 30
    Julia-May 235
    Mary 144
    William Lingan, Gen. 30
Galena, Ill. 113
Gales
    Altona F. 156
    Weston R. 156
Gallagher
    Mary 71
    Mary A. 181
    Rev. 122, 174
    Thomas 261
    William D. 181
Gallaher
    Edward A. 140
    James, Rev. 140
    John S. 52, 165, 253
    Marcellus 180, 253
    Mary Helen 52
    Rev. 94
    Sallie 140
Gallant
    Edward 25
    Mary A. 25
    William Thomas 25
Gallatin
    Albert 119, 271
Gallaudet
    Sophia 207
    Thomas H., Rev.* 207
    Thomas, Rev. 50, 207
Galt
    Fannie Ellen 7
    Grayson Page 222
    John 124
    M.W. 222
    Margaret 43
    Mary A. 7

Mary Jane 222
Sterling 43
Thomas J. 7
Galveston, Tex. 35, 75, 266
Gamble
   John G., Col. 209
   John M., Col. 9
   Julia 209
   Mary L. 9
   Mr. 143
Gambrill
   Amo G. 224
Gangewer
   A.M. 161
   Ann Janet 161
Gannon
   Mary A.O. 228
   Mary F. 70
Gantt
   Ann 68
   Fannie Perkins 259
   John W., Dr. 259
   Thomas T. 68
Gardener
   Catherine Frances 179
   F., Capt. 156
   Frank Alexander 156
   John Henry 179
   John L., Col. 179
   Mathilde 156
   William 152
   William H., Capt. 155
Gardiner
   Alexander 6
   J.C. 100
   J.W.T. 236
   Matilda 37
   Thomas E. 74
Gardiner, Me. 252
Gardner
   C.T. 116
   Charles K., Col. 204, 209
   Frances E. 72
   J.B., Dr. 66
   John H. 272
   John J. 96
   Mary 226
   Sarah McLean 209
   Selden 72
   Virgil H., Col. 226
   William, Comm. 72
Garita of San Cosmo 126
Garner
   H., Capt. 83, 150
   Jane Singleton 83
   Lucy A. 150
   Mary 234
Garnett
   Alex. Y.P., Dr. 183
   Annie 183
   Dr. 29
   Henry F., Col. 107
   Louis A. 147
   Maria Champe 147

Mary W. 183
Muscoe 147
Garratt
   Charlotte 156
Garrison 132
Gartland
   Elizabeth F.X. 45
   Francis Xavier, Rev. 254
Gass
   Charles G. 183
Gassaway
   Hanson 236
   J.G., Rev. 67
   Madison 77, 79
   Mrs. 261
Gassett
   Edward 266
Gassoway
   Rev. 59
Gaston
   Joseph A. 164
Gaston Co., N.C. 127
Gaston, Ala. 224
Gates
   James 245
   Mary E. 245
   Sylvester F. 13
Gatewood
   Mary Kate 97
Gathright
   Cordelia 244
Gatton
   A.H. 196
   Martha W. 196
Gautier
   C. 1
Gawler
   Alfred 123
Gear
   E.G., Rev. 59
   M.C. 59
Gearney
   Michael 139
Gedney
   Thomas R., Capt. 151
Geneva, Switz. 118
Gentry
   Meredith P., Hon. 215
   Mrs. 215
George
   J.W. 244
Georgetown Cemetery 105
Georgetown College 21, 34, 151, 216, 228
Georgetown Heights, D.C. 54, 87, 103, 105-106, 179, 181, 211, 222, 238
Georgetown, D.C. 1-5, 7-9, 11-15, 17, 19, 21, 24, 27, 28, 30, 32, 34-36, 38, 40, 41, 43, 44, 46-49, 53-56, 58, 59, 61-66, 69, 70, 74-76, 78, 82, 84, 86-89, 91, 93-95, 97, 99-101, 103-107, 110-117, 119, 121-124, 126, 128, 130, 131, 134, 137-140, 142, 143, 147-150, 152, 156, 159-163, 165, 167, 169-173, 175, 179, 180, 183, 184, 187-189, 192, 194-197, 200, 203, 206-209, 211-213, 215, 217-219, 221, 225, 227, 228, 231-234, 236-238, 240, 244-248, 252, 255, 257, 258, 260-262, 266, 267, 269, 273
Georgetown, Del. 6
Georgetown, Ga. 242
Georgetown, Pa. 240
Georgia 7, 86, 100, 197, 207, 271
Gere
   John A., Rev. 251
German
   John H. 184
Germania Benevolent Society 156
Germantown 205
Germantown, Pa. 43, 84, 221, 240, 250
Germany 1, 14, 37, 209, 244
Germon
   Elizabeth E. 273
   Francis 64
   Mr. 121
Gettener
   Benjamin F. 221
Gettysburg, Pa. 62
Gibbons
   John W. 233
   Lyman, Hon. 158
Gibbs
   A. Chisholm 173
   Andrew Coyle 212
   Caroline L. 263
   Eliza L. 173
   Emma 155
   John H. 155
   John V. 127
   Lucretia Jane 155
Gibson
   Catharine 256
   David, Col. 49
   Eliza J.A. 49
   Francis J. 46
   Jacob Carter 225
   Maria Louisa 32
   Phineas 176
   R. 256
   Samuel 176
   Sarah N. 179
   Sarah Thompson 166
   Tobias 166
   Walter W. 78
   William, Prof. 179
Gibsonville, Calif. 226

Gideon
    George S. 156
    Jacob 173, 175, 188
    Mary 173, 175
    Mr., printing office of 4
Giesboro, D.C. 180
Gieze
    Henry 115
Gilbert
    Charles C. 269
    Mary S. 269
Gilchrist
    John, Corp. 249
Gildermeister
    Therese 231
Giles
    Rev. 74
Gillespie
    Anna 272
    James A. 272
Gilliss/Gillis
    George 163, 182
    George Marsh 139
    Hannah M. 182
    J.M., Lieut. 139
    L.I., Rev. 173
    L.J., Rev. 19, 22, 189
    Rev. 3, 12, 29, 77
    Thomas H. 8, 10
    Walter V. 163
Gilman
    Cornelia A. 146
    E. 146
    Ephraim 142
    Ernest 18
    George Ephraim 143
    H.P. 18
    Helen Parris 34
    Margaret D. 143
    William H. 143
    Z.D. 18, 34, 222
Girault
    A.N., Prof. 190
    Margaret S. 190
Gittings
    George 85
    John S. 197
    Lambert 95
    Mary T. 95
Given
    Adelaide Carothers 23
    Emily S. 23
    John T. 23
Giveny
    Patrick 154
Gladman
    Mary 138
Glasgow
    Augustus 199
Glasgow, Scot. 40, 110, 127, 141, 162, 230
Glen Wallace, Va. 11
Glencoe, Va. 177

Glenn
    John, Hon. 168
Glorson
    James 102
Gloucester Co., Va. 10, 120
Gloucester, N.J. 3
Glover
    E. Kate 214
    L.M., Rev. 271
Glynn
    Thomas, Dr. 92
Godard
    Matilda A. 201
Goddard
    Andrew 4
    Anna Maria 61
    Benjamin F. 118
    Charles B. 122
    Daniel Convers 122
    Eliza Ann 95
    Henry 142
    John 64
Goddin
    James E. 161
Goggin
    Elizabeth E. 80
    Marcy 92
    Sallie P. 201
    William L., Hon. 201
Gold
    Mary A. 203
Goldin
    Cordelia 247
    John 113, 247
    Robert Latimer 247
Golding
    Charles 154
    Dorothy 103
Goldsborough
    C.W. 22
    Catharine 22
    Charles H. 23
    Charles W. 23
    Frederick 213
    Maria C. 4
    William 228
Goldsby
    Eliza Frances 150
    Thornton B., Col. 150
Goldsmith
    Annie M. 130
    John T. 215
Gooch
    John J. 139
Goochland Co., Va. 161, 244
Goodall
    Mary Ann 70
    Thomas 70
Goode
    Edward P. 247
Goodell
    Mary E. 122
Goodfellow
    Rev. 193

Goodger
    William H. 242
Goodhue
    James M., Col. 111
Goodloe
    D.R. 32
Goodman
    William H. 243
Goodrich
    Mary Ann 208
    Mr. 70
Goodwin
    H.M., Rev. 187
    Julia A. 126
    Stephen R. 169
Goodwood, Md. 27, 58
Gorden
    Martha 19
Gordon
    Emily C. 105
    Franklin Blake 2
    George A. 209
    Glorvina 2
    John M. 105
    Lizzie F. 58
    Mary 53
    S.R., Rev. 203
    Sallie E. 235
    William A. 2
Gordonsdale, Va. 168
Gore
    Jabez 2
Gorham, Me. 53
Gorsuch
    J.S., Rev. 37
    Rev. 1, 18
Goshert
    Lizzie S. 105
Gosnell
    Richard 164
Gossage
    Rev. 3
Goszler
    S.B.B. 169
Gough
    Mary 110
    Stephen 110
Gould
    Anna M. 76
    Stephen 76
    William Henry 76
Governor (title) 15, 35, 50, 51, 90, 98, 121, 125, 199, 206, 218, 227, 228, 236, 239, 271
    Iowa 141
    Kentucky 185
    Maryland 51
    Ohio 141
    Oregon 134
Grace Church 47, 191, 203, 251
Graham
    Charlotte Meade 76
    Col. 142

299

David 18
James D., Lieut. Col. 76
James, Hon. 47
Joseph, Gen. 47
Margaret Campbell 76
Maria 18
Rachel 231
Robert H. 219
Gramlich
   Louisa 37
Grammar
   Annie 126
   G.C. 126
Grand Coteau, La. 74, 96, 113
Granenger
   Caroline 39
   John 39
   Mary Elizabeth 39
Granger
   Clement 141
   James H. 255
Grant
   Ann E. 199
   William R., M.D. 83
   William W. 113
Grantville, S.C. 77
Granville Co., N.C. 11, 40
Granville, N.J. 194
Gratiot
   Gen. 163
   Mary Victoria 163
Gratton
   Robert R. 269
Gray
   Fannie W. 124
   Franklin C. 149
   George W. 121
   Henry W. 96
   Henry W., Col. 256
   Jane 133
   Jennie 256
   Lucy Ann 129
   Mary Melvina 96
   Mrs. 121
   William H. 124
Grayson
   E.B. 265
   Mary Caroline 265
   Thomas W. 22
Great Britain 272
Great Salt Lake 27
Greece 79
Greek language 165
Green
   A. 22, 66
   Albert G. 191
   Ammon 25
   Annie S. 66
   Archibald R. 159
   C.K. 269
   Dr. 234
   Elizabeth Lawrence 258
   Gen. 60
   Jane 91
   Joel C. 71
   Joseph D. 203
   Josephus 71
   Joshua, Dr. 258
   Mary Louise 191
   May Elizabeth 22
   Michael 70
   Robert B. 147
   Samuel, Hon. 15
   William H. 116
Green Hill 231
Greenbrier Co., Va. 18
Greene
   Ann Temple 157
   Fannie R. 125
   Frances M. 217
   John R. 157
Greene Co., N.Y. 191
Greene Co., Pa. 262
Greene Co., Va. 95
Greenfield
   Benjamin Truman 51, 124
Greenfield, N.Y. 47
Greenleaf
   Patrick Henry, Rev. 109
   William C. 178
Greenleaf's Point 29, 99, 216
Greenough
   Agnes Cushing 27
   Francis Clark 146
   J. James 32, 114
   J.J. 146
   James 27
   M.F. 146
   Mary Annie 114
   Mary F. 27, 32, 114
   Mary Lincoln 32
Greensboro(ugh), Ala. 44, 221
Greensboro, Ga. 58
Greensboro(ugh), N.C. 85, 189
Greenville 241
Greenwell
   W.E. 255
Greer
   Georgiana Hill 147
   Henrietta 38, 147
   James C. 38, 147
   Rachel 87
   Susan 87
   William 38, 82, 87, 147, 162, 182
   William P. 182
Greeves
   Amanda 3
   John 3, 169
   Thomas 24
Gregg
   William, Capt. 159
Grey
   Benjamin Edwards 150
Grey Co., Can. 92
Griegsville, Va. 1
Grier
   Maj. 151
Griffin
   Ann 138
   J.H., Rev. 169
   James L. 210
   Lancelot 138
   Sarah 138
   Sinia 210
Griffin, Ga. 56
Griffith
   Chas. G. 24
   Frances E. 252
   George, Capt. 160
   Lizzie A. 160
   Mary Adelaide 252
   Rev. 12, 246
   W.A. 99
   William A. 252
   William, Capt. 241
Griggs
   William L. 186
Grigsby
   James 160
Grimes
   Martha 167
   Robert 167
   Robert Powers 167
   William 32
Gross
   Rev. 239
Gross Isle, Mich. 143
Groton, Mass. 132, 258
Grotz
   Agnes M. 92
Grouard
   Edward St. Pierre 171
   Ellen 171
   George M. 171
Grove, The 245
Grove, Va. 36, 57
Groves
   Eliza 231
Grupe
   William 38
Guatemala 98
Guayaquil, South America 4
Guelph 92
Guernsey 249
Guest
   Job, Rev. 217
   Rev. 122
Guilford courthouse 60
Guinand
   William 66
Gulager's boarding house 217
Gulich
   John S. 241
Gunnell
   Henry D. 122, 210
   James S., Dr. 94
   Maggie Mutter 120
   Martha A. 120
   Mary E. 122
   W.H. 256
   William P., Dr. 5, 120

Gunton
    Dr. 201
    Lizzie Livingston 272
    Mary R.M. 143
    Thomas 201
    William A. 143, 219
    William, Dr. 219, 272
Gurley
    E.M. 31, 35
    Marion Ann Muirhead 35
    P.D., Rev. 255, 268
    Porter Gillet 31
    R.R., Rev. 31
    R.R., Rev.* 35
    Rev. 257
    W.H.F. 209
Guy
    Benjamin F. 199
    Jane Anna 14
    Miranda M. 245
Guyandotte, Va. 104
Guyther
    John S. 264
Gwathmey
    Columbia 46
    H.B. 92
    Matilda C. 92
Gwin
    Mary 107
    W.M., Hon. 107
    William M., Hon. 137

H

Hackett
    J. 221
Haddock's Hills, D.C. 21
Hadley
    Benjamin 252
Hagan
    Henry 235
Hager
    C. 170
    Christopher 34
    Christopher Columbus 34
    Frederick 34
    George Henry 170
    Theresa Elizabeth 170
    W. 170
Hagerstown, Md. 14, 103, 131, 168, 237
Haggarty
    John 165
Hagner
    Alexander B. 161
    E. Louisa Smith 192
    J.R., Maj. 192
    Mary M. 222
    Mrs. 60
    P.V., Bvt. Maj. 134
    Peter 222
    Richard H. 20
Hague 125

Hale
    William B. 37
Haliday
    Mary Jane 136
Hall
    Anna Maria 212
    Caroline M. 245
    Caroline S. 28
    Charles H., Rev.* 267
    Columbus 158
    D., Mrs. 158
    E.J. 28
    Edward 32
    Ephraim W. 204
    Francis M. 27
    G.W. 212
    H. Kent 80
    James A. 266
    Joseph, Dr. 204
    Sarah Jane 46
    Thomas 222
    William J., Col. 80
Haller
    Louisa M. 197
Halloway
    Ransom, Hon. 2
Hallowell 252
    Benjamin 114
    Caroline 114
Halter
    Helen Lucretia 95
    Nicholas 95
Hamburg 31
Hamill
    Stephen 126
Hamilton
    Charles Beale, Dr. 20
    Edward M. 228
    Evan 144
    George S., Dr. 161
    James, Dr. 270
    Mary E. 184
    Mary Grace Dalton 87, 93
    Patrick 40
    Rev. 84, 117, 138
    Robert M. 87, 93
    Sarah 144
    William B. 80
    William, Col. 184
    William, Rev. 49, 53, 66, 90
Hamilton Co., Ohio 208
Hammel
    William 45
Hammond
    Henry 212
    M.A.B. 159
    Nicholas 205
    Sarah Jane 262
Hamner
    Rev. 23
Hancock
    John 111
Hancock, Md. 235
Hancock, N.Y. 52

Hancocktown, Md. 199
Hand
    Anna S. 4
    Catharine Chauncey 253
    Emily Joanna 28
    Joseph W. 28, 253
Handley
    Martha Virginia 190
Hands
    John 16
    Marry Ann 16
    Thomas Dixon 16
Handy
    Ann P. 182
    Charles N., Col. 83
    J.W.K., Rev.* 190
    James H. 83
    Margaret C. 88
    Robert J. Walker 182
    S.W. 88
    Sarah Selby 190
    William 182
Haney
    Hugh 166
Hank
    J. Newman, Rev. 170
    J.W.F., Dr. 170
Hanks
    William, Rev. 231
Hanly
    Edmund 224
    Mary Jane 224
Hannahan
    Elizabeth 32
    Thomas 32
Hannan
    Joanna Louisa 51
Hannefin
    William 53
Hannibal, Mo. 136
Hanover Co., Va. 162
Hansbrough
    G. Woodson 55
Hanson
    Charles, Capt. 185
    Grafton D. 164
    Isaac K. 185
    J.K. 41
    John J., Lieut. 185
    Richard M. 129
    Samuel 127
    Thomas M. 159
    Weightman K.F., Capt. 185
Harbaugh
    Elenor 16
    Joseph 16
    Leonard 254
    W.S. 254
    Winifred S. 254
Hardaway
    Henrietta C. 208
Hardcastle
    Edmund L.F., Capt. 185

Harden
  Lizzie S. 269
  William, Rev.* 163, 269
Hardenbergh
  C.L. 46
  Mary H. 46
Hardie
  James A., Lieut. 14
Hardin
  Augusta L. 211
  Fanny 211
  L.B. 211
Harding
  Eliza Jane 111
  John, Jr. 159
Hardisty
  Thomas J. 225
Hardy
  William G., M.D. 24
Hare
  D.O. 59
  Mary M. 59
  Rev. 230
Harewood, Va. 128
Harford Co., Md. 40, 160
Harkness
  Daniel S. 144
  John C. 173
  Margaret Y. 173
Harmon
  Agnes 238
  James 238
Harney
  Mr. 190
Harper
  Francis 213
  George W. 118
  Hon. 101
  Lucretia 8
  Robert Goodloe 205
  Virginia A. 57
  William C. 264
Harper's Ferry, Va. 14, 40, 46, 56, 178
Harrington
  Caroline 248
  Catharine 139
  George 248
  George W. 155
  Jeremiah 139
  Richard H. 39
Harris
  Angeline Coolidge 164
  Arnold 164
  Auba C. 215
  Elizabeth 190
  Frances A. 237
  Jeremiah 11
  Julia 147
  Lilian Longfellow 215
  Mary C. 74
  Mary E. 181
  Matthias 189
  O.C. 171
  Rebecca J. 68
  S.B. 237
  Samuel L. 215
  Susan 164
  Thomas A., Maj. 40
  Thomas, Dr. 74, 190
Harris, Scot. 107
Harrisburg, Pa. 14, 42, 220, 247, 264
Harrison
  Ann Catharine 5
  Bertram 107
  Betty Carr 51
  Edward Jaquelin, Dr. 51
  Elias, Rev. 40
  Frederick T. 167
  George F. 28
  Gustavus 167
  Hugh T., Rev. 177
  Hugh, Rev. 170
  Joseph 23
  Louisa 23, 161
  Mathew 23
  Matilda 248
  Philip, Sr. 65
  Randolph 161
  Williamson 80
Harrison Co., Va. 199
Harrod
  Mary 253
Harrover
  Eliza 182
  Hiram 182
  James R. 234
  W.H. 182
Harrow
  James D. 42
Harryman
  Ann Rebecca 164
  C.S., Miss 169
Hart
  Amy 37
  John D., Capt. 235
  Mary 54
  Samuel 54
Harte
  Edward 98
  Edward Alfred 98
  Rosina M. 98
Hartford, Conn. 176, 207, 232
Hartford, Ver. 37
Hartman
  Calvin T. 30
Harvard University 7, 214
Harvey
  A.J. 101
  Anne E.J. 272
  J.F. 265
  James E. 223
  John Blan 101
  Margaret 111
  Margaret F. 101
  Miss 193
  William C. 178
William Egbert 145
Harwood
  Edwin, Rev. 260
Haseltine
  Mary K. 219
  William 219
Haskins
  Adelaide C. 101
  Charles 101
  Ralph 140
  Rebecca Jewett 101
Haslam
  Lina 232
  Selina 232
  William H. 232
Haslup
  Henry 104
Hassard
  Samuel Nicholson 157
Hassler
  J.J.S. 166
Hatch
  Anselm, Capt. 181
Hatton
  Henry D. 265
  Mary G. 221
Hauptman
  Emma Almira 106
  John W. 106
  Philip H. 194
  Rachel M. 106
Hausenpflute
  Peter 14
Havana, Cub. 100, 201
Havenner
  Annie 214
  Charles W. 149
  Eugenius Emory 68
  John F. 214
  Mary Cornelia 68
  Thomas H. 68
  William Thomas 214
Haviland
  John 83
Havre, Fra. 60
Hawke
  Julia 180
  Mary 158
  Thomas A. 180
Hawkins
  Ann Alecia 60
  Columbia V. 53
  Delia 62
  Laidler, R. 49
  Philemon, Col. 62
Hawks
  Francis L., Rev. 43
  Rev. 267
Hawley
  Lewis J. 165
  William 273
Hay
  Mary V. 65

Hayden
    H.A. 254
    H.H., Dr. 173
    Virginia Josephine 254
Haydon
    Dudley M. 272
Hayes
    Jonathan 191
    Lizzie 65
    William 193
Hays
    Annie W. West 236
    John 236
    Nicholas 158
Haywood
    Delia 62
    Stephen 62
Hazel
    Zachariah 45
Hazlewood, Md. 189
Hazzard
    Caroline 169
Head
    Frances 118
    George M. 34
Healy
    Mr. 75
Heap
    David Porter, Dr. 257
    Evelina M. 124
    S.D. 124
Heard
    Dr. 189
    Edward J. 54, 264
    Edward J., Dr. 192
    Joseph, Capt. 54
Heath
    Alexander W. Buel 109
    Edmonia 257
    Herman H. 109
    James P., Maj. 195
    Josephine V. 195
    Mary Selden 257
    Richard M. 257
Hebb
    Elizabeth Somerville 166
    William, Col. 166
Hebron, Conn. 52
Hedges
    John W., Rev. 164, 201
Hedgesville, Va. 150
Hedgman
    Hannah B. 23
    John G. 23
Heigl
    William 158
Heileman
    Anne S. 123
    Julius F., Col. 123
Heise
    Joseph L. 196
Heiss
    William H. 4

Heitmuller
    Caroline 112
Hellen
    Johnson 158
    Josephine 158
Heller
    Elenora 171
Helm
    J.J., Rev. 221
Henderson
    Andrew A., Dr. 93
    Archibald, Gen. 196
    Eliza G. 196
    Margaret C. 56
    Orra M. 35
    Rev. 60
    Richard H. 35
    Robert 70
    Thomas 35
    Thomas, Dr. 246
Henderson, Ky. 71, 93
Hendley
    Sophia 53
Hendrickson
    Sarah R. 41
    T., Capt. 41, 160
Henley
    Eliza 270
    J.D., Comm. 270
Henning
    Rev. 79
Henry
    Elvira M. 54
    J.M., Rev. 193-195, 264, 269
    James 77, 238
    John 54
    John Thomas 238
    Lucy Ellen 183
    Nathaniel 45
    P.M., Capt. 183
    Patrick 45
    Rachel 238
    Rev. 221
    Robert V. 273
    Susanna J. 183
Henry Co., Ia. 150, 240
Hepburn
    Annie Leake 257
    David 124
    John M. 257
    Louisa V. 51
    Mrs. 173
Herbert
    Gertrude 55
    Mary Jane 215
    Nathaniel 61
    Patrick 158
    Thomas 266
    William 14
Herbst
    Francis T. 5
Herefore
    William P., Dr. 64

Herity
    Bridget 179
Hermitage, Md. 246, 253
Hermitage, Tenn. 138
Herndon
    T.D., Elder 114
Herrick
    E., Hon. 220
    Rebecca 220
Herrill
    John E. 40
Hesse, Ger. 77
Heston
    Emma 78
    Newton, Rev.* 78
Hevner
    John P. 201
    Peter 201
    Virginia 201
Hewes
    William, Rev. 219
Hewett
    Mary B. 71
    R. 71
Hewitt
    A.K. 202
Heyer
    Jane 226
Heyl
    Mary 230
    William H. 230
Heyne, Ger. 77
Hibbs
    Charles 90
    Eleanor 90
Hickey
    John F., Rev. 228
Hicks
    Pascal 159
Hieskell
    H.M. 33
Higbee
    Rev. 112
Higginbotham
    Elvira M. 54
Higgins
    A. 109
    Charles 110
    Dennis 53
    Edward 109
    Edward, Lieut. 43
    Eudora 252
    Franklin 110
    Patrick 109
Highfield House, Eng. 100
Highlands, D.C. 14, 125
Hildt
    George, Rev. 155
Hill
    Charles Gilbert 212
    Elizabeth S. 225
    Francis M. 225
    Isaac 56, 212
    Isaac, Hon. 15

J.B., Rev. 255
James C., Dr. 122
James Mitchell 214
James N. 112
Johanah 56
Johanna 212
John Augustus 56
John Burley 179
Joseph B. 238
Margaret 148
Mary B. 144, 214
Mary Jane 163
Matilda 24
Mrs. 52
Rev. 54, 57, 105, 176, 248
Richard S. 225
Richard T. 206
Sarah A. 117
Silas H. 144, 179, 214
Stephen P., Rev. 51, 64, 77, 174, 182, 215, 235, 259
Varnum 144
Victoria 137
Hilleary
C.T., Capt. 162
Elizabeth Ann 132
Ellen T. 162
James 132
John M. 132
Sarah O. 12
Tilghman, Sr. 12
Hiller
Ann S. 219
Hilliard
Mary W. 73
Hilton
Samuel 76
Hinds Co., Miss. 118, 235
Hinds County Gazette 118
Hines
A.F. 29
Christina 135
Frederick 135
Henry 237
John B. 168
Rachael 33
Hingham, Mass. 61
Hinton
Annie Forster 86
Catharine J.H. 108
George W. 108
Josiah T. 136
Mary Ann 210
Robert W. 108
Hitaffer
James R. 155
Thomas 148
Hitchcock
Mr. 129
Hitchcox
M.M. 53
Hite
John 237
Sarah 237

Hittle
Rev. 166
Hitz
Margaret 160
Mr. 165
Hoag
Sheldon J. 191
Hoban
Anna Rosetta 173
James 173
Marion B. 173
Hobbie
Mary 207
Selah R., Hon. 207, 218
Hobbs
Christina 255
Elizabeth A. 69
Hobson
B.J. 123
Hockaday
Amelia S. 127
P.B. 127
Hocking Co., Ohio 236
Hodge
A.A., Rev. 173
Emma 8
William, Rev. 37
Hodges
Benjamin T. 95
Ellen 116
Joseph 248
Rev. 2, 4, 6, 8, 24, 26, 37, 46, 48, 50, 59, 61, 64, 66, 72, 79, 80, 87, 88, 91, 92, 95, 104, 113, 116, 118, 122, 125, 129-131, 137, 138, 142, 153, 154, 157, 159, 160, 166, 169, 178, 186, 191, 196, 201, 203, 209, 210, 212, 221, 225, 228, 229, 232-234, 237, 247, 248, 250-252, 262, 267, 269, 273
W., Rev. 271-273
Hodgkins
Rachael 178
Hodgson
Jane J. 198
Joseph 17
Joseph F. 251
Mary Isabel 251
Richard Gormly 251
Susan R. 17
Hodson
Thomas 269
Hoeke
Henry 1
Hoff
J.F., Rev. 204
Hoffman
Henry 209
Samuel 98
Hogan
Jane 143

Sarah 143
William 143
Hogg
John W. 70
Hohman
Carolus 139
Holbrook
Josiah 257
Holcombe
Prof. 188
Holderby
Mary Phenton 104
Holladay
Rev. 191
Holland 229
Edward 5
Elizabeth J. 253
James S. 253
John E. 22, 101
John Sands 253
Mary 5
Mary A. 22
Rev. 95
Susannah 22
Willie 101
Holland Company 229
Holley
Clemenia 126
Clemenia E. 126
John M. 126
Hollingshead
J.S. 69
Mary Ann 98
Hollingsworth
Eliza Kelso 48
William W. 257
Hollins
George N., Comm. 89
Maria R. 89
Hollywood, Ala. 111
Hollywood, Miss. 272
Holmead
Alfred, Rev. 51, 203, 230
Rev. 210
Holmes
Caroline F. 50
John, Hon. 50
P.H. 73
Holroyd
Mary Jane 13
Holt
Mary Margaret 142
Susannah 64
Holton
Sarah M. 264
Holtzman
America B. 79
Emma O. 79
George H. 245
John T. 79
Kate M. 245
William F. 220
Homans
Benjamin 2

Benjamin, Jr. 246
Martha 2
Homewood
   George 20
Honeywood, Va. 262
Hong Kong, China 133, 224
Honolulu, S.I. 100
Hood
   John 173
   John H. 131
   Mary Whartenby 173
Hooe
   James H. 67
Hooper
   Catharine 130
   George R. 130
   Grenville T.W. 130
   Jane 50
Hoover
   Andrew 134
   Charles Edward 60
   Charles P. 134
   Elizabeth A. 60
   J.H., Rev.* 75
   William 60
Hopeten 20
Hopewell
   Walter, Hon. 151
Hopkins
   Elizabeth A. 140
   H.H., Rev. 178
   John 20
   John S. 40
   Mary 20
   Mary Jane 169
   Rev. 29
Horbach
   Albert 124
Horn's Point, Md. 228
Hornblower
   William B., Rev. 247
Horner
   Barbara Lucinda 179
   Emily 93
   Inman 93, 179
   Joseph 49
Hornor
   Robert E. 26
Horry
   Comm. 68
   Elias 68
   Mary Shubrick 68
Hort
   William P. 75
Hoskins
   Elizabeth A. 142
Hot Springs, Ark. 151
Hotel D'Albion 97
Hough
   Lucinda L. 219
   William W. 238
Houma, La. 269

Hourly
   Juliana 19
   Timothy 19
House
   George E. 217
Houston
   Agnes 136
   John 114
   Martha White 114
   Mary Humes 136
   Samuel A., Dr. 136
   Samuel Humes 232
Houston, Tex. 12
Howard
   F., Dr. 126
   Frank 245
   Hannah 245
   Henry 36, 43
   Henry, Prof. 159
   Isabella Leavitt 156
   James 156
   Jane Freeman 213
   Justin H. 87
   Laura P. 43
   Sarah 126
   Virginia 159
   William E. 245
Howard Co., Md. 177, 189, 194, 207, 217
Howe
   Rev. 50
Howell
   George H. 83
   John C., Lieut. 233
   Mary 116
   Mary H. 112
   S. Harrison 97
   Samuel L., Dr. 112
   Virginia A. 259
Howison
   James K. 244
   Mrs. 12
Howle
   Joanna 233
   Joanna Frances 8
   Parke G., Maj. 8, 233
Hoxton
   T.S., Dr. 260
Hoye
   Thomas W. 126
Hoyle
   E. 127
   Margaret E. 127
Hoyt
   Goold 58
Huamantla, Mex. 206
Hubbard
   Mary 116
Hudal
   Mary 256
Huddleston
   John E. 5
Huegez
   Rev. 188

Huggins
   F.B. 146
   Francis B. 157
   Joseph 171
   Joshua 55
   Sarah 146
Hughes
   Christopher, Hon. 33
   Eliza Frances 247
   George A. 33
   James 50
   James E., Rev. 161
   John Somerfield 247
   Margaret A. 137
   Margaret Smith 33
   Maria Sidney 33
   Nathaniel 137
   Rev. 189, 229
   Robert B. 247
   William 155
Hughlett
   Sallie D. 185
   William, Col. 185
Huguenots 23, 38
Huidekoper
   Harm Jahn 229
Hull
   Nannie Innes 131
   Randolph Pomeroy 131
   Robert 105
   William H. 131
   Wm. H., Capt. 3
Hulse
   Rebecca 269
Hume
   J. 194
   Jesse W., Rev. 209
   Margaret M. 175
Humes
   Alexander 188
Humphrey
   Mary 158
   Susan 174
   William 174
Humphreys
   Ann Rebecca 81
   Clement 123
   Eliza M. 67
   Elizabeth 230
   Guy C. 81
   John 230
   Joseph A. 166
   Louisa 67
   Mary 230
   Rev. 180
   Rev.* 67
Humphries
   A. Rebecca 70
   Frederic Carlten 70
   G.C. 181
   Guy C. 70
Hungerford
   Annie M. 20
   Dr. 20

Henry 167
John P., Capt. 194
John Pratt 194
John Pratt, Capt. 180
Sarah A.W. 167
Hunnicutt
  Annie Eliza 15
  John A. 15, 268
Hunt
  Amos 247
  Bettie M. 213
  Catharine A. 88
  Charles Amos 247
  Clara Jane 88
  Edward B., Lieut. 120
  Harvey J. 129
  Henry J., Maj. 62
  R. Finley 88
  R. Finley, Dr. 247
  Tabitha 50
Hunter
  Andrew 114
  Anne Morrison 261
  Eliza Cecil 74
  J. Brooke 184
  J.B., Col. 100
  James, Col. 74
  John C. 207
  Margaret 14
  Margaret C. 100
  Mary 114
  Oceana 189
  William 261
  William, Col. 177
Huntingdon, Eng. 73
Huntington
  Rev. 272
Huntoon
  Jonathan G., Hon. 50
Huntsville, Ala. 209
Hurdle
  Grace M. 102
  Kate Alberta 102
  Mary A. 62
  Samuel V. 102
Hurley
  John 44
  John P. 234
  Mary Ann 44
Hurly
  Theodore 113
Hurst
  George, Lieut. 48
  John H. 270
  Mary L. 9
  Rev. 101
  Robert 85
  William D., Lieut. 9
Hurtado & Co. 119
Hutchinson
  Betty S. 78
  William E. 5
Hutchison
  C./E. Nye, M.D. 94, 97

Caroline C. 65
Hutter
  E.W., Rev. 105
Hutton
  Rev. 116, 266
Hyatt
  Alpheus 138
  Lucretia 87
  Margaret Ann 242
  Richard 204
  Richard G. 242
  Richard Grafton 242
  Wesley 87
Hyde
  Elias G. 12
  George A. 139, 143
  Richard A. 235
  Samuel Gridley 118

I

I.O.O.F. (also see "Odd Fellows")
  Central Lodge No. 1 76
Iardella
  Edward Francis 244
  I. Andria 244
  J.A.C. 2
  L.A. 138
  M.A. 244
Iberville Parish, La. 35
Ide
  George B., Rev. 123
Illinois 100, 146, 147, 240, 271
Indian Agent 15
Indian Bureau 21
Indian Springs, Ga. 232
Indian Town, Md. 4
Indian treaties 165
Indiana Co., Pa. 113
Indianapolis, Ind. 101
Indianola, Tex. 181
Indians 151, 210
Ingersoll
  Charles M. 91
  Colin M., Hon. 191
  Elizabeth Ann 133
Ingle
  Adeline 237
  Edward 237
  Henry 91
  John P. 125, 164
  Joseph 12
  Maria 164
  Mary 12, 125
Ingleside, Va. 107
Ingman
  William 95
Ingraham
  Sarah Ann 243
Iniguez
  Don Manuel 77
  Ecarnacion 77

Inman
  Maria S. 72
  William, Capt. 72
Innis
  Anna 26
  Henry, Hon. 26
Iowa 13, 141
Iowa City, Ia. 141
Ireland 7, 15, 23, 38, 62, 100, 154,
  215, 218, 257, 262
Ironside
  George E., Dr. 115
  Mary A. 115
  R.B., Dr. 173
Irvine
  Callender, Gen. 92
  Patience Elliot 92
Irving
  David E. 246
  George Washington 246
  Sarah A. 246
  William 242
Irving House, D.C. 85
Irwin
  Francis G. 190
  Henry 162
  Hester A. 162
  J.W. 159
Isaac
  Joseph C. 262
Isherwood
  A.H. 87
  B.F. 87
  Julian 87
Island (southwest part of D.C.) 1,
  10, 21, 83, 124, 133, 135,
  162, 168, 169, 200, 204,
  211, 213, 220, 247, 253,
  272
Isle Harris, Scotland 21
Islington, Eng. 94
Israel
  Ann Maria 71
  F., Rev. 228, 231, 235, 238,
    249, 257, 266, 270, 273
  G.W., Rev. 23
  George N., Rev. 62
  Martha A. 23
  Otho 71
  Robert 122

J

Jack
  James 7, 252
  Susan 7
Jackson
  Ada Augusta 12
  Andrew 138, 224
  Cornelia Augusta 171
  Gen. 15, 165, 218, 244, 261
  George C. 144
  Henry R., Hon. 171

Jonathan E., Dr. 258
Jonathan Edwards, Dr. 256
Maria Catharine 29
Mary A. 12, 144
Rachael 138
Rev. 2
Susan Lowndes 32
William B. 32
William S. 12
Jackson Courthouse, Va. 21, 44
Jackson, Miss. 22
Jacksonville, Ill. 271
Jacobs
    Henry, Dr. 69
    S.D., Hon. 96
Jagiello
    Apollonia 40
jail 13
Jalapa 190
Jamaica 11
James
    Frances Anna 231
    Frances R. 231
    Israel E. 239
    Lavinia J. 101
    Mary F. 54
    Mrs. 18
    William 101, 259
Jameson
    Eliza 176
Jamieson
    E. Theresa 91
Janney
    Jonathan 98, 212
    Margaret 98
    Phineas 212
Janvier
    Benjamin A. 245
    Margaret B. 245
    William Stanhope 245
Japan 239
Jardin
    Agricola Armand 34
    Armand 34
    Honorine 34
Jarvis
    N.S., Dr. 223
Jasper, Tex. 114
Jaudon
    Lawson White 110
    Marguerite Peyton 110
    Samuel 110
Jay
    John 205
    Josephine 65
    Peter Augustus 65
Jeffers
    Mrs. 177
    William R. 213
Jefferson
    Fannie A. 156
    Ferdinand 215
    Hamilton 156
    Mary E. 253
    Thomas 90, 198, 221, 245
Jefferson City, Mo. 13, 119
Jefferson Co., Ky. 101, 193
Jefferson Co., Va. 8, 9, 11, 31, 41, 67, 108, 125, 157, 162, 230, 242, 252, 255, 259
Jefferson Inquirer 13
Jenifer
    James L. 41
    Louisa R.T. 41
Jenkins
    Ambrosia M. 171
    Charles J. 222
    Elisha, Col. 159
    Hannah 159
    Leoline 13
    Mary Gertrude 13
    Rosina L. 13
Jenks
    Sarah E. 193
Jennings
    John 77
    Robert C. 112
    Samuel K., Rev.* 260
    Thomas R. 44
Jesup
    Jane Findley 71
    Lucy Ann 214
    Maj. Gen. 71
    Thomas S., Gen. 214
Jett
    Elizabeth I. 248
    Elvira Lane 268
    James 268
Jewell
    Catharine 161
    Ellen 149
    Fannie Isadora 167
    James Gray 167
    William 161
    William, Maj. 167
John
    Reuben C. 53
    Thomas 200
Johns
    Bishop 268
    H.V.D., Rev. 133, 138
    John, Rev. 197
    Margaretta Jane 268
    Rebecca 228
    Rev. 9, 134, 219, 230
    Thomas 228
Johnson
    Addel 147
    Amanda 234
    Amelia 246
    Ann Eliza 22
    Anne Love 88
    Bradley T. 36
    Bryant 246
    Carter P., Dr. 88, 103
    Catharine 112
    Catherine S. 84
    Cave, Hon. 55
    Chancellor 106
    Charlotte P. 105
    Elizabeth 55
    Emily Contee 82
    George 78, 81, 266
    Greenleaf's Point 144
    Henry 125
    Henry D. 212
    Henry Forrest 103
    Henry Galileo 125
    Horace Holmes Moss 265
    James 144
    James A. 32
    James W. 84
    John B. 144
    John Harrison 60
    John M. 265
    John, Hon. 33
    John, Rev. 104
    Joseph 46
    Joseph, Hon. 199
    Laura 106
    Martin H., Dr. 95
    Mary 26
    Mary Ann 125
    Mary T. 33
    Matilda N. 96
    Rebecca 81
    Reverdy, Hon. 82
    Reverdy, Jr. 133
    Samuel 65
    Sarah 199
    T.W. 105
    Thomas 35
    Thomas R. 26
    Thomas W. 60
    W.P.C., Rev.* 22
    W.R., Prof. 251
    Walter R. 87
    William C. 166
    William H. 78
    William O. 57
Johnston
    Cyrus, Rev. 94, 97
    Elizabeth 101
    Ellen Augusta 242
    Emily Newman 120
    J.T., Rev. 80, 159, 199
    James T., Dr. 120
    John 27
    Margaret 211
    Margaret M. 120
    Rev. 87
    Samuel 272
    William P., Dr. 242
    Z.F., Comm. 120
Johnstone
    Rev. 267
Jolly
    Bushrod 23
Joncherez
    Louis F. 64
Jones
    Annie S. 31

Arnold E., Col. 24
Bernard, Jr. 37
Beverley R. 230
Clement F., Rev. 203
D.R., Lieut. 140
David, Maj. 241
Edward 145
Edward, Lieut. 196
Elizabeth A. 55
Elizabeth Jackson 24
Emma 177
Emma Blanche 177
Hannah Maria 42
Harriette L. 23
Hugh 71
Isaac D., Hon. 105
J. Anderson 247
James 131
James H. 80
John C., Capt. 247
John D., Col. 241
John R. 104
Mary Elizabeth 225
Mary Frances 99
Mary Sophia 31
Olivia E. 132
Paul 35
Peter, Capt. 96
Rebecca 271
Rev. 91, 96
Robert 246
T.D., Dr. 132
T.G., Rev. 125
Thomas, Rev.* 31
W. Brooke, Dr. 177
Walter, Gen. 23
Warner P. 268
William H. 41
William, Dr. 42
Jonestown, Pa. 95
Jordan
   Thomas 247
Jordon
   J.W. 31
Joselen
   Ellen E. 77
Josetti
   Martin L.B. 33
Journal of Commerce 92
Joyce
   Andrew J. 227
   Ann 113
   Frances M. 227
   George William 227
   John 113
   John J. 270
   Margaret A. 214, 222
   Michael Joseph 113
Judd
   S. Corning 101
Judge 3, 15, 44, 69, 73, 77, 80, 90, 94, 96, 101, 103, 107, 116, 125, 132, 147, 151, 158, 165, 168, 171, 192, 194, 196, 197, 200, 205, 208, 220, 222, 225, 241, 251, 266, 268
   John 139
   William 246
Julledy
   Rev. 2
Jullien
   Augustin 96
   Catharine 96
   Gabriel Winfield 96
   Mary Margaret 262
Julme
   Peter 36
Junkin
   D.X., Rev. 76, 115, 147, 155, 163, 168, 172, 177, 204
   Dr. 105
   Rev. 146
Justice (occupation) 43, 73, 97, 143
Justice of the Peace 222

K

Kahoe
   William 251
Kane
   Elias 148
   Elizabeth 148
Kankey
   Araminta Montgomery 146
   Zebulon, Rev. 146
Kaufman
   David S. 5
Kavenaugh
   Alice 177
Kearney
   James, Col. 174
   Louisa 174
   Medora 174
Kearns
   Mary Ann 64
Keasby
   A.Q. 108
   Elizabeth 108
Keating
   Margaret E. 72
Keck
   Ann Eliza 43
   James 43
   Jane 43
Keech
   Catharine A. 233
   James 120
   W.S., Dr. 233
Keefe
   William N. 93
   William, Sr. 208
Keenan
   Joseph A., Dr. 252
Keene, N.H. 54

Keener
   Anna M. 170
Kehler
   John H., Rev. 181
   S. Ella 181
Kehoe
   Sarah E. 136
Keightley
   Archibald 185
   Isabella 185
Keith
   John 264
   Margaret 264
   P. Tapier, Rev. 157
   Ruel 54
   Sarah J. 264
Keithley
   John 25
Kellen
   Robert, Rev.* 24
Keller
   Ann Margaret 56
   Charles 230
   Charles M. 260
   Cornelia M. 161
   Felix 89
   Frank 252
   Frederick L. 109
   J.P. 127, 252
   Jonas P. 89
   Margaret Jane 260
   Michael 214
   S.A. 252
   Sarah 89
Kelly
   Bell 145
   Catharine Harriet 243
   Egbert B. 80
   John 145
   Margaret 25, 41, 145
   Mary Eliza 94
   Mary W. 243
   Michael 143
   Moses 243
   Robert 153
   Sarah Ellen 41
   Thomas 55
   William Henry 41
Kemble
   James 90
Kemp
   Mary A. 198
Kempton
   Rev. 43
Kendall
   A., Hon. 203
   Adela 25
   Amos 117
   Amos, Hon. 25
   Charlotte S. 129
   George M. 129
   John 258
Kendrick
   George H. 2

Kennedy
   Alfred W., Dr. 29
   Andrew 242, 255
   Anne R. 242
   Anthony 33, 255
   John 255
   John C. 159
   John P. 255
   Letetia 121
   Nancy Clayton 255
   Pendleton 255
   Wesley 29
Kenney
   Jane 203
Kenny
   Rev. 22
Kenrick
   Rev. 191
Kent
   Gov. 52, 54, 87
   James 128
   Joseph 114
   Kate L. 52, 54
   Sarah F. 87
   Thomas H. 114
Kent Co., Md. 52, 54, 157, 205, 231
Kent Island, Md. 32, 34
Kentucky 3, 26, 28, 41, 53, 56, 71, 83, 103, 127, 150, 159, 189, 193, 197, 218, 245, 272
Keokuk, Ia. 16, 78, 219, 265
Kepler
   Rev. 64, 92
Ker
   Leander, Rev. 171
Kerby
   John 253
Kerr
   Chapman 112
   David, Rev. 52, 57, 59, 160
   Elizabeth 33
   Henrietta Earle 160
   John 199
   William W.S. 52
Kersey
   Virginia A. 215
Kessler
   Peter F. 211
Ketchum
   Sarah Elizabeth 249
   William H., Capt. 249
Key
   H.G.S., Hon. 128
   Sarah Ann 128
Key West, Fla. 227, 240
Keyes
   William C. 225
Keyworth
   Emma 114
   Kate 189
   Robert 114, 189

Kibby
   John B. 73
Kidwell
   Sarah E. 6
Kieckhoefer
   A.T. 163
   Julia Augusta 163
Killen
   Rev. 26
Killmon
   Samuel, Capt. 43
Kinchey
   Paul 72
Kinchy
   Paul 78
King
   Ann C. 94
   Charles Collins 94
   Charles Francis 194
   Daniel, Dr. 218
   Edward 7
   Eleanor H. 84
   Eliza Anthoinette 77
   Elizabeth C. 147, 190
   Elizabeth Seaver 147
   Fannie Landon 191
   Francis 54
   Genevieve Agnes 224
   George G. 147
   George G., Hon. 3, 190
   George H. 106
   George, Hon. 3
   George, Rev. 52, 54
   Harriet 70
   Henrietta Landon 191
   Horatio 94
   James 116
   James A. 231, 263
   James D. 161, 224
   John 123
   John A. 209
   John H. 84
   Levi G. 271
   M.D.V., Mrs. 263
   Martin 195
   Mary 116
   Mary A. 161
   Mary Ann 205
   Matilda S. 41
   Mr., Hon. 3
   Nancy 62
   Orson 77
   Roswell 7
   Samuel D. 41
   Sarah 115
   Sarah Virginia 41
   Thomas 186
   Thomas Grosvenor 231
   Thomas Worthington 7
   Vincent 115
   W.W. 54
   William 62, 123, 218, 236
   William P. 163
   William, Hon. 98

   Z.M.P. 191
King and Queen Co., Va. 124
King George Co., Va. 41, 67, 77, 79, 83, 108, 151, 177, 180, 181, 190, 223, 263, 270
Kingsford
   Edward, Rev. 192
Kingston, Scot. 40
Kinkle
   William H., Rev. 201
Kinney
   Mary 129
Kinsolving
   O.A., Rev. 191
Kip
   Jane 63
   Rev. 266
Kirby
   Charles T. 251
   James 60
   M., Mrs. 60
   Samuel 211
   William Wallace 126
Kirk
   Ed. N., Rev. 120
   G.E. 162
   Silas 190
   Thomas A.M. 162
Kirkpatrick
   Catharine P. 34
   John A. 34
   Mary Alice 34
Kirkwood
   Wallace 180
Kishacoquillas, Pa. 221
Kleiber
   Ann 255
   Jacob 255
Kleindienst
   John P. 108
Kleipstein
   William, Dr. 34
Klemann
   William 171
Klinehanse
   George D. 250
   Susan C. 250
Klopfer
   Benjamin 53
Knapp
   Auren 248
Knight
   Edward, Rev. 155, 206
   Elizabeth 159
   Rev. 110, 155, 231
Knighton
   Elizabeth E. 172
Knights
   Lydia 170
Knobloch
   Harriet 17
Knowles
   Frances 24
   Hazard 24

Martha E. 220
Knox
 Caroline F. 50
 Gen. 50
 Henry, Maj. Gen. 260
 Lucy F. 260
 S.B. 70
Knoxveille
 James 179
Koffman
 Mary Ann 125
Koones
 Frederick 123
Koontz
 Dorothy 65
Korff
 H.G. 156
Krafft
 George P. 249
Kranth
 C.P., Rev. 119
Kreamer
 Elizabeth 84
 John 84
Krebs
 William, Rev. 60
Kuhl
 Henry 67
Kurtz
 Catharine 273
 Daniel 273
Kyle
 Alexander 117

L

LaBarre
 Francis 176
Lacey
 John 55
Lacton, Ia. 237
Lacy
 Drury, Rev. 83, 86
 William Henry 133
Ladd
 Mary Josephine 61
Lafayette Station 184
Lafayette, Ind. 258
Laird
 George B. 32
Lake Catahoula, La. 54, 264
Lake Drummond, N.C. 9
Lakemeyer
 August Frederick 201
 Elizabeth 201
 Frederick 201
Lamb
 Theodore L. 216
Lambert
 Rev. 116
 William H. 156
Lambeth
 Job W., Rev. 133

Lambright
 George 134
 Margaret Elizabeth 134
 Mary 134
Lanahan
 John, Rev. 27, 58
 Peter, Rev. 64
 Rev. 1, 2, 5, 27, 59, 76, 87, 112
Lanark, Can. 141
Lancaster
 Alexius 195
 Letitia 195
Lancaster Co., Pa. 20
Lancaster, Ohio 153
Lancaster, Pa. 222, 234, 239
Land Office 221, 253, 266
Landen
 Daniel 71
Landon
 Sarah F. 260
Landstreet
 William T. 228
Lane
 Ann E. 83
 Ann Elizabeth 218, 257
 Charles 103
 Charles H. 83, 218, 257
 Ellen 26, 103
 Henry Turk 26
 Lillie 83
 Thomas H. 26, 103
Laneghan
 Peter, Rev. 45
Laneville, Va. 213
Langfitt
 Martha 145
Langley
 Aloysius 154
 Margaret E. 228
 Sylvester D. 142
Langston
 Mrs. 52
Langton
 Alexander Thomas 188
 Mrs. 116
languages
 French 91
 Spanish 91
Lanham
 Harriet E. 19
 Julia A. 66
Lanman
 Charles James 59
 Julia Woodbridge 59
Lanphier
 Elizabeth 162
 William 23
Lansdale
 Cornelia 168
 Mary 127
 Thomas Lancaster, Maj. 168
Lapeyre
 Michael 113

LaPointe 241
Lapolt
 Louisa 37
Lapsley Hall, Ky. 56
Larcomb
 James M. 256
Larker
 Virginia 234
Larned
 Benjamin P., Lieut. Col. 42
 Elizabeth R. 42
Larner
 A.J. 70
 Christiana 76
 Gideon W. 155
 John Smith 76
 Josiah Hicks 70
 Mary L. 70
 Michael 76
 Noble D. 56
Latham
 Catharine C. 170
 Franck Pinckney 242
 John E. 174
 R.P., Prof. 272
 R.W. 242
 Robert 68
 Robert W. 170
 Sarah M. 248
 William Fillison 248
 Woodville 248
Lathrop
 Caroline Huntington 265
 J.H. 265
 Mariana B. 265
Latimer
 Edwin W. 109
 Mary 22
 Rebecca M. 91
 Samuel 36, 91
Laub
 Martha Virginia 31
Lauck
 Isaac S. 57
Laural Hill cemetery 263
Laurel, Md. 216
Laurence
 John 5
Laurie
 Alexander Shepherd 116
 Dr. 146
 James, Rev. 37, 101, 116, 131, 146, 148
 James, Rev.* 153
 Rev. 44, 63, 99, 110, 115, 125
 Shepherd, Dr. 110, 116, 119
Laurieston, Scot. 162
Lavender
 James 149
 Mrs. 108
Lawrason
 Elizabeth 19
 Thomas 19

310

Lawrence
   Cornelius W. 98
   James 93
   John Marshall 138
   Jotham 269
   Sarah 269
   T. Bigelow, Col. 216
Lawrence, Mass. 73, 89
Lawrenceville, N.J. 72
Lawrenson
   James 209
   Sophia Smiley 209
Lawrie
   Rev. 3
Lawson
   William 269
Lawyer (occupation) 132, 143, 205, 208
Lay
   Albert Henry 94
   Richard 94
   Susan 94
Lazenby
   Ann Maria 25
   Charles Burnett 7
   Elisha 128
   Mary 215
   Sarah A. 7
   Sarah Amanda 200
   Thomas A. 7, 200
Lea
   Luke 162
   Mary 162
Leachman
   R.C., Rev. 263
Leadbitter
   D., Lieut. 60
   Elizabeth Waterman 60
   Nathan, Jr. 60
Leamington, D.C. 70
Leaner
   Louisa 186
   Mary Maria 186
   William 186
Leavel
   Rev. 268
Leavenworth
   Harriet 252
   Henry, Gen. 252
Lebanon, Pa. 105
Leclerc
   Rev. 168
Leddy
   Owen 70
Lee
   Bishop 92
   Eliza 204
   Eveline P. 169
   F., Col. 136
   Francis, Col. 204
   George Sibley 136
   H.W., Rev. 18
   Harvey 187
   Henry 147, 155
   Mary Elizabeth 125
   Mary J. 231
   R.B., Maj. 169
   William 125
Lee, N.H. 77
Leeds, Va. 230
Leehy
   Honora 8
Leesburg, Va. 35, 38, 44, 124, 146, 166, 196, 210, 246, 253
Leib
   Thomas J., Comm. 35
Leigh
   William 262
Leland
   Amos 50
   Caroline Augusta 50
Lemoine
   Fanny 122
Lenaghan
   Peter B., Rev. 91
   Rev. 27
Lenox
   Walter 206
Lenthall
   Jane 107
   John 107
   Mr. 102
Leonard
   A. 41
   Mary 41
LeRoy
   Alexis 219
   Cora 219
   Robert 44
Leslie
   Anna M. 224
   Ellen L. 11
   Henry P. 121
   Robert 224
   Robert H. 11
Leuth, Ire. 119
Levin
   Myer, Rev. 268
Lewis
   Amelia 44
   Benjamin Ernest 20
   Betty 90
   Catharine E. 217
   Charles 250
   Daingerfield 263, 270
   George Washington 82
   Harrison P. 250
   Henry Bocock 217
   James 28
   Joseph C. 20
   Joseph E. 13
   Joseph Knowles 259
   Lizzie B. 250
   Mary K. 20
   Mary Willis 263, 270
   Rachel 13
   Robert A. 196
   Samuel 184
   Samuel L., Col. 217
   Washington 13
   Willam G., Dr. 12
   William D. 44
   William D., Jr. 117
Lewisburg, Va. 269
Lexington, Ky. 154, 166
Lexington, Mass. 225
Liberia 125
Liberty Co., Ga. 7
Liberty Fire Company 143
Liberty, Tex. 169
Lightbourn
   J.H., Rev.* 217
Lighter
   John T. 64
Lightford
   Ann Matilda 245
Lilly
   Edwin 154
Lincoln
   A.B., Lieut. 88
Lincoln Co., N.C. 47
Lincolnshire, Eng. 73, 269
Lincolnton, N.C. 127
Lindenberger
   Annie Eliza 11
Lindsay
   Anna 210
   D.R. 210
   George F., Capt. 109
   Maria Amos 46
   Robert John 210
   S. 120
Lindsey
   Martha A. 5
Lindsley
   A.B. 11
   E. 70
   Mary Ann Augusta 70
Lindsly
   Fanny H. 232
   Harvey, Dr. 232
Linkins
   William, Sr. 27
Linnard
   Maj. 22
   Thomas B., Maj. 20
Linton
   Thomas A., Maj. 141
Lipphardt
   John 101
Lippincott
   Addie W. 270
   William 270
Lipscomb
   M.J.C. 147
   R.M., Rev. 96, 196
   Rev. 161
   W.C. 147
   William Corrie 147
Lisbon, Md. 194
Litchfield Co., Conn. 77

Lithuania, Pol. 40
Littele
    J. Debarth 230
Little
    Amelia Elenora 57
    Arabella Florinda 6
    Araminta 6, 57
    Catherine Frances 86
    David 86, 249
    James 6, 57
    Margaret D. 239
    Mary Elizabeth 126
    P.C. 8
    Peter 159
    Peter, Jr. 206
    Peter, Sr. 99
    Samuel I. 239
    Sarah E. 86
Little Falls 225
Little Hackney, Md. 39
Little Rock, Ark. 110, 116
Liverpool, Eng. 73, 128, 173, 185
Livingston
    Nora Carroll 1
    Robert LeRoy, Hon. 1
Livingston Co., N.Y. 14, 49
Llangavellach, South Wales 149
Lloyd
    Edward, Hon. 228
    Jasper S. 272
    Sally Scott 228
Lochbie, Fla. 218
Lochobar, Va. 267
Lochrey
    Hugh 175
    Jane 175
Locke
    Catherine Isabella 120
Locker
    Sarah E. 201
Lockett
    Thomas F., Rev. 44
Lockhart
    James R. 77
Lockor
    Anna 272
Lockport, N.Y. 66
Lockwood
    Rev. 20, 122
    Richard J. 67
Locust Grove, Md. 16, 156
Locust Hill 223
Locust Hill, Md. 220
Locust Hill, Va. 124
Logan, Ohio 236
Loker
    William H. 132
Lomax
    Elizabeth 49
    John 118
London, Eng. 24, 38, 94, 129, 139,
    186, 216, 220, 258
Long
    Caroline V. 223

Long Bridge 44
Long Island, N.Y. 24, 200
Longford Co., Ire. 165
Longford, Ire. 103
Longstreet
    James, Maj. 239
    William Dent 239
Longwood, Md. 251
Looker
    Allison C. 104
Loomis
    L., Gen. 255
    Martha B. 255
    Mary S. 198
    Nathan 198
Lord
    Elizabeth 74
    Ella 74
    W. Blair 265
    William 74
Lothian, Md. 168
Lott
    Gerrit V. 186
Louck
    Robert M. 140
Loudoun Co., Va. 44, 51, 55, 66,
    74, 95, 101, 106, 124, 153,
    177, 190, 191, 246, 254
Louey
    Boudinot S. 211
Loughborough
    Caroline E. 1
    David Augustine 236
    Emilly Rebecca 236
    Hamilton 236
    J.H., Dr. 1
    Louisa 236
Louisa Co., Va. 6, 57
Louisiana 122, 244
Louisville Courier 56
Louisville, Ky. 25, 36, 41, 42, 48,
    93, 163, 178, 182
Love
    Martha 186
Lovegrove
    William R. 189
Lovejoy
    John N., Sr. 267
Lovell
    Helen A. 111
    William S. 111
Lowd
    Maj. 270
Lowe
    Alfred 49
    Barbara 51
    E.L., Hon. 51
    Nathan 138
    Warren 254
Lowndes Co., Ala. 158
Loyed
    Elizabeth C. 91

Lucas
    Charles B. 36
    Eliza 36
    Ellen 111
    Emeline 125
    Fielding 163
    Fielding, Jr. 163
    Margaret 266
    Robert 141
    Robert, Col. 125
    Thomas 111
    William 36
Luce
    Stephen B. 270
Lucey
    Margaret 225
Lucymont, Md. 150
Ludlam
    Mary 232
    Nicholas 232
Ludlow
    Ezra 206
    Rachel S. 206
Lum
    A. Stewart 184
Lundstreet
    Samuel 187
Lunt
    Julia 57
Luray, Va. 223
Lusby
    A. Francis 129
    Elizabeth E. 214
Lush
    Lucius Y. 127
Luskey
    Serg. 157
Lusky
    Charles 245
Lutz
    John 3
    Mary 3
Lyddane
    William 163
Lyford
    William Gilman 95
Lyles
    Annie Elizabeth 124
    Eliza 46
    Thomas C., Col. 46
Lyme, Conn. 10
Lynch
    Daniel, Rev. 21
    George J. 258
    Henry 198, 257
    James 63
    Jane 63
    Johanna 139
    John 142
    John A. 88
    Julia 198
    Lynch 142
    Mary Ann 63
    Mary H.B. 257

Rev. 65
William 195
Lynchburg, Va. 201, 257, 267, 268
Lyndall
   George 42
Lyne
   Lavinia H. 177
   Leonard H. 267
Lynn
   John W. 273
Lynn, Mass. 73
Lyon
   Jacob 59
   Jane 59
Lyons
   Amanda 110
   Henningham H. 33
   James 33
   John 110

M

M'Knight
   Charles, Capt. 146
MacAllister
   Anna J. 32
   Christopher, Rev.* 32
MacDaniel
   Ezekiel 253
   Virginia 253
MacElfresh
   Rev. 47
Macfarlan
   Allan, Col. 209
   Rev. 126
MacFarland
   John 162
MacGill
   Maria L.B. 262
   Thomas 51
Machinist (occupation) 55
Mack
   Martin 87
   Rev. 117
Mackall
   Louis, Dr. 10
Mackenheimer
   Rev. 27, 58, 117
MacLeod
   Aggripina 107
   Alexander Norman 21, 107
MacNamara
   Daniel 225
MacNeill
   Eliza W. 47
   William, Gen. 47
Macomb
   J., Mrs. 143
   John N., Capt. 97
   Maj. Gen. 15
   Sarah 15
   William Henry 97

Macrae
   Ann Amelia H. 20
   Eliza Westwood W. 78
   Emily Virginia 249
Maddox
   Alexander 91
   Elizabeth F. 146
   John A. 83
   Sarah A. 83
   William R. 146
Madge
   Thomas, Rev. 94
Madison
   James 198, 207
Madison (Ind.) Banner 268
Madison Co., Va. 11
Madison, Conn. 28
Madrid, Spain 107, 205
Maffit
   A.B., Mrs. 111
   William, Rev.* 111
Maffitt
   John N., Lieut. 108
Magee
   Ann 193
Magrath
   L.O. 92
Magruder
   Caleb C. 151
   Edward 8
   Eleanor B. 1
   Fielder M. 140
   Hon. 205
   James A. 261
   John Holmes 208
   John R. 236
   Margaret 164
   Oliver B. 92
   Thomas Belt 151
   Virginia T. 83
   William B., Dr. 212
Maguire
   James 270
   Mary Elizabeth 270
   Mrs. 117
   Sue B. 117
   Thomas F. 231
Mahon
   Alexander 211
   D.N., Dr. 62
   Mary G. 211
   Richard Coxe 211
Mahorney
   Henrietta Q. 40
mail-boat 163
Maine 50, 75, 225
Malvern, Va. 268
Manahan
   Charlotte Packard 36
   Joseph, Capt. 36
Mangham
   John C., Jr. 56
Mangum
   Rebecca T. 187

Mankin
   Deborah 102, 247
   James 102, 247
   Margaretta Grace Dent 102
   William Clarance 247
Mankins
   Adeline 15
   John M. 15
   Theodore F. 15
Mann
   Charles 151
   Lucy Amanda Frances 31
   William 151
Manning
   Elizabeth H. 48
   Ignatius 48
   Ignatius, Maj. 26, 87
   Infant 26
   Margaret 255
   Nathaniel 66, 255
   R.C. 26
   Rosa M. 66
   Rosette Caroline 26
   W. Wilfred A., Dr. 26
   W.A., Dr. 26
Mansion House Hotel, Va. 40
Maple Hill, D.C. 31
Marbel
   Caspar 139
Marbury
   Cora 134
   James Somervell, Rev.* 44
   John 44, 56
   John H. 234
   John, Jr. 28
   Mary Ann 56
Marbury's Landing 108
Marcellus
   A.A., Rev.* 214
   Robert H. 214
Marceron
   Louis 35, 218
   Peter T. 45, 114
Marcy
   Edmund 176
   Samuel 67
   William L., Hon. 176
Marietta, Ga. 77, 78
Marietta, Ohio 152
Marine Barracks 6, 45, 82, 136, 157, 243, 249
Marines/Marine Corps 8, 9, 42, 82, 95, 109, 116, 125, 137, 141, 145, 157, 229, 233, 263, 270, 271
Marion Co., Fla. 68
market 131
Markland
   A.H. 41
   Matthew 28
Markriter
   Joseph 171

Marks
    Rev. 8, 33, 41, 50, 64, 75, 143,
        166, 169, 186, 191, 205
    S.A.H., Rev. 13, 46, 205, 207,
        226, 256, 271
Marlatt
    A.G., Rev. 211
Marlborough, Md. 113, 160
Marmeduke
    Martha 131
Marmion, Va. 263, 270
Marquis
    Sarah Emma 247
    William H. 247
Marr
    Maria 179
    Mary 179
    Thomas F. 179
Marrilat
    Charles Henry 103
Marriott
    William H., Gen. 23
Marron
    Eliza Ann 153
    John 153
    Margaret Ann 153
Marsh
    Louisa V. 195
Marshal (occupation) 101
Marshall
    Edward C., Hon. 127
    Eleanor F. 213
    Elizabeth A.L. 198
    George R.H. 213
    James K. 230
    James K., Jr. 251
    Jaquelin A. 47
    Louis, Jr., Dr. 19
    Mary Frances 47
    Nannie Burwell 230
Marshe
    Esther Ann 271
    Thomas 271
Martell
    Elizabeth 19
Marthen
    Rev. 63
Martin
    Albertine 107
    Col. 135
    Elizabeth J. 230
    George Sutherland 72
    George W., Col. 244
    Hester Ann 75
    J., Rev. 46
    Joel, Dr. 272
    John 99
    John S., Dr. 105, 190
    Louisa V. 130
    M.F., Rev. 67
    Margaret Isabella 48
    Martha 135
    Mary 72
    Mary A. 80

Mary King 105
Sarah Selby 190
William 50, 72
Martine
    Andrew 220
Martineau
    Peter 94
    Sarah 94
Martinsburg(h), Va. 11, 28, 33, 51,
    87, 120, 137, 186
Marton
    Cassa Ann 57
Maryland 18, 39, 51, 52, 54, 69,
    87, 92, 94, 98, 101,
    105-107, 111, 112, 123,
    125, 126, 140, 151, 156,
    168, 170, 179, 188, 196,
    213-215, 232, 235, 236,
    255
Maryman
    Ann Maria 4
    Horatio R. 131
Marysville Herald 216
Marysville, Calif., 1, 208
Masi
    S. 16
Mason
    Henry M., Rev. 185
    John M., Dr. 240
    John T. 26
    John, Gen. 229
    Margaret 59
    Mary Virginia 54
    Maynadier 54, 176
    Murray 176
    Nannie R. 79
    R.B., Gen. 14
    Rev. 36, 156
    Thomson F., Hon. 138
    Virginia 138
    W.R. 79
Mason Co., Va. 253
Mason's Island 159
Masonic Hall 153
Masons (also see "Free Masons")
    Washington Lodge 101
Massachusetts 8, 52, 58, 77, 81,
    85, 98, 165, 190, 216, 225
Massachusetts Medical Society
    132
Massey
    Mary Jane 85
    Rev. 23
Massoletti
    Joseph R. 75
    Julietta M. 26
    Rosalia 75
    Vincent Louis 75
Masterson
    Francis X. 149
Mathews
    M. Anna F. 41
    William P., Capt. 41

Matthews
    Elizabeth B. 47
    Henry C. 34
    John H. 34
    John, Gen. 229
    Rev. 188, 190, 196, 199
    Robert A. 100
    William, Rev. 8, 68
Mattingly
    Dorothy 33
    George 10
    Joseph 196
    Zachariah T. 114
Maury
    Dabney H., Lieut. 79
Maxwell
    Andrew G.C. 186
    Helen A. 2
    James 186, 250
    John S. 63
    Mary 186, 250
    Robert 178
May
    Ann Columbia 36
    Anna 230
    James R. 179, 255
    William, Lieut. 138
Mayer
    P.F., Rev. 212
Mayers
    Mathew 139
Mayfield
    Benjamin R. 43
Mayflower 26
Mayhew School 52
Mayhue
    Elizabeth 52
Maynadier
    Catharine Scott 40
    Eliza 185
    Henry E., Lieut. 103
    Kate Eveleth 95
    William Murray 40
    William, Capt. 95, 185
Mayo
    Isabella C. 37
Mayor 28, 206, 266
    Alexandria 131
Mazatlan 269

McAlister
    Alexander, Rev.* 12
    Mary Harriet 12
McAvoy
    Rosanna 82
McBain
    Mary Elizabeth 47
McCaffrey
    Thomas A., Rev. 175
McCall
    E.R., Capt. 187
    Sarah W. 187
McCalla

314

John M. 29
Thomas 29
McCardle
  Elizabeth 3
McCarthy
  Catharine 244
  Charles F. 244
  Florence S. 31
  George 31
  James 236
  Mary Ann 88
  Wenefred 31
  William 76
McCarty
  John Mason, Col. 113
  Olivia Beale 168
McCathran
  Benjamin F. 229
  William W. 234
McCeney
  George 31
  Harriet 31
  Robert S.P. 31
McClasky
  William E. 28
  William T. 28
McCleery
  Mary L. 115
McClellan
  John, Bvt. Lt. Col. 250
McClellan Co., Tex. 256, 258
McClelland
  George W. 119
  Robert, Hon. 267
McClery
  Indiana Irene 100
  James 100
McClung
  John A., Rev. 101
McCollam
  John J. 2
McConnell
  M. Esther 231
McConnellsville, Ohio 257
McCorkle
  Joseph P. 250
  Sallie C. 250
McCormick
  A.T., Rev.* 126
  Charles, Dr. 150
  Ellen W. 150
  James 235
  Jane 126
McCoskey
  S.A., Rev. 164
McCubbin
  Edward 25, 41, 64
  Margaret 25
  Nicholas O. 209
  Susan 41
McCulloh
  Annie L. 163
  James W. 163
McCullough

Nannie L. 193
William 193
McCutchen
  Mary Arkansas 225
McDaniel
  James W. 146
McDermott
  Agnes 99
  John 99
  Martha L. 99
McDonald
  Amanda 106
  Clara Ann 81
  Frances Maria 53
  Mary E. 209
  Matthew 53
  P.W., Brev. Maj. 50
McDonough Co., Ill. 116
McDowell
  A.M. 192
  Frances E.H. 28
  James, Gov. 28
  N.H. 192
  William H. 192
McDuell
  Annie C. 114
  Columbia Saphronia 10
  George 114
  George Henry 148
McDuffie
  J. Thomas 169
McElderry
  John P. 117
McElfresh
  Ariana 11
  Charles, Rev. 43, 66
  Elizabeth 102
  George S. 102
  Henry B. 201
  John H., Col. 11
  Mary Elizabeth 102
  Rev. 188
McElray
  Isabella 227
McFarlan
  Ebenezer, Dr. 126
McFarland
  J., Rev. 104
  John M. 194, 264
  Louisa M. 264
McGarvey
  Charles 152, 179
  Elizabeth 179
  Jane 163
McGee
  Catherine 191
  Owen 191
  Owen Thomas 191
McGill
  Agnes 260
  Henry 232
  Henry Miott 94
  Rev. 107
  Thomas 76

Thomas Milton 76
Thomas P. 230
McGinnall
  Michael 240
McGowan
  William C. 162
McGregor
  Helen 122, 253
  Helen Woods 255
  John R. 231
  Mary 231
  N.M. 82, 122, 253, 255
McGuffey
  Charles S. 47
  Mary H. 232
  William H., Rev. 80, 232
  William H., Rev.* 47
  William, Rev.* 43
McGuire
  E.C., Rev. 79
  James C. 157
  Margaret 157
  Margaret Louise 157
McGunnegle
  Clara B. 32
  George K. 32
  Wilson 180
McHanney
  Harriet 220
  Jacob 220
McHeill
  William Gibbs, Gen. 140
McIlvaine
  Emerson 188
  Joseph, Hon. 188
McIntire
  T.C., Dr. 259
McIntosh
  Eleanor Maria 24
  J.M. 24
  John 112
McJilton
  Daniel, Rev.* 30
McKean
  Bridgett 139
  J.P. 13
  James P. 155
  Laura A. 155
McKelyutte
  Mary Ellen 36
McKendree Chapel 84, 90, 101
McKendree Church 172, 189
McKenney
  Elizabeth 88
  Mary 160
  Samuel 160
  William, Rev.* 81
McKenny
  Chloe Ann 40
  Mary 163
  Samuel 163
  William, Rev.* 40
McKeon
  John, Hon. 229

McKim
- John L., Rev. 6
- John W. 176
- S.A.H., Dr. 263

McKinstry
- William P. 144

McKnew
- Charles 110, 194, 214
- Charles G. 214
- Jeremiah 121
- Maria 214

McKnight
- Cornelia Clinton 170
- G.B. 170
- George Piercy 16
- John, Capt. 16
- John, Rev. 170

McLain
- W., Rev. 114, 206
- William, Rev. 271

McLane
- Allan 30
- Maria C. 30

McLaughlin
- James A. 215
- Rev. 186

McLean
- A. Clinton 204
- Charles 137
- G.W., Capt. 137
- Hon. 225
- John, Hon. 241
- Rebecca J. 137
- Samuel 113
- Susan Wilson 113
- William, Rev. 101

McLeod
- Elizabeth H. 48
- Matthew 48
- Priscilla 30
- Roderick 30

McMannus/McManus
- Rev. 139, 163

McMorine
- Helen 112
- John 112

McMullen
- Robert, Hon. 69

McNair
- Stephen Y. 220

McNantz
- Charles Neal 129
- Julia Anna 129
- Louisa Jane 129
- Patrick H. 129

McNeir
- Elizabeth Guest 122
- George 122

McNelly
- Hester 143
- Matthew 143
- William Thomas 143

McNemara
- John 99

McNerhany
- Catharine 231
- Mary Frances 74

McPeak
- Jacqueline P. 129
- Mary Ann 129
- William 129

McPhail
- G.W., Rev. 33
- Leonard Cassell, M.D. 23
- P.G., Rev. 105

McPherson
- Josephine C. 74
- Mary Augusta 96
- S.C. 74
- Samuel C. 96

McRae
- Cameron F., Rev.* 165
- Daniel 233
- Julia 165

McRea
- Elizabeth R. 148
- James M. 148
- Lydia Lucille 148

McSherry
- James 87

McTavish
- John 98

McVean
- Margaret W. 19

McVeigh
- Maria Louisa 146

McVickar
- J., Rev. 30

McWhir
- Dr. 7

Mead
- Abigail Jane 117
- Delilah 102
- James 102

Meade
- Margaret Coats 82
- R.K., Rev. 43, 113
- Richard W. 82, 116
- Salvadora McLaughlin 116

Meadow Grove, Va. 57
Meadville, Pa. 48, 70, 229, 235

Mechlin
- Bertha 257
- Joseph 152
- Margaretta 152
- William 257

Mecklenburg Co., N.C. 169
Mecklenburg Co., Va. 244
Medfield, Mass. 264

Medford
- James 55

Medford, Mass. 132
Medical Society of D.C. 225
Mediterranean sea 73, 243, 250

Meehan
- Maria 4

Meem
- George A. 56, 134
- James Walter 56
- Rebecca A. 134

Meginley
- Mary Ann 70

Meiere
- Anna Jane 32
- J., Prof. 32

Meigs
- Charles D. 180
- M.C., Capt. 180
- Montgomery C., Capt. 187
- Mr. 61
- Vincent Trowbridge 187

Meily
- John 95

Meinzesheimer
- Lewis, Serg. 229

Melcher
- Andrew D. 217
- Mary J. 217
- William 217

Melham
- Jenny Lind 94

Mellor
- John 263

Melville
- Oliver Henry 234

Memphis and Charleston railroad 184
Memphis, Tenn. 23, 48, 67, 97, 106, 114, 231, 271
Mendota, Minn. 48

Menke
- Meinard 49

Merchant 18, 36, 48, 98, 101, 118, 129, 131, 137, 193, 195, 204, 236

Meredity
- John H. 58

Meril
- Charles H. 111

Meriwether
- Charles J. 171

Merrick
- Joseph J. 232
- Stephen, Rev. 248

Merritt
- Sophia 159
- William H.E. 159

Metcaff
- Eleanor 65

Metcalf
- John C. 26

Methodist Episcopal Church 123
Methodist Episcopal Church South 248
Methodist Protestant Church 113, 123, 242
Mexican forces 190
Mexican War 50, 93, 98, 185, 190, 206, 243, 270

Mexico 30, 141, 148, 181, 206, 263
Meyer
    Joseph 8
Michel
    Lucy 165
Michigan 164, 226
Michigan Territory 239, 241
Mickum
    William Brent 47
Middleburg, Va. 25, 42, 177, 254
Middlesex Co., Mass. 132
Middlesex Co., Va. 153
Middlesex, Eng. 49, 94
Middleton
    B.F. 69
    Elizabeth 69
    Fanny V. 123
    John A. 232
    Mrs. 204
    Robert 123
Midshipman 224
Mifflin Co., Pa. 148, 221
Milburn
    George 210
    George W. 236
    Mary Ann 210
    Pamela 236
    Thomas 236
Mile-end, Eng. 49
Miles
    Catherine 267
    Mary 202
Milford, Va. 25
Military Academy 22, 30, 49, 50, 115
Millard
    Catharine 149
Miller
    Albert S., Maj. 133
    Andrew J. 263
    Ann Eliza 125
    Ann Taliaferro 230
    Anna Judson 99
    Catherine 210
    Charles 182
    Charles, Jr. 198
    Charlotte 182
    Dana 55
    David 127
    Elizabeth 108
    Elizabeth Jane 205
    Francis 114
    George 123, 182
    Harriet 96
    Henry J., Hon. 32
    Jacob W., Hon. 108
    James 205
    James J. 230
    James N. 80
    Janet 39
    John 96, 99
    John A. 99
    John F. 166

    John Irvin 253
    John Irving 254
    Lizzie 244
    Margaret 68
    Margaret A. 131
    Mary 99
    Philip 37
    Rachel Parker 263
    Royal A. 6
    Samuel 125
    Thomas J. 214
    Victoria J. 262
    Virginia F. 32
Millersville, Md. 99
Milligan
    Elizabeth 241
Millington
    Jane E. 64
Mills
    Anna Smith 234
    Armstead T. 273
    E.K., Gen. 77
    Eliza Emily 77
    John 83
    Mary Ann 83
    Mary Jane 196
    Robert 234
    Sarah Hannah 83
    William McCartey 170
Millson
    Susanna P. 228
Millwood, Va. 258
Milton, Del. 6
Milton, Pa. 115
Minge
    John J., Dr. 60
    Sally H. 60
Minister 94, 112, 114, 178, 205
Minister of Chile 14, 165
Minister of Customs 77
Minister Plenipotentiary 99, 121, 163, 271
Minister to China 21
Minister to Russia 191
Minitree
    Catharine 28
Minnesota Pioneer 111
Minnesota Territory 41, 59, 136, 235
Minnix
    Charlotte V. 139
Minor
    Hugh W. 127
    Mary F. 127
    William G., Col. 13
Mint, U.S. Branch 75
Mirror 261
Missionary 35, 148
Mississippi 57, 94, 96, 106, 167, 226, 233
Mississippi river 235
Missouri 88, 131, 138, 156, 158, 184, 189, 253

Mitchel
    Desire 10
    John 10
    Louis 10
    Samuel 10
    Susan 10
Mitchell
    Amanda A. 152
    Cordelia 28
    Emma 28
    George A. 90
    George W. 259
    Georgianna H. 16
    J. Francis 112
    J.D., Rev. 267
    John G. 164
    John M. 208
    John R. 259
    John T. 212
    Joseph Anthony Peck 212
    Joseph T. 52, 54
    Mary 90
    Rev. 26, 162
    Sarah A. 212
    Sarah Ellen 229
    Spencer, Dr. 128
    Susan E. 128
    Thomas A. 37
    Thomas, Maj. 97
    William 28
Mix
    Catherine S. 95
    Charles E. 95, 128, 266
    Ida 95
    Mary V. 128
Mobile Evening News 249
Mobile, Ala. 37, 39, 117, 238, 249, 258
Modisett
    Rev. 136
Mohler
    Ursula 65
Mohun
    Anna 102
    Anna M. 269
    Eliza Hellen 102
    Francis 102, 269
    M.P. 2
    Michael P. 262
Molino del Rey 263
Monkton, Ver. 116
Monmouth Co., N.Y. 129
Monohun Co., Ire. 155
Monongahela City, Pa. 171
Monroe
    James 218
    James, Hon. 98
    Mrs. 98
    T.J.C., Dr. 118
    T.L.C., Dr. 134
Monroe, Mich. 241
Montandon
    Julian 3
Montazile, Md. 247

Monterey, Calif. 115, 126, 263
Montevideo 87, 93, 154
Montgomery 162
    J.B., Capt. 62
    Julia M. 62
Montgomery Co., Md. 1, 8, 12, 23, 30, 34, 39, 64, 82, 84, 87, 88, 101, 109, 110, 114, 116, 120, 122, 126, 132, 133, 155, 156, 163, 164, 168, 169, 172, 173, 182, 191, 198, 201, 204, 208, 209, 213, 217, 223, 225, 227, 234, 238, 241, 245, 247, 251, 253, 262, 266, 268, 270
Montpelier, Va. 144
Montreal, Can. 99, 166
Moore
    Ann Virginia 253
    Bridget 215
    Emily Jane 266
    H.A. 133
    Jacob B. 145
    James 183, 242
    James A. 251
    James Henry 209
    James, Rev. 199
    Joseph B. 119
    Joshua J. 221
    Joshua, Rev.* 221
    Mary Elizabeth 263
    Mary L. 125
    Mary Rebecca 145
    Peter F. 186
    Priscilla 133
    Rev. 2
    Richard H., Dr. 7
    Robert Lowry 242
    Sallie M. 183
    Sarah Jane 64
    Selina M. 223
    T.V., Rev.* 92
    Thomas 216
    Virginia Bokee 161
    Warren 183
    William George 188
    William M. 195, 266
    William W. 161
Moore, Edwards & Co. 186
Moorhead
    J.W. 25
    James 25
    Sidney J. 25
Moran
    Alice 192
    Annina 93
    C. Angeline 266
    Elasah 266
    Mary 192
    Mary C.B. 268
    Samuel C. 268
Morcoe
    Elizabeth Jane 236
    Teresa Ann 236
    William E. 213, 236
More
    James Howard 81
    Lucy A. 81
    Stewart 81
Morehead
    Charles D. 185
    Charles Edwin 185
    Eliza 185
    Emma A. 185
    John M., Hon. 85
    Marie Louise 85
Morehouse Parish, La. 70
Moreland
    John 166
    Octavia 166
Morfit
    Campbell 221
Morgan
    Amanda M. 123
    Ann C. 200
    Charles W., Comm. 160
    Charlotte Eliphel 46
    Edwin C. 169, 233
    Edwin Cecil 233
    Elizabeth Alzera 109
    Evelyn P. 233
    George R. 142
    J.E., Prof. 231
    John R. 165
    Joseph, Capt. 134
    Julia S. 160
    L.F., Rev. 24, 41, 47, 52, 64, 80, 87
    Lieut. 103
    Louise A. 103
    Margaret E. 109
    Mary 142
    Rev. 2, 6, 12, 17, 21, 29, 33, 46, 49, 154
    William 109
    William F., Rev. 59
Morgansburg, Va. 134
Morison
    Alexander 228
Morrell
    Robert B. 250
Morris
    Charles 214
    Charles, Comm. 116
    Comm. 18, 262
    Elizabeth A. 165
    Enos M. 22
    G.W. 155
    George P., Gen. 183
    Gerard W. 97
    Ida W. 183
    Jacob, Gen. 178
    Joseph 22
    Joseph, Hon. 262
    Julia Howe 116
    Lewis Lee 178
    Martha Pyne 97
    Robert 39
Morris, N.Y. 178
Morrisett
    Thomas 142
Morrison
    Anna E. 189
    Anne 261
    B.W., Dr. 84
    Bartlett W. 83
    Catharine Virginia 266
    Mary Virginia 266
    O.H. 162
    Rev. 256
    William C. 128, 266
    William M. 83
Morristown, N.J. 97
Morrisville, Pa. 120
Morsell
    B.K. 34
    Maggie J. 199
    R.A. 223
    Richard J. 125
Mortimer
    John 116
    R. Isabella 116
Morton
    Henry J., Rev. 234
    Mary 267
Morven, Va. 251
Mosby
    John G. 91
    Virginia Cary 91
Mosher
    Harriet 187
    Mary 187
    Theodore 187
Moss
    Alcinda 257
    John T. 256
    William 49
Mothershead
    Margaret 66
    Mary 153
Motzer
    D., Rev. 184
    D., Rev.* 173
    Daniel, Rev. 97, 241
    Elizabeth B. 173
    Lizzie B. 173
Mountain View, Va. 189
Mounts
    George W. 269
Mountz
    Elizabeth 150
    Jacob 150
    John 152
    Mary Ann 152
Mower
    Thomas G., Dr. 214
Moxley
    Hannah M. 182
    Richard 182
Mt. Airy, Md. 230
Mt. Airy, Va. 41

Mt. Calm, Va. 171
Mt. Erin, Va. 53
Mt. Gilead, Ohio 217
Mt. Herman, D.C. 167
Mt. Hermon, D.C. 142
Mt. Hope, D.C. 46
Mt. Hope, Md. 145
Mt. Lubentia, Md. 195
Mt. Oak, Md. 1
Mt. Pleasant, D.C. 86
Mt. Pleasant, Ia. 150
Mt. Pleasant, Md. 2, 83, 92, 176
Mt. Vernon Church 120
Mt. Vernon, Ohio 176
Mt. Vernon, Va. 7, 22
Mudd
    Emily B. 248
    Ignatius 11, 248
    Ignatius F. 93
    Ignatius, Mrs. 109
    Mary Elizabeth 93
    Robert Ignatius 6
    Sarah J. 93
    Sylvester 239
    Theodore, Col. 6
Mullay
    John C. 21
Mulliken
    Elizabeth Ann 27
Mullikin
    Eleanor B. 1
    John B. 1, 143
    Mary R. 143
Mullone
    Thomas 33
Mullowny
    John F. 22
Mulloy
    Jane F. 104
    John 104
    Sarah Elizabeth 139
    William A. 104
Mullrany
    Barnerd 166
Mulraney
    B. 110
    Mary A. 110
Mumford
    J.B., Mrs. 223
Mundell
    Samuel 45
Munding
    Joseph M., Dr. 77
Munn
    Samuel E., Lieut. 268
Munro
    David 162
Munroe
    David 40
    Mary Katherine 40
    Thomas 85
Murns
    Mary 158

Murphy
    Catherine 142
    Ellen 89
    Helena C. 163
    Jane E. 130
    John 99
    Mary Ann 143
    Robert C. 177
    Samuel 117
    Timothy 42
Murray
    A.B. 6, 28, 47
    J.J., Rev. 27, 78
    James 56, 244
    John J., Rev. 3
    Juliet 28
    Mary J. 6
    Nicolaus 67
    Sally 244
    Susan E. 47
    Washington F. 41
Murrey
    A.B. 259
    Mary Jane 259
Murter
    Jane 22
Muschett
    James M.A., Dr. 191
Musician 126
Mustin
    Thomas 31, 219
Mutual Fire and Marine Insurance Company 270
Myers
    Benjamin S. 43
    Edward 246
    Herbert Reginald 246
    Isabella J. 246
    John 184
    Rev. 67
    T., Rev. 66

N

Nadall
    B.H., Rev. 136
Nairn
    John W. 192
Nalley
    Aaron 137
    Elizabeth 137
    Matilda A. 245
    William 215
Napoleon 62
Nardin
    Joseph 85
Nash
    Robert H., Jr. 187
    William 224
Nashville, Tenn. 3, 31, 36, 44, 53, 147, 165, 178, 237
Nassau Hall 165
Nassau, Ger. 201

Natchez, Miss. 194
National Fire Insurance Company 262
National Hotel 29, 82, 110, 120, 147, 218, 256
National Institute 142
National Intelligencer 198, 199, 235, 257
    files sought 42
    office 77
National Observatory 125
National Theatre 211
Naugatuck, Conn. 107
Navajo Indians 151
Naval Asylum 35
Naval School 137
Navy 2, 4, 8-12, 14, 17, 18, 20, 21, 26, 27, 29, 30, 33, 35-37, 40-43, 46-48, 50, 54-56, 59, 62, 64, 67, 68, 70, 72, 73, 77, 80, 81, 83, 87, 89, 93, 98, 103, 106, 108, 109, 116, 118, 120, 125
Navy Department 2
Navy Yard 1, 9, 35, 39, 42, 43, 54-57, 69, 80, 86, 90, 99, 102, 116, 121, 124, 128, 132, 135, 141, 143, 155, 158, 159, 170, 172, 175, 181, 184, 189, 194, 203, 204, 206, 208, 218, 226, 237, 239, 242, 243, 245, 247, 250, 262, 263, 273
Naylor
    Ann E. 109
    Francis Y. 109
Neabsco, Va. 146
Neale
    Ann Elizabeth 101
    Priscilla 136
Nebraska Territory 254
Neely
    Edward B. 90
    John 160
    Mary E. 160
Negroes 43, 117, 118, 224, 244
Nelson
    C.K., Rev. 56, 80, 99, 244
    C.K., Rev.* 222
    Charles Edward 130
    Elizabeth 135
    John 197
    John S. 106
    Margaret 189
    Mary Ann 56
    Mr. 197
    Philip 204
    Rev. 28, 62, 106
    Samuel 135
    Thomas M., Maj. 196
    William C. 244
    William L. 233
    William M., Rev. 259
Nelson Co., Va. 9

Nesbit
    Jonathan 70
    Mary 70
    William Sanford 70
Nesbitt
    Ellen Serena 168
    Isaac 168
Neumeyer
    Leopold 15
Nevada, Calif. 147
Nevins
    Mary F. 152
Nevitte
    John B., Hon. 96
    Matilda 96
New Albany, Ind. 74, 110, 209
New Almaden, Calif. 204
New Brunswick, N.J. 46, 220
New Castle, Del. 197
New Geneva, Pa. 50, 119
New Hampshire 15, 54, 111, 137, 160, 254, 271
New Haven railroad 157
New Haven, Conn. 6, 47, 191
New Jersey 58, 98, 107, 108, 116, 135, 141, 174, 263, 264
New London, Conn. 71
New Mexico 29
New Milford, Conn. 19
New Orleans and Jackson railroad 186
New Orleans Commercial Bulletin 19
New Orleans Picayune 26
New Orleans, La. 3, 7, 16, 50, 65, 75, 77, 79, 80, 90, 108, 116, 123, 127, 149, 150, 176, 178, 179, 185, 195, 198, 212, 221, 226, 244, 245, 251, 265, 268, 271
New Port, Fla. 180
New York 1, 2, 4, 6, 14, 15, 18, 26, 35, 37, 39, 43, 44, 46, 47, 50, 54, 55, 58, 59, 63, 65, 68, 73, 77, 80, 82, 83, 88, 89, 92-95, 97-99, 101, 107, 110, 112-117, 120, 121, 129, 138, 141, 148, 150, 155, 159, 160, 163, 170, 173, 186, 189, 191, 198, 204, 206, 207, 209, 211, 214, 216, 223, 224, 226, 229, 231, 232, 238, 241-243, 248-250, 254-257, 260, 263
New York Evening Post 207
New York Sealpel 214
New York Times 206
Newark, Del. 136
Newark, N.J. 4, 234
Newbern, N.C. 228
Newburgh, N.Y. 104, 207, 218
Newburyport, Mass. 129
Newcastle Co., Del. 12

Newell
    John 160
Newfield House, Scot. 110, 141
Newfoundland 140
Newhouse
    Harvey M. 57
Newport, Fla. 194
Newport, Md. 195
Newport, R.I. 3, 31, 114, 174, 190
newspapers
    Alexandria Gazette 131
    Baltimore American 270
    Baltimore Argus 46
    Boston Traveller 260
    Buffalo Commercial Advertiser 245
    Chambersburg Compiler 175
    Cleveland Herald 254
    Edgefield (S.C.) Advertiser 200
    Evening Post 98
    Fairfax News 38
    Glove 150
    Leesburg Washingtonian 176
    Louisville Courier 56
    Lynchburg Virginian 168
    Madison (Ind.) Banner 268
    Marlborough Advocate 151
    Marysville Herald 216
    Mirror 261
    Mobile Evening News 249
    National Intelligencer 42, 183, 198, 199, 235, 257
    New York Evening Post 129, 173, 207
    New York Sealpel 214
    New York Times 206
    Niles' Register 133
    Norfolk Beacon 141
    North Carolinan 42
    Palladium 261
    Penny Post 258
    Philadelphia Evening Bulletin 223
    Philadelphia Inquirer 72
    Philadelphia Observer 175
    Piscayne 176
    Republic 154
    Republican 141, 143
    Richmond Dispatch 185
    Richmond Enquirer 168, 228
    Richmond Whig 56
    Rochester Amer. 270
    St. Louis Intelligencer 82
    St. Louis Rep. 201
    Telegraph 261
    Toronto Guardian 92
    Union 176, 249
    Washington Union 213
    Winchester (Va.) Republican 52, 155
Newton
    A.L. 152, 215
    Cornelia S. 176
    J.W., Rev. 62

    Mary 215
    Mary Brockenbrough 46
    Thomas Gaston 176
    W.J., Capt. 176
    W.L. 84
    William Giles 126
    William J. 215
    Willoughby, Hon. 46
Newton Co., Miss. 74
Newtown, Md. 162
Newville, Va. 31
Niagara Falls, N.Y. 83, 245
Nicaragua 163
Nicholas Co., Ky. 230
Nicholls
    J.W. 36
Nicholson
    A.A., Maj. 271
    Ann Temple 157
    Augustus S. 71
    Comm. 50
    Helen L. 271
    J.J., Comm. 93
    James W. 50
    John Stricker 93
    Maj. 145
    Margaret 166
    Margaret Virginia 166
    Rev. 5
    Samuel, Comm. 157
    Sommerville 42
    Thomas 147
    Walter 166
Niles
    Hezekiah/Hazekiah 100, 133
    Sally A. 100
    Samuel V. 53
Niles's Register 100
Nimmo
    W.A., Lieut. 134
Noble
    Ellen C. 246
    John 4
    Mason, Rev. 159, 175
Noerr
    Andrew 80
    Catharine 80
    Louisa Elizabeth 80
Nokes
    James 268
    Margaret 196
Nolan
    John, Col. 110
Noland
    C. St. Geo., Lieut. 162
    Mary C. 162
Nolen
    Jeremiah 19
Norflet
    Mary E. 248
Norfolk Co., Mass. 264
Norfolk Co., Va. 36
Norfolk, Eng. 15
Norfolk, Va. 2, 9, 19, 36, 40, 54,

65, 70, 96, 112, 118, 153, 154, 175-177, 246, 248, 264, 270, 272, 273
Normanstone, D.C. 117
Norment
    Richard B. 186
Norris
    Agnes B. 159
    Amanda A. 9
    E.M. 80
    Enoch M. 271, 273
    James 142
    Mary 142
    Mary Ellen 24
    Oliver, Rev.* 80
Norristown, Pa. 126, 220
North
    J. Bartram 47, 270
    Jane Caroline 157
    John Gough 157
    Phebe 47
    Stephen 234
    William B. 234
North American Land Co. 39
North Carolina 1, 27, 32, 36, 135, 157, 181, 221, 238, 252
North Carolinan 42
North Dorset, Ver. 109
North View, D.C. 179, 181
Northampton Co., Va. 178, 199
Northern Market 27
Northwestern Territory 71
Norton
    Ebenezer F. 24
    George, Rev. 57
    George, Rev.* 230
    James William 8
Norwalk 157
Norwich, Conn. 59
Norwich, N.Y. 263
Norwood
    Belt S. 227
    William, Rev. 252
Nott
    Virginia C. 67
    William Edwin 117
Nottingham District 272
Nottingham, Md. 43, 126
Nourse
    Benjamin F. 127
    Benjamin P., Dr. 172
    C.H., Rev. 127
    Charles H., Rev. 172
    Charles J. 28
    Charles J., Maj. 125
    Charles L., Maj. 14
    Elizabeth I. 125
    Elizabeth R. 192
    Emma J. 127
    J.E., Prof. 219
    James, Rev. 192
    James, Rev.* 146, 239, 240
    Joseph Harvey 146
    Louisa Pemberton 28

    Maria 219
    Sarah W. 219
    Susan S. 172
Nova Scotia 174
Nowland
    Adolphus Henry 213
    J.H.B. 213
Noyes
    Albert 119
    Emilie 124
    Helen M. 231
    Joseph C., Hon. 231
    William, Capt. 124
Nugent
    Bridget 61
    Esther A. 264
    Martha 13
Nutt
    Richard 88
Nye
    Ellen Josephine 172
    J.W. 133, 172
    Mary Ann 133
    Mary Norma Theresa 133
    Norman Willard 133
    P. 133, 172

O

O'Brien
    Eustace E. 26
    Lawrence 262
    Mary 26
    Rebecca 26
    Thomas M. 138
O'Bryan
    Catharine 12
O'Bryon
    Rose L. 218
O'Connel
    Margaret 158
O'Conner
    Mary 8
    Michael 8
O'Connor
    Honora 139
O'Donnell
    Charles Oliver 112
    Elleanor 124
    John C. 124
    Sarah M. 64
O'Donnoghue
    Dennis 213
    Margaret E. 99
    Mary A. 213
    Patrick 78
    T. 99
O'Driscoll
    Elizabeth 153
O'Flanagan
    P.B., Rev. 62
O'Flannigan
    P.B., Rev. 4

O'Hare
    John 77
O'Keefe
    Rev. 264
O'Leary
    Ann 98
    Denis 98
    John 38, 108
    Mary 38
O'Meara
    Ann 33
O'Neale
    Elizabeth 158
    T. 82
    Timothy 238
O'Neill
    Rev. 94
    Thomas 61
O'Regan
    A., Rev. 14
    Johanna 254
O'Reilly
    James 13
    W., Rev. 102
O'Toole
    Rev. 154, 178, 179, 223, 228
    T., Rev. 231

Oak Grove, Va. 168
Oak Hill, Md. 241, 262
Oak Lawn, Md. 140
Oak Ridge, Va. 9
Oakdale, Va. 199
Oakleigh, Ala. 221
Oakley
    Charles Henry, M.D. 37
Oaks, Md. 120
Oakwood, Mo. 41
Oakwood, Va. 259
Oates
    Edward H. 218
    George 218
    George, Sr. 127
Oatland, Md. 1
Oatland, Va. 186
Ober
    Charles Vernon 37
    Hannah 37, 56
    Hannah Kettlewell 56
    Henry N. 67
    John 30
    Merrill H. 116
    Mrs. A. 90
    S.J. 37, 56
    Stephen J. 250
Obispado 115
Observatory 166
Odd Fellows 46, 76, 252, 267
Odd Fellows' Hall 55, 246
Oden
    Benjamin 203
    Louisa 223
    Mary 203

Oertly
  Bartholomew 232
Offley
  Helen 59
  John H. 59
Ogden
  Anna E. 90
  Sarah Priscilla 47
  William L. 33
Ogle
  George C. 189
  Richard L. 121
Ogle Co., Ill. 264
Ohio 141, 190, 208, 257, 262
Old Point Comfort, Md. 62
Oldfield
  Granville S., Jr. 112
Oldham Co., Ky. 181
Oliver
  John 96
Olyphant
  David W.C. 35
Omaha Indians 148
Onondaga Co., N.Y. 80
Opelousas, La. 3, 122, 189, 241
Orange Co., N.C. 129
Orange Co., Va. 3, 33, 110
Orange Springs, Fla. 68
Ord
  E.O.C., Capt. 266
Orderly Sergeant 157
Ordnance Corps 51, 166, 174, 226
Oregon 134, 148
Orem
  Andrew 245
  Eugenie 245
  James B. 245
Orme
  Thomas 101
  William 60
  William Ward 193
Ormesby, Eng. 100
Orr
  James 6
  John M. 196, 253
  Orra L. 196, 253
  Sally Moore 253
  Willie Grayson 196
Osbodby
  Thomas W. 146
Osborn
  Francis 251
Osborne
  Elizabeth Ann 258
  Mary 81
Osbourn
  Richard 113
  Sophia M. 117
  Susan H. 227
Osmington, Eng. 142
Ostendorf
  Henrick 139
Osterloh
  John F., Rev.* 208

Mary Anna 208
Oswego, N.Y. 122, 145
Otey
  Charles C. 201
  Rev. 231
Otis
  Mr. 207
Otsego Co., N.Y. 178
Ott
  John D. 16
  Mary Ann 16
  Sally Bogan 16
Otterback
  Benjamin L. 182
  Philip 172
Ould
  Remus R. 104
  Robert 11, 242
  Samuel R.G. 242
  Sarah A. 11, 242
Ourand
  Samuel F.D. 68
Owen
  Edward 37
  John S. 100
  Mary F. 37
  Otwayanna 90
  Samuel W. 243
  Washington Winder 155
  William, Dr. 90
Owens
  Amelia E. 271
  Elizabeth 132
  Mary E. 155, 173
Owensboro, Ky. 72, 178
Owings
  John A. 138
Owner
  Henry 96
  James 13
  James, Capt. 69
  Mary 69
  Sarah Elizabeth 13
  William Henry 13
Oxford, Md. 217

P

Pacific ocean 141
Packard
  Elizabeth E. 74
  Perez 74
Padget
  John 87
Padgett
  Jane V. 87
  Joseph H. 186
  William Henry 160
Page
  Anthony C.W. 30
  Charles H., Rev. 101
  Charles, Dr. 94
  Daniel 245

Elizabeth E. 245
Emma 204
Matthew, Dr. 192
Nathaniel B. 171
Peyton R. 258
Rev. 271
Sally 258
Page Co., Va. 223
Paine
  Elizabeth H. 154
  John 154
Pairo
  Caldwell 58
  Charles W. 58, 221
  Loveday 112
  Mary Jane 58
  Thomas W. 112
Palladium 261
Pallhuber/Pallhuben
  J.E., Rev. 207, 213
Palmer
  Eliza 266
  William 244
  William P., Dr. 266
Palmyra, Va. 17
Palo Alto, Calif. 115, 126, 190, 240
Paluber
  J.E., Rev. 112
Panama 119, 141
Paramaribo, Sur. 81
Pardon
  Henry F.B. 21
Parent
  Peter J. 98
Parham
  John 145
  William J. 138
Paris, Fra. 60, 97, 134, 135, 151,
    170, 255
Paris, Ky. 103, 162
Park
  Jane S. 177
Parker
  George 181
  John E. 6
  Kate P. 199
  Mary Ann 180
  Rev. 99
  S.E., Gen. 199
  Southey S. 180, 265
Parkin
  Elizabeth 273
  W.W. 89
Parks
  Adaline 94
  D. 97
  Mary A. 97
Parodi Singers 90
Parrot
  Abner 234
parsonages
  Foundry Church 188, 235, 246,
    251, 257, 258, 269, 273
  M.E. Church South 77

Wesley Chapel 160, 196, 255, 268
Parsons
  Bernard 4
  James Lawrence 148
  James Washington, Dr. 4
  Julia 148
  Mary Miller 17
  Thomas H. 148
  William 17
Paschall
  Thomas 106
Pass Christian, Miss. 54
Passed Midshipman 46, 59, 77, 120, 148, 163, 180
Pastor 78, 88
Patent Office 102, 123, 151
Paterson
  A.B., Rev. 116
  William 116
Paterson, N.J. 164, 247
Patten
  Emma Hamilton 147
  George 147
  Mary M. 220
  Richard 147, 220
Patterson
  Carlile P. 136
  Carlile, Lt. 4
  Caroline 133
  Comm. 243
  Daniel T., Comm. 50
  Eliza W. 136
  George Ann 50
  Helen Mar 82
  Joseph C. 76
  Joseph N. 69, 76
  Josephine Pearson 136
  Louisa Jane 235
  Rufus Lenoir 85
  Sarah A.J. 151
  Thomas, Dr. 82
Patti
  Amalia 90
Paulding
  Leonard 59
Pawtuxet, R.I. 194, 238
Paxton
  Rebecca L. 268
Pay Department 263
Paymaster 42, 60, 125
Paymaster General 239
Payne
  Ada 178
  America 184, 187
  Charles Borromeo 184, 187
  George W. 176
  Margaret 88
  Maria Ann Quigley 110
  Maud 184, 187
  Rice W. 184, 187
  Robert A. 214
  William MacManus 100
  William McManus 110

Peabody
  Amelia H. 85
  George 129, 173
  John, Capt. 85
Peabody, Riggs & Co. 129
Peaco
  J.W., Dr. 93
  Mary Virginia 93
  William H. 188
Peake
  Joannah 239
Peakland, Va. 201
Pearce
  Catharine 167
  Catharine J. 96
  J.A., Hon. 96, 167
  Sen. 225
Pearson
  Eliza Worthington 4
  Ellen 220
  G.F., Comm. 220
  Joseph, Hon. 4, 65
  Josephine 65
  Mrs. 136
Peck
  Jesse T., Rev. 111, 114, 123, 129, 157, 159, 211
  Jesse T., Rev.* 188
  Joseph 231, 263
  M.D. Virginia 231
  Miss 263
  Rev. 122, 199
  Sylvia 211
  William 36
Peddicord
  Mrs. 227
Pedrick
  John C. 243
Peekskill, N.Y. 271
Peet
  E.W., Rev. 120
Pelermo, Sicily 226
Pembroke, N.H. 219
Pendle
  Thomas F. 127
Pendleton
  Edmund 44
  Rev. 55
  W.N., Rev. 11
  William H., Rev. 230
Penington
  Samuel C. 203
penitentiary, D.C. 76
Penn
  Alexander G., Hon. 122
Pennsylvania 21, 36, 49, 69, 72, 115, 141, 150, 188, 211, 222, 235, 257, 263
Pennsylvania Medical College 83
Penny Post 258
Pensacola Navy Yard 9
Pensacola, Fla. 42, 48, 50, 89, 109, 179, 184, 194, 240
Pension Office 18, 61

Percival
  James 266
  John, Capt. 266
  Maria W. 266
Pereira
  Luizinha Iantha 112
Perkins
  James 207
  Thomas Handysyde, Col. 207
Perrie
  Sophia H. 79
  Susan E. 6
Perry
  Elizabeth 57
  Josephus 267
  William M. 191
Perry Wood, Md. 196
Perryville, Pa. 240
Perseverence Fire Company 267
Peter
  Catharine B. 5
  James F. 5
  Martha Custis 238
  Thomas 238
Peter family graveyard 238
Peterkin
  Rev. 233
Peters
  Cecilia 208
  George W. 237
  H., Miss 159
  Julius A. 237
  Mary A. 237
  Mary Elizabeth 243
  William, Capt. 208
Petersburg, Va. 11, 36, 53, 158, 177, 218, 226, 242, 244, 252
Peterson
  H.W. 92
  Harriet Middleton 92
Petigru
  J. Louis 187
  Thomas, Comm. 187
Pettibone
  Jane E. 182
  Mary Ellen 182
  William 182
Petticord
  Sarah Jane 129
Pettigrew
  Charles Lockhart 157
Pettit
  Charles 20, 195
  Eliza 195
  Mary Elizabeth 195
  Samuel Thomas 20
Petty
  J.S., Rev. 214
Peyton
  Bernard, Gen. 134
  Edward Marshall 168
  Elizabeth 190
  Fanny 25

Henry 25
John Howe 190
Margaret (Sallahue) 25
Nannette 168
Robert E., Dr. 168
Susan S. 134
Walter Jones 168
Pharr
   D.C., Rev. 97
Phelps
   David, Gen. 52
   E.P., Rev. 227, 229, 230, 235, 242, 246, 251, 257, 269, 273
   John T. 6
   S. Ledyard 185
Phenix
   Dawson 77
   Thomas, Jr. 79
Philadelphia Conference 78
Philadelphia Evening Bulletin 223
Philadelphia Inquirer 20, 72
Philadelphia Medical College 260
Philadelphia, Pa. 1, 3-7, 10, 12, 19-22, 26, 30, 31, 34-36, 39, 42, 44, 46, 50, 53, 59, 61, 63, 64, 66, 68, 69, 71, 73-76, 81-84, 91-93, 100, 105-107, 116, 117, 135, 139, 142, 150, 153, 158, 165, 184, 186, 188, 195, 199-201, 203, 204, 209, 212, 218, 221-223, 225, 227, 228, 230, 234, 239, 250, 251, 261, 263, 268, 270-272
Philip
   J. Van Ness 106
Philips
   Janet B. 224
Phillips
   Ann 133
   George Martin 88
   Hamilton 4
   Harvey L. 27
   Isaac, Capt. 133
   James B. 4
   Jonathan 241
   Mary A. 27
   Mary C. 4
   Mary E. 42
   Rosanna E. 26
   William 27
Physician 73, 74, 81, 119, 132, 188, 189, 192, 222, 235, 246, 260, 270
Pianist 90
Pickens
   Andrew, Gen. 140
   Joseph, Col. 140
Pickett
   George E., Capt. 60
   James S., Capt. 114
   John T. 189

Mary Eloise 114
Sally H. 60
Pickrell
   Angelina 116
   John 54, 116
Pierce
   Abner C. 32
   Daniel 2
   Emeline 2
   George F., Rev. 156
   Mary A. 17
   Richard 127
   Thomas 256
Piercy
   Henriette 118
   W.P., Comm. 118
Piggot/Piggott
   Ann Rebecca 81
   Ebenezer Peyton 39
   James Mason 39
   Mason A. 81
   Mary E. 39
   Rebecca D. 82
Pikesville, Md. 166
Pilatka, Fla. 88, 197
Piles
   Julius Henry 33
   Phillip S. 179
Pilgrims 26
Pilling
   James, Sr. 118
   Sarah 272
Pilot Grove, Md. 238
Pine
   Smith, Rev. 27
Pinkney
   Rev. 220
Piqua, Ohio 8
Piscataway, Md. 40, 97, 140
Pise
   C.C., Rev. 206
Pitt Co., N.C. 32
Pitts
   Mary A. 36
   Morgan P., Dr. 36
Pittsburg(h), Pa. 60, 65, 72, 139, 206
plague-ship 185
Plant
   Anadora 81
   Eliza Ann 81
   George H. 81
   Hannah A. 14
   J. William 172
   Joseph J.B. 172
   Julia A. 172
   Nathaniel 27
Planter 125, 153
Plater
   Hon. 94
   J. Rousby 92
   Thomas 3

Platt
   J.M., Rev. 269
   William H., Rev. 158
Plattsburg, N.Y. 256
Pleasanton
   Augustus J., Col. 201
   Mary 20
   Mary Virginia 201
   Stephen 20
Pleasants
   James, Gov. 227
   John Adair 91
   Susanna 227
   William Henry 122
Pleasantville, Va. 120
Pleasonton
   Mary 18
   Stephen 18
Plowman
   Elizabeth A. 249
   Jesse F. 249
   Marian Louisa 64
Plumer
   Rev. 48
   William, Hon. 254
Plummer
   Rev. 92
   S.M., Capt. 53
Plunkett
   Joseph H., Rev. 11, 40
Plymouth, Mass. 26
Poe
   Caroline 244
   George 244
   George, Jr. 206
   Maria 206
Poindexter
   Carter Braxton 65
   John G. 65
   Mary Eliza 65
Poisal
   John, Rev. 164
Poitiaux
   B. Eugene 124
Poits
   Mary 191
   William, Dr. 191
Polglase
   Benjamin 144
Polk
   Caroline E.G. 127
   President 22
Pollard
   J.R. 135
   Margaret C. 56
   Richard, Maj. 9, 56
   Thomas 124
Polley
   Thomas 130
Pollock
   A.D., Rev. 256
Pomonkey, Md. 69
Ponchartrain Railroad 176

Pool
- James 111

Poole
- Elizabeth 141
- Lewis H. 141
- Mary Elizabeth 141

Poolesville, Md. 215

Poor
- Alfred 190
- George H. 94
- Moses 49, 94
- William A. 193

Poplar Hill, Md. 34, 147
Poplar Run, Va. 33
Port Tobacco, Md. 4, 22, 23, 50, 69, 161, 174, 189, 229, 235, 268
Port-au-Prince 142

Porter
- Andrew Jackson 239
- Andrew, Lt. Col. 164
- Bolton S., Lieut. 70
- Comm. 40
- D.D., Lieut. 211
- D.S. 203
- Edward Leroy 81
- George B. 239
- Georgeann 211
- Harriet Amelia 37
- Imogen 40
- John Braddock 203
- John E. 66, 203
- Mary C. 245
- Mary E. 138
- Ogden 83
- Peter A. 245
- Peter Augustus 83
- Sarah 203
- W.D. 36
- W.D., Lieut. 83
- Wright 37

Portici, Va. 148
Portland 178
Portland, Me. 231
Portsmouth, N.H. 14, 43, 140
Portsmouth, N.Y. 220
Portsmouth, Va. 9, 120, 125, 141, 166, 227

Posey
- James H. 253
- John, Capt. 71
- Julia R. 216
- Mary E. 84
- Thomas, Maj. Gen. 71

Post
- Frances A. 92
- R., Rev. 261
- Reuben, Rev.* 92
- William M., Dr. 261

Post Office 115, 173
Post Office Department 30, 61, 69, 111, 155, 215
Postmaster 69, 85, 96, 113, 265
Postmaster General 218

Poston
- Amelia 35

Potomac Aqueduct 225
Potomac River 159

Potter
- Allethia F.F. 118
- George Ourand 118
- Rev. 221
- Thomas L. 118

Potts
- Caroline C. 36
- Mary Ann 191
- Samuel J. 36

Pottsdam, N.Y. 268
Pottsville, Pa. 141
Poughkeepsie Telegraph 80
Poughkeepsie, N.Y. 24, 52, 80

Powell
- Alcinda J. 160
- Burr, Maj. 25
- Catharine 25
- John D., Rev. 257
- Mary Charlotte 195

Powers
- Abigail 150
- Lemuel, Rev.* 150
- Mary 11

Powhatan Co., Va. 143
Powhatan Hill, Va. 41

Prall
- Virginia L. 106

Prather
- O.J. 133

Pratt
- Julia Helen 191
- Rachel 71
- William D. 71
- Zadoc, Hon. 191

Prattsville, N.Y. 191

Prenal
- Virginia J. 201

Prendable
- Catharine 139

Prendergast
- M. 254

Presbyterian Church 3, 21, 26, 32, 42, 48, 51, 62, 72, 75, 77, 78, 82, 95-97, 101, 122, 146, 153, 161, 162, 167, 168, 170, 183, 192-195, 211, 222, 224, 230, 234, 240, 255, 256, 265, 268, 271

Prescott
- Lucy 132
- Miss 132
- Oliver, Hon. 132
- William, Col. 132

President 58, 108
- U.S. 126, 166, 175

Presque Isle 72

Preston
- Henry 113
- J.B., Hon. 134
- Letitia 132
- Mrs. 250
- Thomas W. 117
- W.O., Rev. 1
- William, Col. 132

Preston Co., Va. 1

Prettyman
- Amelia H. 119
- Margaretta F. 176
- William, Rev. 176

Preuss
- Louisa Savary 247

Preuss family burial ground 247

Price
- Bettie M. 2
- Cicero 154
- Francis 2
- Joseph T. 92
- Margaret 92
- Mary A. 169
- Reese E., Gen. 169
- Serg. 151
- Thomas L., Gen. 223

Prichard
- H.F. 68

Prince Edward Co., Va. 91, 191, 233
Prince Frederick, Md. 167
Prince George's Co., Md. 1, 2, 5-8, 10, 12, 16, 19, 27, 30, 33, 39-41, 46, 58, 64, 66, 67, 75, 79, 82-84, 87, 88, 90, 92, 95, 97, 108, 109, 111, 113, 114, 118, 121-123, 126, 127, 129, 132, 134, 139, 140, 143, 146, 147, 155, 156, 162, 164, 169, 171, 175, 178, 180, 186, 189, 194-196, 199-201, 203, 204, 206, 207, 209, 212, 213, 216, 220, 221, 224-226, 230, 231, 233, 234, 236, 243, 245, 247, 248, 252, 254, 256, 260, 261, 265, 269, 271-273
Prince William Co., Va. 24, 25, 36, 49, 64, 69, 86, 91, 106, 109, 110, 146, 148, 191, 245, 253, 255
Princess Anne, Md. 24, 88, 127
Princeton College 65, 258, 273
Princeton Theological Seminary 50
Princeton, N.J. 4, 26, 50, 51, 112, 233, 240
Printer 14, 96, 178, 183, 251, 254, 261

Printz
- Cornelius 213
- Susan H. 213

Prior
- Thomas O. 59

Procter
- Samuel 57

Proctor
    Abner B. 160
Professor 43, 47, 51, 54, 83, 87, 120, 166, 240
Prospect Hill, Md. 39
Prosperi
    Frederick 157
Prout
    Jonathan 68
    Martha Hale 61
    Sarah S. 269
    William 61, 269
Provest
    Alexander 43
    Margaret 43
Providence, R.I. 35, 60, 136, 238, 273
Pruderoski
    Elizabeth 225
Prussia 193
Puebla 190
Puerto Rico 167
Pulaski, Tenn. 68
Pulizzi
    Elizabeth 247
    Venerando, Serg. Maj. 116, 247
Pullin
    John 205
Pulsfort
    Elizabeth 139
Pumphrey
    Arthur G. 226
    Levi 10, 208
    Walter M. 199
Purcell
    John Francis 60
    Mary F.E. 60
    William F. 60
Purify
    James S., Rev. 187
Puritans 174
Pursell
    John F.B. 159
Purser 184, 192, 207, 241
Putnam
    Charles E. 271
Putnam, Ohio 226
Pye
    E. Rudhall 273
Pyne
    D., Rev. 222
    John 89, 97
    Rev. 4, 20, 21, 54, 58, 98, 123, 190, 212
    Smith/Smyth, Rev. 89, 125, 132, 133, 137, 143, 155, 166, 184, 192, 214, 223, 257, 270

Q

Quaker Hill, Md. 198
Quantrile
    A.R. 167
    Mary Ann 167
Quartermaster 143
Quartermaster General 29
Queen
    Eleanor Jane B. 32
    John Theodore 197
    O. Bedingfeld 32
    Sarah 32
Queen Anne's Co., Md. 32, 59, 205
Queens Co., Ire. 99, 168
Queenston, N.J. 26
Quesenbury
    E.R. 181
    George Forrest 181
    Nicholas 181
Quigley
    Ann Amanda 86
    Daniel 86
    John 201
    Maria Ann 100, 110
    Mary 86
Quigly
    Mary 57
    William 57
Quin
    Catherine 154
Quincy, Ill. 132
Quinn
    James 261
    Mary 270
Quinter
    Joseph R. 104
    Rebecca 104
    Virginia 104
Quirk
    John B. 64
Quisenberry
    Amelia Jane 13
    George Nicholas 83
    J.T. 13, 14
    Louisa M. 13
    Louisa Matilda 14
    Louise 14
    N. 83
Quitman
    F. Henry 226
    Gen. 226

R

Radcliff
    J.T. 23
    Joseph 52
    William C. 52
Radcliffe
    Fanny A. 95
    George 54
    Joseph 17, 54
    Julia A. 54
    Mary S. 17
    William 95
Ragan
    John 71
    Michael 45
    Sarah 134
Ragsdale
    Anna Maria McLean 81
Rahway, N.J. 137
Raiford
    Philip H., Col. 156
Railey
    James Green 147
    James, Col. 147
railroad 5
railroad depot 79
Raleigh Register 36
Raleigh, N.C. 36, 62, 86, 93, 156, 189
Ramsgate, Eng. 49
Randall
    Alexander 14, 135
    Alexander, Hon. 69, 125
    Alexander, Jr. 14
    Burton 125
    Catharine W. 14
    Catharine Wirt 133, 135
    Daniel, Lieut. Col. 60
    Daniel, Maj. 125
    Deborah 125
    Elizabeth Wirt 116
    George A.W. 180
    Jane 272
    John 125
    Judge 125
    Lucinda 180
    Richard, Hon. 125
    Thomas, Hon. 116
    William Wirt 69
Randolph
    Bettie 57
    Burwell Stark 265
    C.C., Capt. 57
    James Innes, Col. 131
    James J., Col. 3, 95, 131
    John Brockenbrough 239
    Mary P. 95
    Nannie J. 3
    Peyton 131
    Robert C., Dr. 221
    Thomas Mann 89, 90
    Virginia 89
    William E.E. 11
Rankin
    J. Eames, Rev.* 268
    John W. 95
Ranson
    A.R.H. 259
    Ann Elizabeth 230
    Bettie 9
    George William 252
    James L. 9
    Matthew 230

Rapley
    William W. 169
Rappahannock Co., Va. 55, 144, 268
Ratcliffe
    Joseph 264
    Sarah Amanda 264
Rawlings
    Maria R.M. 195
    Mary 195
    Sarah 141
Ray
    A. Ross 26
    Alexander 11
    Eleanor 11
    Eliza L. 26
    Gabella 180
    Hyde, Dr. 180
    Ida Leslie 26
Read
    A., Lieut. 42
    C.H., Rev. 55
    Caroline Laurens 108
    N.H., Hon. 208
    Thomas 231
Reading, Eng. 118
Recorder 139, 143
Rector 44, 47, 57, 66, 80, 99, 109
    Maj. 38
Red Hill, N.C. 11
Reddy
    Mary Ann 91
Redfern
    Joseph 51
Redin
    Mary Ann 84
    William 84
Redlands, Va. 113
Reed
    A., Rev. 77
    Ann Elizabeth 199
    D.C. 127
    Isaac 84
    Isabella 251
    John 84
    Margaret Ann 268
    Martha Virginia 214
    Rev. 204
    Thomas E. 53
Reese
    D. Evans, Rev. 156, 169, 214
    Hugh L. 158
    John 251
    Joseph 234
    Levi R., Rev.* 45
    Rev. 113, 171, 264
Reeside
    James 23
    Sarah A. 23
Reeve
    Nathan 207
Reeves
    Hannah M. 196
    Martha M. 231

Regan
    James 119
Registrar 92
Reid
    David S. 1
    Robert S. 217
Reiley
    James A. 134
Reilly
    Eliza M.D. 175
    Francis 54
    Mary 54
    Teresa Frances 54
    Thomas 175
Reily
    Barbara 105
    John H. 106
    William 145
    William, Maj. 105
Religious Society of Friends 43
Remington
    James 181, 226
    Mary Elizabeth 226
    Ruth Ellen 181
Reno
    J.L., Bvt. Capt. 192
Rensaelaer, N.Y. 47
Renwick
    Henry B. 98
Republic 26
Resaca de la Palma 115, 126, 240
Revenue Marine 161
Revenue Service 223
Revolutionary War 50, 52, 56-58, 62, 63, 71, 76, 81, 103, 105, 121, 140, 146, 168, 171, 183, 197, 198, 200, 205, 241, 260
Reynolds
    A.W., Capt. 85
    Alberta Otwayanna 41
    Enoch L. 246
    Sally 85
Rheem
    John 184
Rhoads
    Edward 106
    H., Mrs. 106
Rhode Island 30, 35, 140, 273
Rhodes
    Christopher 194, 238
    Edward 88, 103
    Eliza Allen 194
    Sarah Aborn 238
Ricard
    Caleb B. 268
Rice
    Mrs. 29
    Robert R. 137
Rice's boarding-house 29
Richards
    Alfred 4
    Anne E. 50
    Felix 20

    Jane C. 4
    William 244
    William G. 153
Richardson
    Alfred 79
    C.F.E. 196
    Charlotte 196
    John, Maj. 92
    Laura Virginia 16
    Mary 196
    Sarah Ann 252
    Wilmina E. 16
    Wm. A. 16
Richmond Co., Ga. 7
Richmond Co., Va. 168
Richmond Enquirer 102, 228
Richmond Whig 56
Richmond, Va. 15, 31, 33, 37, 46, 54, 55, 65, 73, 88, 91, 92, 97, 103, 107, 124, 134, 140, 143, 161, 165, 176, 182, 185, 186, 192, 209, 227, 228, 235, 252, 258, 259, 272
Ricker
    Lawrence 109
    Mary 109
    Preston 109
Rickerby
    Alfred 52
Ricketts
    Richard 87
Rickey
    Anna S. 5
    R.H. 5
Riddall
    Mrs. 182
Riddle
    Ariana 116
    James, Hon. 116
Riddlemoser
    John B. 50
Ridenour
    Upton H. 244
Rider
    James, Rev. 34
Ridgate
    Benjamin C. 122
    Margaret E. 122
Ridgely
    Absolom 189
    Anna Josephine 154
    Charles Sterett 177
    Elizabeth 189
    Frances Ann 12
    James L., Col. 154
    Mary A. 177
    Mary A. Hopkins 118
    Samuel 217
    William G. 94
    William R. 183
Ridout
    Rev. 227

Riggs
- Elisha 129, 173
- George 173
- George W. 57, 95, 154
- Samuel 129
- Virginia 95
- William 129

Riggs, Hitchcock & Co. 129
Riggs, Peabody & Co. 173
Rigsby
- Mary 25

Riley
- Elizabeth W. 95
- John Blackston 21
- Mr. 141
- Thomas R. 21

Ringgold
- Abel Upshur 178
- Harriet B. 214
- Susan Upshur 178
- Thomas L., Capt. 178, 226

Ringwood, Va. 111
Rio de Janerio, Brazil 30
Rio Grande (river) 44, 270
Riordan
- James 109, 170
- John Francis 170
- Martha 109, 170
- Philip 109

Rison
- Charles E. 39

Ritchie
- Charlotte C. 197
- Thomas 197, 228, 235
- Thomas, Jr. 228

Rittenhouse
- Benjamin F. 146, 209
- Elizabeth S. 209
- Henrietta 204
- Isabel Laurie 146

Ritter
- John F. 212
- Peter 172
- Terese 172

Rives
- Amelie Louise 226
- J.S. 212
- John C. 150
- John G. 159
- Maria L. 159
- Mary Ann 150
- William C., Hon. 226

Roach
- Catharine A. 123
- Edward N. 123

Roane
- Archibald 261
- John J. 183
- Mary A. 183
- Ruth 261
- Spencer 44, 261
- Thomas Fauntleroy 183

Roanoke, Va. 122

Robb
- Ann Eliza 217
- John 217

Robbins
- Margaret 9
- Thomas 9

Roberts
- Edmund, Rev.* 271
- John 131, 243
- Julia 8
- Solomon W. 5
- Thomas Booth 263

Robertson
- James 68, 209
- James M. 48
- Jane Byrd 246
- Mary 68
- Rachel 151
- Sarah Jane 238
- Thomas 246

Robey
- Elizabeth A. 197
- Nehemiah 166

Robins
- Thomas 199

Robinson
- Angelica P. 67
- Catharine A.G. 78
- Eleanor 110
- G.W. 74
- George W. 85
- Henry, Gen. 259
- John A. 120
- John G. 110
- Julia H. 182
- Maria 110
- Mary Ann 85
- Mary Emily 191
- Walter 128
- William 46
- William Y. 211

Roby
- Emma 266
- John H. 72
- Richard S. 137

Roche
- Ellen T. 145
- James R. 128
- John 230

Rochester Amer. 270
Rochester, N.Y. 18, 102, 270
Rochfort, Fra. 178
Rock Creek 32
Rock Creek cemetery 187
Rock Creek Church 14, 42, 74, 112
Rock Creek Parish 52, 57, 59
Rockaway, N.J. 174
Rockbridge Co., Va. 251
Rockerford
- Rev. 96

Rockingham Co., Va. 1, 32
Rockville, Md. 8, 28, 54, 57, 61, 107, 120, 121, 150, 170, 186, 231, 249, 269

Rodgers
- Comm. 243
- Comm., Mrs. 180
- Henry, Lieut. 222
- Ravaud Kearny, Rev. 117

Rodier
- Estelle 259
- Louisa M. 259
- P. Louis 259

Roemmelle/Roemmele
- Ellen 227
- John C. 45, 201, 227
- Mary Ellen 45

Rogers
- Frances B. 89
- George Clarke 49
- Hugh 177
- J. Smyth, M.D. 89
- Jane Teresa 52
- John D. 191
- John, Capt. 56
- Rev. 55
- Thomas, Capt. 56

Rogerson
- Eleanor D. 123

Roland
- John F., Brev. Maj. 115

Rolando
- Henry 21

Roley
- Rev. 9

Rolfe
- A.F.N., Rev. 252

Rollin
- Caroline 255

Rollings
- Caroline 75
- Mary Louisa 75
- Washington 75

Roman states 49
Rome, Italy 232
Romford, Eng. 49
Ronaldson
- Richard 12

Rooker
- Ann Elizabeth 218
- Jabez B. 218
- W.T., Rev. 48

Rooney
- Francis 55

Root
- Gen. 218

Rose
- Adam L. 234
- Lucy 186
- Mary Gideon 188
- Rebecca Elizabeth 188
- Thomas 186
- William P. 239

Rose Hill, Va. 176
Rose Mont, Tenn. 165
Roseland, Pa. 127
Rosemont 259

Rosenberg
    Joseph 155
Ross
    Andrew 220
    Mary Louisa 191
    Rebecca 220
    Rev. 26
    Sarah R. 33
Rosser
    Leonidas, Rev. 60, 77, 81, 84
    Rev. 83
Roszel
    S.S., Rev. 112, 140
Roszell
    Rev. 105
    S., Rev. 84
    S.A., Rev. 6
Rothwell
    Andrew 6
    Ann 6
    Eleanor D. 6
Rowan
    J.W. 260
    Margaret 138
    Margaret S. 145
Rowland
    David 264
    John 272
Rowzee
    Emma Elberta 23
    Greenberry 23
    Thomazine M. 23
Roxbury, Mass. 154
Roy
    James P., Lieut. 259
Rucker
    D. Henry, Maj. 143
    Henry 143
Ruff
    Dolly Ann 257
    Elizabeth 43
    Elizabeth Priscilla 102
    George Nelson 257
    George R. 102
    John A. 257
    Sarah Jane 102
Rumley
    Rev. 44
Rumsey
    James G. 29
Ruppert
    Caspar 102
    Catharine 139
Rush
    Catherine Eliza 218, 228
    James Murray 199
    Julia 230
    Mary A. 238
    Mr. 198
    Richard, Hon. 218, 230
Russ
    Rebecca 90

Russell
    Henry 51
    J.A., Rev. 263
    Jonathan 272
    Rev. 120, 270
    Thomas, Col. 252
Russia 272
Rust
    Sumner 220
Rustin Hill, Va. 110
Rutherdale
    Bridget 141
    John S. 141
Rutherford
    John 252
Rutledge
    Arthur Middleton 53
    Bishop 116
Ryan
    James Emmett 222
    Laurantine 222
    William 222
Ryder
    Rev. 24
Ryland Chapel 37, 210
Ryon
    Julia W. 105
    Richard J. 105
    Samuel Wheeler 105

S

Sabin
    Jesse 267
Saco, Me. 64
Sacramento, Calif. 40, 237
Saffell
    Rachel A. 156
Safford
    H. 226
Sage
    G.A. 3
    H.B. 131
    Henry B. 96
    Mary Ann 3
    Wilhelmina 131
Salem 260
Salem, Ia. 239, 240
Salem, N.J. 108, 221
Salem, Ohio 60
Salem, Va. 161
Saline Co., Mo. 67
Salisbury, Conn. 77
Salisbury, Md. 209
Salisbury, N.C. 46
Sallahue
    Margaret 25
Salt Lake, Utah 27
Sampson
    G.W., Rev. 231
    George W., Rev. 139
    George, Rev. 219
    Rev. 138

    T.W., Rev. 149
Samson
    G.W., Rev. 131, 149, 152, 161,
        174, 210, 255, 259, 266,
        272
    G.W., Rev.* 239
    George W., Rev. 203
    Rev. 139
San Antonio, Tex. 126
San Francisco, Calif. 22, 29, 96,
    101, 123, 131, 133, 141,
    145, 147, 155, 187, 208,
    242, 266
Sanders
    B.C. 242
    G.P. 216
    Nancy A. 216
    Phineas Bradley 242
Sanderson
    Elizabeth Martha 80
    Francis 83
    Hannah Tingey 83
    Samuel 80
Sandusky, Ohio 11, 235
Sandwich Islands 100, 242
Sandy Spring, Md. 35
Sanger
    Martha N. 237
    William A. 237
    William P.S. 237
Sansbury
    Harriet 33
    James T. 75
    Susan 226
Santa Anna 190
Santa Fe, Mex. 38, 44, 111, 143,
    151
Saratoga Co., N.Y. 6, 17, 32, 47,
    59, 75, 247, 254
Saratoga Springs 111, 238
Sargent
    Epes, Capt. 154
    Epes, Jr. 154
    Hon. 251
    John O. 154
    John Osborne 208
    T.B., Rev. 228
Saunders
    Bickerton 6
    Jeannie C. 36
    R.M., Hon. 36
    Susan 199
    Thomas F. 80
    W.H., Capt. 44
    William H., Dr. 62
Saut Ste. Marie, Mich. 141, 253
Savage
    Thomas S., Rev. 54
Savannah Republican 7
Savannah, Ga. 74, 82, 171, 209,
    254, 255
Sawyer
    James, Col. 183
    Lemuel, Hon. 67

    Lydia 183
Saxton
    Charlotte H. 18
    Seth 18
Saybrook Mirror 10
Scanlon
    Patrick 139
Scarritt
    J. Mason, Capt. 240
Scheckels
    Theodore 74
Schermerhorn
    John, Rev.* 15
Schlatmann
    Mary Theresa 36
Schlosser
    N., Rev. 153
Schmid
    A., Rev. 9
Schnappauf
    Canigunda 67
Schneck
    B.S., Rev. 116
Schneider
    Catharine G. 184
    Louis H. 79
Schofield
    Martha 119
Scholfield
    Sarah N. 115
School Teacher 172
Schooler
    William D. 244
schooners
    George Ann 68
    Robert Armstrong 44
    Vixen 185
Schott
    Ann Virginia 256
    Charles A. 231
    John G. 256
Schroeder
    William 262
Schuarzkopf
    Metta, Miss 173
Schussler
    Caroline Emily 77
    Charles 77, 217, 256
    Christiner Moellor 217
Schutter
    Hubert 231
Schwartz
    Joseph Lewis 142
Schwartze
    A.J., Dr. 203, 236
    Augusta M. 203
    Joseph R.B. 112
Schwrar
    Philip G. 80
Scotland 98, 233
Scotland, La. 267
Scotoozsler
    Canratt 37

Scott
    Agnes Jane 105
    Alexander 214
    Alexander B. 57
    Ann M. 105
    Ann Rebecca 250
    Anna R. 227
    Camilla 58
    Elizabeth 214
    Elizabeth C. 122
    Gen. 58, 141
    Henry L. 74
    Marianna T. 161
    Mary Ann 129
    Mr. 216
    Rev. 258
    Sarah 117
    Sarah E. 137
    Sarah Ellen 193
    William A. 105, 250
    William Graham 271
    William H. 57
Scranton, Pa. 26
Scrivener
    John 101
    John, Rev. 248
    Mary Maria 101
Sculptor 179
Seabrook
    Edward W. 238
Seaford, Del. 157
Seaman 35, 154
Sears
    James W., Sr. 167
    R., Mrs. 232
Seaver
    Elizabeth C. 3
    Jonathan 3, 147, 190
    Jonathan M. 43
Second Presbyterian Church 78, 146, 193
Secretary 15, 47, 91, 101, 262
Secretary of Finance 39
Secretary of State 12, 176
Seibel
    John C. 33
Seifert
    Carolina 172
Selden
    Anne R. 242
    Bettie 160
    Cary, Maj. 155
    George W. 29
    James 29, 160, 254
    James M. 70
    John 242
    Kate K. 254
    Margaret 29, 254
    Mary Frances 70
    Virginia 155
Sellman
    John H., Dr. 35
Selma, Ala. 226
Selma, Va. 166

Semens
    Emilie 124
Semmes
    B.J., Dr. 140
    Benedict I., Dr. 140
    Emily 140
    Raphael 203
    Senator 15, 175, 193, 205, 217, 225, 228, 271
Seneca Mills, Md. 238
Sengstack
    Eliza M. 113
    Henry E. 209
    Isabella 209
Senseney
    George E. 52
Sequart
    Charles E.B. 151
Serapis 35
Sergeant
    Albert N., Dr. 235
    John 87, 210
    S. Emma 87
Sergeant-at-Arms 86
Serrin
    William D. 52
servants 117
Sessford
    John, Sr. 228
    Martha 228
Settle
    Henrietta W. 1
    Thomas, Hon. 1
Seufferele/Seufferle
    George J. 195
    J. Jacob 90
    Jacob 5
    Mary Magdalen 5
    Mary Margaret 90
Sewall
    Dr. 225
    Robert D. 147
    Thomas, Rev. 75
Sewell
    Frances Ann 212
    William 223
Sexsmith
    Elizabeth 86
Seymour
    Gov. 191
Shaaff
    J.T., Dr. 268
    Margaretta Jane 268
Shaahy
    John 67
Shackelford
    J.W., Rev. 232
Shackford
    Rev. 73
Shackleford
    Thomas 24
Shand
    Rev. 222
Shanghai, China 177

Shapley
    J.M., Rev.* 78
Sharon, Conn. 52
Shaw
    Alfred C. 71
    Francis N. 216
    Mrs. 197
Shay
    Michael 268
Sheahan
    Michael J. 55
Sheckell
    Rosalie 118
Sheckels
    Mary Ann 203
    Merrit 203
Sheffield, Eng. 127
Sheirburn
    Harriet A. 221
Sheldon
    Harriet W. 224
    Israel 224
Shelton
    E.E. 99
    Mary 99
Shepherd's Hill, Va. 41
Shepherdstown, Va. 125, 157, 181
Sheppard
    J., Rev.* 123
    Josephine B. 123
Sherbertt
    Martha 255
Sherburne
    John Henry, Col. 95
Sheriff
    Levi 214
Sherman
    A. Eliza 17
    C.E. 164
    Charles E. 233
    Charles R. 258
    Sarah Jane 6
Sherrard
    Joseph H. 47
    Mary Frances 47
Sherwood
    Charles W. 230
    Helen C. 184
    John 54
    Rebecca V. 189
Shetlin
    Jacob 160
Shields
    Mary Ann 75
    Thomas 13
Shiloh Baptist Church 227
Shipley
    Benjamin 134
    E. Ada 134
Shipman
    J.W., Rev. 114
Shipper 62

ships
    Antelope 203
    Boxer 243
    Enterprize 243
    Francis P. Sage 248
    French man-of-war 261
    Ocean Queen 186
    Preble 176
    San Francisco 206, 207, 243
Shoemaker
    David L. 139
    Mary R. 139
    Samuel M. 203
Short
    Edward 103
    Elizabeth A. 103
    Mary Agnes 103
Shotwell
    Nathan, Rev.* 115
Shreve/Shreeve
    James H. 212
    John 175
    Margaret R. 27
    Mary R. 175
Shriver
    Hon. 194
    Mary 194
Shuch
    George 160
Shugrue
    Catherine 106
    John 106
    Margaret 106
Shultz
    H.A., Rev. 234
Shyne
    Catharine 241
    Mary Teresa 241
    Michael R. 12, 241
Sibley
    E.S., Maj. 18
    Henry H., Hon. 48
    Henry Hastings 48
Siebels
    Amanda 239
    Edwin W. 239
Siebrecht
    Eliza 185
    Henry 185
Sigourney
    Henry 226
Silliman
    Emily 193
    George 39
    Gold S. 39, 193
Silver Spring, Md. 170
Simmes
    Robert V. 185
Simmons
    David P. 150
    Eliza Jane 159
    Mary Emma 159
    Samuel 163
    Sarah F. 205

    William R. 159
Simms
    Camilla 158
    Charles Carroll 125
    Elexius 158, 211
    John W. 84
    M.L. 41
    Richard E. 138
    Richard H. 35
    Sampson 41
    Selma V. 225
Simoda, Japan 270
Simonds
    Laura A. 112
Simons
    James, Dr. 95
Simonton
    John W. 227
Simpson
    E. Ford 134
    Edward 177
    James A. 175, 179
    Joel 101
    Julia C. 175, 179
    Lucy A. 64
    Marcellus 35
    Mary 107
    Mary E. 101
    Samuel, Col. 269
    T.W., Rev. 162
Simpton
    Ellen 96
    George, Capt. 96
Sims
    Ann Little 118
    Martha J. 193
Sing Sing, N.Y. 30, 108, 260
Singer 90
Sinnott
    B.H. 255
Sinon
    John 91, 216
    Mary 91
Sioussa
    Augustus 125
    Frederick 166
    Harriet 166
Sipe
    Ann E. 155
Sisters of Charity, Md. 145
Sitgreaves
    Lorenzo, Capt. 214
Skelly
    Caroline 175
Skidmore
    Columbia 271
    Margaretta 38
Skinner
    F.G. 144
    Joseph Blount 65
    Joshua 111
Skirving
    John, Jr. 95
    Mary Ann 64

Slagle
    Charlotte 90
    Jacob 90
Slamm
    Jennie 34
    Levi D. 34
    Rittenhouse 34
Slater
    Margaret 50
    William 50
Slattery
    Rev. 8, 12, 36, 52, 55, 64, 70, 73, 87, 98, 100
Slaughter
    Albert G., Comm. 181
Slicer
    Henry, Rev. 163
    Henry, Rev.* 269
    Lizzie 269
    Lizzie S. 163
Sloat
    Jeannette E.W. 229
    John D., Comm. 229
sloops
    Warren 22
Slye
    Daniel W. 224
    Edwin D. 142
Small
    George 231
Smallwood
    Gen. 205
    Richard L. 114
Smallwood's brigade 168
Smedberg
    Jane R. 223
Smedes
    Rev. 189
Smets
    Alexander C.N. 78
Smith
    Albert Hebard 258
    Andrew 230
    Ann E. 55, 253
    Annie 34
    Annie Ellsworth 258
    Azariah, Rev.* 35
    Benjamin 26
    Benjamin P. 190
    Catharine Matilda 9
    Catherine 113
    Charles W. 41
    Clara E. 49
    Clarence Cyrillus 106
    Cynthia W. 67
    David P. 194
    Dennis A. 62, 251
    Dorsey Brown 253
    Dr. 273
    E. Delafield 46
    E. Goodrich 243
    E.C. 129
    Edward A. 29
    Emma 194
    Fanny 26
    Fleet 21, 44
    Flodoardo Howard 105
    Francis H., Col. 246
    Frederick A., Capt. 117
    George H. 81, 168
    Henrietta 145
    Henry C. 195
    Hugh C. 185
    J. Bowen 199
    J.B.H. 145
    J.L. 169
    J.S., Rev. 209
    James 253
    James H. 66
    James K. 204
    James L. 219
    James R. 10, 34, 196
    James S., Hon. 129
    Jane H. 21
    John 163, 255
    John A. 79, 117
    John C., Rev. 13, 19, 23, 26, 30, 32, 33, 40, 52, 53, 56, 57, 61, 64, 67, 76, 77, 80, 81, 83, 86, 90, 95, 96, 100, 106-108, 110-113, 117-119, 122, 124-126, 129, 133, 142, 144-146, 149, 151, 155, 156, 161, 164, 167, 174-176, 183, 188, 191, 194, 199, 201, 203, 214, 215, 217, 219, 224, 225, 227, 228, 230-234, 243, 255, 256, 265, 266, 268, 272
    John L. 105, 106
    John P. 165
    John, Rev.* 17
    Josephine 187
    Lewis 49
    Lucy Wadsworth 145
    Malinda 160
    Marcia Augusta 24
    Margaret F. 182
    Mary Ann E. 186
    Mary Elizabeth 87, 119
    Mary Ellen 160
    Mary Kate 10
    Mary Rebecca 251
    Matilda M. 249
    Mr. 68
    Mrs. 268
    Rebecca 67
    Rebecca M. 79, 106, 169
    Rebecca Maria 105
    Rev. 238, 249
    Richard 24
    Richard H., Lieut. 207
    Robert, Dr. 113
    Roswell C. 258
    Sophia L. 42
    Susan W. 243
    T.A., Gen. 67
    Thomas, Rev. 160
    Wilfred 56
    William H., Rev. 49
    William Joseph 249
    William M.W. 243
    William R., Hon. 232
Smith's Row 126
Smithson
    Lelia McNutt 135
    Martha E. 135
    William T. 135
Smithsonian Institute 37, 61
Smithtown, N.Y. 24
Smoot
    Annie 237
    Edwin K. 51
    Emma 51
    John H. 9
    Joseph 192
    Joseph, Capt. 2
    L.R. 236
    Mary J. 192
    Minta E. 122
    S.C., Dr. 51
    Samuel 122, 236
    Victoria 2
Smyth
    Mary Isabella 195
Snape
    Thomas W. 17
Snethen
    Charles C. 176
    Nicholas, Rev.* 176
Sniffen
    Theodore 96
Sniffin
    Susan A. 6
Snow Hill, Md. 68, 83, 105, 190
Snowden
    George 190
    Letitia 190
Snyder
    Gov. 121
Society of Friends 43, 59, 114, 164, 198
Sodre
    Chevalier de 112
Solomon
    Josiah, Rev. 239
Solona, Va. 17
Somerset Co., Md. 10, 24, 62, 66, 88, 127, 133, 199, 202
Somervell
    James 229
Somerville, N.J. 83, 164
Sommerville
    Anne 40, 149
    John 149
    Portia 40
    Robert A. 40, 149
Sonoma, Calif. 148
Sons of Temperance 85
Sotherland
    S.B., Rev. 131

Sothoron
- William, Dr. 41

Sourin
- E.J., Rev. 201

South America 7
South Bend, Ark. 137
South Carolina 71, 95, 97, 99, 140, 170, 197, 200, 239
South Salem, N.Y. 38

Southall
- A.G. 227

Southard
- Samuel L., Rev. 4

Southeastern Asia 79

Southgate
- Rev. 264

Spalding
- B.D. 133
- George Washington 34
- Maria P. 34
- William E. 34

Spanish Legation 107
Spanish Secretary 31

Sparrow
- Rev. 78, 163, 241
- Wilhelmina 241

Speakes
- John W. 61

Speaks
- Ann Eliza 264
- W.F., Rev. 264

Speer
- Alexander, Dr. 234

Speiden
- Marian Eliza 192
- William 192

Speir
- Caroline Elizabeth 23
- Robert 23

Speischer
- Frederick 244

Spencer 146
Spezzia, Sardinia 250

Spicknall
- John W. 150
- Lucy A. 150
- William H., Col. 83

Spignul
- Aliey 49
- William B. 49

Spotsylvania Co., Va. 13, 167

Sprigg
- Caroline Lansdale 121
- D. Francis, Rev. 28, 262
- John B. 2
- John C. 177
- Martha Rebecca 177
- Mrs. 79
- Osborn 121

Sprigg's boarding house 228
Spring Park, Va. 170
Springfield, La. 186
Springfield, Mass., 112
Springfield, Tenn. 31

springs 151

Sproat
- Mary S. 60

Sprole
- W.T., Rev. 102

St. Alban's Parish, D.C. 252, 254
St. Alphonsus Church 9
St. Ame's Church 244
St. Andrew's Church 22
St. Ann's Church 67
St. Anne's Church 80
St. Augustine, Fla. 85, 263, 265, 270, 271
St. Bartholomew's Church 89
St. Charles Hotel 20
St. Charles, Mo. 52

St. Clair
- James W. 269

St. Domingo 85
St. George's Church 49
St. James Church 252, 259
St. John's Church 16, 21, 49, 58, 60, 69, 76, 98, 105, 122, 140, 148, 155, 177, 179, 181, 187, 189, 195, 201, 222, 232, 235, 237, 257, 258, 266, 270
St. John's College 67
St. John's Lodge No. 11 153
St. John's, Berkley 99
St. Landry Parish, La. 192
St. Louis Co., Mo. 88
St. Louis Intelligencer 82
St. Louis University 82
St. Louis, Mo. 12, 14, 16, 30, 32, 35, 42, 44, 59, 67, 81, 96, 127, 131, 139, 143, 146, 163, 168, 169, 201, 217, 235, 251, 267
St. Luke's Church 18
St. Marin, La. 54
St. Martin Parish, La. 264
St. Mary's Church 8, 19, 22, 36, 37, 45, 55, 67, 71, 75, 89, 102, 129, 139, 158, 232
St. Mary's Co., Md. 26, 39, 44, 48, 49, 65, 84, 110, 120, 124, 128, 132, 149, 168, 183, 224, 237, 256, 264, 271
St. Mat(t)hew's Church 9, 19, 33, 112, 122, 134, 147, 163, 186, 196, 203, 211, 218, 224, 230, 255, 265
St. Matthew's Lutheran Church 105
St. Michael's Church 157
St. Michael's, Md. 220
St. Patrick's Burial-Ground 45
St. Patrick's Cathedral 112, 121
St. Patrick's Church 8, 11, 15, 68, 100, 102, 110, 122, 142, 149, 154, 165, 177-179, 181, 188, 203, 205, 218, 228, 229, 231, 233, 242, 248, 269

St. Paul, Minn. 111, 235, 238, 251, 263
St. Paul's Church 2, 10, 44, 48, 91, 109, 143, 154, 164, 176
St. Paul's English Lutheran Church 49, 184, 195
St. Paul's Lutheran Church 68, 72, 89, 112, 227
St. Peter's Catholic Church 136
St. Peter's Church 2, 20, 45, 57, 59, 95, 131, 203, 228, 252, 256, 265
St. Peter's Parish 271
St. Petersburgh 183
St. Philip's Church 99
St. Rose's Chapel 223
St. Stephen's Church 204
St. Thomas's Church 203
St. Vincent de Paul Female Academy 217

Staats
- J. Allanson 77

Stabler
- Edward 114
- Mary 114
- William 114

Stafford Co., Va. 3, 23, 44, 156, 187, 269

Stahl
- Cornelia 132
- Daniel, Dr. 132

Stallings
- Elizabeth Rebecca 170

Stallions
- Rebecca 212

Stamp
- John 206

Stanfield
- Margaret K. 273

Stanford
- Henry 29
- Leah Ann 188
- Sarah E. 29
- Wm. H. 29

Stanforth
- Elizabeth 178
- Levin 178

Staniford
- T., Col. 223

Stanley
- Henry, Rev. 159
- J.M. 224
- Rev. 127, 164, 215, 260
- Sarah 160

Stanly
- F., Lieut. 27
- F., Rev. 111
- Henry, Rev. 113
- Marion Eckford 27

Stansbury
- Arthur J. 75
- Charles F. 75
- Howard, Capt. 75
- Martha R. 2

333

Martha Rebecca 177
Rebecca 177
Susan 75
Thomas 177
Stanton
  Henry W., Lieut. 15
Staples
  Elizabeth 137
Starling
  Jane G. 256
Starr
  Harriet 166
State Department 91
Staten Island, N.Y. 67, 181
Staunton river 244
Staunton, Va. 25, 105, 124, 163, 190, 192, 199
steamboat wharf 96
steamers 173, 175
  Fremont 30
  Pacific 129
  Palmetto 157
  Tennessee 141
  Thomas Collier 219
Stearns
  Fanny L.G. 138
Steedman
  Charles, Lieut. 12
  Ellen Duane 12
Steel
  W.C., Rev. 234, 245
Steele
  D., Rev.* 89
Steen
  Constance 42
  E., Maj. 42
Steer
  Laura 156
Steffin
  Margaretta 102
Steinman
  John F. 234
  Rebecca 234
Stelle
  Beulah 58
  E.B. 58
  Pontius D. 58
Stephen
  Hon. 205
  Rev. 199
Stephen's Church 71
Stephens
  Rachel A. 40
Stetson
  John, Capt. 58
  Mary A. 47
  Mary Douglas 58
Steuart
  Ariana 116
  John, Dr. 116
Stevens
  Augustus R. 191
  Catherine 138
  Cordelia 113
  Emma Maria 170
  John 220
  M.H. 39
  Mary Virginia 112
  Meury White 39
  Susan B. 39
  Thomas H., Comm. 112
  Thomas Holdup, Comm. 170
  William 220
Stevenson
  Carter L. 262
  Frances Annette 262
  Isabella H. 262
Stewart
  Agnes C. 214
  Andrew, Hon. 39
  Anna Payne 194
  Caleb 160
  Charles 157, 257
  Charles S., Rev. 93
  Charles W. 266
  Cloye Ann 78
  G. Thomas 125
  George M. 157
  George W. 78
  John H. 106
  John J. 195
  Louisa M. 194
  M., Rev. 87
  Margaret 214, 242, 254
  Mary Elizabeth 254
  Richard P. 194
  Sally M. 194
  Samuel 242
  Samuel K., Rev. 88
  Thomas F. 214, 254
  William Walker, Dr. 232
  William, Col. 187
  William, Dr. 88
Stickney
  Jennie 247
  Kendall 247
  William 247
Stillings
  Mary 80
Stinchcomb
  John Henry 229
Stipes
  Henry 14
Stockbridge
  J.C., Rev. 228
Stockbridge, Mass. 81
Stockholm, Sweden 124
Stockton
  Mary 233
  Robert F., Hon. 233
  Thomas H., Rev. 80
Stockton, Calif. 4, 100
Stoddert
  Ann 68
  Benjamin 68, 178
Stoke Newington (Green), Eng. 38, 94
Stokesley, Eng. 100
Stone
  Charles P., Bvt. Capt. 174
  James H. 138
  Julia Ann 77
  Malinda 79
  Maria H. 191
  Mary Jane 227
  Sallie R. 183
  Sarah 156
  William B. 156
  William H. 139
Stonestreet
  Edward E., Dr. 121
Stony Arbor Farm, Md. 27
Stony Harbor, Md. 40
Storer
  Dorothy H. 41
  John 41
Storrs
  A. 196
Story
  John T. 131
Stott
  Charles 264
  James 131
  Sally 131
Stover
  Solomon 27
Strakosch
  Maurice 90
Strange
  Robert, Hon. 189
Stratford-upon-Avon, Eng. 94
Stratton
  J., Rev. 272
  James B., Rev. 194
streets
  1st 4, 54, 55, 76, 94, 126, 141, 155, 161, 219, 224, 262
  2d 5, 44, 83, 84, 93, 119, 143, 155, 157, 160, 183, 213, 214, 216, 219, 223, 224, 233, 251
  3d 3, 5, 21, 34, 38, 44, 58, 79, 104, 109, 115, 119, 145, 146, 157, 161, 165, 167, 170, 172, 180, 183, 184, 191, 193, 214, 223, 228, 233, 237, 245, 250, 255, 256, 259, 266
  4th 45, 51, 74, 90, 95, 99, 103, 104, 133, 142, 146, 158, 161, 170, 172, 178, 191, 219, 237, 238, 250, 253, 261, 266
  4½ 7, 16, 28, 38, 45, 58, 61, 68, 75, 78, 79, 81, 84, 91, 95, 98, 108, 115, 129, 136, 144, 155, 181, 183, 185, 206, 210, 217, 227, 228, 232, 234, 256, 266
  5th 20, 24, 36, 43, 70, 74, 78, 79, 86, 90, 99, 104, 108, 129, 133, 137, 144, 155,

174, 178, 195, 220, 222, 238, 251, 253, 257
6th 4, 7, 20, 22, 23-25, 28, 31, 36, 43, 45, 52, 56, 60, 62, 71, 76, 81, 83, 86, 88-90, 98, 105, 108, 113, 117, 120, 129, 130, 133, 135, 136, 144, 145, 155, 162, 167, 168, 172, 178, 181, 185, 188, 196, 201, 206, 210, 214, 215, 218, 220, 222, 227, 232, 236, 238, 239, 245, 250, 251, 257, 262, 263, 267, 269
7th 3, 6, 11, 12, 15, 17, 22, 25, 27, 31, 38, 45, 49, 54, 56, 57, 60, 73-77, 88, 92, 93, 101, 111, 113, 120, 121, 126, 131, 133, 135, 140-142, 148, 158, 162, 167, 172, 173, 178, 182, 189, 194, 210, 215-218, 222, 227, 234, 238, 243, 245, 246, 248, 250, 251, 256, 262, 263, 265, 267
8th 25, 51, 54, 64, 81, 93, 102, 103, 119, 121, 123, 124, 130, 132, 141, 145, 162, 184, 193, 201, 211, 213, 219, 222, 226, 232, 241, 247-249, 262
9th 4, 12, 16, 21, 26, 52, 59, 62, 66, 71, 73, 81, 84, 94, 99, 103, 104, 107, 109, 111, 124, 127, 128, 145, 148-150, 152, 158, 162, 165, 169, 172, 174, 178, 196, 210, 212, 224, 227, 247, 249, 253, 256, 259, 164
10th 16, 19, 24, 26, 35, 36, 52, 59, 75, 80, 82-86, 88, 90, 95, 103, 104, 109, 111, 112, 115, 118, 123, 126, 128, 139, 148, 149, 153, 156, 158, 160, 162, 165, 169, 172, 174, 185, 200, 201, 225-227, 249, 256, 263
11th 1, 5, 32, 46, 51, 65, 72, 77, 78, 97, 111, 143-145, 147, 152, 156, 185, 199-201, 204, 211, 213-215, 222, 223, 242, 244, 246, 257, 262, 263, 267
12th 1, 3, 9, 15, 17-19, 31, 35, 55, 57, 65, 75, 77, 78, 82, 87, 97, 106, 124, 127, 132, 137, 144, 152, 199, 215, 216, 228, 232, 246, 247, 250, 256, 257, 261
13th 3, 14, 15, 17, 18, 23, 27, 29, 39, 43, 57, 61, 91, 110, 113, 118, 121, 132, 135, 139, 149, 152, 153, 171, 207, 208, 211, 216, 219, 228, 257, 259, 262, 270, 272
13½ 9, 23, 34, 139
14th 14, 39, 57, 74, 89, 91, 97, 118, 121, 124, 125, 152, 160, 200, 218, 219, 259, 267, 268, 270
15th 13, 14, 28, 69, 98, 118, 124, 149, 153, 188, 189, 205, 240, 272
16th 60, 63, 69, 205
17th 67, 102, 104, 166, 208, 218, 237, 239
18th 21, 27, 59, 100, 102, 107, 130, 170, 201, 208, 213, 237
19th 15, 17, 22, 51, 59, 69, 96, 100, 102, 107, 152, 200, 237, 254
20th 51, 83, 96, 104, 118, 120, 141, 228, 254
21st 13, 34, 37, 50, 188
22d 13, 34, 37, 40, 237
26th 147, 236
27th 152, 163, 236
34th, N.Y. 159

A 69
B 1, 13, 20, 37, 40, 85, 111, 135, 154, 174, 200, 213, 222, 244, 248, 256, 272
Beale 115
Boundary 142
Bridge 15, 19, 47, 63, 64, 100, 152, 156, 171, 197, 200, 217, 269
C 1, 10, 13, 17, 21, 27, 31, 34, 40, 73, 79, 80, 83, 85, 103, 109, 113, 124, 135, 143, 152, 154, 168, 181, 193, 213, 228, 250, 251, 256, 257, 265, 266
Cathedral 133
Congress 13, 48, 200, 218, 236
D 23, 26, 34, 44, 61, 73, 75, 80, 83, 87, 93, 111, 124, 139, 144, 145, 149, 152, 158, 170, 172, 193, 199, 207, 210, 211, 219, 220, 222, 237, 239, 241, 248, 249, 256, 261, 262
Dunbarton 104, 131
E 12, 16, 19, 20, 27, 29, 35, 43, 46, 61, 65, 75, 77, 83, 87, 109, 111, 115, 116, 124, 137, 144, 145, 149, 152, 153, 156, 158, 164, 165, 196, 201, 211, 214, 215, 218, 219, 222, 227, 228, 236, 239, 241, 249, 250, 253, 257, 269
East Capitol 3, 4, 52, 53, 76, 84, 86, 109, 151, 165, 219, 224, 248, 255
F 3, 10, 12, 14, 18, 22, 29, 31, 35, 36, 38, 39, 50, 52, 55-57, 61, 67, 75, 76, 83, 88-91, 94, 100, 104, 113, 118-121, 126, 135, 137, 144, 145, 147, 156, 162, 164, 165, 196, 205, 211, 216-218, 220, 222, 223, 232, 239, 242, 243, 245, 250, 254, 257, 268-270
Fairfax 149
Fayette 5, 82, 87, 147
Franklin Row 2, 17
Frederick 110, 160, 262
G 5, 19, 28, 39, 51, 54, 57, 69, 74, 78, 79, 91, 95, 97, 102-105, 107, 110, 113, 130, 137, 145, 147, 151-153, 155, 162, 188, 194, 200, 204, 208, 211, 213-215, 219, 222, 223, 226, 232, 245, 246, 259, 261, 264, 267
Garrison 6, 39, 204
Gay 11, 17, 246
Georgia avenue 172, 218
Green 17
H 4, 16, 17, 19, 21-23, 34, 37, 45, 51, 69-72, 78, 79, 95, 98, 103, 105, 113, 133, 137, 141, 144, 145, 147, 148, 153, 156, 158, 162, 167, 170, 177, 180, 188, 194, 201, 204, 208, 211, 213, 215, 220, 222, 223, 225, 232, 237, 238, 245, 246, 248, 253, 259, 261, 263, 264, 270
Half 42
Harding, Liverpool 128
High 12, 17, 56, 88, 89, 95, 187, 203, 266
I 16, 50, 59, 60, 62, 63, 74, 78, 102, 104, 118, 133, 140, 145, 152, 155, 158, 160, 165, 167, 170, 172, 174, 178, 191, 195, 213, 216, 232, 237, 238, 245-248, 250, 253, 254, 256, 261, 263, 267
Indiana Ave. 121
Indiana avenue 161, 233
Jefferson 142
John (London) 220
K 11, 36, 39, 74, 78, 90, 97, 102, 152, 155, 156, 169, 189, 195, 201, 226, 232, 236, 244, 250, 251, 253, 266
King 199

335

L 24, 27, 36, 56, 59, 74, 81, 99, 119, 133, 139, 141, 143, 148, 149, 153, 156, 163, 165, 169, 172, 178, 185, 189, 205, 215, 244, 247, 256, 259
Lafayette Square 89
Louisiana avenue 31, 69, 76, 79, 266
M 24, 36, 51, 59, 69, 96, 100, 119, 121, 124, 128, 143, 149, 153, 159, 184, 210, 215, 240, 249, 256, 262
Market 14, 47, 86, 175, 245
Maryland 109
Maryland Ave. 11, 25, 28, 32, 38, 60, 91, 93
Maryland avenue 129, 142, 155, 183, 191, 214, 251, 262, 263, 267
Massachusetts avenue 9, 13, 14, 36, 84, 90, 131, 158, 178, 207, 215, 251, 258
Missouri avenue 21, 95, 109, 136, 177, 232, 239, 243, 266
Montgomery 104
N 4, 14, 24, 84, 99, 104, 108, 127, 146, 159, 184, 210, 228, 249, 262
New 105
New Jersey Ave. 47, 50, 61, 98, 114
New Jersey avenue 137, 180, 193, 244
New York avenue 15, 49, 56, 59, 66, 104, 117, 145, 146, 161, 172, 173, 193, 217, 226, 235, 250, 253
North Capitol 29, 175
O 25, 174
Ohio avenue 179
Oxford 162
P 25, 130, 193
Paterson 40
Patrick 199
Pennsylvania avenue 1, 3, 7, 15, 25, 34, 35, 38, 39, 45, 51, 52, 55, 58, 60, 51, 81, 82, 85, 88, 98, 102, 108, 111, 115, 127, 132, 135, 141, 157, 161, 162, 166, 167, 171, 184, 185, 188, 201, 210, 218, 219, 221, 236, 237, 241, 245, 250, 268
Philadelphia place 245
Poppleton 252
Potomac 47, 235
Prospect 58, 137, 221
Q 154
R 257
S 200
South Capitol 4

T 200
Vermont avenue 16, 167, 191
Virginia avenue 57, 104, 180, 204, 242
Warren 255
Water 192, 213
West 173, 261
Stribling
  Ann Taliaferro 230
  Cornelius 127
  Taliaferro, Dr. 230
Stricker
  John, Gen. 93
Strickland
  George 18
Strider
  Mary L.K. 31
  Samuel 31
Stringfellow
  Horace, Rev.* 46
  Rev. 158
Stringham
  Edwina H. 250
  S.H., Comm. 250
Strong
  Edward N. 117
Strother
  E., Capt. 184
  George W. 237
  Milley 46
  Sarah A.E. 184
Struthers
  John 239
  Mary 239
Stuart
  Charles Calvert 261
  Ellen C. 261
  Frederic D. 141
  James Douglass 141
  Mary C. 261
  W.D. 237
Sughrue
  Honora 139
  Timothy 139
Sullivan
  Abbe 193
  Jeremiah 75
  John 89
  John T. 6
  Marshall C. 101
  Mr. 207
  William 36
Sumatra 157
Summerfield, Ark. 150
Summerfield, Md. 231
Summers
  Albert 137
  Edward 64
Sunbury, Ga. 7
Sunderland
  Byron, Rev. 175, 243
  Rev. 227, 234
Supreme Court of Louisiana 3

Surgeon 23, 26, 29, 30, 98, 100, 214, 223, 224, 234, 243
Surgeon's Mate 20
Surry Co., Va. 15
Surveyor 123, 263
Surveyor General 134
Sussex Co., Del. 92
Sussex, Eng. 163
Sutherland
  Annie 145
  Capt. 145
  Idabella 219
  Rev. 273
Sutton
  Elizabeth 152
  Georgianna B. 161
  J. Robert 152
  James 120
  Margaret 53
  Rebecca 152
  Robert M. 128
  William 152
Swaim
  Moses R. 170
Swan Point, Md. 232
Swann
  Annie H. 139
  Helen M. 106
  Richard 139
  Samuel Stanhope 139
  Thomas W. 106
  Thomas William 106
Swearingen
  Charles E. 39
  Elizabeth Stewart 39
  Mary E. 39
Sweeney
  Patrick H. 158
Sweeny
  A., Mrs. 61, 63
  John F. 63
  Mary 88
Sweeting
  Ellen 208
Swift
  Emily 117
  Joseph 117
Switzerland 52, 72, 78, 102, 103, 118, 165
Sydenham, Pa. 218, 228, 230
Sykes
  George, Capt. 249
Sylvester
  Ann Jane 134
  Emma Jane 134
  George 134
Synge
  William Webb Follett 137
Synott
  Mary 128
  Thomas 128
Syracuse (N.Y.) Star 101

T

Tableman
　William G.F. 42
Taconey 223
Talahatchie Co., Miss. 244
Talbert
　Elizabeth 186
　Tobias F. 57
Talbot
　Josephine Truxtun 176
　M., Rev. 176
　M.R., Rev. 176
　Susan McKenzie 216
　Thomas 199
　Thomas J. 216
Talbot Co., Md. 23, 205, 217, 220
Talbot settlement 174
Talburt
　Alexander 194
Talcahuano, Chil[e] 77
Talcott
　George H., Lt. Col. 232
Taliaferro
　Norbourne M., Hon. 168
Tallahassee, Fla. 116, 165, 209
Talley
　William D. 5
Tampa Bay, Fla. 190
Tampa, Fla. 197
Taney
　Augustine, Dr. 172
　Maria Key 73
　Mr. 205
　Roger B. 73
Taneyhill
　Erickson H. 26
　Mary E. 26
Taneytown, Md. 43, 127
Tangiers 22
Tanner
　Mary E. 171
Tansil/Tansill
　Charles Montgomery 157
　Charles R. 157
　G.S., Serg. 157
Tanye
　Hon. 97
　Sophia Brooke 97
Taos, N.M. 151
Tarbel
　Henrietta H. 21
　Joseph, Capt. 21
Tarlton
　Jane Elizabeth 76
Tarman
　Richard Henry 201
Tarring
　Henry, Rev. 134
　Rev. 40
Tasistro
　Louis F. 154

Tastet
　Joseph M., Dr. 219
　Nicholas 219
Tate
　Andrew 117
　Mrs. 262
Tavenner
　Charles H. 172
　Charles Richard 172
　Maria 172
Tayloe
　Edward T., Col. 41
　John 270
　William H. 41
Taylor
　Alexander F. 54
　Bushrod, Dr. 268
　Edward, Jr. 96
　Frances 72
　Francis Harwood 229
　Francis, Lieut. Col. 97, 229
　Gen. 30, 44, 190, 240, 270
　George 31, 38
　George, Maj. 206
　J. 126
　J.P., Col. 140
　James 15, 215
　John 136, 263
　John F. 169
　John W. 254
　Joseph 75
　Julian 135
　Julian, Dr. 134
　Louther 235
　Margaret 108
　Margaret E. 3
　Mary 75
　Mary A. 34
　Mrs. 207, 210
　President 12
　Rebecca 34, 140
　Richard 72
　Robert J. 134, 135
　Rosalie B. 121
　Samuel 143
　Stark B. 24
　William Jaqueline 258
　Zachary, Gen. 108
Tazewell Co., Va. 132
Teasdale
　Rev. 114
　T.C., Rev. 110, 121
Teeple
　John B. 153
Telegraph 261
Telfair
　Mary M. 30
　William B. 190
Temple
　William G. 48
Temple Michael parish 165
Templeman
　George 70

Temps
　William Henry 53
Ten Broeck
　A., Rev. 125
Tench
　Thomas P. 69
Tennessee 19, 70, 96, 116, 207, 215
Tenth Street Baptist Church 259
Terre Bonne parish, La. 166
Terre Haute, Ind. 29, 182
Terrett
　Burdett A., Capt. 263
　Colville 41
　George Hunter, Capt. 263
　George, Bvt. Maj. 263
　John Chapman, Lieut. 263
　Julia 267
　Washington 263
Texas 5, 50, 218
Thackara
　Owen, Rev. 1
Thaft
　Louisa W. 102
Thames 241
Thatcher
　H.K., Lieut. 260
　Lucy F.K. 260
Thaw
　Columbia 230
　Joseph 64, 230
The Hive, Md. 14
Theilich
　Friederich 102
Theological Episcopal Seminary 20
Theological Seminary 241, 268
Thibodaux, La. 268, 269
Thomas
　Abel C., Rev. 54
　Ann 237
　Ann Salony 224
　Catharine 10
　Charles Edward 19, 177
　Charles, Col. 235
　D., Mrs. 89
　Edward 84
　Eleazer 146
　Eliza 48
　Francis William 10
　Gen. 235
　Henry 224
　John H., Dr. 264
　John Handy 84
　John Hanson 165
　John M., Dr. 188
　John W. 177
　Joseph 213
　Mary A. 228
　Mary Ann 177
　Moses 181
　Sarah 171
　W.H. 10
　William 97

Thomaston, Me. 50, 90, 260
Thompson
   Allen A. 14
   Charles Clagett 135
   Egbert, Lieut. 248
   Elizabeth Ann 204
   Elizabeth D. 15
   Estella M. 126
   George 126
   George W. 259
   Georgianna 126, 210
   Henry 15, 104
   Hon. 266
   James R. 129
   Jane 38
   John A. 212
   Joseph A. 193
   Julia 128
   Lucas P., Hon. 105, 192
   Lydia 93
   Mary Ann 135
   Mary C. 194
   Mary Clare 194
   Mary Mercer 266
   Nancy 64
   Pishey 38
   Richard Henry 124
   Richard R. 4
   Robert 198
   S.W. 26
   Smith 135, 194
   Susan Amelia 24
   Susan Caroline 192
   Susan R. 105
   Virginia 107
   Waddy, Gen. 241
   William 204
   William H., Lieut. 22
Thomson
   Alexander Peterkin 161
   Caroline M. 79
   Estelle E. 139
   Estelle M. 161
   George 161
   Hon. 200
Thorn
   John H. 222
Thorndike
   Anna D. 114
   Charles 114
   Mary A. 31
Thornton
   Fannie H. 259
   Howard F. 259
   J.B., Col. 106
   James B. 231
   Jane 79
   John S., Col. 231
   Marianna T. 106
   Philip, Dr. 144
   Susan Stuart 231
Thoroughfare, Va. 49, 106

Throom
   J.W.N. 26
   Sarah Hale 26
Throop
   Dr. 26
Thruston
   Alfred B. 58
Ticer
   James 219
   Lewis 219
Tidball
   Alexander S. 40, 230
   Alfred Howell 40
   Jane Scott 230
   Rebecca J. 230
Tilley
   Barbara 34
   E.M. 227
   Mrs. 109
Tillinghast
   N.P., Rev. 59, 258
   Rev. 17, 31, 117, 128, 140, 142, 195, 206, 237, 257
Tillou
   F.R. 27
   Marion E. 27
Tilson
   J., Rev.* 61
Tilton
   Warren 11
Tingle
   Mr. 18
Tinkle
   Rev. 5
Tippett
   Mary M. 188
Tochman
   Gaspar, Maj. 40
Todd
   Elizabeth G. 250
   James, Rev. 32
   John 86
   John Payne 70
   Mary Hammond 250
   Rev. 232
   William B. 250
Todd Co., Ky. 190
Todhunter
   Emma 236
   I. Edmondson 114
   J.E. 236
   Joseph 236
Toldeo, Ohio 141
Tomes
   Charles, Rev. 53
   Rev. 3, 53
Tonge
   Elizabeth 135
   Richard 12
   Thomas 135
Toombs
   Mary Louisa 156
   Robert, Hon. 156

Toomey
   Ann 154
Topographical Engineers 52, 54, 102, 250
Topping
   Ann Maria 114
   Mary E. 233
   Nathan H. 114, 233
Toronto Guardian 92
Toten
   Joseph S., Lieut. 157
Totten
   Catlyna 48
   Gen. 48
Towers
   John T. 114, 266
   Mary M.M. 122
   Richard Wallach 122
   Susan B. 114
   William 122
Towles
   Rev. 49, 106
Towner
   Fannie E. 95
Townley
   Mr. 179
Townsand
   Mary A. 64
Townsend
   John K., M.D. 6
   Lemuel R. 238
   Matthias B. 197
   Miss 191
   Sarah 264
Towson
   Nathan, Maj. Gen. 104, 239
   Sophia 104
Tracey
   Frances Maria 53
   James Francis 53
Trail
   Charles E. 11
Train
   George Francis 48
Travers
   Hester A. 27
   Jabez, Capt. 27
   Sidney 132
Trayer
   Mr. 200
Treadwell
   W.H., Capt. 220
Treasury Department 6, 10, 15, 18, 27, 29, 52, 62, 68, 78, 91, 220, 233, 242, 246, 250
Tredway
   Louis Demos 90
Trego
   Eliza 211
Tremain
   Augustus, Hon. 80
   Porter 80
Trenholm
   Rose Frances 19

Trenton, N.J. 58, 252
Tretler
   John 264
Trinidad 113
Trinity Church 19-21, 23, 47, 54, 62, 91, 93, 94, 109, 112, 114, 115, 122, 138, 157, 160, 163, 180, 181, 203, 204, 207-209, 213, 214, 216, 223, 225, 257, 264, 265, 270
Trinity College 176
Triplett
   Eliza H. 72
   John R. 267
   Philip, Hon. 72
Tripoli 18
Trowbridge
   Charles C. 222
   Kate S. 222
Troy 99
Troy, N.Y. 71, 154, 212
Truckson
   Martha Cordelia 122
True
   Edwin E. 48
Truman
   Elizabeth 88
   Josiah 88, 145
Trunnell
   Henry 147
   Richard H. 76
Tryer
   Henrietta 123
Tschiffelly
   Elizabeth A. 110
Tuckahoe, Va. 89
Tucker
   Capt. 7
   Charles C. 154
   Durbin 249
   Elizabeth A. 235
   Enoch 97, 228
   Henrietta 186
   James 186
   James Henry 186
   M. Virginia 228
   Samuel W. 80
   Sarah R. 7
   W. McKendree, Dr. 252
Tuckerman
   Edward 228
Tudor Hall, Md. 128
Tudor Place, D.C. 238
Tuleries, Va. 112
Tuley
   Col., Mrs. 256
Tunis 124
Tunstell
   George N. 140
Tuomy
   Timothy J. 253
Turkey 18

Turnbull
   Kate 223
   William, Col. 223
Turner
   Catherine J. 213
   Margaretta S. 67
   Rev. 117
   Richard H. 67
   Thomas B. 214
   William H.F. 193
Turpin
   Amanda L. 22
   James S. 207
Turtin
   Elizabeth M. 212
Turton
   Annie Booth 37
   Jane 79
   John B. 37
   Sarah A. 37
Tuscaloosa, Ala. 193
Tuscumbia, Ala. 210
Tustin
   Septimus, Rev. 127
Tutor 124
Tweed
   C.A. 237
   Emily J. 237
Tweedy
   Julia E. 96
   Robert 96
Twiggs
   David E., Gen. 50
   Gen. 50
Tyler
   Frances Annette 262
   Grace C. 66
   Grafton, Dr. 66, 156
   President 6, 203
   Trueman 66
   William W. 262
Tyng
   Dudly, Rev. 8
   Rev. 9
Typographical Society 104

U

U.S. Hotel 5, 57, 75, 92, 140, 165, 178
Ulerich
   H., Mrs. 28
   Maria S. 28
Ulrick
   Michael 36
Umstead
   J.T., Rev. 265
Undertaker 265
Underwood
   J.R., Hon. 49, 53, 56
   Jeanie 49
   Light 53
Union Chapel 105, 128, 135, 224

Union M.E. Church 228, 235, 238
Uniontown, Pa. 39
Unitarian Chapel 94
Unitarian Church 145
United Empire Loyalists 174
University of Maryland 192, 260
University of Pennsylvania 66, 71, 179, 258
University of Virginia 43, 47, 159, 188, 232
Upham
   Henry 84
   Sarah Maria 84
Upper Marlboro(ugh), Md. 66, 117, 142, 151, 171
Upper Platte river 210
Upperville, Va. 23, 30, 33, 145, 251
Utica, N.Y. 166
Uxbridge, Mass. 94

V

Vail
   Elizabeth 97
Valentine
   Arthur S. 82
   Mathias 82
   P.J. 82
Valparaiso, Ind. 30
Van Horne
   J., Maj. 269
Van Kleeck
   Elbert Herring 116
   Rev. 154
Van Patten
   Amelia C. 108
   Charles H., Dr. 108
   Priscilla Louisa 108
Van Rensselaer
   Solomon 71
Van Reswick
   Wilfred 237
Van Riswick
   John 237
   John E. 237
   Mary 237
Van Santwoord
   Henry Coolidge 167
   John 167
   Susan M. 167
Van Tassel
   Clara 48
Van Tyne
   J.P., Dr. 135
   Thomas R. 135
Van Vallenburg
   Charles Eugene 19
Van Vassel
   Sarah 215
Van Wyck
   Abraham 212
   Sarah 212

Van Zandt
- Nicholas H. 190

Vandalia, Ill. 263

Vanscriver
- William 245

Vantine
- John P., Dr. 9

Varden
- Josiah, Rev. 199

Veiro
- William A. 156

Venable
- A.W., Hon. 11
- Joseph G. 65
- Mary Grace 11
- William 8

Venecia, Calif. 174

Vension
- William 234

Vera Cruz 44, 126

VerMehr
- Rev. 96

Vermont 100

Vessey
- Leonard 195

Vibber
- Phoebe Ann 255

Vick
- Bushrod W. 252

Vicksburg, Miss. 235

Vienna 95

Villard
- Mary Ann 21, 22
- R.H.L. 21

Vincennes, Ind. 104, 219

Vincinanza
- Rev. 221

Vineyard Farm, Md. 236

Vinson
- Ann Mary 107
- Anna M. 137
- Charles 27
- T.F.W., Col. 107

Vinton
- Francis, Rev. 83

Virginia 19, 23, 24, 28, 29, 31, 37, 53, 67, 70, 71, 74, 82, 87, 88, 90, 92, 94, 96, 98, 101, 102, 106, 107, 112, 122, 123, 131, 139, 140, 151, 156, 160, 164, 171, 174, 182, 186, 190, 192, 193, 195, 197-201, 206, 208, 213, 215, 218, 221, 224, 225, 229, 231, 243, 252, 253, 255, 257, 258, 267, 273

Virginia Herald 42

Virginia Military Institute 246

Vivans
- Josephine 51

Vonderlehr
- Barbara 45

Voss
- Augustus 31
- W. 167

W

Waco Village, Tex. 256, 258

Wade
- Edgar F. 130

Wadsworth
- Alexander 112
- Alexander S. 17
- Comm. 132, 133
- Louisa D. 132, 133

Waggaman
- Floyd 195
- Martha J. 203

Wagoner
- Louisa Ann 113

Wahl
- John 179

Wailes
- I.H. 93, 146
- Isaac H. 13, 237
- Mary N.H. 147
- Nancy H. 237
- Nannie H. 146

Wainright/Wainwright
- Col. 137
- Henrietta Mary 137
- Jonathan Mayhew, Rev. 254
- Mrs. 137, 213
- Rev. 223

Waite
- Edward 47
- Matthew 84
- Sarah Brett 84

Wake
- Margaret T. 149

Wake Co., N.C. 187

Wake Forest 187

Wakefield, Va. 67

Walbach/Walback
- Gen. 166
- Louis A.B., Capt. 51, 166

Wald
- James E. 133

Waldron
- N.S., Maj. 95

Wales
- John, Hon. 256
- Mary Josephine 256
- Stephen C. 188

Walker
- Albert Morgan 53
- Angelina 116
- Ann H. 30
- Ann Rebecca 230
- Anna M. 138
- B., Maj. 168
- Benjamin, Maj. 267
- C., Rev. 230
- Caroline C. 171
- Catherine 63
- Charles Carroll 79
- Charles E. 53
- Dorcas 59
- Eliza Josephine 193
- Elizabeth H. 79
- George A., Maj. 42
- George H. 268
- Hannah M. 193
- Harriet L. 168
- Henry 63
- Isaac P., Hon. 79
- J.C. 171
- James C. 19
- John 193
- John Christian 171
- John H. 26
- John M. 116
- Letitia McCreery 24
- Maria C. 188
- Mary Jane 53
- Mrs. 243
- Nathan 227
- Reuben 63
- Sallie A. 267
- Samuel 55
- Samuel Purviance 24
- Thomas Douglas 230
- Zachariah G. 201

Wall
- C.O. 69
- J.H.D. 224
- James E. 267
- Mary Ann 224
- R.J. 156
- Rachael L. 199

Wallace
- Ann K. 120
- George W. 37
- Mary A.K. 12
- Michael 11
- Robert 12, 120

Wallach
- Richard 119
- Robert R. 119

Waller
- A.B. 113, 231
- Amelia Maria 93
- Fanny E. 113
- Henry 260
- J.D. 34
- James D. 93, 148
- Maria H. 34

Wallingsford's boarding-house 227

Walsh
- J.C. 187
- Julia E. 71

Walter
- Anna Pauline 129
- Carolina 22
- Mary S. 239

Walton
- Coates 139

Walworth
    William B. 256
Wampler
    J.M. 94
Wands
    Margaret B. 134
Wannall
    Charles P. 98
    Thomas 11
War Department 109
War of 1812 146, 197, 207, 221, 229, 235
Ward
    Emily R. 264
    Horatio M. 146
    J. Thomas, Rev. 186
    J.Y., Rev. 21
    John B. 21
    John, Dr. 87, 93
    Lauriston 64
    M., Mrs. 95
    Margaret Anna 186
    Rev. 168
    Sarah 249
    U., Rev. 40
    Ulysses, Rev.* 186
    William 15, 264
    William Harrison 27
Warden 76
Warder
    Barney 192
    Helen Cornelia 195
    Walter, Capt. 195
    William 198
Ware
    Henry A. 256
Waring
    Ann M. 48
    Col. 2
    Edmund H., Rev. 213
    Eliza Genevieve 2
    Elizabeth 236
    F.G. 169
    Henry 48
    Henry H. 243
    James, Dr. 48
    Mary E. 32
    Sarah C. 7
Warley
    A.F. 148
    Emily C.W. 148
Warm Springs, Va. 102, 182
Warner
    John 100
    Sally A. 100
Warner, N.H. 190
Warren
    John 117
    John G. 46
    Mary H. 46
    Susan W. 117
Warren Co., N.C. 62, 239
Warrenton Springs 241
Warrenton, N.C. 229, 238, 239

Warrenton, Va. 7, 25, 49, 57, 93, 103, 149, 179, 181, 184, 187
Warring
    M.L. 5
Warrington
    Comm. 20
    Lewis, Comm. 49
Warsaw, Poland 40
Warwick
    Ellen Virginia 230
Washburn
    C., Rev. 160
    E.A., Rev.* 232
Washington
    Bailey, Dr. 243
    Bushrod 22
    George 58, 76, 85, 90, 125, 146, 174, 198, 205
    George C., Col. 238
    George, house of 7
    George, tomb of 56
    John Marshall, Maj. 206
    Lund 151
    Mary Lizzie 108
Washington (Pa.) Examiner 22
Washington Academy 66
Washington Asylum 105
Washington Benevolent Society 118
Washington Club 238
Washington Co., D.C. 19, 71, 122, 180, 214
Washington Co., Md. 238
Washington Co., Va. 113
Washington College 205, 220
Washington County Court 103
Washington depot 81
Washington Infirmary 14, 20, 92, 209, 211, 230, 232, 253, 270
Washington Lodge 101
Washington Preachers' Meeting 188
Washington Union 94, 213
Washington, Ga. 156
Washington, Ind. 184
Washington, Ky. 261
Washington, La. 192
Washington, Pa. 66, 90, 220, 261
Waterford, N.Y. 32
Waterford, Va. 95
Waterloo Co., Can. 92
Waterman
    Edwin 46, 234
    Maria A. 234
Waters
    Amelia R. 262
    Courtney 209
    Cyrus, Dr. 168
    David S. 178
    Dwight R. 83, 262
    Elkanah 97
    Isabella 265

    John 96
    Marceila 262
    Mary Melvina 96
    Rebecca 186
    Rev. 189
    Warren S. 129
    William 43
Watervliet 81
Watkins
    Caroline 2
    Caroline H. 77
    Eliza B. 2
    George L. 77
    George S. 2
    Margaret 56
    Mary 107
    Mary Agnes 252
    Simon, Rev. 130
    T., Dr. 252
    Tobias, Dr. 107
Watson
    Benjamin T. 123
    Dr. 177
    Elizabeth Coates Love 109
    Elizabeth Courts 200
    Emeline R. 216
    J. Carlson 155
    J.N., Rev. 213
    James 69, 200
    James W. 109
    John 267
    Laura Van Lear 177
    Mary Elizabeth 123
    Rev. 134
    Sarah Ann 112
    Sophia E. 256
    Thomas P. 228
    Virginia C. 80
    William 169
Watterston
    George 210
Wattles
    Elizabeth T. 199
    Henry Starr 232
    Nathaniel 199
Waugh
    Bishop 81
    Kate 81
    M.M. 160
    Mary 160
    W.B. 81
Waverley, Va. 241
Wayland
    Anna Mead 50
    Charles 50
Waylen
    Rev. 216
Wayman
    A.W., Rev. 147
    Rev. 57
Wayne
    Anthony, Maj. Gen. 121
    Isaac, Hon. 121
    Mr. 71

Waynesboro, Va. 186
Waynesburg, Va. 33
Wayson
   Matilda F. 211
Weaver
   Anne 178
   Clarence S.M. 24
   Helan M. 219
   Henry 211
   J.G. 21, 24
   John George 21
   John T. 253
   Lydia 21, 24
   Mrs. 153
   William H. 46
Weaver burying ground 211
Webb
   Pollard 252
   Thomas T., Capt. 153
Weber
   Christian H. 69, 159
   Magdalene 159
   Mary 159
Webster
   Daniel L. 224
   George N. 78
   Mr. 75
   Rev. 16
   Webster 225
Weed
   Edwin C. 47
Weems
   Elizabeth 189
Weightman
   R.H. 266
   Richard Hanson 266
   Susan B. 266
Weir
   W. Tasker 91
Welch
   Alice 212
   Ann 148
   Harriet 165
   Jane 8
   Maria Josephine 73
   Sarah 74
Weller
   Sen. 208
Welles
   Benjamin 208
   Georgiana 208
Wellesley
   Family of 229
Wellford
   Parke Farley 191
   Rebecca Parke 213
   William N., Dr. 191, 213
Welling
   Genevieve Hamilton 107
   James C. 107
Wellington Co., Can. 92
Wellington, Va. 122

Wells
   Elijah 50
   Richard A., Dr. 119
   Sarah 186
Werner
   Charles 227
Wesley Chapel 22, 23, 28, 66, 85,
   122, 140, 144, 160, 196,
   201, 224, 231, 255, 268
Wesleyan Female College 31
West
   Benjamin F. 178
   Benjamin Oden 158
   Charles Blodget 107
   Charles S. 41, 156
   Covington O. 1
   Helen M. 158
   Isabella Leavitt Howard 156
   John 41
   William H. 107
   William Henry 210
West Baton Rouge, La. 96, 110,
   194
West Feliciana, La. 80
West Hoboken, N.J. 107
West Liberty, Va. 115
West Point 100, 140, 151, 197,
   206, 207, 240
West Point, N.Y. 30, 102
West River Landing, Md. 212
West River, Md. 7, 168, 173
West Springfield, Mass. 198
Westchester, Pa. 91
Westcott
   Bayse Newcomb, Lieut. 54
   Elizabeth 217
   Geo. Clinton, Capt. 141
   J.D., Hon. 217
   John, Dr. 263
   Judge 141
   Rachel Parker 263
Westerfield
   Mary Elizabeth 31
Western States 15
Westmeath, Ire. 61
Westmoreland Co., Va. 67, 72, 73,
   141, 243
Westmoreland, Va. 46, 107
Westover 128
Westwood, Tenn. 44
Wethered
   John 231
   Sarah J. 231
Wetherill
   Martha 123
   Samuel M. 123
Wexford Co., Ire. 256, 257, 262,
   270
Wexford, Ire. 45, 192
Whaley
   F.N., Rev. 17
   Harriet 4
   Thomas 4

Wharton
   Rev. 167
Wheat
   Annie H. 79
   Annie May 79
   J.H. 162
   John 29, 216
   John M. 29
   Joseph H. 182
   Lemuel C. 79, 216
   Mary Ellen 6
   R.W., Dr. 260
   Rachel 260
   Thomas 6
Wheatleigh
   Charles 258
Wheatley
   Andrew J. 100
Wheeler
   Ann Mary 107
   Arabella 71
   Elizabeth B. 27
   H.A. 215
   Hester A. 137
   Isabella E. 71
   J.H., Col. 27
   John 107
   John P. 137
   Sarah 137
   Simeon, Col. 227
   T.T., Gen. 137, 215
   Thomas, Rev. 159
Wheeling, Va. 6
Wheelock
   Edward B. 271
Whelan
   Mary 100
Whipple
   Edward A. 158
   Mary J. 251
Whitall
   Joseph Ellis 35
   Samuel 35
Whitcomb
   Mary 149
White
   Ann 225
   Anna Catharine 61
   Charles E. 111
   Ellen 115
   Florilla 32
   Georgie 204
   Henry 117
   Henry Clay 167
   Hugh, Hon. 32
   J. Jefferson 129
   James 164
   James L. 34, 35, 167
   James Lawrence 35
   James, Capt. 86
   John P. 61
   Joseph, Rev. 8
   Lucinda 77, 79
   Martha 206

    Martha Ellen 86
    Mary Frances 12
    Mary Kate 10
    Mathias M. 115
    Patrick 158
    Rachel W. 167
    Robert 44
    Sarah M. 61
    Thomas P. 271
    W.G.W. 10
    William G.W. 34, 129, 204
    William Henry 115
    William Taylor 70
White Plains, N.Y. 220
White Sulphur Springs, Va. 18, 46
Whitehorn
    M.C. 59
Whitele
    F.N., Rev. 259
Whiting
    Levi, Col. 107
    Washington J. 193
Whitney
    Asa 115
    James O. 183
    Joseph 257
    Julia 166
    Julia Bradley 189
    Louis F. 189
    Reuben M. 166
    Sarah Ann 257
Whittaker
    Margaret 131
Whittemore
    Jeannette E. 229
Whittingham
    Bishop 10
Whittle
    F.M., Rev. 161
Whittlesey
    Adah Blair 114
    C.S. 67
    Elizabeth 114
    George Beal 67
    Granville 77
    Oliver 114
    Virginia 67
Whittlesy
    J.H. 171
Wickham
    Elizabeth S. 176
    Elizabeth S.M. 182
    John 176, 182
Widdicombe
    Mary 108
    Mary Louisa 108
    Robert 108
Wigg
    William Hazzard 170
Wilcox
    Ann 191
    Asa F. 109
    Charles G. 127
    John A., Hon. 94
    Roger W. 208
    Samuel, Lieut. 161
    Zuleima Forrest 127
Wildes
    George, Rev. 129
Wildman
    C.G. 269
    Elizabeth Allen 269
Wiley
    John 19
Wilkerson
    Mary Elizabeth 77
Wilkes
    Charles, Capt. 257
    John, Jr. 223
Wilkesbarre, Pa. 246
Wilkins
    Benjamin F. 9
    Charles P., Hon. 148
    Mr. 181
Wilkinson
    Alfred Berry 117
    Mary 117
    Sarah 154
Willard
    Agnes E.H. 94
    George, Dr. 94
    Mr. 89
Willard's Hotel 9, 150, 221, 252
Willett
    America 51
    Charles R.A. 51
    John 51
Willey
    America 48
    Annie H.R. 48
    Calvin, Jr. 85
    John 48
William and Mary College 153
Williams
    Ann M. 136
    Caroline 215
    Charles S. 184
    Charlotte 165
    Charlotte J. 66
    Edney 170
    Elisha W. 217, 251
    Eliza M. 271
    Elizabeth M. 62
    Ezra 165, 264
    Fanny Ellen 246
    George 66
    Henry 126
    Hiram Opie 97
    James 23, 84
    John R. 187
    John S., Col. 259
    Joseph L. 261, 265
    Joseph Zadock 116
    Kate Douglas 265
    Lemuel 215
    Lemuel D. 64
    Lewis 225
    Maria S. 97
    Martha Plater 217
    Mary Ann 84
    Mary E. 184
    Meeta Dashiell 215
    Melinda 261, 265
    Mr. 67
    Nathaniel F., Jr. 246
    Otho Holland, Gen. 103
    Penelope R. 51
    Rebecca Jane 261, 265
    Rev. 20, 231
    S.S. 97
    Samuel K. 51
    Sarah 271, 273
    Sarah Ann 223
    Sarah E. 259
    Thomas J., Capt. 177
    Virginia 183
    Virginia Josephine 252
    William A. 136, 252
    William D. 9
    William P. 59
    Zadock 170, 267, 271
Williamsburg (L.I.), N.Y. 115, 126
Williamson
    Albert A. 8
    Benjamin 156
    James 8
    Jane Larned Macomb 97
    Lizzie B. 173
    Mary 8
    Virginia Elizabeth 86
    William 97, 173
Williamstown, Mass. 267
Willis
    Louisa L. 265
Williss
    Lizzie S. 217
    Nellie M. 217
    William B. 217
Willow Glen, Md. 46
Willson
    Ellen 104
    John J. 104
    Leah Summers 104
Wilmington, Del. 31, 92, 99, 178, 221, 256
Wilmington, N.C. 241
Wilson
    Agnes 239
    Amanda S. 72
    Amanda S.D. 67
    Anna A. 145, 172
    Charles 194
    Clarendon J.L., Lieut. 151
    Cornelia M. 263
    Ellen 116
    Ellen G. 58
    Frances 226
    Frank Stakely 263
    Frederick T. 201
    George Gideon 64
    Henry William 48
    J.E. 72

J.F. 72
James 8, 154
James Osmond 167
James, Hon. 54
Jesse B. 145, 172
Jesse Webster 172
John E. 67
John E., Lieut. 227
John F. 67
John P. 104
Joseph S. 110
Laura E. 8
Margaret 104
Mary 194
Mary Elizabeth 54, 145
Mary H. 52
Mary L. 63
Mary S. 110, 235
Mattie A. 204
Mr. 200
Nelly 62
Norval, Rev. 108
Osborne Sprigg 110
P.R. 263
Patrick 104
Peter F. 161
Rev. 98, 108
Samuel, Dr. 15
Sarah C. 265
Sarah Catharine 61
Sarah Louisa 108
Thomas 8
Thomas N. 116
W. Bruce 8
Wilson 239
Wily
   John S., Dr. 98
Winans
   Jacob W., Rev. 172
Winchester Republican 52
Winchester, Ky. 49
Winchester, N.H. 37
Winchester, Va. 40, 46, 47, 51, 57,
   60, 119, 155, 214, 230
Winder
   Sally R. 59
   William H., Gen. 205
Windle
   Catherine F. 178
   George 178
Windsor
   Henry J., Rev.* 19
   Jane Catharine 256
   Mary 155
Wineberger
   Jane Elizabeth 49
Wines
   Charles Mason 220
   E.C., Rev.* 220
   Emma S. 220
Wingate
   Edward 196
   Henry T., Lieut. 225

Wingenroth
   Amelia Bertha 149
   F. 149
   F.F. 201
   Susan 149
Wingerd
   Ann 17, 115
   J.P. 115
   John 17
   John P. 17
Wingfield
   Rev. 227
   Sidney 58
   Thomas 58
Winn
   Rebecca 248
Winslow
   Rev. 67
   Zechariah L. 227
Winston
   Mary H. 194
Winthrop House, Mass. 109
Winthrop, Me. 73
Wirt
   Catharine 133, 135
   Ellen 150
   John L. 3
   William 135, 150
   William, Dr. 133
Wisbeach, Eng. 73
Wisconsin 79, 216, 255
Wise
   __cer Sergeant 29
   George D. 235
   Harriet Ann 113
   Henry, Hon. 29
   Irvin Augustus 113
   James A. 113
   Jane Elizabeth 207
   Julia May 235
   Mrs. 103
Wishart
   J. Wilson, Dr. 66
Withers
   James 174
   Margaret 174
   Virginia 174
Wittenauer
   Alexander 206
Witter
   Henry F., Lieut. 183
Wolcott
   Arthur 265
Wolfe
   Eliza B. 6
   William W., Dr. 6
Wollard
   Samuel 64
Wood
   Ann Eliza 272
   Charles Temple 264
   Edward, Sr. 272
   Elizabeth 167
   Hanna 7

   Henry S. 45
   Lenore 167
   Lydia 45
   Robert Serrell 142, 167
   Sarah E. 242
   Silas 101
   Thomas 233
Wood Cot, Md. 248
Wood Grove, Va. 190
Wood's Hole, Mass. 108
Woodbridge
   Dudley 152
Woodbury
   Levi, Hon. 43
Woodbury, Md. 149, 219
Wooddall
   Laura A. 131
Woodfield, Pa. 117
Woodford Co., Ky. 166
Woodhull
   Ellen F. 108
   Maxwell, Lieut. 108
   William Maxwell 108
Woodlands, Md. 184
Woodlawn, Md. 266
Woodlawn, Va. 67
Woodley
   R.D., Rev. 183
Woodruff
   Absalom B. 247
Woods
   James S. 127
   John 88
   Rev. 14
Woodsfield, Ohio 22, 262
Woodstock, D.C. 91
Woodstock, Va. 136
Woodville, Ohio 235
Woodward
   Catharine H. 224
   Esther 84
   James M. 248
   Mary Ann 174
   Mr. 68
   Rosewell 224
   Sedley 159
   Virginia C. 62
   William 84, 159
   William R. 84, 174
woodyard 236
Woolfolk
   John 41
Woolford
   John 127
Wootton
   Flavel S.M. 150
Worcester
   Samuel H., Rev. 106
Worcester Co., Md. 65, 66, 162,
   190
Worcester, Mass. 214
Wormley
   Ralph 114

Worth
    Gen. 44, 190
Worthen
    Charles 36
    Mary Ann 36
Worthington
    Nathan E. 67
    S. 208
    Thomas H. 62
    Zachariah H. 133
Wotherspoon
    Alexander S., Dr. 225
Wright
    Annie 269
    Benjamin D. 48
    Catherine B. 8
    Clintonia Gustavia 138
    Emily 48
    Emma Elizabeth 229
    George H. 149
    Harriet J.C. 92
    Harriet Rebecca 51
    James M. 51
    Joseph H. 204
    Mary A. 207
    Mary Rebecca 51
    Rev. 191
    Robert 92
    Sarah 30
    Susan 30
    Thomas C. 8
    W.H.D.C. 138
Wroe
    Everet 12
    Julia Ann 157
    Samuel C. 114
Wroth
    William G. 191
Würtemberg, Ger. 5, 129
Wyatt
    C.C., Rev. 187
    Rev. 33, 82, 95, 246, 251
Wyche
    B.G., Dr. 235
Wye river 205
Wyman
    Nancy 257
Wysong
    Rev. 162, 167, 195, 213
    T.T., Rev. 165, 166

Y

Yale College 52, 99
Yates
    Mary E. 206
Yeatman
    Henry 24
    J.H. 208
    James E. 67
    Robert W.S. 208

Yerby
    A. Oscar 33
    A.F. 168
    Adonis L. 17
    Bettie 33
    George William 42
    Oscar 33
    William G. 33
York Co., Pa. 106
York, Pa. 9, 67
Yorkshire, Eng. 100, 118
Yorktown, Va. 174
Yost
    Elizabeth E. 272
Young
    Abner 24
    Adelaide 123
    Alex. H. 186
    Anna Barbara 180
    C.B., Rev. 162
    Charles Richard 109
    Euphemia Jane 24
    Ezekiel 46
    Frances Corlis 175
    George A. 147
    Guilford D., Col. 212
    I. Fenwick 180
    J. Fenwick 1
    Jabez 227
    Jacob 64
    James, Rev.* 175
    Jane Lawrence 123
    John 186
    John A. 76
    John Y. 269
    Joseph N. 8
    Kate 194
    L. Huntington 212
    Margaret 255
    Margaret Ann 46
    Matilda 100
    Nicholas D., Rev. 53
    Noble, Dr. 123
    Nora C. 180
    Richard 109
    Richard M., Hon. 100
    Sarah T. 53
    Serena S. 186
    Thomas H., Dr. 269
    Walter B., Dr. 268
    William P., Col. 194
    William W. 123
Young Men's Christian Association 216
Yreka, Calif. 173
Yuba Co., Calif. 1
Yulee
    Elias 29
    Jesse William 29
    Rachel 29
Yunganz
    Martin 45

Z

Zanesville, Ohio 122, 166, 269
Zantzinger
    H.A. 238
    Harriot 238
    Louisa F. 226
    William C. 238
Zappone
    A. 222
    Almericus 214
Zimmerman
    Anna Maria 43
    Henry F. 123
    J.R. 249
    John C. 43
    Margaret 123
    Mary M. 249
    Susan 249
Zungel
    Ernst 102

No Surname

[ ]
    Betty 118
    Jenkins 44

Other Heritage Books by Wesley E. Pippenger:

Alexandria (Arlington) County, Virginia Death Records, 1853-1896

Alexandria City and Arlington County, Virginia Records Index: Vol. 1

Alexandria City and Arlington County, Virginia Records Index: Vol. 2

Alexandria County, Virginia Marriage Records, 1853-1895

Alexandria Virginia Marriage Index, January 10, 1893 to August 31, 1905

Alexandria, Virginia Marriages, 1870-1892

Alexandria, Virginia Town Lots, 1749-1801, Together with the Proceedings of the Board of Trustees, 1749-1780

Alexandria, Virginia Wills, Administrations and Guardianships, 1786-1800

Alexandria, Virginia 1808 Census (Wards 1, 2, 3, and 4)

Alexandria, Virginia Death Records, 1863-1896

Alexandria, Virginia Hustings Court Orders, Volume 1, 1780-1787

Connections and Separations: Divorce, Name Change and Other Genealogical Tidbits from the Acts of the Virginia General Assembly

Daily National Intelligencer *Index to Deaths, 1855-1870*

Daily National Intelligencer, *Washington, District of Columbia Marriages and Deaths Notices (January 1, 1851 to December 30, 1854)*

*Dead People on the Move: Reconstruction of the Georgetown Presbyterian Burying Ground,
Holmead's (Western) Burying Ground, and other Removals in the District of Columbia*

Death Notices from Richmond, Virginia Newspapers, 1841-1853

District of Columbia Ancestors, A Guide to Records of the District of Columbia

District of Columbia Death Records: August 1, 1874-July 31, 1879

District of Columbia Foreign Deaths, 1888-1923

District of Columbia Guardianship Index, 1802-1928

District of Columbia Interments (Index to Deaths), January 1, 1855 to July 31, 1874

District of Columbia Marriage Licenses, Register 1: 1811-1858

District of Columbia Marriage Licenses, Register 2: 1858-1870

District of Columbia Marriage Records Index, 1877-1885

District of Columbia Marriage Records Index, October 20, 1885 to January 20, 1892: Marriage Record Books 21 to 30

District of Columbia Probate Records, 1801-1852

District of Columbia: Original Land Owners, 1791-1800

Early Church Records of Alexandria City and Fairfax County, Virginia

Georgetown, District of Columbia 1850 Federal Population Census (Schedule I) and 1853 Directory of Residents of Georgetown

Georgetown, District of Columbia Marriage and Death Notices, 1801-1838

*Husbands and Wives Associated with Early Alexandria, Virginia
(and the Surrounding Area), 3rd Edition, Revised*

Index to District of Columbia Estates, 1801-1929

*Index to Virginia Estates, 1800-1865
Volumes 4, 5 and 6*

John Alexander, a Northern Neck Proprietor, His Family, Friends and Kin

Legislative Petitions of Alexandria, 1778-1861

Pippenger and Pittenger Families

Proceedings of the Orphan's Court, Washington County, District of Columbia, 1801-1808

The Georgetown Courier *Marriage and Death Notices:
Georgetown, District of Columbia, November 18, 1865 to May 6, 1876*

*The Georgetown Directory for the Year 1830: to which is appended, a Short Description of
the Churches, Public Institutions, and the Original Charter of Georgetown, and
Extracts of the Laws Pertaining to the Chesapeake and Ohio Canal Company*

The Virginia Gazette and Alexandria Advertiser:
Volume 1, September 3, 1789 to November 11, 1790

The Virginia Journal and Alexandria Advertiser:
Volume I (February 5, 1784 to January 27, 1785)

Volume II (February 3, 1785 to January 26, 1786)

Volume III (March 2, 1786 to January 25, 1787)

Volume IV (February 8, 1787 to May 21, 1789)

The Washington and Georgetown Directory of 1853

Tombstone Inscriptions of Alexandria, Volumes 1-4

www.ingramcontent.com/pod-product-compliance
Lightning Source LLC
Chambersburg PA
CBHW081416230426
43668CB00016B/2249